The Best of ROLLING STONE

The Best of

ROLLING

STONE

25 YEARS OF JOURNALISM ON THE EDGE

Edited by ROBERT LOVE

MAIN
STREET
BOOKS

DOUBLEDAY
NEW YORK LONDON TORONTO SYDNEY AUCKLAND

A MAIN STREET BOOK
PUBLISHED BY DOUBLEDAY
a division of Bantam Doubleday Dell Publishing Group, Inc.
1540 Broadway, New York, New York 10036

MAIN STREET BOOKS, DOUBLEDAY
and the portrayal of a building with a tree
are trademarks of Doubleday,
a division of Bantam Doubleday Dell
Publishing Group, Inc.

Library of Congress Cataloging-in-Publication Data

The Best of Rolling Stone : 25 years of journalism on the edge
/ the editors of Rolling Stone. — 1st ed.
p.   cm.
"A Main Street book" — T.p. verso.
1. Journalism — United States — History — 20th century.
2. Rock music — Periodicals — History.
3. United States — Popular culture — History — 20th century.
4. Rolling Stone (New York, N.Y.)
I. Rolling Stone (New York, N.Y.)
PN4867.B44   1993
051 — dc20   93-16607
CIP
ISBN 0-385-42580-5
Printed in the United States of America
September 1993

1 2 3 4 5 6 7 8 9 10

First Edition

ontents

Introduction

JANN S. WENNER

When I started ROLLING STONE in 1967—in a second-floor loft above a small print shop in San Francisco—I wrote that the magazine "is not just about music but also about the things and attitudes that the music embraces." As time went on, I began to interpret that charter rather broadly. We understood that music was the glue holding a generation together. And through music, ideas were being communicated about personal relationships, social values, political ethics and the way we wanted to conduct our lives. The mainstream media at that time—movies, television, newspapers and magazines—were paying scant attention to what turned out to be one of the biggest stories of the times: the emerging generational upheaval in America.

The paths that led editors and writers to ROLLING STONE are a part of that story. They came from all kinds of places in all kinds of ways. David Harris wrote to me from prison, where he was serving two years for defying the draft; Eric Ehrmann wrote from his fraternity house in Ohio. When Joe Eszterhas, then a reporter with the *Cleveland Plain Dealer,* came to the loft offices to purchase back issues, the mailroom guys were certain he was a narc. (Naturally, he went on to write major exposés of narcotics officers in ROLLING STONE.)

Hunter S. Thompson showed up in my office wearing a gray bubble wig, carrying a huge satchel full of God-knows-what in one hand and three six-packs in the other, and talked for an hour straight. After his first assignment, "Freak Power in the Rockies," about his nearly successful attempt to be elected sheriff in Aspen, Colorado, he went on to write "Fear and Loathing in Las Vegas," excerpted here, and many other memorable pieces. They would change the fate of ROLLING STONE and the face of journalism.

Within a few years we had assembled a legendary writing and reporting staff. In addition to Thompson and Eszterhas, there were Tim Cahill, Jonathan Cott, Tim Crouse, David Felton, Ben Fong-Torres, Howard Kohn and Michael Rogers, to name a few. At just that time, I was finally able to get Tom Wolfe to write for ROLLING STONE. He covered the Apollo space program in a series of articles that were expanded and published later as *The Right Stuff.* (How this assignment came about is a yarn he tells in vintage style in these pages.)

Over the years many writers have come through the portals and delivered great pieces. As you will read in the essays that introduce these excerpts, the story behind the story can be as remarkable and telling as the story itself. A double-edged dissection of the gantlet facing reporters in recent years can be found in Bill Zehme's encounters with the notoriously cagey actor Warren Beatty and Mike Sager's attempts to report on the life and death of porn icon John Holmes in the face of deal-seeking lawyers and agents.

In the last decade, ROLLING STONE has leaned heavily on the talents of columnists P.J. O'Rourke and William Greider. P.J.'s pen is his sword, and he uses it to drive liars, cheats, thieves and scoundrels out into the open. His conservatism springs from his need to conserve common sense. Bill Greider has been articulating ROLLING STONE's political conscience—and his own—with eloquence since he came to us from the *Washington Post* in 1982, the first years of his lonely political mission through the Reagan-Bush decade.

Having published some four thousand major features over twenty-six years, we have had to leave a lot of fine writing unrepresented here. So I must say that I am immensely proud of *all* the talent that has worked at ROLLING STONE over the years—in Lawrence Wright's words, "literary hellcats who brushed aside journalistic conventions and social taboos to get at new ways of telling the truth." Larry, who joined us as a contributing editor in 1985, describes, the responsibility a serious writer feels in accepting an assignment from ROLLING STONE: "Not only must it be the final word on a subject," he writes, "it must be freshly seen and powerfully told."

The criteria I set forth from the first issue, expressed less elegantly and less succinctly, went like this: The story has to be about something interesting and important, not duplicating what you can read elsewhere; you have to get out there and report the hell out of it, meaning be passionate and get involved, take chances; write it well—long if necessary—and be accurate in every detail; and in the end, tell the truth about what you think. That is the charge I gave to the writers and the editors of ROLLING STONE.

A few words about the editors: Although the writer always gets the credit for the story, the truth is that nearly every article is a collaboration between writer and editor. We have had at the magazine some of the finest editors I have ever known. While I ask our writers to do their very best work for ROLLING STONE—on deadline, of course—I've made this mandate the responsibility of the editors who work for me. Without them, none of this would have been possible.

This collection is the best of what we do. It is an eclectic look at events, people and ideas that shaped our lives and our view of the world. I think of it as an impressionistic history of the past quarter century. These are true tales of journalism—how it really happens, out on the road. The delightful essays, in which the writers tell their own stories, provide valuable context for each excerpt. How they got the story, even how they got the opportunity to *do* the story, are tales of our times; taken as a whole, they are also the true backstage history of ROLLING STONE itself.

—1993, New York City

Preface

ROBERT LOVE

Back in the days when ROLLING STONE's paper was serrated at the edges, our features averaged more than 10,000 words in length. Many of the magazine's signature stories, like Hunter S. Thompson's "Fear and Loathing in Las Vegas" and Tom Wolfe's "Post-Orbital Remorse," rolled out at over 40,000 words—more like books waiting for their hard covers. In recent years, although we've tended to run shorter pieces, some of the finest examples of the ROLLING STONE style of reporting, like David Black's "Plague Years" and Tom Horton's "Paradise Lost," were nearly as big as those giants from the days of newsprint.

If you've already noted the *number* of writers represented in this anthology, it won't come as a surprise to learn that their pieces have been abridged. Only four, in fact, are reproduced at their original length: Robert Palmer's "Up the Mountain," Greil Marcus's "Blue Hawaii," Anthony DeCurtis's "Anarchy in the U.S.S.R.?" and William Greider's "Lonesome Drifter." The rest have, once again, been edited.

What does that mean? For readers who are not familiar with the duties of a magazine editor, we do a variety of things: from trimming a piece to fit, as is the case here, to conceiving the idea for an article. We tend the mothership while the reporter is out researching the story. When the piece comes in, we examine it, word by word, to make sure that the language is precise and elegant—that it says exactly what the writer wants it to. We write the headlines and picture captions, put through the expenses, talk to the lawyers, fight for space to run it, and, of course, see that the writers get paid. Oh, and one last thing: We represent the interests of the readers.

At ROLLING STONE, where we've never had editing by committee, writers and editors tend to forge intense, stormy relationships while deciding "what works best" for the reader. This is an eyeball-to-eyeball process, usually right at the computer terminal, and you cannot hide behind someone else's opinion when you ask for a third rewrite.

Since the magazine has been around now for more than twenty-five years, we're often approached by writers who believe passionately that they have a ROLLING STONE story. Sometimes they're right. The editors, however, must decide that; we are the appointed guardians of the style. In giving us his charge, Jann has also encouraged us to have faith: in a quirky idea, a powerful young voice, a new way of telling a story that better gets at the truth.

No subject is out of bounds, but no subject is in itself interesting enough—unless it has a strong narrative and sharply drawn characters. Readers might have liked Howard Kohn's 1975 article on the failure of the nuclear industry to police itself; what they'll never forget is the story of a courageous young woman named Karen Silkwood.

Editing often comes down to making choices. And with such a wealth of material available for this book, we chose to include many excerpts instead of a few famous pieces at full length. In our judgment then, this collection represents the best of the best. While we were refitting the stories to this new context, we set out not only to preserve the flavor of the writing but to retain enough of the story that first-time readers will find them as compelling as we did.

So here they are, thirty-seven examples of the art of journalism as practiced at ROLLING STONE. Along with each piece you'll find a first-person essay by the reporter telling how he, she or the story first came to the magazine's attention. The Contributors section on page 505 tells where the writers have gone since—some pretty impressive destinations.

Working with such a redoubtable roster provoked anxious delight, but I didn't work alone. ROLLING STONE editors Bob Wallace, Tom Conroy, Eric Etheridge, Karen Johnston, Sid Holt, Peter Travers, Anthony De-Curtis, David Fricke and Corey Seymour all contributed their time and effort. Jacqueline Onassis and Bruce Tracy at Doubleday were gracious taskmasters. If you, the reader, still find that these stories tingle in your hands, we have been successful. If not, don't blame the writers; blame the editors.

Toking Down with the MC5

Eric Ehrmann

A DETROIT QUINTET SET OUT TO FUSE ROCK AND RAD-
ICAL POLITICS. A STUDENT JOURNALIST FROM CLEVE-
LAND WENT TO OBSERVE THE EXPERIMENT.

Twenty-four years ago, I traveled to Ann Arbor, Michigan, to
write the article that put the MC5 on the cover of ROLLING
STONE. The band exploded on the Midwestern music scene like
a Molotov cocktail, mixing high-octane Detroit rock with a vir-
ulent strain of radical politics.

I was a student at Miami University, in Oxford, Ohio, at the time and
a columnist at the *Miami Student*, the campus newspaper. The Sixties cultural revolution was slow to take hold at Mother Miami, as we called it.
Coats and ties were mandatory at dinner. Women lived in their own dorms
and had to be home from dates by midnight. Pot parties were taboo, and
the nearest liquor store was across the state line in Indiana, making road
trips the order of the day.

Finding a copy of ROLLING STONE was like finding a Solzhenitsyn
book in Siberia. I spent much of my free time pounding down Stroh's
long necks at Mac and Joe's bar with my Deke fraternity brothers and my
pal P.J. O'Rourke. Three Deke brothers played in the Lemon Pipers, the

bubblegum band that won a gold record for "Green Tambourine." They would bring copies of ROLLING STONE with them when they came off the road, and we'd sit around the bar reading them.

As an aspiring journalist with an interest in music (I began studying classical trumpet when I was eight and financed most of my college education playing in a Dixieland band), I was drawn to ROLLING STONE. The early issues featured a small box inviting journalists to submit articles for consideration. In the spring of 1968, I sent a query letter to ROLLING STONE expressing my interest in writing. Copy editor Charles Perry replied, asking me to submit a list of article ideas.

That summer, I traveled to London and Paris and wrote my first ROLLING STONE article, a review of Savoy Brown at the Marquee Club, the mecca for the British blues revival in London's Soho district. I received a check for $25, which back then seemed like $250. But money was hardly the object. More important was contributing to a publication that spoke for my generation. Enclosed with the check was a note from editor in chief Jann Wenner asking me to keep him posted on developments, musical and otherwise, in the Midwest.

Quite frankly, my writing the MC5 piece was very much an accident of time and place. When I returned to school in the fall, two of my Deke brothers told me about getting blown away by the band at an outdoor concert in Chicago during the Democratic National Convention. Knowing of my connection to ROLLING STONE, they told me the MC5 had to be seen to be believed. Indeed, the band's linkage of politics and music had the makings of a powerful national story. I did some homework and sent a proposal to Jann in San Francisco; he asked me to draft a 2500-word piece.

Jann sent me a laundry list of editorial requirements. He wanted a story that went beyond music to discuss the band's lifestyle and philosophy. But getting the story posed the classic rock-journalist's dilemma: how to penetrate the band's inner circle. Fortunately, Brother J.C. Crawford, the band's resident political orator, was from my hometown, Shaker Heights, Ohio. Being a homeboy to Brother J.C. provided an opening. I took a week off from classes and drove up to Ann Arbor to visit the MC5 early in October 1968.

I thought the Miami Dekes were the original *Animal House* guys until I met the MC5. The band members wore shirts made from American flags, bullied their girlfriends like cave men and had the balls to preach violent revolution. The action inside their big house on Ann Arbor's fraternity row had more to do with Michoacán than with Michigan. (As you probably know, Michoacán is a major marijuana-producing state in Mexico.)

Although the band members were on friendly terms with local underground journalists, they were suspicious of ROLLING STONE, which they viewed as being "soft" on politics. My first night was spent answering their questions. They chided me about being a square from a conservative school in Ohio and asked me why I lived in a frat house instead of a commune and why I liked bourbon more than pot. As an acid test, several of them tried to toke me under the table with marijuana and filled my head with horror stories about their scrapes with the narcs in the Detroit underground.

Passing the test meant passing the pipe. After countless toke-downs, I began to feel like the last one standing at a Deke house purple-passion party. When Wayne Kramer and Brother J.C. Crawford started smiling at me and calling me "scribe," I figured I had passed the test.

Then came the propaganda: a doctrinal harangue from band manager and spiritual leader John Sinclair on "kicking out the jams," the MC5 philosophy of free love, revolution and rock & roll. In a tribal ritual typical of communal houses of the period, we would sit around a long harvest table, eating food prepared by the "old ladies" of the band. The emancipation of women didn't have a high place on the MC5's revolutionary agenda, and the old ladies seemed more than happy to defer to the macho behavior of their men.

Looking back, it seems like one big outtake from Rob Reiner's film *This Is Spinal Tap*. Interviewing required me to play through the politics of the communal pecking order. John Sinclair wanted the story told his way. When I would put a question to the band members, Sinclair would butt in. Singer Rob Tyner's comments reflected Sinclair's philosophy of revolution through rock & roll. Guitarist Wayne Kramer tried hard not to let Sinclair's politics get in the way of his reputation as the house wise guy. Drummer Dennis Thompson, the band's best natural talent (on a par with Keith Moon and Ginger Baker), was outspoken about police repression. Guitarist Fred "Sonic" Smith and bassist Michael Davis were quiet guys who let the others do most of the talking.

We would rap until the wee hours, and what was left of my nights was spent crashed out in a sleeping bag on their living-room floor. The band spent much of the week building me up for the main event, the "destroy experience," a Saturday night concert at Michigan State University's Union Ballroom.

Watching the MC5 get ready for the ballroom concert was like watching a football team pad up for a playoff. The dressing room at the Union was full of smoking and joking and camaraderie with a couple of tough-looking MC5 bodyguards watching the door. Sinclair and Brother J.C. Crawford raised the mood to a fever pitch with their inspirational preconcert harangues. Sinclair wrote the band's song list on strips of tape, which he stuck to the members' wrists or instruments. Then, after Brother J.C.

had worked the crowd into a frenzy with his political jive-rap, the band made its frenetic run onto the stage.

The MC5 lived up to its reputation as an incredible live act. It worked harder than James Brown, mesmerized you more than the Doors and took you higher than Sly Stone, when he was on. Surrounded by MC5 fans in the front row, I watched the band deliver a show that blurred the distinction between entertainment and politics. When I returned to the dressing room after the concert, the band invited me to a party. But after a week, I had had my fill. I blew off the party and made the all-night drive home down Interstate 75.

Back in my own world, I opened a bottle of J.T.S. Brown and sat myself down in front of a typewriter. Translating the high-energy world of live music and radical politics to the two-dimensional print medium meant going above the tree line. Getting away from the political hotbed of Ann Arbor helped; the bourbon did, too. What came out was an attempt to give readers the feeling of what it was like to visit the MC5 house and have a front-row seat at a live concert. I tried to reveal the band for what it was at the time: a group of working-class heroes who played hard, partied harder and were true believers in Sinclair's notion that revolution was rock & roll's bottom line.

After the MC5 piece, Jann expanded regional coverage, creating opportunities for Midwestern writers like Joe Eszterhas in Cleveland and Dave Marsh in Detroit. David Felton defected from the *Los Angeles Times*. Paul Scanlon came out of Palo Alto, California, to join the staff.

In 1969, I went out to San Francisco to work on article development at ROLLING STONE; I wrote pieces on Iggy and the Stooges, the Wild Thing (a biker band from Boston) and the funeral of writer Jack Kerouac. The sprawling Brannan Street office was a classic, well-lit place, a magnet for talent and ideas. On any given day, Annie Leibovitz would show up in her air-force fatigue jacket, cameras dangling from her neck, armed with proof sheets. Hunter Thompson would be stalking the corridors.

During the Seventies, I lived in Europe, but ROLLING STONE was never far from my mind. I would see it on sale at newsstands on the Champs-Élysées, in Paris, and on the Kurfürstendamm, in Berlin. Smuggled into Eastern Europe, ROLLING STONE became one of the symbols of cultural freedom and democracy that helped break down the Iron Curtain. The MC5 projected that freedom, and in doing so, it helped open the door for much of the music we can enjoy today.

RS 25

The overflow crowd of 1,800 at Michigan State University's Union Ballroom is up on its feet, shouting "get down" and waving the familiar "V" for victory, as Brother J.C. Crawford articulates the MC5's gospel, a radical harangue for freedom.

"Are you ready brothers and sisters? Are you ready to make all those problems start becomin' solutions?"

"Yea!" The crowd responds.

"OK—Everybody's gettin' down . . . eatin', smokin' dope and makin' love in the streets . . . so let's *kick out the jams Motherfuckers*—the MC5!"

At that instant, lead singer Rob Tyner runs onto the stage and leaps high into the air, his body writhes amidst the strobe lighting for a split second and when his feet hit the ground, the MC5 begin to "Kick Out The Jams."

This is how the MC5 experience starts off. From then on, hold your head because you are in for a total destroy experience.

The MC5 are attempting to politicize and liberate the minds of our culture. This radical musical action stems from the one-dimensional automobile factory environment of their Detroit home (their name stands for Motor City Five) and it is spreading rapidly with the popularity of the band.

"Wherever we play we walk through the crowds and rap with the people on the way up to the stage . . . we tell 'em to kick out the jams and get down on it . . . everybody's gotta get down!"—Lead Guitarist Wayne Cramer, 20, born in Detroit of a lower middle-class background—digs wearing brown Stetson Saratoga shoes with the white stitching penciled in.

"It's the high energy, man! Little Richard screamed his ass off and Chuck Berry got his split kick dance steps from Harlem tap dancers like Baby Laurence . . . ever dig him?

"We do it our way."—Drummer Dennis Thompson, a 20-year-old pincushion for Detroit's pricky politicians. Wears only a leather vest and jeans on stage, but plays with such intensity that he takes the vest off after the first song and must have the equipment man wipe the sweat off him while playing.

"Fuck everything else man . . . just get down!"—Lead vocalist Rob Tyner, 23, lifelong Motor City inhabitant. Teases his hair and wears bench-made dancing boots—often wears mini-skirts and tights on stage. "It's all here, just get down/get down/*get down!*"

Rhythm guitarist Fred Smith and bass guitarist Mike Davis have also spent all of their twenty years in Detroit and are the relatively subdued members of the group. The "5" (as they prefer to be preferred to in the vernacular) got together around three years ago and began doing hard blues and R&B. They gigged around Detroit and gained a reputation as a good blues band, doing John Lee Hooker, Little Richard, Chuck Berry and their own original topical blues material.

When Uncle Russ Gibb, a radio station entrepreneur, opened his Grande Ballroom, he used the 5 to play on his concert dates with nationally known groups. Late in the fall of 1967, John Sinclair, who was instrumental in the development of the Detroit scene, became interested in the 5's music. Sinclair, writing for Down Beat at the time and hosting his own local TV jazz show, would rap after gigs at the Grande with Bob Tyner, who shared his interest in the free form of Sun-Ra, Pharoah Sanders, Rashid Ali and John Coltrane. A self-styled poet-philosopher, Sinclair was a close friend of the late saxophonist Coltrane. The 5's conception of blues was beginning to branch out and Sinclair's fresh conception of free form jazz created a synthesis of ideas when it met the 5's basic blues-rock roots.

"High energy is a total and environmental involvement of the musician and the audience. It happens when your senses and emotions spew themselves completely onto a medium." — John Sinclair, 26, mentor-manager of the MC5. A native of Detroit, dropped out of college after becoming fed-up with his master's thesis, accomplished jazz trumpeter — a big shaggy-haired soft-spoken bear.

"Sure, it's a political thing, just dig the energy . . . not just white power or black power but everybody's power. We were the only group to play up at the Battle of Chicago . . . Burroughs dug us, Genet dug us and check out what Mailer had to say in Harper's." In quest of a conducive environment, the MC5 have found communal living to have a profound influence upon their ability to communicate and more readily share ideas. Similar examples of this benefit can be found in Traffic, the Grateful Dead and the Band (Big Pink). These groups are proving that the best creativity is not always generated when five musicians live in different places, think different things and try to gain recognition on their axes whenever they play.

"To express the total environment through music, the musician must break away from the ordinary everyday and put himself in a place where he can devote all his time to thinking and playing." — John Sinclair.

The 5 are a part of Sinclair's dream come true, Trans-Love Energies. A completely liberated communal environment where people can live and create. The commune was originally established in Detroit but shortly after the King assassination, police repression became so harsh (arrests, drug busts, brutality and general pigshit) that Sinclair and his fellow communards chose to move their energies into Ann Arbor, incubator of SDS and hotbed of political activism. Now the MC5 live in an 18 room house, ironically located along Hill St. and Ann Arbor's "Fraternity Row," with about ten other individuals who contribute to Trans-Love's energies.

Next door is another large house which Trans-Love rents; another band, the UP, resides there along with fifteen additional communards. The 5 bring in most of the dust (bread, money) to pay the $550.00 monthly rent tab for the two big houses. Trans-Love's magic light show also gathers in the dust because it generally goes along with the 5 wherever they play. Recently, the band just purchased three new panel trucks with communal earnings. The commune is quite a successful endeavor and it welcomes anyone who wants to participate and do their thing.

Chicks live with the 5 and also provide the domestic energies to make clothing for concert wear, keep the place tidy and make some of the most destroy barbecue ribs and chicken that you can chomp on. Anyone from the area can walk in, sit down at the 30-foot long harvest table and scarf down some really destroy food, absolutely free.

One warning, the MC5 is a unique subculture. All of the communication inside of the 5 house is game talk, which to the ordinary observer would sound like double talk . . . well brothers . . . it ain't. It's like this — to quote Brother J.C. Crawford, Exalted Preacher of Zenta International, the political arm of Trans-Love Energies:

"May I warn you, may I make it known that I warn you, the pipe of power is to be passed . . . let it be lit and let it pass, brothers and sisters . . . this is the pre-dinner toke-down, brothers and sisters, toke this scribe [meaning myself—MC5 jargon for all writers] down into the hallowed and exalted halls of Zenta . . . let the pipe be passed and bring on the food."

Everyone barbarically devours the ribs and potatoes. Brother J.C. begins his gospel once more in a W. C. your friends. A little instant anarchy for you power Fields-1890's politician fashion.

"Brothers and sisters, this is the pre-after-dinner toke-down, after this toke-down comes the after-dinner toke-down and after that comes the pre-post-after-dinner toke-down and finally the post-after-dinner-toke-down."

Wayne Cramer passes the pipe after puffing on it and smiles.

"Actually, you've gotta toke down to get down and in order to toke down you gotta get down and if you get down, we all get down."

"Yeah, just like Alice in Wonderland," says John Sinclair.

John Sinclair and the MC5 don't care about being busted. He once gave a narc a free joint, just for kicks, thinking the pig would want to get off. That caper was his third offence for possession. It is now in the courts on appeal and a decision is pending. Sinclair is not sweating jail though. He spent his first wedding anniversary in the Wayne County Jail (Detroit) and wrote a poem for the pig that busted him. If John Sinclair gets sent up the river, Detroit will burn. The city politicians know this and they still can breathe the smolderings of Summer 1966. When the police became heavy handed in the Plum Street hip community late in the Spring of 1968, the white and black militants made a pact to stick up for each other. John Sinclair was one of those cats who brought the forces together, and if he is sent to jail, Detroit will burn once again. There are more politicized hippies in Detroit and its surrounding areas who have helmets, gas masks, teargas and homemade Mace along with other ordnance paraphernelia than any other city currently in insurrection.

While the guerrillas wait in hiding, their band the MC5 helps them get money by playing political benefit concerts. Whether it be for a bail party, rent party, fund raising benefit for Black UAW workers trying to organize their independent local or an underground paper in need of dust to continue circulation, the 5 will play.

"If you need bread or are in jail, just call us and we'll try and help the best we can . . . we know the feeling brother."

The Grande Ballroom is the mecca of the Detroit rock scene. It was once the sight of stately waltzes and high-priority social affairs. Now the neighborhood has changed into a depressed area, but if you are over 17 and able to pay, you can still dance. The Grande itself is a similar scene to the old Avalon in San Francisco. It has a definite gaudy midwestern hippodrome look. Trans-Love artists provide the poster work for the national artists that owner Russ Gibb books in. Gibbs has recently opened a Grande Ballroom in Cleveland and plans to co-ordinate his bookings once he gets Cleveland Grande together. Usually the ballroom is publicized in Detroit's two underground papers, the Fifth Estate and John Sinclair's SUN.

The Detroit scene has also been responsible for the S.R.C. (Scott Richard Case) now on Capitol and presently touring the country; The Amboy Dukes, who recently had the single "Journey to the Center of Your Mind"; and the Stooges. The Stooges are a totally bizarre experience and will have a bizzaro-destroy impact on the music world when Elektra releases a Stooge album next spring. Also hailing from Ann Arbor, the Stooges practice macrobiotics and live on their own communal farm. Stooge Vocalist Iggy Osterberg leaps off stage into the laps of surprised girls and plays a game of Reverse-rapo, taking off his shirt, pulling down his pants, then goofing on the girl and walking away. He has the potential to make Jim Morrison look like a tame puppy. Often Iggy injures himself in his violent movements to which he comments, "Yeah, we watch a lot of TV at the house."

Iggy was once a protege of ex-Butterfield drummer Sam Lay and is presently living in Ann Arbor with Nico.

Elektra Records caught wind of the 5 and signed them along with the Stooges to recording contracts. Elektra gave two free recording concerts at the Grande in co-operation with Trans-Love and Zenta International on October 30 & 31st. Bruce Botnik of Sunset Sound and Wally Heider were flown in to record the sessions in a portable 8-track housed in a truck.

Most important was the fact that this event marked the first time that a unique cultural form has been captured in its own midwestern environment without having to migrate to an east coast or west coast cultural center. Their album should be available shortly after the first of the year.

"We had to do it live—the whole thing is energy, audience rapport. It is no longer a question of just getting your head into the music, but letting the energy liberate every cell in your body. I guess you could say our thing is a condemnation of everything that is false and deceitful in our society."—John Sinclair.

"Yeah, that's the middle class alright."—Wayne Cramer.

When considering the lower middle class from which the 5 eminated, it isn't difficult to understand the high energy which they put into their music. J.C. begins to explain: "The Motor City . . . dedicated to the production of the automobile—symbol of Western Man's mobility and affluence."

Gargantuan assembly lines at River Rouge discharge wastes through the bowels of the city. These wastes do not dissipate, they accumulate.

"It's all accumulating to make a machine that goofs on you two years after you sweat your ass off to buy it."

Wayne begins singing . . .

"Everyone's a junkie, na na-na na na."

"Toke this boy down."—Brother J.C.

"And then there's always Junkie Uncle Bill Burroughs."—Wayne.

What William Burroughs has done to writing, the MC5 are doing to music. There are all into Burroughs very deeply. His LP is often heard on the Trans-Love stereo.

"Yeah, we're with Burroughs. Junkie, junkie, who's the real junkie . . . nobody knows. We're all junkies. Listen to our music—that's why we say get down and kick out the jams. Everybody's gotta shuck his junkie thing, man," says Sinclair.

Wayne forcefully adds his comments:

"Get down, get down, what about the poor dope junkie who is really hooked because he can't handle the scene . . . he gets jail man."

MC5 sees Detroit as a personification of junkie society and themselves as the rejection of this society through high energy environmental experience.

"People really get uptight if you tell them they don't have to work and hack the straight world. They say . . . well, what would we do. They don't know how to read, they don't know how to listen to music and they don't know how to touch each other."—John Sinclair.

"Sure, lots of folks will say that we are un-music . . . but what kind of junkies are they?"—Dennis Thompson.

"When the 5 is playin' and everybody's down . . . there ain't no junkies."—Brother J.C.

When the MC5 plays, everyone participates. Musicians hop on stage to wail with their axes and there is always a free microphone. When the 5 played a benefit for The Paper at Michigan State, one dude came up and beat drummer Dennis Thompson's ride cymbal for five minutes and had to be helped off stage. Thompson is as powerful as Ginger Baker, but with a different motive. Baker is playing to prove that he is the Cream of rock drummers . . . and it looks as if he is killing himself in the process. Dennis Thompson is playing with such fierceness because he has, along with the rest of the 5, experienced twenty years of repression in the middle class rut. He says this with every pulsation of the band.

"Now, we don't think we're obscene," says Wayne.

"Just go down town Detroit and look at the books they sell . . . all about success and workin' hard and that bullshit."—Brother J.C.

"So far, we've never been busted for obscenity, but as we get around, some ego-tripping pigs will make some kind of scene just like the Doors had in New Haven."—John Sinclair.

"I really don't know what obscene means . . . the only people that talk about it are the freaks and they are the ones that are the most obscene things going."—Rob Tyner.

At first meeting the 5 come on somewhat aloof, and since I was a scribe, there was a short period of feeling each other out. Brother J.C. eased the communication gap and when the pipe began to pass, we really got into things. The gaming and double talk is great amusement for themselves and their friends. That is all they do aside from their political music. Their subculture is very tight and if one does something, the others are fraternally obliged to follow suit. When they practice a new song, everyone takes part, not just one guy doing the lyrics and another doing the music.

"It's everybody's thing, we all do it and if we all didn't do it, we wouldn't be."—Wayne Cramer.

Narc busts are an inconvenience to all of us, but few rock bands have actually *reveled* in them the way MC5 does. Here's MC5 publicist-etc. John Sinclair's account of a bust in mid-1968—as it appeared in an MC5 publicity *handout*. The scene was the Grosse Point Hideout, an east-side teen dance joint, and: "MC5 drummer Dennis Thompson and manager John Sinclair stepped outside during the second set for a smoke and met some fans in the parking lot next to the building. The young rock and roll addicts produced some grass, and while the sacrament was being ingested two rent-a-cops strolled on the scene, surprising one young man with a joint in his hand.

It's the kind of press release that would give a Hollywood flack an instant stroke. But MC5 occupies another universe, another sensibility, where narcs are figures of fun.

From the cross-section of people observed at the Union Ballroom at Michigan State, it seems all kinds of people dig the MC5. A straight fraternity type with a crested blazer commented:

"Jeez, they sure are crazy, but their music really gets to me . . . it is really hard for me to identify with anything after hearing this."

A quiet little girl with long auburn braids lamented:

"I'm so useless, what will happen to me when the revolution comes. They have so much energy. I'll never do anything."

What is so exciting about the MC5, according to Sinclair, is that "the whole thing is very blues and R&B oriented . . . but we've taken our own energies and exposed them to Trane and Sun-Ra and Pharoah . . . you can't predict it . . . either can we."

There is a little bit of something for everybody in the 5 . . . if you dig Little Richard, they've got "Tutti-Frutti" . . . if you dig Screamin' Jay Hawkins, they "Cast A Spell On You" . . . if you dig Chuck Berry, they do his moves and if you dig freaky clothing, they've got lots of it that you'll never see any place else because they make it themselves. If you are a girl and you dig sex, you might even get one of them (or all of them) to ball you (depending on how much you like Hubert Selby backseat ball scenes).

There is no telling what will happen when the 5 hit the stage . . . just as there's no telling what will happen when you get down and kick out the jams. You may start putting the make on the girl next to you, or you may go out and blow up your local draft board. If you dig cheap thrills, you'll never get more for your money. Go to their house, eat their food, smoke their dope and play their games . . . their games are your games, and we all play games!

The 5 are condemning society and anyone who is plugged in to its system and they are a bit skeptical of themselves as they stand on the brink of success. "It's nice that this is happening but if it didn't happen we'd be doin' the same thing . . . no different," says Wayne.

"As long as we move people, we'll be doin' what we want to do. As long as they get down and kick, we'll be happy."—Dennis.

The Rolling Stones on Tour

ROBERT GREENFIELD

OH, TO BE YOUNG, FANCY-FREE AND WORKING IN THE
LONDON BUREAU OF "ROLLING STONE" WHEN MICK
JAGGER AGREES TO LET YOU TRAVEL WITH THE BAND.

Twenty years ago, London was a different city in nearly every way. I could hail a black cab on Haverstock Hill, in Hampstead, not all that far from the tiny garret without central heat or a lavatory on Primrose Gardens where I lived, and have it take me all the way through Hyde Park, past Chelsea, and then out beyond World's End for less than a pound—and still have enough change left over at the end to tip the driver.

The trip itself took almost no time at all. Traffic was always light in the city back then, for one very simple reason: Virtually no one in London owned a car. At least no one that I knew, despite the fact that they cost so little used (at the going rate of $2.20 to the pound back then, an old blue Bedford van could be had for around 120 bucks).

Even had I wanted to drive on the wrong side of the road, I could never have afforded anything quite *that* grand. As the associate editor of the London bureau of ROLLING STONE, located up the stairs at 28 Newman Street, in the West End, I earned the princely sum of fifteen pounds a week. Five quid a week went for rent. I spent as much again for food. The rest I banked in order to have something set aside for a rainy day. It rained every single day while I lived in London. Every single bloody day.

On a daily basis, there were only four of us in the tiny two-room office on Newman Street, each one as much a friend and a family member to the other as a fellow worker. Andrew Bailey was the editor. On ads, Brian Cookman of Bronx Cheer, a pub band that was either ten years ahead or ten years behind the times. On phones, Fiona Bower, who had been raised to be a lady but could, when the occasion demanded, curse like a stevedore on the docks in Woolwich.

Chris Hodenfield was there playing the part of the boy reporter as only Jimmy Olsen had ever done before. Ray Downing dropped in only when the mood struck him and he could find a spare moment to take care of all those things that no one else could do.

Late indeed though it may have been for flower power in the U.S. of A.—what with Janis Joplin and Jimi Hendrix and then Jim Morrison dying off in fairly rapid succession and the National Guard shooting white middle-class kids on the campus at Kent State for no good reason other than they just happened to be there protesting the war—in London to some degree the hippie thing still held sway. By 1971, the operative concept over there had become that of "the underground," reflecting what was going on in America but in a very English way.

It was before any American show ever became a regular favorite on English telly. There was no MTV. Telephone connections to the United States were so bad as to make airmail the most effective means of communication. Yet on a regular basis, rock & roll bands kept departing from Heathrow in order to seek their fame and fortune on tour in the U.S.A. Like some kind of weird lend-lease program in reverse.

No band ever had done this with more success than the Rolling Stones. Having caught the buzz about the coming tour, Andrew Bailey arranged for us to have lunch with Jo Bergman, then nominally in charge of the Stones' London office, located at 46A Maddox Street, in the West End.

At lunch that day, we all drank a good deal of very good wine. Boldly, I told Jo, a lady who pioneered the concept of big hair on both sides of the Atlantic, that all I wanted to do on this particular tour was "just kind of hang out, man, and see what happens." God only knows why she bought it. It was a far more innocent time in the world and in the business as well. In London, credentials were easier to come by, tending to be entirely personal rather than professional. That I wanted to try to do something a little different was good enough for Jo. Giggling as no one else ever could, she said yes, and I began an association with the Stones that over the next two years took me from London to Los Angeles and through North America with them on their 1972 tour.

For me, the English tour began as I walked behind Charlie Watts down a platform at King's Cross Station, in north-central London, in order to board the train to the first show. Charlie's father, then still alive, worked for British Rail. He either just happened to be on duty in the station that day or had come especially to see Charlie off. I know he was in uniform. I may be wrong, but I believe he was also carrying some sort of brakeman's lantern in his hand. Casually, as only the British ever could, father and son said hello and then goodbye, wishing each other the best as Charlie stepped on the train. The train pulled out. We were off.

All the way to Newcastle, I sat in a first-class compartment with people who *belonged* on the tour. People who had real jobs and crushing responsibilities. None of them had the faintest idea who I was. No one even bothered to ask. I was there? There *had* to be a reason. Soon enough, my specific function would be revealed. If not, well then, that was all right, too.

In Newcastle, we all went to the very modern hotel with a view of the city where everyone on the tour was staying. In the lobby, someone put a room key in my hand. I remember putting the key in the lock, shutting the door behind me and leaping around with a kind of happiness I have known only a few times since. I felt as though I were on my way somewhere fast. I was twenty-five years old. It was the first time in my life I was staying in a hotel room by myself.

After the second show of the night, perhaps the best one of the entire tour, everyone repaired to a hotel banquet room for a midnight meal. I happened to be sitting next to Charlie Watts. The conversation turned to jazz, Skinnay Ennis and "the cat" who played the solo on "And the Angels Sing." Only no one could remember his name. Anyone coming up with the answer would score bonus points.

The song had been one of my mother's favorites, always playing on the radio in the kitchen as I ate breakfast before going off to school. "Ziggy Elman," I said. Charlie Watts shot me a significant look. As the English liked to say back then, "Nice one." At least *some* of my credentials were in order.

The Stones played in Manchester, Coventry, Leeds and Glasgow. Just the way the Stones ordered food in even the most ordinary places knocked me out. They always knew *exactly* what they wanted to eat and *just* how it should be cooked. In their hands, any menu became a work of art.

"Bitch" and "Brown Sugar," two songs the Stones performed for the first time on that tour, played constantly in my mind. I heard them as I rode with Jo Bergman in a car driven by the late Ian Stewart through the Pennines, a range of hills in the north of England. From behind the wheel, Stew kept looking up suspiciously in the rearview mirror at me. I had a beard. My hair was long. Was I not a bloody hippie after all?

Steadfastly, in his most stubborn and infuriatingly lantern-jawed, tight-lipped Scots manner, he refused to stop the car to let me go to the bath-room until I finally made it very plain that this was a *real* emergency that could in fact result in something *very* dire happening in the back seat of the car. Right *now*. That, Stew liked. I had just threatened him, as no true hippie would have ever done. He said I reminded him of Brian Jones, another traveler who could never hold his water for very long.

I remember laughing like crazy while riding in limousines with Marshall Chess, then just beginning his time of service with the band. In time, I got to talk and hang out with Nicky Hopkins, Bobby Keys, Jim Price and even Chip Monck, the onstage "Voice of Woodstock" (or V.O.W., as he was sometimes referred to by those jealous of his position behind the piano, stage left, where in full view of the audience, he would dance throughout the entire set each night while calling light cues for the band).

The only person I never got to meet was Keith Richards. Little wonder. Along with Anita Pallenberg—a woman for whom back then the term *sex bomb* could have been personally created—their infant son Marlon and the late Gram Parsons, they formed a little subtour of their own, never arriving anywhere on time. Although I did not know it then, Keith's long and very difficult bout with heroin had only just begun.

I finally made contact with him near the very end of the tour in Brigh-ton, where the Stones had been booked to play an oversold, smoky, hellish disco called the Big Apple. For some reason, probably a mistake on their part, Keith and Anita actually arrived at that gig on time, only to find the dressing-room door locked. The corridor was deadly cold. Cold as only a corridor in England could be.

Keith began to curse. As only Keith Richards could. The bloody *nerve*. Who did these people think they were, after *all*? Here in his arms lay poor Marlon. A poor and pitiful orphan of the storm. A tiny, suffering child whose cough at any moment might become the croup. Who, just like Tiny Tim on Christmas Eve, might soon be praying for the Lord above to God bless us every one. Sod the bloody promoter. The filthy *lout*. How dare he? Who *did* these people think they were, after all?

Keith worked the scene for all it was worth. He squeezed every possible drop of blood from every last line of dialogue that left his then still-unreconstructed mouth. Then he decided the time had come. The time for action. The time for Keith to take matters into his own hands.

The next thing I knew, Keith Richards and I were breaking into the dressing room by using a variety of small implements, a metal comb and a Swiss army knife among them, to take all the screws out of the door hinges so we could then throw the door itself onto the floor. While in the act, he and I never spoke. There was no need. We were partners in a crime being committed in the name of justice, rock & roll style.

The night wore on, getting ever weirder. At one point, a very loaded and deathly pale Gram Parsons asked me to take him upstairs so he could look at the stage. Out we went together into the still-freezing corridor. I pushed open a door that I thought would lead us to the crowded dance floor on which thousands of sweaty kids were smoking hash in order to prepare themselves for the Stones. With me in the lead, the two of us began going up flights of stairs. Endless flights of stairs. There was a door at each and every landing, but all of them were locked. It was like being trapped while changing classes in some high school of the perpetually damned.

By my side, Parsons began to lose it in a serious way. His breathing became labored, his face even more pale than it had been before. This was not cool. At *all*. Finally, I found a door that was not locked. I shoved it open, and out we both stepped into the completely deserted second balcony of a huge, cavernous movie house. Above our heads, on a screen that had to be twenty feet high and twice as wide, the movie *Myra Breckinridge* was being shown in very lurid living color. We had gone beyond. We had just entered another dimension. We were now both in the twilight zone.

By this point, reality had become an entirely subjective concept. How could it not be so? I was on the road with the Stones. Doors that I had never before seen were now wide-open to me. I possessed a certain power that could not be explained. Yet everyone felt it all the same. I was somebody by association.

Throughout the entire tour, I made it my business never to let anyone ever see me take any notes. Not a single one. My aim was simple: I did not want anyone to be conscious that I was listening to and recording everything they did and said.

Just before the tour ended in London, Mick Jagger felt the need to challenge me on this point. Nothing personal, mind you. Just Mick being Mick (a full-time job if ever there was one), rattling the bars of my cage in order to find out if anyone was in fact alive inside. Call it my final exam for personal credentials in a world where he was the final judge of everything and everyone.

Backstage at the Roundhouse, Mick Jagger let me know in no uncertain terms that he had my number. I hadn't fooled him at all. For the past ten days, I had done nothing but enjoy myself. I had run as wild and full-out as anyone else on the tour, when in fact it was to work that I should have put my hand. The truth was that I had no real idea what *any* of this was about. Now, *did I?*

I mumbled something in my own defense. Then I went home and wrote the piece that's excerpted here. Concerning one thing of course, Mick himself was dead right. God, but I had fun. Staying up through the night while careening from town to town with a bunch of crazy people who laughed all the time as the Rolling Stones played kick-ass rock & roll in tiny little trade-union halls, ballrooms and university auditoriums. It was far less a job than a unique shot at experiencing something that I think I knew even then would not come again.

Recently, I found myself at a funeral with someone else who had been on that journey through England with the Stones twenty years ago. The only difference was that since then, he had been on every single tour that both the Rolling Stones as a band and Mick Jagger as a solo performer had done. And by that I mean every *single* one.

"Wot?" he said in a manner so English that there is simply no way to get it on the page. "That last one we did round England? Gettin' on buses and ridin' ordinary trains? Best tour ever. That's what tha' was. Best tour there ever *was*."

I thought so then. I still think so even now. Which only goes to show that no matter how thoroughly this world of ours sometimes threatens to go to hell in a handbasket, at least some things *never* change. One of them being the memories we carry around within us like a raincoat. Even when there is no rain.

RS 80

APRIL 15TH, 1971

"**B**oogie, Bobby, boogie," Marshall Chess is saying over and over to Bobby Keys in the seat next to him, slamming out the phrase and laughing as they talk about old-time saxophone rides.

"Booo-gey, Booo-gey," Anita Richards, née Pallenberg is singsonging in the back of the plane, making the word sound like an errant German nickname for Humphrey Bogart.

Boogie, a small brown and white puppy, is about to fall asleep in the arms of Anita's husband, Keith. The doors of the midnight flight from Glasgow to London are about to close. Conversations buzz and hum. Only the tops of heads and the outsides of elbows are visible.

What could be nicer? Flying home from Glasgow in the midnight hour after two good shows before packed houses of people out of 1957 (brass-blonde ladies screaming and clutching at their heads whenever Mick showed his ass to the audience).

Contentment positively flows from seat to seat, the engines are about to rev, it's five, four, three, two minutes to takeoff. When down the aisle comes a blue-jacketed airline official, all the way to the back seat where

Keith and his dog recline. And the official says: "That dog flies by prior arrangement only, sir. You'll have to get off the plane."

"What?"

"I'm sorry, sir, I warned you in the airport. How you managed to slip by me on the plane I don't know, but you'll have to get off *now.*"

"Look, I've flown BEA, TWA, Pan Am"—Keith Richards, singer, composer, lead guitar player, Rolling Stone, is reciting a list of every airline he's ever been on—"to San Francisco, to places you or this airline have never been . . ."

"You have to supply a box, sir."

"I happen to know that section of the Geneva Convention very well. *You* have to supply the box. This is ridiculous. It's an emergency. My wife and family are here, we have to get home and take my child to a doctor tomorrow."

"I'm very sorry, sir."

"We just want to get home. Is it that important? Just let us leave."

"The rules, sir."

"I know the rules. Get this plane going, we're not moving."

Exit the official. Reenter the official with two large blue Scottish policemen.

" 'Ere, wot's the law doin' 'ere? Come to arrest us all, have you? Oy, you you, oy." One of the cops is doing his best to ignore Mick Jagger, who is lying flat on his backbone in a seat, naked to the waist save for a blue nylon windbreaker someone has thrown over him after he gave his sweaty T-shirt away onstage.

"Oy, Oy," Mick says loudly, a saucy schoolboy trying to get the police to notice. He reaches out to jangle at the cop's sleeve.

"Now, now, chummy," the cop says, leaning over. "No one's done nothin' yet, why should we arrest anyone?"

"He's come to arrest the dog," Keith says.

"Wot you doin' here," Mick demands of the cop. "A little dog like that. A puppy." His face falls. "You should be ashamed. Ooo called the law?" he wails. "Arrest us."

"Chummy," the cop says, "I wouldn't give you the publicity."

" 'Chummy'?" Mick demands.

"Sir . . . look . . ."

"Don't curse me, I saw you say fuck, don't go curse me . . ."

Beautiful, Mick. All they have to do is search the luggage and it's twenty years in the Glasgow jail.

"Anita," Mick says, "go find the captain."

Beautiful, Mick. Mata Hari Anita, all crocheted stockings and tiger hot-pants, sent to seduce the captain of the airplane as it sits on a runway in Glasgow.

"Goooo," Mick googles. Marlon, Keith's eighteen-month-old son, googles back and laughs. The cop is outflanked, bewildered, surrounded by little kids, slinky ladies, rock stars. Mick . . . beautiful.

"We'll put him in Charlie Watt's orange bag," Marshall Chess the solution-maker says, meaning the dog. "Is that okay?"

"Yes," says the cop.

"No," says the airline official.

"You brought him on this plane and now the two of you can't agree," Keith shouts.

"How about mah vulture," Bobby Keys yells out. "Can ah keep him up hyeah?"

In the five years since the Rolling Stones last toured England, they have made so much money through album sales and concert tours of Europe and America that they find themselves in a tax bracket of their own. They have become the first rock & roll band to be forced into stylish Somerset Maugham-type exile in the South of France.

Along with Crosby, Stills, Nash, and Young, they are the last of the absolute superstar bands—modern-day lords who are totally cared for and looked after, whose only responsibility is to keep their heads in a place that enables them to keep on making their music.

It's been a year since Allen Klein had anything to do with representing their corporate interests. Their recording contract with Decca has lapsed.

Marshall Chess, the son of the good Jewish businessman who established and ran Chess Records, was along on their European tour, and his presence on this one (their farewell tour of the U.K.) meant the start of something new for the Stones—incorporation on a scale no band except the Beatles has ever undertaken. Or, as Bobby Keys shouted one sweaty night in a Newcastle dressing room, with his arm wrapped about Charlie Watts's head, "Gawdammit Chawlie, rock 'n' roll is on the road *agayn*.

Empty King's Cross Main Line station on a cold, clear Thursday that feels like November in New York. One penny for the toilets and the pay phones don't work. The twelve o'clock train for Doncaster, York, Darlington, Newcastle, Dunbar, Edinburgh, and Aberdeen leaving from Track 8.

Nicky Hopkins, who went to California for a week and stayed two years, is on board and off again, and again, snapping pictures of anything that doesn't move—the station, Cadbury chocolate wrappers—as long as it's typically English. Mr. Sessions Man, with a beautiful hangdog face and a camera always hanging from his neck. Bobby Keys and Jim Price, the Texas Horns, most recently on the road with Delaney and Bonnie and Joe Cocker's Mad Dogs and Englishmen, Bill Wyman and his lady, Astrid. Charlie Watts, dapper, being seen off by his father: "Awrite, Charlie, I don't wanna go. Let me off."

A trainman with a green flag in his pocket comes down the line closing doors. The two Micks, Jagger and Taylor, catch a later train. Keith misses that one too and is driven up. Sudden small flake snow comes swirling, as the train eases out of the station to the north and Newcastle.

Newcastle, a gray, scruffy city located on the Tyne River in the part of England that is nearest Scotland. Without any sound tests and only one week of rehearsal, the Stones begin the tour there with two concerts. They are still one of the killer bands of all time.

Opening with "Jumpin' Jack Flash," Mick in a pink sateen suit and a multicolored jockey's hat. Then into "Live with Me," "Dead Flowers" off *Sticky Fingers,* "Stray Cat Blues," and "Love in Vain" with Mick Taylor doing two totally controlled solos that soar nightly. Then "Prodigal Son," Keith picking and stringing on an acoustic guitar as Mick stands next to him and sings. Then "Midnight Rambler," which, as it breaks down, is six, eight, ten or twelve bars of basic blues, depending on how long it takes Keith to sling one guitar over his head and get another on and tuned and launch the song's driving riff. Then everybody pushing to one ending, and the psychodrama begins, with just the bass pulsing away and the lights blue and eerie in Mick's face.

Off comes the studded black belt; Mick is down on his knees, "Beggin' with ya bay-bay, uh, uh . . . Go down on me bay-bay, uh, uh." Rising slow and sinister to "Wahl, you heard about de Boston . . . ," stretching and stretching the second syllable, dangling the belt up behind his shoulder, then slashing it to the floor as the band crashes it in back of him and all the lights come up.

"Honey, it's not one a those."

"Oooooooooooooooooh."

Every night, there's this sharp intake of breath, nervous giggles, little girls finally getting hip to what it's all about as that belt crashes down and the band hits everything in sight and the lights come up on Mick, hunched over and prowling like an evil old man.

Then "Bitch" with Bobby Keys and Jim Price blowing circles you can stomp in, "A song for all the whores in the audience." "Honky Tonk Women," followed by a long, unrecognizable intro that always fools everyone because it leads into "Satisfaction."

Most nights the crowd is solidly crazed by this point, rocking down the aisles, idiot dancing in the balcony, middle-aged ladies bumping obscenely in toreador pants (1957!), skinheads gently waltzing ushers around in circles. "Little Queenie," "Brown Sugar," and then "Street Fighting Man" with Mick flinging a wicker basket of yellow daffodils into the house, petals floating down through spotlight beams as he leaps four feet in the air and screams.

*   *   *

The concert over, there's a long white starched table set for forty people back at the hotel. A beggar's banquet trailing away in the middle of a ballroom. Forty clear glass tumblers all in a line. Knife, spoon, fork set perfectly and repeated forty times. At two in the morning, surrealism, Rolling Stones variety.

Marshall Chess sits across from Jagger. Mick's lady, Bianca, sits next to him in a white linen cape and a wide-brim pushed-back hat. She has a face so beautiful as to be insolent; high cheekbones, sweeping facial plains, a cruel mouth, features that become Oriental in repose.

"More than twenty minutes on a side and you lose level," Marshall is saying. "You know that. It's how they cut the grooves. So we have to work out the running order . . ."

Down the table a ways, Jim Price asks Charlie Watts, "You dig Skinnay Ennis and the cat who blew that solo in "And the Angels Sing?"

"Fantastic," Charlie says, sounding a little like Cary Grant.

"That was Ziggy Elman," someone says.

"He's from mah home town." Jim Price smiles.

"Who?"

"We can begin distribution right away to key spots throughout the States. We're gonna use one picture worldwide to advertise it and it'll have an international number. That's a first," Marshall says proudly.

"He's dead," Jim Price notes.

"Who?"

"Skinnay Ennis."

"You mean Ziggy Elman, man?"

"They're both dead," Charlie says sadly, shaking his head.

"Henry Busse too," Jim says.

"Fantastic," Charlie says, exploding it like a soft cymbal crash with brushes.

"We'll send you a test pressing by air," Marshall says.

"And you send me back a dub . . ."

"You'll send me one too," Charlie demands loudly.

"We will, Charlie," Marshall says, a little surprised.

Charlie smiles. "Just addin' to the bravado."

"Ah am going to burn down this goddahmn hotel if ah don't find mah suitcase," Bobby Keys says, in a voice made louder by the fact that it's in England. "Goddamn, ah'll throw Chawlie Watts out a window. What's that, slide one of them on mah plate, lady," he orders a waitress. "You know what these rolls are good for?"

"Oh-oh," Jim Price says softly.

Whang, a roll comes spinning through the air.

"You know what these glasses are good for?" Bobby asks rhetorically.

"Will you do it that way, Mick," Marshall asks. "Will you? If we cut

'Moonlight Mile' to four verses and make up a running order so that the guy in the States can get started on the sleeves?"

Mumble, mumble, Mick's head is down, speaking to Bianca. It's 4:00 A.M. He raises his head, he looks a little glazed. He says, "What, Marshall?"

A very proper BBC interviewer asked Mick Jagger, "Ahah, ahem, John Lennon, in his interview in ROLLING STONE magazine said that the Rolling Stones always did things after the Beatles did them. Are you then too planning to break up?"

Mick's face widened and he broke into his haw-haw laugh. "Charlie, are we goin' a brake up then? Are you gettin' tired of all of this?" As Charlie crept around the outside circle of cameras asking, "Who's he? Who is that?"

"Naw, we're not breakin' up," Mick said. "And if we did, we wouldn't be as bitchy as them."

The Stones are separately becoming the people they want to be. Charlie could be drumming with a jazz quartet, playing nightly gigs in small clubs in Sweden or Denmark. Bill, who's the oldest, wears fine clothes, likes white wine, smokes small cigars. Mick Taylor is younger than anyone, as much a part of things as he wants to be, a fine blues guitarist. Keith drives the band onstage, pushes the changes. He and Anita are undisputed king and queen of funk and inner space. Mick Jagger, twenty-eight years old, very much the man of the world, always whoever he wants to be on a given night, is in the process of becoming European.

Bianca is talking about going gambling somewhere. A few nights ago in Manchester, Mick, Marshall and Bianca found a casino that only let you lose and Mick dropped more than anyone, about three hundred quid ($720).

"You even play gin rummy in another language," Marshall tells Bianca. So far on the tour he owes her eight thousand dollars in rummy debts. "But the dealer in Manchester, he was terrible . . ."

"Dealing out of a shoe, probably had three decks in there," someone offers.

"Ah, if we had won, we'd be sayin' how good he was, wouldn't we, Mick?" Marshall asks.

Mick looks up, pauses, and says, "I really don't care."

And there is this silence that seems to grow around the phrase, before and after, like when the Stones sing "Wild Horses" onstage and no one knows what to do with it. It stops everyone cold. They have to think.

Mick *doesn't* care.

"Oh, that was last night, huh?" Marshall says, picking up on it.

"Tu vas changer le choix?" Bianca asks Mick. The first show was notable.

A quiet country audience in peaceful Coventry sat politely and watched. Mick didn't throw them the flowers in "Street Fighting Man," and Chip Monck played them "God Save the Queen" as soon as it was over.

"Drunken bitch," Mick notes, as one of the band's ladies wobbles by. "She won't lose weight that way, will she?" He sighs. "There's nothing to do but bitch, is there?"

"Intermission's over," a manager says. "Time to go."

"No," Mick says flatly. "Don't wanna. Oh, fucking why. They sold all the tickets here in three hours and then they come and just *sit* there."

"Let's go and tread the boards then, Mick," Charlie says, doin' a little soft shoe, making him smile.

"Yeah. A tap dance. Oh, it's all right. Why do they have to sit there though? C'mon then. Same show, if it's the same audience. Maybe we'll even knock out a number and go home early."

And of course, just like in the movies, the second show is a *bitch* and Mick and the boys incite the crowd to riot. Charlie cooks. The lights all go purple and green against a white-painted wooden stage floor. Everyone sweats and goes home happy.

In Bobby Keys's dressing room before one show, his ever-present cassette recorder is spooling out Buddy Holly singing, "Are you ready? Are you ready? Ready, ready, ready to rock and roll."

"Mah golden saxophone is comin' up now," Bobby says as the next song comes on. Indeed. Bobby Keys, who looks about eighteen after a good night, actually played with Buddy Holly, recorded with him at K-triple-L radio in Texas, and claims to have appeared at the Alan Freed shows at the Brooklyn Paramount which featured the Everly Brothers, Clyde McPhatter, Buddy Holly and the Crickets, and Sam "The Man" Taylor's big band. Bobby is pushing twenty-nine. 'Ah been on the road sixteen goddahm years," he says. "That's why I am the way I am."

And so saying, he pulls on his black tiger-skin and velvet jacket over a special ruffled black shirt, and goes out onstage to blow with one of the last real rock 'n' roll bands around.

"Oh, OK, who listens to Berry anymore?" Mick Jagger asks on the flight to Glasgow. This day, he is wearing a long brushed-grey suede maxicoat, a tight, ribbed sweater and a blue printed cap perched on the back of his head. He's looking very French.

"I mean, I haven't listened to that stuff in years. Rock 'n' roll has always been made by white suburban kids, bourgeois kids. Elton John is a fine example. For God's sake, I listen to the MC5."

"Rock 'n' roll's not over. I don't like to see one thing end until I see another beginning. Like when you break up with a woman. D'y'know what I mean?"

In Glasgow, one of life's cheap plastic dramas. Green's Playhouse. Paint peeling off all the walls. Six inches of soot in the air vents. Bare bulbs backstage and fluorescent tubes for house lights. The third balcony is closed to "keep the raytes doon."

A group that's been together for a week is filling in before the Stones' first set and the first two numbers they do are Jagger/Richards compositions. Third generation rock.

The lead singer, on his way into the dressing room, passes Mick Jagger on his way out. A hot, seedy, cramped corridor in the basement of a Glasgow theater. They actually brush shoulders.

Mick misses the train to Bristol even though he's on the platform when it pulls out. He doesn't want to run for it. No one expects Keith, Anita, baby and dog to make trains. Along with Gram Parsons they've become a separate traveling entity.

The kids in Bristol may be sharp as a pistol but the ushers are thick, bearded wrestlers in silk suits who stand facing out in front of the stage and stop anyone from dancing. Mick celebrates "Street Fighting Man" by placing small mounds of flowers on each of their heads, a baptismal offering. The kids dance. The Stones do an encore.

During the second show, an usher drags a pretty painted young girl offstage; Mick kicks him in the shoulder.

In Liverpool, Mick shows up with his hair cut. Glyn Johns is along to record. Keith has missed the train. The jet that will get him to the theater in plenty of time breaks down. So does the 'prop they replace it with. He arrives an hour late with Anita, who is essentially naked in silver lamé and a push-em-up-'n-grab-em bra over what looks like bare skin.

Mick and Bianca slouch on a couch waiting. "You been on the road for eighteen months now, Marlon," Mick says. "How do you like this life?"

U*p the Mountain*

ROBERT PALMER

BRIAN JONES AND WILLIAM BURROUGHS TOLD TALES
OF THE ANCIENT TRANCE MUSIC PLAYED BY THE MAS-
TER MUSICIANS OF JAJOUKA. OUR REPORTER GOT
CAUGHT UP IN THE SPELL.

L ike any budding beatnik growing up in the twilight zone between *On the Road* and Woodstock, I always made it a point to
read anything by William Burroughs. I kept noticing cryptic
allusions in Burroughs's work to Jajouka, a mountain village
somewhere in Morocco, home of the Master Musicians (who were they?)
and their mysterious Rites of Pan (what was *that?*).

Being a Stones fanatic, I was intrigued when I heard that Brian Jones
had visited the village with Burroughs's longtime friend and frequent col-
laborator Brion Gysin. Then Gysin published a novel called *The Process,*
which described Jajouka, its music and the lifestyle of the Master Musicians. They were the sons of sons of musicians, and apparently they sat
around all day playing music and smoking kif when they weren't driving
possessed tribesmen into mass Dionysian frenzies. It sounded like my kind
of scene.

I reviewed *The Process* in ROLLING STONE and mailed a copy to Gysin, care of his publisher. He wrote back from Tangier, saying, "Drop in any time." Meanwhile, Rolling Stones Records announced plans to release an album called *Brian Jones Presents the Pipes of Pan at Joujouka*. I contacted label honcho Marshall Chess, and he showed me footage of Jajouka on Robert Frank's Moviola. The place looked like Paradise. One night Marshall and I listened to Jones's tape. I don't think we ever figured out whether we were playing the tape backward or forward, but we had a lot of fun trying. Later, I learned Jones had subjected some of the music to studio processing, including overdubs involving tracks running backward *and* forward.

In 1969 and 1970, Ed Ward had written glowing ROLLING STONE reviews of two albums by the band I played with, Insect Trust. We met after a show, and when he became the magazine's record editor and found himself in a jam for a jazz reviewer, he remembered me. I had a journalism background, played sax and clarinet, claimed to know something about jazz, had long hair and was under thirty. Obviously, I could be trusted. I began writing reviews, but Jajouka was still on my mind.

By 1971, I was living in Manhattan, and among my friends was Michael Herr, recently returned from Southeast Asia and in the early stages of writing the best book on Vietnam, bar none, *Dispatches*. One night Michael called and insisted that I be at his apartment no later than ten the next morning. We were both cheapo-horror-trash-movie buffs, and some New York channel was showing the cult classic *Carnival of Souls* at that ridiculous hour. I'm glad I went. I saw a truly outstanding movie, listened to a bunch of Stones records for about the billionth time and met Jann Wenner.

Naturally, Jann wanted to get Michael into ROLLING STONE. But since I was already writing reviews for the magazine, he also asked me if I had any feature ideas. By this time we were strolling down Seventh Avenue South, and a shop selling Oriental rugs captured our attention. It reminded me of my imaginary Morocco, and I started barraging Jann with secondhand Jajouka lore. When I told him about hearing the Brian Jones recordings, Jann said: "I'll tell you what. You go over and get that story, and I'll pay you $500 for it."

That was about five times as much as I'd ever been paid for a story. I agreed instantly, right before Jann shelled out several thou for a Persian rug without batting an eye. It didn't occur to me that travel expenses hadn't been mentioned. The deal was $500, period. But even though it was the Seventies, it was still the Sixties, if you know what I mean. This was going to be an adventure.

I booked passage on a Yugoslav freighter. My fellow passengers fell into two groups: hippies running away to Morocco and parents going to Morocco in search of their runaway sons and daughters. This state of affairs made the communal meals somewhat tense, and the freighter's five-ways-to-cook-potatoes cuisine did little to soothe frayed nerves. On the other hand, you could sit right up in the bow of the boat, party all night and watch the sun come up out of the Atlantic. It was, like, spectacular.

Instead of looking up Gysin and going after the story, I ended up traveling south with some hippies from Kansas City. I soon found myself in the walled city of Essaouira, ravaged by dysentery, with a spider bite on my arm that swelled to baseball size. The local doctor, a Foreign Legion veteran who had survived the carnage at Dien Bien Phu, checked my vital signs, lunged for his bag and shot me up with digitalis. "Since there is nothing in your system to counteract the poison, it is making your heart beat quite irregularly," he said cheerfully. "You could die at any moment. If you stay in this hotel, I cannot assume responsibility; I suggest you check into the hospital."

The expatriates around town all told true-life horror stories about the hospital. My companion asked the doctor, "If your wife was in this condition, would you check *her* into the local hospital?" The doctor huffed: "Certainly not! I would put her into my car and drive her to Casablanca." I elected to take my stand amid the echoing stone halls of the Atlantic Hotel. After two weeks of spider venom and no food or drink other than water, I noticed I was still alive and caught the train for Tangier.

This was the fabled Marrakech Express, but it wasn't exactly what it was cracked up to be. It stopped in every outpost and often, for no apparent reason, in the middle of nowhere. My first night on the train I awoke from a fever dream to find the car I was in deserted. The train was sitting—somewhere. All I could see outside was a single halogen light set too far up on a pole to illuminate anything at ground level. All else was darkness. Thinking absently about trying to find something to eat, I stepped down off the train, without seeing or hearing a soul. I walked a few yards into the pitch-black night; as I neared the light pole, I noticed what looked like a dozen pairs of demon eyes coming my way. Before I could decide if I was dreaming, the demon eyes resolved into a pack of wild dogs, all snarling, salivating and bearing down fast. There was something to eat out there after all: me. I made it back to the train, but only just.

In the middle of the second night, the local from hell finally wheezed into Tangier. I got a taxi and headed straight for Gysin's. He was hospitable and charming and lived conveniently near the city's all-night pharmacy. Before long I was back on my feet and listening to Gysin's own unadulterated tapes of the Master Musicians. The double-reed horns set up a buzzing field of harmonics, and the drumming sounded like an earthquake. Before long, I was ready to go.

The article excerpted here, filed from Tangier, gave me a feeling of accomplishment and, eventually, the $500. But my involvement with the Master Musicians was just beginning. The ancient moon-goddess/horned-god religion of the Mediterranean basin wasn't just *celebrated* in Jajouka, it was *alive,* and it drew me. I returned a few months later and spent some time, studying the traditional music and the magic of the old souls there. In 1973, I returned again in the company of saxophonist Ornette Coleman. We recorded a so-far-unreleased album at the height of the Pan festival, with the screaming and shrilling of hundreds of hill tribesmen in trance overlaying the elemental ritual music.

After a 1988 visit I wrote "Into the Mystic" (RS 548), an article recounting trance experiences, light visions, strange nights in high-mountain Phoenician temple ruins and running with Bou Jeloud—the village's Pan—through the mad riot of the Rites. "You sent them *that?*" my friends asked incredulously after reading the manuscript. "Nobody will ever believe this stuff. You think they're going to *publish* this?" To my surprise, the editors told me they loved it; they paid me more than $500 for it, too.

It does seem curious—though not by Jajouka standards—that this article is resurfacing now. Bill Laswell recently released *Apocalypse Across the Sky,* a splendid album featuring the Master Musicians, on his Axiom label. Bachir Attar, son of Chief Jnuin, who taught me much in the Seventies, led a Jajouka contingent on "Continental Drift," a track on the Stones' *Steel Wheels;* a fanfare from the track introduced shows on the *Steel Wheels* tour. The Tangier expatriate scene has inspired a number of recent movies (*The Sheltering Sky, Naked Lunch*) and books (Michelle Green's *Dream at the End of the World,* Stephen Davis's *Jajouka Rolling Stone*). You can call this synchronicity or happenstance; I call it that old Jajouka magic. I have only one question: When do I get to go back?

RS 93

OCTOBER 14TH, 1971

Hamri, the painter, went up the mountain to the village of Jajouka because he had family there. Hamri took Brion Gysin up the mountain and Gysin wrote about it in *The Process.* Gysin took William Burroughs up the mountain, and Burroughs described it in *The Ticket That Exploded.* Brian Jones heard Gysin's tapes of the Master Musicians of Jajouka and went up the mountain with a Uher and a recording engineer. He heard half the music and made a tape that is now a record; but that isn't half the story.

We went bouncing up the mountain in a VW with Sanche and Nancy de Gramont and their son Gabriel, out of the Tangier afternoon and south along Morocco's Atlantic coast, where cattle and sheep graze down to the ocean's edge and cork forests crowd the roadside. Turned inland at La-rache, blank bungalow siestas, dusty streets with children and dogs, had left the paved road at Ksar-el Kebir, squatting on a hill, white-walled and old with Coca-Cola signs.

From there the narrow cowpath of a road climbs steeply into dramatic green hills and broad expanses of tall grass, past lean-to settlements walled with dried reeds and sudden vistas opening off into the beginnings of the Rif. Nearing the end of the road, the crown of a great hill, we came to the outskirts of Jajouka; houses of mud, plaster and polished dung; roofs made of thatching and corrugated tin; tents pitched among the houses and, off to one side, the red and white carcass of a freshly-killed cow being hacked to pieces a few yards from the tomb of the saint.

The remains of Saint Sidi Hamid Sherk, who introduced Islam to the region sometime around the year 800, give Jajouka a moral authority unquestioned, until recently, by the people of the neighboring villages. This authority is expressed, and sustained, by Jajouka's Master Musicians, the sons of sons of sons of musicians, who play to exorcise the illnesses of pilgrims, to reaffirm the identity of villagers and visitors at festival and feast times, and to entertain and instruct their listeners and themselves, wafting their time-seasoned melodies and handed-down rhythms out across the Jebel on clouds of kif smoke. Hamri says the musicians "want all time play and smoke kif, smoke kif and play," but the sound we drove into our first afternoon in Jajouka was the buzz of hill families gathered for Miloud, amid the smoky smell of sizzling mutton and calves' liver.

So we downshifted through the haphazard houses and tents, into laugh-ing curious crowds and up across the wide, grassy summit of the hill. Just below the summit, we stopped before a lone, white building, two big rooms and a long, tin-roofed front porch: the "school," lodge and living quarters for the musicians. Took a few tentative steps out of the car and spun around in a circle, open space and open sky rushing away into all the degrees of distance, elliptical mountains, rolling fields, valley villages and enormous trees; nothing flat, only heights and depths.

Hamri welcomed us and we went walking across the green and down into the village, attended by a hundred children: sly little boys in brown djellabas and giggling girls in costumes, wide-eyed at my red beard, too excited to keep a respectful distance. The adults studied us with welcom-ing eyes as we walked among the tents, past baskets of almonds, currants, and spun sugar confections until finally, overwhelmed, we sat on a rock in the middle of the surge and the sunlight, utter strangers utterly at home.

"The Mother Ship," was all I could say, "the Mother Ship."

Back at the "school," Hamri was holding court, attended by the coming

and going of musicians, a few of them young, most of them old, all identifiable by the brown djellabas and white turbans that serve as all-purpose
clothing and uniforms. Some of the musicians were preparing mint tea,
cleaning up scraps from lunch, or helping Hamri hang a goat's carcass
from the eaves. The rest sat in groups, talking softly and smoking their
long sebsis, which they filled from pouches made of sheep's bladders, while
Hamri set to work stripping off the goat's meat with his bare hands. We
eased into a corner and looked off into the approaching evening while I
played back, in my mind's ear, selections from the background Brion Gysin
had given us the night before:

"The musicians have papers from the Alaouite Sultans, who came to
power about the same time as Louis XIV in France and Charles II in
England. The text of these, written by a royal chamberlain or official
scribe, addresses them with extraordinary respect, and acknowledges that
they have rights over the Sultan: the right to play him to bed, to play him
to the mosque on Fridays, rights for a group to live in the Palace, and so
forth. Two musicians who are still alive remember being at the court of
the Sultan Moulay Hafid, who was Sultan in Marrakech when his brother
was Sultan in Fez.

"This all broke up with the French occupation in 1912. A pirate called
Raisouli, who set himself up as a would-be Sultan, treated the musicians
of Jajouka royally while he lasted; it was very good for his publicity to
have them. In the Twenties he paid them a hundred dollars a month apiece,
which was a huge sum of money in those days. But then Raisouli was
busted by the Spaniards.

"The Spaniards looked after these things in some ways better than the
French did; they had much more understanding of it, because it's so mixed
up with their own music, their own cultural history. What the music is, in
fact, is the popularization of the classical music that was written around
the ninth, tenth century in Andalusia, court music at the courts of Cordova
and Seville. Around 1492, there was a big expulsion of the Moors from
southern Spain, and a great many of those people settled back in the hills
at that time. The Spaniards were fairly good to those up in Jajouka; they
were allowed to collect a tithe on all of the neighboring villages, who
acknowledged the moral authority of the saint buried in Jajouka. The
musicians would simply travel around to the fields at harvest time, and
people would give them a measure of whatever it was they were harvesting.

"Now the political development of the music in all the countries has
been that, as soon as a nationalist revolution is successful, they immediately want to put down their own music; to get out of their old clothes,
and get into levis. Here, at the moment of Independence in 1956, there
were enormous parades with the entire population streaming through the
streets for several weeks on end. They were beating up any Moroccan

musicians who even dared to make a squeak and started huge samba lines shouting. 'The samba and the rhumba are the national music of New Morocco.'

"All musicians who were caught were taken away and put in concentration camps, along with all the whores who were caught; they were going to be settled down and taught useful handicrafts. Music came back because of the tourist boom, but still . . . last August, September at harvest time the musicians from Jajouka had fights with people, who stoned them when they came to the fields to ask for their tithe.

"Hamri's been most anxious to try and get these things reestablished by the government, but the government just doesn't want to hear about such things anymore. In fact, the really shocking thing is that every one of the musicians up in Jajouka is taxed for his instrument, something like six dollars a year, and his total yearly income isn't more than ten dollars in cash. There was no future at all visible a couple of years ago, when Hamri really rooted around and I gave them money for what he calls the 'school.' They have a place to hang out and meet regularly, and they have a group of young kids who come and learn all the drumming rhythms. So something is going on. Still, it's a terrible scramble."

I awoke from a nap in the darkened school. A bonfire was beginning to crackle outside. "Get the Uher quick," Sanche said. A gigantic sound rent the air. Lining the rock wall that runs across the hill's summit were 15 rhaita players—rhaita is a kind of oboe, a double reed horn with a flared bell—playing a ringing fanfare in outlandish harmony. At right angles to the farthest rhaita player a line of five drummers beat out an incantatory counterpoint. The sound of the band, as I set up the taping equipment in the firelight, was an immense presence louder than any amplifier, filling the hilltop like an amphitheater. The rhaitas shrilled simultaneously into a shrieking falsetto register that seemed to trail off into dog-whistle frequencies and sounded like thousands of Arab women screaming, "yuyuyuyuyu."

The musicians call this opening piece the "Kaimonos." It begins as a slow processional march, with the horns phrasing freely over an almost quizzical rhythm, and then accelerates, the rhaitas building kinetic phrases to a pitch of hysteria that signals the arrival of Bou Jeloud. Bou Jeloud means "the Father of Skins"; Gysin has identified him further as "the Father of Fear"; he is none other than a continuing survival of the Horned God of antiquity, the goat-god, Pan.

When Marc Antony, dressed in animal skins, ran the race of the Lupercal in Rome, Caesar asked him to strike his barren wife Calpurnia, as he ran. Bou Jeloud dances in Jajouka today sewn naked into the skin of a freshly-slaughtered goat, a huge straw hat tied over his ears, his hands, face and feet blackened with charcoal, and it is said that the women he flails with his two leafy switches become pregnant within a year.

"Bou Jeloud is always taboo," says Gysin. "The boy who dances Bou Jeloud just automatically never comes and sits down and shares the kif pipe with other people, or when they're sitting around the tray of tea, he's always sitting ten feet away. Slimou, the boy who's been dancing him these last few years, is a very wild creature. He never comes into a house, not even the musicians' house, he just comes under the porch, sits on the very edge of the circle of people."

When Slimou isn't dancing, he often seems to vanish; occasionally you can spot him, far off down the hillside, meandering along with a herd of goats. He appeared out of the darkness one night in Jajouka, while I was rummaging in the back seat of the VW, and in halting French bummed a cigarette, disappearing with it into the blackness outside the perimeter of firelight.

When he leaps into the circle of celebrants, half-man and half-goat in the half-light, Slimou is no longer Slimou; he is Bou Jeloud. He stands before the row of rhaita players, his entire body vibrating with the energy of their music, drinking up the concentrated force of ancient pandemonium and feeding it back into a pyramiding intensity that wants to send the hilltop spinning off into space. The musicians respond with a new propulsive phrase that catapults him across the grass and through the bonfire, attacking men, women, and children with his sapling arms. The crowd scatters before his lunges, screaming their own counterpoint to the antiphonal interplay of drums and rhaitas.

The head piper leads the horns into a blaring announcement of Aisha Hamouka, "Crazy Aisha," a personage so powerful she must be danced by a crowd of little boys dressed as women. The villagers say that Bou Jeloud was enticed to Jajouka by promises of prolific sex, but that Crazy Aisha was always there, dancing in the trees.

"Sounds a lot like the Bacchae and other such ladies who danced around an oak tree," says Gysin. "Hamouka, that's the same word as amok. It's thought that in Punic maybe Aisha is Asharat, or Astarte." Whoever she is, Bou Jeloud flails her into frightened parts; we can hear the saplings connecting with their bodies from across the field.

The musicians have been wailing nonstop for an hour and a half with a controlled abandon that raises questions about the limits and force of human breath. At any given moment two of the horn players are laying out, drawing on their sebsis. When they finish the pipe, they spit the coal onto the ground and roar back into the melee, giving two others the chance to lay out for a smoke. They phrase together in section, trade patterns between sections, and then rise together into that piercing, high-mountain unison, fingers sliding up and down the horns quicker than the eye can follow.

The chief drummer, unable to contain himself, dances into the circle, strutting and prancing and whirling around and around without missing a beat on his drum. Both he and Bou Jeloud make rushing approaches at our little enclave on the porch, the drummer smiling and inviting us to the dance, Bou Jeloud growling and grimacing, a wild animal battering ram storming the doors of our Europeanness.

Suddenly, the pipers fall into a single held tone and the drums rumble and roar to the climax; they stop on a dime, seconds before the end of my reel of tape. Gabriel de Gramont, age 7, has been looking from the dancers to the musicians to the Uher and back again. "The tape recorder has a very good memory," he says, as the musicians drift down to the house and the temporarily spent crowd disperses. "It remembers everything it hears and tells it back to you whenever you want. But it's too bad it doesn't have any eyes."

There is something special about the chief drummer, who teaches the rhythms to dancers and drummers alike, some extra-linguistic communication line that is reading me loud and clear. After the evening meal, when most of the musicians have left to play Bou Jeloud out into the thickets and between the cottages in the village proper, the head drummer, the head piper, and two of the other musicians stay behind to play for Hamri and for us at the house, with cane flutes, taut skins, and a dancing boy. Some part of my mind is wondering, as they play, how the pipers can hold tones for so long, since they aren't doing the cheek-puffing, Roland Kirk-style circular breathing routine I've seen reed players in Marrakech using, but my body is far from any such considerations. I'm weaving and bobbing to the music, the flutes floating free over a piledriver 6/8 rhythm straight down from remotest Near Eastern antiquity, and the drummers shouting "Aiwa" — "Everything's groovy."

The chief drummer suddenly drops his drum, jumps into our little circle, and dances right over to the space I am shaking, smiling broad as a river and flashing deep eye contact, vibrating saucer sightings back to Elijah's Air Force: The Mother Ship. After the music he says to me through Hamri, "Sometimes the musicians cannot play together; is the same music, the same musicians, but sometimes is apart. Then sometimes is all together, all playing and going high, high . . . Tonight I see you with the music, I see you in the rhythm. I know you are a musician." I am found out, I am recognized, and I can see that putting away the tape recorder and getting out my horn is the only way I am going to get *this* show on the road.

Whatever vibrations Brian Jones may have felt his one night in Jajouka, we know that he spent the next few weeks in Tangier, listening and relistening to his tapes, finding his way in the music. He heard it running forwards, he heard it running backwards, he heard it overlaid upon itself, and he recreated his multi-directional hearing with considerable expertise

in a London studio. Since he visited Jajouka at an off-time, between festivals and full moons, he heard only a few pieces which a small group of
musicians played especially for him: parts of the "Kaimonos"; parts of
Bou Jeloud's music and none of Crazy Aisha's; plus some of the inter-
planetary after-dinner music performed with flutes and one or two drums.
He added to what he heard with a backward drum track here, a backward
melody there, an electronic undercurrent that suggests the menace of the
darkness outside the circle of firelight. The basis of the unusual stereo
effects achieved was the positioning of the recording engineer, who stood
with his Uher 4400 in the center of the musicians, crossing his two microphones in one hand while they marched around him in a revolving
figure 8.

Jajouka, the first commercial recording of the Master Musicians (to be
released by Rolling Stones Records), thus emerges as a kind of hybrid, a
melange of funky hill music and sophisticated studio techniques. A note
from Brian Jones on his reasons for making the album is included in the
package, which an anecdote from Brion Gysin may help clarify:

"We were sitting on the ground with Brian, under the very low eaves
of this thatched farm house, and the musicians were working just four or
five feet away, ahead of us in the courtyard where the animals usually are.
It was getting to be time to eat, and suddenly two of the musicians came
along with a snow-white goat. The goat disappeared off into the shadows
with the two musicians, one of whom was holding a long knife which Brian
suddenly caught the glitter of, and he started to get up, making a sort of
funny noise, and he said, 'That's me!' And everybody picked up on it right
at once and said, yeah right, it looks just like you. It was perfectly true,
he had this fringe of blond hair hanging right down in front of his eyes,
and we said, of course that's you. Then about twenty minutes later we
were eating this goat's liver on shish-kebab sticks."

Hamri, who contributed a cover painting to the *Jajouka* LP, hoped it
would help the musicians out of their present dilemma, but so far this has
not been the case. (Trevor Churchill, of Rolling Stones Records, contacted
by telephone late in May, said, "We probably wouldn't be paying royalties
directly to the musicians because the LP came to us through Brian Jones'
estate.")

Meanwhile, many of Jajouka's finest young musicians have already left
to work at industrial jobs in the cities. The musicians have always been an
aristocratic group—Arabic rather than Berber-speaking, set apart from
the majority of the villagers. They share the family surname Attar, which
means "the perfume maker." The name belonged to a well-known Persian
poet of the 13th century, and is a password in Sufism implying the divine
essence. According to Gysin, "at certain moments of mystical experience
induced by music, instead of hearing you smell this divine perfume."

Only the son of a Master Musician can become a Master Musician, and considerable esoteric knowledge is doubtless passed on along with musical secrets, but mystic masters are rarely breadwinners in the American Century, and though Hamri, Gysin, and other friends of the community have ideas for survival procedures, ranging from sending the musicians on concert tours to turning Jajouka into a sort of overnight theater, the practical choices are limited.

With more and more pop musicians wandering about Morocco, the irresistible rhythms and sounds of the cannabis culture bid fair to become a major musical influence during the next few years, but no one is sure how this will affect Moroccan musicians.

The Moroccan government's belated recognition of the wealth and diversity of native musical folklore has resulted in their sponsorship of an annual Moroccan Folklore Festival, a mixed blessing. Held in Marrakesh, the festival attracts a number of tourists and music lovers and gives numerous groups a week's work, but each group is allowed only five minutes on stage. In this competitive atmosphere, with only the best received groups coming back night after night, the crowd-pleasing techniques of the most popular performers are quickly adopted by groups from other regions. Consequently, the power and depth of the music and dancing, its intimate connection with the earth and the local culture is being plasticized into a sort of Ed Sullivan common denominator.

Whether because of a long-standing North-South rivalry or religious-political reservations, the musicians from Jajouka have yet to appear in the Festival, now in its tenth year. Interested parties in Tangier are plotting a rival festival using northern groups who haven't been invited to Marrakech, but even half a dozen festivals will scarcely support the countless musicians who are being replaced by radio and television programming aimed at an urban, essentially rootless and "Europeanized" population.

The Jamaa-el-F'na, the great public square of Marrakech, offers musicians and dancers a stage of sorts the year round, and troupes of drummers and dancing boys, rhaita virtuosos, and small bands made up of gimbris, violins, rebabs, and hand drums are playing strong, exciting music there almost any sunny day, competing for the crowd's attention with tricksters, clowns, whores, short-change artists, magicians and beggars, some broadcasting their spiels through portable P.A.s powered by auto batteries. Lined with merchants in tiny stalls selling everything from clothes to household utensils to endless piles of sebsis and hookahs, the Jamaa-el-F'na is the tourist's Mecca, but admission is free and only the most determined dancing boy can squeeze enough pennies out of a besieged crowd to pay for a trip down from the hills and back.

Many groups that were once towers of power fold up under the barrage, splintering and then disbanding as the players marry Europeans, take menial jobs, drift back to the country, or drown in the shark-infested hustle. New groups come to take their place, the tourists disappear, replaced by ragged hippies left over from the summer influx, and the cycle repeats itself.

Many of the groups that are holding together are connected with one or another of Morocco's musical brotherhoods, mysterious organizations whose origins, rituals, and other secrets are as inaccessible to outsiders as the sources of power that lie just under the surface in Jajouka. All anyone seems to know about these brotherhoods is that each has its own peculiar rhythm, and that each of these rhythms produces trance.

Many members of brotherhoods think of themselves as doctors who happen to be using music rather than pills to effect their cures, and devotees say they awake the morning after a night of trance-dancing refreshed and rested in body and soul. A person in a trance may do almost anything: jump ten feet in the air, speak in animal languages, walk on red hot coals, cut or otherwise mutilate himself. An extreme case is the devotees of the Hamadcha brotherhood, centering in the region around Meknes, who chop fissures into their own skulls with small axes, but these and other trance-induced wounds heal with a rapidity that baffles European physicians.

Why do certain rhythms produce trance states? There are no real answers, only clues. In a rural, tribal life, babies are liable to hear the rhythms, and sense their parents' reactions, even in a pre-natal state. A Moroccan from Tafraouet told us that those who fall into trance most easily often were cured of a childhood fever by musicians from the local brotherhood. Still, there are a growing number of new converts, many of whom were never exposed to the music during childhood. These new devotees join a particular brotherhood by ear; according to Gysin, "One day you hear the music and you start to dance, and then you know that you belong to that brotherhood. You dance until you can't stop and then, when you've passed out and been brought around again, you realize that you've established a contract with them for life." Paul Bowles notes that all trance rhythms are polyrhythmic and/or polymetric, and Gysin has suggested that these rhythms play back and forth on the alpha-wave rhythms of the brain. No clear-cut conclusions are possible.

The most public, and currently popular, of the musical brotherhoods is the G'naoua. G'naoua musicians are usually black, as opposed to the lighter Arab and Berber people who make up the plurality of Morocco's population. Their following is largest because their rhythm is both irresistible and easily accessible to native and westerner alike.

One G'naoua troupe toured the United States several years ago and this troupe, composed of drummers and of dancers who play qarqaba (dumbell-shaped pieces of iron that maintain a clacking, metallic rhythm), tears up the Marrakech Festival every year, storming onstage for five minutes of sheer ecstatic insanity, sandwiched between elaborately costumed but static processionals and abstractly folksy courtship dances. Other G'naoua groups sometimes employ the gimbri (a three-stringed lute, often with a tortoise-shell resonator) for more intimate gatherings, and these groups often work "G'naoua parties," given by visiting freaks or hippies-in-residence in towns like Essaouira, Marrakech, or even Tangier.

We attended one G'naoua party, in the tiled courtyard of an old Portugese house in Essaouira. A young gimbri player, two drummers, and several hand-clapping devotees made up the G'naoua contingent, together with a 13-year-old dancing boy high on LSD. Pipes passed around the circle, the conversation welled up and subsided, and then the gimbri player hit a handful of notes, establishing an eternal-sounding pattern like the bass riffs that introduce a Pharoah Sanders record.

The drummers and handclappers locked into the pattern, and they were off for an hour or more with the dancing boy gliding around the room, his hand gestures turning to animals and birds on the candle-lit walls. The music had no melody, no harmony, neither theme nor variation, no beginning and no ending. It traveled down a straight, narrow, infinitely continuous road, and we traveled with it, spacing into the drone and out of time. The "monotony" established a hypnotic effect, as it does in much Moroccan music, so that each slight shift in emphasis, and each change in the drum and gimbri patterns, caused parallel shifts in planes of consciousness, amplified by the absence of distracting surface decoration. The devotees fell to their knees, rolling their heads about wildly at the feet of the drummers, the dancing boy whirled around the circle, his feet barely touching the floor, and while nobody went into trance (a definite experiential state that takes hours to complete and must be played on through to unconsciousness, at the risk of psychic damage to the ecstatic should the music end prematurely), a good time was had by all.

Tangier, of course, is an old hand at trance-dancing parties and stoned-out cultural interchanges, moody old whore of a Scorpio city with as many psychic ups-and-downs as hills. The city's expatriate colony includes several Americans whose vast, though largely unpublished, knowledge of Moroccan music comes from years of first-hand experience. There is Randy Weston, genial giant jazz pianist with numerous African musical acquaintances, whose African Rhythms Club is a sort of Tangier equivalent to the Village Vanguard. There is Paul Bowles, author of *The Sheltering Sky, A Hundred Camels in the Courtyard*, and numerous other books, and a trained composer/musician as well. Bowles recorded the Library of Congress collection of Moroccan music, and his tape library, which lines the walls of his apartment near the US Consulate three reels deep, contains extensive samplings of music from every corner of North Africa. He was generous with musical information, recorded examples, and explanations shot through with his remarkable, intuitive intelligence, but Brion Gysin, who first came to North Africa with Bowles in 1937, was our one-man crash course, filling our heads with sounds from his own tape library and telescoping his 20 years of field recording and speculation into a few intensive weeks of talking and listening.

The tragedy of the Tangier scene is that its comprehensive collective knowledge sits, for the most part, on shelves or in drawers, wrapped in layers of plastic to ward off dampness and decay. Gysin and Bowles played us samplings of the hill music of the Jebel, with its gimbris, lutes, flutes, and violins; of the rebab players of the south, who saw at their banjo-like instruments with a short bow; of the wailing, nasal vocal music, accompanied by gimbri or lute and common to all Islam; of monastic choirs from the high Atlas, overpowering drumming cadres from the Sahara, and the drum-dominated trance music of each of the Moroccan brotherhoods. There are the twisting, winding rhythms of the Aissaoua, who subjectively become snakes when far into the trance state; the Hadaoua, who spice their kinetic drumming with a dash of theater and smoke enormous amounts of kif; the D'kaoua, who dance and breathe together in the Sufi way, stomping and repeatedly shouting *Allah! Allah!* until they fall unconscious; and the previously mentioned G'naoua and Hamadcha.

Of all the brotherhoods, only Jilala, who are numerous in and around Tangier, have been commercially recorded. The album *Jilala,* issued a few years ago in a limited pressing under the Trance Records logo, is poorly balanced, and the group included a G'naoua infiltrator whose qarqaba is foreign to Jilala music and works at cross-purposes to the predominating rhythmic thrust. The album cover confounds the confusion; it depicts a group of Hamadcha streaming down a hillside.

The tapes painstakingly recorded over the years by collectors like Bowles, Gysin, Christopher Wanklyn, and others are more valuable than ever today, with the continuing dearth of commercially available recordings, the breaking up of traditional Moroccan cultural patterns, and the concurrent splintering and adulterating of musical groups and styles. The earliest of these tapes are already beginning to decompose, but the painters, writers, musicians, and other artists who recorded them are neither equipped for nor inclined toward the kind of painstaking study, systematization, and preservation that is necessary if the Moroccan musical legacy is to survive intact.

Meanwhile, far off in the hills that ring Tangier from the coastline to the bay, the Master Musicians of Jajouka play their rhaitas, flutes, and drums, smoke their kif, guard their chain of secret knowledge unbroken since pagan times, and wonder about their luck and their future. Change is in the air, as more and more outsiders step through their space-time doorway and their legend grows, but their friends wonder, while they think and talk and work toward the community's survival, whether concert tours or tourist invasions will undermine the music's roots in the hill country, whether culture shock will paralyze the music's strength and growth as surely as the starvation that seems to be the only other alternative.

I am wondering now, on the road back down the mountain, what part, if any, I am playing in this karmic cycle. Sunlight is pouring down, like the energy that poured into me when the musicians played and I played and we fell through each other, weightless, into the sky. Our VW passes groups of villagers, returning homeward from the feast and stopping here and there along the road to look off into the hills.

The music lingers in their bodies and in each synapse of their minds, spreading its ripples across the meanest particles of matter, and each ripple vibrates the shape of the Mother Ship that landed on the mountain ages ago, disgorging Bou Jeloud and the first of the Master Musicians, shutting down its motors and waiting, overgrown with foliage and trees and layers of dung and earth, losing its shape in the gentle rising oval of the hilltop. When the last of the Master Musicians dies and the last Musician's son moves on to find work in new industries or to hustle new jungle streets, that Mother Ship is going to come to life with a low, barely perceptible hum, increasing in volume and in force until she soars off into the void with Crazy Aisha dancing like mad around the deck and Bou Jeloud at the controls.

Fear and Loathing in Las Vegas

HUNTER S. THOMPSON

A SAVAGE RETURN TO THE HEART OF THE AMERICAN
DREAM . . . A LOST MEMO FROM THE WRONG DESK . . .
WARM AND DRY AT THE BATES MOTEL . . . THE MEANING
OF MY ART.

MEMO FROM THE NATIONAL AFFAIRS DESK
TO: *Bob Love*
FROM: *HST*
SUBJECT: *Rolling Stone 25th Anniversary Issue/Book*

Dear Bob,
I WAS TOUCHED by the witless innocence of your recent
query in re: MORBID FLASHBACKS, STRANGE MEM-
ORIES AND OTHER TIMELESS CLASSICS FROM
THE VAULTS OF 'ROLLING STONE' ($666, Leather
bound, Limited Edition, two pounds)

Jesus! I can almost *feel* the slab-like little fucker in my
hands right now, like a Spanish-leather tombstone. Impreg-
nate the leather with some kind of oily Essence of Blood that

will seem to glow and emit a dank scent if left too long in the sun.

Get it, Bobby? That is the smell of *burning blood!* Hell *yes,* it is! And it's *our* blood, Bob. We know that goddamn smell, don't we?

Whoops . . . Maybe not, eh?

This story I wrote about Las Vegas went to press twenty (*twenty*) years ago, Bobby. *Twenty years.* That's a long time. Twenty years is a *generation* in Politics.

Jesus, Bob. You're just a kid. No wonder you act nervous when you have to ask me what it was like to "work" for ROLLING STONE back then. . . . Of course! How could you know? You were *not there.* You were *another person,* a child. . . .

Please forgive me, Bob, for my rude presumption vis-à-vis your personal knowledge or memory of what it feels like to suddenly and unexpectedly recognize the smell of your *own blood* in the air of a summer afternoon twenty years later.

Weird, eh? Yeah . . . Especially if it's coming from a goddamn *book* . . . Naw. That *could* happen, but it would be wrong. . . .

Wrong. That is the word. That is what it was like to work for ROLLING STONE twenty years ago. . . . It was Wrong. Or at least it looked that way. Yeah. It *seemed* Wrong, and that was the terrible Joy of it. . . . Hell, on some days you could even *get paid* for being Wrong. And let me *tell* you, Bobby—that was *serious* Fun. (See attached Exhibit 1/Vegas, 1972.)

You will never know that elegant feeling, Bob. Because now it is Right to work for ROLLING STONE. . . . Hell, I worked as hard for ROLLING STONE as I ever did in my life, before or since. . . . (Well, shucks . . . like the *New York Times* says, some things are *not* Fit to Print—and this may be one of them.) There is an ancient Chinese curse that says, *"May you live in Interesting times."* This is an *interesting subject.* . . .

Indeed. And I understand that your hobby, Bob, is *alchemy.* Which is wonderful. It must be a lot of Fun—especially when you get into that business of turning lead into gold. (Ho, ho . . . Real Magic, right?) Hell, turning lead into gold is a king-hell serious *trick.* Damn few people can do it, and I'm sure as hell not one of them. . . .

But try *this* for fun, Bobby. I learned to turn Wrong into
Right. . . . Hot damn! How's *that* for a trick?

Like a candle in the wind
Like a lizard in the limelight
They snuffed you out forever
  —F.X. LEACH,
     1971, HOLLYWOOD

You probably don't remember *Leach,* either. Do you? Fuck
no, you don't. You probably don't even remember Marilyn
Monroe. . . . You're like a goddamn *newt,* Bobby. You have a
one-cell brain . . . (which is not *technically* a crime) and believe
me, I'm proud of you for the way you can actually *handle*
yourself and act normal when we work together. . . . Hell, the
only difference between us, Bob, is that I'm crazy and you're
dumb.

But so what? It's only a Generation Gap. No fault of your
own . . . Fuck these people. They are trying to drive a wedge
between us.

They hate us because we are *happy* when we work, and
they're *not.* . . . No. They are not like us, Bob. They are not
immersed in Art like we are. They are Hyenas. They *like* the
smell of blood . . . and you can bet they got plenty of blood
from Marilyn, just like they expect to get plenty from You
and from Me.

Why is it, Bob, that these days all of our highest and finest
stories seem to involve *blood?* It has always been that way for
me—especially back then, in the early days, when almost
everything was so painful that finally you couldn't stand it
anymore, and that's why we had to do drugs.

I remember one particularly ugly night down there in
Jann's basement in Ord Court when we got so excited about
the Salazar story that we stabbed each other with scissors and
locked Jane in the garage with a pack of mongrel dogs.

There was plenty of blood in the Salazar story. The pigs
blew Salazar's head off on a dead-end street in East L.A., and
then they tried to kill me, too. What the hell, if you didn't
bleed on the story, it wasn't worth doing. We believed it back
then. . . . Our operative ethic was the law of irreversible
mutation.

MEMOS FROM
THE WRONG DESK — 1992

*Even a man who's pure at heart and says his prayers by night may
become a wolf when the wolfsbane blooms and the moon is full and
bright.*
                    — 'FRANKENSTEIN MEETS THE WOLF MAN'

*What shall it profit a man, if he shall gain the whole world, and
lose his own soul?*
                                              — MARK 8:36

*The Past belongs to the Living
The Future belongs to the Dead.*
    — F.X. LEACH
        1992, SAN FRANCISCO

I have always encouraged the reader to approach and *meet* my
Work, as it were, from the outside to the inside (as in a zoom
lens, or a neon sign, like the friendly WELCOME at the foot
of the driveway up the hill to the Bates Motel . . .). It looks
very inviting — indeed, very warm and dry and somehow
Comforting — at that hour of the night, in a rainstorm. . . .
    Ah, yes. We will know, soon enough, about Norman. . . .
He is weird, but friendly. Right. *"Thank God for the Bates
Motel, honey, we were almost out of gas."*
    Norman was a sot and a Sadist, a flesh-slitting crazy psy-
chotic who stabbed huge puncture wounds in the backs and
brains of his victims — (*repeatedly,* by *surprise,* from *behind*) —
and then sucked out their brains, in a frenzy.
    Why? Who knows why? He was Criminally Insane. . . .
    Norman was Wrong, deeply wrong — But so what? He was
good at his work, and he enjoyed it. He was *successful* at it, in
the main — despite his serious handicap. He killed for his
Mother, they said, and who can blame him for that? Hell, it
was Norman who said, "A boy's best friend is his mother."
    That was what it all meant, to Norman. . . . Yet, he *killed,*
like a Monster — stabbing *repeatedly,* through the cheap
shower curtain, over and over again — without soiling his reputation as a fine Innkeeper. Because he continued to lure them
in. Strangers *flocked* to his place — especially on cold and rainy
nights.
    Because he had the best Front Door in the business, and
his business was luring them in. . . . "They said his place

looked like Home," a rival innkeeper explained. It was eerie. He was worse than Dracula, but he did a bang hell of a lot of business! Because he was friendly, and he stayed up late, and people *smiled* when he called them "cousin" and gave them Refuge from the Storm, when it was late at night and they needed him.

Which was often. And he often met their needs. Not *all* were found stabbed to death thru the eyeballs from behind. Not *all* were thieves and fornicators. Not *all* were lewd and Stark Naked doing the Wild Thing all by themselves in a steamy, cheap tin shower stall at midnight in a thunderstorm somewhere on the outskirts of Needles. . . .

Hell *no*. What kind of person is that?

We may *crawl*, Bob, but we will never get as low as that . . . and certainly not in the public pages of a slick-paper magazine that publishes my Work(s). No. We could do that—but it would be Wrong.

Or maybe Fun, on some days . . . And that is the Tragedy of it. That is the business we have chosen.

To wit: We *must* come face to face with the terrible Fact that there is a Brutal, Overweening *violence* somewhere near the Core of my Work(s), which the first-time reader should not necessarily be forced to embrace and confront *all at once.* . . . Or at least not *immediately*. No. Not everybody is comfortable on this plane.

That is the *art*. That is the Crystalized Vision. I am only the medium, the channel, a human lightning rod for all the smoking, homeless visions and the horrible Acid flashbacks of a whole Generation—which are *precious*, if only as Living, Savage *monuments* to a dream that haunts us all.

In our secret dreams, we were brutes. We wallowed in Murder and Sodomy. . . . But we also wallowed in Beauty, and we knew that Beauty was Truth. Even when it fried you to a cinder or blew off the top of your Head . . . and we still live in fear of these flashbacks, which come in the night without warning and cause us to scream in our sleep.

Art is long and Life is short, and success is very far off. . . . Joe Conrad said that, and he suffered more grievous flashbacks on any given Sunday than most men will know all their lives.

I, too, am haunted by visions cruel and splintered and primitive—but I have no choice. They are *graven images,* foul outbursts of madness and brainless violence that will always remain Unspeakable, unless we make it Art. . . .

Or Music. Or Bombs. Or anything else that blows up or burns or explodes in a meaningless fireball . . . Until we give it the Dignity of Resurrection, the Shock of Recognition and the wondrous glow of Love . . .

When the going gets Weird, the Weird turn pro. That is the Dogma. That is all Ye know, and all Ye need to know.

Take it from me. I understand these things.

Owl Farm
February 7th

Dear Jann,

Thanks for helping me put the whack on those flaky suck-fish bastards up in New Hampshire. They had hoped to exploit me, for all the wrong reasons. There is no money available for the *fun fringe* on the Campaign Trail these days. They have cut back to Basics. Like Whores, etc. . . . What the hell? It's the Nineties.

Anyway, here's the lead for my Vegas Excerpt intro. This is the first three (3) of seven (7) very dense, legal-length pages—*about 1700 words, so far.* I can have it finished and camera-ready by Sundown, your time tomorrow, January 31st.

Just in time, eh? Right on schedule. Hot damn.

Meanwhile, I need $5000 today. . . . Or let's say my banker needs it. There are indications of a vacuum in my personal account, he says—strange sucking sounds when he tries to feed my outstanding checks into it. . . .

Probably a quick wire transfer would be best. That will impress the brute. He gets edgy when he can't hear the constant hum of the Revenue Stream, just like any other Junkie. . . .

Hell, we *know* these people, Jann. They are *our Creatures.* . . . Yeah. You and Me, Bubba. We *did* it. . . . Christ, how Horrible, eh? On some days I am Haunted by it, and I'm sure you feel the same way. . . .

(Whoops. No more Plagiarism.) Nevermind . . . and thanx in advance for your *expeditious processing of the $5000*—the remainder of which shall be due Sundown tomorrow.

Laughs don't come cheap, these days, do they? . . . Anyway, I think we should put Public Enemy on the cover, right away, as soon as possible. I figure that enemies of Evan Mecham's have to be friends of mine. Okay.

—HST

W e were somewhere around Barstow on the edge of the desert when the drugs began to take hold. I remember saying something like "I feel a bit lightheaded; maybe you should drive. . . ." And suddenly there was a terrible roar all around us and the sky was full of what looked like huge bats, all swooping and screeching and diving around the car, which was going about 100 miles an hour with the top down to Las Vegas. And a voice was screaming: "Holy Jesus! What are these goddamn animals?"

Then it was quiet again. My attorney had taken his shirt off and was pouring beer on his chest, to facilitate the tanning process. "What the hell are you yelling about?" he muttered, staring up at the sun with his eyes closed and covered with wraparound Spanish sunglasses. "Never mind," I said. "It's your turn to drive." I hit the brakes and aimed the Great Red Shark toward the shoulder of the highway. No point mentioning those bats, I thought. The poor bastard will see them soon enough.

It was almost noon, and we still had more than 100 miles to go. They would be tough miles. Very soon, I knew, we would both be completely twisted. But there was no going back, and no time to rest. We would have to ride it out. Press registration for the fabulous Mint 400 was already underway, and we had to get there by four to claim our soundproof suite. A fashionable sporting magazine in New York had taken care of the reservations, along with this huge red Chevy convertible we'd just rented off a lot on the Sunset Strip . . . and I was, after all, a professional journalist; so I had an obligation to *cover the story,* for good or ill.

The sporting editors had also given me $300 in cash, most of which was already spent on extremely dangerous drugs. The trunk of the car looked like a mobile police narcotics lab. We had two bags of grass, 75 pellets of mescaline, five sheets of high-powered blotter acid, a salt shaker half full of cocaine, and a whole galaxy of multi-colored uppers, downers, screamers, laughers . . . and also a quart of tequila, a quart of rum, a case of Budweiser, a pint of raw ether and two dozen amyls.

All this had been rounded up the night before, in a frenzy of high-speed driving all over Los Angeles County—from Topanga to Watts, we picked up everything we could get our hands on. Not that we *needed* all that for the trip, but once you get locked into a serious drug collection, the tendency is to push it as far as you can.

The only thing that really worried me was the ether. There is nothing in the world more helpless and irresponsible and depraved than a man in the depths of an ether binge. And I knew we'd get into that rotten stuff pretty soon. Probably at the next gas station. We had sampled almost everything else, and now—yes, it was time for a long snort of ether. And then do the next 100 miles in a horrible, slobbering sort of spastic stupor. The only way to keep alert on ether is to do up a lot of amyls—not all at once, but steadily, just enough to maintain the focus at 90 miles an hour through Barstow.

"Man, this is the way to travel," said my attorney. He leaned over to turn the volume up on the radio, humming along with the rhythm section and kind of moaning the words: "One toke over the line . . . Sweet Jesus . . . One toke over the line . . ."

One toke? You poor fool! Wait till you see those goddamn bats. I could barely hear the radio . . . slumped over on the far side of the seat, grappling with a tape recorder turned all the way up on "Sympathy for the Devil." That was the only tape we had, so we played it constantly, over and over, as a kind of demented counterpoint to the radio. And also to maintain our rhythm on the road. A constant speed is good for gas mileage—and for some reason that seemed important at the time. Indeed. On a trip like this one *must* be careful about gas consumption. Avoid those quick bursts of acceleration that drag blood to the back of the brain.

My attorney saw the hitchhiker long before I did. "Let's give this boy a lift," he said, and before I could mount any argument he was stopped and this poor Okie kid was running up to the car with a big grin on his face, saying, "Hot damn! I never rode in a convertible before!"

"Is that right?" I said. "Well, I guess you're about ready, eh?"

The kid nodded eagerly as we roared off.

"We're your friends," said my attorney. "We're not like the others."

O Christ, I thought, he's gone around the bend. "No more of that talk," I said sharply. "Or I'll put the leeches on you." He grinned, seeming to understand. Luckily, the noise in the car was so awful—between the wind and the radio and the tape machine—that the kid in the back seat couldn't hear a word we were saying. Or could he?

How long can we *maintain?* I wondered. How long before one of us starts raving and jabbering at this boy? What will he think then? This same lonely desert was the last known home of the Manson family. Will he make that grim connection when my attorney starts screaming about bats and huge manta rays coming down on the car? If so—well, we'll just have to cut his head off and bury him somewhere. Because it goes without saying that we can't turn him loose. He'll report us at once to some kind of outback nazi law enforcement agency, and they'll run us down like dogs.

Jesus! Did I *say* that? Or just think it? Was I talking? Did they hear me? I glanced over at my attorney, but he seemed oblivious—watching the road, driving our Great Red Shark along at a hundred and ten or so. There was no sound from the back seat.

Maybe I'd better have a chat with this boy, I thought. Perhaps if I *explain* things, he'll rest easy.

Of course. I leaned around in the seat and gave him a fine big smile . . . admiring the shape of his skull.

"By the way," I said. "There's one thing you should probably understand."

He stared at me, not blinking. Was he gritting his teeth?

"Can you *hear* me?" I yelled.

He nodded.

"That's good," I said. "Because I want you to know that we're on our way to Las Vegas to find the American Dream." I smiled. "That's why we rented this car. It was the only way to do it. Can you grasp that?"

He nodded again, but his eyes were nervous.

"I want you to have all the background," I said. "Because this is a very ominous assignment—with overtones of extreme personal danger. . . . Hell, I forgot all about this beer; you want one?"

He shook his head.

"How about some ether?" I said.

"What?"

"Never mind. Let's get right to the heart of this thing. You see, about 24 hours ago we were sitting in the Polo Lounge of the Beverly Hills Hotel—in the patio section, of course—and we were just sitting there under this palm tree when this uniformed dwarf came up to me with a pink telephone and said, 'This must be the call you've been waiting for all this time, sir.' "

I laughed and ripped open a beer can that foamed all over the back seat while I kept talking. "And you know? He was right! I'd been *expecting* that call, but I didn't know who it would come from. Do you follow me?"

The boy's face was a mask of pure fear and bewilderment.

I blundered on: "I want you to understand that this man at the wheel is my *attorney!* He's not just some dingbat I found on the Strip. Shit, *look* at him! He doesn't look like you or me, right? That's because he's a foreigner. I think he's probably Samoan. But it doesn't matter, does it? Are you prejudiced?"

"Oh, hell *no!*" he blurted.

"I didn't think so," I said. "Because in spite of his race, this man is extremely valuable to me." I glanced over at my attorney, but his mind was somewhere else.

I whacked the back of the driver's seat with my fist. "This is *important*, goddamnit! This is a *true story!*" The car swerved sickeningly, then straightened out. "Keep your hands off my fucking neck!" my attorney screamed. The kid in the back looked like he was ready to jump right out of the car and take his chances.

Our vibrations were getting nasty—but why? I was puzzled, frustrated. Was there no communication in this car? Had we deteriorated to the level of *dumb beasts?*

Because my story *was* true. I was certain of that. And it was extremely important, I felt, for the *meaning* of our journey to be made absolutely clear. We had actually been sitting there in the Polo Lounge—for many hours—drinking Singapore Slings with mescal on the side and beer chasers. And when the call came, I was ready.

The dwark approached our table cautiously, as I recall, and when he handed me the pink telephone I said nothing, merely listened. And then I hung up, turning to face my attorney. "That was headquarters," I said. "They want me to go to Las Vegas at once, and make contact with a Portuguese photographer named Lacerda. He'll have the details. All I have to do is check into my suite and he'll seek me out."

My attorney said nothing for a moment, then he suddenly came alive in his chair. "God *hell!*" he exclaimed. "I think I see the *pattern.* This one sounds like real trouble!" He tucked his khaki undershirt into his white rayon bellbottoms and called for more drink. "You're going to need plenty of legal advice before this thing is over," he said. "And my first advice is that you should rent a very fast car with no top and get the hell out of L.A. for at least 48 hours." He shook his head sadly. "This blows my weekend, because naturally I'll have to go with you—and we'll have to arm ourselves."

"Why not?" I said. "If a thing like this is worth doing at all, it's worth doing right. We'll need some decent equipment and plenty of cash on the line—if only for drugs and a super-sensitive tape recorder, for the sake of a permanent record."

"What kind of a story is this?" he asked.

"The Mint 400," I said. "It's the richest off-the-road race for motor-cycles and dune-buggies in the history of organized sport—a fantastic spectacle in honor of some fatback *grossero* named Del Webb, who owns the luxurious Mint Hotel in the heart of downtown Las Vegas . . . at least that's what the press release says; my man in New York just read it to me."

"Well," he said, "as your attorney I advise you to buy a motorcycle. How else can you cover a thing like this righteously?"

"No way," I said. "Where can we get hold of a Vincent Black Shadow?"

"What's that?"

"A fantastic bike," I said. "The new model is something like two thousand cubic inches, developing 200 brake horsepower at 4000 revolutions per minute on a magnesium frame with two styrofoam seats and a total curb weight of exactly 200 pounds."

"That sounds about right for this gig," he said.

"It is," I assured him. "The fucker's not much for turning, but it's pure hell on the straightaway. It'll outrun the F-111 until takeoff."

"Takeoff?" he said. "Can we handle that much torque?"

"Absolutely," I said. "I'll call New York for some cash."

II

The seizure of $300 from a pig woman in Beverly Hills

The New York office was not familiar with the Vincent Black Shadow: they referred me to the Los Angeles bureau—which is actually in Beverly Hills just a few long blocks from the Polo Lounge—but when I got there, the money-woman refused to give me more than $300 in cash. She had no idea who I was, she said, and by that time I was pouring sweat. My blood is too thick for California: I have never been able to properly explain myself in this climate. Not with the soaking sweats . . . wild red eyeballs and trembling hands.

So I took the $300 and left. My attorney was waiting in a bar around the corner. "This won't make the nut," he said, "unless we have unlimited credit."

I assured him we would. "You Samoans are all the same," I told him. "You have no faith in the essential decency of the white man's culture. Jesus, just one hour ago we were sitting over there in that stinking bagnio, stone broke and paralyzed for the weekend, when a call comes through from some total stranger in New York, telling me to go to Las Vegas and expenses be damned—and then he sends me over to some office in Beverly Hills where another total stranger gives me $300 raw cash for no reason at all . . . I tell you, my man, this is the American Dream in action! We'd be fools not to ride this strange torpedo all the way out to the end."

"Indeed," he said. "We *must* do it."

"Right," I said. "But first we need the car. And after that, the cocaine. And then the tape recorder, for special music, and some Acapulco shirts." The only way to prepare for a trip like this, I felt, was to dress up like human peacocks and get crazy, then screech off across the desert and *cover the story*. Never lose sight of the primary responsibility.

But what *was* the story? Nobody had bothered to say. So we would have to drum it up on our own. Free Enterprise. The American Dream. Horatio Alger gone mad on drugs in Las Vegas. Do it *now*: pure Gonzo journalism.

There was also the socio-psychic factor. Every now and then when your life gets complicated and the weasels start closing in, the only real cure is to load up on heinous chemicals and then drive like a bastard from Hollywood to Las Vegas. To *relax,* as it were, in the womb of the desert sun. Just roll the roof back and screw it on, grease the face with white tanning butter and move out with the music at top volume, and at least a pint of ether.

Getting hold of the drugs had been no problem, but the car and the tape recorder were not easy things to round up at 6:30 on a Friday afternoon in Hollywood. I already had one car, but it was far too small and slow for desert work. We went to a Polynesian bar, where my attorney made 17 calls before locating a convertible with adequate horsepower and proper coloring.

"Hang onto it," I heard him say into the phone. "We'll be over to make the trade in 30 minutes." Then after a pause, he began shouting: "What? *Of course* the gentleman has a major credit card! Do you realize who the fuck you're talking to?"

"Don't take any guff from these swine," I said as he slammed the phone down. "Now we need a sound store with the finest equipment. Nothing dinky. We want one of those new Belgian Heliowatts with a voice-activated shotgun mike, for picking up conversations in oncoming cars."

We made several more calls and finally located our equipment in a store about five miles away. It was closed, but the salesman said he would wait, if we hurried. But we were delayed enroute when a Stingray in front of us killed a pedestrian on Sunset Boulevard. The store was closed by the time we got there. There were people inside, but they refused to come to the double-glass door until we gave it a few belts and made ourselves clear.

Finally two salesmen brandishing tire irons came to the door and we managed to negotiate the sale through a tiny slit. Then they opened the door just wide enough to shove the equipment out, before slamming and locking it again. "Now take that stuff and get the hell away from here," one of them shouted through the slit.

My attorney shook his fist at them. "We'll be back," he yelled. "One of these days I'll toss a fucking bomb into that place! I have your name on this sales slip! I'll find out where you live and burn your house down!"

"That'll give him something to think about," he muttered as we drove off. "That guy is a paranoid psychotic, anyway. They're easy to spot."

We had trouble, again, at the car rental agency. After signing all the papers, I got into the car and almost lost control of it while backing across the lot to the gas pump. The rental-man was obviously shaken.

"Say there . . . uh . . . you fellas are going to be *careful* with this car, aren't you?"

"Of course."

"Well, good god!" he said. "You just backed over that two-foot concrete abutment and you didn't even slow down! Forty-five in reverse! And you barely missed the pump!"

"No harm done," I said. "I always test a transmission that way. The *rear end*. For stress factors."

Meanwhile, my attorney was busy transferring rum and ice from the Pinto to the back seat of the convertible. The rental-man watched him nervously.

"Say," he said. "Are you fellas *drinking?*"

"Not me," I said.

"Just fill the goddamn tank," my attorney snapped. "We're in a hell of a hurry. We're on our way to Las Vegas for a desert race."

"What?"

"Never mind," I said. "We're responsible people." I watched him put the gas cap on, then I quickly poked the thing into low gear and we lurched into traffic.

"There's another worrier," said my attorney. "He's probably all cranked up on speed."

"Yeah, you should have given him some reds."

"Reds wouldn't help a pig like that," he said. "To hell with him. We have a lot of business to take care of, before we can get on the road."

"I'd like to get hold of some priests' robes," I said. "They might come in handy in Las Vegas."

But there were no costume stores open, and we weren't up to burglarizing a church. "Why bother?" said my attorney. "And you have to remember that a lot of cops are good vicious Catholics. Can you imagine what those bastards would do to us if we got busted all drugged-up and drunk in stolen vestments? Jesus, they'd castrate us!"

"You're right," I said. "And for christ's sake don't smoke that pipe at stoplights. Keep in mind that we're exposed."

He nodded. "We need a big hookah. Keep it down here on the seat, out of sight. If anybody sees us, they'll think we're using oxygen."

We spent the rest of that night rounding up materials and packing the car. Then we ate the mescaline and went swimming in the ocean. Somewhere around dawn we had breakfast in a Malibu coffee shop, then drove very carefully across town and plunged onto the smog-shrouded Pasadena Freeway, heading East.

III

Strange medicine on the desert . . . a crisis of confidence

I am still vaguely haunted by our hitchhiker's remarks about how he'd "never rode in a convertible before." Here's this poor geek living in a world of convertibles zipping past him on the highways all the time, and he's never even *ridden* in one. It made me feel like King Farouk. I was tempted to have my attorney pull into the next airport and arrange some kind of simple, common-law contract whereby we could just *give* the car to this unfortunate bastard. Just say: "Here, sign this and the car's yours." Give him the keys and then use the credit card to zap off on a jet to some place like Miami and rent another huge fireapple-red convertible for a drug-addled, top-speed run across the water all the way out to the last stop in Key West . . . and then trade the car off for a boat. Keep moving.

But this manic notion passed quickly. There was no point in getting this harmless kid locked up—and, besides, I had *plans* for this car. I was looking forward to flashing around Las Vegas in the bugger. Maybe do a bit of serious drag-racing on the Strip: Pull up to that big stoplight in front of the Flamingo and start screaming at the traffic:

"Alright, you chickenshit wimps! You pansies! When this goddamn light flips green, I'm gonna stomp down on this thing and blow every one of you gutless punks off the road!"

Right. Challenge the bastards on their own turf. Come screeching up to the crosswalk, bucking and skidding with a bottle of rum in one hand and jamming the horn to drown out the music . . . glazed eyes insanely dilated behind tiny black, gold-rimmed greaser shades, screaming gibber- ish . . . a genuinely *dangerous* drunk, reeking of ether and terminal psycho- sis. Revving the engine up to a terrible high-pitched chattering whine, waiting for the light to change . . .

How often does a chance like that come around? To jangle the bastards right down to the core of their spleens. Old elephants limp off to the hills to die; old Americans go out to the highway and drive themselves to death with huge cars.

But our trip was different. It was a classic affirmation of everything right and true and decent in the national character. It was a gross, physical salute to the fantastic *possibilities* of life in this country—but only for those with true grit. And we were chock full of that.

My attorney understood this concept, despite his racial handicap, but our hitchhiker was not an easy person to reach. He *said* he understood, but I could see in his eyes that he didn't. He was lying to me.

The car suddenly veered off the road and we came to a sliding halt in the gravel. I was hurled against the dashboard. My attorney was slumped over the wheel. "What's wrong?" I yelled. "We can't stop *here*. This is bat country!"

"My heart," he groaned. "Where's the medicine?"

"Oh," I said. "The medicine, yes, it's right here." I reached into the kit-bag for the amyls. The kid seemed petrified. "Don't worry," I said. "This man has a bad heart—Angina Pectoris. But we have the cure for it. Yes, here they are." I picked four amyls out of the tin box and handed two of them to my attorney. He immediately cracked one under his nose, and I did likewise.

He took a long snort and fell back on the seat, staring straight up at the sun. "Turn up the fucking music!" he screamed. "My heart feels like an alligator!

"Volume! Clarity! Bass! We must have bass!" He flailed his naked arms at the sky. "What's *wrong* with us? Are we goddamn *old ladies?*"

I turned both the radio and the tape machine up full bore. "You scurvy shyster bastard," I said. "Watch your language! You're talking to a doctor of journalism!"

He was laughing out of control. "What the fuck are we *doing* out here on this desert?" he shouted. "Somebody call the police! We need help!"

"Pay no attention to this swine," I said to the hitchhiker. "He can't handle the medicine. Actually, we're *both* doctors of journalism, and we're on our way to Las Vegas to cover the main story of our generation." And then I began laughing. . . .

My attorney hunched around to face the hitchhiker. "The truth is," he said, "we're going to Vegas to croak a scag baron named Savage Henry. I've known him for years, but he ripped us off—and you know what that means, right?"

I wanted to shut him off, but we were both helpless with laughter. What the fuck *were* we doing out here on this desert, when we both had bad hearts?

"Savage Henry has cashed his check!" My attorney snarled at the kid in the back seat. "We're going to rip his lungs out!"

"And eat them!" I blurted. "That bastard won't get away with this! What's going on in this country when a scumsucker like that can get away with sandbagging a doctor of journalism?"

Nobody answered. My attorney was cracking another amyl and the kid was climbing out of the back seat, scrambling down the trunk lid. "Thanks for the ride," he yelled. "Thanks a *lot.* I *like* you guys. Don't worry about *me.*" His feet hit the asphalt and he started running back towards Baker. Out in the middle of the desert, not a tree in sight.

"Wait a minute," I yelled. "Come back and get a beer." But apparently he couldn't hear me. The music was very loud, and he was moving away from us at good speed.

"Good riddance," said my attorney. "We had a real freak on our hands. That boy made me nervous. Did you see his *eyes?*" He was still laughing. "Jesus," he said. "This is good medicine!"

I opened the door and reeled around to the driver's side. "Move over," I said. "I'll drive. We have to get out of California before that kid finds a cop."

"Shit, that'll be hours," said my attorney. "He's a hundred miles from anywhere."

"So are we," I said.

"Let's turn around and drive back to the Polo Lounge," he said. "They'll never look for us there."

I ignored him. "Open the tequila," I yelled as the windscream took over again; I stomped on the accelerator as we hurtled back onto the highway. Moments later he leaned over with a map. "There's a place up ahead called Mescal Springs," he said. "As your attorney, I advise you to stop and take a swim."

I shook my head. "It's absolutely imperative that we get to the Mint Hotel before the deadline for press registration," I said. "Otherwise, we might have to pay for our suite."

He nodded. "But let's forget that bullshit about the American Dream," he said. "The *important* thing is the Great Samoan Dream." He was rummaging around in the kit-bag. "I think it's about time to chew up a blotter," he said. "That cheap mescaline wore off a long time ago, and I don't know if I can stand the smell of that goddamn ether any longer."

"I *like* it," I said. "We should soak a towel with the stuff and then put it down on the floorboard by the accelerator, so the fumes will rise up in my face all the way to Las Vegas."

He was turning the tape cassette over. The radio was screaming: "Power to the People—Right On!" John Lennon's political song, ten years too late. "That poor fool should have stayed where he was," said my attorney. "Punks like that just get in the way when they try to be serious."

"Speaking of serious," I said. "I think it's about time to get into the ether and the cocaine."

"Forget ether," he said. "Let's save it for soaking down the rug in the suite. But here's this. Your half of the sunshine blotter. Just chew it up like baseball gum."

I took the blotter and ate it. My attorney was now fumbling with the salt shaker containing the cocaine. Opening it. Spilling it. Then screaming and grabbing at the air, as our fine white dust blew up and out across the desert highway. A very expensive little twister rising up from the Great Red Shark. "Oh, *jesus!*" he moaned. "Did you see what God just did to us?"

"God didn't do that!" I shouted. "*You* did it. You're a fucking narcotics agent! I was on to your stinking act from the start, you pig!"

"You better be careful," he said. And suddenly he was waving a fat black .357 magnum at me. One of those snubnosed Colt Pythons with the beveled cylinder. "Plenty of vultures out here," he said. "They'll pick your bones clean before morning."

"You whore," I said. "When we get to Las Vegas I'll have you chopped into hamburger. What do you think the Drug Bund will do when I show up with a Samoan narcotics agent?"

"They'll kill us both," he said. "Savage Henry knows who I am. Shit, I'm your *attorney*." He burst into wild laughter. "You're full of acid, you fool. It'll be a goddamn miracle if we can get to the hotel and check in before you turn into a wild animal. Are you ready for that? Checking into a Vegas hotel under a phony name with intent to commit capital fraud and a head full of acid?" He was laughing again, then he jammed his nose down toward the salt shaker, aiming the thin green roll of a $20 bill straight into what was left of the powder.

"How long do we have?" I said.

"Maybe 30 more minutes," he replied. "As your attorney I advise you to drive at top speed."

Las Vegas was just up ahead. I could see the strip/hotel skyline looming through the blue desert ground-haze: The Sahara, the landmark, the Americana and the ominous Thunderbird—a cluster of grey rectangles in the distance, rising out of the cactus.

Thirty minutes. It was going to be very close. The objective was the big tower of the Mint Hotel, downtown—and if we didn't get there before we lost all control, there was also the Nevada State prison upstate in Carson City. I had been there once, but only for a talk with the prisoners—and I didn't want to go back, for any reason at all. So there was really no choice: We would have to run the gauntlet, and acid be damned. Go through all the official gibberish, get the car into the hotel garage, work out on the desk clerk, deal with the bellboy, sign in for the press passes—all of it bogus, totally illegal, a fraud on its face, but of course it would have to be done.

"KILL THE BODY AND THE HEAD WILL DIE"

This line appears in my notebook, for some reason. Perhaps some connection with Joe Frazier. Is he still alive? Still able to talk? I watched that fight in Seattle—horribly twisted about four seats down the aisle from the Governor. A very painful experience in every way, a proper end to the Sixties: Tim Leary a prisoner of Eldridge Cleaver in Algeria, Bob Dylan clipping coupons in Greenwich Village, both Kennedys murdered by mutants, Owsley folding napkins on Terminal Island, and finally Cassius/Ali belted incredibly off his pedestal by a human hamburger, a man on the verge of death. Joe Frazier, like Nixon, had finally prevailed for reasons that people like me refused to understand—at least not out loud.

. . . But that was some other era, burned out and long gone from the brutish realities of this foul year of Our Lord, Nineteen Hundred and Seventy One. A lot of things had changed in those years. And now I was in Las Vegas as the motor sports editor of this fine slick magazine that had sent me out here in the Great Red Shark for some reason that nobody claimed to understand. "Just check it out," they said, "and we'll take it from there. . . ."

Indeed. Check it out. But when we finally arrived at the Mint Hotel my attorney was unable to cope artfully with the registration procedure. We were forced to stand in line with all the others—which proved to be extremely difficult under the circumstances. I kept telling myself: "Be quiet, be calm, say nothing . . . speak only when spoken to: name, rank and press affiliation, nothing else, ignore this terrible drug, pretend it's not happening. . . ."

There is no way to explain the terror I felt when I finally lunged up to the clerk and began babbling. All my well-rehearsed lines fell apart under that woman's stoney glare. "Hi there," I said. "My name is . . . ah, Raoul Duke . . . yes, *on the list,* that's for sure. Free lunch, final wisdom, total coverage. . . . why not? I have my attorney with me and I realize of course that *his* name is not on my list, but we *must* have that suite, yes, this man is actually my *driver.* We brought this red shark all the way from the Strip and now it's time for the desert, right? Yes. Just check the list and you'll see. Don't worry. What's the score, here? What's next?"

The woman never blinked. "Your room's not ready yet," she said. "But there's somebody looking for you."

"No!" I shouted. "Why? We haven't *done* anything yet!" My legs felt rubbery. I gripped the desk and sagged toward her as she held out the envelope, but I refused to accept it. The woman's face was *changing:* swelling, pulsing . . . horrible green jowls and fangs jutting out, the face of a Moray Eel! Deadly poison! I lunged backwards into my attorney, who gripped my arm as he reached out to take the note. "I'll handle this," he said to the Moray woman. "This man has a bad heart, but I have plenty of medicine. My name is Doctor Gonzo. Prepare our suite at once. We'll be in the bar."

The woman shrugged as he led me away. In a town full of bedrock crazies, nobody even *notices* an acid freak. We struggled through the crowded lobby and found two stools at the bar. My attorney ordered two cuba libres with beer and mescal on the side, then he opened the envelope. "Who's Lacerda?" he asked. "He's waiting for us in a room on the 12th floor."

I couldn't remember. Lacerda? The name rang a bell, but I couldn't concentrate. Terrible things were happening all around us. Right next to me a huge reptile was gnawing on a woman's neck, the carpet was a blood-soaked sponge—impossible to walk on it, no footing at all. "Order some golf shoes," I whispered. "Otherwise, we'll never get out of this place alive. You notice these lizards don't have any trouble moving around in this muck—that's because they have *claws* on their feet."

"Lizards?" he said. "If you think we're in trouble now, wait till you see what's happening in the elevators." He took off his Brazilian sunglasses and I could see he'd been crying. "I just went upstairs to see this man Lacerda," he said. "I told him we knew what he was up to. He *says* he's a photographer, but when I mentioned Savage Henry—well, that did it; he freaked. I could see it in his eyes. He knows we're onto him."

"Does he understand we have magnums?" I said.

"No. But I told him we had a Vincent Black Shadow. That scared the piss out of him."

"Good," I said. "But what about our room? And the golf shoes? We're right in the middle of a fucking reptile zoo! And somebody's giving *booze* to these goddamn things! It won't be long before they tear us to shreds. Jesus, look at the floor! Have you ever *seen* so much blood? How many have they killed *already?*" I pointed across the room to a group that seemed to be staring at us. "Holy shit, look at that bunch over there! They've spotted us!"

"That's the press table," he said. "That's where you have to sign in for our credentials. Shit, let's get it over with. You handle that, and I'll get the room."

IV

Hideous music and the sound of many shotguns . . .
rude vibes on a Saturday evening in Vegas

We finally got into the suite around dusk, and my attorney was immediately on the phone to room service—ordering four club sandwiches, four shrimp cocktails, a quart of rum and nine fresh grapefruits. "Vitamin C," he explained. "We'll need all we can get."

I agreed. By this time the drink was beginning to cut the acid and my hallucinations were down to a tolerable level. The room service waiter had a vaguely reptilian cast to his features, but I was no longer seeing huge pterodactyls lumbering around the corridors in pools of fresh blood. The only problem now was a gigantic neon sign outside the window, blocking our view of the mountains—millions of colored balls running around a very complicated track, strange symbols & filigree, giving off a loud hum. . . .

"Look outside," I said.

"Why?"

"There's a big . . . machine in the sky, . . . some kind of electric snake . . . coming straight at us."

"Shoot it," said my attorney.

"Not yet," I said. "I want to study its habits."

He went over to the corner and began pulling on a chain to close the drapes. "Look," he said, "you've got to stop this talk about snakes and leeches and lizards and that stuff. It's making me sick."

"Don't worry," I said.

"*Worry?* Jesus, I almost went crazy down there in the bar. They'll never let us back in that place—not after your scene at the press table."

"What scene?"

"You bastard," he said. "I left you alone for *three minutes!* You scared the shit out of those people! Waving that goddamn marlin spike around and yelling about reptiles. You're lucky I came back in time. They were ready to call the cops. I said you were only drunk and that I was taking you up to your room for a cold shower. Hell, the only reason they gave us the press passes was to get you out of there."

He was pacing around nervously. "Jesus, that scene straightened me right out! I *must* have some drugs. What have you done with the mescaline?"

"The kit-bag," I said.

He opened the bag and ate two pellets while I got the tape machine going. "Maybe *you* should only eat *one* of these," he said. "That acid's still working on you."

I agreed. "We have to go out to the track before dark," I said. "But we have time to watch the TV news. Let's carve up this grapefruit and make a fine rum punch, maybe toss in a blotter . . . where's the car?"

"We gave it to somebody in the parking lot," he said. "I have the ticket in my briefcase."

"What's the number? I'll call down and have them wash the bastard, get rid of that dust and grime."

"Good idea," he said. But he couldn't find the ticket.

"Well, we're fucked," I said. "We'll never convince them to give us that car without proof."

He thought for a moment, then picked up the phone and asked for the garage. "This is Doctor Gonzo in eight-fifty," he said. "I seem to have lost my parking stub for that red convertible I left with you, but I want the car washed and ready to go in 30 minutes. Can you send up a duplicate stub? . . . What . . . Oh? . . . Well, that's fine." He hung up and reached for the hash pipe. "No problem," he said. "That man remembers my face."

"That's good," I said. "They'll probably have a big net ready for us when we show up."

He shook his head. "As your attorney, I advise you not to worry about *me.*"

The TV news was about the Laos Invasion—a series of horrifying disasters: explosions and twisted wreckage, men fleeing in terror, Pentagon generals babbling insane lies. "Turn that shit off!" screamed my attorney. "Let's get *out* of here!"

A wise move. Moments after we picked up the car my attorney went into a drug coma and ran a red light on Main street before I could bring us under control. I propped him up in the passenger seat and took the wheel myself . . . feeling fine, extremely sharp. All around me in traffic I could see people talking and I wanted to hear what they were saying. All of them. But the shotgun mike was in the trunk and I decided to leave it there. Las Vegas is not the kind of town where you want to drive down Main Street aiming a black bazooka-looking instrument at people.

Turn up the radio. Turn up the tape machine. Look into the sunset up ahead. Roll the windows down for a better taste of the cool desert wind. Ah yes. This is what it's all about. Total control now. Tooling along the main drag on a Saturday night in Las Vegas, two good old boys in a fireapple-red convertible . . . stoned, ripped, twisted . . . Good People.

Naked Lunch Box

ROBIN GREEN

DAVID CASSIDY, THE NUMBER 1 TEEN IDOL OF THE EARLY SEVENTIES, HAD HIS HEART SET ON A COVER STORY. SO WE GAVE IT TO HIM.

The first time I opened up a ROLLING STONE, I was living in New York. This was in 1968. I was working at Marvel Comics as Stan Lee's secretary. It was pretty much my last straight job for a good many years.

ROLLING STONE came out of the Bay area in those days. Maybe I moved out to Berkeley partly because the magazine made it sound like such a party out there (it was). Or maybe ROLLING STONE had nothing to do with it. I can't remember. Whyever, my boyfriend and I got into his Pontiac Firebird convertible (overhead cam 6, Cony shocks—how and why do I remember such details?) and headed west, stopping to visit friends in New Mexico, camping naked like savages for a week near some caves in the Jemez Mountains by a natural hot spring.

A couple years later I was still reading ROLLING STONE, stoned, cover to cover. I'd had it with waitressing and jewelry lessons, and my old college roommate gave me the name of someone at the magazine, Alan Rinzler, the associate publisher. I borrowed a jeans jacket from a friend that had an emblem of people fucking on the back and took my dog and went across the bay to ROLLING STONE, which had its offices in a converted brick warehouse. If they didn't want the fucking jacket and they didn't want the fucking dog, fuck 'em. Alan had his dog at the office, too. Now *this* was hip.

I told Alan I'd do anything to work there—secretary, receptionist. He said they just hired a receptionist. Was there anything else I could do? I'd written some good short stories in college (Brown), so I said, "Well, I can write." (Interestingly, a receptionist who came soon after, Harriet Fier, rose to be managing editor of the magazine.) Alan arranged for me to meet Jann Wenner.

My meeting with Jann lasted about three minutes. He was short, cute, endomorphic, a nail biter who talked fast and thought fast (a speed freak?) and sent me out the door with an assignment to write about Marvel Comics.

I came back with 10,000 words, for which Jann paid me five cents a word. What's that—$500? So what? My rent was $60 a month. By then I had broken up with my boyfriend and was sharing a house in Berkeley I found off a bulletin board at a food co-op. They put Hulk on the cover of ROLLING STONE.

My price went up to ten cents a word, and I was made a contributing editor—the only woman writer on the masthead for some years, years in which Joe Eszterhas, for instance, arrived at the magazine from the Cleveland *Plain Dealer* with a bowie knife hanging from his belt and a pipe in his mouth, writing prose like "the great stone canyons of New York City." And Hunter Thompson, high on mescaline, swilling down Wild Turkey, drove Route 1 on the wrong side of the road at night with the lights out. (What was I doing in that car? Well, I lived.) Years in which it didn't seem all that unusual to hold an editorial retreat at Big Sur or all that untoward for most of the editors and writers to drop mescaline and bathe together naked in sulfur baths at Esalen at night in a cave in the side of a cliff overlooking the moonlit Pacific while in the distance whales migrated south.

Writer David Felton (a.k.a. the Stonecutter, because he was slow, very slow) was my editor. I never thought of working for any other magazines. Well, once I did have a meeting with *Esquire* in New York. The guy wanted me to write about a woman who kept winning blue ribbons at cat shows because she had the only cat of its breed. He thought he was giving me a chance to move into the big time, but I thought, "Huh?" It sounded so . . . straight.

My beat, if I had one, was irony. I wrote about a cut-rate yet evil guru (way before Jim Jones), Dennis Hopper in his good old, bad old unreformed days (*Esquire* called after the article came out and said, "Who's the new bitch?"), a whorehouse in Nevada and the following story—a fairly thorough exploration of the marketing and selling of a teen idol, David Cassidy (who actually was in his twenties).

David Cassidy's PR man had approached ROLLING STONE about the article. David was getting old for the Partridge Family, the Partridge Family was getting old period, and David wanted now to be considered an adult talent. Since the media had created the teen idol he was in the first place, it seemed logical, I suppose, to call on the media to transmogrify his image. And what groovier vehicle than a cover of ROLLING STONE? So we gave it to him.

I spent five days on tour with the fellow—first-class flight to New York, rooms at the Plaza, a pleasant, actually uneventful five days. But still . . . other ROLLING STONE writers were traveling with the Stones, Dylan, the Dead, Neil Young, for chrissakes, and here I was with this kid and his mom, Shirley Jones, who always seemed to be somewhere around. Go be ironic.

After the article ran, there were a few unhappy letters from young girls because photographer Annie Leibovitz had persuaded David to pose naked—he wanted to be hip, didn't he?—and one photograph revealed David's pubic hair, which his young fans said he couldn't possibly possess.

I heard David's PR man got fired as a result of the article. David himself, after *The Partridge Family* got canceled, dropped out of sight for four or five years. He went to Hawaii, I think. But he had a small comeback in 1990, even reaching the Top Forty with a song called "Lyin' to Myself."

As for the title, "Naked Lunch Box," Cassidy's people marketed a line of David Cassidy lunch boxes. But it's also important to note that the article ran in the same issue as an interview with William Burroughs.

The article ran 10,000 words. I counted every word. I always did. It was one of the most satisfying parts of the job.

As for me, my ROLLING STONE career pretty much ground to a halt around 1974. It had been four years, and it wasn't fun anymore, and I was blocked on this article I was trying to write on the children of Robert Kennedy. I'd been taking months, and Jann said now or never, and even this failed to move me to the typewriter. I moved instead to Iowa City for a couple years of R&R at the Iowa Writers Workshop.

It was an amicable parting. Jann and I both happened to be in Israel at the time. We were at a nightclub with some people, and we went outside on the patio, and Jann said, "You realize I have to take you off the masthead." Kind of like a sergeant being stripped of his stripes. I shrugged and said, "Okay." He put his arms around me, and we hugged, and then he said: "Do me a favor, Robin, will you? Don't ever write about me, okay?"

"**D**rive over to the Hippopotamus," Henry instructed.

"Aw, Henry, let's go back to the hotel," pleaded David Cassidy, who sat slumped down in the back seat.

"Heeey," chided Henry. "We're in the Big Apple. Let's just see what's happening."

David slumped further in the joyless back seat, muttering his consent. He was exhausted, stoned and drunk, and dizzy from the antibiotics he was taking to drive away a flu. It had been a busy day—two hour-long interviews in the morning; a press conference at New York City College; a rehearsal all afternoon; a session with gossip columnist Earl Wilson; and pictures for the Cancer Society. Then an impromptu tap dancing lesson in his hotel room with a lady he'd met at rehearsal that afternoon. Then dinner, dope, wine, and now this climbing in and out of the back seat of a car looking for what? New York action?

Well, he had his action and he wanted to go to sleep. But that wasn't what the others were into, except for Jill, who sat close to him. The Lincoln limousine pulled in front of the third discotheque they'd been to that evening. They hadn't stayed at the others because Henry didn't think they were quite right.

"We'll just go in and check it out," said Henry. "Just one more. If we don't dig it, we'll leave."

David mustered a small protest.

"*Try* it," laughed Henry. "You'll *like* it."

So David was herded into the Hippopotamus.

"Wait here," said Ron, David's valet. "I'll go take a look."

Ron climbed the steps to a room which poured out music and cigarette smoke, lit purple and pink.

"Where do you think you're going?" demanded the doorman, who barred Ron's entrance to the room.

"You don't understand," Ron said. His voice had a bitchy edge on it now. "I'm here with Mr. Cassidy, my employer. I have to see if the place is all right. You see, there he is right there, standing with those people just inside the door. David Cassidy."

"Where?"

"Right there," Ron was almost screaming. "In the blue coat."

The doorman squinted at the slight figure in the dark hallway, then looked back at Ron.

"That's David Cassidy!" Ron said.

The doorman looked at David again. He shrugged. "Who's David Cassidy?"

Only three weeks earlier that same David Cassidy had set an attendance record at the Houston Astrodome, selling 56,723 tickets to two matinees on the same day.

I

Baboom, Baboom, Boys and Girls, Zing!

Madison Square Garden was filled five balconies full an hour before the matinee with 20,650 excited females—the same girls who more than 20 years ago would have wept for Sinatra and 10 years ago for Elvis. Average teen age girls who keep diaries, go steady and chew gum. And many younger ones, eight- and nine-year-olds, some with their mothers. David Cassidy's audience—who never miss a Partridge Family episode, who devote scrap books to him and wallpaper their bedrooms with his face and body.

Now they held up banners reading "David Spells Luv."

"I hope I brought enough Kleenex," worried a 16-year-old wearing a tight sweater and hot pants. "I'll probably cry. I cried when I got my ticket."

"Ooooh!" cried one small voice inside the hood of a pink and red snow suit. Eight-year-old wide-eyed Amanda Lewis clutched a $2.00 David Cassidy program to her undeveloped bosom. "He's so sexy."

One fan didn't know if David was sexy. "I'm a boy," explained Elliot Fain, age 11, from Forest Hills. "I think he's a very interesting person though."

The girls were there to scream. They screamed whenever so much as an equipment man mounted the stage. One news photographer approached a cluster of ladies. "Scream!" he directed. They screamed. He took a picture.

Aproned vendors coursed through with screams of their own: Posters! Programs! Hot dogs! Popcorn!

When the lights dimmed, the show's MC—a fave DJ on WABC radio—strutted onto the stage, long-legged and agile as a circus barker. "I just saw David backstage!" he announced.

"EEEAAHHH!" went the crowd.

"Now, when I count to three I want you to say 'Hi, David!' One, two, three!"

"HI, DA-VID!" The auditorium shook.

"And now I want you kids to show the world that children your age can behave and not go crazy. Yell and scream, but stay in your seats. Let me hear you say 'I will.' One, two, three!"

* * *

In a windowless cinderblock dressing room, all David's people were assembled. Wes Farrell, record producer; Ruth Aarons, manager; Jim Flood, PR man; Steve Wax, A&R man; Sam Hymen, David's roommate; Ron the valet; Henry Diltz, pop photographer; Steve Alsberg, road-manager. No Jack Cassidy, David's father, but Shirley Jones, his stepmother, with two of her three sons, and his mother Evelyn Ward with David's grandfather, 84 years old, in a grey three-piece suit.

In a corner, a pile of gifts from fans four feet high: stuffed animals, plastic flowers, incense and scented candles, shirts and hand-printed messages of undying love.

David signed autographs for promoters' and policemen's daughters, and chatted with well wishers. It was a high moment for him; a triumph, he called it. "Here I am," he said. "I've arrived."

"Think about it," said Henry Diltz. "The karma is fantastic. David was an actor, looking for a break, and then this Partridge Family TV show comes along. He wasn't a singer, but he evolved really nicely into one. Take the Stones, or Cream. After being into folk music, the blues, and rock and roll for ten, 12 years, they fill Madison Square Garden. Well, David's filling it, too, and *he's only been singing in front of people for a year!*"

Minutes before showtime, Ron helped David into his costume, a $500 white crepe jump suit slit to the navel and decorated with fringe, beads, bells and sequins around the waist.

"I wish," said David, "that anyone who has ever put down someone in my situation—the Beatles, or Presley or anyone—I wish that they could be where I am, could jump into my white suit for just one day. It's such a rush, they'd never come down to think about it.

"It's a high going out on that stage. You look around and it's all there for you, people loving you like that. My friends are there with me, I'm doing what I love to do most, singing and I'm singing for people who would rather have me sing than anybody else in the world.

"There's one song I do, 'I Woke Up in Love This Morning,' and I find a little place where I can sort of point to them. And they each think I mean *them*, and I do. Whew, I can't wait. Let me get out there. Let me do it!"

David sang into the mirror as he applied pancake make-up to his face, chest and arms. He said he didn't think of anything before a concert. "I'm in a state of, 'Well, here I go,' like a runner before a race, an athlete before he takes the big dive. The roll of the drums, baboom, baboom, and then, 'Ladies and Gentlemen, boys and girls!' And I take the baton and zing . . . !"

Flanked by his valet and his road manager, David was off and running. He leapt onto the stage, welcomed by a blood curdling screech. The continuous blinking of flash bulbs gave the place a strobelit effect.

"I love you, I love you," David screamed back at them. "I love *everybody.*"

On stage this mild, quiet guy was transformed into a glistening white superstar. He gave it everything, his 5'7", 125 lb. body had. Like a young and healthy animal of no particular gender he moved as he sang, in a graceful, almost choreographed way.

"I never get tired of watching David's act," said his roommate Sam Hymen, looking on from the sidelines. "And I've seen it 50, 100 times. Something's happening out there. The white costume, the big band behind him." The band played perfectly, wearing sedate matching maroon blazers. "I like to watch the audience, too, they're so turned on and happy."

In the first row, Shirley Jones sat with David's family. "It's like a revival meeting," she said, "the way he excites the audience, then calms them down."

Fans tossed stuffed animals and dolls onto the stage, and one girl managed somehow to elude guards and climb up there herself. Once there, she froze. David jumped when he noticed her, a plump girl in a blue chemise. Gracefully, he took her hand and kissed her cheek.

Though no one fainted, as 24 had in Detroit, the energy was high. The girls went wild in place. The young ones grew restless when David crooned the slower ballads in a small, but soothing voice. Many older girls wept.

If David was emanating heavy vibes, they escaped one 24-year-old observer. Jill watched the show on a backstage TV screen. "It's so weird," she said. "Last night, he was really nice. He was a really good fuck." Jill shook her head. "But seeing him doing his act, I can't believe it's the same person. This act is so Las Vegas. He's like a male Ann-Margret."

Twenty thousand girls were satisfied, though, transfixed by their idol. When the hour set was over, they sat in darkness and groaned in disappointment. But not for long.

When the lights went up, they recovered and set to furious but businesslike pursuit of their fantasy. Guards blocked off the backstage area, but some fans were small enough to race under their arms and between their legs, overturning one cop.

Finally, they swarmed through, searching for David, who had made good his frantic escape covered with a blanket on the back seat floor of a Japanese sedan. One vendor sold programs along the escape route, getting in a few last-minute sales.

II

Twitchy Thighs and Sticky Seats

In two years, David Cassidy has swept hurricane-like into the pre-pubescent lives of millions of American girls. Leaving: six and a half million long-playing albums and singles; 44 television programs; David Cassidy lunch boxes; David Cassidy bubble gum; David Cassidy coloring books and David Cassidy pens; not to mention several millions of teen magazines, wall stickers, love beads, posters and photo albums. Among many things, including those wet theater seats.

As David himself puts it, "This is very filthy, but when the hall empties out after one of my concerts, those girls leave behind them thousands of *sticky seats.*"

Virtually unknown in the older world of rock audiences, David is an idol to television multitudes and teenage millions. The rise to fame began more than two years ago when he appeared in television programs like *Ironside, Bonanza* and *Marcus Welby MD.* And when he landed the role of a dying boy on *Medical Center,* he unmistakably began to capture viewers' hearts. Then came Keith Partridge, a weekly situation comedy role in *The Partridge Family.*

When *The Partridge Family* started, David was 20 years old. But with his exceptionally pretty face and tiny voice, he passed as the bouncy 16-year-old son in a family of four children who lived in the suburbs and made their living as a rock and roll band.

Only two years before, the show's producers had created the Monkees. With *The Partridge Family* they planned to dub the singing when the band performed, but they soon discovered — to the delight and surprise of everyone — that David himself could sing.

Soon, the television company began putting out Partridge Family records, which sold well. Soon enough, David emerged as a solo performer, cutting his own records, on tour with his own band.

"I was an actor," David explained later, thinking back to his decision to forget Broadway and return to Hollywood. "I was out to earn the bucks. I wanted to be a working actor — one who works all the time, who other actors look at and say, 'Well, he's pretty good.' Honestly, my goal was not to be a star."

Five weeks after his return to Hollywood he went from earning $150 a day to television guest-star roles. And then came the script for *The Partridge Family.*

"When I first read the script, I thought it was terrible," David recalled. "I was thinking about saying these dumb lines like 'Gee, Mom, can I borrow the keys to the car.' I just couldn't bring myself to do it after doing all those heavy things I'd done.

"I called Ruth and said, 'You gotta be kidding with this.' And she said, 'Read it over again and call me back.' Well, I'm so soft. I read it over — twice — and then I called her back and I said, 'I guess it's not so bad.' Only because I'd gotten used to it."

And he had the same reaction to the music he was being asked to perform, first as part of the Partridge Family and later on his own. "When I first got in the studio, I said to the producer, Wes Farrell, 'I don't want to cut bubble gum records.' And he said, 'No, man, we're not going to cut bubble gum records.' Me and my friend Cookie were jamming at the time, the blues, and all of a sudden I'm gonna sing, 'I Think I Love You!' "

At first, radio stations hadn't liked the song either. But it has now sold over five million copies. "When that record came out it was only Wes and Larry Uttal, head of Bell Records, who thought it was going to be a smash.

"What happened with that record was we got secondary air play on it, small towns. The primary stations didn't want it. They said, 'Let the TV show break it,' which I can understand."

Finally one town, Cedar Rapids, Iowa, played the record, and it went from 40 to one in two days.

"Now everybody cuts it. Percy Faith, the Boston Pops. And it was written for *me*. I've got good writers writing for me.

"I want people to know that I like to sing that song. I stand naked — that's the best word I can think of — and say 'This is how I am.' "

Interlude:
A Fig Leaf Doesn't Fall

Both teenaged girls wore hot pants, silver stars pasted on their red-polka-dot cheeks under heavily painted eyes. The two had camped out in front of the elevator door on the sixth floor of the Plaza Hotel all evening, waiting for David to return to his suite. When he appeared with his entourage, the girls rose. They didn't rush to David, but ran instead into each other's arms where, according to some apparent plan, they arranged themselves in a provocative pose. They smiled.

"Hi," David smiled. "What're you girls up to?"

"You!" they squealed, and kissed each other passionately. Arms around each other, the shorter girl moved one leg between the other's thigh, and with her free hand began to caress her friend's bosom.

David took Jill's arm and led her past them down the hall. The two girls stared after him, disappointed. They pleaded with Henry to intercede for them.

"David," Henry ran down the hall. "Where are you *going?*"

"Aw, Henry," David said, "Chicks like that don't turn me on."

Henry talked to him in earnest tones, gesturing occasionally towards the two girls who smiled hopefully at David each time Henry pointed their way.

"But Henry, I mean, after I got done making love to that, I'd feel shitty. I couldn't look at them. I couldn't wait to get them out of my bed so I wouldn't have to see them there, and face them, and myself, too."

When David emerged from his hotel room the next morning he saw that the two bizarre would-be groupies still stood draped around each other leaning against a wall outside the sixth floor elevator door.

"You think they were there all night?" David asked Henry in the limousine en route to Madison Square Garden.

"Naw," said Henry. "I let them camp out in my room on the floor. They were strange little girls. I had to drag it out of them, but they're from New Jersey. Just two ordinary girls during the week. The big one with the moustache is a telephone operator, and the little feminine one works in a store."

"Oh, no!" groaned David, "there they are in that cab behind us." From the yellow cab following them they could see two excited females waving and smiling.

"Get rid of them Caesar. See if you can lose them." David's voice was urgent. "I don't want them around me. I don't want them near the dressing room. My *family* is going to be there."

Smoking a joint and drinking wine ordered from room service at the Plaza Hotel, David watched the March 10th episode of *The Partridge Family*.

Keith and his family were driving to the country for a week's vacation from their busy schedules as rock and roll stars. En route, their psychedelic painted bus breaks down. They seek help from a country couple, who recognize them and plot to keep them there so that they'll perform at a benefit for a neighboring Indian reservation.

"Watch," David predicted. "Here's where I do my pouting schtick. I always have to do one of these things."

On the screen, Keith is annoyed at the delay, and puts up a fuss when his mother suggests he take his younger brother Danny fishing. While cleaning the fish in their captor's garage, Keith finds a case of the stuff needed to repair their bus. He realizes that the couple is lying to them. Holding one of the fish he has caught in his hand, he says to Danny, "There's something fishy here." Laughter, on the television and from David's corner.

Keith stalks into the couple's house to confront them. But the two still hide their intentions, and Keith is chastised by his mother for being suspicious.

The next day, the couple takes the Partridge Family to the Indian reservation, where they see the plight of the Indians.

"Someone should do something," says Keith's mother.

"That's what everybody says," moralized the country woman.

Keith's mother apologizes and asks what she can do to help.

"Well," replies the woman, "there is going to be a fair for the Indians this afternoon. Perhaps you could entertain."

Just then, the younger son, Danny, finds a leaflet announcing that his family was scheduled to perform that afternoon. Everyone laughs, realizing that there has indeed been a plot all along.

The plot thickens when the Partridge Family manager finds one of the leaflets, which has reached him somehow, in Las Vegas. He drives out to prevent the concert which is against the terms of the family's contract. Discovering this, the couple send the manager on a wild goose chase.

"Watch this," David laughed. "This is really funny."

In full color the manager is scared foolish by a band of Indians pretending to be on the warpath. Meanwhile, the Partridge Family performs on a stage atop their bus, and everything works out for the best.

Post-Orbital Remorse

TOM WOLFE

THEY WERE CAGEY SOULS, ALL RIGHT, BUT THE RE-
PORTER HUNG IN UNTIL THEY TOOK HIM UP INTO THE
CAPSULE AND LAID OUT THE SECRETS OF THE BROTH-
ERHOOD. BUT FIRST THERE WAS THAT RACK-JOBBERS'
CONVENTION.

I n the fall of 1969, Jann Wenner was twenty-three years old and still
had long hair, fluffed out and tucked under in a pageboy bob, and
ROLLING STONE was still referred to as an underground newspaper,
and the Sixties were still the Sixties. Woodstock had occurred (in
the same sense that the Krakatoa tidal wave occurred) a few months before. Therefore, it looked unseemly when Underground Editor Wenner,
whom I had never met, arrived for our appointment in a stretch limousine
with enough steel strung out in the wheelbase to modernize Guatemala. It
was out of character, or so I thought at the time. It wasn't until twenty
years later, in the decade some anonymous genius has forevermore
branded as yuppie, that I realized the spirit of the age may change, but all
Rising Generations are alike. Given the slightest slack in the velvet rope,
they'll take everything.

The windows of the limousine were tinted deep raspberry. The driver was a Keith Richards look-alike with a ponytail, a fringed leather jerkin and a pair of smoked glasses. The car service was Head Limo, specializing in ferrying rock musicians and other heads. (*Heads*: A Sixties expression. You could look it up.) It was the most terrifying ride I ever took, and I had once been on a bus driven by Neal Cassady. As we careened through the streets of Manhattan, it became obvious that the driver couldn't see out of this raspberry coffin any better than I could and cared a great deal less. Purely from an urge to shorten the trip, I agreed to it when Editor Wenner proposed the lamest assignment I had ever heard of in twelve years of American journalism: the annual meeting of the National Association of Recording Merchandisers.

To my amazement, the NARM convention (for thus it was called) was spellbinding. There in Miami Beach, in the Americana Hotel, which had a tropical forest encased in a glass cone in the lobby (all designed by Morris Lapidus), I saw the music business with no clothes on. Which is to say, I met the rack jobbers, and I met them in the presence of the artists, namely, the reigning rock musicians, composers and record producers. The young rockers and composers, in the invigorating wake of Woodstock, talked in manifesto language about stripping away the bourgeois bullshit and telling it like it is, Mr. Jones—they actually used expressions such as "bourgeois," "bullshit," "telling it like it is" and "Mr. Jones"—but it was the rack jobbers who did such stripping away as was actually done.

The rack jobbers were the wholesalers who brought the records (today, the tapes and CDs) to the racks, the wire racks that held the records and albums in the malls, K Marts, Wal-Marts and all other places where recorded music was sold. If the rack jobbers didn't "push the product out the end of the pipeline," it didn't get sold. And a rack jobber was a rack jobber. His music appreciation depended on one thing: how many dollars a record or album would generate per square foot of rack space. A rack jobber would suffer in the name of art, youth, rock and the doors of perception for perhaps thirty seconds. I saw that for myself. On the night of the NARM convention's grand banquet, a dinner for some 1200 souls, the featured performers were the Chambers Brothers. They made the mistake of beginning their act with a ten-minute instrumental number that had been highly praised, extravagantly praised, by all the record reviewers. When the houselights came up, the vast hall was deserted. Or almost deserted. At one table a rack jobber had caught one of his pant legs between the seat and an upright of his chair as he arose to flee, and his wife, his daughter, her husband and five associates were still struggling to free him.

But when all was said and done, the entire business hummed to the rack jobbers' tune. The music business was like the movie business. Art was fine, but the pipeline was the pipeline, and if you couldn't push the product through the pipeline, what difference did art, youth, the generation gap, the war in Vietnam, race riots in the cities and the fatuousness of the bourgeoisie make? The rack jobbers came first. Peace, love, civil rights and the legalization of marijuana could take a number and wait their turn.

Alas, I was fated never to write this revelation of the music industry in the raw. Shortly thereafter, with the idea of gathering material for a non-fiction book about New York City, I attended a party given by Leonard Bernstein and his wife, Felicia, for the Black Panther Party of America. That evening was so bizarre I put the rack jobbers aside and wrote an article (for *New York* magazine) entitled "Radical Chic." Then I did a companion piece about the poverty program entitled "Mau-Mauing the Flak Catchers." And by then the rockers and rack jobbers of yore were hopelessly old news.

Being a Calvinist at heart, I couldn't get my guilt to lie down and die. So when Young Wenner—his youth is one of the longest on record, having lingered now for countless decades—approached me almost three years later with another assignment, another Florida assignment, in fact, I assented before he had even finished the sentence. The idea was to go to Cape Kennedy and cover the launch of Apollo 17, NASA's final mission to the moon, and the antics of all the people who are drawn to such events, all those who insist on being at heavyweight-championship fights and the World Series and bicentennial celebrations in New York Harbor, those who show up, in short, wherever *things are happening.*

The whole swarm materialized at the cape. In the VIP grandstand on the night of the launch was everyone from Jonathan Winters, George Wallace, Jacob Javits, the 136-year-old ex-slave Charlie Smith and Frank Sinatra to King Hussein of Jordan, who insisted on flying into the cape at the controls of his own military jet. The air controllers sent their women and children to north Georgia. In fact, the king merely ran off the runway and came to rest harmlessly on the banks of the Banana River. Half the content of the New York tabloid gossip columns was there. Ahmet Ertegun and Billy Rayner were playing backgammon in the wire grass in front of the grandstand during the pre-launch holds, bravely enduring the Florida littoral's no-see-um bugs, minute insects that went after the ankles with a bite as vicious as a mink's. Also on hand was a young photographer named Annie Leibovitz, who had just started doing work for ROLLING STONE and looked like twelve people, all of them identical and born with batteries included. It was as crazy a scene as any chronicler of the social tableau could wish for.

But my eyes kept wandering to the rocket, the Saturn V rocket that would launch Apollo 17, a stupendous thing, thirty-six stories high, a white shaft gleaming in a bath of arc light against the night sky. Three men (Eugene Cernan, Ronald Evans and Harrison Schmitt) were perched up on top of it in a little thimble known as a command module. The rocket was gorged with a highly volatile fuel called liquid oxygen, and the three men were waiting for someone to light the fuse. Who on earth were they? Or, rather, what were they? Why were they willing to do such a thing?

It was a pretty obvious, wide-eyed question, but I couldn't get it out of my mind. I told Young Wenner I wanted to make the story a study of the psychology of the astronauts themselves. And since I had a good ten days or so until the deadline, why not include *all* the astronauts who had signed on for the Mercury, Gemini and Apollo programs? No stranger to folly and the delusions of journalists, Young Wenner said go ahead.

At first I thought my task would be easy, because this, the final mission to the moon, had turned into a reunion of all the astronauts, and they were in a jolly mood and quite approachable. Or they were approachable up to a certain point. Unfortunately, that point was my key question: "What does it take to be an astronaut?" The very subject seemed to violate a taboo. The taboo had to do with a secret code of conduct among military pilots, which I decided to call "the code of the right stuff," since they wouldn't even talk about it, much less name it. I can remember flying from Florida to Texas and from Texas to Colorado and from Colorado to San Jose, California, frantically in search of some stray astronaut somewhere who would break the code and spill the beans. My one article for ROLLING STONE turned into four, each written against some yet more hellish deadline. I can remember feeding typed pages into a machine attached to a telephone in a suite in the Sherry-Netherlands Hotel, in New York, that somehow transmitted them to the ROLLING STONE office in San Francisco. The machine was known as the Mojo, so named by its previous user, Hunter Thompson. Later, a variation of it would be produced and sold as the fax. After some six or seven Mojo weeks and four dreadful Mojo deadlines, 50,000 words had gone into this series, which Editor Wenner entitled "Post-Orbital Remorse," referring not to the astronauts, as everyone thought, but to the author.

By now it was March of 1973. After three months of couscous, fluids and bed rest, I decided to rewrite the series in book form. I figured this might take five or six months. It took a little longer. In the summer of 1979, I completed the rewrite and, trying to overcome the remorse, renamed it *The Right Stuff*.

I swore I would never go through any such experience again. Therefore, I can't fully account for what happened next—which is to say, how I then got involved with writing serially for ROLLING STONE, over a period of sixty relentless weeks, meaning twenty-seven consecutive hellish deadlines, a book entitled *The Bonfire of the Vanities*. All I know is that only Jann Wenner is mad enough to have let such a thing happen.

Heeeeee-yuh-yuh-yuh-yuh-yuh-yuh-yuh we're not laughing at *you*, Tom. It's just that the question you're asking always used to be such a joke to us. Every time one of us went up, right from the beginning, even before the lunar missions, here would come a bunch of reporters with a look on their faces like the twelve-year-old boy asking the fourteen-year-old boy about . . . *it*. And they'd say: "Yes, but what is it *really* like?" It became a joke. You could tell that they thought we were holding out on them or else that there was something about being an astronaut that we didn't know how to put into words. Actually, it wasn't a bad question. At least it is one that nobody has ever answered. Nobody ever *has* described what we experienced. But it became a joke, all the same.

As you can gather, we never had a particularly high opinion of the press. The press mainly hovered, like the fruit fly. Oh, there was the occasional good soul here and there that we liked, such as some of the people from Life . . . perhaps because they were our captives, come to think of it! Right! But taken as a whole . . . my God, what a swarm of silverfish and second-raters.

You should have been at the party that Life gave last week on the night before the launch [Apollo 17]. The "Life Luau," they called it. It was on a parking lot out back of the Wakulla Motel in Cocoa Beach. They had a striped tent and a steel band and those woven Island hats and a catered Polynesian buffet, but the parking lot was all dirt and cinders and the smoke from the burnt catered Polynesian roast pineapple stew started drifting out into the red ants and the armadillos and the gate crashers and the palmetto bugs, as the locals call the roaches, as they all came creeping up the crest from out of the palmettos by the beach stinging, devouring and butting into all in their path—one thing is still a certainty in this world: it remains humanly impossible to do anything with class in Cocoa Beach, Florida. But Life gave it their best shot, and it was their Last Luau, as one might say. You can't beat Cocoa Beach! That's the beauty of it; it's so Low Rent—and nothing on this earth or in this galaxy will ever change that. It's gorgeous. It's an eternal 1953 DeSoto coupe with venetian blinds in the rear window rusting in the salt air out in the back by the septic tank. Anyway, this party was the last fling. Deke Slayton was there, and Wally Schirra was there, and John Swigert and Rusty Shweickart and Al Worden, and then Alan Shepard showed up. Al was wearing a sport shirt and his new *hep* haircut. He's grown it a little longer and he combs it forward over his forehead in little bangs, like he's Glen Campbell.

But he hasn't changed. Some kid with a big head of electric hair named Bob Schwartzman from a paper called the Boston Phoenix comes up and says, "Mr. Shepard"—that's his first mistake, since it's Admiral—"would you be willing to talk to me sometime about the relationship between the astronauts and the press?" So Al gives him a look you could exterminate head lice with and says, "Sure, if you're willing to listen to a bunch of four-letter words." Gracious to the last, Al! Al's OK. He's indestructible . . .

It is entirely possible, of course, that we misjudged and underestimated the press. God knows they misjudged us. I don't know how they could ever buy the idea that a bunch of test pilots and combat pilots would turn into programmed Merit Badgers as soon as they were given the title Astronaut. The shell protecting that particular image was about as substantial as a Baggie. In the old days they cringed every time Deke Slayton got near a microphone. The Deke Slayton you see today is. Ronald Coleman and Franchot Tone compared to the Deke Slayton of five or ten years ago. Deke was what you might call *basic*. His vocabulary leaned heavily on certain key words. Deke came from out of that military atmosphere where it seems like you're always sitting around somewhere listening to two good old boys from Valdosta, Georgia, talking Army Creole. That's a language in which even simple words like "right" and "correct" have been removed. All day you're hearing the conversation that goes:

"I tol'im if he messed wif me again, I was gonna kick his ass, didn' I?"

"Fuckin' A."

"So all that happened was, he messed around wif me again and I kicked his ass like I tol'im I was gonna do, iddn'at what happened?"

"Fuckin A."

"So how come all of a sudden they getting ready to th'ow my ass in the fucking stock-ade?"

"Unfuckinbelievable."

Or how could the press really believe that our wives were all Doris Day sitting at home wearing her pageboy bob and playing *Moonlight in Vermont* on the upright in the family room while the fleet's deployed? Do you know those marvelous scenes on television during a mission, where the man—or half the time it's a woman—is holding a microphone and saying:

"Inside this trim, modest suburban home tonight is Trudy Cooper, wife of Astronaut Gordon Cooper, sharing the anxiety and the pride of the entire world at this tense moment, but in a very private and very crucial way that only she can understand. Trudy Cooper has told this reporter that one thing has prepared her for this test of her own courage and will sustain her through this test, and that one thing is faith: faith in the ability of her husband, faith in the efficiency and dedication of the thousands of engineers and other personnel who provide his guidance system and ground support . . . and faith in Almighty God . . ."

In the picture on the screen all you see is one reporter standing in front of a little house with the shades drawn, and it all looks very cozy. In point of fact, the lawn would be Nut City. It would look like the clay flats three hours after the Marx Midway carnival pulls in. There would be four or five mobile units with cables running through the gumbo. It would look like Nassau Bay and Timber Cove had been invaded by giant toasters. All these people would be out there wearing bush jackets with leather straps going this way and that and knocking back their Tab and Diet-Pepsi out of pop-top cans and yelling to each other and mainly just milling around . . . hovering . . . like the fruit fly . . . They were desperate, of course. Give us a sign! Give us anything! Give us the diaper service man! The diaper service man comes in with his big plastic bags and smoking a cigar to provide an aromatic screen for his daily task—and they're all over him when he comes out of the house lugging his steamy load. He locks himself in the front seat, choking on cigar smoke and protecting his precious load, and they're banging on his panel truck. "Let us in! We want to see!" They're on their knees. They're slithering in the ooze. They're interviewing the dog, the cat, the rhododendrons. They're making rubbings of the Lith-o-Loid Brix that line the barbecue pit.

Naturally if you happen to be inside that house and peeking out from behind the drapes and witnessing this lunacy in your own yard, and then you look over at the TV set and there is a picture of Nancy Whoever standing alone in front of your little homey cottage like an illustration from out of *Honey Bear* and saying those unbelievable things on top of it—well, then, naturally everybody in the house just cracks up, that's all, and it doesn't matter what is happening at that moment to Mr. Wonderful up in space. Our wives used to enjoy this. They'd all get together in the house of whoever's husband was up, the house that was under siege by the fruit flies, as it were, and they had their Squarely Stable routine they would go through. In the very moment when the woman with the microphone was outside delivering one of those recitations on faith, the wives would be breaking up. One of them would be standing up with her fist up to her chin as if she were holding a microphone and saying:

"We're here at the trim, modest suburban home of Squarely Stable, the famous astronaut, and we have here for our NBC viewers his attractive wife, Primly Stable. Mrs. Stable, I'm sure our viewers would like to share your thoughts and feelings at this moment. You must be very prayerful but very hopeful and very proud at this time, halfway through your husband's mission."

And then she'd shift her fist over underneath the chin of whoever's husband was up there, and she'd answer:

"Yes, Nancy, that's true. I'm very prayerful but very hopeful and very proud at this time, halfway through my husband's mission."

"Tell us, Mrs. Stable—may I call you Primly?"

"Certainly, Nancy, Primly."

"Tell us, Primly, tell us what you felt during lift-off, at the very moment when the rocket began to rise from the earth to take your husband on this historic journey."

"To tell you the truth, Nancy, I missed that part of it. About ten minutes before, I ran out of diapers."

"Well, would you say you had a lump in your throat as big as a tennis ball?"

"That's about the size of it, Nancy, I had a lump in my throat as big as a tennis ball."

"And finally, Primly Stable, I know that above all right now you are praying for the safe return to earth of your husband. But if you could make one other wish at this moment and have it come true, what would that one wish be?"

"Well, I would wish that all the babies in the world and all the diaper servicemen in the world could be in this house right now to share this wonderful moment with me and my children."

—as the voice of the earnest chick out in the yard—in your own yard! at that very moment!—winds up her little speech pouring it into hundreds of thousands of little cottages around the world: ". . . and ground support . . . and faith in Almighty God . . ." And everybody cracks up all over again.

I didn't mean to get off on all that, Tom. You want to get down to the main business, to Apollo 17. You want to know what it's *really like* . . . We've always been willing to describe it, all of it, but so few people really wanted to listen, or else they didn't really know the nature of the question itself. That's what makes it so hard to describe—and that's why you've got to bear with us. I'll take you right inside the capsule with Evans, Schmitt and Gene Cernan, if that's what you want. I can give you a pretty exact idea of what they're experiencing. It would be hard to believe they're that different from the rest of us. Certainly Gene isn't. The interesting case is Jack Schmitt, not because he's a scientist, but because he isn't a scientist—not any more—but we can get back to that. The main thing to know is that the capsule right now is filled up with three colossal egos.

Ti*tanic* egos, one might say, but of a type you've probably never known in your life, Tom, because it is extremely doubtful that you have ever been involved in a particular competition known as *The Right Stuff*. That's what flying happens to be about. It's a vast competition, which no one involved will acknowledge the existence of, we being such cagey souls, called *The Right Stuff*. The main thing to know about an astronaut, if you want to understand his psychology, is not that he's going into space but that he is a flyer and has been in that game for fifteen or twenty years. It's like a huge and very complex pyramid, miles high, and the idea is to prove at every foot of the way up that pyramid that you are one of the elected and anointed ones who have *the right stuff* and can move ever higher and even— ultimately, God willing, one day—that you might be able to join that very special few at the very top, that elite who truly have the capacity to bring tears to men's eyes, the very Brotherhood of The Right Stuff itself.

The right stuff is not bravery in the simple sense; it is bravery in the most sophisticated sense. Any fool can put his hide on the line and throw his life away in the process. The idea is to be able to put your hide on the line—and then to have the moxie, the reflexes, the talent, the experience, to pull it back in at the last yawning moment—and then to be able to go out again the next day and do it all over again—and, in its best expression, to be able to do it in some higher cause, in some calling that means something. Gus Grissom once mentioned that when he first went out to Korea to fly in combat, they used to go out to the field before dawn, in the dark, in buses, and the pilots who had not been shot at by a Mig in man-to-man combat had to stand up. At first he couldn't believe it and then he couldn't bear it—those bastards sitting down were *the only ones with the right stuff!* The way Gus told it, and he wouldn't have lied about a thing like that, the next morning, as they rumbled out there in the dark, he was sitting down. He had gone out there the first day and had it out with some howling supersonic Chinee just so he could have a seat on the bus.

The truth is that unless you have flown in combat, you can never be truly accepted into the Brotherhood, no matter what else you may do. There were plenty of pilots in their thirties who, to the consternation of their moms, dads, wives, bosses, Buddy & Sis—they just couldn't freaking believe it—who confounded all by volunteering to go active and fly in Korea. In godforsaken *Korea!* But it was simple enough. Half of them were flyers who had trained during World War II but never seen combat, and this was their last crack at it—at the ascension, at the Right Stuff. This may be hard to believe, but there are astronauts—including some of us who have been to the moon—who have it gnawing at our hearts that we are not truly accepted into the Brotherhood of The Right Stuff because we have never stood that particular trial, which is combat. And there are others of us who have felt worse than that, who have felt the breath of the hairy bear, namely, Guilt, because we spent five or six years training to go to the moon—while good buddies of ours have been flying in Vietnam.

We have been at that beautiful perfect ripe age, the mid-thirties, when the craziness is gone and you have logged three thousand hours or so in jets and you're still alive, which proves something right there, and you've still got the reflexes to hang your hide on the edge, right up to the Halusian Gulp, and then pull it back, which means you would have been the perfect wing commander, flying over North Vietnam from Thailand in the F-105s or off a carrier in a F-4 or F-8. Instead, you're flying nice and sweet and serene in your T-38 from Houston to Akron, Ohio, to have your Astronaut Couch molded to your very own body, for the capsule you will be going up in, which is one of the sweet secret moments in astronaut success—yet somewhere in the back of your mind you can hear that lunatic locker room scene where they're all young and insane and crazy for danger and the F-4 pilots have scrawled on the face of their lockers, GO PARK YOUR BUSES, F-8S, THE F-4S ARE HERE! and the F-8s have written on theirs, PULL YOUR DAISIES, F-4S, IT'S A MAN'S JOB!—the F-4s being the fastest Navy planes, the Phantoms, the ones that can take on the Migs, man-to-man, at 1400 mph—but the F-8s being something still hairier, in a way, the fighter bombers, no match for a Mig, and yet they have to fly in low, right over the SAM sites and all the other shit, with the Migs coming in, too, and try to lay their loads in the cradle . . . and all of them, F-4 freaks and F-8 freaks, training on shore duty by going out all night and getting totally wrecked and coming into the field in the morning not hungover, you understand, but *drunk,* and going over to the oxygen tanks and clapping the cones over their faces and just burning the alcohol out of the system with brute pure-oxygen resuscitation and then going right out to the plane and going up and telling you later: "I don't recommend it, you understand, but it *can* be done" (—provided you have *the right stuff,* you miserable pud-knockers!).

We are sometimes depicted as being such mechanical creatures, we astronauts, super-rational, "programmed" men of NASA, when the fact is that most of us still have that original magical faith in and yearning for The Right Stuff. If we do much reading at all, most of us have read Antoine de Saint-Exupery from cover to cover. He was the super-mystic of all the mystics who ever flew. He is the only one who ever wrote it down, but even he was a cagey, modest fucker like the rest of us when it came down to calling it by its real name. He talks about the whole sensation of soaring above the earth, of the fragile and vulnerable appearance of civilization down below, and of men who in the moment of the shitfire show not only personal courage but a sense of duty, honor and mission— which are merely grand names, one soon realizes, that he is strewing, like lilies, around The Right Stuff. The archetypical Saint-Ex figure is his buddy Sagon, whose cockpit is in flames and so he crawls out on the wing and sits there, in mid-air, as if in some weird picnic excursion coasting leisurely toward the Gulp, saying, "Let's see—what can I do now?" (Other than parachute to earth, of course, which any fool could do!)

What can I do now? (in this moment when the very Jaws are opening!) And in that is the essence of truly *having it.* At the very top of the pyramid, in the US at any rate, has always been the combat pilot who passed that test and also showed the intelligence to go one step further and become a test pilot, preferably at Edwards [Edwards Air Force Base, in California], which, believe me, has always been Right Stuff City, perhaps even more so than the Astronaut Office in Houston. Deke Slayton and Neil Armstrong both flew as test pilots at Edwards. Neil flew an X-15 at 4000 mph to 200,000 feet, which is right on the edge of space. The X series, the rocket planes—that was the sheer frothing grizzly in the history of this little competition we're talking about. Test pilots were buying the farm, as they used to say, at a rate that approached five percent a year. They'd send you up riding a chimney loaded with liquid oxygen, the same thing they fuel the Saturn-Apollo with, of course. Sometimes those goddamned things turned out to be a brick with fins on it that some maniac at a drawing board down there figured would fly. You'd be hauled up to 30,000 feet under the wing of a B-52 and cut loose, at which point you were supposed to ride the monster until it squealed or blew up.

In those monsters you had to be *afraid* to panic—and that is not a joke. The field of consciousness is very small, as Saint-Ex says, and there was only one thing you could let yourself think about when the tear-up came: *What do I do next?* You used to have the perfect test pilot described as the man who, when he is strangling on a rope and has thirty seconds left, can still concentrate on: Hmmmm—the bastards had to loop that knot, so there must be a way to *un*loop it. Sometimes they used to play tapes of pilots into the final dive, the one into the Gulp, and the guy would be tumbling, going end over end like a brick, with not one prayer left, and he knew it, and he would be screaming into the microphone, but not for Mom, or God or the nameless spirit of Ahor but for one last hopeless crumb of information about the loop: "I've tried A! I've tried B! I've tried C! I've tried D! Tell me what else I can try!" and then that truly spooky click on the machine. *What do I do now?* (in this moment when the very Jaws are opening!) And everybody around the table would look at one another and nod almost imperceptibly, and the unspoken message was: Too bad; there was a man with the right stuff. There was no national mourning, you understand. Nobody outside of Edwards knew the man's name. If he was well-liked, he might get some dusty stretch of road named for him down on the base. He was probably a junior officer doing all this for ten or eleven thousand a year. He had maybe two suits, only one of which he dared wear around people he didn't know. But none of that mattered—not in the Brotherhood! Hah . . . Oh would that we astronauts might have remained so lucky. . . .

In the 1960s, of course, being an astronaut became the apex of the pyramid; or to put it more precisely, if you had been a combat pilot, test pilot, and then became an astronaut—and were one of those who went up—then that was *it*. You were in the Brotherhood for sure. That was why it was such a bitter thing for Deke Slayton when they chose him as one of the original Mercury astronauts and then washed him out for that minor arrhythmia [of the heart]. When it came to being a combat pilot and a test pilot—the two rungs next to the new apex [astronaut]—Deke was known as the best of the original Mercury seven. But that is the nature of The Right Stuff. It was a test of the whole creature, your mind, psyche, nerve and body, and the whole goddamned thing could blow at any seam. Very *bitter* stuff!

This business of the Right Stuff is a very primitive and profound thing. It is not something that only pilots respond to. When the space program brought it a little more out into the open, it actually brought tears to people's eyes. Back in 1963, or maybe 1962, anyway when Kennedy was still President, he brought a group of us to the White House. I can't remember exactly why, because he used to bring us there all the time, privately as well as publicly, which was another interesting thing. . . . Anyway, this particular time his father was there, Joseph Kennedy. He had had a stroke, you will recall, and half his body was paralyzed and he was sitting in a wheelchair. The President takes us into this room to meet him, and the first one he introduces him to is John Glenn. This was the old, pure John, the first American to orbit the earth, and the old man reaches up with his one good hand to shake hands with John and suddenly he starts crying. But the thing is, only half of his face is crying, because of the stroke. One half of his face isn't moving a muscle. It's set, like iron, which was more like the real Joe Kennedy used to be, of course. But the other half—well, it's blubbering, that's the only way you can describe it. His eyebrow on that side is curling down over his eye, the way it does when you're really bawling, you know, and the tears streaming out of the crevice where his eyebrow and his eye and his nose come together, and one of his nostrils is quivering and his lips are writhing and contorting on that side, and his chin is all pulled up and trembling—but just on the one side! But the other half is just staring at John, absolutely calm, impassive, like iron, as I say.

The President would lean down and put his arm around his shoulders and say: "Now, now, Dad, it's all right, okay." But Joe Kennedy was still crying when we left the room.

I'll never forget that sight. Well, obviously if he hadn't had a stroke, he wouldn't have been crying. Nevertheless, the emotion is there, and it would have been there whether he had had a stroke or not. That was the way the Right Stuff affected people. Plenty of people cried when they saw John in those days. Even the Presidents were affected by the Right Stuff. It's that primitive; man can't escape it. All of them, Kennedy, Johnson, Nixon—they're all a little mousey around us at first. Any astronaut can dial the number of the White House and ask for the old man and he'll answer, although I don't know of any astronaut who hasn't been up who has had the nerve to try it. The weird thing is that here you are, still a junior officer in the Air Force or the Navy, making $10 or $11,000 a year, with two suits to your name, one of which you might risk wearing around strangers—and suddenly you have entree all over the world. I'm not kidding! If an American astronaut goes to Rome and wants to dial the Pope, the Pope will answer. It's the truth. Now, this little realization can twist a man in some weird ways, Tom. In fact, therein lie the seeds of something I'm going to tell you about, "post orbital remorse."

History is going to look back on that series of successes, Tom, and marvel, absolutely *marvel*.

The odd thing, though, is that I have to say that *History* will look back and marvel. The public really stopped marveling pretty early in the game, and this created some curious problems among us, particularly those of us in the second, third and fifth groups of astronauts [the fourth group was made up of scientists, including Schmitt]. A lot of us and a lot of other people in NASA started wondering why the enthusiasm for the space program started tailing off so much after John Glenn's flight in 1962. We were making amazing headway, but the public was obviously getting bored. That showed up in the television ratings for the flights and everything else. You'd hear all sorts of explanations . . . The war in Vietnam had ruined national morale, also known as patriotism . . . Americans were becoming too fat and too cynical and were all wrapped up in their charge accounts . . . The new generation of kids was more interested in exploring the inner space of consciousness and the liberation of the self than in any bureaucratic program the government could put together . . . Well, I don't think it was that complicated. The problem was . . . we were *too* successful! Let's face it, the suspense in John Glenn's flight and most of the Mercury flights was: *this man is liable to get wiped out.*

But here we were, sailing on into the Gemini and Apollo programs, and everything was going like clockwork. Those rockets were no longer settling back on their asses and blowing up or heading off toward Sarasota or even going off into dicey orbits, like the Soviet cosmonaut Komarov's. We seemed to have all the problems knocked. The public turned its nose back into the great shopping plaza of life. Perhaps they would take another glance our way the day we actually put somebody on the surface of the moon. Our big PR trouble was: *nobody was getting killed!*

Even the fact that six astronauts had died in accidents in one year [February, 1966–January, 1967] didn't generate any suspense, because none of the accidents were space flights, and the public was barely even aware of half of them. Gus Grissom, Ed White and Roger Chafee died in

January, 1967, in the fire in what would have been the first manned Apollo flight, and of course most people remember that, but they were on the ground, in a simulated flight situation. Ed Givens died in an automobile wreck after a Birdman party [the Birdman Club, an Air Force pilots' fraternity]. Two—neither of whom had been up—Charlie Bassett and Elliot See—were killed in a T-38 in February, 1966. Two more men from the third group [of astronauts] also died in their T-38s, Ted Freeman back in 1964 and C.C. Williams, in October, 1967. And I bet there is not one American in ten thousand who remembers the name of any of them. We all went to their funerals in a group, just as if we had all been in the same wing in the Air Force—but to tell the truth, not even we brooded over the fact that four of the 49 pilots selected so far had died in the ship we all flew every week, the T-38. An Air Force general from the Air Safety Command was once talking to a group of us, and he said that there were three to four "serious accidents" for every 100,000 hours of flying T-38s, which he was citing as a pretty low figure. There are only two kinds of "serious accidents" in a T-38, the one where you bail out in time and the one where you buy the farm. There is not much in between. Well, among the whole group of us, the 49 pilots [i.e., not counting the 17 science astronauts], we had run up just about 100,000 hours . . . and so we were keeping the statistics right on the button. Three or four per 100,000 hours . . . Most of us didn't even mull over it to that extent. *These things happen* . . . and after C.C. Williams' funeral in a little town in Texas called Dickerson, the moment the service was over—the very moment, in fact, that we all stepped outside—there was a tremendous *crack,* and four T-38s came from out of nowhere, in close formation, came barreling right over that little church within a hundred feet of the steeple, roaring the full-bore roar of Fate, turning the very air into one vast infinite roar, and then vanished, four white streaks disappearing into the heavens, and there you had it all: Hail to C.C. Williams, he was pilot, and he is dead, and his soul flies on with the Right Stuff, which will defy the Gulp forever. And with that you just put every death behind you.

But the public, Tom, didn't even see that much of it. After a while they weren't looking at us as individuals anymore: you made it, you went *up*— and those fuckers out there didn't even know who you were!

If anything, what you're doing seems to be bigger, and a bigger thing to the world, because you're getting closer and closer to the moon, and then you're landing on it. Not only that, by the time we got into the Apollo series, they had the on-board television camera perfected and people all over the world were watching us in real time, via satellite. This isn't something that you are consciously dwelling on during a flight, but it is a part of the whole configuration that you are well aware of. Then you come back, splash down, and the television networks are waiting, and there is a whole aircraft carrier full of people beaming all over you, and you get messages from the President and famous people of every description. Even during the two weeks of debriefing, when you are isolated, you're seeing yourself on television and you're seeing your picture in the paper everyday, papers from all over the country and all over the world. And well, I mean, shit, Tom, you're trying not to be carried away by the whole thing, but let's face it: you're *famous!* The whole world seems to have been watching . . . you! You've got a worldwide . . . *face!* It's a funny feeling, it's like candy for your soul, and you find yourself laughing and smiling a lot, over nothing, and chuckling with your wife and, what is more amazing, *talking* to her for a change, and she is so happy and is telling herself and the therapist: "Our relationship certainly has improved since Joe got back."

Then comes the worldwide tour, courtesy of the US Information Agency. You have a trip coming up that goes to perhaps two dozen countries and five continents, one of those things, and a relatively new thought comes across your mind: "Well, I'd better go out and get myself some goddamned clothes!" And that you do. You go out and spend $2000 to $3500 on clothes, which is money you don't have at the time, by the way, but your credit seems awfully good, and you buy up these clothes, including half the things you used to laugh at in the ads. You put on your $20 pajama-stripe shirts and your diamond-check doubleknits and your patent leather fruit boots, and you go into the bathroom alone and check it out and make faces into the mirror and talk to your own grinning mug, out loud, and say: "If you weren't such a world-famous stud, I'd say you looked *sweet!*" And then you go back out into the living room, where your wife is waiting, and you do some more chuckling for no goddamned reason in the world and you talk to her some more, even saying something nice about her goddamned friend, Raven Sue, who you know has been sniping at you to your wife for the heartless brute that you are, and your wife floats into another happy spell: "Things are going to be better now, Dr. Weiskopf."

Then you go across the country, where there are all kinds of banquets and press conferences, and then you head overseas, and there is one thing about these tours that you should understand, Tom. The schedule is very tight, which means you are not doing much wandering about on your own. You are always being led before people who have been briefed on your coming and are waiting for you and know about what you have just done. That's all you see for a couple of months, people all over the globe who are intensely aware of the extraordinary feat you have performed and who know your face and your name. You really seem very goddamned famous. You'll be in some really backward part of the world, like Indonesia, and a little kid who doesn't look 12 will come up and call you by name and ask, very seriously: "Would it be possible, sir, to launch the rocket from the

South Pole, because would it not be true, sir, that one would in that manner, sir, avoid the belt of radiation?" And the kid is right, theoretically, and you come away telling yourself: "12 years old! and already he's absorbed in this thing I'm doing." . . . Indonesia! . . .

Then you return to the United States, and . . . now what? You're back and you begin to notice that in your absence has occurred some incredible . . . *memory decay*. When you left it seemed as if the whole country had been following your adventure . . . and your face . . . but now . . . nobody's head is swinging around on the sidewalk as you walk by, people aren't nudging one another and saying, "Hey, that's—" Not only that, outside of NASA, nobody even seems to remember your name!

I mean, let us try out a few names on you, Tom: Richard F. Gordon, John W. Young, David R. Scott, Donn Eisele, William Anders, Michael Collins, Alan L. Bean, Fred W. Haise, Stuart A. Roosa, James B. Irwin, Alfred M. Worden, Charles M. Duke. What did they do? All right, you may get Collins, since he was on Apollo 11 with Armstrong and Aldrin. But what about Gordon? He went up twice, on Gemini 11 and Apollo 12. Scott went up three times, on Gemini 8, Apollo 9 and Apollo 15, but if you remember him it is probably only because of the flap over the goddamned postal covers they took up on Apollo 15. Eisele went up on Apollo 7, Anders on Apollo 8, Bean on Apollo 12, Haise on Apollo 13, Roosa on Apollo 14, Irwin and Worden on Apollo 15, Duke on Apollo 16; and Young went up three times, on Gemini 10, Apollo 10 and Apollo 16. Bean, Irwin, Scott and Duke are four of the twelve human beings who have ever walked on the surface of the moon.

But it's not simply that nobody remembers your name. It's more complicated than that. There's an extra little twist on it. Let us give you an example. On the afternoon before this last flight, Apollo 17, Jim Irwin was down at the Cape with some of his new friends from the Baptist outfit he is now with, the evangelical outfit, High Flight—and with some of his new friends from, shall we say, the lay side of the Ledger of Life, some directors and other 150-watters from Johns-Manville. Jim and these people and perhaps 25 other random souls who had managed to get VIP badges for the launching took one of the last bus tours of the Space Center before the launch that night. The VIPs were piled up in lines out at the Visitors Information Center, and the buses were making the circuit right up until sundown. Jim and his wife Mary were sitting in the second seat from the front, on the left. All of five feet from them, in the very front of the bus, was the tour guide, wearing the white officer-style cap and one of those little stem microphones around his neck. Now, this guide was really well versed on the Kennedy Space Center. He's rattling off facts and figures about the Redstone rockets and the Atlas rockets and the Titan rockets and the Saturn rockets and Al Shepard's flight and John Glenn's flight and the pads they used to use and the pads they use now and the automatic abort systems and the flight crew training for the moon landings. He's pointing out the cinder ring, the little clearing where the astronauts who went to the moon had practiced on a simulated lunar surface—this guy has it all at his fingertips, and he's never at a loss when somebody asks a question. At one point the bus stops and he leads everybody inside one of the old bunker-style buildings they used for the early flights and he's pointing out the way the flights used to be launched and so forth. Then everybody gets back on the bus and sits down, and the guide gets up and says:

"Ladies and gentlemen, I've just been informed that one of our former astronauts, Jim Irwin, who was on the crew of Apollo 15, is on this bus!"

Then he turns to Jim with a huge embarrassed smile on and says: "Believe me, if I had known you were on board, I'd wouldn't be the one standing up here with this microphone on trying to tell people what this is all about!"

Well, Jim does the right thing, he says the right thing, he says: "Listen, you've probably forgotten more than I ever knew about this place. You're doing fine."

Except for the High Flight and the Johns-Manville people, nobody else on this bus knew that Jim Irwin, one of the twelve mortals to walk on the moon, was on this bus, either, but now they're all picking up. They're all craning about. Toward the back a woman from Colorado is saying to the man she happens to be sitting next to, some dude who is all in white except for a blue blazer, white winged-tip shoes, the whole bit, a guy who looked a bit like you, Tom, as a matter of fact—she's saying to him:

"Excuse me, but do you know which one is Irwin?"

So the guy points him out, and she says: "Is that him?"

"Yes."

"And which one was he on?"

"Apollo 15."

"Well, I get them so confused!"

We'll grant you that Jim is wearing a white polo shirt and sunglasses, and he has his hair combed forward just a bit, in the Modified Groovy manner, like Al Shepard now wears it, but this man, this face, watched by millions on television just 16 months before, never registered with her or anybody else except his own religious and commercial cohorts—not even with the tour guide, the man whose very job was knowing all about the space program and who obviously took pride in his work!

Are you beginning to comprehend the picture, Tom? Almost any of us, even those of us who have been to the moon, can walk into a room and be introduced by name to all sorts of people, even prominent, well-educated people, and you're just another face in the man-swarm—until some-body says: "He's an astronaut. He went to the moon." Then it changes—like that! They light up! They're all smiles! Their pearly mouths are gleaming! They're all around you! The room has come alive! You're Mr. Wonderful again! They've turned the Fame circuit back on! They've switched on the sun lamp in your soul!

Except that you also overhear the questions they ask each other behind their hands . . . "*Who?* What did he do?" It doesn't take long for the truth to sink in. You can't go on for very long believing that it is *you* who are famous, that it is *you* who have become something extraordinary in the hierarchy of mortals. It is you as a figure who is really known only as Astronaut, as a symbol of space exploration itself, of the program itself, of the rockets and the countdowns and the mighty fireballs of the launch and of the whole idea of the space voyage and of walking on another heavenly body.

Which is not a small role, after all! . . . You've enabled millions to love the Power and behold it as man's glory. . . . Remember, Tom, that at the very outset the engineers wanted to do this thing without manned flights; go to the moon and explore with machines. They figured they could ac-complish it in half the time and at one-tenth the cost. They argued against manned flight for a long time. And yet the decision to put men on top of those rockets was a decision of incalculable value. Only 34 of us have ever been up, but our presence on those flights took the whole human race out into space and up onto the moon and into the far reaches of the galaxy. We turned it from an experiment into an adventure. In terms of the pres-tige of this country, our presence on those ships built up a credit rating that could survive a hell of a lot of debts, including the war and the race business and a hell of a lot of other things. . . . You will all appreciate that 20 years from now. . . . The moment that Neil Armstrong set foot on the moon—well, it just spun out the cortex of everybody in the world. They looked away from their TV sets and then up at the moon, and they said with one of the few notes of true wonder they will ever know in their lives: "There's a man walking up there."

And so we think about all that—and we understand it—and yet we still can't believe that somehow that glory and wonder hasn't transferred to us as individuals. After all, there have only been 34 of us! Oh, perhaps Neil can be said to possess it personally . . . and perhaps John . . . perhaps it will attach to them, personally, as individuals, forever. But as for the rest of us: we are . . . Astronaut, a composite figure . . . we stand for the program, for the great effort, for the great machine, for the Integral. . . . But a man can't look at the world as a composite figure, that is a stunt the ego cannot perform . . . I—Ego—am always on top of the world. If you or I could peer around the curvature of the horizon and see people in Chile and Peru, we would break out laughing. They would seem to be stuck onto the globe at such a crazy goddamned angle, trudging over South America at a 90-degree tilt . . . Ever since we came back, we have had to look at the world as *I*—not as Composite, Astronaut, Integral— and we get scarcely a single responding glance.

Ask a Marine

DAVID HARRIS

THE ASSIGNMENT BROUGHT THEM TOGETHER: THE
WRITER WHO HAD BEEN JAILED FOR DEFYING THE
DRAFT AND THE WAR HERO WHO WOULD NEVER WALK
AGAIN.

It was 1973, I was twenty-seven years old, and "Ask a Marine" was
my first assignment as a professional journalist. I had spent the
previous seven years as an organizer against the Vietnam War; for
two of those years, I was incarcerated in federal prison for refusing
to be drafted into the army. The war had only been "over" for several
weeks when I got the assignment. I had already written two books about
my experiences, but this was different. I was setting out to join a profession and enter the workaday world where my less adventurous peers had
long since been ensconced. Now, twenty years later, it all seems old hat
and matter-of-fact, of course. I've spent the intervening decades publishing dozens of stories for ROLLING STONE and the *New York Times Magazine*, as well as four more books, but then it was an immense moment. I
was divorced, broke, a single parent and making what the "adult" world
described as a late start in an altogether unfamiliar environment.

That I even had this opportunity sprang from having written Jann Wenner, ROLLING STONE's founder and plenipotentiary, a week earlier. I had first been introduced to the magazine in 1971, when it ran a short feature about my release from the penitentiary. By the time I made contact, the STONE had solidified its reputation as the ongoing voice of the Sixties generation out among the big boys of the information world. I had already decided that I wanted to make a living with my typewriter, and for the last six months, I had been writing radio editorials for use by local antiwar broadcasters. I sent Wenner several of them, suggesting he might be interested in publishing them. He came right back with a note that he had no use for these pieces but he'd be interested in having me write some longer reportage. Why didn't I come up to the office and talk it over?

I was game for whatever he had in mind. I had never taken a course in journalism, but I was used to presenting information; I could write, I knew how to tell a story, and in the immediate moment, I had no trouble recognizing a golden opportunity when it fell into my lap. I called Wenner's office immediately and scheduled an appointment.

In those days, ROLLING STONE was still headquartered in a remodeled four-story brick office building on San Francisco's Third Street, just north of China Basin. It was nothing special according to the prevailing standards of big-city commerce, but coming out of the scruffy settings I was used to, it seemed quite fancy.

My first human contact at the magazine was Judy, the receptionist who oversaw a carpeted anteroom off the third-floor elevator landing. Judy recognized my name and thought it was just great that I might do something for the magazine. As I waited to be summoned to Wenner's office, she and I talked and then talked more. I told her I hoped this meeting would be the beginning of my career as a journalist.

In that case, she advised me, I should pay attention to my size when I got in there with him. Jann was a good guy, she said, but he was a little self-conscious about being short. A tall person like me could make him nervous, and that might spoil everything. She suggested that I stoop when standing and sit down as quickly as possible.

After a fifteen-minute wait in the lobby with Judy, a secretary ushered me into a large, bustling, high-ceilinged work space, divided only by low partitions, and across it to a walled office in the building's back corner. Jann was inside, sitting at his desk. He stood up in his chair and reached across to shake hands. I bent a little at the knees, gave his hand a squeeze and sat down immediately. He was in his shirt sleeves, with his tie undone, and I was wearing no tie at all. I slouched in my chair so that my head was lower than his.

Neither Jann nor I was much for small talk, and in five minutes the meeting was over. He asked if I had any story ideas. I said I knew a great one about a paralyzed former marine down in L.A. He said the magazine would cover my expenses, as long as I kept them close to the vest, and pay me ten cents a word, if the story was accepted.

I had no idea if it was a good deal or a bad one, but I never considered saying anything but yes. It was confirmed with a handshake, and when I left his office, I felt anointed — and suddenly professional.

"So," Judy asked after I got back to the waiting room, "how'd it go?"

"I'm on my way," I said, chortling. "Ten cents a word."

Getting the story was easy. I already knew Ron Kovic from having shared a speaker's platform with him on a couple of occasions. A week after I met with Wenner, I spent three days in Los Angeles, talking to Kovic during the afternoon and sleeping on a friend's spare bed at night. I collected a dozen hours of his taped recollections.

Back home at the house I rented in East Palo Alto, I began poring over the tapes, taking longhand notes and transcribing. This process is now so familiar to me I could do it in my sleep, but then it was fresh and very different. The principal object was, of course, to catalog the information and quotes that I'd collected. But by instinct, I also used it to immerse myself in the world and the being of this person I wanted to bring to life on the printed page.

I used the ritual of listening and relistening to each word he had spoken as a way of insinuating myself far enough into his person that I could command it into sentences and paragraphs. For me, this almost meditative ritual of concentration remains an intense one, even after repeating it for almost twenty years, but never was it more intense than while working on "Ask a Marine."

Listening to Kovic's voice rambling out of my tape recorder, I felt the stirrings of the young man headed to boot camp and the dead weight of the body in which he'd returned from Vietnam. Sometimes my stomach tied in knots. At other moments, my eyes filled with tears. I could feel myself becoming my subject, making his experiences at least momentarily my own. At night, I dreamt marine dreams and awoke to the antiseptic smell of long hospital corridors dominating my imagination. Such immersion is a heady process that I have since learned, if done right, always takes a writer just a step away from being overwhelmed, but this first time it was positively disorienting.

The feeling was only magnified by an allergic reaction that descended on me at the exact moment I began reviewing the tapes. I'd never had such a reaction before, and the sudden appearance of a bright red rash all over my upper body, inexorably expanding into puffy scarlet welts, was quite terrorizing. Even after my doctor diagnosed the condition, I was half-convinced it had grown out of my intense concentration on Kovic, as though I had somehow assumed a fraction of his disability as I captured his persona. Sitting at my typewriter, searching for words, trying to resist the urge to scratch the long red eruptions on my arms, I wondered if I would ever be able to extricate myself from this psychosomatic jungle. I spent the week and a half it took to produce the story's final draft wondering each night as I went to sleep if my obsession with this wheelchair-bound marine would leave me paralyzed when I woke the next morning.

As terrorized as I sometimes was, however, I did not stop writing.

By the time I filed the story with the office in San Francisco and heard back from Wenner, of course, I could laugh at my fears. The eruptions on my skin had vanished, and I felt as good as new. The word from Jann's office was nothing but excellent. Jann called me personally to let me know. Everyone loved the story about Kovic, he said, and wanted me to do more. I should come back up again and talk to him.

This time, the office seemed remarkably less alien. After another session with the boss, during which I received marching orders for my next article, Judy took me across the street to Jerry's Inn, the bar where everyone on the magazine hung out and ate lunch. She introduced me around the room, and soon the regulars were buying me drinks and telling me what good things they'd heard about my piece on the paralyzed marine.

I soaked it all up. I was never much for drinking in the middle of the day, but by the time I left Jerry's and went marching down Third Street for my car, I had a warm alcoholic glow. I was starting another chapter in my life, and it all seemed to be working out just as I'd hoped.

I was a journalist now, I told myself, squinting into the bright afternoon sky, and I hadn't paralyzed myself along the way, despite my ordeal of the previous week. At the moment, it seemed all anyone could ever want.

RS 139

JULY 19TH, 1973

Ron Kovic was born on the Fourth of July, 1946, and spent much of his youth laying cap pistol ambushes for the Long Island Railway trains that clanked in and out of Massapequa. In those days, the Fourth of July still meant something in the state of New York. Every year the American Legion marched and Ron's birthday shone through it all as a blessing, if not a small miracle, in the family. Being born like that wasn't something the Kovics took lightly. Ron's father had left the family farm to

work for A&P and Ron's Uncle Jim fought all over Korea with the United
States Marine Corps. The two of them sat in the kitchen behind beers
and talked. Uncle Jim said he'd seen good men splattered for the birthday his nephew had been given as a gift from God. Ron's dad nodded his
head.

After overhearing a few of these family discussions, Ron had his heart
set. He ran his body until it was a young bunch of ropes. He was Massapequa High's finest wrestler and the American Legion cannon's biggest
fan. The sign by the road said, MARINE CORPS BUILDS MEN: BODY,
MIND AND SPIRIT, and Ron knew it was true. No one in the neighborhood was surprised when Ron Kovic finished high school and joined up.
He was meant for the marines. They were just in his stars.

When Ron signed his life over to the bald eagle, he went to Parris
Island with all the others just like himself. His dream commenced with
the drill instructor lining all 82 up on the parade deck. Their heads
were shaved and they wore their first khaki in wrinkles and lumps.
The DI introduced himself and told them they were a bunch of maggots.
He would address them as "the herd" and they would respond with "aye,
aye, sir." They would say aye, aye sir when they opened their mouths and
aye, aye sir before they closed them. If they did everything he said and did
it quicker than he could say it, then he would transform them from lowly
maggots into something the Marine Corps could use. That was the DI's
first promise. His second promise was to beat their asses if they didn't.
Ron listened hard. The walls of his stomach grew hair and he settled into
his life. He was going to be a marine. For goddamn sure, he was going to
be a marine.

After boot camp, Private Kovic was sent to Camp Lejeune and then on
to Radio School at Norfolk Marine Barracks. When he was done in Norfolk, the private was a private first class and assigned to the Second Field
Artillery. It chafed Ron a little. He wanted to charge up a hill but mostly
he cleaned radios. It was getting hard on him, being ready and not asked,
and then he heard about Vietnam. Right away he wanted to go. That's
where the marines were fighting and that's what a marine is supposed to
do.

PFC Kovic requested immediate transfer to WESPAC, Vietnam.
When the form asked why, he wrote, "to serve my country." It's so much
later now that it's hard to believe, but back then Ron and everybody in
the battalion office had no doubts. PFC Kovic got orders in ten days and
flew to Camp Pendleton to Okinawa to Da Nang Airfield and into his
dreams.

Ron Kovic really did like it. Just like he knew he would back in Massapequa. He liked it so much he went right for its middle. After three months,

PFC Kovic was a lance corporal and he volunteered for what was called "Recon." It was April and Sgt. Jimmy Howard and a platoon from Delta Company had been surrounded on Hill 488 west of Chu Lai. Only eight grunts got back so the reconnaissance outfit had to be what was called "rebuilt." The sergeant asked for volunteers and Ron was the first to step forward. He'd heard about Recon.

Recon were studs. They were jungle thugs and said they ate Cong for lunch. Every mean thing Ron had ever heard, he'd heard about Recon. They were the light of the West in an ocean of darkness. Ron was ready for it.

When he got home, the Marine Corps gave Ron Kovic a Commendation medal with a combat V and a promotion to E-4.

Ron had a good taste in his mouth right up to the time he left. He was tied in a knot with the second platoon and he loved them the same way he loved his gun. It was tight, hairy, silent work they did together and made them close. Only one last memory had an edge on it.

Ron was sitting on his sea bag in the middle of base camp waiting for the jeep ride to his plane. He was right by the sign that said DUNN'S RAIDERS. That was his outfit, Dunn's Raiders, like the sign said: WE CAME TO KILL. NEVER HAVE SO FEW DONE SO FOUL TO SO MANY. There was a skull and crossbones on its bottom edge.

The heat was burrowing into his back when someone called him.

"Hey Kovic," they said. "Come here and see what we got."

Ron walked over to one of the tents with three marines inside. The grunt in the middle had a jar in his hands. Inside the jar there were two fingers and an ear.

"Look at this," he said. "Nice, huh? I'm gonna mail 'em back to the States. Wheatstraw says he knows how to get them through."

Ron got stiff and a strap tightened around his gut. The fingers hung half way up in the fluid and the ear was floating on the top. Since he was about to leave, no one held his reaction against him. It was to be expected.

Charging up the runway to the plane back to the States, Ron forgot about the jar and sailed home to Massapequa to show the neighborhood his yellow boots.

The C-130 took him to a different world, miles away. It got old quick and Ron missed Recon. His memories burned at him. Ron Kovic was stationed with a Hawk Missile Battalion and his buddies were getting cut up in the jungle. That was no good. It pushed at him and pushed at him until it finally pushed him over.

A copy of the New York Daily News did the trick. The front page was covered with four longhairs burning a flag in Central Park. That pissed Ron off so bad, he sat on his foot locker and cried for the first time since he'd become a marine. When he finished, E-4 Kovic went down to the Admin office and requested a transfer back to Vietnam. Transfer was denied four days later. Going back had come to be thought of as insane and the sergeant stared when Kovic came in 14 more times to repeat his request. By then he was considered crazy enough to return.

His new orders made Ron Kovic a full sergeant with three stripes on his arm. When the sergeant was honest, he copped that his future had him worried. His orders wouldn't let him join his old outfit. He was going to the Third Division in the DMZ instead. From what he'd heard, the DMZ was a different kind of place from the one he remembered.

It sure enough looked that way on the plane he took to Dong Ha. No one talked. The only sounds were the marines loading their ammo magazines. When speaking broke out, the dirty ones said there was lots of "arty" up there and Ron had never been under arty before. Not that it took long to find out what arty meant. He looked out the window and Dong Ha airfield was full of rocket holes. People there said the shit was coming in every day, a hundred at a time.

Ron's base was at the mouth of the Qua Viet River, past Geo Lin. The country was all sand and stumpy pine trees and the marines worked mostly off amtracs: steel boxes with a cave inside big enough to carry a squad. The camp was dug into bunkers, eight sandbags high. At night, Ron led a scout team outside the perimeter and laid ambushes 1000 meters from the wire. They sat in the rain and watched for the NVA. During the day, the scouts slept. At least they tried to. They had to ask arty's permission first. When it was arty's turn to talk, nobody slept.

As soon as the marines heard the crack with the whistle on the end of it, every son of a bitch with any sense ran for the bunkers. The rounds came in right on top, each one sounding like it had a ticket for the hairs on your ass. Noses bled and ears ached. A lot of the Third Marines got to keeping rosaries close by, to use in the shelters. It was nothing but scary. The worst Ron ever saw was when they took 150 hits, right after lunch.

As soon as the arty lifted, Ron grabbed a medic bag and ran out on the compound. He saw his own tent first and it was just shrapnel holes held together with canvas threads. Past that there was a crowd where Sgt. Bodigga's supply tent had once been. Ron pushed through the ring of marines and found a hole. No tent. Just a hole. In the bottom was something that looked like five or six bodies. They were all powder-burned and torn up. Ron reached in to find IDs and could only find Bodigga's wallet. After looking again, Sgt. Kovic realized that Bodigga was all there was in the hole . . . all those pieces were just Bodigga. Ron stacked Sgt. Bodigga on a stretcher and cried. Over his shoulder, in the motor pool, someone was screaming.

"McCarthy," they screamed. "They got McCarthy. Those motherfuckers. Those rotten motherfuckers. They got McCarthy."

McCarthy was from Boston and he had blue eyes. When he was laid out with the rest of the dead, stripped naked in front of the command bunker with his loose parts piled next to him, McCarthy's eyes were open and looked straight up into the rain.

Ron saw him there and wanted to kill somebody. He wanted to kill somebody and use them to paste McCarthy and Bodigga back together.

It didn't turn out that simple. As soon as Ron Kovic got to wanting that way, something happened to make him feel just the opposite. It was a night patrol.

A lieutenant took Ron's detail out to search for sappers across the river. There was a village on the far bank and the colonel was worried someone would dive in and put a mine to the marine boats. A hundred meters from the village, the patrol saw the light of a small fire. It was inside a hootch and it wasn't supposed to be there. The village had been ordered to keep lights out. The platoon spread out along a paddy dike and watched. Word was passed to hold fire and the lieutenant set off an illumination flare. Just as the flare lit, someone to Ron's left fucked up and let go. That shot set the whole line on fire for 30 seconds at full automatic. When they finished, Ron and Leroy were sent up to check the hootch.

Inside the broken bamboo, there was an old man with the top of his head shot away. Two kids were on either side of him. One's foot just dangled. The other had taken a round in the stomach that came out his ass. The hootch's floor was covered with blood.

When the platoon crossed the paddy and saw it, the marines melted into lumps. Some dropped their weapons and only Leroy talked.

"Jesus Christ," he whined. "What'd we do. We've killed an old man and some kids."

The lieutenant yelled to form up in a 360 but Leroy kept moaning and no one else moved. The villagers started to come out of their huts and scream at the marines. It took the lieutenant five minutes to round the patrol into shape. After they called a chopper for the kid who was still breathing, the platoon went inside the wire. Sgt. Kovic laid in his bunker all night and wanted to give it up. He wanted the referee to blow the whistle and call time out until he'd had a chance to think it over.

But wars don't work that way. Ron reported to the colonel in the morning and asked to be taken off patrols. The colonel said no. Instead the platoon got a week in camp and Sgt. Kovic was ordered to get his shit together and act like a marine.

The platoon didn't go back to action until January 20th. When they did, it was in the afternoon. January 20th started late but turned into a big day, about as big a day as there will ever be in the life of Sgt. Ron Kovic. It was a day that made all the ones after it very different from the ones that went before.

"The people on the amtracs got hit first" is the way he remembers it. "I heard the pop . . . pop . . . pop as the mortars left their tubes and the crashing as they hit around the tracks. Then rounds started cracking around us. I couldn't tell if they were coming from the village or the treeline, so I fired both places. I was completely out in the open.

"All we could do was take ground and return fire. After a little bit, I heard a loud crack right next to me and my whole leg went numb. A .30 caliber bullet had gone in the front of my foot and come out the heel. It took a piece out the size of a silver dollar. My foot was all smashed. I stayed standing as long as I could but then it began to feel like it was on fire. I went to a prone position and kept using my rifle until it jammed from the sand.

"When I couldn't get a round into the chamber, I decided to stand and see where the rest of my platoon was. I slammed the rifle down and pushed myself up with it. Just as I got my arms straight, I heard a huge crack next to my ear. It was like getting hit with an express train. My whole body started vibrating. Another .30 caliber bullet had hit my right shoulder, passed through my lung and severed my spinal cord into two pieces. My whole body seemed to have left me. I felt like I was somewhere up in the air."

"I closed my eyes for just a second, then I started to breathe. My lung was collapsed so I just took little breaths. Slow little sucks. All I could think was that I didn't want to die. I couldn't think of nothin' else. I waited to die. I mean I just waited for it all to black out, for all the things that are supposed to happen when you die. I couldn't believe what was going on. Where was my body? I must've been hit with a mortar. That was it, a mortar. It had ground up everything below my chest.

"Then I moved my hands behind me and I felt legs. I felt legs but they didn't feel back. They were my legs. There was something wrong but I couldn't explain it. My body was there but I couldn't feel it. Then I got real excited. It was still there. I wasn't going to bleed to death. My body was still there.

"I lay there for what seemed like hours. Once, somebody ran up in back of me. 'Hey,' he said. 'Hey Sarge, you all right? Then I heard another crack and he seemed to fall on the back of me. I couldn't feel it but I heard. Someone from my left yelled, 'He's dead, Sarge. They shot him through the heart.' He was a marine from the company who'd run all the way up. I yelled for everybody to stop coming. I don't know if they heard, but I yelled. I was being used as bait. Other than that, I felt nothing. I just wanted to live. I tried to calm myself. I felt cheated. I felt cheated to die. Twenty fucking years old and they were taking my life away from me.

"Then a black man came running up. He grabbed me and threw me over his shoulder. He started dragging me back. He was a big black man. Big black arms. Big black hands. All I can remember is staring up at the sky and the sky sort of spinning and jumping. I could just feel the top of my body. I felt the sun in my face and him picking me up and throwing me down. All the time he was yelling, 'you motherfuckers. Fuckers. Fuckers. Goddamn motherfuckers.' And me screaming the same thing. 'Motherfuckers. Motherfuckers.' "

By the next morning, Sgt. Kovic had been given the last rites of the Catholic Church and gone on the operating table. He was in the intensive care ward at Marble Mountain in Da Nang. He'd been brought there by choppers with tubes in his lungs and IVs all over his body. There was a Korean (who'd hit a booby trap) in the bed to his left. When he wasn't babbling in sing-song, the Korean waved his two remaining fingers over his head until he died. Then a black pilot took the Korean's place. Ron watched the pilot die too.

After that, Ron was sure he'd die if he stayed at Marble Mountain. Living meant doing everything right, so Sgt. Kovic listed his dos and don'ts on a Red Cross pad. The nurse turned him over every four hours and Ron never complained. He was going to be the perfect patient who recovers miraculously. The morphine helped. He got his syringe every 120 minutes. When he was waiting for his shot, Ron Kovic noticed that he couldn't feel his dick anymore. All day long, he explored his floppy body and checked to see if it had come back while he was asleep. It never did.

Ron Kovic lay three days in Yokuska Naval Hospital with his catheter and his striker frame and then he demanded a wheel chair. "I'm ready," he said. The doctors thought it was early but Ron insisted. They brought the chair and lifted Ron into it. He was still being Marble Mountain's best patient and didn't make any noise. For half-an-hour he tried the chair. At the end of it, Sgt. Kovic puked all over himself and passed out. When he recovered, Ron decided to wait on the chair until he reached the States.

In the meantime, he'd concentrate. Ron kept a little chart of his progress each day. He swore to the doctors he was going to walk out. "If it's the last thing I do," is the way he said it. "Right out the fucking door." The doctors said that wasn't possible, but Ron wouldn't listen. He had to have something to want and that was it.

When he wasn't wanting, Sgt. Kovic watched. There was pain all around him but Ron knew it would pass. He figured out that most of the other lumps under the covers would heal. The pain would become a memory and then they'd leave, tall and strong again and whole. But he wouldn't. His wound couldn't. His shoulder would close up and so would his foot but that was all. The life in Sgt. Kovic's head would never touch his feet again.

After a while, the war had almost disappeared. The radio said everybody'd be home soon and hospitals were just about the only thing Ron remembered. There was a short one in Anchorage, another in Virginia, one in New York State and then another that looked out on New Jersey. The last one was the Kingsbridge VA. It was summer by then and Ron stayed at the Kingsbridge hospital 11 months the first time and then again for six more.

Sgt. Kovic now belonged to the Veterans' Administration. The marines discharged him with a bronze star and wished him well. The VA's job was to retrain certain kinds of ex-soldiers and Sgt. Kovic was 100% retired. The first thing the VA tried to teach him was how to shit slowly and once every three days.

That's when they gave the enemas, every third day. Other than that you had to shit in your bed and lay on it. The enemas started at five in the morning. Tommy the Enema Man came by with his tube and dangled it under their noses. When everyone was awake, they each got a striker frame. Tommy and his helper rolled them all, 24 para- and quadriplegics, half the ward, into what was called the blue room. When it was full, the two white coats pumped all the stomachs up with soapy water. All 24 lay in there with their withered bodies and listened to their bowels hit the buckets like cow flop. When it was done, Tommy wiped each of their asses and rolled them into the shower.

Ron called it the car wash. The attendant ran a thin white strip of pHisohex down the middle of Ron's body and then hosed it off. When they were shorthanded, the attendant sometimes had to leave in the middle of the scrub. The second time Ron got washed, he lay in the Kingsbridge shower for an hour waiting for the attendant to come back. All Ron did was try not to scream like he wanted to. He learned to lie on the tile and watch his body that wouldn't move and had started to shrivel.

Every third day Ron wanted to scream and he never did. After a couple of months, the screams didn't even bother to cross his mind. Ron lay there and felt he'd been used up and thrown away and no one was treating him like the marine he had gone out and been.

The more he looked around the ward, the more Ron felt it. C-3 was the sign over the door and it was one big mirror. He saw his friends and there he was. Propped up and flopped over, they weren't much to look at.

Ron noticed Mark more than anybody else. Mark was a 19-year-old head. He'd been a six-foot marine once. But then his truck hit a mine on the way to Khe Sanh and Mark went out the window. He was paralyzed from the neck down. Mark got around by pushing his chin on an electric button that made the wheels on his chair spin. It was Mark who taught Ron how to fight the rats.

The rats were smallish, brown, and came out at night. Just past 2 a.m., one crawled up on Mark's chest. He screamed. Then he screamed again. No one came. He screamed for three hours until an aide arrived and told Mark he must be drunk. From then on, Mark got Ron to lob his dinner rolls behind the radiator. That kept the rats eating all night and off their chests while Mark and Ron talked. Mark had been a high-school football player and asked Ron to look at the team picture and pick him out. Mark was proud and didn't take to being a loose sack of flesh very easily. He fought it as hard as he could. He lay up all night and listened to his plastic piss bag slop over onto the floor and he hated it. He kept hating it until the day he would talk his friend in Chicago into sticking a needle through his vein. Mark would die with his eyes full of heroin and his body full of empty space. But that was much later, after Ron left the VA for the first time.

When Ron reached the doors, he left just the way he'd promised back in Japan. He walked. It wasn't like he'd pictured it but it sure wasn't in a chair. He trained every day with braces until he could move on crutches and drag his strapped-up legs along. He scraped out the door to his mom and dad and he felt proud. Every time he got up on his crutches he felt that way. To Ron Kovic, he was tall and pretty even if his spine did have a new bend to it. Ron walked like that all over the backyard in Massapequa. The doctors said he did it too much. He finally broke his femur when he was out on a walk and had to return to Kingsbridge.

This time there was an operation. When he got off the table, his right leg had a plate in it and was shorter than the other. The leg turned in, too, and wouldn't fit in his braces anymore. Ron screamed at the doctors.

"You ruined it," he said. "Now I can't walk anymore. I'll never get to stand up."

"It's all right," the doctors said. "You couldn't really walk anyway."

The second time Ron left Kingsbridge he was pissed. He remembers it today and he still gets angry: His jaw freezes up and he talks louder than he means to. "It was like I'd swallowed a lie," he explains, "and then they rubbed my face in it. America made me. They made me and I gave them everything I could give and then I wasn't good enough to treat like a man. I didn't want to be a good patient anymore. I was proud and they wouldn't even let on I was still alive. I was something for a closet and a budget cut. I didn't feel lucky anymore. I was gonna live and I knew how I was gonna live. I was living with a body that was already dead. That had to be worth something, but it wasn't. All it could get me was a seat out by the pigeons and the old men from World War II."

After a while, Ron couldn't sit on his anger any more. He moved to Los Angeles and called the office of Vietnam Veterans Against the War.

When the phone answered, Ron said he wanted to join and do anything he could to stop the war.

Ron meant it. He manned tables and spoke at high schools. He told them how he'd been the Massapequa flash. He told them how he'd sung about the "Halls of Montezuma" and the "Shores of Tripoli" and how it was a lie. He told whoever would listen and half those who wouldn't.

Ron felt better than he'd felt in a long time. He liked the folks, like he was one of them. He didn't feel like a freak and he wondered why it had taken so long for him to find out. His new life gave Ron a chance to meet his country again. One such meeting on Wilshire Boulevard drove the last of the bald eagle from Ron Kovic's mind. It happened in front of the headquarters for Richard Nixon's re-election.

The picket started at 11 a.m. and by noon there was quite a crowd and almost as many cops. And these weren't any run-of-the-mill-bust-a-drunk-on-a-street-corner cops. It was the L.A.P.D. and anybody west of Barstow knows the L.A.P.D. doesn't take no for an answer.

The ones Ron met were young, undercover, and tried special hard. They moved in the crowd and took notes. Ron was up the block with a line of people who had wheeled over the cross street and blocked traffic. The blue line of police moved their way and they scattered back to the sidewalk. As soon as the cops leaned to the cross street, the people on Wilshire did the same thing and the police scurried back. It didn't take long for the L.A.P.D. to tire of the game. The captain gave an order to disperse and the people decided to take it. The blue men had their clubs out and their goggles on: two very bad signs. The decision was made to go to McArthur Park. Ron wheeled the word up to the cops.

"We're leaving," he said. "We're going to obey the order to disperse."

With that, the line of signs made its own slow way back down the boulevard. Ron stayed at the back, making sure everybody got out all right. It was then that he met the L.A.P.D. up so close there was no way to mistake what he saw. The two longhaired ones came up from his back. The first grabbed Ron's chair. The second said, "You're under arrest," and started banging the handcuffs on Ron's wrists.

"What are you doing?" Ron said. "We're leaving."

The back of the crowd saw what was happening and ran to help. That set off a whistle and the blue line charged into a big circle with Ron inside. He was dumped out of his chair and onto the street. All Ron could think to do was shout.

"I'm a Vietnam veteran," he yelled. "I fought in the DMZ. I'm paralyzed. Don't you know what you're doing?"

The L.A.P.D. didn't shout back. The red-haired one pulled Ron's hands behind his back and locked them. Then the blue circle made a wedge and headed across the street with Ron in tow. A cop had each shoulder and Ron's head bobbed up and down off the asphalt. The people who tried to help said they saw the police beat Ron's body with their sticks, but Ron didn't feel it. He felt the curb when his forehead hit it and then all of a sudden he felt lifted up and into a squad car. They propped him up in the front seat. He immediately flopped over into the dashboard and panted.

"I have no stomach muscles," he said. "With my hands in back of me, I can't sit up. I can't hardly breathe either." Ron had to talk in a grunt.

The cop shoved him up straight. "Sit up," he said.

Ron flopped back over. "I'm a veteran," he wheezed. "Don't you see what you're doing to me? I'm paralyzed."

"Sit up," the cop said and rammed Ron against the Ford's seat. Ron flopped back. "I said sit up you commie son of a bitch." The L.A.P.D. bounced Ron back and forth all the way to the station. At the booking desk, the cop asked the turnkey where to put the crippled one.

"Take him up on the roof and throw him off," the turnkey said.

They didn't. But it wasn't because they didn't want to. When Ron left five days later, the turnkey looked at him from behind his jowels.

"They shoulda let you die over there," he said. "You shoulda died and never come back."

If you want to find Ron Kovic just go to the VVAW office in L.A.: take the Arlington off-ramp from the Santa Monica Freeway and head for Pico Boulevard. The letters are painted on their storefront. I went in and found him. He looked up from writing a leaflet and I asked him how he felt.

"In the last five years," he said, "I've felt tremendous pain and bitterness both. I felt a closeness to no one but myself and my chair. I felt an anger I could never describe. I also felt a humility and a compassion I could never explain. It was a tremendous sense of loss and a tremendous sense of gain. I felt I had lost a great portion of my body but I'd gained a good deal of my soul. It was like I had to trade the one for the other."

Then I asked what he was going to do now that the war was over.

He laughed. He laughed the way he does: letting it run out to the ends of his lips and vibrate there.

"The war's not over," he said. "The war is between those who catch hell and those who give it out. Just 'cause it's not on TV don't mean they stopped giving it out. Ask somebody who's fought one. They'll tell you a war don't end just because somebody says so. A war isn't over until you don't have to live with it anymore."

For a lot of us that's going to be a long old time. Like Ron Kovic. Sometimes when he sits up at night, he can hear the war rumbling down in his legs. It makes a sound like the Long Island Railway flashing through Massapequa and heading west.

The Wild Side
of Paradise

MICHAEL THOMAS

AN AUSTRALIAN JOURNALIST—AND FORMER CHILD
RADIO STAR—FOUND HIMSELF IN JAMAICA JUST AS
REGGAE WAS STARTING TO CATCH A FIRE.

The first brothel to take credit cards opened for business in Nevada in the summer of 1973. This struck some of us as an important event at the time. You knew that somewhere out on Route 66 there was some poor bozo who was going to be the first man in the history of usury to pay interest on a blow job. Jann took the bet. I was on my way. . . .

But I had to go to Arthur's wedding. Arthur and Susanna had decided to get married in Jamaica, and seeing as Susanna was about eighteen months pregnant there was no time to lose. A few of us turned up to make matters worse. It was a charming ceremony in the hills above Montego Bay. Then we met Dickie.

Dickie's idea of a good start to the day was to pick up where you left off the night before. He'd blink, groan, curse, ratchet his eyes open, climb over Sylvia or Vonetta or whatever her name was, some damp-eyed beauty who'd just been standing there looking stunning, sucking her thumb and making eyes at the traffic on the road up to Strawberry Hill the day before, and he'd fix a spliff. This took some time. It took a lot of brown paper bags. Dickie's idea of a spliff was no skinny little thing, no limp little reefer; it was more like a loaf of French bread. He kept weird hours. You'd have breakfast at 4:00 p.m. in a nightclub on the Spanish Town Road. All the chairs were on the tables. *Portia Faces Life* was on the radio in the kitchen. . . .

Dickie had something to do with Island Records. Nobody knew what. He held no specific portfolio, but he had the keys to the car. He and Chris Blackwell *go back*, to "My Boy Lollipop" and beyond, to the days when Island was just a load of 45s in the back of a van. They cut a classic silhouette, like Leporello and Don Giovanni. In a town like Kingston in the state it was in at the time, you haven't got a hope unless you know a man who knows a shortcut. It was Dickie's genius to make everything possible. Four days late. He dragged us down to Trench Town to find Bob Marley. It was Dickie's idea to take a ride out to the beach at Hellshire and introduce us to Countryman.

Who needed no introduction. Countryman spoke for himself. He spoke in rhyme. He looked like an angel. He had the grace and stealth and quickness of an antelope, the negligent Nureyev-like arrogance of an aristocrat, the diabolical cunning of a Jesuit, the bottomless compassion of a High Lama, a master's degree in Upper Niger consciousness and a laugh like a waterfall. He was made in heaven, and I can show you proof. Dickie and I made a movie in Jamaica a few years later starring Countryman. It could have hung together a lot better than it did, but you still meet blind people who've seen it 200 times. There was something wrong with the story. But there was nothing wrong with the idea.

What was going on in Kingston at the time, the random slapstick slaughter, was what came to be known in places like the bar of the New Stanley Hotel in Nairobi or the Travelodge in Port Moresby or the roof terrace of the Caravelle in Saigon as Post-Colonial Pubescent Trauma. This is what happens ten, fifteen years after the gassy euphoria of Independence Day wears off and all the big promises fall flat and things just keep going from bad to worse and the trigger-happy jobless cease to believe there is life after twenty-one and start shooting back. What was unique to Jamaica, where the real rude genius of Jamaica lay, and this was hatched in ganja, was in the solution they found. They abandoned all reason. They turned suffering into an ideology. They turned misery into bliss. They turned alienation into an independent spiritual republic. Bob Marley put it into words, and the rest you know. Perry Henzell said it: The Rastas were the conscience of Jamaica. And Countryman was all that Rasta allowed. He could juggle live fish.

When you needed a breather, after a hard day in Babylon debating

Ethiopian metaphysics with the Tribes of Judah, when you felt like Peter Tosh had chopped your head off and swapped it for a custard apple, then there was Strawberry Hill. Strawberry Hill had been a hotel in the plantation days. It sat high in the hills above Kingston, buried in bougainvillea, like a forgotten figment of the Raj. They still served roast beef on Sundays. The tea was from Harrod's. Island used it as a funny farm for its British acts experiencing personal problems, so there was always a passing trade in anguish: deranged half-naked Scotsmen staggering round foaming at the chops and clawing at clouds of unseen gnats, et cetera. I wrote this story there. The bananas outside the window grew before my eyes. *Portia Faces Life* was on the radio in the kitchen. . . .

Just imagine my embarrassment. Those deep dark unctuous chords on the Wurlitzer, and then the oily intro: "Episode 1234 of *Portia . . . Faces . . . Life . . .* Dedicated to those who are in love . . . and those who can . . . re-*member*." *Portia Faces Life* was the most popular soap in Jamaica. I suppose the JBC got it for a buck and a half at a fire sale. It was ten years out of date, it had nothing remotely to do with the life of the woman in the kitchen, it was made at the Grace Gibson Studios, in Sydney, Australia, and every woman in every kitchen in Jamaica hung on Portia's every word. Portia was a lawyer. She had a son who never grew up who was always falling off his bike. His name, by one of those amusing flukes, was Dickie, too. I couldn't believe my ears. Put yourself in my shoes. It was *my* bike! I'd missed five years of cricket practice Wednesday afternoons at the Grace Gibson Studios playing Dickie on the radio when I was at North Sydney High. I did it till my voice broke. I made enough money to buy my first TR4. Walking into the kitchen at Strawberry Hill was like walking through a wall ten years thick, like falling through a mirror. Dickie and the Scotsman had to hold me down, they had to stick a soupspoon under my tongue. . . .

Strawberry Hill's gone now, blown away by the hurricane. Peter Tosh got shot. Bob Marley died, leaving untold millions and untold kids by untold different women and no will. The House That Rasta Built came tumbling down, and years later they're all still fighting over the bones.

ROLLING STONE put Countryman on the inside cover. Arthur took the picture. Susanna had a daughter, a marvelous girl who just started at UCLA, so we know how long ago this was. Bob's dreadlocks were just starting to sprout. . . .

This was when we practiced what we preached. Her name was Carla. She wore green socks. She worked at ROLLING STONE, the word on the rails was she was married to the Mob. She had a place downtown. She had a water bed that slept six. There was nothing to fear but the clap. . . .

JULY 19TH, 1973

They can take a loss in Jamaica and shrug it off; they're used to it, they've been let down and shut out all their lives. Anybody on the street will tell you it's been that way for 400 years, they've been pushed and shoved and left to their own dangerous devices, and there's a lot of menacing talk going around shantytown about the *pressure*. About how you can push a man just so far, lean on him for just so long, slam too many doors in his face and then the pressure's going to peak and short-circuit and a man is going to have to turn around and cut somebody's throat. Everybody down here in paradise is carrying a knife, everybody, even the kids.

But as soon as the cricket winds down, Bulldog the Rude Boy lights up a splif the size of a sno-cone and the music comes on again, the reggae, something by Bang Hugh and the Lionaries called "Rasta No Born Yah," Number Ten this week, and everybody all over the island's plugged into the same shuffle, the same stutter guitar and choppy drums and, most of all, the bass. All over the island windows are shifting in their sills and cups are rattling in their saucers and the gold fillings are humming in Bulldog's teeth, and one way or another everybody from the two-year-olds crawling in the garbage in Ghost Town to the 135-year-old Rasta out at the beach awaiting the imminent apocalypse, everybody's got the beat, the upbeat, everybody's all hooked up to the common throb.

Nearly two-thirds of the people in Jamaica can't read or write, so all they know is what they're told, what they hear—and they hear it on the radio. Tell a farmer up in the Cockpit Country that there are men riding 'round in golf carts on the surface of the moon, and he'll laugh. He's no fool, he's not about to credit such a rash and ignorant blasphemy. But if it's on the charts, if he can hear Big Youth or The Scorpion fussing and hollering and skanking over the bass line, telling about the moonshots, then it goes down easy. If it's on the charts in Jamaica, it exists. If it isn't, then it's just hearsay—some alien, suspicious, irrelevant and hostile reality fraught with shameful deceptions like birth control which any street Ja-maican knows is a lot of rass disguising a barbaric plot to kill off the black race—and he isn't falling for it.

The music, the reggae you've been hearing here and there when a loose one slipped through customs and showed up in Cashbox, the kind of feel Johnny Nash gets close to but never quite grasps belly to belly—the music is the root language of the Jamaican poor, and just about everybody in Jamaica is dirt poor and downtrodden.

It's what the besieged Jamaican middle class used to write off as a raggamuffin music—"reggae," Bulldog says, is just an uptown way of saying ragga, and ragga is just a lazy way of saying raggamuffin, or rather *not* saying it, flinging it back rude. Which sounds OK and may or may not be strictly true because there are no facts in Jamaica, everybody has his own version of everything. But whatever it's been called, ska, blue-beat, rocksteady, reggae—it comes red-raw, rude and ragged out of the shantytowns of West Kingston. Wretched little ghettoes like Ghost Town and Trench Town and Greenwich Farm and the Dungle, where all the pressures threatening to hemorrhage Jamaican society meet and combust in a slow burn that might any day boil over into riot and revolution and slaughter in the streets.

So far though, mostly what happens is a couple of Rude Boys get ripped on Red Stripe beer and too much ganja and the *pressure* starts to nag and one of them turns nasty and they start cutting each other. Or else they go cut somebody's uncle, some Chinaman who runs a bar, anybody, it's pure free-form desperado violence and mad-dog anarchy. Just the other night some Johnny Too Bad came through Ghost Town doing 90 down a one-way street, and the police gave chase and the kid spun the car into somebody's living room, seized a sleeping two-year-old as a shield and came out shooting everything that moved. He shot six cops before they mowed him down. The *pressure* got him.

He was most likely some Christian kid from the country who'd hit shantytown with high hopes and all he found was too many hungry people living in oil drums and garbage cans and fruitcrates and one-room plywood outhouses with nothing inside except a formica dinette suite and a glass cabinet for the family china and a radio blasting. For West Kingston, literally, is a garbage dump. It used to be a fishing village outside of town, and then the city started reclaiming the harbor and they turned it into a dump. Pretty soon the Israelites appeared—lost tribes of dirt-poor, unemployed, homeless losers and scavengers and boogooyaggas and vagrant Rastas—the "sufferers" they call themselves, the pariahs of paradise. They all started living there, in the stench and rot of it all; they built shacks and huts out of cardboard and plywood and rusty old iron and the place spread like a disease till now it's a teeming suffering tropic slum. In the Sixties the bulldozers came in, the builders chased the squatters off Akee Walk and put up a few concrete highrises, but already they look like they're getting ready to fall down and bury whole families alive. West Kingston remains a bomb-site landscape of live garbage and boxwood and unlikely tropic greenery. It's Jamaica's dirty secret, a few acres of simmering living hell deep down in the heart of paradise, and nobody who doesn't live there ever goes near the place if they can help it. Chances are you'd get killed. The police travel in packs.

*   *   *

Bob Marley missed *The Harder They Come:* He's seen it up close. He's been making records for nearly ten years on and off. The Wailers must have had 70 or 80 singles out and just about every one of them made the charts; Marley wrote "Stir It Up" and "Guava Jelly" and taught Johnny Nash everything he knows about Jamaican rhythm, but he's still down in Ghost Town sitting 'round half-naked and flat broke. He's probably the most gifted street poet on the whole scene because he gets it first-hand— and the thing about reggae is that it's always been upbeat shantytown blues, the songs are storm warnings from the suffering Israelites crying to be heard after 400 years of slavery and neglect, and Marley pleads their case better than anybody. Songs like "Slave Driver" and "Concrete Jungle" sound sweet and catchy, but they're as bitter as wine gone to vinegar. He sings in a loose rheumy way, the guitar player plays lovely sinister atmospherics, and the whole thing is so stylish and goes down so easily you might miss the message first time through, you might miss the dire threat—

> *Every time I hear the crack of a whip,*
> *My blood runs cold,*
> *I remember on the slave ship,*
> *How they brutalized my very soul—*
> *Slave driver,*
> *The tables have turned,*
> *Catch-a-fire,*
> *You're gonna get burned . . .*

Bob's been burned and cheated and spun out and spit on so many times it's a wonder the pressure hasn't got the better of him by now, but it hasn't. They can't touch him. He's a Rasta. And the Rastas don't even speak the same language.

It's not just the inscrutable Jamaican patois. That's the dialect—a matter of mischievous and insolent tropic scansion that sounds like 17th century gutter English back to front and fed through a mangle. But the language of the Rastas is a matter of attitude. It's pure unfettered speech. "I and I," they say, meaning you and me, meaning we're all in this together. You can never tell if a Rasta's telling you lies or whether he's just gone off the rails without a map into the psychic rapids of Upper Niger consciousness or whether he's just plain touched by the sun. He can't tell either and he doesn't care. The Rastas are operating on a completely different metaphoric level according to a secret deranged logic that makes perfect sense only if you abandon all reason. It takes a while to get the hang of it. It's a state of mind.

You've got to see through the facts here, because the facts are mad. The Rastafarian brotherhood surfaced in Jamaica about 40 years ago in the wake of Marcus Garvey. Garvey was a fire-breathing Jamaican evangelist who went 'round Harlem in the Twenties prophesying the coronation of a black king in Africa who would redeem the lost tribes and carry them home. It's all in the Bible, in Revelations, Chapter 5, verses 1–10, and when Haile Selassie was crowned Emperor of Ethiopia in 1930, the Rastas in Jamaica recognized him as Ras Tafari, the one true God of the prophecy, the King of Kings, Lord of Lords, the Conquering Lion of Judah. Or just *Jah*. Haile Selassie's flattered. He's not a modest man, but he's never acknowledged his divinity, on the contrary he's been trying to phase the whole thing out. The Rastas appreciate the political niceties of his diffidence, but they worship him regardless. And they want to go back home to ancestral Africa where they belong.

Until that big day comes and it probably never will, they consider themselves to be exiles stranded in Babylon. So they take no part. They have disenfranchised themselves, they don't vote, they don't get counted in the census, they reject the whole sprawl of Jamaican society as it has rejected them. They are pariahs.

The early Rastas kept to the hills and the remote black sand beaches of the south coast—mad half-naked hermits caked in mud with their hair sprouting in thickets and tangles stiff with grime and running with lice. When they came to town and started raving in the streets, they scared the living daylights out of people. They were penniless black vagrants with no stake at all in the capitalist mobility of Babylon and they took pride in it. They beat their empty stomachs. They flaunted their poverty and that made the middle class mad. Somewhere in their midbrain it made them uneasy and that uneasiness grew as the Rastas got wilder and filthier and their numbers increased and they were making a bizarre public display of pissing on everything upward that the middle class believed in, rejecting wholesale their entire earthly existence, and upsetting the children, leading them astray, turning them on to the dread ganja. The middle class has got a lot of Mercedes and fully staffed hilltop villas at stake in Jamaica, even a guy who runs a filling station has a couple of maids. So they panicked. They busted the Rastas for everything. They became the scapegoats and the whipping boys of a frightened society—a black African society with a light tan middle class hooked on the conventions of a white colonial aristocracy and losing ground. The Rastas, on the other hand, were going back to Africa—proud to be black, glad to be hairy and half-naked like the East African tribesmen they saw in magazines. They plaited their locks in greasy imitation. And there were more and more of them.

You didn't have to do anything too drastic to go Rasta if you were down in the dirt anyway, so it was a good cover for a lot of thugs and spies wanted by the police. Rasta offered an alternative outcast nationality beyond the law. They gave shelter to fugitives because they were fugitives themselves. Whenever some Chinaman got cut or a building caught fire, the police blamed it on the Rastas. The pressure backfired though. They just closed their ranks. When a bunch of black revolutionaries from America moved in in the early Sixties and tried to take charge of the Rastas and recruit them for guerrilla warfare, they found they'd badly misread the movement. A couple of English soldiers got shot, there were isolated shootouts and one gang of apache Rastas wasted a small town near Montego Bay and chopped up a few people with machetes. Official retaliation was brutal. But it was all a false alarm. The Rastas *are* revolutionaries, that's why they've got Jamaica spooked, but they're not getting ready to come pouring down out of the hills waving machetes and sack the Sheraton-Universal. The Rasta revolution is on a completely different level. They reject violence altogether. They have simply defected.

The orthodox litany is the softcore of Rastafarianism. They *do* insist most passionately on the divinity of Haile Selassie, they *do* ache and yearn to go back to Africa and they vigorously deny the evidence that those few zealots who actually did make it to Ethiopia in the Sixties are finding the parched deserts of their ancestors a bit grim and inhospitable. But Ethiopia, in truth, is just somewhere over the rainbow, a spiritual nationality, and it doesn't matter that chances are they'll never get there. The dream of redemption is all the nourishment they need to support them in their day-to-day rejection of Babylon. Like the Christian heretics and martyrs of the Middle Ages, their agony feeds and fortifies them.

They profess a strict Nazarene code of conduct: They don't drink booze, they don't eat meat, they live communally and share what they've got, they never beg and never steal. They do their Christian best to be upright and compassionate Samaritans. And they smoke about a pound and a half a week each. The smoke never clears. They don't let a pause go by without loading up the cheloom for an almighty lungful of the sacramental weed. They smoke so much ganja they understand each other.

And when you've got half a dozen Rastas out at Cunchyman's shack at the beach, all fired up and arguing full steam about something they can really get their teeth into, like whether or not electricity is more powerful than lightning—something deep and fraught with metaphor like that so they can really cut loose and rave and rhapsodise—another night we were discussing whether or not a shark is faster than a porpoise—anything at all really. Once they get going the Rastas hit sustained heights of pure lunatic rhetoric that's so fluid and has such sheer velocity that eventually your earthbound linear systems pack it in, and your eyes begin to play tricks, and your tongue feels like a lizard and if you don't pass out cold on the floor, you begin to realize that what Perry Hanzell says is true: The Rastas run Jamaica. They are the black conscience of paradise.

*   *   *

An ax can kill 13 men, Cunchyman says. It will still be sharp after 13 men have chopped wood with it all their lives. But Cunchyman captured an ax, he says, and hung it on the wall and it rusted away. The Rastas, by such simple enigmatic equations, have freed themselves from earthly care. Cunchyman lives like a wild animal on a beautiful stretch of deserted paradise miles from anywhere, and nobody can touch him. He has rejected rejection. He came upon this spot out here about 15 years ago—he was walking along the beach one day smoking a splif and he found a piece of plywood lying around so he stuck it up against a palm tree and called it home. He's got a woman and a couple of kids now, so he's put up something more permanent—a thatched lean-to, just a couple of rooms and an outdoor fireplace and a radio. He cooked us dinner: Parrotfish fried in coconut oil and a fish stew that had 34 different species of seafood in it; he'd walked 16 miles that afternoon to make sure he had all the things he needed. When he's feeling a little uncomfortable, he says, he swims straight out to sea as far as he can, till he's fighting for air and his arms are like lead and his toes cramp up, and then he sees if he can get back alive. He gets a good laugh out of that; he rocks back on his haunches and laughs fit to burst. He gets a good laugh out of everything. "Peace and love," he says when you meet him; that's the Rasta greeting, it has been for 30 years.

The Rastas are imaginary beings. They are exiles, not just from a distant and misunderstood past, but from the grim and banal realities of the present day as well. They live in the imagination. And the imagination is immortal.

"When you check death," says Cunchyman, "how you feel?"

"We don't check death," says Bob Marley. "It's life I leadin'. If I good all through then I live life everlastin'. When death see we, death flee."

Jah-man, one of Cunchyman's neighbors out at the beach, reckons he's 135 years old and never felt better.

The sad part of it is the city's building a road out here, it's already just a couple of miles away. Cunchyman will move around the next headland to another beach, but sooner or later the road will come that far too and he'll have to move again. And Jamaica's a small island. The Jamaican economy feeds on tourists who are so bored and so wired up and twisted they're willing to spend a hundred dollars a day to see how a barefoot illiterate like Cunchyman can live for free and be happy, eating off the trees and out of the sea, in perfect sync with the tides and the winds and the stars in the sky.

"You need us more than we need you," says Perry Henzell. "And the tragedy is that by the time you're prepared to come to us to learn how to relax and be happy, every pressure in our society, from government, from media, is telling us we must get to where you were 20 years ago, and that's exactly where we're going to be."

The main vein of the Jamaican economy these days is not sugar, not bananas, not even tourism. It's bauxite. They use it to make aluminum. Bauxite is dirt. They're not just selling space on the island, they're selling the island itself, the very earth, for a few cents a ton.

King
of the Goons

JOE ESZTERHAS

HOW A HELL'S ANGELS SHOOT-OUT LED A MIDWEST-
ERN NEWSPAPERMAN TO THE COSMIC GIGGLE AND
THE PLEASURES OF GETTING NAKED, WATCHING
WHALES AND FILING 37,000 WORDS ON EVEL KNIEVEL.

I t was a newsstand on Cleveland's Short Vincent, a little street where
flagpole sitters once perched and where, in 1969, Midwestern Ma-
fiosi came out of the Theatrical Bar and Grill to nuzzle their platinum honeys and sparkle their pinkie rings. It was the only newsstand
in Cleveland that sold out-of-town papers.

I was a general-assignment reporter for the morning daily, and I would
go down to the newsstand periodically to see what was happening out of
town—a good idea if you were interested in writing and interested, too,
in staying alive. Most of the reporters I was working with were dead. Oh,
sure, they did their daily breathing, and at one time in their lives they may
have had *ambitions*, but over the years their ambitions had reduced them
to their weekly paychecks. I wanted to write. . . . And I didn't want to die.
. . . And so I made my periodic treks to Short Vincent.

I saw my first copy of ROLLING STONE there, bought it, took it home
and felt like Saint Paul falling flat on his ass on the way to Damascus. It

had a life force. It tingled in my hands. It didn't squirm around wearing a straitjacket of "objectivity." It told, subjectively, what it saw as the truth. And there was writing in it. Not the homogenized, deodorized crap most other magazines were dishing up but real *writing*. Writing that went for the funny bone, the cortex or the jugular. Writing that — holy shit! — didn't seem to have many space limitations.

I kept going back and getting new copies and did my job at the newspaper, becoming increasingly frustrated because reading this little magazine that proclaimed itself to believe in "the cosmic giggle" underlined the stultifying nature of what I was doing day-to-day. I was getting so frustrated at the paper that I found myself sneaking off in the middle of the afternoon on certain especially bad days and seeing a movie. I was twenty-five years old. Is that how the others in the city room around me had begun to die? I wondered. In some cheesy little theater on Euclid Avenue, their mouths stuffed with popcorn?

My wife and I drove out west for a vacation. I'd never been west before. She wanted to see the Grand Canyon and the Petrified Forest. I wanted to see Big Sur, the Haight-Ashbury and, oh, yes, one other place. It was down on Brannan Street, in San Francisco. She gave me a very knowing look.

I went down to Brannan Street on a Monday morning. The ROLLING STONE offices were upstairs. I was wearing a suit and tie (from Sears) and very short hair. I walked into the place and got very suspicious looks. What exactly did I want? Well, I exactly wanted all their back issues. All of them? All of them. The receptionist was no longer suspicious; now she was hostile. She went into an office, forgot to close the door and was whispering to someone else. I heard the word *narc* several times. Other heads soon popped out from behind the door and looked me over. I got my big stack of back issues and fled.

In a little motel near Carmel called the Tickle Pink, I read all of the back issues. I didn't really read them; I *devoured* them. There was a dramatic, crashing sea cresting and breaking outside the picture window. I was barely aware of it. There was a massive stone fireplace against the wall. I never even built a fire. I read this magazine — every word of every issue.

Shortly after we got back to Cleveland (we never did see the Grand Canyon; we'd spent too much time at the Tickle Pink; my wife still won't forgive me), I covered a bar shooting for my paper. The Hell's Angels had gone into a steelworker bar and turned it into the O.K. Corral. The *Chicago Sun-Times* had sent a Pulitzer Prize winner to Cleveland to cover the same story. The Pulitzer winner was a friend of mine more interested in Jack Daniel's than Hell's Angels, and at the end of the day he asked if he could borrow my notes for his story. Well, what the hell, I gave him my notes.

He called me a few weeks later from Chicago. This magazine had called him from San Francisco, he said. Had I ever heard of it? Some weird name—ROLLING something. They'd liked his Hell's Angels story so much they wanted him to write a 3000-word piece for them. I tried to be low-key. "What did you say to them?" I said. He was equally low-key. "I told him there's this guy in Cleveland who knows the story much better than I do," he said. He gave me the name and number of an editor in San Francisco.

I called the number. I got the assignment. I thanked all the saints I no longer believed in. I worked harder on that story for ROLLING STONE than on anything I'd worked on for years. I realized as I was doing it that I was excited about something that I was writing. I realized, too, sadly, that it was a new sensation.

I sent the story off. They liked it. They printed it. They sent me a check with a Boy Scout on it. A few weeks after the story appeared, I got a letter at the paper. It said: "I thought I was the only writer in America able to write well about Hell's Angels. I was wrong." It was signed Hunter S. Thompson and came from someplace called Owl Farm, in Colorado. I stared at the letter a long time, folded it up finally and put it in my wallet. It stayed there for months. I was high. A story of mine in a magazine that believed in the cosmic giggle! A check with a Boy Scout on it! A fan letter from an Owl Farm! From Hunter Thompson himself!

A short time later I got a call from the editor in San Francisco. They knew I'd written a book about the shootings at Kent State. Would I be interested in doing a piece about Kent State one year afterward? I asked the editor how long a piece they wanted. "Oh," he said casually, "not longer than 15,000 words." *Fifteen thousand words? In* ROLLING STONE? *Me?*

I played hooky from the paper and wrote 15,000 words. It was published in toto, nearly unedited. It got mentioned on the cover. I went back to the newsstand on Short Vincent and bought up all of the twenty copies they were getting. I didn't give any copies to anyone. I just liked holding the stack.

Things at the paper, meanwhile, were not going well. My personal life was getting a little . . . screwy. I wasn't wearing suits at work anymore. I was wearing jeans and tight tops. I had lost thirty pounds. I had grown a beard. My hair was long—not really, but certainly considered long in Cleveland. I was not only writing about antiwar protesters but joining them on the street, kissing off "objectivity." I was in trouble with my editors, who just didn't like my new attitude and who, I heard, suspected that maybe . . . just maybe . . . I was smoking something . . . *funny*. I wrote an article for another magazine about my editors, and when I sent it off, I told my wife I'd probably get fired. I was the paper's star reporter, she said. They'd never fire me. She was wrong. I got fired.

The day after I got fired, I got a phone call. Would it be possible for me to take a leave of absence from my paper and go out to San Francisco to do an investigative piece about narcotics agents? Would it be possible? Sure, it'd be possible. It wouldn't be any kind of problem. I didn't really have to take a *leave*, either.

My wife was . . . more than skeptical. I'd been this hotshot on a big-city daily. I'd won awards. I had a column with my picture next to it that sometimes ran on the front page. Now I'd gotten myself fired. Now I'd grown this damn beard. Now I wasn't eating right. Now I was going to go out to . . . ROLLING STONE? Is this what I'd had in mind all along? Well, I answered sheepishly, I didn't . . . think so . . . at least not . . . *consciously.*

They flew me out there. They had moved to new offices on Third Street. The train station was just down the street. The smell of freshly roasting coffee was in the air. There was a little bar across the street where a lot of the creative business seemed to be done. The women were young, intelligent and beautiful. On very special warm days they took off their tops. There was rock & roll in the walls. There was a lot of . . . smoking.

I met some of the other writers. One of them lived in the office, sat in a barber's chair and used the men's room to wash up in the morning. Another had hot brandies for lunch, seemed to have read everything and dazzled you with literary allusions until the moment he passed out (usually at the cigarette machine). I saw the same writer, in another bar, go up to the jukebox and get very pissed off when it wouldn't give him a pack of Camels. I met Hunter, a mythical presence rarely in the office, usually at a motel called the Seal Rock, running up his expense account. I saw him with a monstrous hypodermic needle at a party. He took the needle, plunged it deep into his navel and shot himself up with ether.

And, of course, I met Jann Wenner, who seemed to single-handedly galvanize the place and somehow, miraculously, make it work. He would appear periodically in a cape and Sherlock Holmes cap, a bag of Doggie Diner cheeseburgers in hand, ready for either a late breakfast or an early lunch. His attitude was that he *expected* great things from all of us. His eyes said, "Don't disappoint me."

Shortly after I got there, we had an editorial conference at Esalen, which is at Big Sur. Writers came in from all over the country. We talked about story ideas and future goals. I realized, as the days went by, that I felt more alive than I had in years. I felt so alive and excited inside that I was numbed into silence.

It's possible that I was in shock. Here I was, a part of the cosmic giggle, a lifelong Midwesterner, an immigrant raised in a strict, ethnic household. And these were the things I was seeing:

At dinner at Esalen one night, a woman at a neighboring table took a piece of chicken and smeared it across her face, smiling beatifically. She said that she wanted to "relate to what she was eating."

In the middle of an editorial meeting one day I glanced out the window and saw whales offshore, their flukes up, gamboling about. I was told we were taking a group photograph one day. I showed up. Everyone was naked. Oh, boy. I got naked, too. Even Annie, who took the photograph, got naked.

What amazed me was this: The immigrant Midwesterner finally felt . . . very much . . . at home.

It is more than twenty years later now. Jann wants me to write an introduction to an anthologized article about Evel Knievel. I have missed several deadlines, and he's angry. He faxes me a memo because I have been avoiding his calls. It ends this way: "Don't disappoint me."

Damn him. More than twenty years later, and it still works. The introduction is done.

RS 173

NOVEMBER 7TH, 1974

I

Evel Knievel comes down the anthill, revved-up and overheated, sees the crowd and says to a shotgunned deputy: "If those goddamned sonsofbitches come up here, blow their goddamn heads off!" The gunman nods and says nothing. The look in his eyes says he won't have to be told again.

As he heads toward his trailer Bob Arum tries to soothe him and the star yells: "Look at this! Sunday is the greatest day of my life and it's being run by a bunch of goddamn Jews!" And Arum backs away from him, laughs, tries to make a joke of it—"It's hot up there, he's tired and he probably needs his salt tablets." Arum graps for his manhood and adds softly with the ever-present smile: "If there's one thing I can't stand, it's a longhaired loudmouth cowboy."

The star is in his trailer next to the launch ramp and his press conference will begin any minute now. Newsmen swoop around the steps outside the trailer door and the Mud Man and the Hollow Lady and the Goiter are leading a rhythmic and unchanging jungle chant: "We want Eeeeevel! We want Eeeeeeevel! We want Eeeeeeevel!"

Jim Watt, an NBC cameraman from Los Angeles, a thirtyish veteran of wars and riots, a little man with a monstrous camera slung over his shoulder, is talking to media advisor Shelly Saltman. Somebody yells: "Hey, Shelly, let some of the sound crews in here!" Jim Watt tells Shelly he would appreciate it if the star stood during his press conference. Watt is a pro and his request is not only to give NBC good footage (since Watt is a short-sized pro) but also to give the star good exposure. If he sits down and other newsmen stand in front of the little cameraman, parts of the star's presence might be obscured.

But the star has overheard Watt talking to the promoter. He explodes through the trailer door and rants: "If I wanna siddown, I'm gonna siddown!" Watt stands there bearing the cross of his heavy camera, his mouth open, as though he'd been kicked in the gut. "Out!" the star yells, halfway back inside his trailer. I am standing right behind the dumbfounded Watt, who is a stranger to me. The star is back inside his trailer now, but remembering that last "Out!" the news-pack takes a step away from the door.

For 18 seconds, nothing happens. I am conscious of the Goiter's screams and the dust blinding me and the sweat wetting my beard and then . . . Boom! Here he comes again, out the trailer door, the original Bobby Knievel, the scourge of Butte, as he-man a hero as you will ever see, his face splotched with color and exuding a hellbent ferocity—and all of this, I suddenly realize, is aimed at the stupefied Watt, whom his NBC colleague, Jack Perkins, sometimes calls the "Dwarf Photographer."

"Tell him the next time he looks at me to have a smile on his face!" Bobby Knievel yells, pointing now to the Dwarf Photographer. "I'm not an actor, Mr. Cameraman, do you understand that?"

"That's right," the Dwarf Photographer says, staring into Bobby Knievel's glare.

"All right," the star says as Watt looks at the ground . . . and for a second I think that it has blown over . . . but Bobby Knievel won't let it alone. "I said—'Have a smile on your face!' "

And then, as I gape, inches away from the two of them, the scene speeds up and lurches wildly because Jim Watt, an ordinary man with an ordinary man's sense of dignity and self-respect, suddenly shows the world that he will not be pushed around. The Dwarf Photographer will not be bullied.

"I don't smile for anybody," Watt says.

The star comes at him. I am so close to them that I can see the sweat trickling off Bobby Knievel's face and I can see the anger and fear in Jim Watt's eyes. Bobby Knievel stands inches taller than Watt and he has that damned cane in his hands and he is using it now on Watt's camera and on Watt's shoulders. The little man tries to defend himself—which is not easy with that cross over his shoulder.

"Get him out!" the star yells. "Out! Out! Get out of here! I don't need any crap from any cameraman like you!" and then Bobby Knievel jams the camera into Watt's face and hits him with the cane and Watt is on the ground, the camera smashed out of his hands.

"Out! Get out!" Bobby Knievel yells, standing over him.

"I can't go without my camera!" Watt yells, still on the ground.

And above him, waving that cane, Bobby Knievel yells: "I'll stick it in your ear if you're not careful!" The news-pack gets between them finally and Watt is led away toward the fence, red, shaken and bruised, and Bobby Knievel roars back inside his trailer.

"We want Eeeeeeevel! We want Eeeeeeevel!" the Mud Man and the Hollow Lady and the Goiter cheerlead. The Dwarf Photographer is on his way to see a doctor and from inside the trailer I can still hear Bobby Knievel's muffled shouts.

After four or five minutes he comes outside, calmer now but still out of breath and I wonder whether he's gobbled some of his trusted Compoz. He very emphatically sits down on the steps (that Dwarf Photographer he damned!)—more exactly, he sits down on a fancy red-white-and-blue rug and I wonder whether he was so insistent on sitting down simply because he wanted to display his patriotic little carpet.

"I wanna tell you something!" he says. "I think that all of you that are here right now know, regardless of what two or three jackasses might say or have said, out of the legitimate millions of press people in the world, what this thing is. It's a monster. I think you all know now looking at me that I wish I didn't have to be here and didn't have to do this. But I'm going to. I'm trying to keep my wits about me and . . . you're welcome to film whatever you want, as long as you try to help me. If anybody doesn't wanna help me, I'll go after them and throw them out just like I did the last guy!"

A few of his musclemen cheer that last threat and, I notice, the newsmen have taken it to heart. There are no embarrassing questions asked here—"It's selective intimidation," a newslady says to me, "just like Nixon, and it works!"—and while everyone here has just seen a little man shoved to the ground and roughed up, no one seems to remember. The questions remind me of the sort of bullshit some sports announcers specialize in after important games—all about technique and strategy, all of it warm wind and piss. The star trots through his paces, mumbles a few words about God's help, and says, "We had two test failures. They say the third time's a charm."

The force of the blastoff, he bemoans (his face sad but his chin uplifted), will probably give him a red-out and cause a "nose hemorrhage." "I know that," he says. Some of the reporters shake their heavy heads. Jesus God, a red-out! A nose bleed! And the guy's still going to do it!

The guy has real balls! And I think about Watt at the doctor's office and see that camera getting jammed into his face and the hero standing over him—not even with his fists, but with a cane. Real balls.

That damn swarm of filth keeps screaming, though, and chanting his name, and tugging at the swaying fence, and Something Has To Be Done or the shit sandwich will smash the fences down days before the cathartic climax of this holy week. As I watch the star now, it finally makes sense to me . . . the whole day . . . all of it . . . the chaps and the violence and the fiery heat are all reduced to a single scene where it all comes together.

The star has gone to the fence to meet his swarm. There he is, holding hands with the bare-titted Hollow Lady, throwing her a kiss. There he is, with the Mud Man and the Goiter, slapping their backs. He's going to walk across the pasture to the Motocross stand, a few hundred yards away, to make a speech.

The swarm sets off across the field, over the horseshit and the beercans and the loblollies, and he is its center! The Lord of the Abyss with his faithful! And the Hollow Lady and the Goiter and the Mud Man are his lieutenants! The swarm sweeps across the field like a black wind and a kid in a wheelchair who is trying to keep pace hits a chuckhole and sprawls to the ground. His chair is kicked out of the way and then broken while he sits in a crumpled heap, terrified, begging for help, shielding his twisted body with his arms, yelling: "I'm a cripple, help me!"

But who has time for cripples at a time like this, when Evel Knievel is making a speech?

"In the next few days we're going to have in here a crowd of 50,000 or more," the star says. "And all of America and the North American continent will be looking at me and at all of you. I've got to have your help! Believe me, the only way we're going to be able to do it is to respect the mothers and fathers who brought kids here and respect the people who came here to see me make that One Last Fly. If you never did anything before in your life, pull together in this thing and help us make it something everyone will respect. And please make sure that the fences are not knocked over under any circumstances so we don't have any problems and please make sure this is an orderly thing. Because I need all the help I can get from you!"

"*You've got it, baby!*" the Goiter yells and he and the Hollow Lady and the Mud Man lead the star back toward his trailer. A few minutes later he is on his helicopter with the red-tuxedoed Watchamacallit next to him. The Goiter stares into the sun and waves. The shotgun-toting cowboys guarding the Skycycle stare at the Goiter and say nothing. Black Jack Swank stares at the cowboys and smiles approvingly.

Evel Knievel is up there in that chopper, above his swarm, and his arm is out the chopper door and he is holding a beercan like a flag. Then he tilts the beercan and pours it on his constituents. A thick slow-motion stream drifts through the hot air onto the crowd.

"He's blessing them," a reporter says.

"He's pissing on them," another laughs.

"Go fuck your mom!" the Hollow Lady screeches.

Thousands of fists flail the desert-dry air. Thousands of voices, hypnotic and obsessed, howl at the sun.

"Eeeeeeeeeevel! Eeeeeeeeeevel! Knieeeeeeeeevel!"

Then with a whoosh that beer-bottle-shaped rocket zooms the blue sky and the cheap picket fences come creaking down and swarms of shrieking bodies are hurtling wildly through the duststorms of their own demented creation toward . . . the abyss, a few hundred feet from them, where the earth stops and there is nothingness, a headlong suicidal swan dive into the vomitgreen waters of the forsaken Snake.

The dust clouds with the howls inside them have hovered over me these weeks and in certain moments I have tried to frieze the turbulence that took place in that arena of desolation, that doom-constructed place of black buttes, jagged rockclots, lava and dinosaur teeth.

I remember that in the feverish moments before they played the national anthem and "The Ballad of Evel Knievel," I stood watching a girl with doe-soft eyes and layers of babyfat as she stripped her T-shirt away (obeying the scrawled sign that said, "Chicks, Show Your Tits!") and was then lifted by hundreds of inflamed and horny hands into the scorched air. The hands moved over her, scratching and squeezing and twisting her nipples, and the hands moved down, tearing away her jeans, and the hands grabbed and mauled her buttocks, ripping away her panties, and the girl ascended on high into the swelter again. More and more hands wriggled in for yet unsullied pieces of her pale skin until, a human fleshball, her nakedness debauched, her tongue lolling, she was discarded—thrown over the fence and into the press compound. I was a few feet from her and I will always remember the bleeding and bruised wounds that were her breasts.

In the moments after the jump . . . after he had been rescued from the depths of that void and after he had pranced and paraded before his fawning faithful and after he had mumbled a grudging few pietisms to his own peculiar god . . . I remember that Knievel hurled his legendary cane into a still hungry crowd. Oh, how they battled for it! This was it, wasn't it? The gold-tipped and diamond-studded magic wand worth thousands of dollars. So a group of men fought wild-eyed over it, clenched their fists and threw their elbows, and the guy who finally won stood with blood shooting from a cut over his eye and with the world's biggest grin on his face. Jesus, he couldn't believe it! And then he looked at it. And Jesus, he couldn't believe it again! It wasn't the magic wand. It wasn't gold. There were no diamonds in it. It was a substitute. A cold piece of steel thrown from that red, white, and blue Erector-set mountaintop for the sheer showbiz of it. And the guy had fought bravely for his treasured souvenir and had been given nothing but a cheap prop. He was himself nothing more than an extra.

II

"Every hype-and-hoopla man in the country is here," Jack Perkins of NBC News says to me, and by Wednesday the hype-hoopla offensive has turned into a full-scale rocket (watertank?) barrage. It is commanded by Bob Arum, guided by Shelly Saltman, a copromoter and former Hollywood PR man, and its foot soldiers are people like Harold Conrad and Margaux Hemingway.

Conrad is an aging boxing hype with a Man-tanned pallor who wears Miami Beach hep and whose considerable puffing talents in the past have been devoted to such spectacles as the Liston-Patterson bout. Hemingway is the famous suicide's granddaughter, a gangling girl from Sun Valley who works very hard distributing press releases for the star she privately terms "a real asshole."

I watch these people at the press briefings — there is a cadaverous, failed playwright among them, too, and I sometimes glimpse him laughing sardonically over his colleagues' efforts at prose — and I am made to understand that everything is Rosier than Rosy. . . . Tickets for the closed-circuit telecast are "selling like hotcakes" all across the country — though exact figures are, regrettably, impossible to obtain. People are "pouring" into the site, though, regrettably, the gate hasn't been tabulated yet and crowd projections would be "misleading." Security problems at the site are "not anticipated," although, regrettably, there are those who are voicing "hysterical fears." Many celebrities will attend, though, regrettably, a complete list is not yet available. "Unofficially," however, "it is understood" that these personages will include Elvis Presley, Burt Reynolds, Dustin Hoffman, Steve McQueen, Ali McGraw, John Wayne, Andy Williams, A.J. Foyt and Parnelli Jones.

Everything Is Go, as they used to say at Cape Canaveral, at Four Days Minus Zero. All of Twin Falls County's specifications have been met and, Bob Arum says, sometime between three and four o'clock Sunday afternoon "our star will make history." Among the Twin Falls specifications which the star has met, I discover, are these: Six vapor lights have been erected at the site; 15 pay phones have been installed; 200 chemical toilets have been set up; 65 security officers have been hired; and 50 drinking water outlets have been provided.

It occurs to me that this is some mad joke. None of these numbers makes sense. They are zany. They are absurd. Two hundred thousand people, the star says, will come here . . . and they will have 15 telephones? And 200 toilets? And 65 cops? And 50 water fountains? One telephone for every 13,000 people? One toilet for every 1000 people? One cop for every 1700 people? One drinking fountain for every 4000 people?

After one of the rose-colored press briefings, I run my statistics down for Shelly Saltman, a sugar-coated man who is "delighted" to meet every new reporter here—"I'm happy you could come," Shelly croons—but who somehow forgets most of their names five minutes later.

"Two hundred thousand people?" Shelly says. "Where did you get that figure?"

"Evel said so," I tell him. "It's even on his record album."

"Oh, that!" he grins. "That's just public relations."

"Well, how many people, Shelly?"

"Knievel said he'd bet anybody a million dollars there will be at least 50,000 here."

"Yeah, but he said 200,000 before that."

"Yeah, but he didn't offer to bet anybody a million dollars on it."

"I gotta go," Shelly says, dancing away, "they need me at the site."

At every press briefing, I notice, one subject is a raw nerve: television coverage of the jump itself. There will be no television coverage, Bob Arum says over and over again. "Absolutely not." The only way his fans will be able to see Evel's historic jump is to plunk down $10 for the closed-circuit telecast.

It is a raw nerve in part because CBS went to the Idaho Land Board a few days ago and offered $50,000 for use of the north rim (across from the jumpsite) to televise the event. CBS argued the jump is a "news event" and belongs to the American public. Top Rank Inc. argued the event is a "private performance," not news, and should be entitled to its "right of privacy." Top Rank added that if CBS was given use of the north rim and persisted in its intent to televise the event, the jump would be canceled. CBS abandoned its plans and a spokesman said the network didn't want its involvement to be cause for cancellation of the jump. NBC and ABC issued statements they would not attempt "unauthorized" coverage of the jump. Bob Arum said anyone attempting to film the jump would face "serious legal consequences," adding: "If any of the locals try to rip us off, we'll get them too."

Walking around the site a few days before blastoff, I see the Skycycle flanked on the east by gigantic vans which are marked ABC-Television. If ABC isn't going to televise this, what are these vans full of ABC equipment doing here?

I ask Arum about that and he replies: "We have hired ABC crews to do our closed-circuit telecast for us. They will use ABC equipment but they won't be working for the network, they'll be working for Top Rank."

"Will the jump be shown at some future time on ABC? On *Wide World of Sports,* maybe, a week later, the way a lot of the closed-circuit fights you've promoted were shown a week later?"

"Absolutely not," Arum says. "There will be no home television showing. Period. The only way anyone will be able to see the jump is either to come here or to watch it closed-circuit at a theater."

Later that afternoon I ask an ABC cameraman walking gingerly around the rim if Top Rank is paying his salary.

"What?" he says.

"You're not working for ABC," I say, "you're working for Top Rank, right?"

"What the hell's wrong with you?" he says.

Later in the week, ABC devotes two prime-time programs to Evel Knievel—a documentary, *One Man . . . One Canyon* narrated by Jules Bergman, and the official George Hamilton film version of the star's life. The network's timing intrigues me. Days before blastoff, the programs seem a part of the public-relations blitz. The content and nature of the "documentary" are even more intriguing. There, onscreen, is Jules Bergman, who has covered most of the astronaut missions, and he is almost hugging Evel Knievel as they walk up the mound toward the Skycycle and Bergman is saying the star's jump will be more dangerous than any of those space shots and he calls Knievel "a heckuva guy."

I think about those big ABC vans next to the Skycycle and how, according to Bergman, the star will take a step for mankind greater even than Neil Armstrong's and all the time I am going over my list. . . . The million-dollar party that wasn't a million-dollar party and the jump cycle that isn't a cycle and the test-failures that weren't failures and the $6 million check that turned into rubber and the 200,000 people who turned into 50,000. . . . Will the fans who'll pay $10 to see their hero this Sunday in theaters everywhere be wasting their inflation-ravaged money? Will the jump be seen on television after all?

I seek out the promoter who told me about the rubber check and buy him a Chivas Regal on the rocks and offer to buy him another and he says:

"All right, what do you want now?"

"ABC is going to televise the goddamn jump, right?"

His eyes are big. "I don't know how the hell you come up with that?" he says. "You know what Evel said. He said if he saw a TV cameraman he'd throw the guy off the edge of the canyon."

"ABC is going to televise it, right?"

"Goddamn you!" he says and takes me through his song and dance again. Yeah, the story won't come out till afterwards. Yeah, I won't tell anybody. Yeah, it's a deal. Yeah, we can shake.

"Okay," he says, "here's how it works. Evel's always been close to ABC's *Wide World of Sports*. They've always given him a lot of coverage and he's got a friend there named John Martin from *Wide World*. Martin knew Arum through the boxing closed-circuits ABC always runs a week later. Well, when Evel first started planning the jump, he asked Martin for advice about closed-circuit and it was Martin who recommended Arum to him. Not only that, but ABC gave Arum and Top Rank some of the $250,000 which was Evel's front money.

"So this is the deal. ABC will show the jump on *Wide World of Sports* the Saturday after the jump. The network is providing the equipment and the camera crew to Top Rank to show the jump on closed-circuit—for free. Top Rank will let the network show the jump for the free crew and equipment and the bucks ABC chipped in for the front money. It's a trade. The documentary and the movie they showed is going to help Evel and Top Rank and ABC. More people will come out here and pay 25 bucks, more people will go to the theaters and pay ten bucks, and more people will watch *Wide World of Sports* next week.

"It's beautiful. The only hitch is that nobody can find out about it before the jump because you know how the schmucks are. If the schmucks find out they can watch the whole thing a week later in their living rooms while guzzling their beers, then they won't pay a dime. Then Evel loses and Top Rank loses and the schmucks win."

III

A few hours before blastoff Sunday, Don Branker stands red-eyed near the Skycycle with horror in his eyes. He has been up all night. The scum-swarm went on a rampage till dawn this morning. Five hundred of them. They burned down concession stands. They looted all the beer they could find. They gunned their motorcycles through bonfires. They vandalized a fire engine. They threatened to torch the Skycycle itself. Only the shot-gun-toting cowboys kept them back from the launch ramp.

On the day of the Event of the Century, Don Branker explains, this is the situation: Many of the concession stands have closed down. Many of the security guards have left in disgust. There is little food, little beer and little security.

It is a blistering day. The temperature is in the high 80s and there is a 20 mph wind. The dust is so thick that some people look gray. Photographers are covering their equipment with plastic bags and crying about the cost of ruin.

New security guards have been hired to replace those who've abandoned the site. They are standing in a group near the Skycycle, the brave men who will keep the horde from going over into the abyss. They are motorcycle outlaws from Colorado and California, my Lost Soul Nomads and Molochs among them. They wear chains for belts and there are official red badges tied onto their beards. They are being paid exactly nothing—except the chance to get a close-up look at the jump and at the abyss. They are led by . . . the Goiter! The Goiter waves his fat arms a lot and shouts a lot of commands. He has been legitimized. The Hollow Lady, who watches him perform, sits on the highest perch of the VIP bleachers. She has been beatified.

Many of the reporters hiding from the dust and the sun under the big top are hung over and reading newspapers. An editorial in the Butte *Montana Standard,* signed by the publisher, says: "I admire your raw courage, Bob Knievel. . . . I admire your cool confidence. . . . I admire your red-white-and-blue Americanism. Our country certainly needs a hefty shot of unabashed pride in its colors, however presented." An editorial in today's *Twin Falls Times-News* says: "People searching for the deeper significance of Evel Knievel's leap might consider this one-liner—Evel's jump is an exclamation without a point."

A UPI newsman next to a telephone in the tent is moaning. "Oh, Jesus Christ! I just talked to my boss. Fucking Ford just pardoned fucking Nixon. Why does this always have to happen to me when I'm on a big story? It's going to knock my byline off the front page!"

Outside the tent P.T. Arum is shaking his head. "Why did he have to do it today?" he says. "Who the hell ever heard of the White House doing anything important on Sunday? At least Ford won't be elected president now."

"Hey Bob," I say to him, "I hear that after all this hoop-dee-doo, Knievel's gonna change his mind. He's going to back out today, huh?"

"Motherfucker!" Arum snaps.

He has more pressing worries. Just a few hours before the jump, there are no more than perhaps 15,000 people here. It is apparent to everyone that the crowd size speaks of financial loss. None of the promoters is talking about 50,000 people "pouring" in here today. Nothing is said about closed-circuit tickets "selling like hotcakes." Bob Arum says simply: "The crowd looks okay to me."

None of the reporters can find the superstar celebrities who are supposed to be here. "Where the hell are Elvis and John Wayne and Steve McQueen and Dustin Hoffman?" I ask Bob Arum.

"I haven't seen them," he says, "but I'm sure they're around." It is a line that Arum will repeat many times today. He hasn't seen them. As a matter of fact, no one in this entire crowd will catch even a glimpse of them all day. But sure, they're around somewhere.

A group of reporters is lined up beside a stand near the Rock of Ages monument. They are writing their names and addresses in a book. They are signing up for free Evel Knievel toys, courtesy of the Ideal Toy company. "These guys really have class," a happy reporter from Salt Lake City says. "I can have toys sent to my nephews and cousins. It's one of the nicest freebies I've ever gotten."

Another reporter is berating one of the star's aides. "There's no beer," he says. "What happened to the damn beer? And the sandwiches are stale. You guys said you'd have fresh sandwiches out here and all the beer we'd want. You broke your promise!" The aide says more sandwiches are on the way but there will be no free beer today. "A lot of the beer got ripped off last night," he says. The reporter yells: "Well, what the hell am I supposed to do?" The aide says: "Have a Sprite!" The reporter walks dejectedly into the crowd. "Anybody wanna sell a beer?" he says.

A reporter from Chicago has overheard the beer and sandwich dispute. "Sure," he says, somewhat philosophically. "No beer and stale sandwiches. That's because they don't need us anymore. They needed us until today to write stories that would get more people out here and into the theaters. But we can't do them any more good today. They don't care what we write for tomorrow. They'll be counting the money tomorrow. So we get no beer and stale sandwiches."

The swarm behind the fence protecting the launch area and the press/VIP compound is growing restless. It is trying to pull the fence down. The Goiter and his outlaws secure the fence. "We want in!" a kid yells at the Goiter. "We want in right now!" The Goiter yells: "You get off that motherfucking fence you cunts or we're gonna kick your ass!"

The star has arrived in a helicopter with Watchamacallit, his wife Linda and his kids. He waves to the crowd and parades to his trailer. The swarm screams: "Eeeeeeeeeeevel! Knieeeeeeeeeevel!"

The swarm has nothing to do and not much to see. The closed-circuit telecast has begun but the swarm can't see any part of it. The Wallendas do their pyramid, Sensational Parker does his sway, the Great Manzini does his leap and Gil Eagles is doing his psychic ride. But the swarm can't see any of this. The swarm is dusty and hungry and relatively beerless. It has but one thing to do and it throws itself militantly into this task. The swarm screams and tugs at the fence.

Black Jack Swank stands near the fence and stares defiantly at the crowd. "Sir, can you come over here, please?" a kid yells to him. Black Jack takes a few steps in the kid's direction. The kid spits at him and laughs. The spit misses and Black Jack steps away, turns his back and doesn't look defiant anymore.

The star is up on the anthill in his Old Glory jumpsuit talking to David Frost. "If I have to hit that wall over there on the other side," he says, "I think that I would rather do that than become the victim of a senseless tragedy. I'd rather be busted into the wind like a meteorite and not become just dust."

A kid watches them outside the fence but can't hear what they are saying. "Cut the shit!" he yells. "Get it the hell on!"

The star comes over to the press area and gives a little speech. He has been thinking it over, he says. He has thought about the newsmen who are here to help him and he has thought about the newsmen who are jackasses. He has totaled it up and it has come out "about a million to three." Jack Perkins and I grin. We know we're not part of the million.

The swarm is really crunching into the fence now and screaming at the newsmen. "You cocksuckers! Let us in there!" one kid yells. "Get the press!" says another. "Kill the goddamn press!" Some of the reporters are becoming very . . . concerned . . . and flee inside the big top. While they are no safer there if the swarm knocks the fence down, they can at least watch Gil Eagles on the monitors and not have to deal with dying.

Father Jerry Sullivan, still in his rumpled suit, solemnly says the benediction. "We all pray that he'll have a successful landing," Father Sullivan prays, "whether that may be on earth or in heaven." Linda, the woman with the size 46 double-D breasts, wears a T-shirt today that says: "Built like a Mack Truck." Linda says she camped out here all night with some of the Mack guys. "Boy," she says, "after all this heavy foreplay this thing better have a juicy ending."

The star is in his trailer saying goodbye to his wife and family. He sees Bob Arum's two little boys. "If I die," he tells them, "it ain't your daddy's fault. He put the money up but I would've jumped anyway."

The Goiter is having an increasingly difficult time dealing with the swarm. "You're a pig just like those press creeps!" a kid tells him. The Goiter doesn't know what to say. He takes a punch at the fence and hurts his knuckles.

The teenaged lovelies in the Butte High School Marching Band stare as the girl who has been stripped by the crowd is thrown into the press compound. "Did you see what they did to her?" a frecklefaced tuba player says to her girlfriend. "Yeah, and I just bet she loved it!" the girlfriend answers.

In the center of the swarm a longhaired Jesus freak wearing a silver cross is delivering a sermon. "Our Lord Jesus Christ is the savior!" he says. "Let us pray to the Lord Jesus Christ for Evel Knievel." Some of the swarm actually start saying the Our Father.

There is a fierce assault on the fence and the Goiter and his special outlaws cannot deal with it. A middle-aged guy with an Evel Knievel haircut is driving his new Cadillac into the fence and trying to knock it down as the swarm readies to charge behind him. The Goiter starts screaming and one of his men materializes out of the dust with a rifle. The outlaw raises the rifle and aims it at the driver. The Cadillac backs away. A few of the Goiter's friends, outside the fence now, swiftly slash a couple of the Cadillac's tires.

One of the Goiter's goons has a microphone in his hands and is telling the swarm to back off. "You gotta be cool," he says, "we don't want anybody to get messed up."

"Fuck you!" a kid yells at him.

"Fuck you too!" the goon answers with the microphone.

The Hollow Lady hears the "Fuck you too!" booming across the site and turns loftily from her perch high atop the VIP bleachers.

"Go fuck your mom!" she screeches.

The preliminary acts are over now. The moment has come. The star begins ascending toward the Skycycle in his Freedom Crane. The swarm howls.

A guy outside the fence grabs his girl by the hair, forces her on her knees and unzips his fly. He is hanging out there in the hot air at the very moment Evel is ascending and she is sucking his cock. The guy yells: "For you, Evel! For you, man!" The girl stops resisting and gets into it.

He is up by the Skycycle now and the loudspeakers blare a recording of his poem. It is called "Why" and it is the voice of Evel Knievel through clouds of dust and chunks of hot air. His voice is softer than I've ever heard it. "It seems that everywhere in the world I go, no matter who or what I know, the people, they look and most of them stare, and I wonder if they really care. They see this king with his golden crown. Some of them smile but most of them frown. I hear them laugh and I hear them cry. No matter what, they all ask why. Why? Well, I'm just like you and you and you. We all have a special purpose in life and my way of life I'm glad I found, for like you I too make the world go round. We're all alike, oh yes we are, we all have a dream of some faraway star. . . ."

When the poem ends, as he begins to climb into the Skycycle, the loudspeakers blare "The Ballad of Evel Knievel" by John Culliton Mahoney. "He lives from day to day, never thinking about tomorrow. His body shows the scars fate has dealt his way. This strong yet simple man walking along the edge of danger, secure in prayers that God has heard him say. . . . Once he's made up his mind there's nothing he won't try. There's something deep inside him . . . yet he knows someday he's gonna have to face that canyon in the sky. . . ."

The teenaged ladies of the Butte High School Marching Band play "The Star-Spangled Banner." The star waves to his wife, then flips a thumbs-up salute to his masses.

"Bob," the star says to Truax, his engineer, "you and your men have done every single thing that you could do. The rest is up to me."

"Cut the shit!" a kid screams again. "Get it on!"

He's strapped into his Skycycle. There is a long silence, then a *whoooooooooooooosh!*, orange smoke, and the rocket-watertank cycle is off.

The moment it goes up, the Goiter and his deputies abandon their fence. Fuck the security! They can't see from here! They turn from the fence and start running across the press compound toward the fence in front of them only a few feet from the rim. The Goiter leads. His outlaws follow. The swarm knocks the abandoned fence down and follows the outlaws. The Goiter is the king of the swarm once again.

But something is very wrong up there in the sky. The drogue parachute on the Skycycle opens when it is not yet two-thirds of the way up the ramp. The rocket goes up too slowly and then, as it heads toward the sun, the main parachute opens and the rocket stops dead. It is like a ball which has come to the end of a rubber band . . . turns upside down, and drifts slowly into the abyss.

The Goiter and his swarm trample the fence only a few feet from the rim. They want to see! The Skycycle is still drifting down.

"He's gonna drown," someone screams.

The girls of the Butte High School Marching Band are sobbing.

"He's dead!" several people yell.

On the other side of the Skycycle, standing at the rim near her family's trailer, Linda Knievel is shouting: "Oh my God! Oh my God!" She can't see down there.

"Where is it?" she yells.

"Below the rocks," someone says.

The Skycycle has landed down there. No one knows whether it's in the Snake or on the rocks. No one really knows whether Evel Knievel is dead or alive though there is a tornadic feeling in the air that the One Last Fly has turned into the One Last Fly. Helicopters flutter over the abyss.

"Tell them to get their asses in gear!" Linda Knievel says, looking at the choppers. "Get your asses in gear!"

Next to the rim, the swarm has taken out its anxiety on an ABC crew. It slashes the crew's wiring, smashes equipment, and yanks headsets from the soundmen. The ABC men run for their lives.

The swarm has totally occupied the rim. The Goiter stands arm-in-arm with the Hollow Lady, who has descended from her VIP perch. They have assumed a stiff ballet-like position. Their legs are planted firmly on the ground, but their heads crane over the abyss. The Goiter's belly hangs over the abyss too.

In the press tent, everyone is watching the monitors. Bobby Riggs is sitting by a TV screen pounding his fists and saying: "Come on, Evel, come up from there!" Jimmy the Greek says: "You never see this kind of crazy shit at a heavyweight fight." Jack Perkins says: "I'll tell you one guy who's hoping he's alive. Watt. You can't sue an estate."

The first word comes on the monitors from a member of the closed-circuit team. "It landed on some rocks! He's not in the river! He's alive! He's standing up! He looks all right!" The reporters cheer. The swarm cheers. Jack Perkins and I cheer. The Goiter and the Hollow Lady are doing a jig on the edge of the abyss with their fists jabbing the air.

A 43-year-old man named John Hood, from Trenton, New Jersey, an old friend of the star's, is one of the first to reach him. He lowers himself out of a helicopter by rope, helps the star from his dented Skycycle, walks with him to the Snake's edge, and helps him into a boat. From there the star gets into a helicopter. Hood stays at the bottom of the void and waits for the chopper to come back for him.

The star is rising from the abyss and ascending toward the rim. His face is slightly bloody, scraped by some underbrush. He seems dazed. Within moments he is being interviewed by David Frost.

"Thank God you're all right!" Frost says,

"I am glad to be back in one piece, thank God!" the star says. He looks bewildered and worn out. He looks a bit like a man who has eaten too much Compoz.

Bob Truax explains what happened: "The parachute blew open too soon. Evel didn't do anything wrong. He didn't pull the chute. What happened had nothing to do with him."

The reporter who has been complaining all day about the lack of beer says: "If the wind would have been stronger the damn Skycycle would have blown all the way back here. It could have landed right on top of the press tent. I bet he planned the whole thing this way. If he would have made it over to the other side, people would have said it was a snap. If he would have died, they would have forgotten him in a year. This way he's a bigger daredevil than ever before. He went crashing down there and lived to tell about it."

The star spends a few minutes with his family, then comes out of the trailer and showboats for the crowd. He tosses them the cheap imitation of his cane. He goes along the fence power-shaking outthrust hands. He has bodyguards everywhere and at one point the guards hold hands and form a circle around him. The guards are Goiter and his outlaw friends. One of his bodyguards, I notice, is the same outlaw who said "Fuck him in the ass!" when I asked him about Evel Knievel at Jan's Lounge.

The star goes back inside the trailer to sit a few moments but will come out soon for a picture-taking session. I look at the photographers who are getting ready and there, with a monstrous new camera over his shoulder, I see . . . Watt, the Dwarf Photographer, back from L.A. The trouble, though, is that Bob Arum has seen him as well.

"Evel doesn't want you in here!" Arum tells Jim Watt. "You'll have to get out of here!"

"I have to get out?" Watt says, shaking his head.

"It's Evel's area," Arum says. "Yes, I'm sorry. Please."

"Why do I have to get out?" Watt asks.

"You know why!" Arum says. "Look, I'm sorry. It's none of my doing. But he wants you out of here. He's not going to come out of the trailer until you're out of here!"

"That's discrimination against NBC," someone says.

"Evel's got no problems with NBC, it's with this guy!" Arum says, pointing to Watt.

"You'll have to go!" Arum says. "*Anybody* else from NBC can stay here," and the Dwarf Photographer says "Jesus Christ!" and, banished once again, lugs his heavy camera away from the star's trailer.

Evel Knievel comes out after a while and gets his picture taken and says: "It wasn't a Truax failure. It wasn't a Knievel failure. It was a metal failure." He says he doesn't think he will try jumping the Snake River Canyon again.

"Let's bet," the beerless reporter says (softly). "Let's bet a million dollars."

After a few minutes, with two or three thousand people still there, Evel Knievel climbs into his helicopter, waves, and Watchamacallit takes him back to the Blue Lakes Inn.

Sunday night, John Hood of Trenton, New Jersey, who helped Evel Knievel out of his Skycycle, is still at the bottom of the canyon. He is cold and hungry. He is waiting for the helicopter which will take him out of the abyss. John Hood thinks: Certainly they're not going to just forget about me and leave me here!

Sunday night, a part of the swarm is still at the site. The swarm is not happy. Where's the free beer? Where's the party Evel promised? The swarm shows it isn't happy. The concession stands are knocked down and burned. So are all the fences. So are the telephone and the utility poles. So are all the toilets. The Evel Knievel Snake River Canyon jumpsite is burning to the ground. The swarm discovers the Cadillac which got its tires slashed trying to bust through the fence. The Cadillac is driven to the launch ramp and is set afire. The Skycycle launch ramp is in flames.

At daybreak Monday, John Hood comes out of the abyss. He has climbed out of there. They just abandoned him. He was the one who helped Evel Knievel out of his wrecked Skycycle and they just left him down there all night in gratitude for his efforts. It was so cold down there that John Hood had to wrap himself in the Skycycle parachute.

Monday morning, when Evel Knievel is heading for the Magic Valley Airport to head back to the Richest Hill on Earth, his driver stops the car. Something is wrong. The driver goes out to look. Both of the rear tires are flat. Someone has vandalized Evel Knievel's car.

Monday morning, the day after the Event of the Century, the headlines are splashed over the top of the front page of every newspaper of every city in the land. The headlines are the focus of much of the whole world's attention. FORD PARDONS NIXON, the headlines say, TERHORST QUITS IN PROTEST.

The Search for the Secret Pyramid

KEN KESEY

WE KNEW THE MERRY PRANKSTER COULD DIG UP
SOMETHING IN EGYPT, BUT KEEZ NEEDED A GUIDE
FOR THIS TRIP. ENTER CHARLIE PERRY, A.K.A. SMOKE-
STACK EL ROPO.

> "Bukra fil-mishmish *is kinda the Egyptian version
> of the Mexicans'* Mañana. *It translates as 'Tomorrow,
> in the time of the apricots.' But dig: There isn't any
> apricot season on the Nile. . . ."*
> —CHARLIE PERRY

Pleasant Hill, OR
St. Pat's Day, 1992

Charlie Perry
Camp Mogen David, CA

Dear Charlie:
  Downwind by a couple decades, peeking back through
cracked mind mirrors. You see, ROLLING STONE is publishing a chunk of "The Search for the Secret Pyramid" they

sent us on in '74, and Jann has asked me to come up with the Most Memorable Scene from that historic assignment. A grand gallery of Egyptian etchings comes flapping to mind:

—like that first night in Cairo, when Ramadan ended and 7 million uproarious believers broke out in a teeming rash of discordant harmony, heralding the rise of global Muslim might . . .

—or that afternoon our motor-mad taxi driver T'ud (*"Thud?"* you screeched from the back seat. "This gear-grinding tire-burning pedal-to-the-metal maniac's name is *Thud?"*) drove us out to Sakara, where a tunnel beneath the sand led us past hundreds of stone boxes big as Buicks, all of them coffins for the bulls that were elaborately sacrificed every year for hundreds of years thousands of years ago, each of them carved from a solid block of rare black granite, and every one of them empty, enigmatic and depressing . . .

—or that chilly dawn my shadowy little Not-guide, Marag (pronounced with a soft g, remember? Mah-rahzh-zh . . .), guided me down through the dark throb of his ancestral village to score me some hash so you wouldn't have to listen to me complain anymore that I was "highless in Gîza." . . .

Great memories, Charlie, but I'm afraid I'm gonna have to disappoint Jann; the Egyptian memory that stands out most in my gallery actually happens on another trip, four years later, when I finally persuade friends and family to return with me to that fabulous land of the pharaohs . . . when hard-shell Baptist Jimmy Carter is getting hard-nosed Hebrew Menachem Begin to sit down and schmooze with moderate Muslim Anwar Sadat in the name of Peace. . . .

—in the Time of the Apricots, when the Grateful Dead played the Great Pyramid.

Sadat's old lady helped put the gig together, explaining to unenthusiastic Arab allies that she understood their concern about infidel Rok'n Rolies playing the World's Most Ancient Temple, but she did not consider it blasphemous in as the promoters agreed that all prophets from the concert would go toward the construction of a soccer field for the under-privileged children of Cairo.

Right. Prophets zero, lions ate, as usual. But the Arab elders went for it. How could they have known what rough beast was lurching toward them across the desert by the truckful? How could they have imagined the prophet-gobbling appetite of a Rok'n Rol army on a full-scale campaign?

Even the gig's promoters never dreamed how *un*prophetable the gig was gonna be. Only 700 tickets sold, mostly to hardcore Deadheads, government operatives and spoiled Saudis who motored over by the limo load. Local sales are zip.

"Oh, well," the promoters sigh as they strap on their most philosophical Woodstock Grin, "some things you gotta write off as the Will of Allah."

Bill Graham isn't one of these promoters. He was always too sharp a businessman to back a stone loser. But he shows up anyway, right on cue, for the sound check. This is the Most Memorable Scene I mean. . . .

It has been a hard crazy afternoon. The Dead road crew is about the only thing that's properly wired. The equipment is unfamiliar (it's borrowed from the Who and shipped into Alexandria to save $) and the Egyptian electricity is uncooperative. The stage is a cruel anvil of hot stone, situated right off the right paw of the crouching Sphinx. The sun is pounding like a brass hammer. It's hot it's hard it's a bitch.

The band is prowling around the towers of amps and speakers, trying to find a little shade—"Let's fucking get this over with before this fucking guitar melts!" Hamza el Din, the opening act, is trying to tune his crook-necked instrument in front of a goose-necked mike. The instrument is an eight-stringed oud. Hamza's a Nubian, black as Mystery Itself. His backup group is twenty-five other Nubians, clustered uncomfortably around him on the hot stage. They're Hamza's school chums from his village, to the south. He thought it might be a nice gesture if the Dead flew them in to help with the little Nubian homeboy chant that he was planning to open the show with. Mickey Hart had of course loved the idea: "Twenty-five Nubians doing an African nursery rhyme? Groovy, fly 'em in."

They've never been away from home before; now Yankee sound guys are trying to tell them what mikes to use. The poor nervous Nubians don't speak American they don't speak English they don't even speak Egyptian! Nobody is communicating with anybody. "Yibble *yabble*," the Nubians chant. "*This* mike!" the sound guys yell. "*Eee-e-ek!*" the tortured equipment screams.

It is into this hot and hectic tableau that Bill Graham comes stalking, right out of the Sphinx's gritty armpit.

"Uncle Bobo!" Bob Weir calls. "You just couldn't keep away, could you?"

GRAHAM [*hands on hips, shaking his head at the stir-fry of incompatible ingredients sizzling before him*]: Never thought it would happen, not in a million years.

ME: Quite the mixed bag, huh, Bill?

GRAHAM [*awed but not overwhelmed*]: Never woulda believed it. Seemed insurmountable. What a mishmash.

ME [*oracular and portentous*]: Nobody has any idea what a mixture like this might produce.

NUBIANS [*chanting along with the little tune Hamza is finally coaxing from his oud*]: Yibble *yabble* gobble dobba dobba doom boom . . .

MICKEY [*calling over the backbeat he's adding on his hand drum*]: It's a twelve-tone scale worked into twelve different rhythm sequences, repeated twelve times, got it?

GRAHAM: Mickey's in hog heaven.

NUBIANS: Hotcha motcha gotcha gotcha *zoom* zam . . .

PHIL [*hunched turkey-necked over his bass*]: Thomma *boom* zoom sorta got it—

NUBIANS: Hotcha motcha gotcha gotcha getcha zoom— [I had just turned on my little Sanyo is how come I happen to have this cassette I'm listening to at present, Charlie. Phone my son Zane, 503-484-4315, if you want a copy].

JERRY [*stepping at last into the dangerous desert sunshine, tentative, like a gray old lion in tinted sadglasses*]: Zwangle, squeedle dweedle dorngle gottit *now* zwornk!

GRAHAM: Tasty . . .

And suddenly, at that moment, under that acetylene sun, it all fluxes together—like silver solder fluxing with gold, a bright wire, stringing all these different rhythms and races, these alien scales and ancient civilizations, into a kind of necklace of sound, gaudy yet somehow appropriate, like the sort of bauble that Bo Diddley, say, might mail to, say, Queen Hatshepsut if he had her address. Indeed, a tasty trinket.

GRAHAM [*hot and getting hotter*]: Damn, I hope somebody with a good tape machine has the sense to record this.

Nobody did, as far as I know, except me and my sixty-buck Sanyo. But even on the crappy cassette you can hear how the hectic scene started changing for the better from the moment Bill Graham showed up—as though the bastard were some kind of bad-vibe blotter. The hotter he got the colder the scene became until, at some secret signal, the whole stage full of chanters and drummers and rockers shifted out of Nubian homeboy raga into Buddy Holly rock as smooth as the transmission on one of those Saudi limos, from "Hotcha motcha gotcha gotcha gee" to "I'm gonna tell you how it's gonna be" without nicking a cog.

Now, lo these many years later, listening to the tape, it all seems to flux together again . . . and by golly, you know, Charlie? Maybe it was all part of our ROLLING STONE assignment after all, the same way the concert at the Sphinx was part of Uncle Bobo's business whether he promoted the damn thing or not.

Be that as it may, scenes this tasty and profound oughta always be reported. That night at the gig, for instance, a conjunction of particularly profound events went down: As the Grateful Dead were playing "Dark Star" through the Who's equipment between the paws of the Sphinx at the foot of the Great Pyramid in the Season of the Apricots, the Sahara moon underwent a total and completely unforeseen eclipse (check it out, September 17th, 1978) at the very hour that Keith Moon was blacking out and dying at his flat in London.

What does it all mean, Charlie? Probably nothing. But if I were Jann, I would send out another probe, just to be on the safe side. It's time. He's got to keep his finger on the dark vein of the World Beyond, whether he detects any pulse or not. *Mondo 2000*, for instance, is putting together a team of virtual surrealists to send to that atoll where they found Amelia Earhart's shoe, hoping to channel an interview. We could beat them to it, Charlie. You choose the wine, I'll chart the channel. Hunter has already volunteered his pineal gland, no strings attached.

> At the ready,
> KEEZ

In 1974, Jann Wenner owed me a trip to Lebanon. I had stuck with ROLLING STONE through every crisis since RS 12, and in reward, he'd promised to let me do a story on the Lebanese hash fields.

The idea made sense. I spoke fluent Arabic, and as a sometime pen name, Smokestack el Ropo, implies, I had a passing acquaintance with controlled smokable substances. Almost immediately, however, Jann started hemming and hawing about his promise. He'd heard of gang warfare in the hashish groves, he said. My services as copy editor and all-around deadline trail boss were just too valuable for him to risk my life.

I *was* a busy boy in those days, between copy editing, proofreading, fact checking (in my years we never misspelled a Sanskrit word) and riding herd on the design and editorial departments to get everything in on time, plus writing a lot of the headlines and captions. I was under so much pressure that in the fevered exhilaration of deadline nights, I developed a habit of walking around on the tops of desks—to "get a higher view," as I put it. I came to feel that all colors but bright yellow were an insidious energy drain. Some people found the resulting wardrobe a bit strident.

But I really figured I could have taken care of myself in the hash fields, and the issue was a faintly sore one between Jann and me for a couple of years. Then, in '74, Ken Kesey approached Jann about a story on the Great Pyramid of Gîza. Jann was a longtime fan of Kesey's—in ROLLING STONE's original office, on Brannan Street, there had been only two photos on the wall: one of the Marx Brothers and one of Kesey at a 1965 Acid Test party. Now the great man wanted us to sponsor an expedition to unravel the mysteries said to be embodied in the pyramid. According to the babblings of the famous "sleeping prophet," Edward Cayce, the pyramid was not a tomb but a symbol fraught with occult power. Moreover, adjoining it was the "Hall of Records," which Cayce said would be discovered between 1958 and 1998. Verrry interesting.

Now Jann could honestly discharge his promise. Kesey would need a guide familiar with the land and fluent in the native tongue. Also (a fact not lost on Kesey), Jann wanted somebody from the home office on hand to . . . well, make sure everything was moving along. He may have had in mind the bizarre roomservice bills Hunter Thompson had run up in Las Vegas.

So in place of a trip to the Lebanese hash fields, I got a translator-chaperon job on an occult journey to Egypt. Close enough. As a sort of trial run, Kesey wanted to visit the headquarters of the Rosicrucian Order, in San Jose, California, which boasts a scale model of the Great Pyramid. It was an early clue to Kesey's psychic-matador research methods. When we got off the freeway in San Jose, Kesey refused to use the map to find the place, hoping to be able to sense the pyramid's vibration. (We had to cheat a little on the final approach.)

He spent the next week or so contacting other occult sources around the country, including the Cayceite Association for Research and Enlightenment, in Virginia Beach, Virginia, and someone in the Midwest named Enoch, who had never been to Egypt. We hooked up in New York and flew together to Cairo.

After one night at a decaying hotel on an island in the Nile, we took a cab to Gîza, the Cairo suburb where the Great Pyramid is located, and checked into the Mena House Hotel, just two minutes' walk away. Kesey determinedly talked them into giving us a room, although we didn't have a reservation, but we were clearly told it would be for only two nights.

The next morning, Kesey threw the I Ching and concluded it was time to have our first real look at the pyramid. Terrific recommendation, I Ching. It was a Muslim holiday, and on holidays the poor people of Cairo tend to party at the base of the pyramid (Cairo is short of parks, and it's a cheap bus ride). The place was crowded with hundreds, perhaps thousands, of Cairenes, picnicking and dancing in party clothes, which they traditionally dye lurid Day-Glo colors.

Kesey had been overwhelmed by the seething mob scene that is Cairo ever since we'd arrived. Clambering up the huge stones of the pyramid, surrounded by hordes of people dressed in science-fiction hues, he seemed even more overwhelmed than usual. Then I heard some kids shout, *"El-khawāga byidūkh! El-khawāga byidūkh!"* ("The foreign gentleman is dizzy! The foreign gentleman is dizzy!")

In Arabic "dizzy" is a polite way of saying "throwing up." And so he was—in a sort of vitamin-laden christening, the foreign gentleman was recycling his breakfast orange juice onto the pyramid. Later, Kesey told me he'd taken a little LSD that morning to heighten his perceptions.

That wasn't the only moment he'd regret dropping that acid. A few minutes later, still not suspecting his sensitive condition, I suggested that we go into the pyramid. Kesey raised his eyes to the mob standing in line, a look of mute struggle on his face. The Universe had just laid down a challenge to him; he sighed and said yes, of course we had to go in.

The internal passageways of the Great Pyramid are steep and narrow, not designed to hold scores of people at a time. We found ourselves in a sweating, lurching crush of people struggling in both directions at the same time, panicky from lack of oxygen. I'm not surprised Kesey concluded the pyramid was not a tomb but a place of initiation.

The next day the hotel reminded us we had to turn our rooms over to the people who had reserved them. Kesey refused to leave the vicinity of the pyramid, though. The management, used to the perennial Egyptian housing shortage, eventually threw up its hands and offered to let us sleep in the changing rooms at the swimming pool.

These proved to be the worst accommodations I've ever had. If you closed the windows to keep out the mosquitoes, you could either leave the air conditioning off and suffocate or leave it on and catch cold. I chose the final option and in two days had to go back to Cairo to find a decent hotel room and the kind of ferocious antibiotics that the USDA hesitates to allow Americans to buy but you can easily find, I'm glad to say, in countries where it's possible to get really sick. I left Kesey on his own.

When I got back to San Francisco, I was given the chance to put in my two cents on the edit of Kesey's reports—which wound up running to five installments—but I declined. Kesey had explained to me his theory that it's more important for a writer to discover his personal myth than to relate facts, and from the narrow, fact-bound viewpoint of a reporter, I'd have had to point out where he played fast and loose with quotations (most of the things he has me say in the story are, let's say, literature) and plain old facts.

But go ahead and read about the Great Pyramid. Something may be revealed after all.

—CHARLES PERRY

RS 180

FEBRUARY 13TH, 1975

Left alone I tried to coordinate my impressions of the place with what I know about it as a geodetic phenomenon.

I remembered my trip to England in the weird winter of '69, standing in the center of Stonehenge, watching the sun of the winter solstice dawn slide up between those two rocks directly in front of me, knowing that exactly half a year later it would slide up between those other two rocks exactly to my right, and remembering how it forced you to strain your mind to include the tilt of our axis, the swing of our orbit around the sun, the singular position on our globe of this circle of prehistoric rocks—how it made you feel you were in a place—an exact place, at a particular time. I knew that the pyramid was built in such a place—one of the acupuncture points of the physical planet—but no matter how I tried I couldn't get that planetary sense that Stonehenge gave me.

I was still disoriented by that feeling of dimensions dropping away— everything still seemed flat; even the back of the Sphinx's head. And I couldn't quite convince myself that I was alone. There seemed to be some- one still sitting with me, not at my side but close. (This is no sixth sense— plants know when someone is near, oughtn't we more complex forms of protoplasm be able to detect the same?)

Somebody was near, the feeling grew stronger: corporeally, physically near! The wad of 200 Egyptian pound notes in my pocket was suddenly bleeping like a beacon and I was beginning to glance about for a weapon when the Sphinx's whole head lit up and proclaimed sonorously, in a voice like Lorne Greene to the tenth power:

"I . . . am . . . the . . . Sphinx. I am . . . very old . . . very old . . ."

It boomed this out to the accompanying strains of Verdi's *Aïda*, as Chephren lit up a glorious green, and little Mykerinos glowed blue and the Great Pyramid blazed an appropriate gold.

Mark had been serious about the Sound and Light. It was a show for the benefit of a whole amphitheater of tourists at the bottom of the hill. From tombs and mastabas everywhere banks of concealed floodlights illuminated the pyramids in slowly shifting hues while the Sphinx ran it all down for them in grandly amplified English (I just happened to hit it on the English Night. The other performances rotate through French, German, Russian and Arabic.)

In the reflection from the face of Chephren, I saw the little figure I had sensed, watching me from a few dozen yards away. I took advantage of the light and headed immediately back toward the Great Pyramid road in long strides. Over the sounds of Verdi and the Sphinx's narrative I thought I could hear the scuffle of feet following but I didn't turn and look till I had reached the road.

He was right behind me.

"Good evening, my friend. A very nice evening, yes?" He hurried the last few steps to fall in beside me. He wore a blue gellabia and scuffed black oxfords without shoestrings or socks. "My name is Marag."

I came to know that it was spelled that way but it was pronounced with a soft, gentle "g" so that it rhymed with collage, if you put the accent on the first syllable: *Mah*-rahzhzh . . .

"Excuse me, but do I hear you wish to buy some hashish?"

His face was polished teak brown, alert and angled, with a neat black mustache over tiny white teeth. The corners of his mouth lifted, but the smile was in his whole face. His eyes were set like amused jewels in hundreds of tiny wrinkles. An old amusement. I judged him to be at least 40, as easily 60, and not quite as tall as my 13-year-old son. Hurrying along beside me he seemed to barely touch the ground. So light. When at last I relinquished the five-pound note and shook his hand to seal our deal his fingers sifted through my grip like so much sand.

There is a little outdoor restaurant at the edge of the *aouda* where you can sip Turkish coffee and watch the Pyramid change colors without having to listen to the Sphinx's nocturnal narrative. After three cups of the bitter brew I paid my tab and headed out. I had waited nearly an hour. He had said 20 minutes. Oh well, I reasoned philosophically, I have only myself to blame; I know the rules. They're international: Whether you're in Tangiers or Tijuana, North Beach or Novato, you don't get up off the bread till you see the score. Twenty minutes . . . in the season of the apricots.

But just as I came out of the restaurant I saw a little blue figure come whisking around up the shadowy trail from the village.

Panting and sweating, he slipped five little packages into my hand, each about the size of a .45 cartridge and wrapped in paper and taped over that. I started digging at one with my thumbnail.

"I had to go more further than I think," he apologized. "Five pieces, five pounds. Eh? Is good?"

I realized he wasn't asking but telling me that the score had cost him exactly what I had put out, none left over for his efforts. His face sparkled up at me. Reaching again for my wallet I also realized that he could have packaged five goat turds and be working me for whatever else he could get out of me. He saw my hesitation.

"As you wish," he shrugged, appearing hurt.

I gave him two American bucks, worth about one Egyptian pound at any official currency exchange but about a pound and a half on the black market. After examining the two greenbacks he grinned to let me know he appreciated my logic if not my generosity:

"Any night, at this Pyramid corner. Ask for Marag. Everybody know where to find Marag." Reaching out, he sifted his hand again through mine, his eyes glittering. "And your name?"

I told him, somewhat unnerved by that glitter and suspicious still of the little pellets: Was he going to burn me, bust me, or both, as the dealers were known to do in Tijuana . . .

"*Kee-*zee? Kee-*zee*?" Trying the accent at each end amused him. "Good night to you, Mr. Kee-zee . . ." And was whisked back into the shadows.

Back in the hotel room I found the little packets were bound so tight I could have never opened one with my fingers. I had to dig my buckknife from my valise. After sawing and peeling and grumbling for five minutes I finally cracked the tiny cardboard cartridge. After I had wrenched loose a piece of the Mena House plumbing to use for a pipe I ascertained it contained a ball of the softest, sweetest, smoothest hash known to civilized taste.

October 30th., Wednesday morn., Up before the sun. I recheck my packing (three girls from Oregon are right now serving life sentences for dope in Turkey where my plane lands after Cairo); nothing but the last ball of hash. And the Murine bottle. The hash I can swallow at the airport, but what about this stuff? Just flush it down the toilet? That's like carrying the key through all the long battle to the castle, through the moat and up the wall to the prison tower with the maiden locked behind the massive stone door then losing it down a bottomless crack before it can be inserted in the keyhole.

I've got to try. Never again will I get the chance. There's not enough time left to swallow it; it would be flight time before I took off. But if I bang it . . .

So I'm headed again up the hill for one last desperation try, the Murine bottle in my shoulder bag, the old disposable insulin outfit in its envelope in my shirt pocket. My heart is knocking and my belly tight by the time I reach the *aouda* and I'm shivering all over. I lean against the casing stones trying to reinforce my resolve but I keep shivering. It's chilly and gray. A whirlwind comes winding across the empty *aouda*, gathering a fanatical congregation of scraps. The wind spins, like a new messiah, inspiring corn husks, cigarette packs, the twisted cones that held yesterday's cooked melon seeds for lifting newspapers, gum papers, toilet papers, higher and higher. What a following! Then the spirit evaporates and the wind unwinds and the zealots drift back to the limestone.

"Good morning, Mr. Kee-zee . . . is a nice morning?"

"Good morning, Marag." I had planned to apologize for the fuckup at the hotel; now I realize again there is nothing to say. "It's not a bad morning. A little chilly . . ."

"A new season comes. The winds will now blow from the desert, more cooler and full of sand : . ."

"No more tourists for a season?"

He shrugs: "As long as there are good reliable guides, there will be tourists." His little eyes, so bright and sharp and amused, are already chipping away at my chill. "Maybe my friend Mister *Kee*-zee want a good guide take him to the top of the Pyramid? Guide most reliable? You know how much?"

"Five pounds," I say, reaching for my wallet. "Let's go."

It's like climbing up on 200 tall tables, one after the other. Marag tucks his gellabia in the top of his shorts and leads the way like a lizard. I have to call a stop to him three times. His tiny eyes needle merrily at me, as I gasp for breath:

"Mr. Kee-*zee*, are you not healthy? Do you not get good nourishment in your country?"

"Just admiring the view, Marag; go on . . ."

We finally reach the top and kick the ravens off. They circle darkly, calling us all kinds of foul names before they sail off through the brightening morn toward the rich fields below. Damn! What a valley. What a river to carve it so! What a gift of a glorious world for sailing through!

"Come, friend . . ."

Marag beckons me to the pole in the center of the square of limestone blocks. "Marag show you little Pyramid trick."

He has me reach as high as I can up the pole with a chip of rock and scratch a mark. I notice a number of similar scratches at various heights. "Now have a seat and breathe awhile this air. It is magic, this air on top Pyramid. You will see."

I sit at the base of the pole, glad for a breather. "How does it affect you, this magic Pyramid air?"

"It affect you to shrink," he says, grinning down from his scant five feet. "Breathe deep. You'll see."

Now that he calls it to mind I remember noticing that most of the Pyramid scalers are indeed men of unusually slight stature. I breathe deep and steady watching the sun on the horizon trying to crowd up out of the clouds. After five minutes or so he tells me to take one further breath and stand with my stone and scratch again. It's hard to tell, with all the marks of previous experiments, but it looks to me like I'm scratching exactly next to my first mark. I'm about to tell him his Pyramid air is just another piece of bull when I find myself flashing.

It's an old trick. I use it myself sometimes as a way to get an audience off cheap and easy. I call it the Dong-Dong. I tell them to take 15 deep breaths, hold the last and stand, and *om* together as the flash comes on. Hyperventilation. Every junior high kid knows it. But the business with the mark on the pole and the magic air was so slick I didn't have the vaguest recognition, even when I felt the familiar faint coming on.

I grab the pole for support, impressed. But this is only the beginning, the necessary prep. Now he positions himself in front of me and stands hands on his hips, gazing upward. He's done all this before. He flaps a moment then, as the breeze stills, I look up and out of the hazy sky I see what he is waiting for. I see the thumb of God come down out of the hazy sky and settle on top of Marag's head, bowing him like a deck of cards until his face snaps down revealing another behind it and another and another, face after face snapping forward in an accelerating riffle—some familiar; from the village, the *aouda,* some famous (I remember distinctly two widely known musicians whom I will not name in case it might bring them hamper) but mostly faces I've never seen. Women and men, black, brown, red and whatever, most of them looking at least past the half-century mark in earthly years.

It's a large deck, numbering in the hundreds, and each face is alive, conscious, firmly aware of my onlooking and looking back at me to prove it. The faces are all individual and the expressions completely various—bemused; patient; mischievous; stern—but besides their age there is one quality uniting them all; each face is entirely, profoundly, unshakingly benevolent.

It is a very good trick.

At the last there are a number of blanks, silhouettes. These must be positions available for those willing and qualified. When the last blank is flipped down there is a hole left in the shape of Marag's slight body. I am looking through this hole over the southeast corner. There is the Sphinx, watching the first rays of the sun, and before him and in front of his paw (right paw) I see it clearly and simply. Within those lanes of huts housing these faithful sentries who have for thousands of years simultaneously manifested and guarded the complete records of all our climbs and all our falls, our catastrophes and our climaxes, await openings for every questioning eye, doorways for every archaeologist and technician and diplomat (they *did* lift the stones with lighter-than-aircraft, you slugabeds at NASA; with bags filled with gas got from a beam of sunlight focused through a gem into the water! You *can* take the bus on through, Henry; just have a little more patience with skills developed outside the scope of your expertise. It's gonna take more than diplomacy to convince the sons of Hagar that they are the same folk as the sons of Sarah; it's gonna take magic, Henry, and some magicians, like Joan Bäez and Rahsaan Roland Kirk). But these are not the halls where the true treasure is secured. It is hidden on the very surface, in the cramped comings and goings and sharing of goat's milk and in the hustle, the everlasting hustle by the grace of wheels this ancient society has managed to survive. For thousands of years this people has cared for this irreplaceable article of measurement, tended it and defended it with often no more defense than their bladders and bowels. As long as there's piss in the King's Coffin there isn't going to be a pair of McDonald's arches on the *aouda*; as long as every third stone step is mined with manure this sacred pile of rock is not going to become sublime Vatican for Pyramidiots.

There is a pride in this hustling heritage. Marag wasn't wanting to send his son away to the Land of Opportunity for good, I realize, having seen those blanks available in this arcanum of temple guards, only long enough to prepare the boy to be a Reliable Not-guide to a new kind of tourist that Marag sniffs coming on the winds of changing consciousness. All those scratches on the pole. He can't explain it better than that but he knows . . . there is a new breed of pilgrim coming, perhaps the first of the long-awaited last, and they will need a new kind of guide. And Marag, out of his humble hustler's love, makes ready to give his son into the service to help usher wearily on to the end of this nonsense even if it can't be explained.

"What you think, Mr. Kee-*zee*?" Marag flips back into the space before me. "Is a good trick?"

"Is a good trick, Marag. Is a great trick . . ."

M*alignant Giant*

HOWARD KOHN

KAREN SILKWOOD'S DEATH EXPOSED CORRUPTION IN THE NUCLEAR-POWER INDUSTRY. OUR REPORTER BROKE THE STORY, AND FOR SIX YEARS HE FOUGHT TO MAKE SURE SHE WASN'T FORGOTTEN.

What might Jann Wenner have done had he known all that lay ahead: all the patience required, all the legal fees to pay? Might he have shown me the door or hired me on the spot? Actually, he did hire me, but that is getting a little ahead of the story.

It was the autumn of 1974. Jann and I barely knew each other. He was the editor of a magazine fast becoming the voice of a generation, and I was a young freelancer just scraping by. This was my first assignment for ROLLING STONE. Apart from that, nothing about the assignment led me to foresee that it would change my life or anything else. It appeared to be nothing more than a whodunit. A woman, en route to a rendezvous to deliver secret documents, is killed when her car goes off the road and hits a culvert wall. The documents are surreptitiously removed from her wrecked car, and there is physical evidence indicating foul play. Her name

is Karen Silkwood. She has been employed as a lab technician at a plutonium factory.

This last part, seemingly so incidental, proved to be the heart of the
matter. I soon realized the story of Karen Silkwood was not as much a
question of vehicular homicide as a plunge into a dark side of atomic
fission.

We had known about such darkness since 1945, when Little Boy and
Fat Man were dropped on the Japanese, but beginning in the Fifties, the
U.S. government had been successfully selling Americans on an equally
amazing yet presumably far more civilized techno-miracle. The Plowshare
Program, among others, touted the possibilities of splitting atoms for
peaceful purposes. Nuclear power to produce electricity was yet another
example of the utopian thinking that dominated postwar America. Tech-
nology is certain and omnipotent, the thinking went. You could find this
thinking in everything from the Vietnam War to the Green Revolution
and Plowshare. Even after Vietnam, most of us were believers. I certainly
was, and up until the last few months of her life, so was Karen Silkwood.
In death, however, she was to become a rallying point for a movement of
doubting Thomases.

She had claimed her documents would reveal a dangerous fraud in the
manufacture of nuclear fuel rods at Kerr-McGee, a *Fortune* 500 company
headquartered in Oklahoma. Kerr-McGee was its own kind of god in
Oklahoma, and it did not suffer gladly reporters from outside the state,
let alone someone from ROLLING STONE. I got nowhere trying to talk to
company employees. They were under orders to keep mum, and Karen
Silkwood's funeral was a persuasive argument to follow orders.

I thought about heading home—I had cut short my honeymoon to go
on this assignment—but instead decided to take a chance on finding some
proof, pro or con, in the archives of the Atomic Energy Commission, in
Washington, D.C. I can't say that what I found during ten days of eye-
strain was proof of anything, but it was enough to make Kerr-McGee's
management nervous. When I told company officials I had seen the
archives, they told me libel lawyers would be perusing every word I
wrote.

I had no idea how serious a threat this might be or how intimidated
Jann might be. He listened and then said excitedly: "Start writing. Sounds
like you're onto a hell of a story. I love it!"

"Malignant Giant" was published in RS 183, and for a while things
proceeded extremely well. Jann said to me, "I'd like to see your name on
the masthead." We shook hands, and I got a staff writer's desk. The
article had struck a chord. Two National Organization for Women staffers
who happened to read it, Kitty Tucker and Sara Nelson, contacted Karen
Silkwood's parents, and between them, they made plans to file a lawsuit

against Kerr-McGee. They also lobbied U.S. senator Lee Metcalf and U.S. congressman John Dingell to undertake investigations. Jane Fonda phoned me to inquire about movie rights, and other readers wrote letters to the editor. No story before or for years afterward generated as much mail to the magazine. There might have been even more, but in Oklahoma it was next to impossible to find copies of RS 183 on the newsstands. Our distributors reported seeing a couple of well-dressed guys (representatives of Kerr-McGee, would you believe?) buying up bundles of them.

By the autumn of 1976, however, it seemed we had created a fuss for no good purpose. The lawsuit had not been filed. The congressional investigations had been abandoned. Jane Fonda had cooled on a movie. Every news organization in the country considered the case a dead issue. Off the record, a variety of people were accusing Karen Silkwood of having been a high-strung, vindictive kook, maybe worse, maybe a child-deserting lesbian, maybe a drug addict with suicidal tendencies. The official consensus in politics and journalism, and especially in popular culture, had turned her into an untouchable.

Except at ROLLING STONE. "Those bozos!" Jann said to me, speaking fast, his only speed. "What do they know?!"

A few days later I was off to Oklahoma, taking another crack at the case. I did not bring back any breakthroughs, just more circumstantial evidence in Karen Silkwood's favor. Jann was somewhat disappointed, yet nonetheless gave this second article as big a play as the first. Meanwhile, beating the statute of limitations by minutes, legal papers were at last filed in federal court against Kerr-McGee. "Too bad it's going to be an exercise in futility," I said to Jann. "Karen Silkwood's father doesn't have the money to finance a lawsuit." The next thing I knew, Jann had written a check for $10,000 in behalf of the lawsuit and offered to match dollar for dollar any contributions from ROLLING STONE readers. Not to let matters rest there, he ran solicitations in the magazine, offering reprints of my stories. The checks that came in from readers, most of them for $10 or $15, the largest for $150 (from Julie Christie, as I remember it), totaled out in five figures, and lo and behold, the lawsuit began to take shape.

You could argue we had crossed the line into advocacy. Perhaps we had. But you could argue as well that we were pursuing the highest goals of journalism. The reputation of a woman unable to defend herself was being impugned. Why? Had she been in fact a loathsome creature, or were the accusations against her an attempt to trick everyone away from an unwanted truth about something gone dreadfully wrong inside an industry subsidized and promoted to the hilt by our government?

As it turned out, the case would go on for another ten years, and a great deal of information would appear first on these pages. I would return again and again to Oklahoma and finally find breakthroughs. I would write altogether a dozen articles about falsified record keeping and missing plutonium and industry-wide safety hazards, about an FBI agent provocateur and CIA intrigue and Israel's obtaining the bomb. There would be fundraising concerts organized out of the magazine offices that would culminate with five nights of Bonnie Raitt, Jackson Browne, Bruce Springsteen, Carly Simon and a host of friends at Madison Square Garden.

There would be eleven weeks of sworn testimony in a federal courtroom, the longest trial in Oklahoma history and a jury verdict that found Kerr-McGee responsible for the contamination in Silkwood's apartment, awarding $10.5 million to her family. A drawn-out appeal to the U.S. Supreme Court would end up in a landmark decision supporting the legal underpinnings of that verdict. There would be *The China Syndrome*, with Jane Fonda, and the movie *Silkwood*, with Meryl Streep. I would write a book. There would be a friendship with Jann and an association with the magazine that has reached to the present and looks like it will last a lifetime. There would be an international antinuclear movement whose members, when arrested for civil disobedience, would take to giving the police a single name, Karen Silkwood. Though it was never determined whether Karen Silkwood's death was the result of foul play, the public's confidence in nuclear power would be so undermined that the industry ultimately would become a shadow of its former self.

But now I am really ahead of the story.

RS 183

MARCH 27TH, 1975

She was 28, a slight woman, dark hair pushing past slender shoulders, haunting beauty nurtured in a small-child look. She was alone that chilly autumn night, driving her tiny three-door Honda through long stretches of prairie. The Oklahoma fields lay flattened under the crude brushmarks of the wind, the grass unable to snap back to attention. Every few miles a big-boned rabbit, mangled and broken, littered the roadside. A couple years back she had fired off a round of angry letters when sheep ranchers staged rabbit roundups, clubbing to death the furry army that had sprung up on the prairie. She was like that, poking her opinions where they weren't welcome.

In the early evening darkness of Wednesday, November 13th, 1974, Karen Silkwood was on an environmental mission of another sort. On the seat beside her lay a manila folder with apparent proof that records were being falsified at the plutonium plant where she worked. Waiting at a Holiday Inn 30 miles away were a union official and a *New York Times* reporter who had just flown from Washington D.C. to Oklahoma City to meet with her.

They waited nearly an hour. Then they picked up the phone.

Karen Silkwood's body had already been found in a small rivulet along Highway 74 where rabbits often came to drink. Her car had swerved left across the highway, skittered about 270 feet along an embankment, smashed head-on into a culvert wingwall, lurched through the air and caromed off another culvert wall, coming to rest in the muddy stream.

Her death was ruled an accident; the police decided she was asleep at the wheel. But the union official was not satisfied. The manila folder was missing. And a private investigator discovered two fresh dents in the rear of her car: telltale marks of a hit-and-run.

In downtown Oklahoma City, where Kerr-McGee's square-block headquarters towers 30 stories above the modest skyline, the Kerr-McGee name is as imposing as its building. The late Robert Kerr, the company's cofounder, claimed to have been born in a log cabin and to have worked his way through college selling magazines. As company president he prided himself on staying at cheap motels and eating baked beans in self-service cafeterias—while fighting to keep unions at bay and workers at minimum wage. As Oklahoma governor in the Forties he ran the state with the same frugality and didn't relax his tight fist until moving to the U.S. Senate in 1948. There Kerr became the most powerful man in the Senate, next to Lyndon Johnson; with Kerr's unflagging zeal, the energy industry won millions of dollars in tax subsidies. And nuclear research profited from fat bags of public dollars, to the exclusion of solar and geothermal research, in which Kerr-McGee had no interest.

Dean McGee, Kerr's successor as company board chairman, holds office and influence in such diverse interests as banks, power companies and the National Cowboy Hall of Fame. McGee has yet to run for public office, but few doubt he could fit comfortably in the governor's chair. "People in Oklahoma look at Dean McGee the same way people in New York look at Nelson Rockefeller—they look up," one local politician has observed. When Richard Nixon came to Oklahoma State University last spring in one of his final public appearances, he had to share the podium with McGee, who received an honorary doctorate.

Recently McGee was named to a federal commission studying America's long-range energy needs, and he presumably will push for nuclear power. But McGee is already looking ahead to the day when nuclear reactors will no longer use uranium. Future reactors will feed on a far more potent fuel: plutonium.

Uranium, like fossil fuels, is limited in supply; in 40 or 50 years we are liable to run out. But plutonium is the love child of an ultimate alchemy: It can reproduce itself. An industry brochure puts it like this: "Question—How many pounds of plutonium will you have left after you use three pounds in a nuclear reactor? Answer—Four pounds!"

Plutonium barely exists in nature; our present supply is entirely man-made. It was first discovered in the Forties among the waste products of fissioned uranium. Plutonium can take several forms—but it is usually a gray, soft metal, a slushy liquid nitrate or a fluffy yellow-green oxide powder fine enough to be inhaled. In any form it is "fiendishly toxic," according to one of its discoverers, Dr. Glenn Seaborg.

Plutonium is much more dangerous than uranium. It is incredibly combustible, readily convertible into nuclear weapons and, once let loose in the atmosphere, it stays deadly for a quarter-million years; it cannot be recaptured or destroyed. Swallowing it in a quantity that can be seen would sear the digestive tract, killing quickly and painfully. Plutonium is also a carcinogenic killer but, because only a few hundred people have ever handled it, scientists disagree as to what amount can cause cancer. As little as a millionth of a gram has induced cancer in lab animals and some experts say that a softball-sized bag of plutonium, if properly dispersed, could visit cancer on every home on earth.

For years plutonium was used exclusively for bombs. The nonmilitary inventory wasn't enough to fill a pair of size ten shoes. But at the Atomic Energy Commission (AEC) in Washington D.C., visionaries saw an incipient bonanza. So the AEC, encouraged by money and kind words from Capitol Hill, set out to make plutonium practical and profitable. A special nuclear reactor to breed plutonium, nicknamed the "fast-breeder," was built in Michigan. It proved a $135-million flop. In 1972, after dozens of false starts, it was abandoned, a vast leprous hulk on the outskirts of Detroit. (Early last year the Soviet Union's only fast-breeder closed down after a serious explosion.)

The AEC was undeterred. It decided more tests were needed. Near Richland, Washington, construction was begun on a facility to test "fuel rods," the plutonium-filled tubes used in a fast-breeder. The Richland facility won't be ready for tests until 1978 and a new fast-breeder, scheduled for Tennessee, won't be finished until the Eighties. But for the past four years fuel rods have been trucked into Richland to await the tests.

Most of the fuel rods come from Kerr-McGee's prized plutonium plant 20 miles outside Oklahoma City. It was Kerr-McGee, on good terms with the AEC since Robert Kerr's congressional days, which was awarded a $1.4-million AEC contract to process the plutonium into pellets and pour them into the fuel rods.

Kerr-McGee's plutonium plant, built next to one of its uranium plants (and within five miles of 92 gas and oil wells, two popular resort lakes and the churning Cimarron River), opened in 1970 shortly before 8583 fish turned belly-up in the river following a big ammonia spill at the facility. Raised against the flat harshness of rural Oklahoma, the barnlike plant is unimposing; only a chain-link fence and armed guards hint at the devil's brew within.

Kerr-McGee had assured the AEC it could deal safely and circum-spectly with the plutonium. But the AEC, a government agency in the curious role of both promoting and policing the nuclear industry, soon received numerous reports of irregularities and accidents at the Kerr-McGee plant. In a situation that left no margin for error, things kept getting bungled.

In October 1970, soon after the plant opened, two workers were contaminated when a radioactive storage container was left in the open for three days. Twenty-two more workers were exposed to plutonium in January 1971 when defective equipment allowed plutonium oxide to escape into the air. Less serious incidents were common. The protective "glove boxes" the workers used often had holes. Sometimes the "Super Tiger" and "Poly Panther" drums, specially designed to store the volatile liquid, unaccountably leaked. Improperly designed pipes once sent plutonium sloshing to wrong parts of the plant.

One day a worker bent to adjust a compressor unit; it exploded, ripping through his hand and tearing off the top of his face, spitting tissue over the ceiling. He died instantly. "When I got there," remembers a former lab technician, "they were washing the goo down the drain." Kerr-McGee, he feels, "didn't give a damn about the people who worked there—it didn't care whether its safety program was effective or not."

In April 1972 two maintenance men repairing a pump at the plant were splashed with a rain of plutonium particles, which settled on their hands, faces, hair and clothes. At noon they left the plant for lunch in a nearby town, not discovering their contamination until they returned. They were scrubbed clean, along with their car. But Kerr-McGee neglected to check out the restaurant where the men had eaten.

Nor did Kerr-McGee inform the AEC of the incident, a clear violation of the federal nuclear code. The AEC was finally alerted to the affair a month later, tipped off by an environmentalist who had learned of it from a plant worker. By then there was nothing to be done for the restaurant patrons, short of an all-out search for any who might have gulped down plutonium with their egg salad.

Beyond adding another bulge to the file of violations already logged against Kerr-McGee, the matter was forgotten.

When Karen Silkwood arrived at the Kerr-McGee plant in late summer

1972, she was just divorced and eager to begin a career as a nuclear laboratory technician. But after only three months testing the plutonium fuel rods, Silkwood was outside the chain-link fence, marching with an on-strike placard.

The Oil, Chemical and Atomic Workers International Union (OCAW), representing the plutonium workers, was at loggerheads with Kerr-McGee. The company, a veteran of the wildcat oil rig, had managed to keep the unions out until 1966, three years after Senator Kerr's death. Now the OCAW was demanding a new contract with higher wages, safer conditions and better training. Kerr-McGee had replied with an offer worse than the old contract. Then, as soon as workers went on strike, the company rushed scabs onto the job, barely missing a beat in fuel-rod production.

Even Kerr-McGee officials later conceded, in a letter to the Sierra Club, that thrusting untrained strikebreakers into the plant led to more plutonium spills and leaks. ("Some scabs got only four hours of training when they should have gotten five days," fumed one striker.) Among the inexperienced substitutes hired during the strike was the plant's safety officer.

On the picket lines, meanwhile, 26-year-old Karen Silkwood was spending a lot of time with 22-year-old Drew Stephens, a short-haired, brainy lab analyst with an easy smile. When he first came to work three years before, Stephens had expected to earn his 40-year gold watch from Kerr-McGee. But he had grown disenchanted after the rash of accidents and now lived for weekends when he turned sports-car racer, a hotdog kid on the local auto-cross circuit.

The strike lasted ten weeks. Those picketers whose jobs had not been lost to scabs returned to work in January 1973, reluctantly signing a new contract that stripped away many of their previous rights, including certain protections against arbitrary firings and reassignments. A few weeks later a plant employee was emptying a bag of plutonium wastes when a fire spontaneously erupted, shooting radioactive dust into the air. Seven workers sucked in the junk. But Kerr-McGee supervisors waited a day before calling in a physician. Four days later the seven workers still had not been tested for contamination in their lungs.

Silkwood and Stephens shared in the outrage building in the plant. But they were now deeply in love, Stephens divorcing his wife of four years to live with Silkwood. They were enjoying the good times, tooling around in Stephen's tomato red Austin-Healy Sprite, country-rock blaring on the radio.

Then, in July 1974, Karen Silkwood became contaminated with pluto-nium.

*   *   *

Oklahoma City still listens to Rosemary Clooney, votes Republican and plays host to all the cowboy conventions it can corral. Adolescents favor mail-order miniskirts and the Burt Reynolds look. A popular radio station provides "full-time Christian broadcasting." Okie country is not the kind of place that fathers worry their daughters will run off to.

But for Karen Silkwood, Oklahoma City was full of bright lights and good-time chances to catch up on what she missed as a teenager. She hung out at bars and rock concerts and learned how to get gently stoned. She was happy. Coming home one night she told Stephens: "I feel like I'm in love with the whole world."

But after several months she moved out, jealous for her freedom, unwilling to risk another marriage. She wanted her own place and, after a money-poor marriage, indulged in a color TV, a $600 stereo, a Suzuki cycle and a Honda Civic Hatchback. Silkwood and Stephens remained friends and part-time lovers, but her career was her first love. She retreated from the night scene to work overtime. And she got involved in the union, OCAW Local 5-283.

Silkwood looked to the union as the only outlet for her growing frustration with management. When suddenly exposed to a swirl of airborne plutonium in July 1974, she was not wearing a respirator. For over a year she had been bugging the company to buy a special respirator to fit over her tiny, narrow face; it hadn't arrived.

When union elections came up the next month, Silkwood ran and won one of the three seats on the Local 5-283 steering committee. Fellow workers knew her as the spunky chick who talked back to her bosses. "Goddamnit, I am right and you are wrong," she once raged at a supervisor. "If you want to tell me what to do, you oughta learn how to do the job right."

Despite growing anticompany jabber at the plant, most workers did not want a fight. Many simply quit; the annual turnover rate among the 115 hourly workers, according to the union, hovered around 60%. Some complained of being harassed out of their jobs; three workers who griped to AEC officials about safety conditions early in 1974 were reportedly tracked down and transferred to "shit details" in the chilly warehouse.

Other plutonium workers took their feelings outside the plant, anonymously phoning tips to environmental groups like the Sierra Club and Friends of the Earth. Several calls also went to Ilene Younghein, an Oklahoma City housewife, mother of two grown kids, a hefty woman with a wonderful rococo laugh who had read about the dangers of plutonium in *Intellectual Digest* and had written to a local newspaper about it.

In the fall of 1973 Younghein had begun a one-woman campaign to shut the plant down. Angry workers simply wanted the company to improve training procedures and apply safety precautions rather than lock its doors. But they supplied inside scuttlebutt to Younghein and other environmentalists, hoping the outside pressure would prod Kerr-McGee to clean up its act. Younghein did her best, collecting 500 signatures on a petition for stricter federal controls and penciling two lengthy doomsday articles for the Oklahoma *Observer*, a maverick semiweekly unintimidated by Kerr-McGee.

Karen Silkwood and the other two Local 5-283 steering committee members were preparing a declaration of war against the company. New contract negotiations were due in a few months, and for the first time Local 5-283 was going to confront Kerr-McGee squarely on the issue of safety. The chronicle of accidents, safety abuses and other allegations was to be compiled into a formal list of grievances.

Silkwood helped interview workers in the dangerous production areas of the plant. Most were young, average age about 25, coming from nearby farms and small towns and, Silkwood learned, several had no idea plutonium could cause cancer.

They spun out a grim tale of corporate callousness: New employees often were sent directly into production without safety training (one such worker had been badly contaminated and had quit the next day before receiving medical attention); production schedules sometimes forced workers to stay on the job even when the air wasn't safe to breathe — supervisors ordering them to wear respirators rather than hunting the source of contamination; and plutonium was sometimes stored in such casual containers as desk drawers.

With their grievances in hand, and with the quickening hopes of the union membership, Silkwood and her fellow committee members, Gerald Brewer and Jack Tice, flew to Washington D.C. for a meeting with the OCAW International. They arrived on September 26th and met Steve Wodka, an OCAW legislative assistant, a hard-nosed, stiff-talking man given to curt skepticism and impatient waves of the hand. Though only 25, he is among the OCAW's best troubleshooters. Wodka and his boss, Tony Mazzocchi, had devoted much of the previous year to hassling do-nothing regulatory agencies and exposing health hazards in the asbestos industry, a crusade that had won them praise from Senator Walter Mondale on the floor of Congress.

Wodka and Mazzocchi pumped Silkwood and the others for details, then the next day marched them over to the only place in town that could put the clamps on Kerr-McGee — the AEC. The AEC copied it all down and promised an investigation.

But Wodka was already considering another investigation. Silkwood had confided to him that for months she had suspected that tests on the plutonium fuel rods destined for Richland, Washington, were being fudged. And, she said, she had recently heard about records being doctored, X-ray photos being black-penciled and other tests being manipulated. Kerr-McGee's plutonium plant might be defrauding the AEC, she had concluded, shipping inadequate or unsafe fuel rods to Richland.

"Both Tony Mazzocchi and I felt this was a very serious situation," Wodka says. "But we felt it was premature to bring it to the attention of the AEC. We had to have proof before we could make any accusations. So we asked Karen to go back to the plant, to find out who was falsifying the records, who was ordering it and to document everything in specific detail."

Silkwood agreed to go undercover.

Back in Oklahoma she revealed her new role to Stephens. She stood in his living room, crouching over the radiator vent to shake off the autumn chill, and jabbed a delicate brown finger into the air: "We're really gonna get those motherfuckers this time."

On October 10th, two of the nation's leading plutonium experts arrived in Oklahoma City from the University of Minnesota, summoned by the OCAW International to conduct crash courses for Kerr-McGee's plutonium workers. Their credentials were impressive: Dr. Donald Geesaman, a top AEC scientist for 13 years, had crusaded for stiffer plutonium standards until he was fired; Dr. Dean Abrahamson was both a physicist and a physician.

The two professors were told that 73 workers had been internally contaminated by plutonium during the previous four years. (Dozens more workers had accidentally brushed plutonium or been sprinkled with it, but had washed it off their skin.) The 73 had been exposed to airborne plutonium; any inhaled into their lungs could not be washed out. The probability of cancer in such cases, Dr. Abrahamson warned, "is disturbingly high." Because it takes 10 or 15 years after exposure to detect cancer, no cases have yet been reported at Kerr-McGee. But those workers with internal contamination must live with the threat of cancer for years to come.

Karen Silkwood was one of those 73, and she was shocked by Abrahamson's news. She had assumed she would stay clear of cancer if she did not breathe in more plutonium than allowed under AEC guidelines. But Abrahamson was saying, "If you can measure plutonium in the air at all, it's too high." The AEC guidelines, he said, were meaningless.

Silkwood grew moody and restless, working nights and unable to sleep during the days. She got a prescription for some sleeping pills. And she began to hunt for another job.

But first, she vowed to Stephens, she was going to get proof that Kerr-McGee was sustaining its plutonium plant through false and perjurious records. She had already collected some evidence, she said, and was certain she could get more.

At one point Silkwood reported to Wodka that she had obtained photographs proving the welding on some fuel rods was too weak. "They [company supervisors] are still passing bad welds no matter what the pictures look like," she said in a telephone conversation that Wodka taped. "I have a weld I would love for you to see, just how far they ground it down to relax the weld trying to get rid of the voids, the occlusions and the cracks." (Unsafe fuel rods, according to MIT physicist Dr. Henry Kendall, could lead to "an accident that would result in the release of huge amounts of radioactivity.")

Silkwood spent the weeks of October staying after hours, poring over files, recording every questionable procedure, building a dossier in a dogeared manila folder. She did not know then that other employes had noticed her spying, and that the plant rumormill was abuzz with suspicions about what she was up to.

"I have guilt feelings about those weeks," Stephens says. "I should have talked to her more, been with her more, helped her out. . . . But I just wanted to forget about the place."

On Tuesday, November 5th, 1974, Silkwood discovered she had been contaminated with plutonium again.

Rapidly, as if no time were left on the clock, Silkwood jammed the dime in its slot and dialed long distance. Washington. Steve Wodka. "Hello." An uncertain trickle started down her face. Her voice tottered. "Please come to Oklahoma," she said. "Something very weird is happening here."

Three times in the past three days Karen Silkwood had been contaminated with plutonium, and no one knew where it was coming from. A monitoring device had first discovered flecks of plutonium on her skin and clothing shortly after she reported for work November 5th. She had quickly stepped under a brisk shower. But the next day the monitor flashed on again. More plutonium on her skin. Another shower. On the third day the mystery repeated itself—and a nasal smear indicated she also was contaminated internally.

How much plutonium, she wanted to know, could a person ingest before it burned out her insides?

Wodka tried to reassure her and promised to fly in. Silkwood hung up and sought out her old lover. "She was damn near incoherent," says Stephens. "She was crying and shaking like a leaf; she kept saying she was going to die."

A team of Kerr-McGee inspectors, armed with alpha counters, fullface respirators, special galoshes, taped up gloves and white coveralls, were meanwhile hunting the source of the plutonium. There had been no recent accident at the plant to account for her contamination. So, at Silk-

wood's request, they had trekked to her apartment. There the alpha counters commenced eerie gibberings. Plutonium, in small quantities, was
everywhere. Outside on the lawn the inspectors filled a 55-gallon drum
with alarm clocks, cosmetics, record albums, drapes, pots and pans, shampoo, bedsheets. Alongside they stacked chairs, bed, stove, refrigerator,
television, items to be trucked to the Kerr-McGee plant for later burial in
an AEC-approved site.

The plutonium trail turned hottest in the kitchen, inside the refrigerator. A package of bologna and a package of cheese were the two most
contaminated items in the apartment. Apparently, the plutonium had been
tracked around the apartment from the refrigerator. But no one could
explain how two sandwich foods had become the source of contamination.

The apartment was sealed off and the AEC called in.

Silkwood, however, was more worried about the plutonium inside her
than on the cheese and bologna. She kept popping the Quaaludes that had
been prescribed a few weeks before. "The Quaaludes were just supposed
to be taken for sleeping at nights," Stephens says. "But she was using
them during the day, just to calm down. I'd never seen her so scared."

Wodka had jetted in from Washington and, after talking to Kerr-
McGee and AEC officials, had helped arrange for Silkwood to fly to an
AEC laboratory in New Mexico to be checked out for poisoning. On
Sunday November 10th, five days after her first contamination, she
boarded a Braniff airliner.

That same morning a front-page New York Times story reported that,
according to the AEC's own internal documents, the AEC had "repeatedly
sought to suppress studies by its own scientists that found nuclear reactors
were more dangerous than officially acknowledged or that raised questions
about reactor safety devices." One AEC study, kept confidential for seven
years, predicted that a major nuclear accident could kill up to 45,000
persons and pollute an area the size of Pennsylvania. Times reporter David
Burnham, who in 1970 interviewed Frank Serpico and broke open the
New York police corruption scandal, had sifted through hundreds of
memos and letters and learned the AEC had a ten-year record of blue-
penciling alarming data, soft-soaping test failures and glad-handing an
industry that increasingly appeared not to know what it was doing.

The report gave scant comfort to Silkwood as she flew to Los Alamos,
New Mexico, site of the world's first plutonium explosion during the
A-bomb tests of World War II. With her were Stephens and Sherri
"Dusty" Ellis, her roommate of the past few months, a blonde, rawboned,
21-year-old rodeo champ. Ellis also worked at the plant but had refused
to get involved in Silkwood's efforts to unmask the company.

Now the three shared the same fears; all had been contaminated in the
apartment.

For two days they underwent a "whole body count," a meticulous prob-
ing of skin, orifices, intestines and lungs, urinating at intervals into plastic
bottles and defecating into Freezette box containers.

After the first day, the three had cause for relief. Dr. George Voelz, the
health division leader, assured them they had suffered no immediate damage. Even Silkwood, by far the most infected, was told she was in no
danger of dying from plutonium poisoning.

On Tuesday November 12th, Silkwood called her mother to announce
the good news about the tests, but added, "I'm still a little scared. I still
don't know how I got contaminated. I feel like someone's using me for a
guinea pig."

"I told her to come home," her mother recalled. "And she said she
would. She said she was ready for a vacation . . . she just had to do a
couple things first."

After more body-prying tests at Los Alamos, the three travelers flew
back to Oklahoma City, landing about 10:30 Tuesday night. Because the
women's apartment had been gutted of furniture, they checked in at Stephens's bungalow, now a bachelor's pad papered with four-color profiles
of racing cars clipped from hotrod magazines. Silkwood wandered over to
her favorite radiator vent, squatting and rubbing to warm up, then went
to bed early. She had a busy day ahead. She had told Wodka she would
give him the evidence she was collecting as soon as she returned from Los
Alamos, and Wodka had set up a meeting with her and David Burnham,
the *Times* reporter, who was winging in from the East Coast. The meeting
was scheduled for Wednesday night at the Holiday Inn Northwest in
Oklahoma City.

Wednesday morning Silkwood drove to work. Contract negotiations between Local 5-283 and Kerr-McGee had begun the week before and, as a
committeewoman, she was supposed to take part in the bargaining. She
spent the morning in negotiations, arguing the union demands for better
safety training and higher injury benefits. In the afternoon she met for
several hours with AEC inspectors, who were trying to unravel the mystery
of her contamination.

At 5:15 p.m. she drove to Crescent, about five miles from the plant,
and stopped at the Hub Cafe for a supper meeting, sans supper, to discuss
negotiations strategy with Local 5-283. Jack Tice, who headed the negotiating team, told the assembled union members that, as expected, Kerr-
McGee was not budging off its hard line.

Silkwood excused herself about 6 p.m. to telephone Stephens, reminding him to pick up Wodka and Burnham at the airport and to expect her
at the motor hotel about 8 p.m. She sounded normal, Stephens remembers, perhaps a bit excited about having an audience with the *New York*

Times. At 7:15 p.m. Silkwood left the Hub Cafe and headed for Highway 74 and the Holiday Inn Northwest. A fellow union member would later swear in an affidavit that Silkwood, minutes before she left the restaurant, was carrying a manila folder an inch thick with papers. The folder, Silkwood told the union member, contained proof that quality-control records were being falsified.

Thirty miles away, Wodka, Burnham and Stephens waited for that proof until 8:45. Then they picked up the phone; but for some reason the Holiday Inn lines were out of order, and another hour passed before the three could get through.

Meanwhile, at 8:05 p.m., a truckdriver, sitting high up in his cab and rolling along the two-lane highway, spotted the white Honda, almost hidden in the muddy culvert. Silkwood had traveled about seven miles from the Hub Cafe, a ten-minute drive.

By the time Stephens, Wodka and Burnham learned the news from a local union member, the 1638-pound Civic Hatchback already had been towed to Ted Sebring's garage in Crescent. And Silkwood had been pronounced dead on arrival at the Guthrie Hospital, the victim of multiple and compound fractures.

The three men raced to the culvert, only a mile from the plutonium plant, and prowled about, stepping gingerly through the mud, which in Oklahoma is the color of dry blood. All they could find were shards of aluminum trim, the orange roadside reflectors that had been trampled by the bouncing car and Silkwood's uncashed paycheck.

Later they found the wreck locked up in Sebring's garage and peered at it through the window. They stopped at the home of union committeeman Jack Tice, one of the last to see Silkwood alive; Stephens called Silkwood's parents. Then they returned to the culvert, searching for an explanation in the tire tracks and the scraps of metal.

The explanation the State Highway Patrol offered was that Karen Silkwood, exhausted after driving 600 miles from Los Alamos to Oklahoma City, had fallen asleep and drifted off the road to an accidental death. Almost immediately the police had to alter their official version when they were told Silkwood had flown from Los Alamos and had gotten a full night's sleep only 12 hours before the crash.

The second official version was somewhat more convincing. Sometime during the afternoon of November 13th Silkwood had gulped down at least one of the pasty white Quaaludes from the vial in her coat pocket. Oklahoma City's chief forensic toxicologist, Richard W. Prouty, discovered .35 milligrams of methaqualone in her bloodstream, conceivably enough to lull her to sleep on the highway.

But that was not sufficient for Steve Wodka.

Silkwood had swallowed several Quaaludes in the past week without nodding out. Why would she fall into a trance on her way to an extremely crucial meeting? And the proof of fraud she was supposedly carrying had disappeared. Her personal effects, listed by the medical examiner, included an ID badge, an electronic security key (for the plant), two marijuana cigarettes, a Kotex pad, two used Kleenexes, a Bradley Mickey Mouse pocket watch, a small notebook, her clothes, $7 in bills and $1.69 in change. But there was no manila folder heavy with Kerr-McGee documents.

Trooper Rick Fagan, however, had mentioned finding dozens of loose papers blowing about the accident scene when he first arrived. Fagan had plucked up the papers, he told his superiors, and shoved them into the Honda. According to the highway patrol's information officer, Lieutenant Kenneth Vanhoy, the papers were in the Honda when Ted Sebring hauled the car away.

Presumably they were still there at 12:30 a.m.—five hours after the accident—when Sebring unlocked his garage for a group of Kerr-McGee and AEC representatives who said they wanted to check out Silkwood's car for plutonium contamination.

But by the next afternoon when Stephens, Wodka and Burnham claimed Silkwood's car from Sebring, no papers were inside.

Wodka called Tony Mazzocchi at OCAW International. Mazzocchi agreed: An outside expert was needed to investigate the crash.

Three days after Silkwood's death an auto-crash expert arrived in Oklahoma City from the Accident Reconstruction Lab of Dallas. A.O. Pipkin, an ex-cop, is a veteran of 2000 accidents and 300 court trials, a no-nonsense pro considered the best man around for piecing together an accident scenario.

Dressed in a Day-Glo orange jumpsuit, Pipkin examined the Honda and found two curious dents, one in the rear bumper, another in the rear fender. They were fresh; there was no road dirt in them. And they appeared to have been made by a car bumper.

At the scene Pipkin noted that the Honda had crossed over the yellow lines and hit the culvert on the left side of the highway. If Silkwood had nodded into a stupor, he reasoned, she would have drifted to the right. In the red clay, Pipkin found something else the police apparently disregarded: tire tracks indicating the car had been out of control before it left the highway.

Pipkin's disconcerting conclusion: Karen Silkwood's Honda had been hit from the rear by another vehicle.

On December 20th, five weeks after Karen Silkwood's death, Kerr-McGee temporarily closed its plutonium plant. These were trying days for the company. Supporters of Kerr-McGee found it necessary to print ads reminding Oklahomans that Dun & Bradstreet had recently named it among the five best-managed corporations in the country. But headlines kept popping up all over, thanks to the *New York Times* wire service, telling of a mysterious death, falsified records and ill-trained workers sent in to handle one of the world's most dangerous poisons.

Nuclear proponents were worried, especially those of the nuclear elite like Dean McGee, who had been helping babysit plans for a multibillion-dollar "nuclear park" near flag-waving Muskogee in northeastern Oklahoma—it would be a carnie midway of over 20 facilities, the boldest assortment of nuclear props ever assembled. Even Muskogee's proud-to-be-Okies were beginning to flinch. "The bad publicity," complained Senator Henry Bellmon, a big McGee booster, "is making it more difficult to get what we want in the Muskogee area."

But the controversy around Kerr-McGee would not quit. Hints of strange goings-on salted the news. Robert G. Bathe, a plutonium worker, reported to police that a motorist had "harassed" him as he drove home from the plant a few nights after Silkwood's death; when Bathe's statement leaked to the press, he and the police suddenly refused to discuss the incident. Shortly afterwards, however, *Times*man David Burnham reported that security at the plant was so atrophied that 60 pounds of plutonium—enough for five Nagasaki bombs—were unaccounted for and possibly missing, an allegation Kerr-McGee heatedly denied.

The most prickly burr in the wind, though, was the AEC investigation, which promised a full report on Kerr-McGee.

On December 17th, at the height of the AEC investigation, Kerr-McGee was forced to announce that five more employees had been contaminated at its plutonium plant. The company claimed it had evidence the accidents were contrived, a modest slander suggesting that workers sniffed poison to embarrass their bosses. Though Kerr-McGee said it had given its evidence to the FBI, the FBI denied receiving it. Nonetheless, three days later, Kerr-McGee handed out lay-off slips, announcing the plant would not reopen until the payroll was checked for security.

Predictably, the plant shutdown ruptured the tentative alliance between the plutonium workers and local environmentalists. To Ilene Younghein, the shutdown was a first step to victory; to Frank Murch, a middle-aged man with seven years invested in Kerr-McGee, it was a slap in the pocketbook: "You're damn right I'm bitter about this. I'm bitter at the environmentalists. It's a hell of a thing, putting this many people out of work." Some took to blaming the dead—one worker who earlier had talked about honoring Karen Silkwood with a special grave marker now spat at the mention of her name.

"Attitudes changed," says Gerald Brewer. "People started to blame Karen for getting thrown out of work right before the holidays." Brewer was one of the two union committee members who accompanied Silkwood to Washington in September. He had worked at the plant three years.

In early January, after plutonium production resumed, Brewer was demoted from his job and transferred to an isolated warehouse. Two weeks later he was fired. There was no official explanation; a company spokesman was still denying the firing five days later.

Brewer's apparent sin, besides his role in compiling the grievances, was his refusal to submit to a polygraph test that asked questions like: "Have you ever talked to the media?" Although of questionable legality, the polygraphs were required of most plutonium workers as a "security precaution" before they could return to their jobs. A Kerr-McGee official described company strategy in a conversation with Jack Taylor, ace reporter for the *Daily Oklahoman:* "We're going to tool back up slowly and hire people who are trustworthy and are not involved [in the union]." As for undesirables—"You don't have to tell them [anything]. You can just say, 'You didn't clear security.'"

Along with Brewer, five other workers who snubbed or failed the polygraphs were handed pink slips. Jack Tice, the third union committeeman to make the trip to Washington, has been transferred to the most isolated part of the plant. "This action was taken in retaliation for union activities," the OCAW International has charged in a formal complaint to the National Labor Relations Board, "and to prevent [Tice] from discussing grievances or other union business with other employes." The OCAW also is challenging the six firings.

Among the six was Dusty Ellis, the cowgirl who shared the contaminated apartment with Silkwood. After her roommate's death Ellis initially cooperated with Kerr-McGee, refusing to talk to either the OCAW or the media. At one point she was seen, red-eyed and distraught, being escorted by two company detectives away from the Edmond Broadway Motor Inn where she had been staying, compliments of Kerr-McGee. Then Ellis— without explanation—aired a suggestion that Silkwood may have been pilfering plutonium from the plant. Shortly thereafter Kerr-McGee reportedly offered Ellis $1000 as payment for any claims she might have against the company.

But Ellis turned down the offer. She began worrying that she had been more seriously contaminated than she had been told; her gums bothered her and she had trouble sleeping. In late December she hired a lawyer and threatened to sue the company for copies of all her health records. Three weeks later she was fired. (Two weeks after that, in early February, Ellis told friends that twice someone had tried, and failed, to break into her new apartment.)

During the month between the plant shutdown and the firings, the AEC had published the results of its investigation. (According to a *Daily Okla-*

homan story, Kerr-McGee officials received a copy of the report well ahead of its official release, apparently in violation of AEC rules.) Company officials, who had been refusing comment since Karen Silkwood's death except to say, "We will let the AEC speak for us," pronounced themselves pleased with the findings.

On the question of falsified records the AEC did locate one former worker who admitted using a felt-tip pen to touch up photo negatives that measured the welding on plutonium fuel rods. The worker, however, said he acted only to make his job easier and not under orders from Kerr-McGee. Without Silkwood's documents, the AEC reported, it could find no other hard proof. But the OCAW questioned whether the AEC was really looking. According to the OCAW, the AEC lied when it claimed to have interviewed a worker who disputed Silkwood's allegations of fraud. This worker, the OCAW says, has given the union a sworn affidavit that the AEC never interviewed him — and that he believes quality controls are not adequate.

Whether Kerr-McGee's plutonium fuel rods are safe and adequate for use is still unknown; they have yet to be tested at the AEC facility in Richland.

On the question of plant safety, the AEC reported that 20 of the 39 grievances it examined were true or partially true: Plutonium had been stored in a desk drawer instead of a prescribed vault; in various incidents, employees had been forced to work in areas not tested for contamination or where leaks remained; in another, the company failed to report a serious leak that had forced it to close the plant in May 1974; generally, respirators had not been checked regularly for deficiencies; few workers had been properly trained.

Such disregard for safety, the AEC decided, merited no censure beyond adding these new citations to the trove already in the Kerr-McGee files. Kerr-McGee was free to resume its role in the AEC's fast-breeder program, a program that might have been seriously compromised had Kerr-McGee been forced to close up shop permanently.

All her old clothes were under quarantine, suspected of plutonium contamination, so Karen Silkwood was buried in a new dress. No Kerr-McGee officials made the journey to Texas for the funeral, nor any AEC officials.

Afterwards Karen's parents returned to the green frame house where she grew up. An old high-school friend of Karen's came over to comfort the Silkwoods and spent the evening weeping in anger. Karen's youngest sister, a high-school junior, said that what happened to Karen had inspired her to become a career woman who would call her own shots.

At OCAW headquarters Steve Wodka has found it difficult to return to other chores. The Silkwood case keeps nagging him. There are too many unanswered questions. For instance, how did Silkwood become contaminated a week before her death? For weeks afterwards Wodka kept the results of her Los Alamos tests scribbled on an OCAW blackboard, trying to puzzle out the mystery. The most logical explanation, he decided, was that Silkwood had been contaminated at the plant and unknowingly carried the plutonium home with her. But then the AEC reported that this would have been virtually impossible, given her duties at the plant during the time immediately preceding her contamination.

So now Wodka has come reluctantly to believe she was poisoned. "Someone must have entered her apartment and placed the plutonium in her refrigerator. That's the only way it could have gotten on the cheese and bologna. We've heard from several sources, including the AEC, that Karen had been seen going through the files, looking for records. Someone apparently figured out what she was up to. One sure way of preventing her from gathering any more evidence would have been to poison her, maybe scare her into leaving."

Wodka also cites another AEC finding: Extra plutonium apparently had been added to four of the urine samples Silkwood gave to Kerr-McGee for analysis in late October and early November. "I think someone tampered with these samples, hoping to get her out of the plant or at least confuse the issue."

Kerr-McGee officials have advanced a different conspiracy theory, passed along in off-the-record conversations with local reporters. Kerr-McGee suggests that Silkwood contaminated herself to embarrass the company. According to this theory, Silkwood smuggled a plutonium capsule out of the plant, either by swallowing it or slipping it up her vagina or anus—all suicidal maneuvers. Cited as evidence is the coincidence that Silkwood was first contaminated November 5th, the day before the company was to begin new contract negotiations with the OCAW. But, even assuming that Silkwood had become a frenzied zealot, this theory does not explain why she thought getting contaminated in her apartment would embarrass the company, or why the company would get red faced over *any* contamination after 73 cases in four years.

Nonetheless, Oklahoma City media has popularized this theory. One state representative, a liberal, shakes his head. "I can't understand that dame, shoving plutonium up her ass like that." And some townspeople have added their own twist, announcing with a wink that "I hear she was a drug-crazy hippie who put this plutonium junk in her mary jew anna."

The OCAW International has pledged not to give up until the case is solved.

"Karen was a very unusual person," Wodka says. "She stood up to the company. She was outspoken. She was very brave, now that we look back on it; in many ways she was a lone voice. She was willing to go ahead when other people were afraid."

"She died for a cause," agrees Ilene Younghein. "She will be remembered as a martyr."

At NRC, the regulatory division of the new AEC, she will be remembered, too. The commission has begun a file on her. It reads: "Silkwood, Karen . . . Former employee, Kerr-McGee."

Tania's World

HOWARD KOHN
AND DAVID WEIR

EVERYBODY IN AMERICA, INCLUDING THE FBI, WAS LOOKING FOR KIDNAPPED HEIRESS PATTY HEARST. IT TOOK A COUPLE OF FORMER COLLEGE RADICALS TO GET THE INSIDE STORY OF HER LIFE UNDERGROUND.

The inside story? Who would have the chutzpah to put such a baldly unexplained headline on a magazine cover? And in blaring type! Yet by the time RS 198 hit the newsstands on a Tuesday in October 1975, no explanation was necessary. The whole country and half the world knew what it meant, to exaggerate not at all.

Until the moment of publication, Jann Wenner went to great lengths to keep this one a secret. Even at the magazine offices it was known only inside a small circle. On the previous Saturday the issue had rolled off the presses under the watchful eye of guards, hired by Jann to make sure no one walked away with a copy. The precautions just helped agitate rumors, of course, and the radio buzzed with them all day Sunday. Finally, after nineteen months, here was everything there was to know about heiress Patty Hearst's kidnapping and disappearance! The scoop of the decade, to be published by that underground music magazine in San Francisco! Everyone wanted to know what had happened to Patty Hearst, from the time when she was stolen away in her nightclothes by members of the Symbionese Liberation Army (SLA) to the shocking flash of her ten weeks later on a bank surveillance camera as the beret-wearing, machine-gun-wielding "Tania" and through the many months after she had dropped completely out of sight.

On Monday morning the *Today* show devoted twenty-two minutes to the scoop. On Monday evening, NBC and CBS led off their news broadcasts with "The Inside Story." The ROLLING STONE cover flashed up on the screen as big as life. By the following morning, the story had become a banner headline on newspapers throughout North America, Europe and Asia.

But if you want more details about all the hoopla, don't ask us. We don't remember. We were too busy trying to keep our jobs. We had made a foolhardy and very public promise to write "The Inside Story: Part 2," and we were a long way from delivering. The truth was, we had no "Part 2." Talk about chutzpah.

We do remember Jann toasting us with champagne in his office and then saying, "Okay, back to work, boys." For two weeks we hardly slept, and most of the sleep we did grab was in airport terminals or in parked cars or at our desks. Our notebooks show we conducted more than thirty interviews, ten on a confidential basis.

These many years later we'd have to say that getting the story was not the hardest part, though. Most other reporters seemed to be waiting for the FBI to break the case and then leak them the information, and it happened that the FBI, more than a year and a half after the kidnapping of Patty Hearst, still did not have a clue. The only people who were able to clear up the mysteries that had transfixed so much of the world (Was Patty an SLA stooge from the very beginning? Had she converted to the SLA? Or was she the consummate victim?) were former college radicals like ourselves who knew someone who knew someone. It was our good luck that both for "The Inside Story" and for "Part 2" we were able to locate and talk to some of the people who had been hiding out with her.

No, the hardest part was dealing with the fact that we ourselves were suddenly in the spotlight. During those same two weeks, we were interviewed by more than thirty other reporters looking for the inside story behind "The Inside Story." Local TV editors assigned crews to tail us, hoping we would lead them to a new scoop they could seize on. When one of us checked his wife into a Sacramento, California, hotel, a TV station went on the air to report our association with "an unknown woman." It was a mad time. A representative of the FBI's San Francisco bureau approached us with a proposition. He would break us apart "at the kneecaps" if we did not give the FBI an advance look at "Part 2." He did not sound like he was kidding around.

Meanwhile, the New World Liberation Front (NWLF), a gang of armed leftists who believed it was their mission in life to carry on the vendettas of the SLA, issued a communiqué to say we'd been placed on their hit list alongside FBI bureau chief Charles Bates. Communiqués were then an accepted means by which underground groups made their wishes known to the larger community of the left or to any psychopaths who might be interested. The surviving members of the SLA, who were by this time under arrest, had expressed unhappiness over their portrayals in "The Inside Story." One of the lawyers in their camp also was issuing threats of ruin to us and the magazine.

For some time there had been a bitter debate over what the proper political perspective on the SLA and the NWLF should be. Were they a genuine expression of Sixties-era dissatisfaction with the status quo? Or were they acting out of a personal dementia? The answer wasn't really hard to come by, but the two groups had a certain genius for public relations. For instance, the ransom demand sent to the Hearst family for Patty's release was not for a bag of money to be dropped off in the dark but rather was for truckloads of food to be handed out to Bay Area poor people in a spectacularly staged media event. Strange as such good Samaritanism might have seemed, there was considerable praise for it on the left. Our piece, on the other hand, had made it clear that based on their overall conduct, these self-styled revolutionaries were no more than criminal thugs.

No one at ROLLING STONE doubted that the situation had become dicey. Recent history in the Bay Area favored violent political retaliations. Everyone on staff stayed away from the windows in the old brick warehouse that served as our offices, and Jann brought in extra security. Yet, in order to do a thorough job for "Part 2," we had to try to get in touch with the NWLF, and through intermediaries we were told we would receive a communiqué in response to questions we had posed. Sure enough, a call to the magazine switchboard said a message would be waiting for us taped to the bottom of the metal ledge in a phone booth several blocks away. We borrowed a van and drove to the site, noticing right away that the booth was in a highly exposed position under a freeway overpass. A small army could have been concealed behind the cement abutments. There was nothing to do but jump out, fumble under the ledge and tear away the communiqué.

In the late summer of 1975, Patty Hearst and her SLA traveling companions, Bill and Emily Harris, returned to San Francisco and were recognized by local residents, who alerted authorities. Captured and held under tight security, the fugitive trio was prosecuted for armed robbery in the Hibernia-bank case. Publication of "The Inside Story" caused the Hearst family to hire high-powered F. Lee Bailey and change legal strategies for Patty's trial. Nonetheless, she was convicted by jurors who did not believe she had acted wholly under duress. The Harrises also were convicted. All three served time behind bars; Patty was pardoned in 1979 after serving almost two years.

Looking back, it's obvious we might have considered dropping the whole idea of a "Part 2." At the time, however, we were too far caught up in the action, and the possibility of calling it quits simply did not occur to us. Nor, we dare say, did it occur to Jann. "You write it, and I'll print it" was his operating slogan, his *axis mundi*. So "Part 2" was printed in RS 200 and was followed by weeks of additional controversy. Francis Ford Coppola, then the publisher of another San Francisco magazine, sicked a team of interviewers on us. The result appeared under the headline ROLLING STONE SUPERSTARS EXAMINE THEIR CONSCIENCES. Another SLA lawyer persuaded a judge to hold us in contempt of court for refusing to name the people who had talked confidentially to us. In the end, however, everything blew over. The contempt citation was dropped; the NWLF never struck; the SLA was thoroughly discredited; and no FBI agents showed up to break our knees. Oh, yes, we also wrote "Part 3."

RS 198

OCTOBER 23RD, 1975

Patty Hearst and Emily Harris waited on a grimy Los Angeles street, fighting their emotions as they listened to a radio rebroadcasting the sounds of their friends dying. On a nearby corner Bill Harris dickered over the price of a battered old car.

Only blocks away, rifle cartridges were exploding in the dying flames of a charred bungalow. The ashes were still too hot to retrieve the bodies of the six SLA members who had died hours before on the afternoon of May 17th, 1974.

Bill Harris shifted impatiently as the car's owner patted a dented fender. "I want five bills for this mother."

The SLA survivors had only $400. Reluctantly Harris offered $350. The man quickly pocketed the money.

Minutes later Bill picked up Patty and Emily and steered onto a freeway north to San Francisco. They drove all night—the Harrises in the front seat of the noisy car and Patty in back, hidden under a blanket. They were too tense to sleep, each grappling with the aftershock of the fiery deaths.

They exited twice at brightly lit service station clusters that flank Interstate 5, checking out each before picking what looked like the safest attendant. They made no other stops and reached San Francisco in the predawn darkness.

The three fugitives drove to a black ghetto with rows of ramshackle Victorians—and sought out a friend. Bill and Emily's knocks brought the man sleepy-eyed to the door.

"You're alive!" Then he panicked. "You can't stay here. The whole state is gonna be crawling with pigs looking for you." He gave them five dollars and shut the door. "Don't come back."

The Harrises returned to the car and twisted the ignition key. Patty poked her head out from under the blanket. "What's the matter? Why won't it start?"

The fugitives had no choice—to continue fiddling with the dead battery might attract attention—so they abandoned the car. Walking the streets, however, was a worse alternative.

"C'mon Tania," said Emily. "You better bring the blanket." Bill and Emily both carried duffel bags. Inside were weapons, disguises and tattered books.

A few blocks away, under a faded Victorian, they spotted a crawl space, a gloomy cave for rats and runaway dogs. As Patty and the Harrises huddled in the dirt under the old house, the noise of a late-night party began in the living room above. Patty gripped her homemade machine gun. "The pigs must have found the car!"

"Shhh," came a whispered response. "Shut up, goddamnit. Please shut up!"

They survived that night and spent the next two weeks in San Francisco, hiding in flophouses. Bill posed as a wino, Patty and Emily as dirty-faced old women. On June 2nd they boarded a bus, dropped 55¢ into the coinbox and headed across the Bay Bridge toward Berkeley. They were on their way to scout out a rally called to commemorate the death of SLA member Angela Atwood. It was there that they got their first break.

The fugitives had only a few crumpled dollars left. The rally seemed their best chance to find a benefactor. So Emily, wearing a tie-dyed shirt, cutoff jeans and a wig, melted into the crowd at Ho Chi Minh Park in Berkeley, the town that helped launch the Movement in the early Sixties.

Emily recognized several faces from the California prison reform groups that had served as the crucible for her and most of the original SLA members. But one of the speakers, Kathy Soliah, attracted her attention. Soliah, who had become friends with Atwood when both quit waitress jobs because they felt the uniforms were demeaning, told the crowd she now considered herself part of the SLA.

Afterward Emily approached her and a few hours later the three fugitives were stashed in a small Berkeley flat, sipping tea and contemplating their next move.

"You can only stay here a few days. But maybe I can find someplace else you can go."

That hope soon faded. Other former SLA sympathizers wanted no part in the new underground life. A few contributed money—but not enough to buy another car. The fugitives were pale and weak from months of being away from sunshine—and eating a diet of carryout hamburgers.

Patty paced about the flat, putting her arms around her, dark eyes staring out the windows, measuring each passer-by as a potential enemy. They felt it was only a matter of time before they would be discovered— in a few days they might be facing a police siege like their friends in Los Angeles. They kept their guns loaded, always within quick reach.

Then after a week at the Berkeley flat, a friend stopped by with an announcement: "I think I found someone who might help you. His name is Jack Scott and he wants to write a book about the SLA."

On February 4th, 1974, while Patty Hearst was being kidnapped, Jack Scott was confronting his own private crisis. A few months earlier he had considered himself a Movement radical working successfully within the system. As Oberlin College's athletic director he had hired the school's first black coaches, opened its athletic facilities to poor people from the community and shocked the alumni by declaring his unconcern for football scores. He also had authored three controversial sports books and founded the Institute for the Study of Sport and Society (ISSS). The sports world regarded Scott as a daring and influential pioneer.

When Oberlin's administration changed hands in early 1974, however, he had been forced out of his job. He had dedicated nearly ten years to his work in sports. Now at age 32, he began to wonder if all that time had been wasted.

Jack and his wife, Micki, moved to an apartment in New York where they continued to run the ISSS and Jack signed a contract to write his autobiography for William Morrow Publishers.

But Jack remained despondent. He stayed indoors, watched television and slept 12 hours a day. Twice a day he went out to corner newsstands and bought copies of the *Times,* the *Post* and the *Daily News.* Judging by the headlines, the only thing happening was the advent of an off-the-wall political militia calling itself the Symbionese Liberation Army.

"SLA Kidnaps Newspaper Heiress"

"SLA Demands $200 Million in Food for Poor"

The SLA's rhetoric and tactics seemed to parody what the Movement had become. But Jack's initial scorn turned to curiosity as the headlines piled up.

"Patty Hearst Joins SLA"

"Patty Helps Rob Bank"

The media also was unable to make up its mind. Were they crazies? Or young idealists fed up with working through the system? Did their tactics signal an emerging guerrilla violence in the United States? Was Patty Hearst in fact an SLA soldier now?

Jack's own doubts about the viability of peaceful reform began to crystalize in the continuing media debate over Patty Hearst and the SLA. At dinnertime he flicked the television knob from one network news show to another so he could monitor each bizarre twist in the case. By early May he was a walking encyclopedia on the subject.

He began spending his days in the offices of New York's book publishers. Jack was persuaded that the SLA symbolized the pent-up frustration of the Movement. He wanted to write a book that placed the SLA in a historical perspective.

But the publishers weren't interested in Jack's theories. A Doubleday editor told him he'd have to talk to people who knew how the SLA was formed before he could get a book contract.

Then Jack's book negotiations and his television watching were interrupted by live camera footage of the six flaming deaths in Los Angeles. He felt the SLA had been executed without a trial.

Flushed by anger, Jack boarded an airplane two weeks later and headed for Berkeley. He had spent six years there studying for his doctorate in educational psychology. He'd been a Goldwater supporter when he first arrived but, like thousands of others, had been radicalized.

Now he sought out old Movement friends who had ties to the underground. They introduced him to a friend of the Harrises. He explained his book idea and asked about the couple. He was told of Emily's disappointments as a teacher in Indiana, Bill's disgust after a military tour in Vietnam, their migration to California, their attempts to hold classes at prisons, the harsh reaction of prison officials to their suggested changes, their disillusionment that grew into cynicism and violence.

Then the friend cautiously introduced a possibility that had seemed a million-to-one shot.

"How'd you like to meet some people who could tell you even more about Bill and Emily—and about Patty?"

Jack understood the question's implications. He was intrigued. If a meeting with the three surviving members of the SLA actually could be arranged, he was willing to go along.

At 2:00 the next afternoon he was at the corner of Telegraph and Dwight Way. For nearly an hour he stood uncomfortably in the sun. He was easily recognized—thinning hair, professorial beard and wire-rimmed glasses. But no one approached him. Then, as he began to walk away, he was stopped by a short dark man dressed in a white tennis outfit and carrying a tennis racket. The man gave Jack an address and told him to come by that evening.

Jack wasn't sure the man was Bill Harris. He wasn't sure he wanted to know. Apprehension began welling up. He circled the block several times before finally knocking on the door. A face looked out from behind a curtain. The door opened and Jack walked into a room prepared for a police invasion. Mattresses were piled against the doors and next to the windows. Rifles that had been converted to automatic machine guns were lined up next to a pair of duffel bags. Grenades were stacked in strategic corners. One gun was cradled by a short unsmiling woman.

She was Tania, Patricia Campbell Hearst, the granddaughter of William Randolph Hearst. Emily Harris was the only other one in the room. She came forward and smiled tentatively, "I'm Yolanda." Then the man in the tennis outfit emerged from another room and gripped Jack's hand, "I'm Teko."

The fugitives said nothing further for a few moments, absorbed in watching their impact on the visitor. They noted Jack's apprehensive glance toward the guns leaning against the walls. He seemed suitably impressed with their military accouterments.

"You said you were interested in the SLA," Bill said. "That's why we invited you here. The most important thing at this time, you must understand, is to help us."

Jack sat down and went through a long nervous explanation of how and why he had agreed to this meeting. He was collecting information for a book. He wanted to present an accurate portrayal of the SLA that probed beneath the screaming headlines. They could help by telling the full story of their involvement.

"Okay," Bill answered. "We know you want to do a book. But right now we don't know if we're gonna be around long enough to read it. Aren't our lives more important than your book?"

Jack nodded. He had over $40,000 that he'd been paid by Oberlin College after he'd threatened to sue for breach of contract. The fugitives were welcome to some of that money.

For Patty and the Harrises this was an incredible offer. "That's just what we need," said Emily. "We can take the money and rent some place out in the country and lay back while things cool out."

But Jack was already having second thoughts. He felt equivocal about the SLA's previous tactics. And he didn't want to be involved if they were planning more violence.

"There is one condition." Jack's quiet voice was firm. The fugitives turned quickly in his direction, their faces stiff and challenging. Jack ignored the sudden change and plunged ahead.

"I can't help you unless you get rid of those guns."

"Who the fuck are you!" Patty stepped forward, her mouth tight with contempt.

Jack was red in the face but he did not retreat. "I won't help you unless you give up your weapons."

The mood in the house went electric with tension. The fugitives had gambled on Jack by inviting him to their hideout. They were pretending that their act was more together than it was. Realistically, they could not leave Berkeley without the kind of money Jack had.

Bill spoke. His tone was taut and blunt. "Listen, we can't stay in this house much longer. Like Yolanda says, we need a place in the country where we can get our shit together. I'll be honest. We need your help. We'll work with you on the book. But our weapons are our only protection. We all feel the same way. When we joined the SLA we understood we'd have to be armed at all times."

The discussion continued. The fugitives were weary. But they clung to the SLA tenet of armed struggle. Jack could not make up his mind. Seven years before, during a "Stop the Draft Week" in Oakland, he and his wife, Micki, had converted their van into a makeshift medical center to treat students who had been clubbed and bloodied by the police. That had been their introduction to the Movement and had set a pattern for their style of radicalism: Their house was open to draft resisters, evicted tenants and others needing a sanctuary.

It was past midnight. Maybe the morning would bring a clearer decision. Jack rose to go.

"You can't leave." Emily's command was precise. "You might attract attention."

Now Jack was scared. In his fantasies the police had the house surrounded and were moving in for another climactic fusillade.

But the fugitives gave him no choice. He was told to sleep sandwiched between Emily and Patty. Positioned at the head of their bed was an arsenal of guns and grenades. Bill turned out the lights and Jack lay back, staring at the ceiling.

He couldn't sleep. Thirty minutes passed. It seemed like decades. Then a loud crash jarred everyone upright. Patty rolled over and grabbed a gun in a single motion that she had practiced many times in the dark. "It's the pigs," she whispered.

Someone had knocked over a garbage can in the alley. Nobody said a word as the three fugitives trained their guns on the entrances. Slowly Bill pulled back a curtain and peered out. He turned to the rest and grinned. "It's only a cat."

Jack forced himself to laugh. The others joined in, a trace of hysteria showing in their smiles.

Beneath the bravado in the gun-filled room, Jack realized, there was a sense of deepening desperation. His mind was made up. If the SLA survivors surrendered their guns, he'd help them find a haven, spend some time with them, get to know them — and write his book.

He settled into a fitful sleep, his nightmares filled with roaring flames and exploding cartridges. His face still felt hot from the dream flames when Bill shook him awake. The fugitives had gotten up early and had reached their own decision.

"We've talked it over. If you'll help get us out of here, we'll leave our guns behind."

Once Jack's wife, Micki, found the fugitives a farm house in a secluded part of Pennsylvania, the next major problem was transportation. Too many wanted posters had been circulated to risk planes or trains. They would have to split up and travel by car. Bill and Emily would get rides from two friends. But Jack would have to chauffeur Patty. None of their other friends was willing to drive 3000 miles with the most famous fugitive in the country.

Jack's curiosity outweighed his fears. He wanted answers to the questions that had been nagging him. Why had Patty converted to the SLA? Had she been tortured? Or brainwashed? Or was she still a hostage? She had been the most hostile to Scott's demand that the fugitives disarm and she had yet to speak a friendly word to him. But maybe that was a ploy to fool the Harrises. Once free of them, she might want to return to her parents and boyfriend.

Emily and her escort left on Friday night. The fugitives felt there was some chance the FBI had the group under surveillance and was waiting to pick them up separately on the highway. So they set up a signal. The others wouldn't leave until Emily called from Nevada.

They expected her call by Saturday afternoon but the phone was silent all Saturday. Jack listened to the radio. There was no news of Emily's apprehension. But that did not calm him. If the feds were laying an ambush, there would be a news blackout.

By Sunday noon Emily still had not phoned. There had been a prearranged deadline. If she didn't call by five o'clock Sunday afternoon, they'd be sure she'd been caught. At five minutes to five the phone rang.

"Hi," said Emily cheerily, "we're in Iowa."

Emily and her companion had misunderstood the signal. They thought the plan was for her to call *at* five on Sunday. Bill started to rebuke Emily for breach of orders. But he was too relieved to hear she was safe. "Stay strong. We'll see you in about a week."

An hour later Jack and Patty were on the freeway outside Berkeley. They were dressed in sports clothes and carried tennis rackets on the back ledge of their car. Tennis rackets somehow seemed a perfect complement to any well-mannered disguise. They were still only across the bay from the Hillsborough mansion where she grew up. As far as Jack knew this was the first time since her kidnapping that Patty had been away from the SLA. He stopped the car and awkwardly began a conversation he'd been rehearsing in his mind.

"Please don't take this the wrong way. But I want you to know that I'm willing to drive you anywhere you want to go. You don't have to go to Pennsylvania. I'll take you anywhere . . ."

Patty looked incredulous. She shifted into a corner of the car farthest from Jack.

He wasn't sure how to interpret her fear. "You can go anywhere you want," he repeated.

"I want to go where my friends are going."

Patty eyed Jack suspiciously. She was ready to bolt if he turned the car toward Hillsborough. Jack's embarrassment rushed across his face. He rammed the gear shift into first and silently resumed their journey east.

Patty stayed in her corner of the car and held herself rigidly, as if waiting for Jack to apologize. He offered small talk, unwilling to concede her opinion that he had blundered inexcusably.

The tension building between them kept them both awake. They were in Reno before Jack suggested stopping for sleep. Patty nodded assent. She stayed in the car while Jack registered for a motel room.

The room was furnished with only one bed. Patty gave a wary glance to it and then to Jack.

"I don't want you to get the wrong idea about me," he tried to reassure her. "I got a room with one bed because we're registered as a married couple. But I don't want you to think you have to have sex with me. In fact, I don't think we should have sex. I don't want you to feel later that you were coerced in any way. All I'd like is to have a warm body next to me."

The hardness around Patty's mouth softened and she smiled for the first time since he'd met her. "Don't worry about it. I'm not into sex with anybody right now. I loved Cujo too much . . ." Cujo—Willie Wolfe— had been killed in Los Angeles. They went to bed exhausted and fell into an uneasy sleep.

The next day Patty ate her meals in the car. Even standing in line at a McDonald's was a risk. Millions had seen her picture on the evening news and the cover of *Newsweek* or heard her soft, distinctive voice on radio broadcasts of the SLA communiques.

For most of the previous four months she had been cooped up inside. Her excursions outside twice had ended in gunfire. Now she was driving across country through an FBI dragnet that already had employed more agents than any other civilian case.

The strain of the past months was showing. To Patty the passing world was populated by an army of undercover agents. Once, as Jack slowed up to ease past a construction site, she ducked and whispered in a half shriek: "Did you see that guy? I know he's a pig."

"C'mon, he's a highway flagman. Don't be so uptight."

When Jack pulled in for gas she frequently demanded he speed away as an attendant approached. "I don't like the way he looks," she'd explain. "He looks like a pig."

Patty's repeated reviling of "pigs" soon led to a discussion about the political criterion for such a classification. Patty took the position that a pig was anyone who did not give wholehearted support to the SLA. Jane Fonda and Tom Hayden, for instance, were pigs because they'd criticized the SLA tactics. Patty sounded like what she was—a new convert to radical thinking.

Jack pointed out Fonda and Hayden's untiring work to end the Vietnam war. "It's one thing to disagree with them but it's another thing to call them pigs. We have to recognize who our friends are and who our enemies are."

Patty sneered and changed the subject. What sort of author was Jack Scott? She had never read any of his books.

He had written about sports, he explained. He believed that athletes had a right not to be treated like cows at an auction. His books challenged those attitudes.

"I don't see how sports is relevant to anything at all," Patty said. "Certainly not to the revolution."

Jack did not reply.

For the rest of the trip they reached an uneasy accord.

The Pennsylvania farmhouse which Micki had rented stood on a bluff overlooking miles of rolling farmland. But the 87-acre spread had seldom seen a plow. The previous owner had spent 30 years trying to raise small-mouth bass in three small ponds that lay 100 yards behind the house in thick stands of alfalfa and timothy grass. An aging windmill that had been used to circulate air through the ponds was the only surviving testament to the experiment. The bass all had been fished out; the fugitives found only bullheads and a few undersized pickerel.

But that served to make the farm more isolated. Fishermen never bothered with the weedy ponds. The few motorists who bumped past the house were introspective farmers who lived down the dusty road out of sight and earshot.

The house also was ideal. From the outside it loomed tall and weathered. Dirty white paint peeled onto waist-high weeds that nearly hid an old and temperamental water tank. On the second floor was a balcony with a wrought-iron railing. Below was a screened in porch with hanging lamp where evenings could be spent listening to the litany of frogs and crickets. Inside were four bedrooms, a kitchen, a living room, dining room and attic — an expansive layout for three people who'd been sleeping on floors in cramped apartments.

Mornings brought rich sunrises flooding over the Pocono Mountains, driving the black flies and mosquitoes into the shade of a clump of trees that bordered the rear of the farm. By midmorning the fugitives were out lying in the sun like three white-bellied bass tossed on the banks of the ponds. Patty spent long hours on a grassy hummock. The Harrises adapted to the sun more slowly. Within days, however, all three were a crimson brown.

The Pennsylvania summer seemed to relax and rejuvenate the fugitives. They read Marx and Debray during the morning cool, then went sunning and swimming, chasing each other into the water. They picked wild blackberries from bushes growing across the road and dropped hook and line in search of the scavenger fish they grew to like cooked with butter and onions.

In their political study sessions Emily and Micki were Patty's mentors. "Tania is a sister," Emily told Micki. "But she's still learning." The two older women became close. Sometimes they'd have long conversations about feminism while sitting on the kitchen floor drinking coffee. Micki confided that she'd felt a little jealous when Jack was traveling across country with a woman she had not then met. Emily replied that she and Bill tried not to be so possessive of each other. They were working it out intellectually, she said, but deep down some jealousies were not yet erased. Emily's candor was a welcome surprise. The two women hugged and laughed.

By the end of June the Scotts were at ease with Patty, Bill and Emily. The only squabble was the amount of time the Scotts were spending at the farm. Jack and Micki had decided to resume working a few days each week at ISSS so they could see their New York friends without inviting them to the farm. Because it was a six-hour round trip, they quickly tired of a daily commute and the fugitives sometimes were left by themselves for days at a time.

But while in New York the Scotts sought out Wendy Yoshimura, another fugitive whose friends had helped Jack find the SLA survivors in Berkeley. Wendy had gone underground in 1972 after being accused in the bombing of a Navy ROTC building in Berkeley. She had been born in a U.S. concentration camp — like many Japanese families, hers had been interned for much of World War II — had attended the California College of Arts and Crafts and had worked as a waitress.

Through mutual friends the Scotts arranged a meeting. Wendy explained that she was working as a waitress again and was hoping to save $500 by the end of the summer so she could return to the West Coast. Jack asked her to move into the farmhouse and offered to pay her the $500. She agreed and soon became a senior adviser and companion to the SLA fugitives.

The Scotts tried to provide everything the fugitives wanted, Micki had stocked the house with food, books and other supplies. When more was needed she sometimes accompanied Emily on shopping trips to Scranton. The fugitives also had new disguises. Patty's hair had been cut to affect a boyish look. Both Bill and Emily had lightened their dark hair with red tints.

Jack and Micki had avoided discussing the issue of how far they would go to protect the SLA survivors. But one evening while Jack was driving to the farm a radio news flash suddenly confronted him with the dilemma.

"We have a report that the SLA has been located. Police have surrounded their hideout and Patty Hearst's parents are being flown to the scene to plead with their daughter for her surrender. Keep tuned for further details."

The fugitives were alone at the house. Jack swallowed hard. His hands jitterbugged on the wheel. Should he somehow try to divert the police? Try to negotiate a peaceful surrender? Or should he turn around and flee back to New York?

His foot stayed jammed against the accelerator. He had to see for himself what was happening. From a mile away the farm seemed dark. He couldn't see any police floodlights or red flashers. As he turned onto the dirt road the radio announced a followup report. "From Los Angeles, word has been received that the SLA sighting was a mistake. Police say that a secretary who lived alone was mistakenly identified as Patty Hearst. This has been another false lead in the hunt for the missing heiress."

Jack's heart stopped hammering. But his face was still ashen as he entered the farmhouse. "Good God," Bill greeted him quizzically. "You look like you just got out of prison."

Jack slumped to a chair and told his story of the two radio announcements. Everybody smiled and patted Jack on the back. The camaraderie carried over to the following days. Jack was asked to teach a basic set of exercises. He fashioned weights from concrete blocks for muscle building and led the fugitives through wind sprints to restore their strength and stamina.

Races were held between a rickety barn and a finish line marked by a child's rusting yellow swing set. Patty was surprisingly swift. Jack, once an outstanding sprinter himself, was hard pressed to outrun her. He had begun to like Patty. She enjoyed joking around and displayed an exuberance that had been impossible to imagine two weeks before. Her snappishness had dissipated.

She still chided Jack about the political irrelevancy of sports and his work at the ISSS. But she exercised daily under his rigorous tutelage. During one hard run she stepped in a gopher hole and crashed forward on a twisted ankle. She limped back to the house hanging onto Jack's shoulder. There he massaged and taped the ligaments. A similar injury had ended Jack's athletic career and ruined his shot at the Olympics when he was Patty's age.

Patty spent the afternoon resting on the porch. Jack stayed with her and they began to talk about Patty's conversion to the SLA.

Patty Hearst and Steven Weed were home in their Berkeley apartment watching *The Magician* on TV at nine o'clock on the foggy night of February 4th, 1974. The young couple lived together in something that used to be called sin and smoked an occasional joint. But in Berkeley they were considered straight.

Outside, a stolen 1964 Chevrolet Impala convertible pulled up in front and dimmed its lights. Donald DeFreeze, Willie Wolfe and Nancy Ling Perry emerged and moved silently to apartment number four. Perry rang the doorbell while DeFreeze and Wolfe waited in the shadows. Perry hunched over and held a hand to her face. "I just had a car accident out front. Could you . . . ?"

Weed cracked open the door and DeFreeze and Wolfe burst in, brandishing guns, knocking him to the floor and kicking him in the face with heavy boots. They grabbed Patty and carried her kicking and screaming to the waiting car. There they shoved her into the trunk with a brusque order: "Get in and keep quiet."

Patty was scared and half-naked but she stared hardeyed at her kidnappers. "Don't give me any shit."

Even in those first terrible moments Patricia Campbell Hearst managed to summon up the daring and arrogance that had been her style through 19 years of life as an heiress to the Hearst fortune.

Her parents had provided every indulgence, tolerated her dope smoking, her sneaking out to rock concerts at San Francisco's Fillmore auditorium and her faded blue jeans. When she couldn't accept the Catholic school discipline that required her to scrub toilets for breaking petty rules, her parents transferred her to a more flexible nonsectarian school.

It was there she met Weed, a math teacher and the school's most eligible bachelor. Two years later, when she was 18, she moved in with him. Her parents initially disapproved and Patty briefly worked at paying her own bills, holding a $2.25 per hour job in a department store for four months. But when she gave that up to return to school, her father paid for her books, tuition and the out-of-wedlock apartment as well. Over the next year her father supplied enough money to buy expensive prints from her grandfather's collection, Persian rugs, a tenth-century Persian manuscript and dozens of plants.

Patty was not used to discomfort. Her life had been insulated from real-life drama and pain. She assumed her father would quickly ransom her.

She was kept blindfolded in a stuffy, closet-sized room with a bare lightbulb and a portable cot. There were no windows and it was hot. She lost track of time and didn't feel like eating. She was told her parents loved money more than her.

She was not raped or starved or otherwise brutalized. But Donald DeFreeze, the SLA leader known as Cinque, kept up a constant intimidation. He berated her and her family for being part of a ruling class that was sucking blood from the common people.

"Your mommy and daddy are insects," he yelled. "They should be made to crawl on their hands and knees like insects if they want you back."

Patty tried to defend her parents. They had not hurt anyone. They were good people. Cinque was wrong. He had never met them.

But Patty feared Cinque. He told her she'd be killed if her parents did not meet the SLA's demands, and she believed him.

So Patty grew impatient as the ransom negotiations bogged down. "I felt my parents were debating how much I was worth," she later told Jack. "Like they figured I was worth $2 million but I wasn't worth $10 million. It was a terrible feeling that my parents could think of me in terms of dollars and cents. I felt sick all over."

It angered her when her father visited San Quentin and reported that the living conditions there were fine.

The SLA had informed him that her living quarters were identical to those in San Quentin. Her father seemed to be saying that tiny cells, stale air and gloomy walls were an acceptable environment for his daughter.

And she became alarmed when heavily armed FBI agents raided a house where they thought she was being held. She felt her parents were recklessly allowing the FBI to risk her life.

After a while it seemed that her parents had given her up for dead. "It's really depressing to hear people talk about me like I was dead," she said in her second taped statement. "I can't explain what it's like." Her mother had taken to wearing black and speaking of Patty in the past tense. Worse, her mother had ignored an SLA demand by accepting another appointment from then governor Ronald Reagan as a regent of the University of California.

"I felt like I could kill her when she did that," Patty said. "My own mother didn't care whether the SLA shot me or not."

By degrees her disillusionment with her parents turned into sympathy for the SLA. Cinque was the first to perceive the change. He rewarded her by allowing her to roam about the San Francisco apartment that served as the SLA headquarters. For a month she had been kept in a small "isolation chamber" approximating a San Quentin "hole." She'd become weak and could barely stand up. To be able to walk freely from one room to another seemed the world's greatest pleasure.

Cinque tempered his frequent beratings of her. Patty was urged to attend the SLA's daily political study sessions. She was invited to listen to the SLA national anthem, an eerie jazz composition of wind and string that Cinque had selected. And she was furnished with statistical evidence and quotations from George Jackson and Ruchell Magee that promoted her political development. Less than ten percent of the U.S. population controls 90% of its wealth. Some people eat catered meals while others starve. Some can afford fancy lawyers while others rot in jail. Some live off their inheritances while others live in squalor and despair.

Patty was shown a long list of the Hearst family holdings — nine newspapers, 13 magazines, four TV and radio stations, a silver mine, a paper mill and prime real estate. Her parents clearly were part of the ruling elite. That's why they had quibbled over the ransom money. That's why they had handed out turkey giblets instead of steaks during the food giveaway that the SLA had demanded. Money meant everything to the economic class of her parents. And the only power that could fight that money was the power that came out of the barrel of a gun.

It was a political philosophy that had bored her when Weed and his doctoral student friends had discussed it in their Berkeley apartment. But Cinque's rough eloquence was more persuasive than the abstract talk of graduate students. The SLA's motives made sense. They wanted to redistribute the Hearst wealth to more needy people. It was her parents — and the economic class they represented — who were to blame for her misery and the misery of countless others.

The SLA members encouraged her radicalization. They hugged her, called her sister and ended her loneliness. Patty's conversion was as much emotional as political.

Seven weeks after she was kidnapped, Patty asked to join the SLA.

She began sleeping with 23-year-old Willie Wolfe, whom she called Cujo. Of the three men in the SLA, Wolfe was the closest to Patty in age and background. The son of a Pennsylvania doctor, he'd attended private schools, been a varsity swimmer, sports editor of the school paper and gotten roughed up in antiwar demonstrations. He'd spent a summer working with kids in Harlem, then spurned the Yale family tradition and enrolled at Berkeley, where he'd roomed with SLA member Russell Little and met Cinque.

He subsequently joined the SLA combat unit that assassinated the Oakland superintendent of schools and wounded his assistant. (Patty told

Jack that Wolfe also helped Cinque kidnap her. She said Weed was mistaken when he identified both of his assailants as black men.)

Violence once had turned Patty off. Now she found it appealing. She learned to use the converted rifles, practiced "keeping my ass down" while crawling through Cinque's homemade obstacle course and took part in a bank robbery to prove herself to the SLA.

After the robbery the SLA switched its headquarters from a racially mixed neighborhood to an all-black one in San Francisco. The eight white SLA members moved their clothes, guns and bullets in daylight—they were wearing Afro wigs and a black-face disguise that was smeared on so professionally that several observers mistook them for blacks. They left behind papers and other paraphernalia in a bathtub filled with acid and excrement beneath a spray-painted sign that read: "Here it is, pigs. Have fun getting it."

In early May they moved again, driving south to Cinque's home turf in Los Angeles. On May 16th Patty and the Harrises took the SLA van to shop at Mel's Sporting Goods store in the suburb of Inglewood. Bill walked through the aisles with frequent glances over his shoulder, a nervous tip-off that a security guard misinterpreted. Bill was grabbed and handcuffed as a suspected shoplifter. He escaped when Patty, keeping a vigil outside Mel's, sprayed the store with machine-gun fire. But the shootout separated the three from the rest of the group and left the SLA van in the hands of Los Angeles police.

The next day police located the SLA hideout through an address written on unpaid parking tickets found in the van. Cinque, Wolfe, Perry, Angela Atwood, Camilla Hall and Mizmoon Soltysik had fled. But they were cornered and killed in a bungalow only blocks away.

"Neither Cujo nor I had ever loved an individual the way we loved each other," she said in her taped communique following the shootout.

Afterwards she clung to the Harrises and shared their love. But her pain over Wolfe's death was a long time in healing.

By mid-summer, constant bickering—political and otherwise—had soured interest in the book and reopened a rift between the Scotts and the fugitives. Both sides agreed that the fugitives should leave the farmhouse by September 1st, the day the lease expired.

Back in New York, Jack conferred with Micki. She agreed. They would move the ISSS to Portland and live and work with renegade Portland Trailblazers' center Bill Walton.

But first they had to untangle themselves from the underground.

So the Harrises drove to phone booths in a nearby town where they called friends on the West Coast. A series of calls followed—all from pay phones and to pay phones. The West Coast friends, whom Bill named the "new team," were willing to help. Everything would be arranged—transportation, money, even a ploy to distract police attention.

The Harrises brought back the news. "These people are heavy revolutionaries," Bill pointedly told the Scotts. "They've really got it together. They want to be part of our unit."

The new team included Kathy Soliah, the friend of Angela Atwood's who had helped the fugitives in Berkeley, and Soliah's brother, Steve. Like many SLA sympathizers, the Soliahs had been outraged by the L.A. shootout. During the summer they had talked to other Berkeley area radicals who believed that the SLA's guerrilla tactics should be resumed—perhaps by bombing carefully selected targets.

The Harrises were anxious to rejoin people who shared their belief in political violence. They felt contempt for the Scotts' skittishness—and no longer bothered to conceal it. And although the Scotts had been logistic experts, the new team had some ideas of its own.

What especially pleased Bill was the decoy operation. Patty was to send an identifiable item of hers to the new team. They would plant it in a Los Angeles apartment and tip off the police in an anonymous call. While the government marshalled its forces in Southern California, the new team would pick up the fugitives and ferry them to a new hideout.

The Scotts and the fugitives prepared for their departure, wiping away fingerprints from the farmhouse and tidying up other details. The Scotts packed the van they'd just bought, closed down their New York apartment and waited for the new team to arrive for the fugitives.

A week passed. The fugitives were still at the farm. The Harrises and Patty were beginning to quarrel, their worry spilling out into petty disputes. The only word from the new team was more procrastination. The decoy operation inexplicably had been called off.

"Do you think they'll ever show up?" Micki asked the Harrises.

Emily shrugged. Bill started to say "of course" but then paused and didn't answer.

Patty was more patient than the others. She had matured noticeably over the summer. She'd dropped "pig" from her daily vocabulary. She had spent long hours reading history books, especially on the early days of the labor movement in the U.S. She was quiet; she stopped x-ing the *New York Times*; she seemed to be preparing for a long-term life in the underground.

Each day Patty practiced walking with a pillow stuffed under her dress. She was disguised as a pregnant teenager with freckles. Throughout the summer the fugitives had studied the art of disguise, reading books on techniques for dyeing and styling hair, affecting lisps and limps, attaching artificial moles, scars and tattoos, wearing reversible clothes. Within minutes they could switch from the hippie mode into the young professional, from seedy bum to roughneck hillbilly.

But the preparation seemed beside the point—their West Coast friends were having second thoughts. Finally, Bill insisted that the new team level with him about its problems. Reluctantly they explained the hitch: Patty Hearst.

Bill was unable to convince them that Patty's disguise would be beyond suspicion. Wendy and the Harrises were okay. But the new team did not want the *Newsweek* cover girl to be in the car when they entered the territories of highway patrolmen, toll attendants, motel managers, gas station operators and restaurant cashiers who regulate a cross-country automobile trip. If Patty could get to the West Coast by herself, they told Bill, they would provide her a hiding place, but she was on her own until then.

Jack also was getting agitated. He wanted Micki to meet Walton before the basketball season opened. But she couldn't leave until the fugitives were gone.

Then came a phone call from Pennsylvania to Oregon.

"We need your help again." Bill's voice sounded urgent. "There's no other way we can do it. We need you to drive a friend across country. No one else will do it." If Patty were ever to leave the farm, it seemed, Jack would have to drive the getaway car. He hesitated.

The risks were incalculable. And his first trip with Patty was a bad memory.

But Patty had changed over the summer. She seldom complained—and never about physical discomforts. And she had the half-joking enthusiasm of a daredevil that Jack admired.

He called back. "Okay, I'll drive your friend."

Three days later Jack, Patty, Micki and their German shepherd Sigmund headed west in the van with boxes of books and clothes stacked in back and a mattress tied on top. They had to alternate sitting on a pillow between the van's two bucket seats. Patty was posing as Jack's pregnant wife, Micki as his sister. After a day on the road, though, they adopted a more conservative tack. A couple traveling alone would arouse less suspicion. So Jack and Patty dropped Micki at the Cleveland airport and continued alone.

This was Patty's first venture out in public since her cross-country trip with Jack in June. On their second day Patty accidentally locked herself in a service station restroom. Afraid to call for help because she still feared her voice might be recognized, she began to unhinge the door, banging away with her shoe. She managed to get one hinge off before the door slid open. Jack had been sitting in the van, waiting and worrying under the boiling sun.

They spoke little. When they did the tension and irritation of three months ago crept back into their conversation. Jack tuned in the radio to a football game. Patty groaned and turned her face to the side window.

In Iowa their worst fears came true. A state patrolman turned on his flasher and motioned their speeding car to the highway shoulder. Jack didn't give the trooper a chance to walk to the van. He swung open the van door and sprinted back to the patrol car.

"Sorry, officer, I guess I got a little excited about Iowa winning today. That was some game. . . ."

"You're an Iowa fan?" The trooper seemed doubtful. "Those are out-of-state tags you got there."

"Hey, I'm just a football fan. No matter where I go I love to listen to football." Jack blabbered on. "You wouldn't give a speeding ticket to a football fan, would you? That would be kind of anti-American."

The trooper grinned. He was feeling good. Iowa had been a 21-point underdog in its win over UCLA. "I'll let you off easy this time but be careful when you cross the border into Nebraska. They got upset by Wisconsin, you know." He put his ticket book away without inspecting the van.

That night Patty and Jack celebrated. They rented an expensive motel room and ordered a room-service dinner. The tension was broken. Patty laughed, "Now I understand what sports means to the revolution. From now on, any time you want to listen to a football game it's okay with me."

Three days later they reached Las Vegas. Jack dropped Patty at a prearranged motel and went to visit his parents who live in Las Vegas and manage an apartment complex. The next day he stopped by the motel. The new team still had not arrived. Nor had they by the next morning. Both Patty and Jack grew worried again. Had she been deserted? But then the new team called. They'd be arriving that night.

Jack returned to his parents' home and settled in to watch *Bonnie and Clyde* on television. Suddenly the local station interrupted with a bulletin. Jack tensed. Had Patty been caught?

But the bulletin was from Reno. A bank had been robbed of $1 million.

Jack remained nervous. He decided to stop by the motel. Patty was still there. Both watched television for a few minutes. Then he got up. The new team would be arriving shortly and he wanted to be gone by then.

Patty was returning to the San Francisco Bay Area where she had grown up, been kidnapped and converted to armed fugitive. There she would reunite with Wendy, Bill and Emily to continue living underground. She was still undecided about how she fit into a revolution she had discovered only seven months before. But she was dedicated to her new beliefs and she still called herself Tania.

Jack embraced Patty, hugging her hard, and said good-bye.

The date was September 27th, 1974.

Her Horses Got Wings, They Can Fly

DAVE MARSH

SHE WAS A FACTORY GIRL, A COAL STOVE VISIONARY AND THE SELF-PROCLAIMED SCION OF RIMBAUD AND THE RONETTES. WELL, THAT'S WHAT PATTI SMITH WANTED THE WORLD TO THINK BACK THEN.

Patti Smith saved my job as a ROLLING STONE feature writer, and I never even thanked her. Patti's story and my role in its early moments formed an article called "Her Horses Got Wings, They Can Fly," published in ROLLING STONE's first issue of 1976. The story remains the most complete account of Patti's peregrinations on the way to pop stardom ever compiled and, given that Smith, although absent many years from the pop scene, remains one of the more influential performers of the Seventies, needs no further justification—certainly less than it needed in '76, when she seemed an entirely impossible Rock & Roll Queen for the Bicentennial. What's more curious is why my job was jeopardized. Blame that on Mick Jagger. I always have.

Or maybe Joan Didion and John Gregory Dunne really deserve the blame. See, they were the ones scheduled to tour with the Rolling Stones in the summer of '75. This had nothing to do with me—I'd just been hired away from *Newsday* to replace Jon Landau as associate editor in charge of record reviews. This was a most prestigious role, which had been held by only three others: Landau, Greil Marcus and Ed Ward, all top-notch rockcrit names.

But I come from restless stock. My grandfather hunted deer for seventy-four consecutive years without ever shooting one, not out of animal-rights scruples but because he was constitutionally unable to sit still for five minutes and his gyrating alerted every beast within miles to his presence. This gene lurks within me also, and so, unlike previous reviews editors, who had made the Records section a fiefdom by holding it as their exclusive responsibility, my duties as enumerated during the discursive weekend hiring session at Jann Wenner's house in San Francisco consisted of editing the Records section and the Performance page, writing features, occasionally editing features and editing Ralph Gleason's Perspectives column.

All of this I actually did, with the exception of editing Ralph, because he died the day before I started work. I'd asked to edit Ralph because I knew him a little and liked him a lot. But there was no way to anticipate what his sudden death would mean to the magazine. ROLLING STONE in the mid-Seventies was no more somber than you'd think it was — I distinctly remember being in the offices for the fall of Saigon, the death of Elvis and the arrest of Patty Hearst, and none of those occasions was the least bit funereal. But Ralph's death threw everybody into mourning that approached despair; we were not and could not be prepared for his passing, especially so suddenly. More than any rock star's demise, this one sank in — as deeply as mortality ever sinks in when you're young and feeling invincible, as all of us were.

When I next heard from Jann, he phoned me at home with more trauma; Didion and Dunne had reneged on the Stones assignment. Part of the editorial genius that possesses Mr. Wenner, it seems, is his willingness to run with the hot hand. He'd decided that the new kid on the block — and a salary man, to boot — made the most suitable replacement.

Oh, unhappy day! Jann meant the assignment to be a plum. In those days the magazine covered tours by the Rolling Stones with an attentiveness other publications bring to presidential campaigns. But by '75, the Rolling Stones already struck me as pretty passé; their shows were more like tourist attractions, for people without interest in rock as music, than hard-core rock & roll events. Wenner would want a celebration; the readers would expect one. My jaundiced eye and music-critic's ear suggested that I'd be unlikely to deliver.

To top it off, Jann neglected to tell me that Mick Jagger harbored a (temporary, I guess) antipathy to ROLLING STONE. For six weeks, Jagger creatively (tediously, actually, but hey! he's *Mick Jagger*) evaded my daily requests for an interview. I wound up writing a story called "I Call and

Call and Call on Mick," a morose account and relatively lackluster piece of writing redeemed only by Jann's last-minute amplification of my hard-boiled-detective diction.

Not only had I failed at my first assignment, but when I got back home, things had become unstable at the office. Staying in New York had been an important precondition of my taking the job, partly because I didn't want to move my family but also because I wanted the independence that only a long-distance work relationship offers.

In 1975, ROLLING STONE's New York bureau was the place to be. It harbored Chet Flippo, Joe Klein, Jonathan Cott and my own all-time favorite among the magazine's feature writers, Tim Crouse. Reporters Tom Powers and Howard Kohn were often around. The redoubtable managing editor Marianne Partridge and senior editor Paul Scanlon had been transferred from San Francisco. Jann swore he loved this team, and I do believe he meant it, 'cause he soon announced that he was moving *all* of the magazine's staff to Manhattan. Glum news for a guy like me, who experiences supervision as surveillance.

The Records section and the Performance page chugged along. But the editors displayed all the lack of eagerness that you'd expect when it came to offering me another feature assignment. I've always loved being a critic, but like any writer, in my heart I'm a storyteller. Quite frankly, I needed a story that could be written in my own voice to establish my credentials as a feature writer.

A Patti Smith story was being prepared by a freelancer whose identity now eludes me. Because of my early relationship to Patti (as editor of *Creem*, I actually hold the distinction of being the very first to publish her poetry), Partridge asked me to read it. The story struck me as okay but not nearly good enough. I went to Partridge. Let me redo the story, I pleaded. I promise I can get further inside it than what you've got. Partridge gave me a shot.

Feeling slightly guilty about swiping someone else's assignment, I went to work. The interviews were fine — I remember talking to Patti on a gray day in a rehearsal hall near Times Square and seeing her in the Village at a poetry reading, but not much else. Rereading the story now, what strikes me is the peripheral but crucial role Robert Mapplethorpe played in it. (Patti's celebrity had then outstripped his, though obviously not for good.)

The real point was Smith's fables of her own origins. I must have believed most of the yarn, because I set it down so faithfully. Patti's stories mesmerized everybody who heard them — in fact, I'm sure if she told me the same stuff today, which she most certainly would not, I'd put it down just as plainly. Her claims about artistic independence amounted to little more than the kind of willful myth-mongering dabbled in by every rock star since Bob Dylan. But this time, the artist hadn't adopted a coy and convenient marketing strategy. In all her tale-spinning, Patti never swerved from her purpose, which was establishing the complete integrity, rock & roll authenticity and deep poetic purpose of Patti Smith the Artist. Patti knew she had something new to say, and her intent was to use it to inspire the masses.

About her chances of actually accomplishing this, I could afford to be dubious, since I was totally persuaded of her artistic validity. But I was wrong. "Her Heroes Got Wings" is quite unconsciously set amid the then-stirring CBGB punk scene that the Patti Smith Group inaugurated. Yet it never occurred to me to view Patti as part of anything so orderly as a trend or a movement. For me, her whole attraction stemmed from being one of a kind. If I'd paid more attention to her band, whose members I conceived of—perhaps inaccurately—as helpmates only, I'd probably have been more attuned to what Patti's project shared with the Ramones, Television and Talking Heads.

But ultimately, whether you believe that what became one of the great pop explosions could have been predicted six months or a year in advance depends, I suppose, on whether you think Malcolm McLaren was a true visionary or just a hustler who got lucky. Having watched him "manage" the New York Dolls, I've never had a doubt. One way or the other, I saw where Patti and her band came from far more clearly than where punk and New Wave were going.

Between us, Patti and I ensured that the major themes of punk and postpunk were covered, from the suspect credibility of record execs to the casual racism of the romantic bohemian narcissist.

Not surprisingly, Patti made it clear that she hated the story. "You always get it wrong, even when you get it right," she sneered backstage a few weeks later. I always figured she was annoyed about the part where I'd attacked her theory of the rock & roll boho as "the last white nigger," but it occurs to me now that maybe I'd hurt the feelings of Clive Davis, the head of Arista Records.

No matter. The editors of ROLLING STONE liked it. As well they should have. ROLLING STONE in my day was renowned as a "writer's magazine," but the actual line editors really ran the place quite imperiously. You could struggle with your copy for weeks, but a day before deadline, they'd simply say, "We have to cut four lines to make room for a photo caption." Protest rewarded only those who enjoyed placing themselves on the wrong side of a blank and beady stare. Editing "Her Horses Got Wings" gave me a memorable chill, since it was on this occasion that Partridge offered to discipline me by cutting all the articles (a, an, the) from my copy. I settled down immediately, not because I thought she would but because I knew she could.

Having run this gantlet, I was thereafter able to spend the better part of five years writing an assortment of feature-length articles for the magazine. Eventually, I wound up creating a column called American Grandstand, which was the successor to Ralph Gleason's Perspectives. (Jon Landau wrote one called Positively 84th Street for a few months in between.) By 1980 or so, I was able to do what I'd come to ROLLING STONE to achieve, which was to function as a writer on my own. Not that I left any more willingly than most of my colleagues.

Jann doesn't know this, but a little while after "Her Horses Got Wings" appeared, I overheard him down the hall, talking to someone in San Francisco—probably Ben Fong-Torres—late one evening. He was grousing about an editorial trouble spot. "Well, you know," he said, "Marsh made a mess of the Jagger interview. But that wasn't his story. When he got to do his own, he came through." Praise spoken behind your back is the kind that counts, I figure, and so I thank him now for what I didn't dare thank him for then.

I belatedly thank Patti, too, annoyed as she may have been (and after this account, may become again). But I still figure we're even: Who do you think introduced her to the guy who wrote "Because the Night"? His idea, not mine, I hasten to add. But then, I never have been very good at seeing into the future. Sometimes, though, it's enough just to be in the right place at the right time.

RS 203

JANUARY 1ST, 1976

> I was a little loose in the attic. When I was a kid I
> tied do-rags around my head tight. I was scared my
> soul would fly out at night. Scared my vital breath
> would make the big slip, some ventriloquist. So I
> steered from drugs and drew myself in full frenzied
> dance.
>
> —PATTI SMITH

She'd been dancing awhile when I first saw her. She walked into that Upper West Side party like a Jersey urchin who'd just inherited Manhattan. All in black—turtleneck and black slacks. She seemed more frail than she really was, but not fragile, though you could have counted her ribs, and her jet black hair straggled like waterlogged yarn. Her skin so pale it was nearly translucent, cheeks drawn so tight and thin I was tempted to pull her aside and offer her a decent meal. If only her teeth had been half rotted, she would have passed for Keith Richards's waif sister.

She glided across the room easy as any rock & roll queen in her beat-up Mary Janes, full of sex and innocence; every eye was pulled her way, every blabbing mouth set off in unison. All the women hated her then—the solidarity of sisterhood was not so firm in 1971—but the men were awed.

Even before the party, I had known who she was. Steve Paul, the blue-velvet Winter Brothers impressario, had stopped by my home in Detroit a few months earlier with a tape of a poetry reading. I didn't care much about poems, but Lenny Kaye, a fellow critic, was her backup guitar. Mostly I was intrigued by the idea of a girl Steve said was a ringer for Keith.

> *Have you seen*
> *dylans dog*
> *it got wings*
> *it can fly*

I don't remember what else she read but she took me right over. In her voice were not simply references but the very rhythms of rock & roll. I wanted to know more, maybe publish a few of her poems in the magazine I was editing. Steve thought bigger—he was gonna make her a rock & roll star.

> *Sixteen and time to pay off. I get this job in a Piss*
> *factory inspectin' pipe. 40 hours, $36 a week, but it's*
> *a paycheck Jack. It's so hot in here, hot like Sahara,*
> *I couldn't think for the heat. But these bitches are too*
> *lame to understand, too goddamn grateful to get this*
> *job to realize they're gettin' screwed up the ass.*
> *—"Piss Factory," 1974*

Patti Smith grew up in Pitman, a town in South Jersey, near Philly and Camden. Her father, a former tap dancer, worked in a factory; her mother, who gave up singing to raise a family, was a waitress.

As the oldest of four children, Patti took much responsibility for her two sisters, Kimberly and Linda, and a brother, Todd. To keep the kids interested, Patti made up stories and acted out plays. When she was seven, she had a siege of scarlet fever, during which she lay hallucinating in front of the "amoebic, jewel-shaped indigo flame" of a coal stove. Her imagination improved.

"I grew up in a tougher part of New Jersey than Bruce Springsteen,"

Patti says. "I wasn't horrified by Altamont, it seemed natural to me. Every high-school dance I went to, somebody was stabbed." At the time, Patti was completely infatuated with black music, black style. Her fondest adolescent memory seems to have been harmonizing to early soul records in the back of a high-school bus, or dancing to them in someone's basement.

Her rock & roll breakout began on a Sunday evening: "My father always watched Ed Sullivan, and he screamed at me, 'Look at these guys!' I was totally into black stuff, I didn't wanna see this Rolling Stones crap. But my father acted so nuts, it was like, he was so cool, for him to react so violently attracted me." As she wrote in 1973, "they put the touch on me. I was blushing jelly, this was no mama boy's music, it was alchemical. I couldn't fathom the recipe but I was ready, blind love for my father was the first thing I sacrificed to Mick Jagger."

But the recipe was more complicated. One day, when Patti was still in high school, Patti and her mother had a fight. To make up, Mrs. Smith brought home two Bob Dylan albums, "because he dresses just like you." Like most of us, Patti discovered in Dylan a passion for social injustice, a madness for language and a personal style. But Patti learned more. Like Dylan's, the myth of Patti Smith's origins is intricately constructed and endlessly fascinating. Unlike him, she has managed to keep most parts of it straight through several readings. No one knows how much is invented, how much flat fact. Maybe it all happened, maybe none of it. I'd rather not know—either way.

Unlike Dylan, or rock's other Westchester rebels, Patti was a true working-class girl. When she worked in a factory during and after high school, it was for the cash, not experience. (The experience did provide the basis of her epic "Piss Factory," though.) Still, in a tough lower-class town, she was strange, and so was everything about her, from her family and ideas to her body itself. It was reedy and breastless even then, as much a boy's as a woman's. Patti knew it; maybe she even exploited it: "Ever since I felt the need to choose I'd choose male. I felt boy rhythms when I was in knee pants. So I stayed in pants. I sobbed when I had to use the ladies' room. My undergarments made me blush. Every feminine gesture I affected from my mother humiliated me," she wrote in her 1967 poem called "Female."

Then she got pregnant. The circumstances don't matter—she was in junior college at the time—but she had the baby without getting married and gave it up for adoption. To Patti, the overwhelmingly female sensation of pregnancy was revolting and made her feel defiled. She wrote: "bloated. pregnant. I crawl through the sand. like lame dog, like a crab. pull my fat baby belly to the sea. pure edge. pull my hair out by the roots. roll and drag and claw like a bitch. like a bitch. like a bitch."

After she had the baby, she came to New York in 1967 and hung around Pratt, the Brooklyn art college. She claims she was driven to the city by "Light My Fire," the Doors hit that summer. Maybe she was. A little earlier, in the factory, she had discovered *Illuminations*, by Arthur Rimbaud, the French poet who wrote all his poetry before he was twenty. She spotted his face on the cover of a book and took off.

"He looked just like Dylan," she still says with a sense of wonder.

At Pratt, she met Robert Mapplethorpe, an artist "who looked like George Harrison. I was drawing. And he encouraged me to do bigger drawings and then write on my drawings and then I was writing these poems on the drawings. And he loved the poems. I was so nebulous when I came to New York, I had this total maniac energy and my *Don't Look Back* walk. And I met Robert and he helped me take all this totally nebulous energy and put it in a form."

She wanted to go to Paris to study art. With her younger sister, Linda, she left. "Then I thought, fuck art, I want to be a traveler. And you have to travel with all these paints and shit. And I like to be free. Sometimes, I think I'm a singer so I don't have to carry a drum kit around."

Paris was lonely for two girls who spoke no French. Then Godard's *One Plus One*, featuring the Rolling Stones recording "Sympathy for the Devil," was released.

"Oh God, we were there night and day. We'd come in the morning and watch it over and over and over again, for five days running. It was May and then I started having all this weird stuff happen to me. First of all, I got an English rock paper and it said that Brian Jones might leave the Stones, God! Wasn't that a heavy thing!"

The Smith sisters moved to a farm outside Paris, *Le Puits*, the Wishing Well. *One Plus One* plus the newspaper item created a strange disjunction in her night life; Patti Smith began to dream of Brian Jones.

"They were so real, and every one was the same. The first one, I was riding in this old Victorian carriage with Mick and Keith and they were talking to each other in this funny language. They kept talking about ritual, it reminded me of voodoo, Haiti or something. And Anita Pallenberg was sitting there real nervous, clutching her hands, I kept saying, 'Where's Brian? Where'd Brian go?' They'd say, 'Never mind.' Then I thought I saw him pass by in this big picture hat, like a Victorian duchess or something. It was one of these art dreams, like some Renoir movie with all these pastel colors. And then the rain started coming down, like Noah's rain. I got this weird feeling and I got out of the carriage and it was all Victorian, all English. And I looked and there was water rising about four feet and he was floating in this old Catherine the Great black Victorian dress and this big picture hat.

"So I told my sister about it and I forgot it. Then the next night the same thing happened. Now I don't even remember the dreams. I remember the second one was more Kenneth Anger, more homosexual, with switchblades. At the end, I came into the bathroom and his head was in the toilet. It was always water, you know?

"Then this big pot of boiling water spilled on me. In reality. I was in a lotta pain, had second degree burns or something, all over me, so they gave me belladonna and morphine. I went to sleep and I had this dream that I was crawling in a glass. And there was a whirlpool, rocks and river and ocean and whirlpool, and we were slipping, it was me and Brian, he had my ankle and he was holding on. I was clutching the grass and I felt really sick, and I was banging, banging the grass. I remember the grass being cool and wet. I grabbed something and it was a hem, I looked up and it was Brian. He said, 'Throw up.' He's saying, 'Spit it out. Spit it out.' He grabbed my hair and he says, 'Spit it out.' And I remember this white hem, like a Moroccan djellaba, grabbing it, and spitting up.

"I woke up, I was throwing up, and it was like I woulda . . . You know how they say Jimi Hendrix died? Well, that dream really blew my mind. I said to my sister, 'Let's go back to Paris.' Maybe we could call up—but I didn't know any rock people then, I didn't even know Bobby Neuwirth. That was the whole tragedy, that I was just totally nobody, I had no connections. I had no money, I couldn't fly to London. And I felt like I had this information that Brian Jones was gonna die. So we went back to Paris and the next day, I couldn't even find it in English, it just said, 'Brian Jones Mort.' "

She began to dream of her father now, about his heart. She and Linda decided to go home. When they arrived, her father was in bed. He'd had a heart attack.

She stayed in Pitman only briefly, then moved back to New York, into the Chelsea Hotel with Mapplethorpe. She was trying to write a requiem for Brian Jones. "That's when my life really blew apart. In a cool way." In the lobby of the Chelsea, she met Bobby Neuwirth, who had played Guildenstern to Bob Dylan's Rosencrantz through the middle Sixties. As Patti tells it, Neuwirth accosted her and asked where she had learned to walk. She replied, "From *Don't Look Back*," the Dylan movie in which Neuwirth was a principal, and the friendship was formed.

"He didn't really understand the whole Brian Jones thing," Patti explains. "But the thing was, he recognized something within the pieces, something that I didn't see. I didn't know what I was doing. I wasn't trying to create art or change the world, I was trying to rid myself of my guilt, my mania about it, my obsession." Neuwirth protected her, telling friends she wasn't a groupie, demanding they keep their hands off.

It was a heady time to be at the Chelsea. Throughout 1970, select parts of the Andy Warhol crowd were living there, as were William Burroughs, the Jefferson Airplane and Janis Joplin. So was playwright Sam Shepard. "He saw in me some other kinda thing. Sam liked the way I walked. He always inspired me to start fights in bar. He always pushed this other thing in me." Shepard, a leading figure just then in the Off-Off Broadway theater, and Patti cowrote a book of plays, *Mad Dog Blues*. But she and Shepard didn't last.

At first she worked as a clerk in Scribner's Fifth Avenue bookstore, for seventy-five dollars a week. Later, as she became better known, she wrote for a number of publications (including this one), scuffling for a living. Gerard Malanga, the Warhol acolyte (he rubber-stamped the signatures on the Warhol electric chair lithographs), invited her to share a reading at St. Mark's in the Bowery with him; with the encouragement of the Chelsea crowd, particularly the rock critic Lenny Kaye who backed her on guitar, she gave it a try. It won her a small cult, and the scene makers, ever aware of new faces, courted her avidly for a while. St. Mark's also won the interest of Steve Paul, the former club owner (the Scene, on West 46th Street, had been the biggest rock club in the city in the mid-Sixties), publicist (for the Peppermint Lounge, at seventeen), and now manager of Johnny and Edgar Winter. She aroused his entreprenerial instinct as no one since the blues brothers.

But Patti wasn't malleable, Steve wanted her to drop the poetry and start singing, perhaps with Edgar Winter. Although she was attracted by rock & roll, she wanted her poetry, too. "I've known I was gonna be a big shot since I was four," she said. "I just didn't know it had anything to do with my throat."

In early 1973, the Mercer Arts Center began to function as a focal point for glitter rock bands such as the New York Dolls. Patti hung around; she knew many of the musicians and business people from her Village haunts. And she was reintroduced to Jane Friedman, an acquaintance from the Chelsea days. Friedman was booking rock acts into one of the Mercer rooms and she let Patti open for them. Patti read without a mike or instrumentalist, bellowing through cupped hands or a megaphone at kids who liked to heckle, but both she and Friedman say Patti always won them over in the end, often by heckling back.

Finally, Patti, explaining that Friedman had always been present at the most crucial moments in her career, asked Jane to manage her. Presuming that she had a poet on her hands again—she had worked at the Gaslight in Greenwich Village during the era of beat poetry readings—Jane agreed.

What Patti Smith was about to attempt had been pulled off by no one before her. She fits no female rock stereotype, not the suppliant lover Joni Mitchell epitomizes nor Janis Joplin's brassy but vulnerable Little Girl

Blue. To get the total adulation she wanted, Patti would have to be as much her own creation as the greatest male stars. Like all of them — Jagger, Dylan, Bowie, Stewart — intense sexuality was sped along by gender ambiguity. The fascination with androgynous creativity and her own ability to exchange sexual roles influenced her early works. The aggressive lesbian imagery of her first book, *Seventh Heaven*, gave way to aggressive heterosexual fantasies.

In mid-1974, she and her band went into the studio to record a single on Mer Records, a label that had been invented and financed for the purpose by Lenny Kaye, Robert Mapplethorpe and Wartoke. The 45 contained her two key performance pieces, "Piss Factory" and "Hey Joe." The latter began as a sort of toast to Patty Hearst — "I was wonderin' were you gettin' it every night from a black revolutionary man and his woman," she said in the introductions, calling forth the sort of deep racial fears that inspired rock in the first place — and exploded into joyous cacophony.

Somewhere, Patti firmly believed, there was a place where Rimbaud's intense aesthetic lust met the Ronettes' boyfriend's stud passion. Surer than ever, she began to locate it, not just in her poetry but in her music — discovering ways to rework raunch classics like "Gloria," "Hey Joe" and "Land of a Thousand Dances" to fit her style — and in the look on her audience's face.

Suddenly, interest sprang up in another quarter. Clive Davis, president of Arista Records and formerly of CBS, was on the phone. Signing had one immediate result: at a May date at the Other End, Bob Dylan showed up. (Davis said he went as a personal favor.) "It was neat that I got to see Dylan, got to spend any time with him before I did my record," Patti says. "Even though we never discussed the record, I never discussed nothing. We never discussed nothing. We never talked. I mean we *talked* . . . You know how I felt? I been talking to him in my brain for twelve years, and now I don't have nothing to say to him. I feel like we should have telepathy by now. Me and my sister don't talk."

Through spring and half the summer, Patti sought a producer. Finally, she settled on John Cale. "My picking John was about as arbitrary as picking Rimbaud. I looked at the cover of *Fear* [Cale's 1974 solo record] and I said, 'Now there's a set of cheekbones.' But I hired the wrong guy. All I was really looked for was a technical person. Instead, I got a total maniac artist. I went to pick out an expensive watercolor painting and instead I got a mirror. It was really like *A Season in Hell*, for both of us. But inspiration doesn't always have to be someone sending me half a dozen American Beauty roses. There's a lotta inspiration going on between the murderer and the victim. And he had me so nuts I wound up doing this nine-minute cut ["Birdland"] that transcended anything I ever did before."

Recording *Horses* pushed Patti even further into the scarlet fever fantasy she had inhabited since childhood. And when her sense of mission becomes confused with her sense of fantasy, problems can arise. "I'm into rock & roll right now because there's a place for me. I don't think it's no accident that Bob Marley and me should be coming up at the same time. Not because I have anything to do with Bob Marley—I just feel like a whole new thing's happening. It's time to figure out what happened in the Sixties. What we can get from the Sixties is that people got so far out that old concepts were really dead. Everything that keeps us apart is really old news, man. People don't know it yet, but future generations will figure it out. That's why I'm working on a link—to keep it going."

But what if everything fails? If she is as fragile as some think, she will break and run at the first sign of rejection. If she's as tough as I think, she'll find a way.

As she wrote about a dream of the return of Brian Jones two years ago:

> *I can't help it. I cry out. How are you? Have you*
> *been all right. He smiles. He turns away and says: "I*
> *have everything under control."*

The Method
of His Madness

CHRIS HODENFIELD

WHAT DID IT TAKE TO FACE DOWN THE GREAT BRANDO
AT THE HEIGHT OF HIS MARLONOSITY? A LARGE DOSE
OF HIPNESS OR JUST PLAIN BALLS?

When I first hoisted myself into Marlon Brando's Dodge van, I was struggling badly with the electric shakes. It was the summer of 1975, and in the world of maximum-charisma actors, Brando was the unassailable king. Jack Nicholson had warned me that whatever I imagined Brando was going to be, in person he was going to be a *lot more*. You'd have thought I was meeting Mao Zedong.

I was but a fresh-faced, longhaired punk, just twenty-five, in a psyche-delic shirt out of *Arabian Nights*. I had flown to Montana on the promise of getting perhaps an hour with Brando, who was there filming *The Missouri Breaks*. The reasons for my stroke of good fortune were not entirely clear. Something I had written about director Robert Altman had appealed to one of Brando's allies. But the real reason, I expect, was that I was carrying credentials from ROLLING STONE. In 1975 there were still clear divisions between straight and hip. It wasn't like today, when everybody is clothed in the same vague shopping-mall casual funk. Brando had no interest in talking with a booze-hound Broadway columnist with meaty sideburns and a jazzy necktie, here to ask what it was *really* like to work with Frank Sinatra.

A guy from ROLLING STONE might be different. Brando had a subscription. When Daniel Schorr wrote a big story about the CIA, for instance, Brando would call down for ten extra copies. A ROLLING STONE guy would want to know if the situation was cool.

Being cool was then considered a heightened state of moral sanctity, like being wealthy today. Anyway, the code of cool let you get away with wearing an *Arabian Nights* shirt in public.

That's what helped ROLLING STONE get through its first ten lean and thread-bare years of existence—it was serving as the arbiter of cool. Celebrities and politicians who fell afoul of the code often got brutally hammered. And we who made the decisions at ROLLING STONE were a real Barbary Coast stew pot of infidels and washouts.

Before it settled down in New York in the late Seventies, ROLLING STONE was scattered all over the world. The magazine was like a great flophouse for itinerant wordsmiths. People wandered through the door and drank coffee from your cup. Often in your travels you had to flop on some other writer's couch. I can recall nights at Don Katz's flat in London, Howard Kohn's in San Francisco and Bob Greenfield's in Carmel. And I don't know how many times some visiting ROLLING STONE dignitary bunked on my sofa. We all assumed that Hunter Thompson had the only expense account in the joint.

As I say, it was a good place for migrant writers, and that's how I found myself joining up in 1970. I had been slumming around Spain and Morocco that year. I fell by England, where my brother Jan was running the London office, and the next thing you know I was assigned to infiltrate a recording session where Howlin' Wolf was mixing it up with Eric Clapton. As I would find over the next fourteen years, in places such as the door to Brando's van, being from ROLLING STONE got you inside.

Nothing about the magazine was secure. The whole staff was a shipload of transient poets and fools on a voyage of self-discovery. I moved along with it. After a couple of years in London, I spent a season in the bare-bones New York office. Then I packed all my gear in a $300 Cadillac and moved to the L.A. office, which was also an open-door kind of down-home precinct. The main office at that time was in San Francisco, and it was a raunchy old factory, a palace of intrigues, the nerve center of sudden and inexplicable decisions, the Plato's Retreat of surging excess.

Visiting writers would hit the San Francisco office like sailors on leave. You never knew if you were going to strike it rich or if you were going to get rolled, bitten and tattooed and lose your watch in the fun house.

All writers need something resembling a home, and ROLLING STONE was a natural asylum. Some writers, like Robin Green, Bob Greenfield, Julia Cameron and Tim Ferris, lit up the magazine famously for just a few years before moving on to books and movies. Then there were guys like Robert Palmer, Cameron Crowe, Tim Cahill, Charlie Perry, Joe Klein, Mikal Gilmore and Tim Crouse, who like me revolved in and out, year after year, doing the work of our lives one month and then the following month wondering what the hell comes next. You couldn't easily leave it. In all the anarchy, though, the writers had that fiery central point of inspiration—each other. You couldn't risk writing like a jerk, because all these other guys would run the table on you.

My province became the movies, and I had to abide by the standards set down at the magazine by Grover Lewis, a Texas poet with troubled eyes that still saw everything. Grover *heard* everything, too. In his stories on *The Last Picture Show*, Lee Marvin and Sam Peckinpah, Grover's people rose off the page in clouds of limelight. His sweeping, strong-arm prose showed us that even if we were only writing about showbiz, it was worth it if your writing glowed in the dark.

And that was just Grover. I think all of us ROLLING STONE writers were teaching each other lessons every two weeks. Then Hunter Thompson hit the bigs, and we all had to learn a few more moves.

This camaraderie, this group hauteur, is what gave an unlettered sap like me the fiber, the temerity, to face down someone like Brando. The only other person I would meet with an equal physical force field would be Kareem Abdul-Jabbar, who is seven feet tall. As I sat with Brando for what turned out to be a week of conversation, I was hanging on to a runaway train. But I had the ROLLING STONE writer's attitude to remind me that, loud shirt and all, I was in charge.

For years after the Brando story came out, it proved to be my footlong, jewel-encrusted calling card. Theater people treat Brando's utterances as if they were Holy Writ, and I was hailed as an apostle.

I remember one aspiring actor who had to know, *had to know*, what Brando was really like. I cranked up a few more stories about Brando's intense way of paying attention, his way of boring right into people's skulls. "Brando really listens to people," I concluded.

The actor heard this and got a little defensive. "Well," he said, "I really listen to people, too." Then he shrugged it off. "But, you know, most of the time they don't have anything to say."

The poor dope had written his own epitaph. In a way, he spoke for all Hollywood, a place where long ago, in a delirium of cash, they just stopped listening to people.

At ROLLING STONE, I got lucky. I had fallen in with people who could see and who could listen. They helped me get the moments down on paper.

Marlon Brando's body was going through the motions, awaiting the return of his personality. It was miles away. He was reeling it in like a dancing sailfish.

His van was parked by the trees in a grassy field. Inside it was quiet. The air conditioner diced the air. Minutes had passed since our introduction, but he just sat on the edge of the bed, hands in a drawer fumbling aimlessly with a hank of wires. He picked up a screwdriver and turned it over carefully.

Here was a hero whose vanity had surrendered. Beneath those wide oakstump shoulders was a vast rippling cargo hold, 240 pounds on a 5-foot-10 frame. It was neat enough in here, a small brown space piled high with books on solar energy and Indian history, and his two congas. Cupboards were stacked with fresh T-shirts, clean towels, and the icebox was filled with Tab.

When at last he found what he was looking for—a cassette tape of Caribbean drum music—he eased across the bed and rested his head against the curtained window. The silvery blond hair rolled over his ears.

That face. He looks an old medicine man. He appears as unmovable as the city planetarium. The concentration level is so high that when his distant manner suddenly evaporates and he has questions about your mother, ah, the arena gets hot.

He is, indeed, a presence. On the cowboy movie set of *The Missouri Breaks*, shot on the hot dry plains of Montana, people seemed to be no more deferential to the actor than they'd be to any pharaoh about to exact tribute.

Which is not the normal attitude for a hard-boiled movie crew. They'd see him walking in their direction, with that head balled up like a clenched fist, that forehead all knotted and complicated. People were embalmed with awe. Beethoven must have had the same air. The costar here, Jack Nicholson, had to laugh: "The man does scorch the earth, right? I mean, for 200 miles in any direction. Not much leavin's."

I wasn't in that van five minutes and I was playing catch-up ball. He does not take up a point and extrapolate to the far measures. He *starts* on a virgin asteroid and winds his way back to earth, free versing and free associating, leaving behind his poetic blur of images about the Russian troops hovering at the Mongolian border, and what starvation does to a baby's brain, and the time we drove through the African riverbeds during monsoon season. . . .

Even if the Pakistanis are the haughtiest people in the world, this is a planetary community, and Wendell Willkie saw it coming, the One World concept, but they laughed him off the stage. Anyway, atolls are notoriously short of nitrogen layers unless you go down below the coral reefs. . . .

He sat absolutely still, his shoulders parked on the pillow like a grand piano. The sad, brooding eyes drank in all the details. And as for the relationship between his body and the space around him, Bernardo Bertolucci's observation was very true. "We are usually dominated *by* space," the *Last Tango* director told Jonathan Cott, "but Brando strangely *dominates* space. Even if Brando is absolutely still, say, sitting on a chair . . . Brando has already taken for himself that privileged space. And Brando's attitude toward life is different from that of other people because of this fact."

Any mention of moviedom would be sidestepped very neatly. Finally I asked if he loathed the subject. "No," he said, shaking his head with no great commitment. The eyes darted and the great train pulled into a distant station.

"Films . . . it's funny. People buy a ticket. That ticket is their transport to a fantasy which you create for them. Fantasyland, that's all, and you make their fantasies live. Fantasies of love or hatred or whatever it is. People want their fantasies over and over. People who masturbate usually masturbate with, at the most, four or five fantasies. By and large.

"Most people like the same food and they like the same kind of music, they like the same kind of sexual fantasy for a period of time, then maybe it changes. As it is in children. Who is it?" He drummed the dashboard. "Bruce Lee. That's the hero. Then you grow up and grow out of your Bruce Lee period, or your Picasso Blue Period, and go into another period.

"But with kids, because they outpower us, because they have no representation, because they are so dependent, all they think about is power. Dinosaurs or the Million Dollar Man, because they feel so helpless, because they have no way out of it, except fantasy. Because they are only that tall.

"And that's all films are." He had a concerned knit to his voice, like a preacher talking about his poverty. "Just an extension of childhood, where everybody wants to be freer, everybody wants to be powerful, everybody wants to be so *overwhelmingly* attractive that there's just no doing anything about it. Or everybody wants to have comradeship and to be understood.

"They become lullabies. They're 'tell-me-again-Daddy' stories. That's all television is: 'Tell me again, Daddy, about the good guy and the bad guy and the strong guy and Kung Fu and Flash Gordon.' "

His voice grew soft. "People love to hear the stories, they love to hear the lullabies.

"Tastes change, but the function doesn't. I might as well be Jimmy Cagney in *White Heat*. The same story, the positive and the negative, the yin and the yang, the antihero.

"You know, so often, creative or positive things are accomplished for reasons that are totally irrelevant. They're done out of vanity, or out of anxiety or fear. There's a book written by Joseph Campbell. He was fascinated by symbols, not unlike Jung. He psychoanalytically treated the hero. The name of the book was *Hero with a Thousand Faces*." He gestured with an open hand, as if smoothing the ruffled air. "But *evil* has a thousand faces.

"There's no fooling. People are sheep. They'll just do any fucking thing. Anything. I mean, the sum total of everything I believe is the sum total of everything I've read, seen. I'm not told how to do it, it's just . . . something's influenced me. James Joyce or Schopenhauer or my Aunt Minnie.

"But everybody's looking for the man on the white horse, everybody's looking for the one who will tell the Truth. So you read Lao-Tzu, you read Konrad Lorenz, I don't know who else, Melville, Kenneth Patchen, somebody you think is not a bullshitter. Somebody who has the eyes of a saint and the perceptions of a ghost.

"They're gonna tell us the way, they're gonna show us. They never really do, and we run around being cheap imitations of all those influences."

He arrested his thought and glanced at my hands. I was twirling my sunglasses.

"What you're doing now, playing with your glasses and looking at me. Shaking your head in moments you don't plan on."

I stopped playing with my glasses, blinked and smiled.

"And blinking and smiling, moving your head. You see, all those are unplanned things. You don't know what you're going to do in sequence. Now the mere fact that I mentioned it set off a whole bunch of movements on your face. Because in some small measure you were frightened by it. Everybody has a very low threshold of fear, and they carry it around and they don't know it. They don't know that they're being afraid if they do something like that. You talk to some people and they'll hang on your eyes for maybe a 12-count and they'll just *have* to get away. They can't stand eye contact. They'll look everywhere . . . and once in a while they'll give you a little flick just to make it look real.

"But they can't stand it. They're the only ones who know it, unless you're aware of patterns of gestures.

"Shakespeare said something that was remarkable. You don't hear it very often. He said, 'There is no art that finds the mind's construction on the face.' Meaning that there is the art of poetry, music or dancing, architecture or painting, whatever. But to find people's minds by their face, especially their face, is an art and it's not recognized as an art."

You're in the business of storing up memories.

"Well, we're just big computers is all. You inevitably store stuff up, and for no reason at all; right in the middle of a conversation, you'll start thinking of a short-handled hoe. It won't be related to anything, except something in your dreams has to do with a rubber telephone. 'Why was I thinking about a rubber telephone?' " He shrugged it off.

I had the impression that you were dredging up your own memories for *Last Tango*. Were they painful?

"No, because after a while it becomes a technical thing. I was putting things in my eyes to make tears in my eyes. I was making the right noises, the sounds of sobs. But, ah, I used to do that stuff straight. But it's too taxing."

He emphasizes such a point with a pincerlike grab at his chest. "For instance, now I don't even learn the lines. I don't learn them for a very specific reason, but . . ." He groped for a reason, and his eyes rested on me: "You see, you didn't know you were gonna look down just then."

I interrupted myself in mid-glance.

"You didn't plan on it, you just did it. And if you know your lines, very often, most of the time it sounds like, 'Mary-had-a-little-lamb-its-fleece-was-white-as-snow.' And people intuit, they unconsciously *know* that you have planned that speech. And they know, for instance, that when you get up to leave, and walk a certain, say, five steps to the doorway and then stop"—he pulled himself up and stopped at the bathroom door, suddenly a punk, and slouching—"they *know* that you're gonna turn around and say, 'Why, don't you ask Edith, then you'll find it in the shoe box.' And then walk out the door."

He disappeared into the bathroom. The theatrical voltage arrives at such a leisurely pace that it successfully dismantles your defenses.

He bounced back out of the bathroom. "But they already beat you to the fucking scene! So that doesn't keep them outta the popcorn. You always have to be ahead of the audience, or the audience is always ahead of you."

Still, I said, *Last Tango* seemed like more than mere technique.

He waved it off. "No, when you . . ." Suddenly, his face clenched and turned away.

Jesus, I thought, maybe I hit a sore spot. He was definitely disturbed. His lips taut, his eyes torn. A sob gurgled in his throat and his shoulders shook. For an instant I was paralyzed. I stared at him.

Abruptly, his grief collapsed into a smile. "You just do that, you know. It just sounds like a bunch of tears. You make your face to go happy or to get mad. It's too costly to crank up. It's just too costly. If you can get by with a technical performance, nobody knows the diff. They can't tell."

I guess not, I said, wiping my palms on the bedspread. The key to his emotions seems to be in his upper lip. He has a very expressive upper lip. It lifts with a challenge, purses down when the irony of this earth gets serious. He cushions himself with irony.

I asked him if the *Last Tango* details were autobiographical.

"Oh, well he [Bertolucci] had some cockamamie notion. What he wanted to do was sort of meld the image of the actor, the performer, with the part. So he got a few extraneous details. Played the drums, I don't know . . . Tahiti . . . so that the man is really telling the story of his life. I don't know what the hell it's supposed to mean. He said, 'Give me some reminiscences about your youth.' That made me think about milking a cow, my mother's getting drunk, one thing and another. He went, 'Wonderful, wonderful.'"

Brando grinned at the thought, leaned back and joined his hands behind his head. I said that several of my friends were upset because the elements were too outrageous. They couldn't take Brando in the role. It was too close.

"Not as far as I'm concerned. I would never, I'd never . . . there's a certain line you draw . . . I mean, in the days when I used to have to crank up emotionally, I would think of things that were very personal, but I would never exploit those in a film. For some goddamn check that came in at the end of the week. Or a director. He wanted to give that impression, so . . ."

He ruminated on a distant cloud. His jaw flexed.

"I don't think Bertolucci knew what the film was about. And *I* didn't know what it was about. He went around telling everybody it was about his prick!"

The laugh sounded like an asthma attack. "He looks at me one day and he says, you know . . . something like, 'You are the embodiment, or reincarnation . . . you are the . . . symbol of my prick.' I mean, what the fuck does that mean?"

When you're around Brando for a while, you think not only of his comedic timing, but that he'd probably be a perceptive director. He's only directed once, a western called *One-Eyed Jacks* (after Kubrick was fired from preproduction).

Do you have any more taste for the job?

"I did it once," he said, shaking his head. "It was an ass-breaker. You work yourself to death. You're the first one up in the morning . . . I mean, we shot that thing on the run, you know. You make up the dialogue the scene before, improvising, and your brain is going crazy."

You wrote the script, I take it.

"Yes. But it's better if you make it up, of course. Unless you're doing Eugene O'Neill. You can't wing that." He pulled up a dimply grin. "You can do it to Tennessee Williams, somebody that can write something. But you get in a picture with six guys like that, it's like an old whore in a lumber camp who's been fucked till she can't see straight."

The question is, how deep do you go with your improvisation?

"Well, it depends on what you're doing. If you're doing a hit-the-roof scene, you have to gas up, sorta. You don't have to kill yourself. When I first started, it was in a movie called, ah . . . *The Men*. And I got there at something like 6:30, and by 9:30, when they were ready to shoot, I had shot my wad."

You were that psyched up?

"In the dressing room, yeah. I was all set to go. I had music," he waved and snapped his fingers, "and I had poetry, everything to transport me into another realm. So I came out dry as a bone.

"If you do a scene any number of times, you just go dry. Unless you crank up very slowly to it. And then snap out of it at take 13. It all depends on the director; if he's fiddling around with this technical issue, there's no sense in cranking up. Because you know he's not going to print anything until the seventh take, he's just rehearsing himself.

"The trouble is, when you're playing one part, the director is playing another, and the writer is playing another part. Everybody's got a different idea. That's why it's better to get the signals straight up front. A lot of directors want to know *everything*. Some directors don't want to know anything. Some directors wait for you to bring everything to them."

John Huston, who did *Reflections in a Golden Eye*, he was supposed to be a free-swinging guy.

"Ah, well. Yeah. He gives you about 25 feet. He's out in the background. He listens. Some guys listen, some guys are auditory; some guys are visual. Some guys are both. He's an auditory guy and he can tell by the tone of your voice whether you're cracking or not. But he leaves you alone pretty good.

"It's the no-talent assholes who get on your back, who all think they're Young Eisenstein Misunderstood, or Orson Welles, or somebody like that. And you know fucking well when they say 'print,' that it's just thumbs-up-the-ass place. Those are the guys that are tough to work with. Chaplin you got to go with. [Charles Chaplin directed him in *A Countess from Hong Kong*.]

"Chaplin is a man whose talent is such that you have to gamble. First off, comedy is his backyard. He's a genius, a cinematic genius. A comedic talent without peer. You don't know that he's senile. Personally, he's a dreadful person. I didn't care much for him. Nasty and sadistic and mean . . ."

His voice trailed off. "*Oh God.* He's like aaa!!!! . . . You got to stop them because they'll get on you. You got to stop them dead. But nevertheless you have to separate that personal life from that artistic life. One has *nothing* to do with the other. It's like writers, or anything else.

"You can't think that understanding people, or perceptive and sensitive people, are going to be perceptive and sensitive in other areas of human relationships. It just doesn't hold true. Talent has nothing to do with it, that's all.

"There are shits who are very understanding and extremely talented, and there are shits who are without a shred of talent. There's good guys on both sides."

That night he was anxious to scram.

Get out of town, wash off the makeup, pull on the T-shirt, get this van moving. He knew there was a good place to camp out by the next day's location, an isolated ravine.

The blue shadows of scrub prairie pines grew in the long light of evening. We swung on to the Interstate. Marlon steered the lumbering van in his own way. Slow and confident.

Spending a week around the guy, it was easy to stew about his massive acting talent going to waste. All those years he was making dog movies, and now he's got offers for every role going, from Aristotle Onassis to Papa Hemingway. When I asked about his present work ethic, he expelled a large, grudging sigh.

"I built a little house in Tahiti," he said at last. "Out of sticks and grass and palm trees, droppings. That gave me an enormous sense of satisfaction. Whenever I can physically achieve some simpler way of doing something.

"Work ethics are funny things. The Tahitians couldn't give three-ninths of two pieces of lizard shit about working.

"It's such a small planet now. I *used* to think that up in the hills of Afghanistan, where the Kurds were, it was light-years away. You go to the interior forests where the Pygmies are now getting shafted. Same with the Masai, now split right down the middle between Uganda and Tanganyika. And Tanganyika says, listen, you can't show your dick anymore."

The road gave way to rutted farmtracks. The tension seemed to be easing away from his shoulders. "I mean, where do you find hope?

"On the island, there's an ample opportunity to demonstrate that it can be done . . . to put these technologies together . . . with wind and methane and solar energy. I want to build it in my own house and then just make a little flick about that.

"I've got a little community developing down there, for an experimental hotel. I dropped a considerable amount of money in research and development. I invented a windmill, but to actually produce wind is quite a trick. My wife and kids are there."

We pulled up on a rise. Somewhere on these yellow fields was the campsite. "Do you have 'journalist' on your passport?" he asked, scanning the plains. My passport doesn't say anything, I said. You mean the immigration cards?

"It must say something. I got so sick of writing 'actor' down on my passport that I wrote 'shepherd.' And it didn't make any difference. Except one dry English immigration officer." He set down the glasses and struck a Commander Schweppes pose. " 'Haws your flawk, Mr. Brando?' I said, 'Doing very well.' 'I'm delighted to hear it.' Didn't smile at all."

He dropped back into gear and shoved off.

Brando had only a few days of moviemaking left. His 15-year-old son, Miko, was to join him for a slow drive back to Los Angeles. They had plans together for the desert, the woods and the rivers. Father was just about finished building a river raft out of inner tubes and two-by-fours.

That night, while he camped alone, the thunderheads rolled overhead. He sat in the dark with a pocket computer, counting and estimating the proximity of the lightning strikes. It travels 1100 feet per second. Enough, he said, to make him feel religious.

Notes on a Native Son

JOE KLEIN

ARLO GUTHRIE TALKED ABOUT HIS LEGENDARY FA-
THER, HIS CRAZY CHILDHOOD, GOD AND DOUBT TO A
VISITOR WHO ARRIVED AT HIS DOOR THROUGH A
TWIST OF FATE.

This is a long story. It began sometime in 1975, with Ralph Nader. I'm not sure it's over yet. It began when Jann Wenner asked
me to do the ROLLING STONE Interview with Nader—not the
most thrilling job, I thought at first, but Ralph was burbling
with ideas and statistics (his normal state of grace, I later learned). One
of his stats had to do with the number of American workers who die of
job-related disease or injury each year. It was a terrible number, and I
decided to make the statistic human by finding and writing about one of
them. He turned out to be a fellow named Charlie Arthur. He was dying
of a rare form of liver cancer, traceable to the polyvinyl chloride gas he
breathed on the job (the gas, it turned out, was a high; the workers liked
getting juiced on it—a moral complication that made the story less politically correct but more human).

It should be noted that Jann and associate editor Marianne Partridge
encouraged me in this, even though the story (*a*) did not involve a celeb-

rity, (b) was bound to be depressing and (c) was time-consuming in the extreme. I would remember their enthusiasm with amazement years later—deep in the Eighties—when most magazine assignments (a) were inevitably profiles of soulless, self-centered celebrity ciphers, (b) had to be bubbly enough to please a press agent and (c) could entail no more "research" than lunch.

Anyway, I spent months on this. It was compelling, emotionally overwhelming work. But it was not, to put it mildly, an up. Indeed, I was wiped out when Charlie Arthur died; I spent weeks moping around the old ROLLING STONE office on East Fifty-sixth Street. Eventually, Dave Marsh, an editor and writer, noticed my dismay. "You've been working here for years," he said. "Don't you think it's time you lightened up a bit? You should write a music piece—you've never done that. Do Springsteen. Hang out at the beach with him. Have fun."

I had to admit, it sounded pretty good. Marsh said he was about to go up to Massachusetts to do a piece about Arlo Guthrie. "He's the last of the line," David said. "He's the end of that whole folk tradition."

Marsh said he'd take his story idea and mine to Wenner. And then Jann made one of those eerie, inexplicable moves that great intuitive editors sometimes make: "No," he told Marsh. "You do Springsteen. Klein does Guthrie."

The result, of course, was that Marsh spent the next decade explaining Springsteen to the world—and I spent the next few years writing a book on Arlo's dad, Woody Guthrie, which eventually would have some impact on Springsteen's life and music (which eventually Marsh would write about). I told you this was a long story.

First, though, there was Arlo: I liked him from the start. He was smart, funny, sensitive, vulnerable (to Huntington's disease, which had killed his father) and refreshingly sane about the difference between his own—substantial—talents and Woody's genius. The research for this, my first and last music "celebrity" profile, involved a bit more than lunch. Arlo invited me up to his farm in Massachusetts—and into his family—for one of the most memorable Christmases I've ever spent. As it happened, the folk-singing son of a bitch also was using me to send a message to his mother: He had converted to Catholicism (Marjorie Guthrie was Jewish). His method of announcing this was curious and, in the family tradition, ironically understated. We came in from grocery shopping on the afternoon before Christmas, and a monk ("in full battle dress," I wrote at the time) was vacuuming the living-room rug. He was a Franciscan, and so, as it happened, was Arlo.

Anyway, we stayed in touch after Christmas, and six months later, Arlo came down to New York for one of his sister Nora's dance programs. The entire Guthrie clan was there, including Harold Leventhal—agent to all Guthries, a fabulous human, perhaps America's only former communist brassiere manufacturer—who approached me during the intermission: "No one has ever written a book about Woody," he said. "Would you be interested?"

No, I said. I was a political writer. I didn't even like folk music very much.

"Weird thing happened," I told Arlo later. "Harold asked me if I wanted to write a book about Woody."

"Do it," he said. "And tell the truth. Anyone else they'd get would be full of shit."

I agreed to think about it some more: Woody's life was a great story. He'd been born on the frontier; lived in the Dust Bowl; moved to Hollywood in the Thirties, New York in the Forties; and died in a mental hospital in Queens. His life also was a way of writing about politics: the cultural history of the American left, especially the Communist party (to which Woody had been informally appended) and the ultimate failure of the socialist dream. I went to speak with Arlo's mother about it. "You really want this done?" I asked. "It could get pretty painful."

"There's nothing you could write that would be more painful than telling me my son had turned Catholic," Marjorie Guthrie said. "Anyway, you're the first one Harold's come up with who seems mature enough to handle my sex life."

Oh. It did turn out to be an interesting sex life—and a wonderful two years, writing *Woody Guthrie: A Life.*

There are several footnotes of interest: Years later I bumped into Jon Landau at the party for Chet Flippo's book about Hank Williams. "You know, Bruce loved your book," he said. "He's been obsessed with Woody ever since—wait till you hear his next album."

It was *Nebraska.* Springsteen's work ever since has proved that Marsh was wrong: The tradition of telling the stories of average folks in song— whether the medium is folk, rock or whatever comes next—remains as strong as it ever was. (I have no doubt, by the way, that if Woody were alive today, he'd be heavily into rap; he always loved words better than music—in part because he couldn't sing a lick—and was, along with Leadbelly, one of the popularizers of the "talking blues" form.)

And finally: Years passed. One day I got a call from a miniseries producer at CBS: "We'd like to do your Guthrie book," he said. I told him it wasn't a bad idea. "But," he continued nervously, "there's one thing: Could you get Springsteen to play Woody?"

Well, I'd never met Springsteen and still haven't. But, Bruce, if you're interested, I'm sure the offer is still out there. This is a story—and a tradition—with legs.

Arlo picked me up at the Pittsfield airport a few days before Christmas in his beige Checker touring car, outfitted with a CB radio and a massive German shepherd named Max-Two-Million. The car, at once bizarre and unassuming, seemed a perfect reflection of Arlo's lifestyle.

He lives with his wife Jackie, their three children and an apparently limitless supply of dogs and pet ducks on a 260-acre farm overlooking a placid valley deep in the Berkshire Mountains. Officially, the farm is located in the town of Washington, Massachusetts, population 486. The land is classic New England, rutted and rocky, with stands of white birch, pine and maple. The air is so sharp it almost crackles in winter. Around Christmas, the sun shines briefly and obliquely, casting long shadows on the ground and wild color patterns in the sky. Often it snows.

Arlo, at age 29, appears stronger and ruddier than he did in the late Sixties when, for a brief while, he was America's favorite hippie. His face is rounder now, less chipmunky. There is a thin wisp of mustache that seems more a halfhearted attempt at camouflage than anything else. His hair, still wild and curly, is speckled with a surprising amount of gray. His speaking voice hasn't a hint of the nasal resonance that makes his singing so distinctive.

"I'm on vacation so there isn't much happening now. But then there's never all that much happening up here," he said when we reached the farm that first afternoon. "Jackie and I are probably the two most lazy people on earth."

Not having anything else to do, Arlo and I immediately fell into a clumsy, rather disjointed discussion about the state of the world. Arlo spoke elliptically—another shower of pronouns—but the basic thought seemed to be that life, especially in the cities, had gone berserk and was about to come crashing down around our ears. He was safe with his family, up on the farm. They could produce food if everything collapsed. Then he said, "People are going to have to make a choice soon. You see, I think things are black and white. I think you make an absolute choice in your life between right and wrong."

An idyllic childhood, as Marjorie describes it. The musical Guthries facing adversity together. The stories—about the $80 guitar, playing the harmonica for Leadbelly—have grown stiff and inflexible over time. Other stories: Arlo's hootenanny bar mitzvah (Marjorie is Jewish), held in a loft on Second Avenue and featuring Pete Seeger, Lee Hays, Cisco Houston and the rest of the folk community that drifted in and out of the Guthrie home. The walks on the beach at Coney Island where they lived, poor but happy, in a tiny house. Woody playing games with the kids.

But Woody just wasn't around that much after the children were born—the memories have been stretched to cover the horror—and when he was there, it could be frightening when he stumbled about, slurring his words, or when he flew into a rage. His Huntington's Disease was already quite advanced, but no one knew.

And so they'd all go to the hospital together on weekends, or the current surrogate would go out to the hospital and fetch Woody and they would all be together—Marjorie, her friend, the children and Woody, watching it all as his nervous system deteriorated and he gradually lost control of his wildly flailing arms and legs, and then his ability to speak . . . finally a mute presence, cigarette dangling from a corner of his mouth.

Arlo watched it quietly too, no doubt confused by all that was going on around him. It wasn't until he went to a private school in the sixth grade and heard the kids singing "Pastures of Plenty" that he realized other people knew Woody's songs. The school, Woodward in Brooklyn, was an integral part of the New York left-intellectual culture and one of the few places where people *would* know Woody's songs in the Fifties. Arlo grew up in that culture, with all the awkward advantages and disadvantages that accrue to the son of a celebrity. He was naturally shy, lousy at sports, disinterested in schools, a loner. There was money in the family for the first time—Harold Leventhal had begun to copyright Woody's songs and royalties were starting to flow, especially after the Weavers recorded "So Long It's Been Good to Know Yuh".

The amazing thing about "Alice's Restaurant" was how it just kept growing; each time its popularity seemed to crest, something new happened and it began to grow again. Even before the album was released, Arlo had blown apart the 1967 Newport Folk Festival and a tape of the song was getting airplay on underground radio stations. Then the album and a sold-out concert tour. At the age of 20, Arlo had achieved a commercial success that dwarfed anything Woody had ever done. Woody, by then, was near death at Creedmoor State Hospital and was physically unable to do much more than smile when Harold Leventhal brought a copy of the record and played it for him. "He looked at the cover," Harold said, "and you could tell he was enjoying it." Several months later, in October 1967, Woody was dead.

The Alice's Restaurant phenomenon continued to grow: there would be a movie of the song. But not just some commercial rip-off—a sensitive movie, directed by Arthur Penn, that seemed, as the song itself did, to sum up all the wonders and horrors of the time. Now *Look* and *Life* and the *New York Times* were chasing Arlo for interviews. *Newsweek* put him

on the cover as the ultimate hippie, the voice of the "Woodstock generation." Elsewhere he was described as "a stringy, now-generation genius
who looks as though he has stepped out of a Modigliani portrait." An
astrology magazine (and Arlo was usually reported as being obsessed with
astrology and the occult) bannered: MOONCHILD ARLO GUTHRIE: TELL
THEM TO GET READY, THE SPACESHIPS ARE COMING. Almost single-
handedly he changed the meaning of the word "freak," and the *Newsweek*
reporter, among others, was driven to distraction by the strange new way
of life he encountered: "Arlo and his friends talk very little . . . good
things are either 'outasight,' 'far out' or 'groovy'; bad things are invariably
'plastic' or 'bring downs' and . . . this argot is used to cover practically
every reaction."

Arlo managed to survive it all by retreating into that perverse, obstinate
sanity that Pete Seeger calls his "self-discipline." He simply refused to
take the hoopla seriously. "I loved it because it was absurd," Arlo recalled.
"All that attention because of a VW bus filled with garbage."

About once a year, a new Arlo Guthrie album would appear. As time
passed, his music seemed to become more traditional. The hippie image
faded, but the hippie sensibility—innocent and yet ironic—remained his
greatest strength. The albums were unfailingly pleasant, good-natured and
intelligent. The reviews usually were respectful. In addition to his own
songs and usually one of Woody's per album, Arlo probed the edges of
the folk tradition, including cowboy songs, nonsense tunes, gospel . . . and
even, on his latest album, the Rolling Stones' "Connection," which he
calls "a great modern folk song." It took a pretty sophisticated mind to
see the links between Woody Guthrie and Mick Jagger, and Arlo managed
to pull all the diverse musical strands together in a way that empha-
sized their similarities. In the process, he grew past all the buttonholes—
Woody's son, hippie commedian, Dylan imitator—to become a singular
voice. In addition, he learned how to sing.

Even though he's played more than his share of benefits (and hard-core
benefits, not soupy ones in favor of clean air or Jimmy Carter) and even
though he's one of the few major performers to sing songs against things
like fascism in Chile, Arlo isn't a very radical person. His politics seem
intuitive, a part of the tradition he was born into. He does what he feels
is right and doesn't have much patience with the purists who expect, because of the songs he sings and the family heritage, that he'll follow a
strict anticapitalist line. "I did a Craig car stereo ad last year just to piss
those people off," he said. And the morning of the Hoyt Axton discussion
he was going to appear in an industrial development film for the state of
Massachusetts—not because he believed in industrial development (in
fact, he opposed it) or the state of Massachusetts, but because it seemed
like it would be fun.

*   *   *

After the filming, we returned to the farm for a small Christmas party Jackie had arranged. "Just some of our friends who live nearby," Arlo explained. The party had already begun by the time we got back—the guests were mostly young people who were not exactly counterculture types. Most of them brought something for the dinner: a salad, a cake, deviled crab, brownies. Jack provided a precooked turkey. The food was set out on the dining room table and candles were lit. It was a pretty casual crowd and no one seemed to care very much when Arlo went upstairs to take a nap for about an hour. The talk was mostly country stuff. Kids cooking, the weather, hunting and fishing, some speculation about the oil tanker aground on the coast. When Arlo returned, he moved on the periphery of the party, finally joining the conversation when it turned to the local schools. He knew all the vagaries of the regional school system and had very strong feelings about keeping Washington's elementary school kids in Washington, rather than sending them over to Becket and paying more money. "We can teach them cheaper and better here ourselves. The money's just going to bureaucrats."

Later, as the party began to thin out, Arlo and I began to talk about Woody. He said he was thinking about doing an album of songs by Woody that no one had ever heard, and said that while most people consider the Thirties Woody's most creative period, he thought the Fifties were his most amazing.

"You know what I remember? I remember him coming home from the hospital and taking me out to the backyard, just him and me, and teaching me the last three verses to 'This Land Is Your Land' because he thinks that if I don't learn them, no one will remember. He can barely strum the guitar at this point, and . . . can you imagine? His friends think he's a drunk, crazy, and they stick him in a puke green room in a mental hospital with all these crazy people.

"Even after he knows he's got this disease, he keeps on fighting it. He keeps typing on the typewriter, writing some of his best stuff. You should read *Seeds of Man*. It was about a trip he took when he was a kid and 30 years later he remembered every detail exactly . . . down to the rock formations along the road. An editor from Dutton went down to Texas and retraced the trip and he couldn't believe it. The book was like a road map. Exact.

"Anyway, he keeps on typing until he can't get it together to use a typewriter anymore. And then he starts writing by hand. And the handwriting gets bigger and bigger until he can only fit one word on a page. And those last songs—you know what they're about? They're about Jesus. About carrying the cross.

And then—and this is so weird you can't really even begin to figure it—when he can't talk or write or do anything at all anymore, he hits it big. All of a sudden everyone is singing his songs. Kids are singing "This Land Is Your Land" in school and people are talking about making it the national anthem. Bob Dylan and all the others are copying him. And he can't react to it. Here's this guy who always had all these words and now that he's making it really big, he can't say anything. But his mind is still there. The disease doesn't affect his mind. He's sitting there in a mental hospital, *and he knows what's going on*, and he can't say anything or tell anyone how he feels. It's Shakespearean. Only Shakespeare could write something like that. . . ."

That would have been a splendid place for the conversation to end. But it didn't. It meandered into politics and eventually back into the same state-of-the-world nonsense we had been talking about two days before. Arlo told a long story about King Antiochus of Judea who ordered all the Jews to convert and singled out one family of a mother and seven broth-ers—the most righteous family in the neighborhood—and one by one he asked them if they believed in the god of the Jews and one by one they each said yes, and he chopped them up and put them in a steaming pot. "That's what it all comes down to," Arlo said, "whether or not, when the time comes, you decide to jump in the pot."

That afternoon, when we came home from shopping and I saw a Francis-can monk in full battle dress vacuuming the living room carpet, the story about jumping into the pot (and all the other hints Arlo had been dropping about making big decisions) began to make a little more sense.

The monk's name was Michael. "I met him five or six years ago on one of those little airplanes that fly into Pittsfield. We met in the air, so to speak," Arlo later explained. "He didn't know very much about me or music and I didn't know about Catholicism. I mean, it started out with me saying, 'Tell me nun stories,' but gradually it became something else."

Michael learned about music and Arlo learned about Catholicism and on Christmas Eve Arlo played the guitar for the children's service at the church over in Haydensville, and he took Communion. The whole busi-ness seemed to confuse the young Guthries as much as it did me—it was obvious that Arlo hadn't tried to impose his new religion on his family. In fact, that night seemed the first time he'd ever brought them to church. Abraham asked, "Why do you come to this church, Daddy?" And on the way home, after hearing all the Christmas stories about angels and such, Cathy said, "I think I hear voices in the sky talking to me."

Around midnight, the inevitable religious conversation began, Michael asked me about being Jewish and I said it was pretty much a cultural thing. He said he thought the logical end product of being Jewish was to believe in Jesus. "I believe I'm Jewish," he said.

I told him I thought Jesus was a pretty impressive figure but, being a writer, I figured the guys who wrote the gospels had gotten a little carried away. Arlo had moved in close by now, and was itching to join the conversation. "Then you have to believe Jesus was the greatest hypocrite in history," he said.

"Why? Why can't I just believe all the writers got carried away?"

"Because of all the prophecies he fulfills. To believe what you do, you gotta believe that there was a conspiracy that lasted over centuries and included all the guys who wrote the Old Testament."

Not knowing the Old Testament too well, I didn't have a comeback.

"You see, it's all or nothing," Arlo continued. "Either you accept Jesus or you don't."

"So that's why you've been saying all that stuff about things being black and white? . . ."

"Yeah. I mean, this whole thing has been as surprising to me as it must be to you," he said. "What do you think of when you think of the Catholic church? You think of oppression, right? But you got to get beyond that. See, I've been through all the other things — all the gurus and things you pick up one week because TV is boring or your old lady is pissed, and then you drop them. But this is different. This is the real thing. And you got to remember that in the beginning I was as skeptical as you."

"So how did it happen?" I asked. He smiled, still wearing the blue Santa Claus cap. "Did it happen in your head or in your gut?"

"It happened . . . well, it's still happening. I'm still learning. But there's a moment that comes when you just accept it."

Nora and Ted, by now, were into the conversation. "What do you do?" Ted asked.

"You love God," Arlo said.

"What does that mean?" Ted pressed.

"It means you love God."

"Yeah, but how do you . . ."

"You decrease," Arlo said.

"God keeps growing in you every day," said Michael.

The conversation fragmented, Michael and Ted talking about the nature of doubt, Jackie beginning to wrap Christmas presents and arrange the tree, Arlo and Nora arguing about religion. Finally, in the midst of a delicate theological point, I blurted, "What's the difference between you and Rennie Davis?"

Arlo leaned back. Thought about it. Finally said, "I don't know."

(Later, of course, I realized that the difference between them was that only one of them would have said, "I don't know.")

With all the singing and theology on Christmas Eve, we didn't get to bed until about five. The kids were up and tearing away at the Christmas presents an hour later and we sat, trying to keep our eyes propped open, watching them. Arlo even made a groggy stab at putting together Abraham's train set. By late morning, though, everyone except the kids was back asleep again.

The plan had been that Arlo was going to make one of his famous too-hot-to-rationally-contemplate Indian curries for dinner. But he was in no shape to make it and we were in no shape to eat it, so he suggested, "Why don't we go over to Alice's for dinner?"

Alice's Restaurant has changed somewhat over the years. Now it is a fancy gourmet place, in a big white house near Tanglewood, complete with a motel and live music on weekends. The tables have white linen tablecloths, there is candlelight; the silver and crystal glistens. There is a wine list. Alice, though, looks pretty much the same. She was wearing a blue turquoise shift and came over and kissed Arlo as soon as he walked in.

We sat down at a big table off in a corner, looking out the window at trees strung gaily with white Christmas lights, and proceeded to get reasonably drunk. In the conversation that followed, some very important things were said, most of which I can't begin to remember . . . although a few do stick out:

"Remember when I said that I became a Catholic because my mother was Jewish and my father was Protestant?" Arlo said. "Well, I wasn't kidding. See, from my mother, I got the whole Jewish mind thing, you know, asking questions. From my father, I got the idea that the answers to the questions don't make a goddamn bit of difference. Well, what do you call someone like that? A Catholic!"

And later: "I know exactly what I'm about. There are people who innovate, people like Woody, but I'm not one of those. I'm just a guy who substantiates what the innovators do. I'm just a link between what went before and what's gonna be . . . and I'm honored as hell just to be a link in the chain, just be part of the tradition."

And still later, "You should come around in two years or so. . . ."

"Why?" I asked.

"Things'll be happening then."

"What things?"

"Things."

Alice came over and sat down. Arlo introduced me as the dietary critic from the *New York Herald Tribune*.

"Arlo has this weird sense of humor," Alice said.

"Yeah, my weird sense of humor hasn't done too badly for either of us," he said.

They started talking about a business idea Alice had, but I kept thinking about what might be happening in two years. Was it something professional? It had taken him two years to develop "Alice's Restaurant" a decade before, pruning it down from two hours to about 18 minutes, every word carefully chosen.

Or was it something else? In two years, the 1980s would be approaching — and the thought stopped me cold — were the 1980s going to be Arlo's version of Woody's 1950s? Probably not. It was still too early to tell but did he have some sort of premonition? Did he already *know*? Was that why he had become preoccupied by religion?

I looked across the table at him, leaning back in his chair, surrounded by his family, a patriarch. The kids were running around the table, banging into Arlo on purpose every so often, as if he were a pillow. He saw me staring, smiled.

Another thought began to develop: it didn't matter. Either way, he was going to be all right. He'd made it past an impossible psychological obstacle course already — a legendary father, a crazy confusing childhood, immediate and dizzying success, all sorts of definitions imposed on him by other people — and he'd emerged not only intact, but unique. Somehow or other he'd make it past the disease too. Maybe he'd just slide by because he wasn't intimiated. And that, I realized, was the wonderful thing about Arlo Guthrie and his music: the confidence, not only that he was going to make it through okay, but that the rest of us would too.

We stumbled out the door after dinner, pretty well sloshed, and it was snowing. We looked up into it and the snow tickled our faces and matted our hair. "God, I love snow," Arlo said. "Ain't it pretty?"

Dolly Parton

Chet Flippo

IT WAS A CLASSIC TRIANGLE: THE REPORTER, THE STAR
AND THE WEIGHT LIFTER. WAIT, WE FORGOT TO MEN-
TION THE PHOTOGRAPHER

"Chet, who's Arnold Schwartza, uhm, Schwartzanooger,
Schwartzenhiger, oh, who is this person?"

The speaker was the ever-charming Dolly Parton.
The year was 1977. I had been doing a series of inter-
views with Dolly for a big feature, a possible cover for ROLLING STONE.
I was hard at work on the old Smith-Corona when Dolly called.

"Arnold Schwarza-whoosit?" I replied. "I think he's some weight lifter
from Poland or somewhere." In my mind's eye, I could hazily make out a
recollection of some recent book or documentary flick or something called
Pumping Iron, whose perpetrators had lobbied heavily and at great expense
to hype it to the editors and writers at ROLLING STONE as a great work.
Unsuccessfully, as I recall. Weight lifting was not something that occupied
much of RS's accessible or operating frontal lobes at the time.

"So, Dolly," I said, "why are you calling me at midnight to ask me
about some muscle guy? Are you throwing me over for a *real man*? Is that
the deal?"

She just laughed her famous Dolly little-girl giggle, all whipped cream and maraschino cherries. "*No*, silly. You know you're my steady. It's just that Judy [Ogle, her assistant and friend] said that your photographer—now, what is her name?"

"Annie. Annie Leibovitz."

"Okay. Annie's person told Judy that this Arnold Schwartzehoover is coming to my photo session tomorrow. *My* photo session. Mine. What do you know about this? Am I supposed to show up wearing a *jockstrap*? Am I going to be photographed bench-pressing 300 pounds?" Her tone became a trifle frosty, definitely a chill in the air.

I scrambled to take cover. What the hell was Annie up to now? I had never seen a photographer who could put people through hoops the way Annie could. Working with her was always, always an adventure—one well worth the effort, for there was no better photographer working. Still—keeping up with her was an all-day job and then some. You better pack two lunches if you so much as went out for coffee with Annie. Of course, Dolly didn't know any of this. Her experience had been pretty much limited to daily newspapers and country-music publications. She had enjoyed a more . . . *leisurely* and protected and friendly media experience in the past, shall we say. She was just now beginning to branch out, blossoming as a national and even universal commodity, as it were. She had obviously never been exposed to an Annie Leibovitz. In fact, she had been very wary of the whole RS thing, not at all sure what a rock & roll magazine was going to do with—or *to*—her.

"Trust me, Dolly," I said in my most convincing voice. "Whatever Annie is doing, she has only *you* in mind. Believe me," I said, praying for belief.

"Well, we-yull. You *sure*, now?"

"Trust me, darlin'."

"Okay." The purr returned to her voice. "But—one thing, mister. You're going with me to *my* photo session. Deal?"

"Deal," I said with relief. God only knew what was going to happen, but if I was there I could at least have some measure of control over whatever level of madness might obtain. I could always, as I once did, threaten to have Annie deported, or worse, if things got too much out of hand. Besides, I would never pass up the chance to hang out with Dolly again.

And it had been only about four hours since she and her limo had dropped me off at my Manhattan apartment and she had motored off for the Waldorf. We had been in Connecticut for a week or so, where she had played several small venues around the state. She was perched at a crucial crossroads in her career, and that was why I had been able to convince the magazine's editors that the time was right for the rock bible yclept ROLL-

ING STONE to do a major take on a five-foot-tall, bewigged, rhinestoned country singer who hadn't been anywhere near electrical-powered instruments since the Tennessee Valley Authority ran power lines into the remote holler where she lived with her family in Sevier County, Tennessee, way back in the Forties.

Dolly had been country music's best-kept secret for years: one of the most original and most sensitive songwriters since Hank Williams and blessed with an achingly sweet voice to boot. And a mischievous, playful mind. All of that was often overlooked because of her hourglass figure, which was exaggerated by skintight, flamboyant Nudie outfits and her cascading wigs and outlandish makeup. It took her years to get over her original image—fostered by her too-long partnership with country singer Porter Wagoner—as Miss Big Tits of the twentieth century. Who can forget that when she made it onto *The Tonight Show*, the best that Johnny Carson could come up with was that he would give a year's salary to look under her blouse?

At any rate, she was bound and determined to break out of the country-music ghetto and find a national audience and carry her music and her message to the world at large. "Crossover," it was called at the time. Part of the campaign involved revamping her media image. That's why she was happy, when I called her people to see about an interview, to submit to the "RS treatment," as she called it, whatever it might turn out to be: growing a mustache or bench-pressing 300 big ones or whatever. As she always used to say, "I'm a brave little soldier."

We were both pleased to discover that the interview experience was actually fun for both of us. She was surprised and grateful to find that I actually knew her music quite well, all the way back, and knew what all she had been through. I was happy to find an interview subject—whose music I loved—who lived up to her work. You would be surprised to discover how seldom that happens in pop and rock and country and jazz. But Dolly fit the bill, all across the board. I *knew*, as I seldom know with an artist, that she could accomplish whatever she wanted to accomplish. It was only a matter of will.

In the meantime, we were out there in the lush green countryside of Connecticut, staying in a little motel (in separate rooms, of course) and tooling around in my fast, sky blue rent-a-Mustang and going to her shows and brunching and going antique browsing. Her husband, Carl, was back in Nashville, and my wife, Martha, was back in Manhattan, but no funny business was going on. Just a meeting of the minds. Talking late in the night about music and writing and writing and music.

We went out grocery shopping and loved watching people's reactions when they recognized her as we pushed our cart up and down the aisles of the supermarket. We read the tabloids to each other out loud at the checkout. We went for a picnic in the local graveyard, mainly because it was the greatest and quietest place around.

Anyway, I had a hell of a lot more fun than I ever had interviewing Mick Jagger, and I told her so. "Do I look like Mick Jagger to you, Chet?" she asked in her sultriest little-girl voice. "Well, uhm, no, no, but—" She was of course putting me on. And on. And on.

Back in Manhattan, at midnight, I called a friend at RS who was always in the know and totally *au courant* with everything that was happening at the magazine. There was no point in trying to call Annie, *even if* I could find her at that time of night. I would just get into another argument about writer versus photographer and who had more rights regarding the subject and access thereto, which I certainly didn't need right then. I just wanted confirmation of what I already pretty much thought was going on.

"Of *course*," my friend told me. "Annie is just using Arnold as a prop. What did you think? No, don't tell me. Look—beautiful, voluptuous woman, you put a *hard* muscleman next to her, great contrast, right? Great picture, right?" She laughed and hung up. Hmm.

Dolly came around and limoed me off bright and early the next morning to Annie's rented studio in Chelsea. She nervously held my hand as we shared coffee on the way. I've never felt more like a one-man Reassurance Service: "Everything is going to be all right. *All right*." Kind of enjoyed it, though.

All was harmony and light at the studio. Tables sagged under the weight of doughnuts and English muffins and Danish and melon and coffee urns and cold cuts and cheese and crackers and grapes and this and that. Annie hugged Dolly like a long-lost cousin. Dust motes were dancing in the sunbeams radiating through the skylights. I heaved a sigh of relief. *My* job was done. Except for the little matter of writing the story.

Arnold and entourage showed up. He was very charming to one and all, although I rather got the impression that he was not entirely *sure* just why he was there. Still, like a trouper he changed into his little bikini and began posing with Dolly.

Then something happened that I missed, as I sat in the background and sipped coffee. Dolly and Annie had their heads together and were giggling helplessly like schoolgirls. Arnold, in his little bikini, was retreating, a trifle red in the face.

Oh. I suddenly figured it out. Graphically. Arnold had been lifting Dolly for a shot. But he had sort of . . . become . . . *aroused*. And his modest tumescence had made two of the earthiest women I have ever met fall out in laughter. I never heard the last of that.

August 25th, 1977

What a grand feeling it is to be heading out of town in a fast, sky blue rent-a-Mustang with a cold six-pack on the floor, the June sun streaming down, the radio turned up loud and Dolly Parton sitting beside me. She's singing along with Jimmy Clanton's oldie. "Just a Dream" and it occurs to me that a certain amount of fantasizing is impossible to avoid. *Let's see . . . we'll find a nice little meadow beside a stream for our picnic and as the day gets hotter we'll want to go for a cool dip in the clear, inviting waters and since neither of us brought a swimsuit. . . .* A battered Chevy pulls up alongside and two pimply teenagers do triple takes at Dolly with her cascading blond wig and tight-fitting shirt. I don't even have to lip-read to get the message: "Hey, what a great-looking chick! She's so *fine*. Lookit the creep with her."

And I realize I'm ten miles out of town and instead of clear streams, all I'm passing is liquor stores.

"Gee, Dolly, maybe I shoulda made reservations somewhere or somethin', I dunno."

"What about this graveyard?" she asks.

"You serious?"

"Yeah, I love cemeteries, they're so quiet. You know, people are *dying* to get into 'em. Really, I write in cemeteries a lot; nobody bothers you there."

I turn off into the Middlefield, Connecticut, cemetery and slowly cruise through. But the caretaker is slashing his way around the tombstones with a 100-decibel ride-a-mower. Clearly, this is not the spot for a quiet picnic.

I break into a slight sweat; adolescent memories. It is not at all cool to take the best-looking girl in school out for a summer picnic and then have to deposit her in a parking lot somewhere behind a Grand Union supermarket. Talk about a last date. *Please, God, find me a patch of grass somewhere.*

Finally, God leads me to a brook, a shade tree and a reasonable facsimile of a meadow. Dolly spreads a yellow blanket and we get down to serious business: the making of big, sloppy bologna and tomato sandwiches and the opening of wine.

Dolly stretches her arms out. "Oh, I just love it outdoors. You can just feel God all around you."

You certainly can, I reply.

A loaf of Wonder Bread, a jug of Italian Swiss Colony and Dolly Parton beside me in the wilderness. Ah, that paradise should come so early in my young life.

"Ooh, you got cherries for dessert," Dolly says. "Um, good. I ain't had a cherry in a long time." She looks at me mischievously. "I don't think I ever had a cherry. If I did, it got shoved so far back I was usin' it for a taillight!"

I must have looked shocked. "I'm just kiddin'," she winks as she throws a cherry seed at me.

I have heard singers called many things, from four-letter words to 27-letter words, but I have never heard one called a "purifier." I always presumed that word applied only to such items as smog devices, our Lord Jesus Christ and Tareyton charcoal filter tips. But came one recent Friday morning when my own purifying sleep was disturbed by a phone call. I dispatched my helpmate to deal with it, but couldn't help overhearing her end of the conversation, which was mostly astonished gasps.

"What was all that about?" I asked. It was, I was told, an editor of a certain women's magazine and she was just calling to inform us that Dolly Parton had "purified" New York's Bottom Line the night before.

"What'd she do, take an ax to the place?"

"No, her music purified the audience. She's a *purifier*."

Well, damn me. I have known Dolly Parton for some time and known her as someone who writes a hell of a good country song and sings with an achingly sweet soprano and looks like what heaven should be populated with. But I also know her as a good ol' girl you can kid around with and not have to be too careful of what you do or say. Hardly someone, though, to get all misty-eyed or mystical over or go sobbing about in nightclubs. Further callers throughout the day, however, report similar quasi-religious experiences and cleansings of the soul. What is going on?

Butch Rutter has been purified. He gets backstage to see Dolly after her show at London's Rainbow Theater even before Chita Rivera because Butch is a . . . *very* special case. Thus far, he is the only known human being on this planet to have his entire back tattooed with a full-color depiction of a Dolly Parton album cover, topped with her autograph and an inscription of love across his shoulder blades. He shows up in full cowboy regalia, accompanied by fellow members of his Alamo Club, a London group of Dolly Parton lovers. They are carrying, besides an air of puppylike devotion, a lovingly crafted brass plaque of Dolly's entire body in accurate profile. They have come in committee to formally ask Dolly to be official queen of the Alamo. Butch gets a regal kiss for that and then he drops his shirt to exhibit the Parton chef-d'oeuvre: a well-done copy of her *Love Is like a Butterfly* album cover. He had the tattoo started in 1976, and when Dolly played Wembley he got her autograph above the butterfly. He spent 12 hours under the needle. He did it because he loves her.

"You didn't get infected from tattooin' over my ink, did ya?" Dolly asks. "Hmmm, that turned out real good, didn't it." She winks as he pulls up his shirt and makes to leave. "Well, at least you're gonna have *one* woman with you forever."

Back on the yellow blanket in the Connecticut countryside, Dolly and I are swapping tales of childhood indiscretions. I do not feel in the least purified and do not mind it a darn bit.

I take a moment to look at Dolly. She was not always as I see her before me; not always an angelic, creamy-skinned, honey-wigged, golden-throated, flashing-eyed, jewel-encrusted, lush-bodied, feisty enchantress of a songwriter and singer. Back there in Sevierville, Tennessee, she was thought at one time a rather unexceptional, born plain child. The fourth of Lee and Avie Lee Parton's 12 children, she was born in the Parton cabin January 19th, 1946. She matured *early* and by ten ran the family during her mother's illnesses. She had already recorded her first single, "Puppy Love," (she rode a Greyhound bus to Lake Charles, Louisiana, to record it, where an uncle had arranged studio time) and had started appearing on regional TV and radio shows. Her vocal style was set then: a shimmering, childlike trill, influenced mainly by church music and by the Elizabethan ballads her mother sang.

She was also ambitious and knew even then—and still knows—just what she wanted and just how to go about getting it, even to taking an unprecedented step for a country music singer: last year she totally shut down her career to retool for a wider audience. She got a new band, a new management firm, a new booking agency. She changed everything but her mind. And her music.

Back last fall, Dolly Parton was about as hot a country property as there was. Everybody from Patti Smith to Linda Ronstadt and Emmylou Harris was singing her songs. She had already started her independence movement in 1973, when she left the *Porter Wagoner Show* after six years. She and Porter, the lean, lanky, pompadoured epitome of flash and glitter in country music, were as famous a C&W duo as George and Tammy and Conway and Loretta. But Dolly had wider horizons in mind. Then last year, came the shift toward pop audiences.

In person, she is stunning. I have seen people spontaneously break into applause when she enters a room. I tactfully suggest that she was probably the foxiest schoolgirl in Tennessee history and that, as a result, she may have had a tough time in school.

I get a smile of irony with her reply. "Well, I tell you, it was kinda rough for me because I was the most popular girl in school in the *wrong* way. *Everybody* talked about Dolly but I didn't have as many friends as I should have had. My best friends were boys because they understood me and weren't tryin' to find fault. But, you know, I never dated the boys in school. I seemed so much older. I only had a couple of dates with boys from school and I felt like their *mother* or somethin'. I had a lotta stories told on me, a lotta lies, just because I looked the way I did. I always was big in the boobs, small in the waist and big in the butt. I just grew up that way and I had that *foxy* personality, too.

"I mean, I was *real* outgoin', real friendly, I think it was scary to people. But I never felt I belonged. Never belonged in my whole life, even as a little kid. I was just *different* and so I never really found my place till I moved to Nashville and got in the music business. That was my *real* place, so I fit in. I was born restless, I really was. I guess I was born with gypsy fever. Now, there is nothin' I like better than goin' home to have a few weeks off, do as I please, go in the yard half-naked, without makeup and without havin' my hair done, or play with the dogs or romp around with the cows. But when I am ready to go, there is *nothin'* I like better than to pack it up and head it on out. I just couldn't stay, and in my later years when I am writing books and poems mostly I think I will travel around and do that. I really wouldn't want to stay at home all the time; that would be a *bore*."

When Dolly lit out for Nashville the day after she was graduated from high school in 1964, she hit town with little more than a cardboard suitcase full of songs. It didn't take her long to start selling those songs, to get a recording contract with Monument and then to switch to RCA when Porter Wagoner, impressed by her television appearances, tapped her to replace singer Norma Jean on his show.

The first thing she did when she hit town, though, was her laundry. In the Wishy Washy laundromat she met a man named Carl Dean.

She married him two years later. He is now an asphalt contractor and, so Parton mythology has it, has never seen her perform and their marriage is a very private thing and he is the stabilizing influence in her gypsy life. I teasingly ask her if he really exists.

"You *know* he does," she half-explodes before she laughs at the absurdity of the question. "And the stories are wrong—he has seen me perform. And he liked it. So there."

For a person who looks the way she does, it comes as a surprise when she claims that few men in the music business have ever seriously tried to put moves on her. She attributes that, naturally, to her fiercely independent nature. She does, however, write ingenuously sensuous songs. One of the more explicit ones is "He Would Know." One line is "I would love to love you but he would know."

"That is true," she says. "You couldn't be human, especially in this business, and not run across people now and then that *really* move you.

And you have to be really strong to avoid temptation and even if you don't avoid it you have to be smart enough to know how much of it you can take. So, when it's more than I can stand, I just get my pencil and guitar out and I start writin': 'In my mind I make love to you often/But *only* in my mind can it be so/Because there is someone home who is counting on me/And if I *did*, I'm sure that he would know.' That's not sayin' I ain't made mistakes and won't make mistakes but if I can just write it and say this is a song about our situation, I hope you can better understand how I feel about it and why it can't be."

Another song Dolly wrote, the beautifully crafted "Bargain Store," was banned by some country stations and that still rankles her.

"I just thought," she says, "well, why don't a person compare your body and your mind and your heart to objects, like an old broken heart sittin' on a shelf and some plans and dreams as if they were things you could see." She starts singing: " 'My life is like unto a bargain store/And I might have just what you're lookin' for/If you don't mind the fact that all the merchandise is used/But with a little mendin' it can be as good as new.' That means that I have been in love before and kicked around and banged around and had my head and my heart broke, my cherry stole, but I can grow *another* one if that's what you want." She laughs a loud, exuberant laugh.

"When I said the bargain store is open, come inside, I just meant my *life* is open, come into my life, so I wasn't even thinkin' of it as a dirty thing. I just felt at that time I had been probably kicked around some. Not by my husband—he is the *best* person that ever lived. But you know, me and Porter, we just kind of said things, hurt each other's feelings and, you know, trampled around on territory that was real sensitive, cut each other about songs. It's just—I felt black and blue and I just wanted to heal back up and mend myself back together and get on with my life."

Common courtesy and a sense of fair play prevent me from asking Dolly what her remarkable measurements might be and that her configuration obviously hasn't hurt her career and what does she think about the Blaze Starr song "38 Double D" (which I have just recited to her) and, while I'm at it, did she ever think about being a stripper?

She is somewhat taken aback and pauses to collect her thoughts. For today's session in her motel room, she's wearing a taut black jumpsuit and a hot pink shawl with a matching orchid in her hair. There is a pizza left over from last night and we are just contemplating warming it up a slice at a time on the bottom of her steam iron.

"I have really tried to not promote nothing but my talent, and the way I look is the way *I like* to look. I'm just an extremist and so I like to dress the part—if I have extreme parts of my body, then I might as well have extreme hairdos or have extreme clothes to match the boobs and the hairdo. *And,* my personality is really extreme. I do just as I please, I always have and always will. I try to live my own life; I don't try to live somebody else's life, and I don't like people tryin' to live *my* life. Now there, how do you like that? Buddy, I *mean* that."

It would be an understatement to observe that, through her songwriting and especially her image, Parton is very secure in her femaleness which, despite her fierce independence, is in many ways very traditional. She carries no soapbox, delivers no rhetoric—though she's not hesitant to speak her mind. And she enjoys being a girl.

But how did her own exaggerated feminine image come about? Wasn't she more of a tomboy as a child?

"Yeah, I was mean as a snake. I'm still a tomboy, a lot more than you might think. But I always loved to be feminine, I always liked frilly things and perfume. I used to use Merthiolate for lipstick and there wasn't nothin' daddy could do to get *that* off."

On her lips? Surely that hurt. "It was worth the pain. I was 15 when teased hair came out and I *loved* that and I loved makeup, I always wore tight clothes. When I walked down the hall, everybody was a-lookin' to see how tight my skirt was that day or how tight my sweater was. I never did like to go around half-naked but a lotta people said I might as well be naked, as tight as my clothes were. But even as a little bitty kid, if my mamma made me wear somethin' that was loose on me, I used to just *cry.* I wanted my clothes to fit me. Even though they was rags, I wanted them to fit close to me.

"When people started changin' their hair styles, I wasn't ready to quit—I just kept makin' it bigger and bigger. I just thought, well, somebody is noticin' it and I'm enjoyin' it. I liked it and still do. I teased my own hair for years and years and it's real damagin' to your hair so about three years ago I started wearin' wigs because it's convenient. But people come to expect that of me and I come to expect it of myself, the flashy clothes and jewelry and all the gaudy appearance. I guess I did invent that part of me. I was always fascinated with fairytale images. Half of a show is the lighting and the shine and the sparkle. Stars are supposed to shine and maybe I just want to be a *star.*"

Surely, though, she might become trapped in the carefully sculpted Dolly Parton image?

About her breasts Dolly drops a line on me with her usual smile and a wink. "There are going to be those who will say, 'I know that they're false; I knew her when' and there will be some who say, 'I know they're real.' I say: '*Let 'em guess.*'"

"*Okay,* I thought about bein' a stripper. But I decided that I really better not. I didn't want to get married. All I had ever known was housework and kids and workin' in the fields. But I didn't want to be domestic, I wanted to be *free*. I had my songs to sing, I had an ambition and it *burned* inside me. It was something I knew would take me out of the mountains. I knew I could see worlds beyond the Smoky Mountains."

"I'm always sure of the goals I set for myself," she says, "but I like for them to be flexible because I may get midways and get a big brainstorm. Then I can change. I just set new goals. There will *never* be a top for me—other than the *one* I am famous for." I try unsuccessfully to avoid glancing at her chest while she laughs at me.

"I mean there is no top and no bottom to my career because once I accomplish the things I decide I'm going to, then I want to get into other things. I am a list maker. I like to write my goals and plans down and keep them in a secret place where people can't see them. You'd be *amazed* that even *years* ago the things I'd written down on my list, that I just mark 'em off as they come true and I think, boy, if *that* ain't proof that positive thinkin' is a marvelous thing. I mean if there is something I *really* want, why, I write it down on a piece of paper and I look at the list and I *concentrate* real hard on it, try to visualize it happening, and I just go through all the motions as if it's already been done."

And, I ask, a bit cynically, does it work?

She jumps forward in her chair, excited. "Yes! It *does*! If I get sick, I think myself well. That's why I never did worry when my throat was botherin' me. I tell you, it is strange the way it works."

I get us out two more Buds and ask her if she possesses any . . . *special* mental powers or something.

"No more than anybody else, if they develop and exercise it. I was born with that gift and that great faith and it wasn't until about two years ago that I discovered that there were books written about positive thinking. But, you see, I had practiced that all my life, *that's* what got me out of the mountains. Even as a little child, I daydreamed *so* strongly that I just saw these things happen and sure enough, they would, so it was just a matter of growing up to meet that. We can be whatever we want to be, the Bible says that, that *all* things are possible to those that *believe*. It don't say *some* things are possible, it says *all* things are possible and it says that if you have faith even as a grain of mustard seed then you shall move mountains and that nothing shall be impossible unto you."

Well, I say, beginning to believe, would you please write down on one of your lists that you want me to become a rich and famous writer?

She smiles a Madonna's smile.

"—I ain't *near* where I'm goin'. My dreams are far too big to stop now 'cause I ain't the greatest at what I do, but I become greater because I *believe*. What I lack in talent I make up for in ambition and faith and determination and positive thinking."

*   *   *

We leave the Holiday Inn for the Oakdale Theatre a good two hours before her curtain time—or ramp time in this case. The Oakdale is what is commonly called a hardtop tent. It's a dome that's open all the way around and the inside slopes down to a revolving stage, a feature Dolly is not fond of. "I got to put my band in the pit and I just stand out there like a sore thumb. And I never did like to go around in circles."

Just before she gets on her bus, a cluster of young girls runs up for autographs. She gives them a dozen red roses she's carrying and the next morning comes a letter from a mother, a letter that's almost dripping with tears of appreciation. "I just love kids," Dolly says on the bus. "But I don't really need one of my own. I've written a lot of children's stories, though. I never show them to anybody—not till I get ready to publish 'em. I've got trunkfuls of things I've written. I've been writin' poetry since I was in grammar school. When I was a teenager I wrote a lot of *real* hot and heavy love stories, I was just so horny myself."

Well, I say, she should write a book. Her life story might be interesting and . . .

"I'm *already* doin' that," she says, turning in her seat to train on me the butterfly-encrusted Christian Dior shades that Porter Wagoner gave her. "I'm gonna call the whole thing *Blossom*, 'cause I used to be called Blossom when I was little, which I think will be a great movie and the whole thing—you know, to blossom into this and blossom into somethin' else."

We ride along in silence for a while. This is the least ostentatious and most decorous musician's bus I've ever seen. Country singers' buses are more often closer to being re-creations of Tijuana whorehouses or explosions in a Sears furniture department. Dolly's is very understated—the bus does not even carry her name. All that makes it distinct from any GMC bus is the destination window or whatever those things are that say "Des Moines" or "Salt Lake City." Her's says "Coach of Many Colors," a play on her favorite song. "I just don't like to advertise myself," she says of that. Which is consistent with her inconsistencies. Flamboyant while within the public eye proper, she values solitude (because of oglers she does not go swimming and seldom goes shopping).

She gets up and heads for the back of the bus to put on her makeup and get dressed for the show. It's an unstated thing that she prefers staying on the bus until showtime. Nor does she stick around for the Mac Davis show, nor does she stay for an Oakdale custom: the "Reception Line." At the end of the evening the performers are expected to stand like horses in a stall and shake hands with the public. No autographs, just genteel hand-holding and murmuring of compliments.

"It's a typical Mac Davis audience," she would say later. "But I wouldn't continue this, wouldn't let this be my career. This whole year has been an exception to all rules for me because of needing the money to run an organization. But after this fall I'll be working more to contemporary and country audiences. This is not my type of audience and I say it's good for me because they all remember seeing me. Whether or not they come back is beside the point."

She's certainly right about the crowd. With all the white shoes and burgundy sport coats and gowns it looks more like the clubhouse of a race track. Latecomers linger outside to chat while Dolly gamely tries to get some feeling out of the crowd. She is partially successful and would later joke that "it's too bad we can't pipe marijuana smoke into the place; maybe they'd giggle durin' 'Me and Little Andy.'"

The latter is one of her Gothic children's tales, about a little girl and her dog who run away from a wayward mother and drunken father and show up at the narrator's house to escape the bitter cold. During their sleep, "the angels take them both to heaven."

That's a common thread in many of her songs: unhappy kids dying off left and right and going on to glory. Dolly did not have a happy childhood and she seems destined to continually rewrite it.

That's straight out of her fundamentalist upbringing, of course. She grew up in the House of Prayer, a Church of God in Sevierville where her grandfather, Jake Owens, was the preacher. "Oh," she had told me, "I remember the hellfire and brimstone he used to preach and how I used to be *real* scared of that and I think that inspired me or *depressed* me into writin' all these sad, mournful songs. You kind of grew up in a horrid atmosphere about fear of religion. We thought God was a *monster* in the sky." But then, in the next breath she had a bright smile as she recalled how she would sit in the last pew in church and the boys would come and scratch at the window, trying to get her to go outside. "Sometimes I would go to church just to see who would walk me home."

She finishes "Me and Little Andy"—which *is* corny—and gets moderate applause. From behind me, I can hear oohs and ahhs as Mac Davis arrives at the dressing room. Dolly, a tiny figure on the revolving stage, with a pink spotlight silhouetting the light red pants outfit under her flowing, spangled chiffon, pauses to introduce her most autobiographical song: "This means more to me than any song I wrote."

With that, she begins her haunting "Coat of Many Colors."

She is clearly singing from the heart, her voice constantly on the edge of breaking and I remember what she had told me about the episode that led her to write that song.

"That was a very sad and cutting memory that I long kept deep within myself. I remembered all the pain of it and the mockery. How the kids had tried to take my little coat off and I was just sprouting . . . boobs, you know, and I didn't have a blouse on under it because I had done *well* just to have a little jacket to wear. So when the kids kept sayin' I didn't have a shirt on under it, I said I *did* because I was embarrassed. So they broke the buttons off my coat. They locked me in the coat closet that day and held the door closed and it was black dark in there and I just went into a screaming fit. I remember all that and I was ashamed to even mention it and for *years* I held it in my mind."

When she hits the last note she looks up defiantly and I find that I am glad it is still dark in this hardtop tent, for I seem to have drops of water coursing down both cheeks. Damn you, Dolly, I silently swear. You finally got to *me*, too. Purification, indeed. I'll tell you off about this. But of course I never do.

Blue Hawaii

GREIL MARCUS

WOODSTOCK, ALTAMONT AND THE MURDER OF JOHN LENNON—BREAKING NEWS STORIES THAT HIT US ON DEADLINE RESULTED IN SOME OF OUR BEST WORK. AFTER ELVIS'S DEATH, ONE CRITIC, FAR FROM HOME, HAD TO TRY TO UNDERSTAND.

ROLLING STONE crisis issues—huge news breaks that touched on the magazine's whole reason for being—came with a sense of consequence and mission. The feeling was *If we don't get it right, nobody will.* Too often it was true. In those moments, all chips were called in; the idea was to come up with something worth leaving behind. Woodstock, Altamont, Elvis Presley, John Lennon—those were the biggest stories, when I was around.

Still in San Francisco in 1969, we were lucky with Woodstock. We covered it almost as a foreign story, something happening in *New York*, far away. The New York press covered it as a local story, as an unnatural disaster, primarily a mess (*At least in three days it'll be over* was the subtext). I happened to be there, so I wrote it up as a matter of course. Jan Hodenfield, the New York bureau chief—the New York bureau, actually—wrote a terrific piece, and a prophetic one, though no one mentions it today. "It was like balling for the first time," Jan quoted "one campaigner," that choice of an almost military phrase odd and purposeful. "You want to do it again and again, because it's so *great*." A perfect pull quote, which it was, but it wasn't the prophecy, which followed: "And they will do it again, the threads of youthful dissidence in Paris and Prague and Fort Lauderdale and Berkeley and Chicago and London, crisscrossing ever more closely until the map of the world we live in is viable for and visible to all of those that are part of it and all of those buried under it."

I would give a lot to have written those words. Writing like that—that sort of vision, that kind of romantic, unsupportable insistence on the weight of events that were elsewhere dismissed as anomalous and trivial—was what the magazine was for. The magazine was a field where that kind of writing made sense, with readers (whether they were in the office or outside of it) who elicited writing that went over the borderline, over the top. Think about it: This wasn't merely a prophecy of more rock festivals but of a different world. It was, among other things, a prophecy of the role of the Plastic People of the Universe would play in Czechoslovakia, over the next twenty years, in the struggle to throw off Stalinist tyranny—or of the way demonstrators in Tiananmen Square, in Beijing in 1989, would be so proud to invoke Woodstock, before they were massacred.

But Woodstock was fun; aside from Hodenfield, not too many people caught the truth that any promise made can be broken. Altamont, a few months later, felt like a broken promise; this time the magazine turned around and covered a historical event in its own back yard as a peculiar kind of local story, a crime story, even as the San Francisco papers and the national press celebrated "Woodstock West." There really was a feeling, in the ROLLING STONE offices, that if we did not get the truth of this ugly story out, it would not get out; that it would be simply folded into the instant Woodstock myth already being used to sell so many things to so many people. But people in and around ROLLING STONE—staff members, sometime contributors, casual photographers, a scared eyewitness to a murder, medics, hustlers—felt privileged to be part of this story, to contribute whatever it was they had to contribute, to naively and proudly set the record straight. I don't recall anyone being satisfied with the Altamont story—not Jann Wenner or managing editor John Burks—but no one ever mentioned Woodstock West again. Even if the story was a failure on our terms—somehow too diffuse, too many facts, no elegance, no ringing conclusion—it was also the sort of story few people get to work on more than once: a write-up that for the world at large less reported an event than made it, if only in the negative. As a crime story, the takeout made its case, and no one ever really tried to answer it.

In a way Elvis Presley's death and the murder of John Lennon were bigger stories, because they touched so many people so fast, and so deeply—did violence to millions of lives. The heart of the issue ROLLING STONE devoted to Elvis Presley was in the testimonies of a dozen people from the music world: people whom the magazine called up with the request that they say something. It was a tactic we first used in 1970, when bluesman Otis Spann died. Since Jon Carroll, deputized to cover the story, knew nothing about Otis Spann, he got hold of Spann's friends, whom he knew nothing about either—Muddy Waters, Willie Dixon, Mike Bloomfield—and got their words down instead of his own. It turned out that in circumstances like these, people who ordinarily live their lives by evasion are eloquent. They speak straight-forwardly, but they spin off poetry in spite of themselves, because they want so badly to say just what they mean, to find the word that isn't close but exactly it—and that is what happened when people were asked if they had anything to say about Elvis Presley. Yes, said Roy Orbison. "I hope people remember the impact—it's not only historical fact, but it's definitely lingering fact." What precisely does that mean? Nothing, precisely—but you could spend years getting to the bottom of those words.

I was on vacation in Hawaii when the Elvis issue was decided on, put together, put out, so I received the results like any other reader. I still look at the cover that was chosen: a man about twenty-two, with a smile that's quiet, modest, proud and sexy all at once: *Yeah, you know me*, it seems to say. You can't imagine a less spectacular photograph of Elvis Presley, or a cover that spoke so well with silence. And yet inside, to start off the coverage of the death, the reactions to frame the memories, the elegies, the histories of music, management, movies, there was another picture, completely different, and just as good.

Somehow, a picture of Elvis near the end—fat, dripping sweat that almost smelled through the newsprint—had been found that could be printed without a sneer. Elvis sat on a stage, the spangles and bangles of his ridiculous costume holding in his bulk, makeup smeared, and he looked—pleased. He looked as if he knew something no one else knew, and as if he were about to pass it on. The picture said, *Too bad I died before I got the chance*. In a queer way, I was more moved by the Elvis issue as a reader than as a writer.

John Lennon's death was not like any of the other stories. Late-night phone calls from all over the country; Jann checked in, about 3:00 a.m., New York time, with nothing to say—no more than anyone else had to say, silence again doing all the talking that was necessary. I wondered, as we talked, if friendships are for events like these, or if the events are for the friendships. I thought about how we'd met in the spring of 1964, freshmen at Berkeley, about the pseudo-Bob Dylan-liner-notes column Jann had written for the *Daily Californian* under the name Mr. Jones—I had no idea who was writing it—about a piece he'd written a few years later praising Herman's Hermits, not an obvious thing to do in San Francisco in 1966 or 1967, when people acted as if hipness were a birthright. You can get fatalistic late at night with death; it seemed as if John Lennon's murder, like that smile of his at the end of *Help!*, was meant to sanctify whatever vaguely associated memories one might bring to it.

We hung up. Jann went off to write his piece, and I went off to write mine.

RS 248

September 22nd, 1977

August 18, Maui, Hawaii   There was a message to call the mainland, so I did. When we're here on vacation we don't follow the news much. Especially on the outer islands, the radio is mostly static; this trip we brought along a cassette machine and some homemade tapes and didn't listen to the radio at all. "They want you to write a piece about Elvis," I was told on the phone. "An obituary." What kind of joke is that, I thought. ROLLING STONE isn't the *New York Times*, we don't keep obits on file. "What kind of joke is that?" I said. "Why, he died today," I was told. "A heart attack, apparently."

I didn't accept it at all, not in any way, but at the same time I knew it was true, and even as part of me withdrew from that fact, headlines began to fly through my brain. NUDE BODY OF GEORGE "SUPERMAN" REEVES FOUND. SINGER DROWNS IN OWN VOMIT. JAMES DEAN SPOKE TO ME FROM THE GRAVE, MAN CLAIMS. I went down to the bar at the hotel where we were staying and ordered a Jack Daniel's, straight from Tennessee, just like Elvis Presley's first 45s.

Like most other people my age—thirty-two—Elvis mattered to me in the fifties; I loved his music, bought some of his records, and never went to any of his movies. He was thrilling, but he was also weird, and I kept my distance. Clearly, though, I had some sort of buried fascination with the man, and when he appeared on TV late in 1968 for his comeback, I found I could handle the fascination. In fact I was caught up in it, and for the next five years I spent far more time listening to Elvis's music, from the beginning on down, than to the music of anyone else. I found, or anyway decided, that Elvis contained more of America—had swallowed whole more of its contradictions and paradoxes—than any other figure I could think of; I found that he was a great, original artist; and I found that neither of these propositions was generally understood. So I wrote about it all, feeling, after twenty thousand words, that I had only scratched the surface.

I didn't write about "a real person"; I wrote about the persona I heard speaking in Elvis's music. I wrote about the personalization of an idea, lots of ideas—freedom, limits, risk, authority, sex, repression, youth, age, tradition, novelty, guilt and the escape from guilt—because they all were there to hear. Reading my responses back onto their source, I understood Elvis not as a human being (his divorce was interesting to me *musically*), but as a force, as a kind of necessity: that is, the necessity existing in every culture that leads it to produce a perfect, all-inclusive metaphor for itself. This, I tried to find a way to say safely, was what Herman Melville attempted to do with his white whale, but this is what Elvis Presley turned out to *be*. Or, rather, turned himself into. Or, maybe, agreed to become. And because such a triumph had to combine absolute determination and self-conscious ambition with utter ease, with the grace of one to whom all good things come naturally, I imagined a special dispensation for Elvis Presley, or, really, read it into the artifacts of his career: that to make all this work, to make this metaphor completely, transcendently American, it would be free. In other words, this would of necessity be a Faustian bargain, but someone else—and who cared who?—would pick up the tab.

I thought about all this, sitting at the bar, still believing what I'd written but wondering if I had not somehow turned myself into the most lunatic Elvis fan of all. Suddenly I began to get angry. I thought: DISGUSTING, SORDID, UGLY, SLEAZY, STUPID, WASTEFUL, PATHETIC. I thought of George Reeves again, another childhood hero, the way his death read off of the front page as a betrayal. I still could not make the event real. Every time I focused on it, the idea of Elvis dead, *not here*, it seemed to imply that he had never been here, that his presence over twenty-three years had been an hallucination, a trick—and as a way to avoid the event, I began to glide toward the corpse. I got tough. I played journalist. No one could tell me he died of anything but booze and dope, I said to myself. Isn't that what everyone in showbiz dies from? Why should I think Elvis would be any different? Heart attack, my ass. I dumped the whole affair into Las Vegas. I wanted to cut loose from it all, to cut my losses, but I was still too angry, and confused, not at anyone or anything: not at Elvis, or myself, or "them," or the fans, or the media, or "rock 'n roll," or success. It was simply rage. I was devastated.

The following night I watched two network television specials on Elvis's death. They were strange shows. On ABC one saw Chuck Berry, who has never hidden his bitterness at the fact that it took a white man to symbolize the new music Berry and others, Elvis among them, had created; here he didn't try to hide his satisfaction that he had lasted longer than "the King." "For what will Elvis be remembered among other musicians?" Berry was asked. "Oh," he replied, "boop, boop, boop; shake your leg; fabulous teen music; the fifties; his movies." Not a man you'd want to trade ironies with in a dark alley—but even Jerry Lee Lewis, the madman, the prodigal son of American music, had lasted longer. On the screen, one saw Elvis performing in Hawaii in 1973—we had been here at the time, too, and I remembered feeling like an idiot as I looked for him on the beach—and in this later incarnation Elvis even looked like George Reeves.

On the NBC special, hosted in an even tone by David Brinkley, a panel of experts had been assembled: Murray the K, the famous DJ, introduced, astonishingly, as the "first civilized person [i.e., Northerner] to play an Elvis record"; Steve Dunleavy, the as-told-to of a quartet of authors responsible for a just-published scandal-biography called *Elvis: What Happened?* (his cowriters were former Elvis bodyguards, fired over the last year or so); and Dave Marsh of ROLLING STONE. Murray the K looked subdued and played the insider: Elvis, he informed America, had told him, Murray, that he, Elvis, would "not outlive his mother," who, Murray said, had also died at forty-two (she was forty-six). Dunleavy looked bored, milked his Australian accent for all the British class it was worth, and spoke coolly of Elvis in his last years as "a walking drugstore." "It was a classic case of 'too much, too soon,' " he said, trying to slide around the cliché. Dave Marsh looked shell-shocked. He looked the way I was feeling, and he said things that perhaps not a large percentage of those watching were prepared to understand.

"It's that Elvis has always been there," Marsh said. "I always expected him to be a part of American culture that I would share with my children." And that was it. Elvis was not a phenomenon. He was not a craze. He was not even, or at least not only, a singer, or an artist. He was that perfect American symbol, fundamentally a mystery, and the idea was that he would outlive us all—or live for as long as it took both him and his audience to reach the limits of what that symbol had to say.

Since I had already read Steve Dunleavy's book, though, I could not help but think that Elvis's death might mean that those limits had already been reached, that the symbol had collapsed back on itself, and upon those who had, over the years, paid attention to it. The moment I'd enjoyed most in *Elvis: What Happened?* came when I read that in 1966 Robert Mitchum offered Elvis the lead in *Thunder Road*—a perfect role for Elvis, and one that could have given him the chance to become the serious actor he dreamed of being—and I enjoyed that moment most because I knew that Mitchum had made *Thunder Road* in 1958, and could so conclude that the accuracy of the rest of the book might be suspect. Because while many of the events detailed in *Elvis: What Happened?* are trivial ("The Most Unforgettable Pillow Fight I Ever Had"), and some of the most sensational clearly inflated (the tale of Elvis demanding that his bodyguards set up a hit on the man who took away his wife), what Red West, Sonny West, and Dave Hebler have to say rings mostly true.

The Elvis of *What Happened?* is a man whose success has driven him nuts. As presented here—in, of course, the present tense; the authors make much of their desire to save Elvis from himself; *it is not too late*, they say—Elvis has no sense of the real world whatsoever. He is schizophrenic, a manic depressive, insanely jealous, crazily "generous," desperate to buy loyalty and able to trust no one. Each of these horrors is intensified by huge and constant doses of uppers and downers, by an entourage of paid sycophants, by Elvis's obsession with firearms, and by his paranoid fantasies of vengeance and death. Each of these neurotic dislocations seeks resolution in Elvis's need to test the limits of what he can get away with (Can the near death of a young girl he overdosed be covered up? Sure it can) and in his desire to bring punishment upon himself for breaking rules he knows are right. Commentator after commentator on the night of Elvis's death mentioned that his life was never complete after his mother died, implying that had she lived he would have also; it seems clear, after reading *What Happened?*, that one root of Elvis's pathology was his inability—from, inevitably, the beginning—to be as good a boy as his mother must have wanted him to be.

I thought of this, however, only after Elvis's death; before that, I hadn't taken the book all that seriously. Now I realize that what I read in it was at the source of my anger at his death, my sense of ugliness and waste. The book disturbed me when I read it, but I merely wrote a brief review and forgot about it. It is only now that I can see through the padding and the mean-spiritedness of the thing to what it has to show us: a picture of a man who lived with nearly complete access to disaster, all the time. The stories that illuminate this reality are not particularly important: you can read them or you can make them up, whether they have to do with the onstage freak-out brought on by dope and who knows what else; the M16 that went off at the wrong time; the rage that no one could cool down. There is nothing in this book, I think, that would have ruined Elvis's career had he lived (perhaps today even the worst possibilities imaginable regarding Elvis's Army relationship with the then-fourteen-year-old Priscilla might not have really hurt him with Middle America; he did finally marry her, after all). But the book's last pages, purportedly the transcript of a telephone conversation between Elvis and Red West, occurring some time after Elvis fired him, a conversation in which they discuss the book that has come out as *What Happened?*, are ending enough.

The feeling I had, reading those last pages, was that Elvis may well have wanted the book to appear; that he wanted the burden and the glory of acting the King removed for good; that he wanted, finally, relief. Of course, that may only be what the authors of *What Happened?* want us to think. Peter Guralnick has written often about Elvis; almost every time, he has headed what he wrote with a quote from William Carlos Williams: "The pure products of America go crazy." In Elvis's case both Guralnick and Williams were obviously right. But it still seems too pat to me, as do the detailed explanations and apologies of *What Happened?* Both merely reduced something we cannot quite get our heads around to something that can be laid to rest by a line.

With Elvis in the ground his death is still out of my reach. This isn't, I know, just another rock 'n' roll death; it isn't any kind of rock 'n' roll death, because it is the only rock 'n' roll death that cannot be contained by the various metaphors rock 'n' roll has itself produced. Nor can it be contained, as Steve Dunleavy and, at times, I try to contain it, by showbiz metaphors. The problem—and it may take years to understand this, years during which some of us will have to keep the files straight and the stacks in order, reminding others that Elvis was not influenced by Chuck Berry, but by Roy Brown, and so on—is that there is just too much that has been dumped in our laps, and that all of it—the art, the boy, the man, the emergence in the South, the reward in Hollywood, the recognition and adulation all over the world for more than twenty years—is all mixed up together.

The problem is that Elvis did not simply change musical history, though of course he did that. He changed history as such, and in doing so he became history. He became part of it, irrevocably and specifically attached to it, as those of us who were changed by him, or who changed ourselves because of things we glimpsed in him, are not. And it must be added that to change history is to do something that cannot be exactly figured out or pinned down: it is to create and pursue a mystery. That Elvis did what he did—and we do not know precisely what he did, because "Milkcow Blues Boogie" and "Hound Dog" cannot be figured out, exactly—means that the world became something other than what it would have been had he not done what he did, and that half-circle of a sentence has to be understood at the limit of its ability to mean anything at all. Because of Elvis's arrival, because of who he was and what he became, because of his event and what we made of it, the American past, from the Civil War to the civil rights movement, from Jonathan Edwards to Abraham Lincoln, looks different than it would have looked without him. Because of that event, its moment—the mid-fifties—was convulsed, and started over. Because of that event, the future has possibilities that would have been otherwise foreclosed.

And you see, we knew all this. We knew it, I think, all the time. You can hear it in the music. Somehow, Elvis must have known it, too. That is why, really, his death makes no sense, no matter if he died of "an irregular heartbeat" (as the papers say today), an overdose, as a suicide, in an accident, or in any other way. And this is what, perhaps, Dave Marsh meant when he said that Elvis had always been there, and hinted that, at least for those of us who helped make Elvis's event, Elvis would of necessity have to outlive us. As with the death of FDR for another generation, it is not simply a person's death that makes no sense, and is in some crucial, terrible way not real. When history is personified, and the person behind that history dies, history itself is no longer real.

My wife came down to the bar and we talked about some of this while I watched the ice melt in my Jack Daniel's. She mentioned that she had asked me to tape Elvis's "Long Black Limousine," from the 1969 comeback album *From Elvis in Memphis,* for our trip; for some reason I had never gotten around to it. It is quite a song: the story of a country girl who goes off to make it in the city, sell her soul, and comes home, as she promised, in a fancy car — which turns out to be a hearse. Elvis never sang with more passion; he was bitter, and of what other recording by Elvis Presley can you say that? Of course, Elvis was no fool; he knew the song was about him, the country boy lost to the city if there ever was one, but he sang as if he liked that fact and loathed it all at once. He contained multitudes. His singing cut through the contradictions, blew them up. William Carlos Williams might say that the pure products of America go crazy, but you might also say that the crazy products of America are pure, or something like that. When the stakes are as high as they always were with Elvis, the neat phrase is not to be trusted; always, it will obscure more than it will reveal. So we talked about "Long Black Limousine," and about the only Elvis music we did have along, an outtake of "Blue Moon of Kentucky," from Elvis's very first sessions, in July of 1954, with studio dialogue bouncing back and forth between a nineteen-year-old Elvis, his accompanists Scotty Moore and Bill Black, and producer Sam Phillips. They were jammin' like crazy, they said. And they were.

We sat for a while longer, and I ordered another Jack Daniel's. My wife explained the rationale to the bartender, who seemed amused. There was, he said, a much more appropriate drink. We asked what. "Why," he said, "a Blue Hawaii. You know, the movie?" That was two nights ago, but I still haven't been able to bring myself to try one.

Son of Samurai

CHARLES M. YOUNG

OUR WRITER TAUGHT JOHN BELUSHI ABOUT PUNK
ROCK AND THE DENIAL OF DEATH. BELUSHI TAUGHT
OUR WRITER NOT TO TAKE SHIT FROM ANYONE.

Backstage at the Palladium, spring 1977. The New York Hell's
Angels chapter had just roared up on its Harleys, several celebrities were disappearing behind various doors to get their
noses packed, and the Grateful Dead's road manager made it
clear he wanted me nowhere near the stage while the band was playing,
even if I was officially at work. As an aspiring gonzo journalist, I was
thinking I ought to be exhilarated by all this potential for social climbing
and weirdness. But I wasn't. I was intimidated and lonely.

John Belushi was one of the celebrities. I had seen him hanging out at
ROLLING STONE a few times, so I finally screwed up my courage and
introduced myself. I remember being exceedingly grateful that he seemed
to like me. We started exploring and eventually found ourselves on the
roof. It was raining lightly and was very cold. John took no notice. We
chatted about rock & roll, about coming to New York from the Midwest,
about deadline stress. I ventured that I had it comparatively easy, since my

deadlines were every two weeks in print and his were every week on live TV.

Squinting into the darkness, I was stunned to see tears shining in John's eyes. "I can't take the pressure," he kept repeating.

If John were still alive, he would be deeply embarrassed by the passage above. Except for a few greedhead businessmen and politicians, I never met anyone so reluctant to reveal personal vulnerability. He was truly the samurai warrior of comedy.

I've always been flummoxed in the presence of crying, and I've always been flummoxed by celebrities in a personal context. I can talk to anyone professionally, but on a personal level a little voice in my brain is always screaming, "You're out of this guy's league!" Here was the world's hottest comedian breaking down, and what solace could I offer? Well, back then I had two standard bits of advice for everyone in any situation, and I gave them: (1) Read *The Denial of Death*, by Ernest Becker, still one of my favorite books, and (2) see the Dead Boys at CBGB. Do you discern a motif in the story so far? Anyway, as far as I know, John never took my advice on the former, but within a few weeks we did go to CBGB for the Dead Boys. And that is one of my few contributions to history: Yes, I introduced John Belushi to punk rock. And he loved it for all the reasons I did: It was brutal, unsentimental, riveting, contemptuous of middle-class hypocrisy, often hilarious, sometimes lawless. John knew great rock & roll when he heard it and made friends with the Dead Boys that night. In 1979 he played drums at a medical benefit after their regular drummer, Johnny Blitz, had been stabbed nearly to death.

Over the next year, I saw John occasionally at clubs and parties and once or twice at the Blues Bar, a dive he co-owned with Dan Aykroyd. We weren't close, exactly, but if you were a journalist, just having John not hate you was an accomplishment. A number of reporters speak bitterly of John to this day because he dumped food on their heads or spat on them. So it was with reluctance that I approached the writing of this profile. Sorting out one's obligations as a friend and as a journalist was especially excruciating in his case. The stakes seemed so much higher. Here are a few details that didn't make the article:

I remember checking into the Beverly Hills Hotel with John. My personal dress code at the time was based on the theory that if you worked for ROLLING STONE, most people would assume you were hip, even though you dressed like a slob. What could the Beverly Hills Hotel do to me? I was traveling with John Belushi, who was also dressed like a slob. So what if I had a bad haircut and was wearing grimy, shapeless bluejeans with a T-shirt that said, ROOT BOY SLIM & THE SEX CHANGE BAND: BOOGIE 'TIL YOU PUKE? So what if the desk clerk looked like he was going to puke as I signed the register? John, of course, got a beautiful suite. My room was slightly larger than the broom closet. I have a vivid memory of opening the curtains to a gorgeous view of the garbage dumpsters. They smelled gorgeous, too.

I remember Dan Aykroyd stopping by my apartment one night in search of John. He was pretty drunk, and he immediately went to my bathroom, where he took a leak, all the while conversing with the door open. Thereafter my toilet had a certain magical aura.

I remember playing miniature golf with John, Steven Spielberg, Amy Irving and John Landis. Being socially as well as sartorially inept, I concentrated on the game and beat everyone by several strokes. When I'm in the mood to be depressed now, I think, "If you lost the goddamn match and figured out something ingratiating to say to Spielberg, you'd be worth millions today."

I remember going to Martha's Vineyard with John. We built model airplanes, ate lobster, went swimming, tooled around in the Bluesmobile and smoked opium, and I beat him at croquet. Jesus, I was a moron.

When I returned to New York, I was told that the previously scheduled cover story had fallen through, and I had two days to write a story that I thought would be given two weeks. From an artistic standpoint, I was severely bummed. Writing is a long series of small decisions, and I knew two days wasn't enough time to get them all correct. Duty nonetheless called, and I have never found anything quite as exhilarating as deadline adrenaline. Having the printers at a national magazine await your words, every minute costing thousands in overtime, all the editors and layout artists tearing their hair while you decide between a semicolon and a period—it's a charge.

In this case, I broke down completely the night before it was absolutely-without-fail-due. Stomach cramps, headaches, profuse sweating, uncontrollable shaking, verbal paralysis. I called my editor, Harriet Fier, and demanded that she bring Pepto-Bismol to my apartment and mop my fevered brow. This is why I never quite made it as a gonzo journalist. Where Hunter would have gobbled more amphetamines and a tab of windowpane, I opted for Pepto-Bismol. On the other hand, thanks to Harriet's brilliant editing and brow mopping, I made the deadline. Upon publication, John didn't spit on me, a great victory, although I still wish I'd had a couple more days to think when I reread certain passages.

The last time I spoke with John, I was interviewing Michael O'Donoghue in his town house for a profile that appeared in *Mother Jones*. John telephoned from Los Angeles, and we talked about the emergence of slam dancing at punk shows. Having been fired recently from ROLLING STONE, I was depressed, and John heard it in my voice. "Don't take shit from anyone," he said. And those were his last words to me. The news of his

death, on March 5th, 1982, was devastating but not surprising. I had heard
his addictions were progressing to a frightening degree. The samurai warrior had a lot in common with Sid Vicious. And O'Donoghue had predicted, with typical lackof euphemism, John's demise in my article.

What is John's legacy? Primarily his work on *Saturday Night Live*. In
the mid-Seventies a large portion of energy left rock & roll and exploded
in comedy. Richard Pryor, Steve Martin, Lily Tomlin, Robin Williams,
Monty Python, Second City, the *SNL* cast, were all operating at a level
the music business hadn't seen since the late Sixties. John had the Burn,
that charismatic flame in the eyes that only the greatest artists in any field
possess. If he'd sobered up and spent more time studying his craft, he
could have been another De Niro or Brando. As it was, he never quite
figured out that TV-skit acting and movie acting require different techniques. His movies weren't great. Most movies with the original cast
members of *SNL* haven't been great. The energy went someplace else.

I thought Bob Woodward's biography *Wired* worked as a warning
against drug abuse, but Woodward lacked the perspective to see why
anyone could have loved John. I loved him because he didn't take shit
from anyone. And he was howlingly funny. His tragedy came in never
realizing that drugs aren't rebellious, a common flaw in counterculture
heroes.

So the energy went someplace else. As my old football coach used to
say, "What goes around, comes around." And what's coming around, after
this Eisenhower-style era, is the Sixties. When the Nineties get heated up,
they're going to make the Sixties look like a nursery school. If there's
such a thing as reincarnation, John Belushi has already appeared somewhere in the Midwest and is giving his grade-school teachers hell until the
real action starts.

RS 271

AUGUST 10TH, 1978

"I feel really weird opening up my personal life this way," says John
Belushi. "But what is there to see? Just a lot of old boxes." Hoist-
ing one on my shoulder, I walk downstairs from his Greenwich Village
apartment and dump it in the trunk of the Bluesmobile, a 1967 Dodge
Monaco with a fresh coat of jet-black paint. Belushi has discovered a
unique way of making reporters useful: if they must ask nosy questions,
the least they can do is save you some bucks in moving expenses. Actually,
there is more to see in the apartment than old boxes — enormous piles of

dirty clothes, two Persian cats, an autographed picture of Ray Charles—but the day is hot, my wind short and my eye for the revealing detail concomitantly dull. As if to reward my efforts, he selects a revealing detail for me.

"They'd just shot me up with morphine," he says, indicating a photograph of himself as a dazed cowboy on the set of *Goin' South*, one of three movies Belushi acted in during the past year, in addition to twenty *Saturday Night Live* shows. "A squib exploded in my hand. We were in Mexico, so they just picked out the splinters and shot me up and we went on with the scene."

Did the morphine affect his acting ability?

"I don't know. It was just a gunfight. . . . I think it'll be a great movie. It has Indians, Mexicans, Orientals, gold, railroads, barroom brawls, bank robberies, horse stealing, everything a Western should have—but no heavy violence."

Dressed in army fatigues and a white T-shirt, Belushi looks capable of handling any sort of violence. Or starting it. His face gives the permanent impression of demented anger lurking barely beneath the surface—an impression reinforced just now by an incipient beard (now that he is off *Saturday Night* for the summer) and a potbelly of the sort usually associated with redneck sheriffs. When he plays the samurai or the crazy weatherman on TV, the effect is hilarious, but up close it's disconcerting. I've known the guy for over a year and have never been quite sure he wasn't about to crush my knees with a brick.

"The same violent urge that makes John great will also ultimately destroy him," says Michael O'Donoghue, a *National Lampoon* alumnus and writer for three seasons on *Saturday Night Live*. (This coming season, he is doing his own show, *Television*). O'Donoghue's humor is best exemplified by his infamous imitation of Tony Orlando and Dawn with needles poked in their eyes. He expects *SNL* to fall into "the enema bank" without him to keep the show in the mainstream of American humor.

"I appeared with John once on *Midday Live* [a local New York talk program hosted by Bill Boggs]," O'Donoghue continues. "Boggs kept asking him to do an Elvis Presley imitation, and I knew John had no ending for it. Finally he agreed, and to get out of the bit, he picked up a glass of water, threw it at Boggs, hit him in the chest and knocked over a table full of plants. You should have seen Steve Allen's face. It turned into the Hollywood Wax Museum. I don't see John ever becoming that stable. He's one-hundred percent Albanian, you know, the only one you're ever likely to meet. I tell him Albanians are gypsies whose wagons broke down. I have this vision of him with a goose under his arm, trying to sneak out of the room. Yes, that is John: an Albanian goose thief.

"He's one of those hysterical personalities that will never be complete. I look for him to end up floating dead after the party. Comedy is a baby seal hunt."

Sitting in the backyard of Belushi's new apartment after we have moved a Bluesmobile full of boxes into storage in the basement, Belushi counts the steps on the stairway to his second-floor balcony. He is pleased to discover they number thirteen, the same as on the gallows where he tries to hang Jack Nicholson in *Goin' South*. The huge new apartment has two floors and a chandeliered living room—highly suitable for a television star on the verge of almost certain movie stardom in the coming year. Maybe even the coming month, with *Animal House*, a comedy premiering in New York City July 28th and scheduled for release in 400 theaters by the middle of August. Universal is counting on a hit, having budgeted about $3.5 million for promotion (the movie itself cost $2.8 million). Their faith is well placed. *Animal House* is hilarious. Written by Douglas Kenney and Chris Miller of the *National Lampoon* and Harold Ramis, formerly of *Playboy*, the movie has much the same sensibility that made the *Lampoon*'s high-school yearbook such a hit. The characters are all stereotypes, but such accurate ones that you recognize everyone you went to college with. Belushi plays Bluto, the most animallike member of the animal fraternity that is expelled from Faber College for crimes that amount to having a good time at the expense of good grades. They seek vengeance by destroying a villainous dean (a tad too villainous, probably. The guy uses four-letter words and is overly frank about his evil intentions. I've never known an educational administrator who didn't sleaze through life on an oil slick of euphemism), a villainous mayor and a villainous rival fraternity. The product of people in their midtwenties to early thirties, the film relays a message from a generation that marched against the war and held gross-out contests to a generation that gets congratulated in *U.S. News and World Report* for shutting up and wanting to go to medical school: go out and trash something, people, or you won't have anything to remember at your five-year reunion.

"I've seen *Animal House* two and a half times now at sneak previews with a real audience, and the reaction was great," says Belushi. "Your face ends up forty feet high and if you blow a line during the filming, you can just do it again. If you blow it on TV, it's gone forever. But I want to continue doing both next season. After that, I don't know."

Belushi's schedule this past season was overwhelming. On Sundays after the TV show, he flew to location (Durango, Mexico, for *Goin' South*; Eugene, Oregon, for *Animal House*, and Los Angeles for *Old Boyfriends*) and flew back on Thursdays for *Saturday Night Live* rehearsals. Because three days of stubble was required for two of the movies and outlawed on the show, just keeping his shaving schedule straight was complicated enough, let alone learning his lines. To keep his life together under such circumstances, I suggest he must be on a more even keel than he was during the first two years of the show.

"Those were very hard times . . . uh . . . very tough, dealing with fame and success, while trying to fulfill your responsibility to the audience," he says. "The trick is knowing what you want to do and then resolving to do everything you have to do to get there."

Does that mean his self-destructive tendencies are under control?

"I think it . . . uh . . . I don't know. It comes along with a certain kind of lifestyle, which you don't change after becoming well known. Everything becomes more heightened, takes on more urgency, and the tendency to self-destruct heightens too. I'm learning to cope and not deny my own success, but I still think it's not happening a lot. I get nervous, and I am capable of doing something to blow it on purpose. A lot of actors have that problem."

John Belushi is not your basic great quote. He tends to not finish sentences before moving on to the next thought. He tends to say things like, "The sky is blue," and then five minutes later say, "Uh, lets put that sky-is-blue stuff off the record. It might offend my fans in Brooklyn," leaving the impression his career will be over, his wife will divorce him, and his cats eaten by wild dogs if you don't put your pen down. That's if he likes you. Once, a double-knit TV reporter wearing white shoes got him to sit down on the set of *Animal House* for an interview and asked how it was to work in movies, as opposed to live television. Belushi paused for a moment, shot him an I'll-eat-your-kneecaps-for-breakfast look and asked, "How much do you make, anyway?" A few days later, he talked more politely to a high-school reporter for over an hour, but told her that he got the original idea for *Saturday Night Live* while eating acid in the desert, and that sundry cast members were junkies, among other lies. She printed it straight.

Furthermore, when John Belushi bothers to be funny around reporters, much of the humor depends on him breaking into weird accents at unexpected moments. Black letters on white paper just cannot convey the humor of his Greek restaurant character suddenly showing up next to you in an airplane seat to Los Angeles and demanding, "Shut door! City of New York don't pay me to air-condition streets! What you want? We have good strawberry pie. You just want grilled cheese? You cheap bastard!"

Nor is John Belushi much given to self-analysis. One of his great imitations is of Joe Cocker, the English R&B singer with the stage mannerisms of a cerebral palsy victim. *Saturday Night Live* fans usually do not remember individual sketches that well, but everyone remembers the night

Belushi sang a duet with Cocker. For some it was hilarious, for others, it was cruel. Belushi himself won't even watch the tape. "It was all rehearsed," he says. "So I asked him to do it a long time before. It was just, uh . . . the answer . . . uh . . . I don't know why I did it. It was very emotional. Don't ask me why I did it."

All of this is to John Belushi's long-term advantage. He has as strong a sense of his own emotional integrity as anyone I have ever met. Some part of his mind is simply inviolable, and as long as he is in the public eye, people will want to know what John Belushi is *really* like. And John Belushi won't tell them.

In pursuit of the impossible dream, then, let us consider some biographical facts:

John Belushi was born January 24th, 1949. He is one-hundred-percent Albanian, which he refuses to discuss.* He seems to have been a nightmare to his schoolteachers. In the sixth grade, they demoted him to second grade to sober him out of his antics. Also in the sixth grade, his gym teacher announced in front of his class that he was the worst of her 400 students and kicked him in the balls. "They crushed the spirit out of me by the time I left," he insists.

Attending Wheaton, Illinois, Central High School, he acquired the nickname Wrestling Shoes from his cousins. "They were a couple of years older and much funnier than me," he recalls. "Every time I opened my mouth, they would cut me down. We were playing poker one New Year's Eve, and they won all my money. I left the table and suddenly burst into tears. They asked me what was wrong, and I said, 'That was for my wrestling shoes.' So they called me Wrestling Shoes ever after."

Bored by his classes, Belushi expended most of his energies playing drums in rock bands, acting in school shows and being captain of the football team. They were conference champions his junior year and finished in a tie for second place the following year. "I must have been the laziest captain they ever had," he says. "I was kicked off the team every year for loafing. The coach used to yell at us to do something or turn in our uniforms. If I felt I'd already done my best, I'd just run to the locker room and turn in my uniform. But I was always back the next day. I never missed a practice. It was a very valuable experience. After two-a-day practices at the end of summer, you feel there's nothing you can't do. I probably wouldn't have made it in New York if it hadn't been for that. As the coach used to say, 'No pain, no gain.' "

---

*Belushi expressed great dismay when I told him I'd been planning to use his Albanian heritage as a humorous motif in this profile. Since he is an expert in both comedy and imitating people with strange accents, I took his word that his ancestral homeland is not funny.

Belushi met his wife, Judy Jacklin, now a book designer, when he was senior and she a sophomore. "The first time I saw him was at a party," she recalls. "He was singing 'Louie, Louie' without slurring the dirty words."

Jacklin characterizes Wheaton, a Chicago suburb, as the town where "Billy Graham went to college. It is heavily Republican and totally dry— you're not even supposed to have liquor in your home. Everyone moves there so their kids can go to the right schools; so they care very much about football games and beauty contests."

After graduation in 1967, Belushi took a year to break out of the Wheaton mold. Bored by acting in summer stock and bored by a brief attempt at college, he moved to Chicago and opened the Universal Life Church Coffee House near the university with two friends, Timo Insana and Steve Beshakas. For three years they put on their own comedy productions, serving the mostly student audience mu tea, Kool-Aide and passing around a jug of wine. "They were mostly tripping anyway," says Belushi. "Our subject matter was sex, drugs and violence." Dan Fogelberg was their opening act, for which they paid him seven dollars.

The club was located in a tough part of Chicago, however, and the local greasers were offended by its presence. One night, one of them tried to get in without paying, and Belushi came from backstage to deal with the problem.

"I paid," said the greaser. "You calling me a liar?"

"Yeah," said Belushi, 'I'm calling you a liar. Get out."

"Who are you?" said the greaser. "God?"

So Belushi pushed him out the door, threw him over a car hood and smashed him in the nose. "About fifty of his friends came out of the cracks in the sidewalk armed with boards and pipes," Belushi remembers. "There was a huge fight, but we finally got all our people inside and the show went on."

The greasers pounded on the windows during the performance and Belushi had an ever-growing bruise on his forehead as he acted. The audience didn't laugh a whole lot. Neither did the police when Belushi went to the station house with the kid whose nose he had broken. "Who threw the first punch?" asked the sergeant.

"Ahhhhhh, I guess I did," said Belushi, grabbing the greaser's hand. "What do you say we be friends?"

That was the end of the coffeehouse, but the experience won Belushi a gig with Second City, the improvisational troupe that has served as a sort of college for comedians over the years (Dan Aykroyd, Bill Murray and Gilda Radner are also graduates of Second City). He gives director Del Close much credit for refining his technique. "Del made us explore and work with the other actors," he says. "He wanted us to take chances and not go for cheap laughs. I even took notes when he talked. It's very hard to be a good actor, you know. It's easy to be cute."

In 1973, he got a call from New York to join the National Lampoon's *Lemmings*, a musical production parodying the Woodstock culture, for which he perfected Joe Cocker and created the role of the announcer exhorting the chant for rain. "I chose him because he projected the feeling of a homicidal maniac," says director Tony Hendra. "Watching him act, you were always glad he hadn't taken up something more dangerous. During rehearsals, he went into a blue funk every third day and I would have to talk him out of going home to Chicago, but once he hit the stage, you knew he was in his element. He was always threatening to go over the edge, and the more dangerous the situation, the funnier."

A good example of how evenly balanced are his desires for success and destruction is how he got picked for *Saturday Night Live*. He and Aykroyd were the last hired for the cast—Aykroyd because of a reputation for not showing up at gigs, and Belushi because "I had a big chip on my shoulder. I thought all television was shit, and I let Lorne [Michaels, producer of *Saturday Night Live*] know it. My own set at home was often covered with spit. The only reason I wanted to be on it was because Michael O'Donoghue was writing and it had a chance to be good."

Belushi auditioned with his beloved samurai character (his own invention after watching a Japanese film festival on educational TV) and won a position, but his attitude was little changed. "I'd been wearing a beard for five years," he recalls: "One day Lorne suggested, 'Let's see what you look like with it off.' I came back the next day with the beard and he said, 'Why don't you just try shaving it once so we can see what it looks like?' I told him I didn't like shaving, and the next day he asked, 'Weren't you supposed to do something last night?' I told him I got sick. 'Let's see it off,' he said. So I finally shaved. My face *is* more expressive without it, I guess. And I couldn't play eleven-year-old kids in skits, like I've done, with a beard. I just grow it in the summer now."

John Belushi occasionally dismisses his audience as "the angel-dust crowd," but it seems as if nearly everybody loves the guy. He cannot walk down the street without being recognized every twenty feet and greeted like a long-lost crazy uncle who used to bounce you on his knee (and maybe dropped you on your head a few times).

In nearly seventy shows on *Saturday Night Live*, he has taken part in an awesome number of skits, many of which he wrote himself. He has contributed a couple of comic catch phrases to the American language—"Cheeseburger, cheeseburger" and "But nooooo!"—just in time to replace Steve Martin's "Excuuuuse me!"

But no matter what role he plays, he is always John Belushi—unlike, say, Dan Aykroyd or Laraine Newman, who project little of their own personalities. Perhaps to his detriment, he is often the same violent lunatic character in whatever role he plays. Bluto in *Animal House*, for example, is not a significant departure from what he has accomplished on TV. The almost certain prospect of becoming a major star carries the danger of being typecast as a maniac for the rest of his life and ultimately boring his fans.

I doubt this will happen, because he would bore himself first. He could have spent the rest of his life as a killer bee, but he stopped before it became stale. He also has too many other talents. He and Aykroyd formed the Blues Brothers to warm up audiences before the show, ultimately made an appearance and now have a contract with Atlantic Records. They will open for Steve Martin at the Universal Amphitheatre in Los Angeles in September. The album will be live (the backup band is as yet unchosen) and the cover will probably feature them changing a flat on the Bluesmobile.

Belushi's plans are hard to pin down. Depending on his mood, he will be happy doing *Saturday Night Live* for the rest of his life or never again (he has one year left on his contract). And he might do another movie, depending on if he can stand all the assholes in Hollywood.

His wife, Judy, who ought to know when to take him at his word, says he wants to be a serious actor. "In college I saw him play Danforth in *The Crucible*, and he was so intense that the other actors thought he was going to hurt them," she says. "When he does get a straight role, he will blow people away."

Aerosmith's Train Keeps a Rollin'

DAISANN McLANE

WORDS WERE CHEAP AND THE BANDS GAVE A RE-
PORTER GREAT ACCESS BACK IN THE HIGH-ROLLIN'
ROCK SUBCULTURE OF THE LATE SEVENTIES. A REPORT
FROM THE PRIVATE JET.

Two clunky men's Harris tweed jackets hang in mothballs in the back of my closet, woolly reminders of my first job out of college, my dream job: two years as a ROLLING STONE rock & roll reporter. I don't wear the jackets anymore—nowadays, my work wardrobe leans more in the direction of black taffeta party dresses— but at the time, they were as indispensable to my professional life as a Kevlar vest is to a New York cop. The dozens of profiles I wrote for the magazine between 1978 and '80 wouldn't have happened without the tweed.

Wearing the straight, sexless uniform of the Ivy League to represent the most celebrated anything-goes journal of the counterculture may seem a bizarre fashion statement, but remember, this was 1978. Back then the main roles available to women interested in rock & roll careers were pensive singer-songwriter, lead chick singer, boho androgyne and grossly underpaid publicist. Back then the etiquette, worldview and vocabulary of your average record-biz mogul were not so far removed from that of a boxing promoter or a mobster (sometimes in fact, these particular individuals *were* boxing promoters or mobsters). Back then all the power and almost all the money in the music business belonged to men, the sort of men to whom it might never occur that the single young woman with an ALL ACCESS pass and a seat on the tour bus was the ROLLING STONE reporter on assignment.

The jacket was there to take care of that. It also, as it turned out, accomplished something much more crucial in terms of the work I was doing: It lowered my profile. In a testosterone jungle of egos, the Girl in the Tweed Jacket projected the gangly gee-whiz of a kid sister. Neither sexy nor hip, she all but disappeared. Managers, agents and rock icons usually forgot she was around, forgot why she was there—and most importantly—who she was there for. In time (and there was plenty of time back then) many of them would loosen up and do and say things they never would have thought to do or say in front of ROLLING STONE. Like show up, as Aerosmith's Steven Tyler did for his interview, holding a needle and thread and a ripped spandex bodysuit, shrugging sheepishly: "Uh, hey, like, can you do me a favor? Can you sew?"

In 1978, I was twenty-four, the only female staff writer at ROLLING STONE and, except for Cameron Crowe, the youngest. For about ten minutes every morning, this fact was an occasion for intense head swelling on my part. Then I'd get to the office, a place guaranteed to turn one's vanities to dust balls. For this was no renovated hippie warehouse in San Francisco but 745 Fifth Avenue, New York, New York—an expensive, serious-business address with an expensive, serious-business view of Central Park, rolled out twenty-three stories below like Jann's own carpet. To stroll (or more like it, pace) these corridors was an exercise in humility not unlike that practiced by the *castigates* of rural Mexico during Holy Week. Summoned by my editor, Peter Herbst, to receive my next assignment, I ran a gantlet of legendary bylines: Chet Flippo, Cameron, Ben Fong-Torres, Chuck Young, David Felton. Even my office cubicle was no refuge from the Giants of Rock Journalism; I shared it with (and he was not happy about this) Dave Marsh. Over in the next cubicle loomed the most looming presence of all, Paul Nelson, an eminence aswirl in wisdom and Dunhill smoke.

All of them writers who were stars . . . *personas*. ROLLING STONE in 1978 was one of the last places that encouraged its writers to develop strong, offbeat, personalized voices. Most other national magazines, anticipating the celeb-sucking reportage of the yuppie Eighties, had begun to red-pencil the no-holds-barred, idiosyncratic, first-person writing of the New Journalism. But at ROLLING STONE we maintained our stake in the territory that had been opened by Tom Wolfe, Norman Mailer and, especially, Hunter S. Thompson. At ROLLING STONE it wasn't enough to go out and merely report a story; a writer was supposed to bag it, tie it up squarely, then march it back home at spear point, still alive and twitching. (Chuck Young showed up at the office after his London escapades with the Sex Pistols in '79 with his T-shirt ripped and bloodied, trophy of a job well done.)

Not surprisingly, these strong, off-beat, personal ROLLING STONE voices tended to bleed off the page and into the offices of 745 Fifth Avenue. The office, at times, resembled a boisterous, competitive basketball court where Michael Jordan-size egos lobbed and passed and dunked shoptalk and, sometimes, each other. At 745 Fifth it was risky to neglect one's writerly image. Image building, however, had its own perils. I remember one warm, sticky summer evening when a handful of us had gathered on the outdoor terrace of the twenty-eighth floor for one of those impromptu, raucous end-of-day sessions that usually revolved around genial verbal games of one-upmanship and the consumption of plastic tumblers of white jug wine. I'd had a few of these and was leaning against the retaining-wall ledge, exhilarated by the view from the top and the fresh, cool breeze, when suddenly I noticed that all talking had stopped. I turned around and saw staff writer Fred Schruers tipsily walking along the six-inch-wide roof ledge, on his hands.

In this highly competitive league, I cast around for my edge, my angle, and discovered that despite a total lack of gymnastic skills, I had certain advantages over the boys. For starters, I could sew. I could also, if need be, sit for an hour with Stevie Nicks on the lace coverlet of her antique Victorian four-poster bed in Bel Air and tut-tut over her recently hysterectomized puppy. Being female made me less threatening, encouraged a certain intimacy; sometimes a familiarity that became surreal, as when Steven Tyler said to me, absolutely straight-faced, "Do you remember what it was like when you used to go finger-fuck girls under the aqueduct?" Of course, I said yes. At moments like these, I'd excuse myself and run into the bathroom, scribble notes on my palm with a Flair. Then I'd come back to the office and furiously type these chronicles of the rock & roll road, every last bizarre, ridiculous, telling detail.

"But what was it like?" is the question people still ask me, thirteen years later, when they find out I used to earn my living stalking lead guitarists in the airport baggage-claim areas of Tulsa, nodding asleep backstage at arenas in Salt Lake City, playing poker in Learjets over Dallas and balancing on bar stools in Holiday Inn cocktail lounges in Shreveport, tape recorder ready to grab the least utterings of Aerosmith, Peter Frampton, Heart, Fleetwood Mac, ZZ Top or Cheap Trick. And this is how I always answer: To understand what things were really like for me, you must first remember that the music business in 1978 was a world in which new records by Peter Frampton shipped platinum and where it was not unusual for a concert contract rider to include specifications concerning the number and dressing-room placement of chilled buckets of Dom Pérignon.

In short, it was a fat time, a moment in which rock had moved from the hip margins to the profitable mainstream and was sailing on a (seemingly) endless high tide of promotion, tour support, recording budgets, recreational intoxicants and loose cash (it was no coincidence that ROLLING STONE, which then depended on record-ad revenues for solvency, made its move from the funky San Francisco warehouse to Fifth Avenue in 1977). Of course, we know now that much of the music that came out then was as cellulite-ridden as its production and tour budgets (this was, remember, the era of the three-record set, *Saturday Night Fever* and solo albums from the members of Kiss). But it all sounded great from a seat in first class, which is where most of the musicians, moguls, functionaries — and sometimes tweed-jacketed journalists — got to sit. To be on the rock & roll road was to glide through the universe on cruise control. For weeks, often months, decisions were made and problems resolved by managers, lawyers, publicists and accountants. Wake-up calls came at noon, road managers collected luggage from outside one's hotel room door. I recall that most musicians I interviewed didn't wear a watch. The myth of the rock & roll road was freedom; the reality was that one emerged from this pampered bubble as dependent and querulous as a spoiled adolescent.

This was a seductive world, indeed, but the tweed jacket always served to remind me who I was, a stranger at this party. I didn't — as did some of my colleagues — befriend rock stars. Nor did I pay too much attention to what they actually said to me in a formal interview situation, since what they actually said was so predictable that Cameron Crowe and I used to begin our phone conversations with a parody of it:

ME: Hello, Cameron . . .

C.C.: Fuck NO! We are *not* breaking up. The solo LP is just so that I can, ya know, express some of my identity.

ME: But you canceled the tour, and your manager doesn't return calls. . . .

C.C.: Bullshit. [*Voice lower, cracking with emotion*] Hey, listen. We're a *band*. This new album's gonna be a band album. We've got a new producer, we're goin' back to our roots. You'll see. We love the road. . . .

Words were cheap in the high-rolling rock & roll subculture of 1978; they were as plentiful as white powder and about as long lasting. The stories of these years in the music business — the ones that interested me — lurked between the lines, in what was *not* said, in the nuances. And so, when I was sent out to write about a band, I began my work by listening to what they wanted to tell ROLLING STONE. Then I'd hang around afterward as long as possible, weeks if I could, accumulating details.

Little did I realize that this method of working would shortly become impossible, because it depended on unlimited time with the subject. Here is my itinerary for a 1979 story on Fleetwood Mac, pegged to the release of *Tusk*. October: One week in Los Angeles to hang out at rehearsals and visit band members individually. November: Three days in L.A. to interview Nicks. Late November: Opening tour dates in Idaho, Denver, Salt Lake City—one week. December: Press party in New York, three nights backstage at Madison Square Garden. ALL ACCESS, said my plastic tags, and all access I got; in this pre-MTV era, bands bent over backward for press coverage, and for ROLLING STONE they did cartwheels. I could not have imagined that one day doing a piece on a band would involve weeks of negotiating with publicists, resulting in a two-hour hotel-room session, then—zip. This was not how we worked in 1978. Back then when my editor suggested that I write a 3500-word feature about Peter Frampton after spending only three days with him at his home in the Bahamas— with no tour time, no follow-up visits—I did what any of my colleagues would have done at the time: I complained.

I don't think anybody realized that the all-access days were sputtering to an end, that spin control was lurking around the corner and that the footloose possibilities of the (literary) New Journalism would be supplanted by the orchestrated (televised) media event. Who imagined that the champagne-bright platinum-selling empire of rock would collapse suddenly, in a heap of returns, budget slashing and layoffs? But it did in 1980, the same year that Ronald Reagan was elected president, and my profession began to acquire a new, Eighties style: Celebrity Journalism.

A couple of years ago, the fellow who was writing the unauthorized history of ROLLING STONE called me up for dish, and I told him, "No comment," a response that surprised me. Like everybody else who ever stalked the corridors of 745 Fifth, I'd sustained my share of battle scars— not only that, I'd been awarded the ultimate ROLLING STONE badge of courage: I'd been fired. Like everybody else, I could run it all down: the ominous editorial sessions, the flying bottles of Polish vodka, the private tears, the public insults, the scorecard of breakdowns and rehabs. But presented with the opportunity to settle old accounts (or at least, the chance to get *my* version of the magazine's history between hard covers), I closed ranks. To wave family laundry in front of a stranger seemed, well, wrong.

What had happened was this: Ten years and several jobs down the line, I'd discovered an unexpected loyalty to what was, I now realize, a most singular place to begin a writing career. Sure, ROLLING STONE had been more like a dysfunctional family than a professional workplace; mean words ricocheted around every corner, the house copy of Machiavelli was dogeared, and fear and loathing reverberated whenever someone slammed an office door. Nevertheless, I cannot remember another situation when as a writer I felt so protected, so invincible. A cruel mother, ROLLING STONE batted you around and then shoved you out into the world and said, "Okay, kid, now be a star." And so you tried, because being around the magazine made that and all other things seem possible. That was the gift.

Twenty-eight stories above Central Park, we did handstands on the edge. At ROLLING STONE, in 1978, it never occurred to us, to me, that we might fall.

RS 285

FEBRUARY 22ND, 1979

J oe Perry sticks out his hand and shows me his scar—a round, purplish blotch right over the vein. A year ago he was hit by an M-80 while Aerosmith was performing before 20,000 fans in Philadelphia. "This is it," he mutters cynically. "Battle scars. Drew blood. Miserable. I was definitely disillusioned."

But not scared off. Aerosmith has been touring behind their latest LP, *Live Bootleg*, and "Come Together," their hit single from *Sgt. Pepper*, from August through December. And four nights a week, lead guitarist Perry is back onstage, gamely dodging the usual barrage of Frisbees, hats, coats, scarves, underwear—and worse. When Aerosmith revisited Philadelphia during this tour, Perry was grazed by a fragment of a beer bottle that splayed off lead singer Steven Tyler's monitor.

Sometimes, though, it can't help but bring you down. One night, after a particularly wicked hailstorm of flying objects, Perry turned to a roadie, shrugging his shoulders, and said, "Maybe if I worked harder on my guitar playing we'd attract a better class of people."

Thunk! A kid in an old army jacket lunges, head first, into the cinderblock wall. He caroms off the wall again, bouncing back in front of the security guard who won't let him inside unless he shows a ticket. "Okay, don't let me in," he says. "I don't give a shit." He hurls himself at the wall again, triumphantly. "I just don't give a shit."

The Aerosmith audience in Shreveport, Louisiana (the next-to-last stop) is committed to rock & roll in a serious way: legions of red-eyed adolescents are flopping to the floor, staggering into pillars and each other, twitching and writhing like victims of a neutron bomb attack. Tonight's concert is general admission—no reserved seats. When the final ticket holder is let in, the floor of the stadium is thick with bodies, pressed up against the five-foot-high, custom-designed steel-mesh security fence that's a permanent part of Aerosmith's stage equipment.

Backstage, Steven Tyler is getting ready to go on, meticulously applying cake eyeliner to his lids and blowing it dry with a Conair 1000. His mirror has a sticker on it that says: STEVEN TYLER KICKS ASS. While he's putting on his makeup, he's listing complaints to his stage manager: the monitor mix is lousy, there's a light missing, when are we gonna get it right? He turns the blow dryer on his hair, fluffing the black mane out. He doesn't look like Mick Jagger—he's got the lips, but his nose turns up and his face is unlined enough for him to get away with shaving a year or two off his age (he says he's thirty). Where Jagger is sinister and suggestive, Tyler's cute and obvious. He sprinkles his conversation with lines like Whaddaya mean?" delivered in a Yonkers-cum-dead-end-kid accent. There's just no mystique in that.

"The problem with rock & roll today," Tyler opines, putting the final touches on his eyes, "is that nobody wants to move. I mean, look at them . . . Foreigner, the Atlanta Rhythm Section. Onstage they just stand there. Don't they know how to *move?*" He shakes his head, bewildered. Moving is the thing that Tyler does best.

They'll pick at you any way they can," says Steven Tyler. Pick and pick and pick."

Tyler glances out the window of a rented Lear Jet. The concert in Shreveport is over, and we're heading for an overnight stop in Dallas. It's been a long evening, but Tyler is expansive, friendly. He pulls the aluminum ring on a can of Coors and absent-mindedly picks the lint from his fingernails with the tab.

"You wanna know why I don't like the press?" he says goodnaturedly. "Did you see the last cover story that's been out on us? If I ever see the guy that wrote it again, I'm gonna beat him up. He made us look like wimps! He was around backstage on the last night of our spring tour, and he heard us bitchin' a little about how the road sucks. And he made it seem like we don't like to tour. That we're too big and rich to want to do it anymore. A lot of kids will read that and think it's true!"

You seem to be worried that people will think you're getting old and tired, I start to say. Tyler cuts me off.

"*Seem* to worry?!!" he sputters, giving me this here's-another-press-asshole glare. Then he turns sullen. I'm an outsider again, not to be trusted.

Mark Radice, the keyboard player who is along for this tour, suggests a game of cards. Tyler, bassist Tom Hamilton, rhythm guitarist Brad Whitford and I all take turns trying to guess the top card of the deck before it's turned over. Hamilton, a tall genial blond who looks like he could be your next-door neighbor in Marin County, explains that the game is called ESP; the band made it up to kill time on the road. Perry and Joey Kramer sit up front, looking disinterested. Tyler loses the round, and silently rolls a cigarette.

We touch down, and the limos are waiting. Inadvertently, I wander into the one where Tyler is sitting alone. Before I can figure out what's going on, he lunges for me and starts landing monkey punches on my back and arms. Huh? Two seconds later, he explodes in laughter.

"Sorry about that. I've been on the road too long."

He smiles a winsome, you-know-I-didn't-mean-it grin at me. It's the kind of look your twelve-year-old cousin shoots you after he's attacked your new party dress with the Water Pik. All this roughhousing must be Tyler's way of making up. When we get to the hotel, he follows me to the desk, makes sure my reservations are in order.

"Come up after you've settled in and we'll do the interview," he leans close to my ear and whispers conspiratorially. "I'm in 729." For security reasons, the band registers under phony names. Without the room number, I have no way of finding him. "Can you remember that?" he repeats. "7-2-9."

Five minutes later, I rap on the appointed door. No answer. It's dark inside. I head back downstairs to check the bar and run into Aerosmith's road manager. "Steven's in his room, or he should be," he says. "Did you go up there? He's in 927."

The Dallas Hilton's room 927 looks like a gypsy's lair: ragtag bits of costume are strewn over lampshades, a leopard-skin morning coat hangs in a corner, two gleaming throwing knives in leather cases sit on the bureau by the television. There's a book in the wastebasket: *Strange Monsters — The Werewolf that Sucked the Blood of Hundreds*.

"Hey, could you do me a favor? Can you sew?" Tyler asks. He rummages in a drawer, pulls out a needle and thread and hands me the skintight white satin jump suit he wears onstage. I search his face for some kind of ulterior motive, but there is none. "See, the leg is unraveling here. If you could just take it up or something. . . ."

Sure. Why not? It's three o'clock in the morning; I might as well be mending a rock star's suit.

The Dog Is Us

MARCELLE CLEMENTS

YOU'RE IN YOUR DORM ROOM. YOU'RE STONED. A DOG WALKS IN. WOW. YOU CAN'T STOP WATCHING HIM. HE'S INCREDIBLY RIDICULOUS. YOU START LAUGHING. NOW IT'S YEARS LATER: YOU GET HIGH AGAIN, AND IT'S NO FUN. WHAT HAPPENED?

For a long time, I regretted having written this piece. And it was not just your run-of-the-mill writer's cringing with the fear of having written an asinine piece on the culture, although that certainly would not have been an unreasonable worry, since at the time it was published—1982—asinine commentary on the culture constituted a vast body of literature. (Fortunately or not, this is no longer a concern, since the culture has become so complex, incoherent and incomprehensible that hardly anyone tries to come up with any syntheses anymore.) Rather, I worried about the ideological implications of writing an article about how people my age—so-called Sixties people (not yet an insulting epithet)—had, in great numbers, stopped smoking marijuana. I feared that some of the notoriety the article attained was caused by the jubilation of the growing contingent of neo-cons and crypto-cons. Had I allied myself with the enemy? Was I now a foot soldier in the killjoy brigade?

But let me backtrack. In fact, this essay was connected with regrets right from the start, though Phase I consisted of the banal repentance every journalist feels immediately upon having accepted an assignment — that one phrase bobbing around in the mind: *There's no story here.* The hitch was that I was the one who had proposed it. The circumstances were dubious enough: I had stopped smoking marijuana, and one night at dinner a friend told me he also had stopped smoking marijuana. There was a saying around that time among journalists that ran something like: If you and one other person are doing the same thing, it's a coincidence. If three of you are doing it, it's a story.

It suddenly *seemed* to me that the people I knew were smoking less pot.

It was on that sound basis that I decided there might be an essay to be written on this topic. This was merely fantasy. As it happened, I hadn't written anything in a long time. My father had died a few months earlier, and I was in bad shape. But — and this was the point of the fantasy — who needed insight into my own problem when there was the possibility of voyeuristically inquiring into many other people's problems *and drug habits* (second only to sex, but barely, in exciting prurience)!

Fantasy accidentally turned into reality when I ran into Terry McDonell, then managing editor of ROLLING STONE. Perhaps merely to fill the few moments in which we exchanged greetings, McDonell must have perfunctorily suggested I write something for the magazine. I babbled something of my half-baked idea, and he thereupon asked me to write it.

The next day I entered a dreadful panic state, which I was extremely careful to conceal from McDonell, engaging in the usual freelance writer's tactics, such as avoiding the editor at parties. McDonell didn't directly contact me during this period, which I attributed to his characteristic Ineffable Coolness, but which I now realize may have been due to the fact that he had entirely forgotten that he'd made the assignment (though, needless to say, this sort of absent-mindedness was symptomatic of the aforementioned I.C.). Whatever notions had once glimmered slightly through the fog that surrounds all ideation around the subject of drugs had disappeared entirely. My reaction to the gargantuan, mammoth, Herculean, seemingly invincible writer's block that ensued was a young writer's solution: I researched.

Did I ever research. I became a researching Sherman tank: Nothing could stop me. I called every one of my friends, and many of *their* friends. I called every pothead I could find. I called cokeheads, junkies and speed freaks to talk with them about what they thought of potheads. I called university research departments, doctors, dealers, people who were working on legalizing marijuana, people who put other people in jail for smoking it. I left few government agencies uncalled—no matter how remote the connection—and I guess those government statisticians must have gotten a kick out of this obsessive New York chick who kept bugging them about this marijuana story.

This compulsive quest went on for about four to six months immediately following my fateful encounter with Terry McDonell. I recently came across my files for "The Dog Is Us," and there were thousands of pages of transcripts, notes and research material. My behavior now seems to me suspiciously like that of some obsessive pothead, and my guess is that thinking about the marijuana high so much propelled me into one of those obsessional-stoned-fixated sorts of states. In any case, by the time I was finished, not a single one of my close friends could bear to hear anything on the subject of marijuana. Let alone this obsessive koanlike thing I kept repeating about the dormitories of the Sixties and everybody staring at dogs when they were stoned and about how the dog was now us, and so on.

The strange thing that happened is that it turned out that there really was a story. When I bugged the people in Washington enough, they looked at their statistics in the way I was interested in, and it turned out that my cohort—the impendingly dreadful Sixties people—really had altered its drug habits. While the rest of the country was *increasing* its marijuana use, my cohort, harbinger of things to come, was cutting down. Even I had to admit this answered the first part of the question: Had people stopped smoking marijuana? It *wasn't* just me and a couple of my friends.

The second part was *why*, and the essay was my attempt to answer the question. It's really funny, I guess (or not so funny, considering all the pain it caused me at the time), that it didn't occur to me that my father's death had upset whatever little equilibrium I had. In fact, it was years after I wrote the piece that I arrived at the amazing deduction that it was probably my reaction to my father's death that prevented me from being able to have a good time when I got high. . . . In any event, whatever was wrong with me, in the process of trying to flee from it, I managed to amass an incredible amount of information, quotes, testimonials, statistics, to answer the question *why* for hundreds of thousands of other people.

To my amazement, McDonell liked the story, and once he'd rather deftly chopped off a few structural excrescences (otherwise known as several thousand extra words), to my amazement, Jann Wenner agreed to print it. It got hundreds of letters and quite a flurry of attention in the rest of the press. In fact, soon I was on the *Today* show chatting about how people my age seemed to have stopped smoking marijuana and mumbling this and that about that darn dog.

And that's when my aforementioned doubts and regrets began: Soon the Just Say No Era kicked into high gear, and suddenly there was the horrendous possibility that my article had assisted in the ideological sabotage of my own subculture. And I was loyal, by the way, to that subculture. I still am: I really don't think the so-called Sixties people were dreadful. They were just kids, and it really wasn't such a bad way to be young.

I never did settle my ambivalence on the whole ideological-sabotage issue, but let's say that I determined that it was possible to decide that you didn't want to kill yourself with drugs without turning into an asshole.

And I still believe that, though I do find myself either irritated (on bad days) or amused (on good days) to see how official America has wound up treating the recreational-drug issue. Especially about the really rather innocent grass smoking of the Sixties, there is quite a curious amount of shuffling of memories and artificial adjustment of retroactive barometers of what was or wasn't acceptable. For instance, we now accept the fact that many of our elected officials at least "tried" marijuana—or else there'd be hardly anyone under fifty to elect. But they can't have enjoyed it—or, in some cases, even inhaled it.

But I've given up the thought of any serious argument, because the drug issue has become, like the rest of the culture, complex to the point of incoherence and incomprehensibility. The tragic fact is that at least one entire generation of poor children has been ruined by the crack phenomenon. So all the rest doesn't seem all that worth arguing about.

But it's wrong to defile our memories, such as they are, by distortion. So, as long as we're on the subject, I'm delighted to have this opportunity to say not only that I often had a good time smoking marijuana as a kid but that not long after I published the piece, I smoked a joint, and though it did make me somewhat anxious, it really wasn't the end of the world, one way or another. There. Now I feel better.

But, as I said, it really doesn't matter anymore. And the truth is that the Sixties have now been so thoroughly commercially exploited as a cultural topic that I have come to associate them with dreadfulness myself. But as far as "The Dog Is Us" is concerned, in the end I liked it well enough to make it the title story of a book of essays. The only long-term inconvenience that ensued was that for years I had to hear people's drug stories.

And so, the regrets eventually faded away. Except the one big regret—embodied but never articulated in this piece—for the era evoked for me by the subject of marijuana, which is, of course, the regret for youth. Whether it was wasted or well spent, I don't know, but it was my youth. I hadn't realized that what I was doing with this piece, and why it was so much trouble to write it, was to say goodbye. It must seem ridiculous not to have understood that then, but maybe that was too painful, or seemed too corny according to the youthful ethos I hadn't quite let go of, so it had to be couched in this other elaborate construct. I guess it was ridiculous. But, mind you, I never pretended that I wasn't ridiculous or that the dog wasn't, indeed, me.

RS 377

SEPTEMBER 2ND, 1982

Trying to recall the spirit of a certain epoch is often like describing a dream: it's easy to chronicle the events, but almost impossible to characterize the motivations. Yet every once in a while, one runs into a telling artifact. Rewind to the past. There's a photograph taken in 1965 of Allen Ginsberg at a demonstration to legalize marijuana. He's standing outside the Women's House of Detention in New York during a snowstorm. There is snow on his hair and beard and glasses, and he has on what appear to be earmuffs, but no gloves. His expression is vaguely eupeptic, and he's sort of waving (at the photographer? at America?) with one hand. With the other hand, he holds a crudely lettered sign that says, POT IS A REALITY KICK.

Many of us who started smoking marijuana around that year agreed with Ginsberg, and in any event, the sign is a reminder of the preoccupations of the time: both "reality" and "kicks" were major concerns. And in search of new interpretations of either the former or the latter, thousands of us — eventually millions — turned on.

Fast-forward to the present. About fifteen percent of all Americans are estimated to be marijuana smokers, and 55 million have tried it at least once. The fact that those figures are staggering only makes it all the more surprising that a dramatic number of people have *stopped* using the drug. Remission (as the Washington statisticians call it) is occurring in all age groups and all classes of people. A 1979 National Institute on Drug Abuse Survey found that over thirty-eight percent of marijuana users now in their early twenties had stopped smoking, as had forty-eight percent of the twenty-six-to-thirty-four-year-olds and sixty-three percent of those over thirty-four. These are the categorical pot teetotalers. Add to those figures the vast numbers of former heavy users who now smoke very occasionally — only a few times a year — and you start to get an idea of a remarkable trend.

Yet the phenomenon appears to be unremarked so far in the scientific or popular press. The statisticians and researchers to whom I spoke when

I first set out to write about this subject weren't even aware of the remission-rate figures, which have so far remained dispersed and buried in the masses of government data about current marijuana use.

So what's going on? There are two possible explanations: either different types of people are smoking marijuana, or else something has happened to the people who used to smoke it. Or both. The drastic rise of remission with age seems especially significant; despite the fact that more Americans of all ages are smoking more marijuana than ever, most of the very people Ginsberg was speaking for in 1965—the people who were college students in the Sixties and whose heroes were the Beats and the blacks, the kids who initiated the popularization of marijuana among the middle class, who turned on America—those are the people who aren't smoking anymore.

Paranoia and the Dog

"Why did you stop smoking?" I asked people around my own age, those I personally started smoking with in the mid- to late Sixties. Persons in this group, perhaps in part because they've been so often examined by the media (under the hideously titled category "The Baby Boom Generation"), tend to be both articulate and self-conscious: they provide an unusually loquacious sample for this sort of inquiry.

The people I went to school with were the "heavy users" when it all started; they used to smoke marijuana to come *down* from other drugs. After a fierce LSD trip or a psyche-twisting speed bout, they'd light up a joint to cool out. Many of them would smoke first thing in the morning and last thing before making love to the person they were spending the night with. The Ginsberg sign comes to mind because, as one of my old school friends puts it, "Psychedelics were unreal and real life was unreal; it was when we were high on marijuana that everything seemed most real."

To get the facts straight, despite all the grandiose talk about consciousness-raising, much of our time then was spent simply lolling about in an indigent stupor. Cast your mind back to a typical stoned dormitory scene, one we experienced hundreds of times. Sitting in a shabbily furnished room, or maybe lying under a tree on campus, there's a bunch of people in a state of pleasant quasi stupefaction. They're listening to music and staring at the spaces between one another's heads. Maybe someone said something a few minutes ago, but most of the people there have either forgotten the last remark that was uttered or else are considering, one by one, the infinite number of repartees that might have been made. In any event, at some point in the proceedings, a dog walks in. Wow. Naturally, everybody there looks at the dog. In fact, they become mesmerized by the dog; they can't stop watching him. And then, invariably, they start laughing. It strikes them that the way the dog is walking about, the way he sniffs, his rheumy eyes, his matted fur (fur!), or, especially, the way he sometimes stops and hesitates with one paw in the air, is somehow extremely funny. In fact, for some reason, the dog's appearance and everything he does and even that he's there at all seems *INCREDIBLY RIDICULOUS*.

Of course, there were variations: some people used to watch their cat on catnip, some used to watch their Mom and Dad, others used to watch Lyndon Johnson or Charlie Company hacking their way through the jungle on TV. Almost anything or anyone could be the dog. Some people used to just lie down, look out the window and laugh because the whole universe was the dog, but the point is that this was my generation's idea of a good time: to take note of the absurd and to laugh at it.

But now it appears that many of us can't take it anymore. That's why most of the people I've talked to say they've stopped smoking: it gives them attacks of ego-chewing paranoia. Now that we're in our midthirties, what often happens when we get high is that we see the dog again, but now the dog is us. And it's not funny.

Rather than being directed outward, the anxiety-ridden pot smoker's attention is focused on self-scrutiny, eventually generating a kind of paralyzing self-consciousness. When I asked people why they had stopped smoking marijuana, many responded with wails of misery. It's not that they no longer have a desire for a recreational drug, but that turning on has come to mean opening a file at the emotional hard-case bureau.

One of my friends, a guy who used to buy dope by the kilo, told me: "All the things that I used to like about being high just make me anxious. Every so often, I try it again out of the old curiosity, but as soon as I get high I ask myself, 'Why did I do this?' My lower lip gets so dry it feels like it's hanging off my face. My heart starts beating really hard, and it reminds me that I'm going to die. And I never want to tell the people I'm with how I'm feeling, because no matter how close I may be to them, I suddenly decide they couldn't care less. So I make up an excuse to leave so I can go back to my apartment and be by myself to think how I'm going to die. And I get absolutely compulsive about leaving. The last time it happened, I was in a car. I demanded to be let out and had to walk on the highway all night to get home."

Here's what another of my friends had to say, someone who used to put on earphones and get high every night, just to unwind: "If I get high with other people, I become convinced they think, and have always thought, that I'm pathetic. So I start saying things to prove I'm not pathetic, and then I think about the things I've just said and realize I'm much more pathetic than they even think I am. It's even worse if I'm by myself. I think about my career, and it seems a total sham to me. I start reviewing my relationships with men and decide they're shallow and based on lies. I can't bear to look in mirrors. And the worst thing is that I feel that the perceptions I'm having are the correct ones, and that even when I come down, I'll still feel this way. Fortunately it's not true. And coming down feels *great*. Safety, at last. I'm never going to take it again. Who needs this?"

Pot anxiety has a peculiar characteristic: in its mild form, you can sometimes will it away, or rather remove yourself by making it a sort of mental object to be examined and manipulated or discarded as you choose. Ideally, of course, the *anxiety* should become the dog. But when it strikes in its most ferocious version, many of us aren't able to laugh at our fears and make a mental object of our dread. We're sometimes just too tired or too bored or too sad or too mad or too frightened.

Enough Edge-Consciousness, Thanks

Of course, there's the fact that the THC content—the active ingredient in marijuana—of your contemporary Colombia spliff is now on the average twenty-five times stronger than the Mexican joint kids used to share, the fact that it's become much harder to score, and much more expensive, the fact that marijuana is now no longer the flag for a certain subculture, the fact that this decade's psychoaesthetics may be more compatible with other drugs than grass. There's all that. But there's no doubt that we've gone through a few changes ourselves.

Set and setting—the environment and the mood you're in when you start to smoke—affect your emotional state once you're high. Whether we acknowledge it or not, our present lives may be so filled with stress, repressed and otherwise, that we can't afford to let go. The people I know have a hard enough time as it is without cutting these wide swaths in their emotional-stability quotients. "I don't want to be sensitized!" a friend fairly yelled into the phone when I asked him why he'd stopped smoking. "I want to be *de*sensitized! I'm *over*sensitized as it is. It's the last thing I need!"

Suppose the simple truth is that, as a group, we suffer from deplorable mental health to begin with and that we simply can't afford to make waves. When we were merely youthful neurotics, part of the very point of taking drugs (I refer, of course, to hallucinogens—marijuana was *nothing*) was to prove to ourselves that we could go to the edge and come back. In fact, we learned to live—we deliberately trained ourselves to do so—in a state of perpetual edge-consciousness. But it's not easy to forget that many of our friends either checked out or burned out. Even those of us who managed to claw our way out of the Sixties and its aftermath without either dying or otherwise irrevocably deteriorating always secretly figured we'd be better when we grew up. But now that we are—at least on paper—grown up, we find that we're better only by the most careful management of our unpredictable emotional resources. So even under the once benign influence of marijuana, we simply can't afford to tap into our preconscious (at least not without supervision).

Research has shown that even though marijuana often has a deleterious effect on short-term memory, long-term memory can improve while in a state of intoxication. Now that we're older and have, uh, lived a little, we're carrying much more baggage. Lying dormant behind the bars of reserve memory banks are some grim, long-forgotten events, places in the unconscious emotional landscape that we never want to visit again.

And besides, let's face it—when all you can think of is that you're going to die, that all your acquaintances think you're pathetic and that you are, in short, a dull and worthless speck in the universe, you tend to lose your sense of humor.

No Regrets

Aside from the fact that former smokers tend to be civil libertarians, they are tolerant of other people's marijuana use because they usually have no regrets about their own days of indulgence. "That was then and this is now" is the prevalent position.

This could be due to the fact that whatever the lessons of marijuana use may have been, they are still part of our view of the world whether or not we continue to smoke. In fact, this was the original plan. "Unquestionably, this drug is very useful to the artist," wrote William Burroughs in 1964. "I have now discontinued the use of cannabis for some years and find that I am able to achieve the same results by nonchemical means . . . especially by training myself to think in association blocks instead of words; that is, cannabis, like all the hallucinogens, can be discontinued once the artist has familiarized himself with the areas opened up by the drug."

Carl Sagan suggests in *The Dragons of Eden,* his book of speculations on the evolution of human intelligence, that the effects of marijuana may have a relationship to the cerebral cortex division of a left hemisphere, which processes information sequentially, and the right hemisphere, which does so simultaneously. He writes, "I wonder if, rather than enhancing anything, the cannabinols . . . simply suppress the left hemisphere and permit the stars to come out." Perhaps, if you've smoked enough marijuana over a sufficient period, you can learn to tap this source even when you're not intoxicated.

To put it another way, once you've seen the dog, you don't forget the construct and you remain conscious of its applications.

Lately, I've been thinking of another long-forgotten Sixties expression: "goofing." A product of marijuana-induced double-consciousness, to goof meant to *act* straight in your confrontations with the straight world, while you were imperceivably, you hoped, stoned. Goofing was performed partly because people were afraid of being busted, but also because it was a funny mind game. Kids used to goof all the time in restaurants and bars. They'd goof on their teachers in class and on their parents in the family living room. Lots of temerarious guys went and goofed on their draft boards.

Some of us have never completely relinquished the practice of goofing, even now that we are — ostensibly at least — enacting the "social roles of adulthood." On the negative side, this may well be one of the things that now makes so many of us anxious. After a certain age, it's no longer goofing, it's simply faking. It means we can never take ourselves completely seriously. Sometimes in the middle of the night, we find ourselves inexorably drawn to ask: "What am I *doing* with my life? I must be kidding with this job and this marriage! My whole existence is *INCREDIBLY RIDICULOUS.*" This can be a devastating notion to the individual who's made a conscious commitment to the idea that his or her job or marriage (or whatever) is a better channel to well-being than wallowing in the wrecked crash pads of the mind.

But if we suffer from this sort of disastrous double vision every once in a while, those are the breaks. On the up side, I think that the people in this generation, partly because of their profound and sometimes implacable irony, are infinitely more interesting than their perhaps calmer potential nonalternative selves would have been.

Much of the Sixties marijuana legacy seems banal and stale to us now, especially since it has been so completely co-opted by the former straights. But all the time we spent tantalizing our psyches wasn't wasted. The people I interviewed for this article had often chosen paths and adopted modes of behavior that wildly diverged from their Sixties expectations. But they still had in common a strange, enticing quality that I can only describe as the ability to disturb. This can be manifested in subtle ways: in the midst of a conversation, in the course of the casual encounter, there is the sudden bold remark, the audacious twist. You look into these people's eyes and you think: "This person's capable of *anything*!"

Are You Scared of the Dark?

So we keep our irony from a bygone era, even as we come of age in another. And as for the rest. . . .

"In college, I did my senior thesis on Hesse's characters' search for self-revelation, a hot item at the time," a friend told me recently. "And when I met with my adviser to discuss it, she asked me, 'What would have been the result of these characters' quests if they had achieved it?' I thought about it, and I finally had to answer, 'They'd be dead!' 'That's right,' she said. 'Why wasn't that in your paper?' I didn't have any answer. I guess I couldn't face it at the time, but now I know you have to eventually detach yourself from most everything you wanted so badly then, because achieving it means to die."

"There are truths which are not for all men, nor for all times," declared Voltaire. If we have allowed the Sixties *Zeitgeist* to become diffuse, it's probably, to some degree, a matter of self-preservation.

So maybe we're not incredibly ridiculous after all. We're just doing the best we can.

Michael Jackson

GERRI HIRSHEY

IT WAS THAT RAREST OF POP MUSIC MOMENTS: MICHAEL JACKSON, HOME ALONE AND READY TO TALK TO A REPORTER FOR HOURS. THERE WAS ONE CONDITION, THOUGH: YOU HAD TO FEEL MUSCLES.

Over the last decade my tape recorder has been unfailing in catching the weirdness of a moment: Bruce Springsteen doing Ed Norton imitations at 3:00 a.m. The whir of bat wings over Eddy Grant's Bajan plantation. Sting howling at the moon. But even my hypersensitive Sony was not up to capturing the steady flick of a snake tongue a few inches from my ear during that first long session with Michael Jackson. That whole trip was quietly strange; not menacing, just *out there*.

The reptile in question was Michael's eight-foot boa constrictor, Muscles. For more than an hour, Muscles lay perfectly balanced on a banister beside me, head erect, beady eyes fixed on the small veins doubtless throbbing in my throat. Michael set him there when I declined to have Muscles lounge around my torso. It seemed a fair compromise.

Young Mike wasn't being naughty. He explained it as an exercise in trust, and he was most convincing. If I was scared of snakes, he had a mortal dread of reporters—and maybe we should both get over it. Michael hadn't done an interview in years without one of his sisters screening questions. And in the nearly ten years since our remarkable sessions in late '82 (conducted as he was finishing *Thriller*), he has never again done an interview of this depth. Not that things went badly. It just was . . . *hard*.

Michael shocked everyone—his family, his management and his record company—by deciding to go it alone. He opened the front door of his rented Encino condo looking like a street whack. His corduroys were dirty and rumpled; the scuffed dress oxfords were untied. No socks. No makeup. His hospitality was touchingly inept; having run out of the proffered lemonade, he filled the other half of my glass with warm Hawaiian Punch. There was no food in the refrigerator, just juice. He explained that he was camping out there while his manse on Hayvenhurst was being rebuilt. But as she breezed through to her bedroom upstairs, sister Janet announced that he lived like a beggar, *all the time;* never ate except for some old lettuce leaves; wore raggedy-ass clothes. A *disgrace* . . .

"Right," big brother shot back as she climbed the stairs. "At least I don't have a booty like YOURS."

Janet's presence clearly relaxed him, but she stayed only for a moment—she had a snake to feed upstairs. When Michael and I sat down to talk, there was no mistaking the strain. Sometimes, he shook with the effort. It was no act; the Boogie Monster *was* Bambi outside the klieg lights. He said he could explain the fear—he just couldn't get past it. He was afraid of saying too much, didn't know how to protect himself. Whenever he spoke his mind, people said he was, well, strange.

Ten minutes into it, I could see his point. As he explained the tea party of garden statuary around his coffee table—including a Narcissus figure named Michael—I could hear how it would read. It nearly made me bawl. He was trying so damned *hard*.

We did agree to leave one part of our conversation out of the story, for his protection at the time. It came up as we sat in the condo dining room, and I noticed the school portrait of a young black woman tucked into the frame of an etching. The photo was one of the few personal touches in the place. The face looked like Anyteen's.

"That's the *real* Billie Jean," Michael said. Quincy Jones had just played that cut for me in the studio; I knew the song was about a woman accusing the singer of fathering her child—which was what this woman's letters insisted. Michael explained that he put the photo she'd sent in a central spot so he could memorize the face; it seemed she wanted him dead in a big way. He said she'd just sent him a gun in the mail with detailed instructions on killing himself. In a barely audible voice, Michael explained that the police had told him the gun was rigged to fire backward into the person doing the shooting. Later his mother would tell me that the woman was in an institution, under psychiatric care. When I saw the "Billie Jean" video a few months later—all disappearing tigers and pinpoint choreography—I kept seeing some girl in a green hospital gown.

"You deal with it," Michael had told me. "You just *deal*."

Over the next couple of days, Michael continued to deal with me, gamely, politely and with increasing humor. Janet shook her head in warning as he offered to drive us over for a tour of his house.

"Ray Charles drives better," she cracked.

Strapped into his gold Camaro, I found myself longing for the relative safety of Muscles's fond embrace. The motor skills were there, but Michael admitted that concentration was a problem. Horns were still honking at us as we pulled into the drive of the magic kingdom he was building for himself.

"You wanna go out tonight?"

Another surprise. Michael was going to a slam-jam Queen concert at the L.A. Forum. He wouldn't mind the company. He felt he had to go. Freddie (the late Mr. Mercury, who died of AIDS in November 1991) had been calling him all week. He really should. . . .

Dusk was falling as we left for the show, Michael and his bodyguard Bill Bray walking point through the condo shrubbery toward a waiting limo. I thought they were being a bit silly—this was months before he hit monster status with *Thriller*. But they sensed the girls before I heard or saw them, made a dash to the car as a spiky red tangle of Lee press-on nails drummed against the windows.

"Lock it down!" Michael yelled to me, pointing to a panel at my knees. Limo savy as I am, I hit the skylight button. Before it was half-open, arms reached in, clawing blindly.

Eeeeeeeeeeeeee. The keening drew blue-haired condo dwellers peering from behind their Levolors. Bray was twisting back from the front seat, prying fingers with surprising gentleness. Michael was helpless with giggles. I was flat scared, looking for Billie Jean in those contorted faces stuck against the windows.

When at last we pulled away, I turned to look at Michael. He had "dressed" for this public evening in jeans and a turquoise terry blazer, black loafers and just a tinge of blusher. This precleft Michael looked great—healthy, handsome and robustly African American.

We stopped to pick up Michael's one true friend—a blond teenage skier who was then his partner in Jehovah's Witness fieldwork—and just as much of a Lost Boy. When Bray piloted us into Mercury's dressing room, the boys shrank back until fab Freddie bounded over like a dizzy Rottweiler and damn near crushed tiny Mike in a hug. They fell against a big trunk that opened, releasing a terrifying avalanche of Freddie's industrial-strength jockstraps. Michael's jaw dropped.

"Ooooooooh, Freddie. What are those?"

A gold football helmet fell out and came to rest on the mountain of cups.

"Rock & roll's a *man's* job, little brother," Freddie thundered. Michael smiled and wanted to know if his host had really spent his last birthday hanging naked from a chandelier. The skier blushed. We all had a swell time until Freddie's trainer called him over for a little preperformance spine cracking.

As it turned out, we didn't see much of the concert. Things got too spooky again once Michael was recognized in the beery dark. Hands, notes, eyes, surrounded us. When an unidentifiable liquid began raining on our heads, Bray stood up. "That's it. We're gone."

We spent more time together, in the studio with Quincy Jones, rambling through Michael's unfinished pleasure dome and visiting his menagerie. Toward the end, while we were bottle feeding his twin fawns, he turned suddenly and looked me in the eyes. Finally.

"You know something? You're no better than I am. I mean, you're just as *sneaky*."

"How do you figure that?" I asked.

"You tap-dance in public. Sure you do, all over the page in ROLLING STONE. You need to perform, too. But when you're done, you can run away and hide. Nobody's *after* you."

Michael had me there, dead to rights. He laughed and put a hand on my shoulder.

"Believe me when I tell you—you don't know how lucky you are."

RS 389

FEBRUARY 17TH, 1983

It's noon, and somewhere in the San Fernando Valley, the front shades of a row of condos are lowered against a hazy glare. Through the metal gate, the courtyard is silent, except for the distant splat of a fountain against its plastic basin. Then comes the chilling whine of a real-life Valley girl. "Grandmut*her*. I am not gonna walk a whole *block*. It's *hu*mid. My hair will be *brillo*."

And the soothing counterpoint of maternal encouragement: "Be good pup, Jolie. *Make* for mama."

All along the courtyard's trimmed inner paths, poodles waddle about trailing poodle-cut ladies on pink leashes.

"Not what you expected, huh?" From behind a mask of bony fingers,

Michael Jackson giggles. Having settled his visitor on the middle floor of his own three-level condo, Michael explains that the residence is temporary, while his Encino, California, home is razed and rebuilt. He concedes that this is an unlikely spot for a young prince of pop.

It is also surprising to see that Michael has decided to face this interview alone. He says he has not done anything like this for over two years. And even when he did, it was always with a cordon of managers, other Jackson brothers and, in one case, his younger sister Janet parroting a reporter's questions before Michael would answer them. The small body of existing literature paints him as excruciatingly shy. He ducks, he hides, he talks to his shoe tops. Or he just doesn't show up. He is known to conduct his private life with almost obsessive caution, "just like a hemophiliac who can't afford to be scratched in any way." The analogy is his.

Run this down next to the stats, the successes, and it doesn't add up. He has been the featured player with the Jackson Five since grade school. In 1980, he stepped out of the Jacksons to record his own LP, *Off the Wall,* and it became the best-selling album of the year. *Thriller,* his new album, is Number Five on the charts. And the list of performers now working with him — or wanting to — includes Paul McCartney, Quincy Jones, Steven Spielberg, Diana Ross, Queen and Jane Fonda. On record, onstage, on TV and screen, Michael Jackson has no trouble stepping out. Nothing scares him, he says. But this. . . .

"Do you *like* doing this?" Michael asks. There is a note of incredulity in his voice, as though he were asking the question of a coroner. He is slumped in a dining-room chair, looking down into the lower level of the living room. It is filled with statuary. There are some graceful, Greco-Roman type bronzes, as well as a few pieces from the suburban birdbath school. The figures are frozen around the sofa like some ghostly tea party.

Michael himself is having little success sitting still. He is so nervous that he is eating — plowing through — a bag of potato chips. This is truly odd behavior. None of his brothers can recall seeing anything snacky pass his lips since he became a strict vegetarian and health-food disciple six years ago. In fact, Katherine Jackson, his mother, worries that Michael seems to exist on little more than air. As far as she can tell, her son just has no interest in food. He says that if he didn't have to eat to stay alive, he wouldn't.

"I really do hate this," he says. Having polished off the chips, he has begun to fold and refold a newspaper clipping. "I am much more relaxed onstage than I am right now. But hey, let's go." He smiles. Later, he will explain that "let's go" is what his bodyguard always says when they are about to wade into some public fray. It's also a phrase Michael has been listening for since he was old enough to tie his own shoes.

* * *

"Let's go, boys." With that, Joe Jackson would round up his sons Jackie, Tito, Jermaine, Marlon and Michael. "Let's go" has rumbled from the brothers' preshow huddle for more than three-quarters of Michael's life, first as the Jackson Five on Motown and now as the Jacksons on Epic. Michael and the Jacksons have sold over a 100 million records. Six of their two dozen Motown singles went platinum; ten others went gold. He was just eleven in 1970 when their first hit "I Want You Back," nudged out B.J. Thomas' "Raindrops Keep Fallin' on My Head," for Number One.

If a jittery record industry dared wager, the smart money would be on Michael Jackson. Recent months have found him at work on no fewer than three projects: his own recently released *Thriller*; Paul McCartney's work-in-progress, which will contain two Jackson-McCartney collaborations, "Say, Say, Say" and "The Man"; and the narration and one song for the storybook *E.T.* album on MCA for director Steven Spielberg and producer Quincy Jones. In his spare time, he wrote and produced Diana Ross' single "Muscles." This is indeed a young man in a hurry. Already he is looking past the album he is scheduled to make with the Jacksons this winter. There is a chance of a spring tour. And then there are the movies. Since his role as the scarecrow in *The Wiz*, his bedroom has been hip-deep in scripts.

At twenty-four, Michael Jackson has one foot planted firmly on either side of the Eighties. His childhood hits are golden oldies, and his boyhood idols have become his peers. Michael was just ten when he moved into Diana Ross' Hollywood home. Now he produces her. He was five when the Beatles crossed over; now he and McCartney wrangle over the same girl on Michael's single "The Girl Is Mine." His showbiz friends span generations as well. He hangs out with the likes of such other kid stars as Tatum O'Neal and Kristy McNichol, and ex-kid star Stevie Wonder. He gossips long distance with Adam Ant and Liza Minnelli, and has heart-to-hearts with octogenarian Fred Astaire. When he visited the set of *On Golden Pond*, Henry Fonda baited fishhooks for him. Jane Fonda is helping him learn acting. Pen pal Katharine Hepburn broke a lifelong habit of avoiding rock by attending a 1981 Jacksons concert at Madison Square Garden.

Even E.T. would be attracted to such a gentle spirit, according to Steven Spielberg, who says he told Michael, "If E.T. didn't come to Elliott, he would have come to your house." Spielberg also says he thought of no one else to narrate the saga of his timorous alien. "Michael is one of the last living innocents who is in complete control of his life. I've never seen *anybody* like Michael. He's an emotional star child."

Cartoons are flashing silently across the giant screen that glows in the darkened den. Michael mentions that he loves cartoons. In fact, he loves all things "magic." This definition is wide enough to include everything from Bambi to James Brown.

"He's *so* magic," Michael says of Brown, admitting that he patterned his own quicksilver choreography on the Godfather's classic bag of stage moves. "I'd be in the wings when I was like six or seven. I'd sit there and watch him."

Michael's kindergarten was the basement of the Apollo Theater in Harlem. He was too shy to actually approach the performers the Jackson Five opened for—everyone from Jackie Wilson to Gladys Knight, the Temptations and Etta James. But he says he had to know everything they did—how James Brown could do a slide, a spin and a split and still make it back before the mike hit the floor. How the mike itself disappeared through the Apollo stage floor. He crept downstairs, along passageways and walls and hid there, peering from behind the dusty flanks of old vaudeville sets while musicians tuned, smoked, played cards and divvied barbecue. Climbing back to the wings, he stood in the protective folds of the musty maroon curtain, watching his favorite acts, committing every double dip and every bump, snap, whip-it-back mike toss to his inventory of night moves. Recently, for a refresher course, Michael went to see James Brown perform at an L.A. club. "He's the *most* electrifying. He can take an audience anywhere he wants to. The audience just went bananas. He went wild—and at his age. He gets so *out* of himself."

Getting out of oneself is a recurrent theme in Michael's life, whether the subject is dancing, singing or acting. As a Jehovah's Witness, Michael believes in an impending holocaust, which will be followed by the second coming of Christ. Religion is a large part of his life, requiring intense Bible study and thrice-weekly meetings at a nearby Kingdom Hall. He has never touched drugs and rarely goes near alcohol. Still, despite the prophesied Armageddon, the spirit is not so dour as to rule out frequent hops on the fantasy shuttle.

"I'm a collector of cartoons," he says. "All the Disney stuff, Bugs Bunny, the old MGM ones. I've only met one person who has a bigger collection than I do, and I was surprised—Paul McCartney. He's a cartoon fanatic. Whenever I go to his house, we watch cartoons. When we came here to work on my album, we rented all these cartoons from the studio, Dumbo and some other stuff. It's real escapism. It's like everything's all right. It's like the world is happening now in a faraway city. Everything's fine.

"The first time I saw *E.T.*, I melted through the whole thing," he says. "The second time, I cried like crazy. And then, in doing the narration, I felt like I was there with them, like behind a tree or something, watching everything that happened."

So great was Michael's emotional involvement that Steven Spielberg found his narrator crying in the darkened studio when he got to the part where E.T. is dying. Finally, Spielberg and producer Quincy Jones decided to run with it and let Michael's voice break. Fighting those feelings would be counterproductive—something Jones had already learned while producing *Off the Wall.*

"I had a song I'd been saving for Michael called "She's Out of My Life," he remembers. "Michael heard it, and it clicked. But when he sang it, he would cry. Every time we did it, I'd look up at the end and Michael would be crying. I said, 'We'll come back in two weeks and do it again, and maybe it won't tear you up so much. Came back and he started to get teary. So we left it in."

For his own protection, Michael has rigged himself a set of emotional floodgates, created situations where it's okay to let it all out. "Some circumstances require me to be real quiet," he says. "But I dance *every* Sunday." On that day, he also fasts.

This, his mother confirms, is a weekly ritual that leaves her son laid out, sweating, laughing and crying. It is also a ritual very similar to Michael's performances. Indeed, the weight of the Jacksons' stage show rests heavily on his narrow, sequined shoulders. There is nothing tentative about his solo turns. He can tuck his long, thin frame into a figure-skater's spin without benefit of ice or skates. Aided by the burn and flash of silvery body suits, he seems to change molecular structure at will, all robot angles one second and rippling curves the next. So sure is the body that his eyes are often closed, his face turned upward to some unseen muse. The bony chest heaves. He pants, bumps and squeals. He has been known to leap offstage and climb up into the rigging.

At home, in his room, he dances until he falls down. Michael says the Sunday dance sessions are also an effective way to quiet his stage addiction when he is not touring. Sometimes in these off periods, another performer will call him up from the audience. And in the long, long trip from his seat to the stage, the two Michaels duke it out.

"I sit there and say, '*Please* don't call me up, I am *too* shy,' " Jackson says. "But once I get up there, I take control of myself. Being onstage is magic. There's nothing like it. You feel the energy of everybody who's out there. You feel it all over your body. When the lights hit you, it's all over. I *swear* it is."

He is smiling now, sitting upright, trying to explain weightlessness to the earthbound.

"When it's time to go off, I don't want to. I could stay up there forever. It's the same thing with making a movie. What's wonderful about a film is that you can become another person. I love to forget. And lots of times, you totally forget. It's like automatic pilot. I mean—whew."

During shooting for *The Wiz,* he became so attached to his Scarecrow character, the crew literally had to wrench him from the set and out of his costume. He was in Oz, and wasn't keen on leaving it for another hotel room.

"That's what I loved about doing *E.T.* I was actually there. The next day, I missed him a lot. I wanted to go back to that spot I was at yesterday in the forest. I wanted to be *there*."

Alas, he is still at the dining-room table in his condo. But despite the visible strain, he's holding steady. And he brightens at a question about his animals. He says he talks to his menagerie every day. "I have two fawns. Mr. Tibbs looks like a ram; he's got the horns. I've got a beautiful llama. His name is Louie." He's also into exotic birds like macaws, cockatoos and a giant rhea.

"Stay right there," he says, "and I'll show you something." He takes the stairs to his bedroom two at a time. Though I know we are the only people in the apartment, I hear him talking.

"Aw, were you asleep? I'm sorry. . . ."

Seconds later, an eight-foot boa constrictor is deposited on the dining-room table. He is moving in my direction at an alarming rate.

"This is Muscles. And I have trained him to eat interviewers."

Muscles, having made it to the tape recorder and flicked his tongue disdainfully, continues on toward the nearest source of warm blood. Michael thoughtfully picks up the reptile as its snub nose butts my wrist. Really, he insists, Muscles is quite sweet. It's all nonsense, this stuff about snakes eating people. Besides, Muscles isn't even hungry; he enjoyed his weekly live rat a couple of days ago. If anything, the stranger's presence has probably made Muscles a trifle nervous himself. Coiled around his owner's torso, his tensile strength has made Michael's forearm a vivid bas-relief of straining blood vessels. To demonstrate the snake's sense of balance, Michael sets him down on a three-inch wide banister, where he will remain, motionless, for the next hour or so.

"Snakes are very misunderstood," he says. Snakes, I suggest, may be the oldest victims of bad press. Michael whacks the table and laughs.

"Bad press. Ain't it *so*, Muscles?"

The snake lifts its head momentarily, then settles back on the banister. All three of us are a bit more relaxed.

"Know what I also love?" Michael volunteers. "Manikins."

Yes, he means the kind you see wearing mink bikinis in Beverly Hills store windows. When his new house is finished, he says he'll have a room with no furniture, just a desk and a bunch of store dummies.

"I guess I want to bring them to life. I like to imagine talking to them. You know what I think it is? Yeah, I think I'll say it. I think I'm accompanying myself with friends I never had. I probably have two friends. And I just got them. Being an entertainer, you just can't tell who is your friend. And they see you so differently. A star instead of a next-door neighbor."

He pauses, staring down at the living-room statues.

"That's what it is. I surround myself with people I want to be my friends. And I can do that with manikins. I'll talk to them."

A restless rhythm is jiggling his foot, and the newspaper clipping has long been destroyed. Michael is apologetic, explaining that he can sit still for just so long. On an impulse, he decides to drive us to the house under construction. Though his parents forced him to learn two years ago, Michael rarely drives. When he does, he refuses to travel freeways, taking hour-long detours to avoid them. He has learned the way to only a few "safe" zones — his brothers' homes, the health-food restaurant and the Kingdom Hall.

First, Muscles must be put away. "He's real sweet," Michael says as he unwinds the serpent from the banister. "I'd like you to wrap him around you before you go."

This is not meant as a prank, and Michael will not force the issue. But fear of interviews can be just as deep-rooted as fear of snakes, and in consenting to talk, Michael was told the same thing he's telling me now: *Trust me. It won't hurt you.*

We compromise. Muscles cakewalks across an ankle. His tongue is dry. It just tickles. Block out the primal dread, and it could be a kitten whisker. "You truly believe," says Michael, "with the power of reason, that this animal won't harm you now, right? But there's this fear, built in by the world, by what people say, that makes you shy away like that."

Having politely made their point, Michael and Muscles disappear upstairs.

Checking the front hall upon his return, Michael finds that a test pressing of "The Girl Is Mine" has been delivered. This is business. He must check it before release, he explains, has he heads for a listen on the stereo in the den. Before the record is finished, he is punching at phone buttons. In between calls to accountants and managers, he says that he makes all his own decisions, right down to the last sequin on his stage suits — the only clothes he cares about. He says he can be a merciless interviewer when it comes to choosing management, musicians and concert promoters. He assesses their performances with the rigor of an investigative reporter, questioning his brothers, fellow artists and even reporters for observations. Though he truly believes his talent comes from God, he is acutely aware of its value on the open market. He is never pushy or overbearing, but he does appreciate respect. Do not ask him, for instance, how long he has been with a particular show-business firm. "Ask me," he corrects, "how long they've been with *me*."

Those who have worked with him do not doubt his capability. Even those to whom he is a star child. "He's in full control," says Spielberg.

"Sometimes he appears to other people to be sort of wavering on the fringes of twilight, but there is great conscious forethought behind everything he does. He's very smart about his career and the choices he makes. I think he is definitely a man of two personalities."

In the studio Quincy Jones found that his professionalism had matured. In fact, Michael's nose for things is so by-your-leave funky that Jones started calling him Smelly Fortunately, when corporate rumblings feared the partnership too unlikely to work, Smelly hung tough and cocked an ear inward to his own special rhythms. Indeed, *Off the Wall*'s most memorable cuts are the Jackson-penned dance tunes. "Working Day and Night" with all its breathy asides and deft punctuation, could only have been written by a dancer. "Don't Stop 'Til You Get Enough," the album's biggest-selling single, bops along with that same appealing give-and-go between restraint and abandon. The song begins with Michael talking in a low mumble over a taut, single-string bass bomp:

"You know, I was wonderin' . . . you know the force, it's got a lot of power, make me feel like a . . . make me feel like. . . ."

Ooooooh. Fraidy cat breaks into disco monster, with onrushing strings and a sexy, cathartic squeal. The introduction is ten seconds of perfect pop tension. Dance boogie is the welcome release. The arrangement—high, gusting strings and vocals over a thudding, in-the-pocket rhythm—is Michael's signature. Smelly, the funky sprite.

It works. Such a creature as Michael is the perfect pop hybrid for the Eighties. The fanzine set is not scared off by raunchy lyrics and chest hair. But the R-rated uptown dance crowd can bump and slide right along the greasy tracks. *Thriller* is eclectic enough to include African chants and some ripping macho-rock guitar work by Eddie Van Halen. It is now being called pop-soul by those into marketing categories. Michael says he doesn't care what anybody wants to call it. Just how it all came about is still a mystery to him—as is the creative process itself.

"I wake up from dreams and go, 'Wow, put *this* down on paper,' " he says. "The whole thing is strange. You hear the words, everything is right there in front of your face. And you say to yourself, 'I'm sorry, I just didn't write this. It's there already.' That's why I hate to take credit for the songs I've written. I feel that somewhere, someplace, it's been done and I'm just a courier bringing it into the world. I really believe that. I love what I do. I'm happy at what I do. It's escapism."

Again, that word. But Michael is right. There is no better definition for good, well-meaning, American pop. Few understand this better than Diana Ross, that Tamla teen turned latter-day pop diva. Her closeness to Michael began when she met the Jacksons.

"No, I didn't discover them," she says, countering the myth. Motown head Berry Gordy had already found them; she simply introduced them on her 1971 television special. "There was an identification between Michael and I," she says. "I was older, he kind of idolized me, and he wanted to sing like me."

She has been pleased to watch Michael become his own person. Still, she wishes he would step out even more. She says she had to be firm and force him to stay in his role as producer on "Muscles." He wanted them to do it jointly. She insisted he go it alone.

"He spends a lot of time, too much time, by himself. I try to get him out. I rented a boat and took my children and Michael on a cruise. Michael has a lot of people around him, but he's very afraid. I don't know why. I think it came from the early days."

Michael's show-business friends, many of them women not thought of as especially motherly, do go to great lengths to push and prod him into the world, and to keep him comfortable. When he's in Manhattan, Ross urges him to go to the theater and the clubs, and counteroffers with quiet weekends at her Connecticut home. In notes and phone calls, Katharine Hepburn has been encouraging about his acting.

Michael has recorded much of this counsel in notebooks and on tape. Visiting Jane Fonda—whom he's known since they met at a Hollywood party a few years ago—on the New Hampshire set of *On Golden Pond* proved to be an intensive crash course. In a mirror version of his scenes with the step-grandson in the movie, Henry Fonda took his daughter's rock-star friend out on the lake and showed him how to fish. They sat on a jetty for hours, talking trout and theater. The night Fonda died, Michael spent the evening with Fonda's widow, Shirlee, and his children, Jane and Peter. He says they sat around, laughing and crying and watching the news reports. The ease with which Michael was welcomed into her family did not surprise Jane Fonda. Michael and her father got on naturally, she says, because they were so much alike.

"Dad was also painfully self-conscious and shy in life," she says, "and he really only felt comfortable when he was behind the mask of a character. He could liberate himself when he was being someone else. That's a lot like Michael.

"In some ways," she continues, "Michael reminds me of the walking wounded. He's an extremely fragile person. I think that just getting on with life, making contact with people, is hard enough, much less to be worried about whither goest the world.

"I remember driving with him one day, and I said, 'God, Michael, I wish I could find a movie I could produce for you.' And suddenly I knew. I said, 'I know what you've got to do. It's *Peter Pan*.' Tears welled up in his eyes and he said, 'Why did you say that?' with this *ferocity*. I said, 'I realize *you're* Peter Pan.' And he started to cry and said, 'You know, all over the walls of my room are pictures of Peter Pan. I've read everything that [author J.M.] Barrie wrote. I totally identify with Peter Pan, the lost boy of never-never land.' "

Hearing that Francis Coppola may be doing a film version, Fonda sent word to him that he must talk to Michael Jackson. "Oh, I can see him," she says, "leading lost children into a world of fantasy and magic."

In the book, that fantasy world lies "second to the right star, then straight on til morning"—no less strange a route, Fonda notes, than Michael's own journey from Indiana.

"From Gary," she says, "straight on to Barrie."

"Just here to see a friend."

Michael is politely trying to sidestep an inquiring young woman decked out with the latest video equipment. She blocks the corridor leading to the warren of dressing rooms beneath the L.A. Forum.

"Can I tell my viewers that Michael Jackson is a Queen fan?"

"I'm a Freddie Mercury fan," he says, slipping past her into a long room crowded with Queen band members, wives, roadies and friends. A burly man with the look of a linebacker is putting lead singer Freddie Mercury through a set of stretching exercises that will propel his road-weary muscles through the final show of the group's recent U.S. tour. The band is merry. Michael is shy, standing quietly at the door until Freddie spots him and leaps up to gather him in a hug.

Freddie invited Michael. He has been calling all week, mainly about the possibility of their working together. They've decided to try it on the Jacksons' upcoming album. Though they are hardly alike—Freddie celebrated a recent birthday by hanging naked from a chandelier—the two have been friendly since Michael listened to the material Queen had recorded for *The Game* and insisted that the single had to be "Another One Bites the Dust."

"Now, he listens to me, right Freddie?"

"Righto, little brother."

The linebacker beckons. Freddie waves his cigarette at the platters of fruit, fowl and candy. "You and your friends make yourselves comfortable."

Our escort, a sweet-faced, ham-fisted bodyguard, is consulting with security about seat locations. There had been girls lurking outside the condo when Michael sprinted to the limousine, girls peering through the tinted glass as the door locks clicked shut. This was all very puzzling to Michael's guest, who was waiting in the car.

He is a real friend, one of the civilians, so normal as to pass unseen by the jaded eyes of celebrity watchers. He has never been to a rock concert, nor has he ever seen Michael perform. He says he hopes to, but mainly, they just hang out together. Sometimes his younger brother even tags along. Most of the time they just talk "just regular old stuff," says the friend. For Michael, it is another kind of magic.

At the moment, though, it's show business as usual. Gossip, to be specific. Michael is questioning a dancer he knows about the recent crisis of a fallen superstar. Michael wants to know what the problem is. The dancer mimes his answer, laying a finger alongside his nose. Michael nods, and translates for his friend: "Drugs. Cocaine."

Michael admits that he seeks out such gossip, and listens again and again as the famous blurt out their need for escape. "Escapism," he says. "I totally understand."

But addictions are another thing. "I always want to know what makes good performers fall to pieces," he says. "I always try to find out. Because I just can't believe it's the same things that get them time and time again." So far, his own addictions—the stage, dancing, cartoons—have been free of toxins.

Something's working on Michael now, but it is nothing chemical. He's buzzing like a bumblebee trapped in a jelly jar. It's the room we're in, he explains. So many times, he's stretched and bounced and whipped up on his vocal cords right here, got *crazy* in here, pumping up, shivering like some flighty race horse as he wriggled into his sequined suit.

"I can't *stand* this," he fairly yells. "I cannot sit still."

Just before he must be held down for his own good, Randy Jackson rockets into the room, containing his brother in a bear hug, helping him dissipate some of the energy with a short bout of wrestling. This is not the same creature who tried to hide behind a potato chip.

Now Michael is boxing with the bodyguard, asking every minute for the time until the man mercifully claps a big hand on the shoulder of his charge and says it: "Let's go."

Mercury and company have already begun moving down the narrow hall, and before anyone can catch him, Michael is drawn into their wake, riding on the low roar of the crowd outside, leaping up to catch a glimpse of Freddie, who is raising a fist and about to take the stairs to the stage.

"Ooooh, Freddie is pumped," says Michael. "I envy him now. You don't *know* how much."

The last of the band makes the stairs, and the black stage curtain closes. Michael turns and lets himself be led into the darkness of the arena.

The Strange and Mysterious Death of Mrs. Jerry Lee Lewis

RICHARD BEN CRAMER

"YOU SCARED OF ME?" LEWIS ONCE ASKED HIS WIFE'S SISTER. "YOU SHOULD BE. WHY DO YOU THINK THEY CALL ME THE KILLER?"

How was I out to lunch? Let me count the ways. I was new to magazines, never having written for a national publication, much less for ROLLING STONE. I was a newspaperman, just returned from the Middle East—a bit unsteady, still, in America. The provenance of rock & roll I had traced as far back as the record store. Past that lay a great sea of unknowing.

All of a sudden, I was in Hernando, Mississippi, where no restaurant order was complete until the waitress asked, "You wan' gravy?" Where the leading candidate for sheriff was known as Big Dog Riley. Where Jerry Lee Lewis was a legend and a power, not to mention the spendingest man in the county, which spending had bought for almost a decade the quiet cooperation of local authorities who would perform all kinds of "community service," like towing the Killer's car out of a ditch without checking his blood for alcohol, or bargaining his drug charge down to a simple fine, or shipping off the bruised body of his dead fifth bride for a private autopsy, with no coroner's jury and little public inquiry into the cause of her death.

And I was proposing to penetrate this long-closed world, to find out how that girl died?

Truly, I was out to lunch.

But God looks after his children who were tardy on brain day. He introduced me to a splendid couple of folks who owned the local weekly newspaper, and then to the local prosecutor, who wanted to help me honorably, even though the resulting story could not reflect well on his grand-jury presentation. And then there were the ambulance drivers, the local cops, local merchants and matrons, meetings at midnight, anonymous notes left at my motel. Bit by bit, they made a picture of life where Jerry Lee lived.

Then, too, I was led to Hernando's Hide-A-Way, the Killer's favorite nightclub, fifteen miles north in Memphis, Tennessee, and to the lubricious owner of that nightclub, Kenny Rodgers; in Memphis, too, there was Elvis's old doctor chum, Dr. Nick; there was Jerry Lee's manager, J.W. Whitten, and Whitten's little dogs, Nickie and Kai; there was J.W.'s former wife; and there were former band members, club bartenders, former girlfriends, bouncers, strippers, whores. . . .

Quickly, it became apparent that this unexpected, inexplicable death was not out of the ordinary in the world of Jerry Lee. And not long after, it would become equally clear that the official version of events diverged early and often from the facts. Something went violently wrong at the Killer's mansion on the night of Shawn Lewis's death. And as soon as that death was disclosed, everything went wrong with the investigation. A grand jury was quickly led to conclude that no crime had occurred. But I was sure Shawn's death was no suicide, no mistaken handful of pills. No one would ever prove what happened: Only two people were in the house that night. One was dead and buried before the appropriate tests could be made. The other was Jerry Lee Lewis.

First, I had to learn something about where Jerry Lee's music came from—and about the stark choices presented to a boy at the Assembly of God church in Ferriday, Louisiana. In a hundred times of trouble, he had vowed he would dedicate his soul and his music to the Lord's work, forevermore, but he never could make that stick. And then the millions of miles and the thousands of nightclub dates—the rage they required, the drinks and drugs—took their toll. He ate away at himself. By the terms of his church, Jerry Lee made his living with the devil's dance on his piano. "Great Balls of Fire" was his anthem not by happenstance.

And he ate through the lives of his women. His third wife, his cousin Myra Gale Brown, won divorce with horrific tales of how Jerry Lee beat her up in view of their little daughter. His fourth wife, Jaren Gunn, also won divorce, but she ended up dead, mysteriously drowned in a Memphis swimming pool, just before her settlement came through. Shawn Michelle Stephens was the fifth. A sharp and spunky twenty-five-year-old from Garden City, Michigan, she thought Jerry Lee was her ticket to the good life. They married on June 7th, 1983, and seventy-seven days later, she was dead.

It seemed to me unlikely that the magazine of rock & roll would greet this harsh story with enthusiasm. I thought, in fact, that if I meant to question Jerry Lee's clean escape from this case, I'd have to possess a ton of stone-hard facts and present them as a wall, every stone immovable. It took weeks in Mississippi, Memphis and Detroit—more weeks in New York. It seemed to me a miracle that I never heard a discouraging word from my editor, Susan Murcko. I thought perhaps I hadn't made exactly clear what it was I thought I'd found. I wrote with trepidation. I saw every word raising a wall that might fall back on me. It was months after the assignment when, at last, I presented to Murcko a thick sheaf of pages.

Too thick!

Murcko started thinning the wall. She worked with the infinite patience of a medieval mason. Thousands of words were chiseled to dust. And nothing was lost. Murcko, God bless her, was all dogged delicacy.

Then Jann Wenner looked it over. Too thick!

To hell with delicacy! More thousands of words, whole interviews, whole characters, were dust, mere dust. Murcko brushed the wall smooth again.

Then fact checkers . . .

Then copy editors . . .

Then lawyers!

I was unprepared for this woe. I was a newspaperman. The way I was brought up, you wrote the thing, you sent it in, it ran that night. Next day, it was over. This was months. This was murder.

February 1984, finally, the story was in type. Ten pages in the magazine. I looked it over as if it were some strange geode, compressed as it was by time and tread. I was shocked to discover that it said what I meant.

The county's inquiry into Shawn's death never was reopened. The feds took up the scent for a while, but they never made a case on the death of Jerry Lee's wife. They put all their eggs into the Internal Revenue basket and actually charged Lewis under the tax laws. But as far as I know, nothing much came of it. Some bargaining went on—more judgments against Jerry Lee, more liens. What the hell, he already had enough judgments against him to pave the road to Tupelo.

Jerry Lee got married again—to a cute young thing. The tabloids attended and wrote about her ring.

The Killer's only reaction to my story came through his manager, J.W. Whitten. He said Jerry Lee was "just surprised . . . that ROLLING STONE would do that kind of thing on us."

Well, so was I.

RS 416

MARCH 1ST, 1984

The Killer was in his bedroom, behind the door of iron bars, as Sonny Daniels, the first ambulance man, moved down the long hall to the guest bedroom to check the report: "Unconscious party at the Jerry Lee Lewis residence."

Lottie Jackson, the housekeeper, showed Sonny into a spotless room: Gauzy drapes filtered the noonday light; there was nothing on the tables, no clothes strewn about, no dust; just a body on the bed, turned away slightly toward the wall, with the covers drawn up to the neck. Sonny probed with his big, blunt fingers at a slender wrist: it was cold. "It's Miz Lewis," Lottie said. "I came in . . . I couldn't wake her up. . . ." Sonny already had the covers back, his thick hand on the woman's neck where the carotid pulse should be: The neck retained its body warmth, but no pulse. Now he bent his pink moon-face with its sandy fuzz of first beard over her pale lips: no breath. He checked the eyes. "Her eyes were all dilated. That's an automatic sign that her brain has done died completely."

Matthew Snyder, the second ambulance man, had barely finished Emergency Medical Technician school. He was twenty, blond, beefy, even younger than Sonny, and just starting with the Hernando, Mississippi, ambulance team. Even rookies knew there wasn't anything uncommon about a run to Jerry Lee's to wake up some passed-out person. But Matthew saw there was something uncommonly wrong now, as he caught the look of worry and excitement from Sonny over at the bed. "Go ahead and check her over," said Sonny, and Matthew restarted the process with the woman's delicate wrist. He saw, up on her forearm, the row of angry little bruises, like someone had grabbed her hard. He saw the little stain of dried blood on the web of her hand. He shook his head at Sonny: no pulse.

Lottie knew it was wrong, too. She was a stolid, hard-working black woman who'd taken care of Jerry Lee since before he moved down here from Memphis—more than ten years, that made it. She was crying as she moved down the hall and knocked at the door with the iron bars.

The Killer was there within seconds. If he'd been sleeping on the big canopied bed, he must have been sleeping in his bathrobe. For now, he came into the hall, with the white terry-cloth lapels pulled tight across his skinny chest, and he looked surprised to find Lottie in tears. Then he looked a silent question into Sonny Daniels' eyes.

"Mr. Lewis, your wife. . . ." Sonny averted his gaze. He said: "I just checked her over in there. . . ."

Still, he didn't meet the question in Jerry Lee's hard eyes. He saw the two bright red scratches on the back of Jerry Lee's hand, like a cat had gouged him from the wrist to the knuckles. When Sonny looked up at last, his own eyes grew, his whole face seemed to grow larger, rounder, younger.

"Mr. Lewis," he said. "I'm sorry. Miz Lewis is dead."

The autopsy that cleared Jerry Lee Lewis called Shawn Michelle Lewis, 25, "a well-developed, well-nourished, white female, measuring sixty-four inches in length, weighing 107 pounds. The hair is brown, the eyes are green. . . ." It hardly did her justice. She was a honey blond with a tan, small and full of bounce, with a grin that made everybody smile and had turned male heads since junior high.

"Everybody liked her. She was like the stepchild of the club. Everybody looked out for her," says Mike DeFour, the manager of DB's, a fancy nightclub in the Hyatt Regency Hotel in Dearborn, Michigan, where Shawn Michelle Stephens worked as a cocktail waitress. DeFour treated his waitresses, "the DB's girls," like family—he loved them all, took care of them, saw to it that they made good money—even the new girls, like Shawn, who had started part time about four years ago. "Some of the girls I gave nicknames to. Shawn was 'Little Buzz,'" because she was always buzzing around, you know, half buzzed. . . .

"No, not like that. Drugs weren't a big problem. You know, a hit on a joint or two, no problem. It was around. Or a shot from a bottle of schnapps—okay, I'd look the other way."

Shawn loved working there. The money was great—sometimes $150 a night. But it wasn't just that: It was upscale, crowded with people who dressed and threw money around. It was something more for a girl from Garden City, a suburb of little boxes built for the auto workers of the Fifties. There, *more* was the stuff of dreams.

But somehow, in Garden City, Shawn never seemed to get much more. Her mother's divorce had only made it harder. Shawn had been in and out of jobs, mostly waitressing, since she graduated in 1975. She dreamed of marrying Scott, her boyfriend, but his parents were strict, and they never thought much of Shawn. So DB's was fine for the moment—great, in fact. She loved the people. It almost wasn't like work. The musicians took them to parties after hours—great parties. One DB's girl, Pam Brewer, took up with J.W. Whitten, the wiry bantam of a road manager for the Jerry Lee Lewis band. Pam flew off to Memphis, and when she came back the next year, she was soon to be Mrs. J.W. Whitten, traveling with the band, flying in Learjets and shopping from a limo! That's when it happened to Shawn.

Jerry Lee, performing for a week at the Dearborn Hyatt, picked Shawn out from among the girls. Pam Brewer set it up: She told Shawn that Jerry Lee wanted to take her to a party in his suite. It wasn't like Shawn had been looking for it. In fact, the first time she'd seen Jerry Lee, she'd told her mother: "Mom, he's a lone man, and he's about your age. You ought to come and try to meet him. . . ." Instead, it was Shawn who went. "I always thought Shawn'd be good for Jerry," says Pam. "She was so cute, petite, and he likes little women. And she was so much fun to be with. I introduced them. I thought she was flexible enough to understand his moods."

Jerry Lee wasn't showing his moods the night of that first party. A great party, Shawn told her friends. Actually, it was just a few drinks in his suite. A couple of other women were already up there. Jerry Lee played piano and sang, while Pam's little Chinese Shih Tzu dog sat up with him on the stool. Shawn knew she was looking good, in her jeans, cowboy boots and a huggy little white rabbit jacket. And Jerry Lee treated her so nice! He'd turn away from the keyboard as he'd slow down his rhythm for a snatch of a love song. She felt him sing straight to her. It was February 1981. Shawn was twenty-three.

"Dead. You sure?" said the Killer, as he crossed the hall to the guest room. He grabbed Shawn's wrist, as if to feel her pulse, then dropped it and just stood staring at her.

"Anything you can do?" Jerry Lee said, mostly to Sonny. "In the hospital?"

"No, sir, we woulda took her already," said Sonny. He was real polite.

Jack McCauley, a deputy sheriff, came into the room at that moment. By happenstance, he said, he'd been patrolling on Malone Road as the ambulance made the turn for Jerry Lee's house. Of course, his ordinary patrol area was miles away, but nothing about Jack McCauley seemed to fit the ordinary. McCauley, 48, certainly was the sharpest deputy in De-Soto County: a college man, a Yankee transplanted to Mississippi, a man who said he'd made a small fortune on developments like the industrial park in the northeast corner of the county. John Burgess McCauley lived in a hideaway house that made Jerry Lee's look modest—it must have been worth $200,000, according to realtors who'd seen it. Nobody quite knew what Jack was doing, fooling around in patrol cars with a deputy's job that paid $12,000 a year. And the way he'd take your head off for the smallest little thing, start shouting and get red all the way up to his crew-cut, no one asked Jack.

Sonny was going to explain to Jerry Lee the need for an inquest, but Jack McCauley took over from there. He had that air of command about him. McCauley announced he was going to clear the room. He wasn't real polite like Sonny—more familiar. "Come to think of it," says Sonny, "I don't recall Jack introducing himself. Maybe he knew Jerry Lee."

Maybe, but it's hard to tell now. McCauley won't talk about the case. And Jerry Lee never said much of anything about it, except that day, when he had a long talk with McCauley. They were alone in Jerry Lee's little den for more than an hour before the state investigators or anybody else arrived at the house. McCauley never filed any report on that long conversation. He did write a report that told how he came in the wake of the ambulance, just after 12:30 p.m., August 24th, 1983, and how he got delayed in the driveway by two employees of Goldsmith's department store, who'd come to the house to hang drapes, and then how Matthew Snyder told him "that a female subject was dead in one of the bedrooms." His report continues:

> Upon entering a small bedroom on the east side of the residence, Mr. Lewis was bending over the bed where a white female was lying partially covered by a bedspread. She was clad in a negligee. . . . When I first arrived, Mr. Lewis' speech was heavily slurred, but he was alert and coherent. I telephoned the sheriff's office and requested a justice of the peace if the coroner could not be located, and an investigator. The latter was requested because there were no visible causes of death and because Mr. Lewis' bathrobe contained apparent bloodstains and he had a cut on his wrist.
>
> At 13:51 hours I advised Mr. Lewis that his manager J.W. Whitten had arrived but would not be allowed to enter the residence until the investigation was completed. Mr. Lewis commented we need to "find out who killed—how she died," so funeral arrangements can be made.

So McCauley was the first to report that Jerry Lee's robe was spotted with blood. Surely, McCauley must have seen, as well, the blood on Shawn Lewis, on her hand, on her hair, on clothes and a bra in another room, on a lamp, in a spot on the carpet. He must have seen the film of dirt on her, and the bruises on her arms and hip, maybe her broken fingernails with something that looked like dried blood underneath. None of this was in his report. But it didn't matter much. For McCauley's report never made it into the investigative file, never left the sheriff's department until after the grand jury had decided no crime had occurred.

Shawn hadn't been a great fan of the Killer's, not until that first night in his suite. She was tiny in her mother's womb when his "Whole Lotta Shakin' Goin' On" threatened to knock Elvis himself off the throne of rock & roll. At forty-five, Jerry Lee was still riveting—a star, and he seemed to like her. He'd make funny faces and twist his head around, trying to understand her funny Yankee way of talking. Then he'd understand and try to mimic, and everybody'd laugh—Jerry, too. Of course, girls were never a problem for the Killer. They were always around. Often, Jerry left the details of his trysting to others; now, in February 1981, it was Pam who issued another invitation, this time with a free ticket to Memphis: "Jerry was gettin' ready to go to Europe, and I figured it was a good time to bring Shawn down. Because I figured he'd take her with him. Which he did. . . ."

Clever girl! Pam Brewer is twenty-six now, and although she's split up with J.W. Whitten, she still lives in Memphis. She talks in a molasses drawl (well, a girl's got to fit in!) about Shawn's springtime trip to Europe.

"He bought a beautiful gold watch for her. I don't know how many thousands he spent on it. It was his first gift to her. . . . They'd send her out, and she'd get herself a bunch of beautiful suits, and she'd come back and just look at herself in the mirror, because she couldn't believe that was her in all those beautiful things. . . .

"How could you not get taken by it? I was in heaven all the time I was, uh, involved."

It was heaven—most of the time. Then there were the times Jerry was speeding so bad after a show: He couldn't come down, and he'd bully Shawn to stay up with him. God, they never slept. And then it was kind of disgusting when Jerry would stick that big needle with the Talwin narcotic right into his stomach. He said his stomach was killing him, and no wonder, the way he lived.

It was better, sort of, back in Nesbit, Mississippi, in the big brick house—at least you could relax. There was the pool shaped like a piano, and the lake out back with the Jet Ski, a sort of kicky little snowmobile for the water. Shawn loved the sun, and she'd lie out there all afternoon, before Jerry woke up. Then at night, they'd go to Hernando's Hide-A-Way, Jerry's home club, fifteen miles north, up in Memphis. They'd roll in about midnight, and Jerry Lee would sort of dance to his table, announcing: "The Killer is here." They'd always drink, or have a pipe or two back in a little office by the bandstand. Sometimes, Hernando's owner, Kenny Rodgers, would get up to the mike, straighten his pearly tie under the vest of his gray business suit and announce: "Ladies an' gennlemen! The greates' ennataina inna worl' . . . the Killa . . . Jerra Lee!" And then Jerry'd screw around for hours, while the house band wilted behind him, and Jerry would work to his own private rhythms, singing a snatch of this or that, cutting off songs in midverse, making the whole club dance to his tune. That could get ugly, too, like the time some patrons left the floor in disgust when Jerry Lee cut off another song. "You stupid ignorant sons-abitches," Jerry Lee screamed from the piano bench. "You got a $20,000 show here, and y'all walkin' off from the Killer!"

Shawn said she knew how to handle him. For one thing, you just had to pay attention. Shawn said she knew, too, how to handle other women. A friend and former DB's girl, Beverly Lithgow, says: "Shawn told about one of the first times they went out to dinner down there near Memphis, and this girl came over to the table and asked for Jerry Lee's autograph. So he gave it to her. She came back again and started talking with him. So the third time she came back, Shawn finally just grabbed her by the hair and pulled her down, and said, 'He's with *me* tonight. Leave him alone.' Shawn said Jerry Lee loved it because she was so forceful."

She had spunk — "She wasn't a pansy," says Bev — enough to leave him when her younger sister, Shelley, came down to visit, and Jerry started showing his moods. Shelley, 20, drove down with their brother, Thomas, and his friend, Dave Lipke. Jerry Lee got jealous; he thought Shelley was bringing a young man for Shawn. Then he got mad, according to Shelley, and started knocking Shawn around. Shelley says the real problem was Jerry Lee's insistence that she and Shawn have sex with him.

"I knew what he wanted, and I wouldn't do it," Shelley says. "He made us leave, but he didn't actually tell us to go. He made Shawn tell us. So she said, 'Well, if you're leaving, so am I.'

"It was really crazy. Jerry Lee was wild. He ended up accusing us of stealing his Jet Ski. But the Jet Ski is big, like a snowmobile. I mean, I only had a Camaro. And he saw us drive away. He parted the curtains. We saw him looking through the bars on his window. I kept saying, 'Duck! Duck!' We all thought he was going to shoot us."

The Killer wore a white tuxedo and a red, ruffled shirt to his wedding on the patio of the big Nesbit house. Shawn shone in ivory-colored silk, and she spoke her vows bravely to Justice of the Peace Bill Bailey, who presided. In the rush, they hadn't been able to find a preacher to do the honors. (Well, J.W. Whitten found one, but he was black and Jerry might not have liked that, so J.W. got the judge.) In the rush, no one thought about the blood test for the license and the three days' wait required by Mississippi law, until Lottie Jackson brought it up on the morning of the wedding. For a while, it looked like Jerry Lee would have to pack the whole party off to Tennessee, where things could be done with less wait and bother. But J.W. fixed the license, too. "I made a phone call," he says, with evident pride. "Just somebody I knew down there." J.W. winks. "In the business, it's called 'juice.'"

Shelley arrived in Mississippi in the first days of June, driving a brand-new red Corvette that Shawn had asked her to deliver for her.

Shelley's mother said the family would drive down, too, but Shawn insisted that they spring for one-way air fare. No problem, Shawn said: Jerry Lee could send them home in the Learjet.

When at last they got it together, it didn't seem to want to start. Shawn's mother walked down the hall to find out what was keeping Jerry. He was almost ready: He was sitting in the master bedroom with his friend, Dr. George Nichopoulos. Dr. Nick had his medical license suspended in 1980 for over-prescribing addictive drugs. He was Elvis' personal physician on part of the King's long slide into drug oblivion. Dr. Nick testified at hearings that he also wrote narcotic prescriptions for Jerry Lee Lewis. Dr. Nick was still a frequent guest at the Nesbit house. On the wedding day, Shawn's mother says, she found Jerry regarding three pairs of pills, laid out neatly on a bed table: two of each, three different colors. Jerry Lee said he'd be up in a moment.

J.W. Whitten had invited the *National Enquirer*, which supplied this account of the big day, June 7th, 1983:

> Despite Jerry's experience at saying, "I do," he was a bundle of nerves during the ceremony. . . . And three times the nervous groom flubbed the line "according to God's holy ordinance." Eventually, Jerry held up his hand to the judge and said, "Just a minute, sir. I'm going to get that right," and went on to complete his vows perfectly.
>
> Then he slipped a ring on the finger of the honey-blonde bride. . . . The magnificent $6000 ring glittered with a two-carat diamond surrounded by smaller diamonds, all set in silver.
>
> "Oh, Lord, was I nervous," laughed the legendary hell-raiser, known to friends and fans as "the Killer." . . .
>
> "It was love at first sight," Jerry recalled.

"I've never believed in that sort of thing, but
there it was: The Killer fell in love."

There it was . . . and Shawn, was it there for her, too?

Well, she clipped the *Enquirer*'s story and sent it to friends and family.
On each copy, she crossed out "$6000" and wrote in the margin, $7000."

Her father stood in the hallway shouting: "What's the deal here? You
marry my daughter, then you can't even come out and see us? Thomas
Stephens was steamed; the morning after the wedding, he'd arrived with
the rest of the family at the house at eleven. They'd sat outside the locked
doors at the pool for more than an hour, before Shawn could emerge from
the bedroom to let them in the house. Now, after another hour, Jerry Lee
still hadn't made an appearance.

Jerry Lee showed a half-hour later, with a mumbled apology. He was
buzzed. They couldn't understand him. He wasn't in a very good mood.
"I went into the kitchen," says Shelley, "and he yelled at me, 'What do
you want?' I said, 'I just came in for a couple of beers.' He started
pounding his fist on the counter, screaming: 'You scared of me? You
should be. Why do you think they call me the Killer? How'd I get that
name, huh?' Then he slapped my face. I was trying not to cry. I couldn't
tell my father. Shawn took us to a hotel there, near the airport, and
dropped us off."

The family didn't have tickets home, and they didn't have the money
to buy them. Gone was the easy promise of the Learjet. Shawn's mother,
Janice Kleinhans, says there weren't any rental cars available at the airport
that day. At last, she had to call Jerry Lee. "I said, 'I don't know where
this mix-up come from, but if you can get us home, you'll have this money
back right away.' "

Jerry Lee said: "I don't want no money back from you." He and Shawn
came by a couple of hours later. Shawn was crying as she met her mother
in the airport and laid $1000 cash in her hand. Jerry Lee kept the motor
running.

In phone calls back to Michigan, Shawn seldom spoke of troubles. Still,
at one point, she told a friend that her life with the Killer was just like
jail—she couldn't stand his jealousy, she felt like she was watched all the
time. Once, she called home all excited about her new Lhasa apso—a
$500 dog! In her next call, she sadly reported that she had to give up the
pet because Jerry Lee got jealous. Later in the seventy-seven-day marriage,
most of the calls were about a homecoming, a Jerry Lee concert Sunday,
August 28th, in Nashville, Michigan. The family planned to convene—
even Shawn's grandfather, who'd been too infirm to make it to the wed-

ding, was planning to go. "Don't forget that Sunday," Shawn reminded them a dozen times.

She couldn't wait to see her sister Shelley and called in the middle of August to invite her down for a visit. Shelley, who had left her apartment and had to wait a month before moving into her new one, delightedly agreed to a long vacation. "Perfect," said Shawn. "I'll send you a ticket."

Her first night there, they went to Hernando's Hide-A-Way. Jerry was in a good mood, joking and dancing with Shawn, trying to charm Shelley. When they left at four in the morning, Jerry Lee was still flying. He played some piano back at the house, then put on the cassette of his new, unreleased album. "No one has ever heard any of these before," the Killer told Shelley and Shawn. When the song "One and Only You" started playing on the tape, Jerry Lee smiled and murmured, "This is dedicated to you."

He said it to both the sisters, but Shelley felt he was pressuring her. She didn't want him coming on. She didn't go for group sex. She said she'd better get to bed. Shawn said: "Oh, stay up a little longer." Shelley didn't want to be put on the spot. She said good night and went to bed.

When she got up at two the next afternoon, Jerry Lee was still up, drinking in his den. His sister, Linda Gail, and her children were over at the house for a visit. Shawn and Shelley sat in the sun at the pool, until Jerry Lee came out, looking mean and slurring his words. "He said something like, 'I think you girls better get your shit together,' and then he hit me on the thigh and slapped me across the face. Shawn sat up to say something, and he hauled off and backhanded her across the face. He hit her hard, too. Then he just looked at us really crazy and walked off into the house again.

"I just looked at Shawn, and she asked me, 'Did he hit you hard? Did it hurt?' I said, 'You're damn right it hurt!' I said, 'I'm leaving. I don't care who he is. Nobody can. . . .' And then I started to cry. 'He can't hit me like that. . . .' I said I was going to the police.

"Shawn said it wouldn't be a good idea to go to the police down there, because they were with Jerry, and they'd be trying to find a way to get me for trying to cause trouble for him. So I just said I was going. I was really upset. And she said, 'Just wait a little, Shel, 'cause I'm leaving, too. I'm not staying if you don't. I know what he'll do to me if I go back in that house.' I said, 'Get your stuff, 'cause I'm leaving, with you or without you.' "

They passed through the den on their way in, and Shelley said, trying not to cry, "I think I'm going to go now."

Jerry Lee said, "Go. Get your ass outta here. Get walkin'." He mumbled something about her being trouble.

"Then Shawn said, 'Shelley's been as quiet as a mouse since she's been here.' Jerry didn't hear her. She was over by the record shelf. He started yelling: 'Speak up! Whaddya say about me?' He grabbed some albums out from under her hands, and he smashed them on the floor. Then he knocked her across the room. Linda Gail grabbed up her two kids and left.

"Shawn was, like, whimpering: 'You're so mean. What's wrong with you?' She was sunk down into the big brown chair. He picked up a set of keys and whipped 'em at her, hit her in the forehead. She bent down to get the keys, and she told him: 'I'm leavin' with Shel. I'm not stayin' here with you.' So he tells her, 'I'll show ya leavin'.' He grabs her by the front of her robe, and he hauls her off down the hall. He says, 'You're my wife. I'll kill you before you leave me.'"

Shelley left the house on foot. She hitched a ride to the nearest store and called her father.

Back in Detroit, Shelley called her mother to recount the fight, but she omitted any mention of group sex. "Well, there may be things you didn't know about," her mother said. "Maybe she was making him mad somehow. There's two sides to everything. One night, when you're over here, we'll call her together and all talk about it." But before they made that call, Shawn wakened her mother with a phone call at 3:30 a.m., August 23rd.

"She said, 'I'm leaving him,'" her mother recalls, "if and when I can get away from him. . . .'"

"I said, 'Shawn, it's three o'clock in the morning. Call me tomorrow.'"

"She said, 'I don't know if I can. Whatever you do, make sure nobody calls for me here.'

" 'Honey, call me tomorrow, okay?'

" 'I don't know if I can, but I'll be in touch, Mom.'

" 'Okay, talk to you later. . . .'"

The next day, Shawn was dead.

Sole Survivor

Kurt Loder

IN THE MIDST OF ONE OF THE GREAT COMEBACKS IN
POP MUSIC HISTORY, TINA TURNER BROKE HER SI-
LENCE ABOUT HER ABUSIVE MARRIAGE.

It was the spring of 1985, and I was sitting in a Hamburg hotel suite
watching porn videos with Tina Turner. Actually, I guess I should
start at the beginning. It was the summer of 1984, and I was wedged
in among teetering stacks of records, tapes, books and other journalistic impedimenta in my pathetically disorganized office on the twenty-
third floor of the old ROLLING STONE building at 745 Fifth Avenue,
attempting to determine an appropriate focus for my first meeting with
Tina Turner—a woman whose early records, made with her ex-husband,
Ike Turner, I had revered for nearly a quarter of a century.

Like many another fan of my generation, I could remember lying abed
in pimply adolescence, transistor radio pressed against my ear, pillow
clamped over my head so as not to tip off the dozing folks downstairs,
soaking up the primal sounds of a late-night radio show sponsored by a
mail-order operation called Randy's Record Shop, in the faraway and utterly mysterious burg of Gallatin, Tennessee. On a clear night, the show
beamed all the way up the East Coast to my New Jersey bedroom, bring-

ing with it a galaxy of fantastic black R&B music that white pop radio, in that dim period, assiduously avoided: Bobby Bland, Jessie Hill, John Lee Hooker—even the deep-gospel harmonizing of the Swan Silvertones and the Staple Singers, as I recall. But most spectacular, to my pale teen ears, were the ur-funky offerings of Ike and Tina Turner, released on the Sue label, out of New York City. Beginning in 1960, Ike and Tina unleashed a series of singles—"A Fool in Love," "I Idolize You," "It's Gonna Work Out Fine," "Poor Fool," "Tra La La La La"—that were deeper and darker and altogether more otherworldly in their absolute *blackness* than anything else I'd ever heard. This music changed my life. But who *were* these people?

Over the ensuing decade, their fame spread somewhat. In 1966 producer Phil Spector recruited Tina—but not Ike—to be the vocal centerpiece of "River Deep—Mountain High," a single that bombed in this country but blossomed into a hit in Britain and that is still astonishing in its sheer sonic assault. Then in the early Seventies, Ike and Tina started charting hits with covers of other groups' tunes (the Beatles' "Come Together," Creedence Clearwater Revival's "Proud Mary"). Nothing, however, moved me as much as those early Sue sides.

By 1976—the year that Ike and Tina Turner ended their professional and marital partnership in a bloody punch-out at the Dallas-Fort Worth airport—I had returned from a sojourn of several years in Europe and was living in New York City. Three years later I started working at ROLLING STONE—a dream, if I may invoke the cliché, come true.

Sometime around the end of 1983, Brant Mewborn—an assistant editor at the time—began talking up the Return of Tina Turner. A musician himself and totally wired into the New York dance-club scene, Brant had been bowled over by an English import single featuring Tina's cover of the 1971 Al Green soul classic "Let's Stay Together." No one else, as I recall, shared Brant's enthusiasm for a Tina story, and that included me. As much as I loved the old black R&B music of the Fifties and Sixties, any revival of the careers of the musicians who'd made that music had always seemed to me to be doomed to degenerate into nostalgia of the most dismaying sort. But Brant—alone at the time, I'm afraid—realized that Tina Turner was not a nostalgia act, and he managed to bulldoze a short piece on her into the magazine. And that was that.

Until "Let's Stay Together" became a Top Forty U.S. hit in the winter of 1984. Suddenly, Tina *was* back—no one who heard the record could deny it. She was augmented by all the latest in British synth-pop wizardry, but her voice actually was better than ever, and she was wielding it with formidable assurance. That summer, her classic comeback album, *Private Dancer*, was released, and its lead single, "What's Love Got to Do With It," began its ascent to the top of the charts. Suddenly, Tina Turner was the hottest female rock act on the planet, and the cover of ROLLING STONE was hers for the asking. Brant Mewborn probably deserved to chronicle this unexpected triumph, but he really was an editor at the magazine (he later edited Tom Wolfe's original ROLLING STONE installments of *The Bonfire of the Vanities*), while I was essentially a feature writer. So I got the assignment.

Time was very tight. Immediately, I received a call from a man named Roger Davies, Tina's manager, requesting that I meet him and Tina for dinner that night at a restaurant of my choice. Given the rush, one of the places on nearby West Fifty-sixth Street, between Fifth and Sixth avenues, seemed ideal.

By this point in time, ROLLING STONE had come a long way from its legendarily boho origins in San Francisco, where Jann had started the magazine in 1967. It now inhabited four floors of a sleek office building hard by the Plaza Hotel, where the Beatles had cavorted during their first visit to America twenty years earlier; from the windows, you could look out across Central Park to the exclusive Dakota apartment block, where John Lennon had been murdered four years before. Tiffany, Bergdorf's and other glossy emporiums were only paces away. But it was a duff neighborhood for bars, so whenever RS staffers craved drink—pretty much always, in my recollection of the period—they often wound up knocking it back in one of the restaurants on West Fifty-sixth. There was a Korean joint where we'd all go to get legless on vile concoctions called ginseng cocktails. Then there was Darbar, a semiswank Indian bistro filled with hammered brass and softly clicking bead curtains, which turned out an acceptable line of tandoori chicken and chewy flat breads. Personally, I've never been all that partial to the cuisine of famine-prone Third World nations—a conceptual aversion, I'm afraid. But Roger Davies had told me that Tina was—or at least that she'd eat just about anything that came before her encased in a carapace of tongue-withering fire spices. So Darbar it was.

Her actual arrival at the restaurant was preceded by an almost tangible static of excitement in the air. Heads swiveled and forks slumped in midlift as she made her way up the stairs to the rattan nook where I awaited. She was wearing a simple black dress and her hair was bouffed out to enormous proportions. She radiated a sort of iconic energy that one encounters very rarely, even in showbiz circles. My opening gambit, once I'd recovered what there was of my composure, was to gush glibly about all those great old Sue singles—brilliant, epochal, own 'em all. To which Tina calmly replied that she hated those records—had hated the songs, had hated recording them, hated that joyless part of her life that they represented and would be happy never to hear any of them ever again.

I was considerably deflated by this revelation but pressed on regardless.

Tina was funny—especially after three glasses of wine, which I later determined was very near her limit—in an earthy and utterly unpretentious way. And Davies, who accompanied her, was an enormously engaging Australian whose obvious love of Tina and her music was, in my experience, a rare thing in the music business. Tina would shortly depart for Canada, where she had contracted long before to do a series of shows for the McDonald's burger chain—a bizarre commitment for a woman whose career had suddenly caught fire again, but one, it was decided, that I should fly up to witness. Which I did. The resulting story—accompanied by a spectacular photo of Tina by Steven Meisel—appeared in the October 11th, 1984, issue of ROLLING STONE and was quite well received.

So much so, in fact, that my agent at William Morris encouraged me to approach Roger and Tina with a proposal to write her life story. As it happened, I found myself flying to Australia several weeks later to cover the making of a movie called *Mad Max Beyond Thunderdome*—starring Mel Gibson . . . and Tina Turner. In a sweltering trailer in the sunbaked outback, I put my proposition to Tina and—back in the States once again—to Roger Davies. Aware that some quickie bios of Tina were already in the works to cash in on her renascent fame, Roger was agreeable, and a deal was struck.

To get Tina's story down on tape, it was arranged that I would take a leave of absence from the magazine—for which Jann gave his blessings—and fly to Budapest to hook up with Tina's European tour. The shows were all sold out, the crowds adoring, and as we made our way from Vienna to Munich to Düsseldorf, after each night's concert, I would grill Tina into the wee hours about her extraordinary life. Sometimes we (well, mostly I) would drink champagne through these sessions—Tina had a fondness for Cristal—and sometimes we'd wind up fairly looped. One night in Hamburg, having helped me empty more than a bottle or two, Tina ordered up an assortment of videos of the horror movies she favored, and when they arrived and we shoved one into a VCR, it turned out to be a hard-core porn tape. Tina collapsed into a cackling fit. I fell over onto the floor and had to be assisted to my feet. In retrospect, I'm amazed that we got anything accomplished at all.

Actually, I recall being fueled throughout most of this endeavor by various deleterious substances and that by the time the book, *I, Tina*—written in what seemed an endless series of overnight sessions in my officially vacated office at ROLLING STONE—was finally published in September of 1986, I was a complete wreck. It sold well, though, and—thanks to Tina's unflagging media popularity—spent several weeks on the *New York Times* bestseller list. As this is written, it is being very slowly turned into a feature film.

All of our lives have changed considerably since then. Tina has found a man who appears to be the love of her life, and she and Roger have both bought homes in the South of France. ROLLING STONE inhabits exceedingly spiffy new offices several blocks downtown from its old location, farther away from the restaurants of West Fifty-sixth Street—which, in any event, are all mostly long gone. Brant Mewborn, a sweet and gentle man, died in 1990, and Ike Turner, Tina's lately luckless ex-husband, has spent stretches of the past several years doing time for cocaine-related charges. As for me, I now work for MTV, along with such old ROLLING STONE colleagues as David Felton and Christopher Connelly, and I continue to marvel at the extent to which music—so often alleged to be a passing passion of childhood—has shaped and directed my life. It was the only thing I ever believed in.

I last saw Tina at the Hotel Bel-Air, in Los Angeles, a while back. We had dinner outdoors, by a pond filled with gurgling white swans, and in lifting a glass, we decided we'd both been blessed. True, she had made some unfortunate miscalculations in her life, and God knows, so had I. But I still think we were right. And I'm still a believer.

RS 432

OCTOBER 11TH, 1984

At three o'clock in the morning, in a hotel room high above still-glimmering Montreal, Tina Turner is plugging into the universal buzz: *nam-myo-ho-renge-kyo, nam-myo-ho-renge-kyo, nam-myo-ho-renge-kyo.* The words are Japanese, but shaped by that dark, burnished voice, now pulsing with reined power, they sound like some plaintive native-American lament—an effect perhaps subliminally suggested by the dramatic sweep of Tina's high, part-Cherokee cheekbones. As the words gather speed, her voice rises slightly to a smoothly rippling alto drone, then winds down. The demonstration is done. She raises her head—wigless at the moment and casually wrapped in a white shower towel—and a smile crinkles her otherwise unlined features. The chant, she says, is a Buddhist invocation of "the mystical law of the universe. I'm saying a word, but it sounds like *hmmmnnn.* Is there anything that is without that? There's a hum in the motor of a car, in the windshield wipers, your refrigerator. An airplane goes *rowwmmmnnn.* Sometimes I just sit and listen to the sounds of the universe and to that hum that is just there."

This chanting—plugging into the universal buzz—has lent spiritual structure to Tina's life. These days, you might say, she is like an electric lamp, summoning power and illumination at the twist of a switch. Before, she suggests—back in the dark years—she was more like a candle, self-consuming and finally benighted. Not to mention trapped, battered and generally brutalized in one of the most famous marriages in R&B history. But that's all part of the very painful past. And the past is something Tina Turner has little time for anymore.

Two nights ago in Ottawa, Tina performed the last shitcan gig of her career. Another McDonald's convention. For seven weeks, McDonald's, the fast-food chain, had been rounding up its highest-grossing regional burger merchants for pat-on-the-back brain-fry junkets to centrally situated hotel ballrooms around North America. The Ottawa bash seemed typical: intensive hooch transfusions for the sales hotshots, a swank feed, some semihysterical corporate rah-rah from a presiding exec and then, with more than a few celebrants on the verge of 'facing out into the fruit sherbet, a show—the show being Tina Turner. One last time.

Many months ago, you see, when she really needed the money—a common situation over the last seven lean years—Tina contracted to play fourteen of these functions. At the time, she hadn't the remotest inkling that her comeback single, "Let's Stay Together," would become a Top Five hit in Britain or that her startlingly strong comeback album, *Private Dancer*, would top the charts in Australia and Canada and sell more than a million copies in the U.S. Suddenly, Tina Turner found herself the hottest female act on three continents. Yet in Ottawa, there she was, headlining some fast-food fiesta on a stage framed by two sets of glowing golden arches. *Eeesh*. She had attempted to bow out of the McDonald's deal, but the burgerdomos were adamant, and the shows went on. Ottawa was the fourteenth and last of them, and the tech crew and the six-man band were audibly relieved. After hearing eerie massed chants of "beef-steak! beef-steak!" and watching a fiery-eyed burger exec whip the assembled franchisees into a froth with the go-get-'em ethos of "our leader"—the late McDonald's mastermind Ray Kroc, author of that tantalizingly titled memoir, *Grinding It Out: The Making of McDonald's*—guitarist Paul Warren blinked his eyes unbelievingly. "This is like Jonestown," he said.

Tina herself, however, remained uncomplaining. A total pro, she knew the drill and accepted it. Taking the stage, she noted the usual ocean of half-capsized banqueteers bobbling before her in ambiguous anticipation. What would *this* crowd be expecting? How much might it remember? "Proud Mary"? "Nutbush City Limits"? Maybe even "River Deep—Mountain High"? Surely, these people wouldn't recall "A Fool in Love," the first record by Tina and her former husband, Ike Turner, an epochal R&B hit in this same month of August exactly twenty-four years ago. Perhaps they'd remember hearing about the glitterized solo show she'd taken to Vegas and Tahoe a few years back—the one with the boy-and-girl dancers and the big-deal disco interlude. In which case, maybe they were prepared to embrace the inevitable: for what else can one normally expect in the ballrooms of American commerce but the last pathetic flickerings of faded and irretrievable fame?

Imagine, then, the instant of lip-flibbering surprise when Tina's band—which is a real rock & roll band, not some has-been backup crew—whipped out the wild, synth-riddled riff to "Let's Pretend We're Married," a song by Prince, and Tina shimmied out onstage in tight black-leather pants and a punk bouffant so bushed out you almost expected to see breadfruit come tumbling down in mounds around her stomping, stiletto-heeled feet. Kick-stepping up to the microphone at center stage, she snapped the sucker off its stand, and with a smile on her face the size of a sweet new moon and a voice that could fuse polyester at fifty paces, she began to sing. To soar, actually. The effect was electrifying—this was no Vegas act. "What you've heard about me is true," Tina chanted. "I change the rules to do what *I* wanna do." She didn't write the words—she rarely has—but, as always, she made them her own.

And from that moment on, the whole potentially ho-hum gig took an entirely different tack. Because Tina in transit across a stage knows only one velocity—flat-out—and as she kicked, shimmied and soared through most of her album and into a withering rendition of ZZ Top's neoboogie hit "Legs," the burger folk first rose to their feet, then up onto their tables, and finally into the very air, leaping and hooting and flapping their napkins overhead as this fabulous woman with the wraparound legs and the flatware-rattling voice proceeded to grind out an exhilarating hour-plus of artfully adult, but undiluted, rock & roll.

And Ottawa was it: the light at the end of the comeback tunnel. Tina Turner had outlasted her past. Now she could look strictly to the future: Her next single, "Better Be Good to Me," would be released as soon as her current hit, the reggae-spiked "What's Love Got to Do with It," could be pried out of the top spot on the U.S. singles chart, and several other tracks off the LP seemed likely candidates to follow. Six sold-out shows in Los Angeles were coming up, and after that she was off to Australia to confer with director George Miller, who's been waiting for two years to feature her in the third of his celebrated *Mad Max* movies (she'll play a kinkily costumed creature called Entity and may do a tune over the titles). Then it would be back to New York in September for the MTV Music Video Awards and the release of her pal David Bowie's new album—on which she harmonizes a haunting reggae track called "Tonight"—and then . . . well, who knows? If all of this could happen to a woman who didn't even have a U.S. record deal a year ago—who in fact not all that many years ago was feeling so slapped down by life that she almost bought out of it with a bottle of sleeping pills—well, then maybe there is a universal harmony. Whatever that buzz is, it's Tina Turner's theme song.

*   *   *

In her suite at Montreal's Le Quatre Saisons, Tina admits that she thinks a crucial cosmic turnaround in her life occurred when she began to let go of the past, allowing dribs and drabs of it to float to the surface of occasional interviews. But to go back all the way—back to the bad old days with Ike—was hard. "God, you know, when I left Ike," she says, "I left all of those memories behind."

Compared to the more generously fleshed beauties of that period, little Anna Mae Bullock was something of a scrawny kid, and so Ike didn't take much notice when she first approached him about getting up to sing with the Kings. Night after night she'd sit there waiting for the call, but it never came. Finally, one night, when Ike was up onstage playing the organ, Tina grabbed the mike and started to belt out a B.B. King tune.

"Everyone came running in to see who the girl was that was singing," Tina remembers. "Then Ike came down. He was real shy. He said, 'I didn't know you could *really* sing.' " Slowly, Ike began working Anna Mae into his stage show.

"I became like a star," she says. "I felt real special. Ike went out and bought me stage clothes—a fur, gloves up to here, costume jewelry and bareback pumps, the glittery ones; long earrings and fancy form-fitting dresses. And I was wearing a padded bra. I thought I was so sharp. And riding in this Cadillac Ike had then—a pink Fleetwood with the fish fins. I swear, I felt like I was rich! And it felt good."

"You see," says Tina, "I was still in love, but I was beginning to realize I was unhappy. I didn't want the relationship anymore—it started that early. We were two totally different people. When Ike got that record deal, I had already decided then that I didn't want to get involved. That was the first time he beat me up. And I thought, 'Okay, I'll do whatever it is.' Christ, I was afraid of Ike. I would do whatever he said. See, Ike was really very funny—he would joke and play—and I do remember good times and having some fun. But he was always so mixed up with confusion and anger that you could very easily forget the good times."

Ike and Tina had settled in a Los Angeles suburb, but the act continued to work eleven months out of the year. When she wasn't onstage, Tina remained the perfect Little Woman. "Ike was like a king," she says. "When he woke up, I'd have to do his hair, do his nails, his feet. You know what I mean? I was a little slave girl."

In 1965, they were appearing at Cyrano's, a club on the Sunset Strip, when Phil Spector walked in. Spector was impressed. He approached Ike ("No one ever approached me," Tina notes) with a proposition to feature the Turners in a concert film he was involved with, *The Big T.N.T. Show.* That was just the opener, though. He was really interested in making a record with Tina—just Tina. Some sort of deal was cut—Tina's not sure exactly what it was. By that point, she was just going along with the program; after gigs, she would slip away and go home to provide the couple's four children (two of Ike's, one of Tina's, and Ronnie, the son they had together) a modicum of company.

In any case, Spector secured from Ike the right to use Tina, and he invited her to his house to hear the song he wanted her to sing, a composition he'd cowritten with Jeff Barry and Ellie Greenwich called "River Deep—Mountain High." Tina loved it. "For the first time in my life, it wasn't R&B. I finally had a chance to *sing*."

In hippie circles, Ike and Tina Turner became everyone's favorite gutbucket soul revue. Ike bought and decorated an elaborate house in Inglewood—orange carpet, green kitchen, mirror over the bed—and built a studio about five minutes away (with its own sort of playpen-apartment), to which he would summon Tina at all hours for recording work. She still didn't say much, but she was more miserable than ever. At one point, despairing about what her life had become, she procured a bottle of sleeping pills from a doctor and took them all before a show one night, hoping to pass out and die onstage.

"But I didn't make it to the stage," she says. "Ike walked in, and I was so scared, 'cause I knew that if he had to cancel before the show, he'd have to pay the musicians. And I did not make it to the stage, and I mean I was insanely afraid. I mean, he would *beat* me so, I cannot tell you, the choking and beating. And I was in the hospital, and I heard later from the doctors that they could not get a pulse. And apparently Ike came in and started talking to me. He said, 'You motherfucker, you better not die; I'll kill you'—and my pulse started!"

By 1975, the hits had dried up for Ike and Tina Turner, and so had a lot of the live work with which Ike had sustained his lifestyle over the years. And Tina, after nearly sixteen years of marriage, had finally reached the end of her rope. In the midst of what was to be their final tour, en route to the L.A. airport for a flight to Dallas, their whole tormented life together finally fell apart.

"He handed me this chocolate candy, and it was melting, you know? And I was wearing a white suit, and I went, 'Uh.' That's all—and he hit me. And this time, I was pissed. I said, 'I'm fightin' back.' "

When they arrived at the Dallas airport, the fight continued. "When I got in the car, he gave me a backhand, just like that. And I remember pointing my finger in his face and saying, 'I told you. You got the money, you got everything. I'm gonna try to stay—but I'm not gonna take your licks anymore.' And then the big fight started—and I started hitting back. I didn't cry once. I cursed back and I yelled, and he goes, 'You son of a bitch, you never talked to me like this before.' And I said, 'That's right, but I am *now*!'

"Because I knew I was gone. I was flying. I knew that that was it. By the time we got to the hotel, I'm not lying, my face was swollen out past my ear. Blood was everyplace. We walked upstairs, and Ike *knew*. So he went and laid across the bed. And I was still saying, 'Can I get you something?' And I started massaging him, as usual, massaging his head. And he started snoring. And I leaned over and I said . . . goodbye."

Ike was not all that easy to shake, according to Tina. There were a few bullets fired into one of the houses she moved to, and a car was burned. For a while, knowing Ike's own predilections, she took to carrying a gun herself. When she walked out on Ike, she had thirty-six cents and a single handbag to her name, and in the subsequent divorce action she asked for nothing more—no money, no property, no payoff on all the years she'd put into their career. It was the price of disengagement, she says—the price of finally buying her freedom.

For a year after the split, Tina did nothing. Through some women friends who put her up, she became interested in Buddhism and chanting. Eventually, she went back to work at the only job she knew. Unfortunately, since it had been she who had walked out on Ike in the midst of a tour, damages for all the resultant blown gigs were laid by the promoters at her door. A friend in the record business agreed to help, and realizing she needed immediate infusions of cash to begin paying off the hundreds of thousands of dollars of debts she'd suddenly fallen heir to, he steered her into cabaret—Vegas, Tahoe. Tina is not ashamed of those days: she had to work, and she was a pro.

Today, Tina looks better than ever, sings better than ever, and says she's now happier than ever too. She has a new boyfriend—a younger man she'd rather not name—and is now attempting to find the "balance of equality between men and women." She sees herself performing till she's fifty, perhaps, and says she'd then like to become a teacher, a propagator of her beloved Buddhist beliefs. Apparently it's preordained.

"I'm gonna focus on this," she says. "I think that's gonna be my message, that's why I'm here. And I think that's why I'm gonna be as powerful as I am. Because in order to get people to listen to you, you've got to be some kind of landmark, some kind of foundation. You don't listen to people that don't mean anything to you. You have to have something there to make people believe you. And so I think that's what's going on now. I'm getting their attention now, and then when I'm ready, they'll listen. And they'll hear."

K*ids in the Dark*

DAVID BRESKIN

AFTER THE DRUG-INSPIRED MURDER OF A TEENAGER AND THE SUICIDE OF ONE OF THE KILLERS, HOW DO YOU GET THEIR TERRIFIED FRIENDS TO BREAK THE SILENCE?

What does a dead body in the woods mean in 1984? Every story starts with a question, and that's the one I was asking myself on my first drive to Northport, Long Island. The story—the murder of a teenager named Gary Lauwers by two of his friends, one of whom, Ricky Kasso, subsequently hanged himself in prison—had already occupied front-page space in the Sunday *New York Times* and was on its way to setting some kind of continual screaming-headline record in the lurid *New York Post*. I didn't really care about the drug-induced Satanism that the newspaper reports trumpeted, and as for the violence, it was run-of-the-mill by city standards—so what that it happened in the lily white suburbs? What interested me were not the sensations themselves—drugs, Satanism, violence—so much as what they were symptomatic of. And that kept leading me back to my question, which really asks not so much about how these kids died as about how these kids lived.

When I got to town, there were reporters in the trees. Literally. Minivans and minicams, the London *Times* and the *National Enquirer, Good Morning America,* the *Today* show and *The CBS Morning News* were swooping down to see what tasty bits the lion had left behind. I waited for the daily press to migrate to a different corpse and stayed for several weeks more once it did.

My local "office" became the phone booth by the harbor, where frogmen were diving for the murder weapon in the first few days. The fact that I looked younger than my twenty-six years, dressed in T-shirts and holey blue-jeans and sneakers, had grown up in a similar town and could more or less talk the kids' language gave me entree into their world. I blended in so well that I was occasionally mistaken for "one of them" by other reporters and asked silly questions. But my desire to hang out with them — and *not* ask questions for long stretches — also made the kids suspicious. In fact, I had to convince some of them that I was not a narc. What more perfect cover than a longhaired, sunglassed, ROLLING STONE reporter?

The adults had their own suspicions. The police twice asked for my ID as I walked down the town's main drag, and I was later almost arrested for "contributing to the delinquency of a minor" when an officer found two of my sources drinking beer in my rental car late at night in a strip-mall parking lot. Did he expect me to be interviewing them in their kitchens with their parents listening in? The police chief later told me there had been some suspicion I was a drug dealer. What more perfect cover than a longhaired, sunglassed ROLLING STONE reporter?

I talked to everybody I could con into talking to me: friends and enemies of the killers and the killed, schoolteachers, drug counselors and dealers, lawyers, waitresses (they always know a lot), cops, parents, doctors, psychologists, prison wardens. The key, as always with sources for whom there is a natural reluctance to talk, is in convincing them you are seeing the story through their eyes and will tell it from their point of view. I kept a separate outfit in my car trunk — jacket, tie, button-down shirt, dress shoes — to wear whenever I needed to look respectable for the adults. (Unfortunately, my phone booth was not of the closed Superman variety, and changing on the fly was a constant problem.) I took material on the record, I took material on a "not for attribution" basis, and I took a great deal off the record. I ended up with forty-four hours of taped interviews.

Many of the kids I talked to were scared and angry and hurt: There'd been a murder, a suicide, there'd been widespread complicity in keeping quiet (which was the trigger for my interest), and now there was the anticipation of a trial for the remaining defendant. The feeling of alienation and desperate self-dramatization in their lives was pathetic and touching. The fact that every "adult" institution had failed them—family, school, church, work—led me to abandon all my interviews with the adults, the authority figures, and to focus exclusively on the kids' point of view. It was painful to let go of half my research, but I felt that even by their absence, perhaps *especially* by their absence, the world of the adults would be felt in the story.

To tell it, I wanted to push the limits of traditional journalism. As the Eighties wore on, I was becoming frustrated with the limitations of magazines—stories were becoming shorter and more formulaic. ROLLING STONE was one of the few places where you could subvert those formulas and maybe create some of your own. For this story, I used a formula that borrows from poetry—the poetry of the "found" voice. I wanted the entire story to be told through the voices of the kids. No introduction, no transitions, no conclusion. I wanted the readers to go swimming in the kids' world and to draw their own conclusions. My only "take" on the story would be the way I selected and edited my raw material, much like the way Frederick Wiseman makes documentary films. I shaped the piece into thirteen sections and titled it "Thirteen Ways of Looking at a Black Spot in the Woods," after the Wallace Stevens poem "Thirteen Ways of Looking at a Blackbird."

This strategy proved too arty, and perhaps too arch, for my editor, Carolyn White, who retitled the piece "Kids in the Dark" and insisted I write both an introduction and brief background notes to begin each section. I wrote the intro in a purple tone: My goal was to write something that Tom Waits could talk-sing. That kind of feeling.

Three things happened after the story was published that gave it a longer shelf life than most. First, the attorney for the surviving attacker, Jimmy Troiano, subpoenaed all my notes and tapes. Of course, we would not give up the material; it would set a horrible precedent. Besides, my word—and the trust of all those kids whom I'd talked to—was on the line. I didn't feel the need to do the defense's work for it. In paranoid fashion, I split up the tapes and moved them to friends' apartments around New York City. Certain key tapes were copied, labeled BLACK SABBATH and put in a safe-deposit box.

ROLLING STONE's lawyers diligently defended my right to this material, and I sought out other writers who would publicize the matter if it looked as if I were going directly to jail without passing go. Luckily, after much ado and a legal bill that probably dwarfed what the magazine had to pay me to write the damn story in the first place, we won the day in court, and my mother stopped worrying about how to smuggle in a nail file in a bowl of chicken soup.

The second thing was that a young playwright in Chicago named Rick Cleveland was so moved by the story that he contacted me and asked if I would let him concoct a play out of it. Yes, I said, if I could do it with him. A year and a half later, *Kids in the Dark* — the headline was now a title — had a successful run in Chicago. It was a one-act, with the murder coming in the first five minutes, and the rest of the play attempting to unwind it. What about film rights? asked everyone. Well, with perfect timing, the movie *River's Edge* opened just as the play closed, and the stories were, shall we say, very similar.

The third thing happened a bit later. A sleazoid book about the crime appeared, *Say You Love Satan*. The author had used as much of the article as he possibly could have — all without acknowledging the source. Sue! I thought. Settle! said my agent, wisely, and we marched off to Bantam Books (the august publisher) and entered into a conference with — guess who? — the same lawyer who had a few years earlier kept me out of jail and had recently become in-house counsel at Bantam. Everything this writer did was legal, she said; it might not be nice, but it was legal. Sue us! she said. Long live the First Amendment, we cursed, leaving the room and "Kids in the Dark" behind us.

RS 435

NOVEMBER 22ND, 1984

Past Is Prologue

The lawyer who twice represented Gary in Juvenile court told a newspaper reporter, "He wasn't really bad. He was just acting out." Gary's act had no room for role reversal.

MARK FISHER: Ricky was totally dusted out and went unconscious for a while at a party. Gary stole the dust from out of his jacket — ten little yellow envelopes with the words SUDDEN IMPACT on them. When Ricky confronted him with it, he gave him back five and went and worked and paid him back for the rest. Gary was scared of him, 'cause every time they'd get together, Ricky would chew him out or beat the shit out of him. He never let him live it down. 'Cause Ricky had the money, but he didn't have the vengeance.

TEEN DUSTHEAD 2: Gary was an easy target. I always saw Gary getting the shit kicked out of him.

TERRIE ALTO: I knew he was afraid of Kasso. He was scared shitless of Ricky.

PEACENIK GIRL: Jimmy Troiano had just gotten out of jail. It was like

April. He and Ricky were going after Gary, looking for him, 'cause he'd ripped him off. And Albert Quinones made Ricky take off his ring, 'cause he didn't want him to really fuck Gary up. I saw Ricky walking up the street looking for him: happy, psyched and everything.

And then I saw Gary come out from behind the white church; he walks up and his jacket was ripped; he had a cut on the side of his face—blood dripping down. Maybe his lip was bleeding. I think he hadn't paid him back the money yet.

MICHELLE DEVEAU: I fixed his wounds up for him once. His black eye. And he had a bloody nose, too. He told me Ricky was an asshole. He'd bought a knife for protection, but I don't think he carried it around. Gary told me Ricky told him he was gonna kill him. Supposedly. He said, "Last time Ricky beat me up, he says next time he's coming back for more and it's not gonna be just a black eye."

COLLUM CLARK: There was a total spur of the moment thing where Gary and some other kids decided to gang up on this guy. They were beating him up, and then Gary took out a pipe and was lighting it up. And he gave him maybe ten bowl burns, circles with the rim of the bowl, a tattoo, sort of. Very severe, and they *hurt*. It was sick, it was torture. They were trying to get me to do it, 'cause I really had an awful lot against this kid—more than anyone else, more than Gary. I said to myself, No, you'll get in trouble. Gary just had a severe dislike for him.

PREPSTER GIRL: Gary pulled a BB gun on two little kids up at the school, to scare 'em. After that, he comes up to a group of my friends who are sitting, talking, and I guess because now that he broke through his faggot, and he's into his little dirt-bag group that he's so proud of, he calls *me* a faggot! And I said, "Oh, yeah, you're so cool you can pull a gun on someone." And he got all mad, and started chasing me, and getting his girlfriends after me, and saying he was gonna kill me. But not *kill* me kill me, just kill me.

That Night

In Cow Harbor Park, kids were reeling from the year's first punch of summer. Eventually, most everyone headed to a birthday party for Randy Guethler. But not Ricky, Jimmy, Gary or Albert.

MIKE "LION" MENTON, 17: Everybody was fucked up that night. It was one of the first nights school ended, so everybody was out. It was a festive night. You could feel it. We got done with finals. People were tripping, people were stoned. Gary went into the park and came back and said, "I saw cats, man!" I said, sure, maybe he saw a cat in the park, and he said, "No, man, there are cats all over the place." He was flipping out.

One of the last things he said to me, "Well, I guess it's safe for me to come down here now. I'm all paid off, I'm in good, it's safe." Then he said goodbye: "I'm going to get some beers and get fucked up."

DOROTHY AT WAKE: That night, Gary said, "Mom"—he calls me Mom—"I'm going back to school. I got my act together: I paid my debts, and I got a lot of friends, and I really care about myself and I don't need drugs anymore. I'm gonna start over."

RICH BARTON, 15: I was down at the park that night. I went up to Aztakea three hours earlier, with Rick and Jim. We tried to make a fire, but we couldn't. It was wet. And then we tried to get out of the woods, but we couldn't. There was no moon and there's a lot of paths up there, and we had the tunes cranking—Sabbath, Ozzy, Judas Priest. When we got out of the woods, I said, "I'm going home, trip out by myself."

PEACENIK GIRL: That night Jimmy and Albert and Ricky came up to me, wanted me to buy mesc. They were really happy and everything. They were dehydrated, so they asked me where the nearest swimming pool was, 'cause they wanted to go pool hopping. They asked me to go to the deli to get orange juice. I got them the biggest orange juice I could find, and they were so happy. All three of them chugged it down. They were all dosed. They were happy.

SOFTHEARTED GIRL: Ricky gave Gary hits of mesc and bought him jelly doughnuts at Dunkin' Donuts. First Gary didn't want to go, but then Ricky said, "We'll buy jelly doughnuts!" So he was, like, "Yeah!"

MARK FISHER: Ricky had twenty-five hits of mesc in a little stash bottle down at the park. I was gonna go get beers, and I gave them my box, had my tape in it, Black Sabbath, *We Sold Our Soul for Rock 'n' Roll*. I came back, and they had left. Aw, shit! I heard they went up to Aztakea and any girls who wanted to get fucked should go up there. That was the word. So I went up to Aztakea, but I didn't quite make it, 'cause it was so dark, I was bumping into trees and falling down. I heard noises as I was getting closer, but I couldn't tell which way to go, and so I finally gave up.

A Trip

Albert Quinones appears to be the only person who saw what happened, and will be the government's star witness. Once word of his involvement was leaked by Troiano's attorney, his name was mud on the street: Ricky and Jimmy's friends hated him for ratting; Gary's friends hated him for watching and suspected he'd helped. After this interview, his mother sent him out of state to be with a priest.

ALBERT QUINONES, 16: Gary already paid him his money back. Everyone was his friend. I mean, Ricky and Gary were both talking a lot, shit like that. The thing that bugs me out, man, is all of them were pushing me, especially Gary and Ricky, to take a hit of mescaline. They were all tripping. It bugs me out. I didn't want to, but finally I just said, "What the hell," so I took a hit. Ricky treated us to doughnuts at Dunkin' Donuts. To me, Gary was being cool and shit. And then we went up to Aztakea, because they wanted to go to a good tripping area, and they've got a little field where you can trip out.

See, Ricky was getting pissed off, because he couldn't start a fire, so Gary just takes off his socks, puts them in there. After Gary made a fire with his socks, he didn't want to make it bigger. And Ricky comes out with a remark, "Why don't you just burn your whole jacket?" The guy's like, "How 'bout I just cut the sleeves off and use my sleeves?" It was fucked, man. So he took off his jacket and gave it to Ricky, and Gary just chopped off the sleeves. I guess he was going to make it into a vest.

All of a sudden Gary goes, "I have funny vibes that you're going to kill me." And Ricky was saying, "I'm not going to kill you. Are you crazy?" and shit like that. I was just tripping out, man. I was peaking. I was peaking out, tripping out. And they were just fighting, punching each other and shit, and I didn't think anything was going to happen. I mean, I could see Ricky's point, too, which is that he was friends with Gary, and he just turns around and steals ten bags of dust.

So they were just rolling on the ground and shit, and Gary got up to his feet after Jimmy had ran up to him and kicked him in the ribs and shit, and Gary had gotten up to his feet, and Ricky just bit him in the neck, bit him in the ear and then he just stabbed him.

It was a trip, man, I'll tell you, man, it was a trip. I mean, you sit there and stare out, and you look at the trees, and it looks like they're bending down and shit. I don't know—that was a trip. I thought it was a nightmare. I couldn't move, man. My whole body, all of a sudden, it just wouldn't move, it wouldn't function. It was like in shock. I was going crazy, man. I just stood there in my place, like all bugged out.

After Ricky stabbed him, Gary took off, ran, and Ricky got him, just like that. Jimmy picked up the knife after Ricky had dropped it, and he gave it to Ricky. And Ricky made Gary get on his knees and say, "I love Satan." Then Ricky just started hacking away from him, man. He just kept stabbing him and shit, and then Gary was just screaming, "Ahhh, I love my mother." It was really fucked, man. And they grabbed him by the legs and dragged him in the woods, Ricky and Jimmy, dragged him in the woods. They came running out of the woods after they just threw leaves on him and shit. They told me that he started stabbing Gary in the face and shit . . .

I wasn't going to rat them out, because what's, like, another body? Man, it's no big deal. I mean, you see them kill once, you just don't think, like, they're not going to kill you.

Where's Gary?

It was just like Gary to take off without warning. Neither his parents nor his friends notified the police he had vanished.

BRIAN HIGGINS, 16: Gary had disappeared so often, you wouldn't think about it.

PEACENIK GIRL: Just offhand, I said to Ricky, "I know you don't even care, but have you seen Gary? 'Cause we talked to his mother, and she hasn't seen him in a while." He was just like, "No." Later that night we hung out for a while. He started complaining he was getting flashbacks. He didn't feel good. He said he was never gonna trip again. He just said, "I just had a bad trip, a really bad trip." He had poison ivy all over him, and I gave him calamine lotion. It freaked me out after I heard about things—I helped aid him in the cure of his poison ivy gotten burying a friend of mine.

SCOTT TRAVIA, 18: I saw Ricky, and he kept saying, "Yeah, everything's cool between me and Gary." Then I got this phone call from Gary's mom—she was wondering where he was. He used to sleep in my garage sometimes, in my '69 Fairlane. I said I hadn't seen him. She told me someone with this eerie voice called her and said, "You will never see your son again, because I just killed him." Neither of us believed it.

GLEN WOLF, VETERAN DIRT-BAG STREET KID, 21: Gary was helping me fix my car. His tools were here. His hose was here. And some of his tapes were here. And I owed him thirty dollars. And it didn't connect that he didn't come back for all that stuff and ask for the money.

BOY AT WAKE: I was there when they threw the knife in the harbor. I saw Albert and Ricky talking, and Ricky said, "What should I do with it?" and Albert said, "Throw it in the water." And then they went over and they threw it in the water. I said, "What was that?" And Ricky said, "Aw, nothing—it was a rock, man." I didn't think anything about it.

MARK FISHER: I was walking up Main Street, just applied for a job at the ice-cream parlor, and I saw Ricky making faces at a window. It was like a mirror. If you asked him what was he on, he'd just say, "Drugs." After that, Ricky came and slept over on the couch in my room for a bunch of nights. He'd write "666" on steam mirrors when he'd take a bath, and he'd leave at 12:30 in the afternoon, before my mom came home. Jimmy spent a night, too.

One day I asked Ricky if I could borrow a knife. Jimmy and Ricky always carried knives in their jacket pocket. And he said, "I don't carry a knife." I said, "I don't carry one either." He said, "That's good, you'll just end up stabbing somebody." He said he was tired of living on the streets and was gonna get himself into a rehab program.

One night he came back to my house. He was on dust. He went to sleep, and he woke up and thought he saw people in the room, people who had *returned*. He said that maybe people were haunting him.

Another night Albert and two girls held a séance at my house, a satanic ritual in which they tried to call forth the devil. It was probably the twentieth or twenty-first of June. Ricky wasn't there. Troiano was in the next room with his girlfriend. They started out by drawing a five-pointed star — they just traced their fingers. They put a cup in the middle. We put our cigarettes in it. What they did say was "Satan will come forth in the form of fire." And all of a sudden the cup in the middle, after a couple of minutes, started going in flames . . . because there was a piece of paper in there. And they said, "Oh, Satan has arrived! Welcome! Welcome!"

PEACENIK GIRL: Ricky asked me if he could have a ride up to Saratoga to see the Dead. I said, "Sure." I told him Gary might be going, if we could find him.

The Silent Circle

The only institution that mattered was friendship. The idea was to pretend you weren't involved, to hang out and hope it went away.

RICH BARTON: I think it was two days after. I saw Ricky down in the round house. He was *up* that night. He was like, "Rich, come here, I gotta tell you something. I killed Gary." I went, "Bullshit! Get out of here." He's like, "Come on, I'll show you the body." I thought he was kidding. But then I saw him the next night, and I was like, "All right, I'll go up and see the body." 'Cause I didn't think it was true.

And so we go up there, it smelled like shit. I'm like, "Rick, what the hell did you kill, a fucking cat?" And all of a sudden he's like, "There it is." And there's like a pile of leaves, and I'm like, "Holy shit, man." I see all these maggots on him, a thick pile of them on top of the leaves. I said, "Rick, I'm getting the hell out here. I'll meet you back downtown." I just fucking booked out of there.

I met Ricky back in the park. He was calm, and he's like, "See, I told you." I said, "I think you're crazy, man. You're gonna get caught. Why'd you do this, man?" He said, "For kicks," something like that. It's like, now if *he* gets caught, I'm going to get involved. I didn't tell anybody, but I couldn't escape it. It came up every two minutes.

MARK FLORIMONTE, 17: The really gross part was smelling it like four blocks away. It smelled like a swamp that was after a thousand years, something just decaying for a thousand years and there's maggots.

They asked me at the grand jury: Why didn't you tell the police? I don't know. When you're a kid, why don't you tell the police, you know?

RICH BARTON: Afterward, Ricky stayed over four times, I guess. I'd be sitting down in my room, and he'd just come through the back door. He was my friend. He'd sleep on the floor of my room and use his leather jacket as a blanket. He'd get up at two in the afternoon, and I'd cook him some hot dogs. The routine was the same as it normally was.

Ricky thought that because they're gonna build houses up there that they'd stumble across the body in like a year or so. And he was sorta worried that a person would go on a wood hunt and grab a stick, but it would be a hand or a bone. He asked me to help bury it. I said, "Fuck that, man. I'm not getting near that thing. I saw it once, that's enough." I said, "You can have this shovel, and you don't have to give it back." Another guy drove Rick up there to do it, and he did it by himself. After, he just came up to me and said, "I buried the body." I said, "Thank God."

Then this other guy asked me about Gary, up at the loading docks. He's like "You know, I think Lauwers is dead." And I'm like, "Holy shit! Really?" I'm just acting. His friend Scott got a call from Lauwers' mother. Somebody called her and said, "I killed your son." I said, "No, he's probably not dead, he probably just ran away."

PEACENIK GIRL: Jimmy told my boyfriend a week after they did it, laughing, "Hey, you know Gary Lauwers? Oh, we killed him last week," and then went into detail. My boyfriend wasn't gonna say anything to me. I wear the peace signs—no one's gonna tell me about a murder.

ALBERT QUINONES: For those three weeks when I didn't know what to do, I was going crazy. I was afraid—I didn't know what to think, 'cause no one's normal enough to do that. If you do that, man, you gotta have losed it, you know. I'd think about going to the cops and just sort of, No, man, because they'd try to frame me, man. They'd set me up.

I tried to avoid them, and all they did was tag. We hung out. They're *very* persistent. They would laugh about it and shit. They told so many people. They would just make jokes: "Oh, Gary's dead, no big deal. Let's go get another one . . ." They'd say, "Let's go up there and watch him rot. . . ."

MARK FLORIMONTE: See, that day, July 4th, they were searching for the body, and they found it. So they wanted to find out who knew about it. They knew Albert hung with Ricky and him, so they grabbed Albert first. And they tried to find out, and Albert wouldn't tell them anything, so that's why when Albert came home, his lip was all cut, he had bruised ribs and a big bump on his head. They wanted to know the truth.

ALBERT QUINONES: The detectives were beating the shit out of me. See, I don't trust them, man, I don't trust no one anymore. They picked me up at two, and they were beating the shit out of me for like two and a half hours, in Yaphank. They brought me up to this room, and they started questioning me and shit, and they were beating the shit out of me. They didn't tell me they were going for Ricky and Jim. I don't know what to think. My head's screwed up ever since that night—and it's still screwed up, man.

The next day they said they were gonna let me go, 'cause Jimmy was coming in. He looked like he got away with it and shit—he's playing it cool. I told them everything. Maybe Jimmy was probably thinking that I wasn't gonna rat him out.

The July 4th Hangover

Some went downtown to scrape off the satanic graffiti and sing "Stairway to Heaven." Some went to praise Ricky Kasso or to bury Gary Lauwers. Some went into the woods to get a look at the black spot. They were all hung over from chugging reality.

MARK FISHER: My mom brings in the paper, and they're on the front page. She says, "See what your friends do, you've had murderers sleeping over at our house." I was just cold as shit, I never heard a thing about it.

DENISE WALKER: It wasn't shocking. It was disappointing. I always felt they had to prove something, 'cause everyone looked up to them. They had to keep doing things so people would think they were great. They'd wreck fences, rip down signs, beat people up. They stole a car and smashed it up. They just got carried away.

RANDY GUETHLER: Before the murder, I was known as a gravedigger. I did it to see bones, to see history. That's why people go to museums. It's just something teenagers do. But now people give me dirty looks everywhere I was, because I'm known as a Satanist. That's a little different.

PEACENIK GIRL: Rick just went sick with the knife. I don't think they carved his eyes out. Ricky just started stabbing him in the face when he found out he wasn't dead. He probably just stabbed his eyes in.

Jimmy's girlfriend told me at the Fireman's Fair, "Really, I didn't *believe* him. When he told me about it, he was laughing! I feel like I have a disease."

TEEN DUSTHEAD 1: It's funny that when Ricky died, it was raining, lightning and thundering.

TEEN DUSTHEAD 2: My door all of a sudden slammed open. It was shut and locked tight, and it slammed open and banged against the wall. It was two a.m. 'Cause indirectly we were the ones that got him started in this whole thing. It was just his way of coming to my house, saying, "Hey, man, look at this shit."

BAKER: Ricky wanted to be the devil's second hand. He said he was gonna chase Gary's soul and kill himself in jail. Everybody knew that.

DAN PETTY: I think Ricky shouldn't have been able to commit suicide. I think Ricky deserved much worse than that.

SOFTHEARTED GIRL: Ricky wanted the suicide. He always talked to me about it. He always said how much better his life would be if he was dead.

RANDY KORWAN, VIETNAM VET, 33: I honor Kasso. I admire him. Why? Because he's honest. He's another rug rat at someone's house; another one on the floor, eking out an existence; another wolf in a house full of wolves.

KING'S PARK GIRL, 16: Ricky hung out with the kid, and Gary stole from him. But, I mean, he had no right to stab the kid in the head. That's where he was wrong.

KING'S PARK RAPPING BOY: Hey, Ricky, you're so fine, why doncha stab me one more time! Do-de-do, do-de-do. Hey, Ricky, you're a nice guy, why doncha stab me in the eye! Do-de-do, do-de-do. Hey, Ricky, you're so swell, why you hanging in your cell?

TERRIE ALTO: This is the first time somebody I know died, other than people who send me checks on Christmas. It's like, I still don't realize he's dead. I've dreamed about him. He's always in my mind. There's so much shit to remind me: his ID bracelet, GARY; his little marines hat.

BILLY LEASON, PALLBEARER, 16: I'm not scared of death. You can't live life that way. If you're gonna live, I say have good times all the time. Go out and have a party. Push yourself as far as you can go. If I die tomorrow, I can always say that I lived my life to the fullest.

KING SARDONIC, KNIGHTS OF THE BLACK CIRCLE, 20: I have theories about when you die. I think it's what you think it's gonna be. For me, it's gonna be like this really classic *Playboy* cartoon from 1966 that had a group of people sitting around a pool. Girls and guys are drinking, and there's a guy all dressed up in a tuxedo—has the horns on and all, like a devil—and he's saying, "You didn't actually think hell would be all that bad, did you?" Something close to that.

MICHELLE DEVEAU: My biggest problem in life is my friends dying. A close friend was killed at a New Year's Eve party two years ago. He was fourteen. He called this girl a slut, and she freaked out and stabbed him. I was massively depressed. I tried killing myself. Two weeks after that another friend shot himself. First in the gut and then in the heart. He was about sixteen. Then another friend got hit by a truck, riding his motorcycle. And now Gary.

My mom and dad came in. They said, "We have something to tell you." First thing I thought was somebody's *dead*. They said, "Gary's dead." I ran into my grandmother's kitchen, grabbed the biggest knife I could find and booked out into the backyard. And I just started hacking away at a tree, started freaking on a tree. That poor tree. One of these big oak trees. It's gonna die.

I imagined him the last time I saw him: in his denim jacket, a Billy Idol T-shirt (I always called him Billy Idol, 'cause he looks just like him), his jeans, his Led Zeppelin pin—you know, where the thing is blowing up—and his Beatles pin. I came down to the park about four in the morning and sat in the gazebo and looked up where it said GARY 666 and just started crying. My parents have been watching me with a fine-toothed comb—looking at my wrists, making sure I don't come in stoned.

I think, Why Gary? Gary was a skinny little guy, an easy target. He went with Ricky to the woods because he was gullible. He was very insecure. He was a sweet guy, and very funny. He always had a joke about something, even something that scared him. He had a lot of jokes about Kasso. Gary's parents were blind to the drugs. Like most parents. He did them to be accepted. Like most kids.

I was committed to Gary. I was in love with the guy, you know. It's sick: I've seen thirteen-year-old girls running around with RICKY LIVES on their T-shirts. They put around graffiti, RICKY LIVES, DEAD OR ALIVE. So I'm putting around GARY LIVES IN OUR HEARTS. Yeah, we were lovers—that's what takes a lot out of me. I still got one of his hickeys. It won't go away. It's a scar.

They Had Dreams

Two months after the murder, Rich Barton was still sleeping on the living-room sofa, afraid to sleep in the bedroom where Ricky had crashed so many nights. His mother says, "These kids are going to need a hundred years of therapy."

RICH BARTON: We were hanging out in Aztakea, getting wasted. I was standing closest to the grave. We had beer and weed. And all of a sudden someone pops up, grabs me and drags me into the woods. It was Gary, and his face was all mangled and stuff. He took me into the woods, and I woke up. I just stayed up and watched *Benny Hill,* movies and stuff.

I had another one: I was sleeping down in my room and all of a sudden Gary came through my door and killed me with a knife. I was sitting there with my mouth wide-open, saying, "Holy shit!" He just comes in and stabs. Doesn't say nothing. I died right away.

ALBERT QUINONES: I was trying to forget about it, man, and I couldn't. It was like, every time it would hit after twelve, I'd start bugging out. I'd get scared to go in my room, because Ricky used to stay in my room. I had some really wicked nightmares, man. I had nightmares that *I* killed him. It was weird. And I had a dream that I killed another guy. I just started stabbing him in the back of the head. And then a cop came in and scooped him up with this little pick or something and threw him in the garbage. It scared the hell out of me.

MICHELLE DEVEAU: My dream is to get the hell out of here. I want to go somewhere there are no sickos and you don't get hurt by people. I think my generation is a bunch of lowlifes. No ideals. Most of us just bumming around getting stoned. People hate each other for stupid reasons. People have no morals. I'm gonna be a peace freak. I'm more like a hippie-type person than anything else. I'd like to be back in Woodstock.

SOFTHEARTED GIRL: The first night I found out, I had a dream, a dream that Gary talked to me. I apologized to him for something. It was so real. And he said it was okay. And I said, "Can we hang out again?" And he was like, "There's only one problem." And I'm like, "What?" And he said, "I'm dead." I woke up with tears on my face.

The Plague Years

DAVID BLACK

EVEN BEFORE WE KNEW WHAT TO CALL IT, AIDS HAD THE POWER TO CHANGE FOREVER A GENERATION'S WAY OF THINKING ABOUT SEX AND LIFE AND DEATH.

The week the first installment of "The Plague Years" appeared on the stands, I was crossing Fiftieth Street at Sixth Avenue in New York City when two men stopped me. One was someone I'd interviewed for the article. The other, his friend, was a stranger.

"Interesting piece," the man I'd interviewed said. And he shook my hand.

"You're the son of a bitch who wrote that?" his friend said. And he slugged me in the face.

Which just about sums up the response to the article.

By the time the story was published, I'd spent nearly a year and a half of my life on the piece. Every few months my editor would call up and tentatively inquire how the article was going.

"Fine, fine," I'd lie. And ask for another $1000 for research—which the magazine sent. Usually, with a somewhat concerned question about the article's delivery date.

In fact, I was overwhelmed and terrified by the subject. I had obsessively filled a dozen cardboard bankers' boxes with files. For months at a time, I was doing three to five interviews a day. I was so exhausted and disoriented that once I collapsed on a flight out of Los Angeles, roused myself off the plane, ducked into a taxi, asked to be taken to the Marriott and woke realizing something was wrong.

"Is this the Marriott in downtown Houston?" I asked.

"Mac," the taxi driver said, "this is the Marriott in Denver, Colorado!"

It didn't matter. Houston, Denver . . . Everywhere I went, AIDS centers and support groups were springing up, many managing only a precarious existence—like centers of resistance in an occupied country. At the centers, I was treated like a war correspondent, a witness to front-line devastation, someone who could bring the brutal truth home.

When I'd call friends from the road to report what I was seeing and hearing, I was accused of exaggerating.

"You always were an alarmist," one friend said. "If this disease were that bad, we'd hear more about it."

Back then, much of the press was keeping a decorous silence on the subject. And when articles did appear, so much information was couched in euphemisms, it was hard to know what was being described unless you already knew.

The night I read Larry Kramer's play on AIDS, *The Normal Heart,* I was so shaken, for the first time in years I wept, sorrowing for those who were dead, dying and destined to die from the disease—and moved by the heroism with which so many people were responding to the tragedies caused by AIDS. The heroism of everyday life.

Another midnight, after gorging myself on medical terrors, I calculated that at the rate AIDS was reported to be spreading, by the end of the decade everyone would be dead. The only benefit of such a forecast was it put the dread of nuclear war in perspective.

More than any other article I'd ever written, the piece on AIDS shattered my comfortable journalistic detachment and forced me to think about the uses of reporting, the assumptions I shared with others—and my own death.

"I got some cold cuts, bagels, fruit. . . . You want a cup of coffee?"

The guy I was interviewing had been out of work for almost a year, but he'd blown what looked like a hundred dollars at Zabar's to lay out a spread for me. He also had just come back from his third stay at St. Vincent's Hospital. He was the first person I'd met with full-blown AIDS.

This was when some researchers I talked to were still—privately—worrying about how infectious the disease was. I'd been assured that it was "almost certainly *not* casually contagious," but as one doctor said, "We don't know enough yet to give any guarantees."

The meal was a gallant gesture—there was a lot of gallantry back then—and whatever my fears, it would have been insulting to turn it down. Also, I was hungry. Toward the end of the meal, the guy asked me how learning about AIDS had changed me. AIDS, he said, changes everyone.

It was a question I hadn't thought much about. A reporter reported what he learned—and in this case, I also hoped to use the subject to explore what then seemed to be a new public acceptance of homosexuality, the past decade of increasing sexual freedom and the response of the state to both.

I'd thought about the impact the piece might have on the magazine's readers. But not about its impact on me.

Researching and writing about any subject was always an education— but what I was learning while doing the AIDS article was less about the subject than about myself: my own fears, biases, paranoias and assumptions.

AIDS first challenged, then shattered, the journalistic distance I usually kept from a subject. I have not written an extended piece of journalism since.

When ROLLING STONE called me up to ask if I was interested in writing a long piece on this new disease—it was still commonly called GRID— that was spreading amid the gay community, I decided to turn down the assignment. I hadn't had a vacation in years and had promised my family I was going to take two weeks off. But the editor offered a long lead time: six months, nine months, to research and write the piece—which he was convinced was a major story.

At first it didn't seem like a major story to me. I dug up the few newspaper clips I could find on the disease. Very little had been written about it. And I made some phone calls.

"A new sexually transmitted disease?" said a third-year medical student. "Great! That gives me a better excuse than herpes not to fuck around!" That call persuaded me to accept the assignment.

For the past few years, I'd noticed a growing concern about genital herpes, chlamydia, venereal warts—a concern that seemed to be edging into controlled hysteria. The overreaction came with a sense of relief: The generation that had spent the past decade enjoying unprecedented sexual freedom—or license—finally had a reason to put on the brakes.

It's hard to remember the yawning gulf of sexual freedom presented to us back then. Almost everyone was experimenting. At parties couples discussed safaris to Plato's Retreat or more exotic sex clubs. Sometimes it felt like we were taking baby steps back to Eden—a world of nudity and appetite as simple as an infant's. Sometimes it felt like we were depraved—or at least, working hard at being so.

We're healthier, saner now, under the New Puritanism. The Fun Police are there to enforce new rules we have made for our own welfare. In the past decade we've learned to ask what our excesses cost us. Is it heretical, now, to ask what our moderation has cost?

AIDS is not just a story of a disease. Not just a story of medical economics, involving the greed of pharmaceutical companies. Not just a story of medical politics, involving the ambition of researchers. It is also a story about the relationship between the gay and straight communities in America, about the way the medical establishment responded to health emergencies, about the ambivalent attitude of society to the sexual revolution, about America's feelings about death and its obsession with health as a nearly constitutional right, about the growing power of a New Puritanism among both liberals and conservatives and about the connection between public policy and individual freedom.

Most of all, AIDS is the story of a transformation in social attitudes. In a period of a little more than a year, sex changed. Instead of promising life, it promised death.

The story of AIDS, finally, is the story of a profound—and far-reaching—alteration in consciousness.

We are a generation whose rallying cry was "Make love not war! Life not death!"

Because of AIDS—or rather because of our attitude *toward* AIDS—we have deprived ourselves of that alternative. Now, there is only death.

AIDS is a terrible disease. People die horribly from it. But we have been sold a bill of goods. Before World War II and the advent of the miracle drugs, there was no truly successful cure for syphilis—which has killed more people than AIDS and has killed them just as horribly. And yet, despite the ravages of syphilis, people did not succumb to the kind of despair that has made our generation buy the equation Sex Equals Death.

With the medical advances of World War II—wonder drugs, new surgical techniques, improved anesthetics—doctors suddenly could intervene in ways never before possible. And with the next generation's advances in understanding preventive medicine, suddenly it seemed as if humankind was on the verge of, if not immortality, at least a kind of life extension that would make us feel immortal.

Media and advertising fed this myth because it flattered a large, young population just entering the marketplace. Youth became the coin of the realm. It was all we traded in.

But we can't escape mortality. People die. Some die young. Every previous generation has known this. We thought we had a pass.

If we don't smoke, don't drink, avoid cholesterol, jog enough, resist sex, we can not only be immortal but stay forever young. Young and ascetic.

Before AIDS, the sexual instinct was a force for life. It was a specific against all the horrors—political and personal—we endured. It allowed a last refuge of hope.

After AIDS, we have allowed ourselves to surrender that refuge. We no longer have the power to deny death by an act of love. Even making love is tinged with doom.

I don't know how to reverse this despair. But part of the story of AIDS is a tale of social control.

Part of the effect of AIDS has been to end the sexual revolution, hobble the gay-rights movement and increase governmental intervention into private morality.

If we allow ourselves to be frightened enough by death—a fate none of us will escape—we make ourselves vulnerable to the forces that can seduce us by offering to trade some of our freedom for an illusory safety. And we surrender to a hopelessness, a denial of life, a rejection of a liveliness and optimism that was a gift our generation offered the world.

RS 446

APRIL 25TH, 1985

Two Visions

The fear of disease is a happy restraint to men. If men were more healthy, 'tis a great chance they would be less righteous.

EDMUND MASSEY
SERMON PREACHED AT ST. ANDREW'S CHURCH,
HOLBORN, ENGLAND, ON JULY 2ND, 1722

From the very beginning, the search for the cure for AIDS, acquired immune-deficiency syndrome, was complicated by the collision of different worlds: straight versus gay, scientific versus hedonistic. There was also a clash between single-agent theories and multifactorial ones, which has been, as René Dubos pointed out in his book, *Man Adapting*, a constant theme in the history of medicine. The disagreement was rooted in something more than differing analyses of statistics; it was a conflict that divided AIDS researchers into two camps, each of which had a particular vision, not just of AIDS but of reality.

Those who believed AIDS was caused by a single virus—including most of the researchers at the Centers for Disease Control (CDC), the National Institutes of Health (NIH) and Harvard University—betrayed a mind that was, at its extreme, amoral: the virus hit you like a bolt from the blue; what you did had nothing to do with it. Those who believed AIDS was caused by several interrelated factors—like Dr. Steven Witkin at the Cornell Medical Center in New York City and some people connected with the AIDS Medical Foundation, an independent research-coordinating group—betrayed a mind that was, at its extreme, moralistic: the disease was a direct result of how you were living your life—going to the baths, being sexually promiscuous and so on. The argument among AIDS researchers, it was becoming clear, was not so much medical as ontological: an argument between two world views.

Whatever it was that made someone susceptible to AIDS, it seemed, had to be produced by an infectious agent, something similar to hepatitis B, which, because it hit the same risk groups, became a model for AIDS.

But, if AIDS, like hepatitis B, was a virus, was it an old or a new one? If it was a known virus, why was it suddenly making so many people sick? If it was a previously unknown virus, where did it come from and how did it get here? If it was a mutation, from what did it mutate?

Of the known viruses, two candidates stood out as likely: Epstein-Barr virus (EBV) and cytomegalovirus (CMV). But the epidemiological pattern didn't fit well for EBV; the case for CMV was a little stronger.

"To follow up on the possibility of CMV being a contributing cause of AIDS, we recognized that if we just took people who already had AIDS, they were going to have CMV in their tissues or secretions or urine or semen," said Dr. W. Lawrence Drew, the director of clinical microbiology and infectious diseases at Mount Zion Hospital in San Francisco. "That wouldn't tell us what we need to know."

Since looking for CMV antibody in people who already had AIDS would lead to self-fulfilling results, Drew and his associates decided to find a hundred gay men who had not yet acquired CMV. Every month, they intended to check them. If their immune systems became abnormal at the same time they developed CMV, and if they then came down with AIDS, the case for CMV as an agent of AIDS would look pretty good.

Since the incubation period of AIDS can be as long as two to three years, it will take a while before Drew can see if the men who have been infected with CMV and have developed the kind of immune-system abnormalities that appear in AIDS end up getting it. If they do, and if CMV is one of the factors in causing it, the question is, why is it causing AIDS now?

"That's a little more difficult to understand," Drew said, "but I don't think it's impossible. With the advent of the bathhouse lifestyle, you had a change in the environment of the organisms. They were able to transmit much more readily than in the past. For example, we've always had shigella and giardia, but for whatever reason they were not a problem until about ten years ago."

But if CMV is being transmitted in bathhouses with an ease and an intensity previously unheard of, why isn't it following the normal pattern: the body fights back and health returns. Why is it producing AIDS?

"Probably because of repeated infection," Drew said.

This theory fits with Witkin's theory: that the sperm does double duty, both depressing the immune system and infecting the body with the virus.

"If you are rectally receptive," Drew said, "you have bleeding points," where the lining of the rectum has been torn.

Since CMV can cause severe illness, whether or not it is the cause of AIDS, Drew stressed the need for prevention—at least using condoms, which he said help but aren't foolproof. The best precaution, he said, was not to have anal intercourse.

Drew's studies concluded that male anal intercourse was the only sexual practice that correlated with CMV. The correlation was negative: men who didn't have anal intercourse had a significantly lower proportion of CMV antibody than men who did: seventy-four percent compared with ninety-seven percent.

"This accounts for one question," Drew said. "Why don't [more] prostitutes get AIDS?" They're sexually active, but, Drew said, "Heterosexual men don't have the [CMV] virus in their semen to begin with. And it is predominantly heterosexual men who go to prostitutes. And while rectal intercourse occurs in those circumstances, it isn't quite as prevalent."

According to Drew's theory, another reason relatively few women, hookers or not, get AIDS, is that, even if a man does have the virus in his semen, "some vaginal immunological function" in vaginal intercourse "may help in not permitting the [CMV] virus to take root." Also, if a man with the virus in his semen is having vaginal intercourse, it is harder for the virus to enter the bloodstream directly, because the vagina's natural lubrication tends to prevent ruptures.

Despite the evidence that AIDS might be related to CMV, Drew was cautious about drawing a direct connection. If AIDS is caused by a single virus, Drew wondered, why hasn't it spread sexually in the nongay population with as much rapidity as it has been spreading in the gay population? "If it's a one-organism, one-disease situation," he said, "there has been plenty of opportunity; there has been plenty of bisexual activity."

I asked about the Haitians.

"If it were one bug," Drew said, "it would travel across the island [to the Dominican Republic]."

I asked about Zaire, where there's an epidemic of what seems to be AIDS, found roughly equally in men and women.

"There's only one needle in Zaire?" Drew offered.

I was puzzled.

Medical humor. Doctors in Zaire have to reuse needles when they are inoculating people, Drew explained. Sloppy sterilization techniques could spread the disease.

"Kids?" I asked.

Babies born with AIDS have presumably been infected in utero by mothers who picked up the disease through dirty needles. Other kids — who, Drew said, "came from very low socioeconomic groups" — may have picked it up from filthy environments. "CMV antibody is common, because of [poor] hygiene in day-care centers, [where] it spreads quickly through urine."

"What about the case of the old couple in Florida?" I asked.

"I have trouble understanding that," Drew admitted.

It turned out that the husband was a hemophiliac who got the disease through blood products and gave it to his wife during intercourse. Both were in their seventies.

Figuring out what causes AIDS is made more difficult by researchers' ignorance of the subcultures that are affected by it: the elderly as well as gays and Haitians. Young, healthy, white, heterosexual, nonaddicted, upper-middle-class, predominantly male researchers don't necessarily know what goes on in a septuagenarian's bedroom, let alone what goes on in a gay bathhouse.

It would make sense for teams researching AIDS to hire someone who knew, say, both epidemiology and the gay-bathhouse scene, but typically that has not been the case. When one gay man was hired recently by the CDC, he was assigned not to the AIDS Task Force, for which he was qualified and wanted to work, but to another division.

"I was called one time by someone who said, 'Could you tell me whether water sports are dangerous?'" Drew said. "I have kids who are extremely competitive swimmers. And I sail. I started to give some sort of answer based on swimming and sailing, when he said, 'Wait a minute here. I think we're on a different track.'"

If the multifactorial theory had a champion, it was Dr. Joseph Sonnabend, one of the discoverers of interferon and the scientific director of the AIDS Medical Foundation. Sonnabend has been treating AIDS patients since the epidemic began. When his activities as a doctor who researched AIDS and treated AIDS patients became well known, the tenants in his New

York apartment building, terrified that he would infect them all, successfully moved to have him evicted.

Sonnabend started a journal, *AIDS Research,* to publish scientific papers that he believed had been excluded from mainstream scientific magazines because they explored the unpopular possibility that AIDS was a multifactorial disease. He is a South African, trained in England, and is not part of any American old-boy network; this may, in part, explain his difficulty with what some feel is an AIDS mafia, a closely knit alliance of doctors and researchers who, despite their own internal competition, have joined forces to stonewall any theory other than their own. Because he has been outspoken about his beliefs, Sonnabend has drawn fire from nearly everyone, from some scientists of the NIH and the CDC to some leaders of the New York-based Gay Men's Health Crisis.

"Since I've been watching the disease in this city," Sonnabend said, "it never occurred to me, never seemed possible, that this disease could be a specific syndrome, a new infectious agent. The patients getting sick had been exposed to an extremely complicated biological environment" — which *was* new.

"There has never been such a concentration of homosexual men," Sonnabend said, "because only recently have there been cities this large."

And only recently has homosexuality become socially acceptable enough for there to be an efflorescence of the fast-track gay lifestyle. It couldn't be a coincidence, Sonnabend believed, that the cities with the greatest number of AIDS cases had the most active sexual scene. The men coming down with AIDS typically had been exposed to several different diseases and immuno-suppressors: gonorrhea, CMV, EBV, gay bowel syndrome, semen. The obvious question that struck Sonnabend was not how could someone exposed to that environment get sick, but how could he remain healthy?

Like Drew, Sonnabend believed that a new virus by itself was not enough to account for AIDS. Additional factors were necessary, perhaps a disease model that involved repeated infections and interactions among various pathogens. The complex model he drew for me began with the fact of promiscuity — which is why many gays reject his theory.

"There are some gay men who see sexual liberation, coming out of the closet, in terms of promiscuity," Sonnabend said. Any indication that promiscuity is responsible for AIDS would be a threat to their identity as gay men.

Straight scientists were hostile to the multifactorial theory because if it were true, anyone with constant assaults on his or her immune system would be liable to get AIDS, including people living in unhygienic conditions or suffering from poor nutrition — people in slums and in third-world countries. Sonnabend believes AIDS is common among the poor around the world.

"The most common cause of pneumocystis is malnutrition," he said.

He suspects that AIDS may have been a leading cause of death among the babies of Vietnamese refugees and that AIDS may exist in Bermuda and in the Dominican Republic. He starts listing places around the world that may have had outbreaks of AIDS.

"If I could get a simple grant, a small one of only $10,000, to go around the world, I'm sure we'd find AIDS all over," he said.

But even in this country, he can't get access to the evidence he needs.

"I suggested doing autopsies on drug addicts [to look for AIDS]," he said, "but [the authorities] resisted it, because it would suggest that they'd missed it."

We may be missing evidence of AIDS among the poor and dispossessed, because they are below the scientific and media horizon of the Western world.

A paper on AIDS coauthored by Sonnabend, Witkin and David T. Purtilo, a doctor at the University of Nebraska Medical Center in Omaha, stated, "In any group, unless suspected, pneumocystis pneumonia will not be detected, as its diagnosis requires biopsy and special stains in most patients."

In other words, if you don't look for AIDS, you might not find it; and if you don't want to find it—in the third world and in slums—you simply avoid looking for it. The diagnosis becomes, to some extent, a self-fulfilling prophecy. If AIDS is caused in part by malnutrition and miserable living conditions, "to make people well," Sonnabend said, "it is not enough to set up clinics; you must eradicate poverty, hunger and filthy ghettos." Not to eliminate the root causes of the disease in the slums and the third world while trying to cure those in the middle class who have it would be an admission that health is a luxury reserved for the rich.

The American champion of the single-factor theory is Dr. Robert C. Gallo, of the National Institutes of Health, where he is chief of the National Cancer Institute Laboratory of Tumor Cell Biology. In the late Seventies, he was the first to identify a virus responsible for a human cancer, and about two years ago, he reported that a retrovirus called HTLV-1 (the initials stand for *human T-cell leukemia virus*) might be the cause of AIDS. About the same time, French researchers at the Pasteur Institute in Paris were announcing the preliminary results of their work with their candidate for the cause of AIDS, a retrovirus they called LAV (for *lymphadenopathy-associated virus*). Clearly both laboratories—one in Paris and one near Washington—were neck and neck in their research.

Last spring, rumors about a major breakthrough—and about increased competition between the Pasteur Institute and the National Cancer Institute—began circulating. Word leaked that the Pasteur Institute was about to make a stronger claim that LAV was the cause of AIDS. On Friday, April 20th, *The New York Times* reported that the head of the Pasteur Institute AIDS research group had said, "I'm convinced it [LAV] has a role in AIDS." LAV showed up in 80 to 90 percent of the American AIDS patients whose blood they had screened. The same day, possibly to undercut the French claim, the NIH announced that on Monday, April 23rd, it would hold a news conference to report on a new virus Gallo had identified, HTLV-3—antibody to which showed up in forty-three of forty-nine AIDS patients, about 89 percent. In the general population, HTLV-3 antibody appears in about 0.5 percent.

The Pasteur Institute and the NIH were playing a name game. Both LAV and HTLV-3 couldn't be the single cause of AIDS unless they were the same virus—which they probably were. The Pasteur Institute had given the virus a new name to emphasize its claim as the discoverer. Gallo, by calling the virus HTLV-3, was emphasizing how similar it was to HTLV-1, which gave him precedence: the virus was only a variant of his earlier discovery. But to make HTLV-3 an accurate name for the AIDS virus, the words *HTLV* stood for had to be changed from *human T-cell leukemia virus* to *human T-lymphotropic retrovirus*.

On Saturday, April 21st, the day after the NIH announced its upcoming news conference, Dr. James O. Mason, the head of the CDC, stated that he believed the French had discovered the cause of AIDS.

"We cannot know for sure now that the LAV virus is the agent that causes AIDS," Mason said, "but the pattern it follows in the human body makes us believe it is." This preempted any news that might come from Gallo and the NIH on Monday.

By one o'clock in the afternoon on Monday, the scramble to see who would be first to get credit for discovering the cause of AIDS had become a joke among the journalists gathered in the first-floor auditorium of the Humphrey Building, in Washington, D.C. Although the government and the scientists were trying to pretend there was no rivalry—either between the Pasteur Institute and the NIH or between the NIH and the CDC— every denial included a grab for the credit.

The opening statement, delivered by Secretary of Health and Human Services, Margaret M. Heckler, was embarrassingly jingoistic. She gave a nod to "other discoveries . . . in different laboratories—even in different parts of the world"—the *even* tinged with wide-eyed wonder that laboratories "in different parts of the world" could compete with American know-how. She *even* mentioned the Pasteur Institute, but the glory was reserved for the home team.

"Today," she stated, "we add another miracle to the long honor roll of American medicine and science." She predicted the imminent release of a test for HTLV-3 that would protect those in need of transfusions from infected blood. (The test has turned out to be so inaccurate—the false-positive rate can be as high as forty percent—that it is virtually useless. In early March, the Food and Drug Administration approved a different blood test, developed by Electro-Nucleonics of Fairfield, New Jersey, that is purported to be more accurate.)

HTLV-3/LAV wasn't a cure; it wasn't even the definitive cause; but it would be widely reported as such. In the straight media, very few news organizations would get the story right. One that did, National Public Radio's evening news program, *All Things Considered,* cautioned the public not to misunderstand the implications of the announcement. And *The New York Times* ran an editorial pointing out, "The commotion [surrounding the news conference] indicates a fierce—and premature—fight for credit between scientists and bureaucratic sponsors of research. . . . What you are hearing is not yet a public benefit but a private competition—for fame, prizes, new research funds."

Most newspapers and television news shows featured pictures of Gallo and photographs of the virus, which looked like a diagram of a golf green, and reported the news as Margaret Heckler's "miracle . . . of American medicine and science." As a result, all over the country, gays, lulled into a false sense of security, thought, Back to the baths.

One reporter at the news conference asked, "How many deaths do you think this announcement will cause?"

When Gallo was introduced, he approached the podium like the only kid in the school assembly to have won a National Merit Scholarship. He was fastidiously dressed. He wore aviator glasses, a Hollywood touch; his hair was rumpled, but just enough to make it look as if he had recently emerged from handling a crisis. His manner was condescending, as though he were the Keeper of Secrets obliged to deal with a world of lesser mortals.

At the podium, Gallo started by repeating a denial that there had ever been "any fights or controversy" between his group and the Pasteur Institute.

"There was some misunderstanding," he said. "If what they identified . . . a year ago is the same as what we now have produced, then I certainly will say so, and I will say so with them in a collaboration."

"Damn nice of him to offer to share credit with the people who beat him by a year," someone said.

What Gallo, the Henry Ford of HTLV-3, had done, which the French had not, was develop a way of mass-producing the virus protein. He'd also proved that HTLV-3 destroys T-4 cells in vitro. And he claimed that at the beginning of the year he had done a test with the CDC in which he found evidence of HTLV-3 (the presence of antibody to that virus) in 100 percent of the blood samples taken from AIDS patients.

Throughout the news conference, reporters kept asking what Gallo's announcement meant for people with AIDS — without getting a satisfactory response. Finally, someone said, "Dr. Gallo, if you had a patient in private practice, one of the . . . currently diagnosed AIDS victims in this country, what would you tell him this discovery means — if anything — to him?"

Gallo replied, "Could somebody else answer that?"

"No!" shouted the press.

The whole conference was unseemly in its rush to capitalize on Gallo's research. The Reagan administration seemed to be using the breakthrough as a way of thumbing its nose at critics who had been complaining that the federal government wasn't doing enough to solve the problem. Among them was Congressman Ted Weiss, a New York Democrat, who had recently criticized the Department of Health and Human Services for failing to adequately fund federal efforts to fight AIDS: "Tragically," Weiss said, "funding levels for AIDS investigations have been dictated by political considerations rather than by the professional judgments of scientists and public-health officials."

The CDC budget for AIDS research in the fiscal year 1983 would rise to $6.2 million; in 1984, it would rise to $13.75 million. The total budget for government AIDS research — including not only the CDC but also the NIH and the Food and Drug Administration — would be $28.7 million for 1983 and $61.5 million for 1984. But critics claim all the money earmarked was not actually distributed and that the figures were padded by including in them many funds that would have gone to general research even if there had never been an AIDS epidemic. In any case, they considered the amounts relatively low — especially given the severity of the crisis.

After Gallo's news conference, research on retroviruses began to get the lion's share of funds. "What happens," wondered Sonnabend, "if two, three, four years down the line, retroviruses turn out not to be the cause — or not the single cause? It's a big gamble."

Unlike most viruses, which have genes made of DNA (the substance containing the genetic code, the biological legacy passed down from one generation to the next), retroviruses have genes made of RNA, a kind of mirror image of DNA. Usually, genetic information is transmitted from DNA to RNA; in retroviruses, the genetic information is transmitted in the reverse direction, from RNA to DNA. Retroviruses are very adaptable. They can get inside a cell and use that cell's DNA to replicate themselves. The cell then becomes a nursery for an increasing number of the retroviruses, which eventually burst out of the cell, destroying it, and spread throughout the body, each new retrovirus able to invade a new cell and start reproducing itself again.

According to Dr. Max Essex, a Harvard professor who worked with Gallo on the HTLV—AIDS research, retroviruses have been known for a long time in a variety of animal species. For example, he said, retroviruses cause a disease similar to AIDS in cats. Horses and mice can also get diseases involving immunodeficiency. Monkeys are susceptible to an AIDS-like disease (called SAIDS), which was detected for the first time at the New England Regional Primate Research Center in Southboro, Massachusetts, in 1980, about the same time that AIDS was being discovered in humans. Scientists at both the New England Regional Primate Research Center and the University of California at Davis believed SAIDS was caused by a retrovirus. There was no evidence that the animal AIDS-type diseases were transmittable to humans until 1983, when two research teams reported that they had successfully infected chimpanzees with HTLV-3/LAV, one using LAV itself and the other using blood from an AIDS patient. This was the first indication that an AIDS-type virus could affect both humans and animals.

Dr. Walter R. Dowdle, the director of the Center for Infectious Diseases at the CDC, offered an explanation of why such a virus was hard to find in humans: "The virus enters the bloodstream of the patient and affects certain cells. The body's immune system gets rid of it—or it becomes integrated into the cells, into the cells' DNA, just stays there with no apparent harm done.

"With certain people," Dowdle continued, "because of host factors or other factors, the virus is stimulated. But by then the virus is no longer around in any large number," damage has already been done to the immune system, "and the patient dies of an opportunistic infection or Kaposi's sarcoma."

As another doctor said, "People die of the secondary infections. No one's ever died of AIDS."

"A great scourge never appears unless there is a reason for it," said Henry Miller in *The Air-Conditioned Nightmare.*

When a virus is introduced into a virgin population, one that has not built up an immunity to it, the virus can spread with the rapidity and intensity of AIDS. Perhaps a virus originating in, say, Africa, where Gallo speculates AIDS began, was picked up by Cuban troops stationed in Angola (or elsewhere) and brought back to the Western Hemisphere. Or perhaps it spread from city to city and country to country with the advent of the fast-track gay lifestyle.

This new lifestyle reached democratically across the socioeconomic spectrum to the poor—who, some believe, might carry a disease without suffering from its symptoms, because, living in less hygienic conditions than the middle class and being more exposed to pathogens, they tend to be less susceptible to infectious diseases. The Indian division of society into castes may have developed in part as a way of maintaining immunological barriers between classes; the untouchables may have been untouchable for reasons of health.

Perhaps there is immunological sense behind long courtships and monogamy.

"Many mistakenly believe that there is little difference between the multifactorial and the single-virus theories," said one man with AIDS. "Such a belief could not be more dangerous. The single-virus theory is very attractive to those conservative forces who would like to destroy precisely those groups affected by AIDS. The single-virus theory may be used to accomplish what the New Right's political efforts have thus far been unable to accomplish."

A blood test for evidence of HTLV-3 could be misused—especially if the general population starts to panic, which it may do as a result of recent research showing evidence that HTLV-3 is present in saliva and that there may be healthy carriers of the virus. Six percent of a random sampling of the medical personnel at one New York City hospital—presumably a non-gay, nonjunkie, non-Haitian, nonrisk group—had antibody to HTLV-3 upon being tested. All of those tested seemed in good health. None were told of the test results, because the hospital didn't want to cause a panic. Although only eight percent of the people with AIDS in America are heterosexuals, there is increasing evidence, especially in Africa and Haiti, that AIDS can spread to the general population. Researchers like Gallo are warning that it is a mistake to see AIDS as a gay disease. Diseases don't have sexual preference.

If there is still a chance that AIDS could bloom into a general epidemic, that no one is free of risk, how would the country protect itself? Test everyone suspected for evidence of HTLV-3—whether they are healthy carriers or sick—and place them in quarantine centers. Or better yet: fill the quarantine centers with anyone in a high-risk group, whether or not their blood shows evidence of HTLV-3. Hemophiliacs and people who need transfusions would be exempted because the blood they get could be certified AIDS free. But the others, the gays, the junkies, the Haitians and the prostitutes—all of whom are on the margins of society (or perceived as such)—could be rounded up and held against their will *for the general welfare.*

Paranoia?

"The categories we defined as risk groups are sociological categories," said Dr. Celso Bianco of the New York Blood Center. "We simply expect to find a medical or biological marker and then transplant that to a social category. It would almost [be doing] the same thing the Germans did in the Second World War. Eugenics. Saying everyone who is a Jew is bad because he is a Jew and because he has the genetic traits of a Jew."

Misused, the evidence of HTLV-3 could become the AIDS yellow star.

Uncivil Rights

. . . all that could conceal their distempers did it, to prevent their neighbors shunning and refusing to converse with them, and also to prevent authority shutting up their houses; which, though not yet practiced, yet was threatened, and people were extremely terrified at the thoughts of it.

DANIEL DEFOE
A JOURNAL OF THE PLAGUE YEAR

"It was never just about sex," said the man with AIDS. His lips were chalky, as if he'd been drinking Gelusil and had forgotten to wipe his mouth. His eyes were red-rimmed. His skin had the transparency of the paper that is used to cover pictures in old books; it looked as if you could peel it away to reveal more clearly a hidden face underneath. "I enjoyed the sex, but going to the baths was also political."

Gays were hit by AIDS just when it seemed that the fight for gay rights was being won.

The gay-liberation movement started in June 1969, when the police raided a Greenwich Village gay bar called the Stonewall and the patrons fought back. At the beginning, there were two major gay organizations, the Gay Liberation Front and the Gay Activists Alliance. The Gay Liberation Front, which had both male and female members, was a leftist child of the Sixties. It wanted to promote gay liberation through radical transformation of the entire social structure. The Gay Activists Alliance had more limited aims. It didn't want to change society. It just wanted to fight for gay rights. And gay rights came to mean fucking and sucking as much as you wanted.

"We were going to show the straight world what it was missing," one gay leader said.

American homosexuals were cultivating the macho stereotype—the biker-lumberjack-Hemingway-tough-guy—that straight men, under the influence of feminism, were abandoning.

Giving up promiscuous sex would mean giving up a hard-won *positive* identity and going back to the Nellie stereotype—even, for some, mistak-

enly believing that the disease was a punishment for their sexual preference.

"It would be a complete rejection of everything being gay has stood for
for fifteen years," said Larry Kramer, a novelist and one of the founders
of Gay Men's Health Crisis (GMHC), the first AIDS support group in
the country. His recently written play about AIDS, *The Normal Heart*—a
play which is to AIDS what Arthur Miller's play, *The Crucible*, was to the
McCarthy era—is to be performed at Joseph Papp's Public Theater in
New York City.

Twenty years ago, the worst thing a sexually active gay man could get
was crabs, an inconvenient but not serious complaint. Then came an increase in syphilis and gonorrhea, but they could be cured relatively easily.
With the spread of hepatitis, gay men were getting into serious trouble
for the first time. After hepatitis, the gay community was plagued with
amoebas, an epidemic that started in the mid-Seventies and still continues.

"You cannot do what we have done all these years and not get in
trouble," said Kramer. "The gay doctors just kept treating us and treating
us. No one ever said, 'Cool it, fellas.' "

For a few, AIDS took on a fatal attraction. If they hadn't come out of
the closet, it forced the issue.

"When I got AIDS," a gay man said, "it was like my body was telling
me I had to take a stand."

But, for most, it added fear upon fear.

In 1981, Kramer met in his living room with a group of other gay men
who were concerned about the new "homosexual disease." Three of Kramer's friends were ill from it; the others all had friends who were dying
or dead. Every month the list would get longer. They decided to throw a
benefit, which was held at a disco on April 8th, 1982. Two thousand people
attended, and the organizers raised $50,000. No one in the group that
organized the benefit—the group that would become Gay Men's Health
Crisis—realized the scope of what they eventually would have to do. They
figured the existing gay health organizations would step in to deal with the
disease. And so would the government.

"We thought the mayor and the health department would do everything," Kramer said.

After all, New York City has more gays—estimated at almost a million—than anywhere else in the world, a potentially powerful voting block.
In San Francisco, which also has a large gay community, Mayor Dianne
Feinstein allocated $4 million for AIDS in 1983. Kramer felt New York
should be at least as generous. But when the leaders of GMHC tried to
arrange a meeting with Mayor Ed Koch, Koch's liaison to the gay community—who was also the liaison to the Hasidic Jewish community—kept
putting them off. The gay community in New York was invisible: how

many gays were calling to complain about the city's slow response to AIDS?

For a year and a half, Kramer and his colleagues in the gay community sought unsuccessfully to meet with Mayor Koch. (The mayor's office disagrees with this version of the story.) They telephoned, sent messages, mailed a letter signed by sixty gay organizations and, finally, picketed a meeting on AIDS at Lenox Hill Hospital that the mayor attended.

Kramer wanted three thousand protesters. A few hundred promised to show up. The day of the meeting, it poured. About thirty came. Kramer thought they were through. Politically, gays *were* invisible.

But all the television stations covered the picket. The next morning, the mayor's office agreed to meet with ten emissaries from the gay community, including two from GMHC.

The board of GMHC was composed of upwardly mobile gays who had not all been politically active in the past (one board member is even still in the closet), and it tended to distance itself from the scruffier, more radical, more outspoken elements in the movement. As its representatives to the mayor's meeting, it selected the president and the executive director. Kramer, who was viewed by the board as embarrassingly strident, was frozen out.

"I said, 'I go, or I quit,'" Kramer said. "They accepted my resignation."

The mayor's office set up a task force, which included representatives from various concerned agencies and scientists and which met regularly with members of the gay community to discuss problems. But red tape tangles up plans that are heralded as triumphs of civic compassion. Even New York's largest AIDS program foundered: a $1.2 million contract with the Red Cross to provide AIDS patients with home care helped only seven patients in its first six months of operation. For better or worse, GMHC remained the primary source of AIDS support in New York City.

"The question was, who needs panda?": The quotation was tacked to a bulletin board in the old offices of GMHC, a cramped brownstone decorated with stuffed Koala and teddy bears hugging each other; pictures of pandas and panda quotes ("Better butt on small pandas"); a poster used in AIDS literature of two naked men, one white and one black, embracing, with the tag YOU CAN HAVE FUN AND BE SAFE TOO; and a newspaper clip with the headline HOMO NEST RAIDED.

GMHC pioneered AIDS support services. Its outreach programs include a hot line that answers about 3000 calls a week, crisis-intervention counseling, group therapy, a recreation program offering everything from museum trips to writing classes, and financial counseling. The last is a crucial service, since getting AIDS can be expensive—the cost of treating the first fifty AIDS patients at one New York hospital was about $3 million—and many victims who fall outside the strict CDC definition of the disease may not be able to get government help like Medicaid in paying off their bills. But the most successful service GMHC established was its buddy program, in which over a hundred volunteers help people with AIDS, shopping for them, cleaning their apartments and being generally available to do what needs to be done.

GMHC also offers legal advice.

"There are particular legal problems that gay people face in this epidemic that nongay people wouldn't face," said the president of GMHC, who prefers that his name not be used—an extraordinary scruple in an organization that seems to believe no one should be ashamed of being gay. "A lot of nongay lawyers are not even aware of the potential problems," he said. "If you were sick in a hospital and were nongay, your wife would have no problem visiting you. But a gay man's lover is not considered family, and he might have trouble getting in to see the patient."

GMHC also tries to make sure the patient's will cannot be challenged, since many parents will try to prevent their son's lover from inheriting anything.

"A dying gay man's parents will suddenly arrive out of nowhere because they are next of kin," said Judy Kreston, a New York therapist who has done a lot of AIDS counseling. "The lover is shunted aside."

To hide the truth at funeral services, some parents will try to pass off a woman as their son's girlfriend.

Parents see death as a way of reclaiming their wayward children—as though being gay were like joining a cult and death were the ultimate deprogrammer.

"Some parents who really can't stand the idea that their son is gay see the disease as a bad-news, good-news situation," said another therapist. "You know: 'The bad news is that your son is gay. The good news is that he's dying.'"

Death
of a Cheerleader

RANDALL SULLIVAN

IN THE EIGHTIES, WINNING WAS EVERYTHING. ESPE-
CIALLY IN ORINDA, CALIFORNIA, WHERE A KID WOULD
DO ANYTHING TO AVOID BEING CALLED A LOSER.

Murder was the story of the Eighties: Every time you turned around there was somebody out to make a killing. Culprits ranged from the insanely greedy to the desperately needy, and victims in the United States outnumbered the country's KIAs from the Korean, Vietnam and Persian Gulf wars combined. Americans per capita killed seventy-three times as often as Austrians and more than four times as often as citizens of the next most murderous "developed" nation on the planet.

The slaughter that took place during the past decade was not always attended by obvious signs of violence: There was no blood and little gore on Wall Street, and yet the stench of death is rising still out of the junk-bond heap of the Reagan era's leveraged buyout/hostile takeover/green-mail madness, that feeding frenzy for little bald men that succeeded in collapsing many more companies than it created.

Those who find a segue from murder to the money market facile — the same apologist-pundits who insist upon reminding us that without Michael

Milken there'd be no MCI—should be shipped air freight out to Humboldt County in Northern California and made to hike in their Cole-Haan loafers through the stumps of what were once old-growth redwoods, cut down by the thousands to pay off debt accrued during the Milken-financed takeover of Pacific Lumber. All that seems to be resting at peace among those tombstones is the national sense of shame.

As you may have surmised, I was taking the situation pretty personally back in 1985, when Reagan's popularity was at its peak, held aloft by a national delusion that had manifested itself most grossly during the previous summer's Olympic Games in Los Angeles, where Americans celebrated their recent victory over the mighty island nation of Grenada by beating up on the likes of Belgium and Bolivia. What rankles me the most when I engage the political context—a lot more often than I'd like—is the convenient case of amnesia that seems to have come upon the American people in general and the mass media in particular. Back in '85, those seven long years ago, the prohibition on speech was paralyzing: Attacking Reagan personally, debunking the myth of "economic recovery" in general or suggesting the eventual costs of deregulation and deficit financing in particular was either disallowed or derided, set upon by self-appointed patriots or waved away as hopelessly out of touch by those who lived from trend to trend.

It was a time when even ROLLING STONE began running those unfortunate Perception (shaggy Sixties atavist) Versus Reality (natty young professional) advertisements. And yet, while I felt a lot more comfortable with the perception than with the reality, ROLLING STONE remained the only mainstream, general-circulation magazine in America that would consistently publish the discordant notes of such as myself.

I should say straight out that what attracted me to this story was its subversive nature. The one implacable retort to the prevailing theory of the New Beginning (the United States as a nation of Happy Campers with their Puppies all in a row) was the way we kept killing one another, by the thousands, from sea to shining sea. Homicide and suicide claimed the lives of more American teenagers than any other cause during the past decade, excepting auto accidents. And when these early exits took place among those who were not only young but white and well off, it was difficult to deny that the cost of keeping up required an increasingly creative accounting.

Of all the analyses of what it was like to come of age during the Eighties, the one that struck the deepest chord in me was spoken by the mother of the fifteen-year-old prom king/football captain/gang leader Mark Miller. Described by his peers as possibly the handsomest and probably the most popular kid in the San Fernando Valley, her son was shot dead outside a teenage nightclub on Van Nuys Boulevard in August of

1985. "These kids," Karen Miller told me, "they know by the time they turn thirteen or fourteen how it is; you're either a superstar or a slave, there's no real in-between anymore."

Teenagers in Orinda, California's most affluent suburb, were among the handful of young Americans who might yet imagine a comfort zone, somewhere in the high end of the upper-middle class. How to get by on $100,000 a year was the basic stuff of dilemma in Orinda, where no resident had killed another in seven years, since the night when a panicked teenage boy took a hammer to the elderly woman who caught him pilfering her savings. What made the mystery surrounding the murder of Kirsten Costas such a compelling metaphor for the fusion of hysteria and hypocrisy that was the essence of the Reagan era was the way the citizens of Orinda reacted: At first they insisted that the killer had to be an outsider — single-parent trash from out of the East Bay, most likely; later they took the position that if the murderess really were a local girl, she would have to be found among those few juniors at Miramonte High School who had been exiled from the mainstream.

Two of Kirsten's classmates were singled out as principal suspects: One was a heavy-metal stoner whose rebellion had been her way of coping with rejection; the other was the pretty and previously popular daughter of a local MD who assumed her punker persona as an avenue of escape from the suffocating insularity of the suburbs. Both girls had been harassed so relentlessly by their neighbors that they were forced to transfer from Miramonte High and enroll in private schools nearby. Few adults in Orinda wanted to talk about these two girls when it was discovered — six months after the murder — that Kirsten Costas's killer was a sweet-faced and well-liked girl whose shaky self-esteem had been shattered when she was cut from the cheerleading squad that Kirsten made.

The encounter with authority that I recall most vividly was my interview with Miramonte High's principal, Branislav Yaich, whose advice to me was "Don't try to put this off on the community — there's no larger meaning here, just one sick girl with some serious problems."

Most of those girls who had been Kirsten's closest friends echoed Principal Yaich. The other girls I talked to, though, seemed not so sure. "This place does things to you," one told me. "You feel like if you're not the best or the smartest or the prettiest, you don't exist."

I met most of Kirsten's confidantes at the trial of Bernadette Protti in the Contra Costa County Courthouse, where they lined up an hour before the doors opened each morning to scramble for seats in the courtroom. Steeped in this grotesque atmosphere, even as I listened to the horrific descriptions of Kirsten's death, I found myself identifying most deeply with the tragedy of her killer, who after all, was still with us. Amid the swarm of curiosity and the cacophony of recrimination, Bernadette seemed far less the "coldblooded killer" her prosecutor described than the human point at which the accumulated tensions in a community that chose to define itself by ambition and entitlement had finally broken through.

During the ten days I spent haunting Orinda after the trial, I was working out of a motel on the other side of the hills in Berkeley, where the mayor was a black socialist and the city's attention to the needs of the handicapped had attracted so many of them that there were occasional gridlocks of wheelchair traffic on the sidewalks along Telegraph Avenue. I felt like a time traveler heading east each morning in my rented Toyota, taking the fast lane out the Walnut Park Freeway toward Orinda, descending into this World of Tomorrow where Ralph Lauren and Anne Klein were standard issue, where everyone was white and prosperous, where all the children truly suffered were the expectations of their parents and the competition of their peers. And yet one dichotomy after another made itself known to me as I proceeded through the list of two dozen or so sixteen-year-old girls who were the majority of my "sources" for "Death of a Cheerleader." The first duality had to do with the distinction between persona and personality, public selves and private ones. Kirsten's friends were most committed to the former, remarkable mainly for their almost total lack of introspection. They were prettier and more popular, while Bernadette's friends were smarter and more sensitive.

An intimation of how sadly acculturated were Orinda's golden children was provided to me by one of Kirsten's closest friends, who explained that the two of them had taken to taunting and tormenting one of the main suspects (the heavy-metal girl) because "we heard she smoked pot." This was said in the same tone that twenty years earlier had been used to pass the word that a girl put out.

To my surprise, being from ROLLING STONE proved to be a distinct advantage in Orinda. The magazine retained just enough marquee value to be taken seriously by the parents and yet was identified with youth in ways that allowed the children to feel they were speaking to one of their own. Still, I stood out. My first night in town, I ate alone at the nicest restaurant I could find, where my young waitress asked me, seriously, if I was a member of the band U2. She had seen the group's concert in San Francisco only two nights earlier and considered it "as close to a religious experience as I've ever had." I hated to disappoint her, but being from ROLLING STONE was enough for an invitation to a home-cooked meal on her night off, along with a description of the community from one recent Miramonte graduate who wasn't headed for Harvard or Stanford.

It was the affiliation with ROLLING STONE as well that led to my big break during the reporting of this story, when the girl who had been Bernadette's best friend, Kris Johnson, agreed to speak to me after consulting with her father, a subscriber to the magazine for more than fifteen years. After talking to Kris, I realized that yet another dichotomy not only was the essence of this story but should be the structure of the article: It had to do with the voice of an individual murmuring beneath the roar of the mob. In Orinda, what all the adults wanted to believe was that Branislav Yaich had told me the first day I came to town, that the murder on that night in June had been "an isolated event," the lonely act of One Sick Girl. Their children, though, especially those close to Bernadette, seemed to sense that she had been acting almost on their behalf, as the agent of a shame and a vengeance inseparable from the aspirations and accomplishments that were Orinda's official portrait.

For some reason it seems significant to note that during the composition of this piece, perhaps my greatest technical problem was the surfeit of Stacys; there seemed to be at least a dozen in the junior class at Miramonte High. (I always imagined that the authors of the movie *Heathers* must have read this article.) In the end I decided to quote only three Stacys, referring to them at each mention by both first name and last (adding to my continual problems with space in the magazine).

I was deluged with inquiries and offers from film and television producers when the article was published. The best question anybody from the entertainment industry ever put to me was asked by Bill Blinn, the cowriter of *Purple Rain*, who had a development deal at Disney. "What do you think happened," Bill wondered, "during those fifteen minutes when [Bernadette and Kirsten] were alone in Bernadette's car?" "What I don't think happened was a lesbian overture," I told him. "I think Bernadette just very plaintively told Kirsten she wanted to be her friend, was misunderstood and then went over the top when she realized how this was going to sound to the other girls on Sunday morning." "That's what I hoped you'd say," Blinn told me.

I can put Blinn's comments in perspective best by recalling my earlier meeting with the younger and more successful producer who felt that the most "salable element" of the story was its "nubility factor": "This happened in summertime, right? We can have a pool party. Twenty 15-year-old girls in bathing suits! How do they top that? We'll kill 'em. We'll mow 'em down. We'll grind 'em up and do them a line at a time. [*Shouting to his secretary*] Call that cocksucker [studio president's name here] and tell him I have a hard-on." This individual became a studio president himself not long after our meeting and remains one of the many good reasons why I have so much trouble separating my sense of humor from my sense of dismay.

Better than the meetings in Hollywood, though, I remember the letters I received from teenagers all over America—from Pittsburgh, Staten Island, New York, and Norman, Oklahoma, to cite but a few—all wanting to know how they might contact Bernadette Protti. The one that comes to my mind first was postmarked Interlachen, Florida, and written by a fifteen-year-old girl who said she had read the article in English class: "I hope you can understand how important this is. I really put a lot of thought into this, and it's like I've been thinking a lot about it. And I just want to let [Bernadette] know that she does have a friend and one that doesn't think she's some psychopath killer. I don't think she is. I don't even think she's crazy."

Clearly, the article's intent was recognized: No less a mainstream publication than *USA Today* asserted, shortly after "Death of a Cheerleader" was published, that the piece "should suggest to all but the most blinkered that the quest for affluence has its price, most tragically among the offspring of the questers."

It seems to me now that while such stories—modern American tragedies—were the best instruments available for bursting the bubble of self-deception that became American Culture during the Reagan era, conditions have changed. Back then it was essential to attack the Big Lie with every available weapon. As George Bush's first term nears an end, however, the number of people who recognize what we've done to ourselves appears to be approaching some sort of critical mass. The situation is dire, and yet I find myself experiencing a renewed sense of hope. The Nineties are a time so profoundly uncertain and indefinite that anything might happen, and I call that progress, given our recent history. An indictment of the criminals may accomplish less at this point than a clarification of the alternatives, a sense of what might still be possible. I read not long ago a note in a regional publication about an artist in New Mexico who had decided that her masterwork would be to reclaim the west shore of the Rio Grande, ten feet at a time, between now and the year 2000. And I thought, "We'll have turned the corner when she makes the cover of ROLLING STONE."

RS 452/453

JULY 18TH–AUGUST 1ST, 1985

Alex Arnold asked the girl in the plaid skirt where she lived. "Do you know the nursery?" she asked. Arnold nodded and steered north on Moraga Way, toward Orinda. The curving, two-lane road followed a creek bed past wooden-bridge driveways leading through steel gates to houses set in oak groves. Above these were forested hills hung with redwood decks and three-car garages, where land-grant rancheros had been subdivided so skillfully that "four bedrooms on wooded lot with serene view" was "a rare bargain" at $495,000.

The girl beside him told Arnold her name was Kirsten Costas. She was fifteen, and a couple of weeks earlier she had finished her sophomore year at Miramonte High School, where she was a star swimmer and had just been voted varsity cheerleader.

Arnold was thinking that Kirsten seemed very self-assured for a girl her age when he was startled by the sound of an overrevving engine. In his rearview mirror, Arnold saw the gold Pinto—"right on my rear end."

I guess I was angry. I don't really know.

Kirsten turned to look between the Volvo's high headrests, Arnold recalled, and "told me it was all right."

No one was home at the Costas house on Orchard Road. Arnold pulled into the driveway next door. "I said I would wait until she got inside," he recalled. As Kirsten stepped onto the porch, Arnold saw "a female person come swooping" out of the tall hedge.

I ran up, and I said, "Kirsten." I said to her, like, "I was going to drive you home. . . ." And she said, "Just go away. Just go away." And she was banging on the door and, and, I don't know.

"At first, I thought I observed a fistfight," Arnold said. Both girls were screaming. Arnold saw the second girl, a blonde in maroon sweat pants, raise her arm, and then Kirsten fell.

She was talking to that man or something. . . . I think he was starting to drive away, and she was telling me to go away, and I just, you know, she was like, you're like that, you know, and she was turning in towards the door, and I just got angry, and I did it.

Kirsten dropped to the ground and bounced up in one motion—"sort of a frog leap," Arnold said. He saw flailing arms and heard piercing screams, then the girls ran off the porch together. "For a moment," Arnold recalled, "I saw both faces coming at me."

I wasn't pursuing her. I was getting home, and she was—and she was getting away from me.

The gold Pinto peeled south on Orchard Road. Arnold backed his Volvo out of the driveway and gave chase. He followed for maybe a quarter of a mile, Arnold said, before "all this stuff jelled." There had been a flash, he realized, when the blonde girl raised her arm. Arnold "saw the picture": an object in the blonde girl's hand, extending from her wrist all the way to the elbow.

"Then I realized something really wrong had happened back there," Arnold said, and he swung his Volvo around in the middle of the road.

It was like, it was, I was screaming, and I ran, and I got in the car, and I just threw the knife in the back and . . . I just drove away, and I went home as fast as I could.

It was only a few minutes after ten when Art Costas, regional manager for the 3M Company's San Francisco office, and his wife, Berit, returned home from the potluck dinner where the couple had spent Saturday night celebrating the Little League season with their son, Peter.

Art's company car came over the last rise on Orchard Road and dropped into a riot of blue police flashers, red ambulance lights, fire trucks, sirens and several dozen shivering spectators, Berit Costas would remember, "all parked in front of our house."

Her husband jumped out of the car in the middle of the street. Mrs. Costas tried to restrain her son, but the boy broke loose and followed his father. Berit Costas was afraid to move. A neighbor came to the side of the car and said Kirsten had been stabbed.

Art Costas pushed his way to the back of the ambulance just in time to get a glimpse of his only daughter—on a stretcher, swaddled in blood-soaked bandages, no longer breathing—before they shut the doors.

The parents followed the ambulance to the Kaiser Medical Center in Walnut Creek, where Kirsten was dead on arrival.

I really feel like it wasn't me. It was weird. It was the weirdest feeling I've ever had. . . . It was exactly like when you see a dream and you see yourself doing things. It was so much like a dream I thought I would wake up.

It was after 2 A.M. before Berit Costas was able to be interviewed by the lead investigator on what would become the most investigated case in county history, Sergeant Richard Weckel of the Contra Costa County sheriff's department.

Four nights earlier, on Wednesday evening, Mrs. Costas told Weckel, she had received a phone call from a girl who said she was from the Bob-o-Links, or Bobbies, Miramonte High's elite social-service club, into which Kirsten had been initiated a few weeks earlier. The caller knew Kirsten was away at cheerleader camp but said the Bobbies were planning a surprise initiation dinner on Saturday night and wondered if Kirsten would be free, Mrs. Costas recalled. "Don't discuss this with anyone, and don't let Kirsten know what it's about," Mrs. Costas remembered the girl on the phone saying. She asked what her daughter should wear, and the girl on the phone said, "Something nice."

Mrs. Costas picked Kirsten up at cheerleader camp on Friday afternoon. Saturday morning she took her daughter to a swim meet, and afterward they went shopping and bought a new pair of shoes for Kirsten to wear that night. The last time she spoke to her daughter was at 8:20 P.M., when she called her from the Little League dinner and reminded Kirsten to turn on the porch light, then added, "Have a good time."

At Kirsten's funeral, Presbyterian minister Dr. James S. Little posed the question "Where was God when it happened?"

"He gives us the freedom to do and be, and in freedom we are vulnerable," Dr. Little explained from the pulpit, where he stood above several hundred sobbing teenage girls. Carrie Norris and Stacy Bennett and Gigi Kosla looked at the closed gray casket buried under heaps of flowers and began to understand that the minister's god kept secrets.

Stacy remembered talking on the telephone to Kirsten that afternoon, only a few hours before the killing. Stacy said she was going to a couples party at Matt Nishimine's house, and Kirsten asked, "What about the Bobbies dinner?" She didn't think there was one, Stacy said— "unless it's just for you."

She never liked me, but I thought she was okay, and I just thought, you know, it would be okay if we were friends.

Carrie had double-dated that night with another of Kirsten's close friends, Karen Kroll. When she came home at about one in the morning, her mother was waiting up for her. "My mom said Kirsten was babysitting and had surprised a burglar and was attacked," Carrie remembered. "She said they took her to Kaiser, but she didn't make it." Carrie kept repeating the words "didn't make it."

She sat up crying all night and then the next morning was on the phone to her friends. "Nobody knew what had happened, except Mr. Costas said it might be some girl that didn't like Kirsten," Carrie recalled. Investigators interviewed nearly a hundred girls that weekend. "The police were saying, 'It might be someone you know,' " Carrie remembered, "and that scared me even more."

Four days after the murder the weekly *Sun* carried a description of the suspect: a teenage girl, shoulder-length blond hair, chunky but not fat, wearing dark-red sweat pants and a yellow T-shirt.

"There were at least a hundred girls at Miramonte alone who could have fit that description," said Carrie Norris. In fact, she was one of them.

"Everybody was looking at everybody else," Stacy Bennett remembered.

Children of Orinda grew up in a community with the highest mean income in the county with the highest median per capita earnings in the state with the greatest net personal wealth in the country with the largest gross national product on earth. They lived in large houses on landscaped lots in a setting of birdcalls and high-tension wires, where streets without sidewalks wound like leafy tunnels through the dense foliage toward hilltop cul-de-sacs called lost Valley Road and Sleepy Hollow Court and Fallen Leaf Terrace.

Not only were Orinda parents accomplishment oriented, so were their children. In 1983 the school's average scores on the California Assessment Program tests placed it in the ninety-ninth percentile in reading, writing and math. Four years running, Miramonte had won the Northern California Academic Decathlon, and the school annually sent its honor roll east to the Ivy League or across the bay to Stanford.

Young athletes coming out of the Meadows Swim and Tennis Club, where Kirsten Costas had begun taking lessons at the age of four, were nationally ranked. A few weeks after her murder, two young Miramonte graduates won silver medals at the Olympics on the U.S. water-polo team.

Stacey Soares, a Miramonte student who had moved to Orinda from the neighboring suburb of Castro Valley, "was shocked by the change. There's such competition for everything here. It's constant neck and neck." In Orinda, she said, "everyone can afford to go to nice clubs and become such pros at everything. You have to be and have to do the best, or you feel like you're being left behind."

In the game of vague motives and clear associations, where the rules were unwritten but the score was always kept, Kirsten Costas had been one of the winners at Miramonte High School. "A very straight, popular, attractive little girl," Principal Yaich told the newspapers.

"I used to call her a social butterfly," said her friend Carrie Norris. "She would flit around from group to group during lunch, joking constantly."

Stacy Bennett "kept remembering the cute things Kirsten did."

"One that was just so much like her" went back to the winter of their sophomore year when Stacy invited Kirsten to spend Ski Week with her family at Lake Tahoe. "We had four girls in our cabin," Stacy recalled. "And there was this one that we all didn't like. My mom had invited her because she invited me to this thing of hers before." The lonely girl brought a diary. "She would look at us and write something, and it was totally bugging us," Stacy remembered. "So finally she goes to take a shower and puts the book down on the table. Kirsten looks at me and

starts laughing, and I started laughing, and we opened it and started reading. Every time she'd take a shower we'd read it, then put it back in the
same place, and she never knew. We would, like, repeat what she had
written about us to each other, and it was *so* funny."

"She made people laugh," said Carrie Norris. "Some people."

Some other people, though—girls who weren't in the Popular Group,
girls who wore last year's fashions, girls who never saw what was coming
until it was already past—were not amused.

*She just sort of put me down. She just said stuff that made me feel bad, and
so—I remember one time, on the ski trip that we were on together, I mean, we
don't have a lot of money and stuff, and we can't afford a lot of nice ski stuff, and
I just had this real crummy pair of skis and some boots, but, you know, I was
having fun anyway, and she made some comment about them, and it just seemed
like everyone else was thinking that, but she was the only one who would come
out and say that.*

"When Kirsten was killed, it really shocked me," Kris Johnson said.
"But, when I thought about it, I could understand. She was so mean. Her
and her little group made a lot of people feel bad about themselves."

"She was only mean to people she didn't care about," said Kirsten's
friend Liesl Palmer.

"After Kirsten died," Stacy Bennett recalled, "our first reaction was not
to talk about it, not even to say her name. But that was impossible."

Across a network of bedroom telephone extensions, Miramonte students were playing back old tapes, recounting every little episode of enmity
between Kirsten and the girls she had taunted. As the stories got passed
around, some altered, some magnified—many invented—they began to
grow into one another, layer upon layer, until they took their place among
Orinda's environmental features, like the tule fogs that rolled in off the
marshes along the Lafayette Reservoir.

"We lived on rumors," Carrie Norris remembered. "That was our
summer." Most of the rumors concerned two girls who had been in Kirsten's class at Miramonte, Helena Hinton and Kathy Lang.* Heavy metal
and hard-core punk, identified by the *Contra Costa Times* only as "girls
who did not fit the community's values," the two had left the Miramonte
mainstream by almost opposite routes.

Helena in junior high had been a gawky girl in glasses—"very quiet
and out of it," Stacey Soares remembered—with an eccentric English

*Names have been changed

father who rebuilt Volkswagen vans in the driveway of a ramshackle house with a mossy roof.

Judging by the way she looked, the other girls figured she was trying either too hard or not at all, and either way, Kris Johnson said, "Helena really never had a chance. She was a complete loser."

During her freshman year at Miramonte, she fell into the school's lowest caste, the Wanna-Be's, kids unable to find any affiliation, even with one another. Then suddenly Helena had a new look: frizzed hair and spray-on pants, corpse-white complexion under heavy, heavy makeup in shades of dried-blood red and wicked-witch black. She had friends suddenly, too, a group the other kids called stoners, pale boys and ghostly girls who gathered in basement rec rooms to get head-punched by bands like Iron Maiden, at school both suffering and cultivating a reputation as brain-damaged dopers.

"It was strange how fast she changed," Stacey Soares remembered. "Any identity is better than no identity," said Sharene Kacyra.

Helena's relations with Kirsten Costas, never good, got worse. "Get a life," Kirsten would call to her in the hallway. Once Helena ran into a girl's restroom, where she stood at the mirror blinking back black-mascara tears and was reported to have said, "I could just kill Kirsten." There was the story of a crank call, one that Kirsten and another girl from the Popular Group, Diane MacDonald, made to Helena one night, when they asked her questions like "Do you smoke pot? Does it make you feel better about yourself?"

"I thought it was funny," Diane MacDonald would say later. "Helena was a stoner person and kind of weird." Kirsten, she added, "didn't mean anything by it." But Helena took it personally, answering in a voice choked with hurt and rage, "If this is Kirsten Costas, tell her I'm going to get her."

I was really good at blocking it out of my mind, and I still am.

In eighth and ninth grades, when Helena Hinton was so far outside she couldn't even look in, Kathy Lang stood at the center. Kathy was a pretty blonde who had always looked two years older than the other girls in her class. The daughter of a wealthy doctor, she wore the right clothes and made the right friends without apparent effort and always seemed to be the first to know about a new band in Berkeley or a new shop in San Francisco.

Kathy, though, got a little too far out in front of her old friends during the summer after their freshman year. When she came back to Miramonte as a sophomore, her long hair was chopped off and two-toned, all bleached-white roots and black-dyed ends. She wore black clothes and cloth earrings and was into new music that came out too fast to dance and too loud to listen, angry songs about a world that was getting worse and would probably end before it got better.

Kathy was "spooky" to straight-A student Stacey Soares: "I remember one time at Ruthie's, this dance place in Berkeley, I was in the bathroom alone with her for a minute, and she just started talking like she was on drugs or something, saying, like, 'We were put on this earth to accomplish something.' I was scared."

"Kathy threatened people because she was in with the so-called Popular Group and rejected them," said her friend Sharene Kacyra. "She just turned her back on their whole little game."

Just a few days before fall classes were scheduled to begin at Miramonte, and more than two months after their daughter's death, Art and Berit Costas held their first press conference. They began with a personal appeal to the killer. "It's time to come forward, darn it," Art Costas said, "and 'fess up to what you've done." In the space of several sentences, Kirsten's father described the blonde girl, sixteen to twenty-five, as "a psychopath who must be suffering very heavily" and as "an animal" to be "hunted down."

I think I'm a pretty normal teenager.

Capturing the killer "is all we focus on right now," Art Costas told the reporters crowded onto his redwood deck. "We can't seem to focus on Kirsten."

The parents were aware that two girls singled out as suspects had been harassed all summer and would not be returning to Miramonte. "That's unfortunate," Art Costas said, "but the fact remains there was a murder here, and these things will happen."

He and his wife were convinced that their daughter had been killed not for *who* she was, Art Costas said, but rather for *what* she was: "the establishment."

"There were kids," he said, "who didn't agree with the way the majority would think and act."

On Tuesday, December 11th, students began to whisper that someone would be arrested that day. "But we had heard so many things," Carrie Norris said. "We didn't know what to believe or not believe."

The next morning Carrie was riding to school for a student-council meeting when she heard the news on the radio: a suspect had been arrested. "That whole day," she recalled, "everyone was running to radios. I was late to all my classes, and I remember my teacher said, 'I won't make you absent today.' In crafts class we had the radio on, and the teacher didn't even try to stop us. We were trying to get all the information we could. Everyone was checking to see who wasn't in school."

By lunchtime, students had determined that three blonde girls from the junior class were absent. The only one from the Bobbies was Bernadette Protti.

"I remember," Stacy Bennett said, "someone told me Bernadette wasn't in school, and I said, 'No way.' "

"I asked this friend of hers, 'What if it was Bernadette?' " recalled Liesl Palmer, "and she said, 'You don't know her.' "

No one thought Bernadette Protti was a loser, her friend Gigi Kosla would say later, "except maybe Bernadette herself."

She was a B-plus student, with an IQ of 127, who had made many friends at Miramonte and not a single enemy. Both casual acquaintances and close friends described her as "sweet" and "sensitive."

"Bernadette was such a sentimental person," said Stacey Soares. "She took everything very emotional. But she could also be a really fun person. She could be hurt easily, and so you had to watch what you said."

"Bernadette was also sensitive to other people," Gigi recalled. "She really related to people when they were hurt."

"What was good about her was she always knew exactly how to make me feel better," said Kris Johnson.

A struggling swimmer and one of the slowest runners on the track team, Bernadette had transferred from a Catholic school during her freshman year and "spent a lot of time catching up," said Stacey Soares. Yet by the end of their sophomore year she had been initiated into the Bobbies and made it to the final twelve during the cheerleader tryouts. And though she was deeply disappointed — after hours of practice in private at home — not to be among the six girls selected, no one would have said *bitterly* disappointed.

"She told me some people made cheerleader that shouldn't have," Gigi recalled, "but she never said Kirsten's name." In fact, during the drive to the funeral, Gigi remembered, "Bernadette said, 'Kirsten was the best. She deserved to make it instead of me.' "

Bernadette wasn't a glamorous girl, but she wasn't a really homely one, either: a trifle bottom heavy, maybe, but solid, with long blond hair, a slightly pasty but unblemished complexion, round features, a short chin and a small mouth that was a trifle glum in repose.

Though it made no sense at all to her friends, Bernadette was one of the Wanna-Be's, and what she wanted to be was part of the Popular Group. Her feeling she would never make it deepened after the cheerleader tryouts, when her attempts to join the Atlantis Club and the yearbook staff were not successful. "And she was a really good writer, too," Kris Johnson said.

"She said, 'Nothing is working,'" Gigi recalled. "'I don't have anything and some people have everything.'"

Bernadette lived out on La Espiral, in a brown wood-frame house with an unplanted front yard—a more comfortable home than most girls grow up in but decidedly modest measured against most houses in Orinda. She was the youngest of six children. Her father, Raymond Protti, a retired engineer for the city of San Francisco, was a little bald man with an air of diffidence and distraction, who wore horn-rimmed glasses and cheap suits. Mr. Protti spent many afternoons tinkering with an assortment of used cars that sat with their hoods shrouded under black-plastic tarps in the driveway. Bernadette's mother, Elaine, was a devout Catholic who studied the Bible at the dining-room table and gave heavily to the church even after her husband went on a pension.

"Bernadette had pain about her home," said Kris Johnson. "She was embarrassed they didn't have a big house or the nicest furniture or good cars. I had the best times at her house, but she'd say, 'I don't know why anyone would want to come to my house.'"

After the murder, investigators had placed Bernadette high on their list of suspects: she was blonde, chunky, a Bobbie, and her parents owned a gold Pinto. When she passed a polygraph, though, the police virtually ignored her. Not until the FBI composite came back did they take another hard look. On Friday, December 8th, Bernadette was summoned to the sheriff's office for an interview that lasted four and a half hours.

The man who asked most of the questions was FBI agent Ron Hilley. A bland-faced and soft-spoken man with a strawberry-blond beard and pale eyes, Hilley was considered, as prosecutor John Oda would put it later, "the best there is at getting confessions. That's his job. He makes them want to confess. He doesn't even look like a police officer, does he? More like a priest or something."

Bernadette stuck to her story during the Friday interview, Hilley recalled, but at one point she asked if he could understand how a sixteen-year-old girl might be more afraid of seeing her name in the newspapers than of any sentence a judge could give her. Hilley said he could understand.

"Does it have to be settled today?" Bernadette asked, and Hilley told her there was time.

On Monday night she asked her mother if they could talk. "I came to her later in the night," Elaine Protti recalled, "and said, 'I'm very tired. I'll take a rest, and you wake me up, and we'll talk then.'" Bernadette let her mother sleep through the night. In the morning Mrs. Protti apologized. "I know you wanted to talk," she said. It was all right, Bernadette told her, "I've written you a note." The girl placed a folded sheet of college-ruled notebook paper on the kitchen counter and asked her mother not to read it for half an hour. Bernadette went out the door and caught a ride to school with Whitney Davisson. "We used to talk about 'Wouldn't it be neat if we had tons of money and could just go shopping at all the stores we wanted and buy whatever we liked,' " recalled Whitney.

Elaine Protti set her kitchen timer for thirty minutes and sat down to do her Bible homework. When the timer went off, she unfolded the sheet of paper.

> *Dear Mom and Dad,*
>
> *I have been trying to tell you this all day, but I love you so much and it's hard so I'm taking the easy way out. I just can't be near you when you see this because I've already caused so much pain. The reason why it took so long on Friday is because the FBI man Mr. Hilley thinks I did it. And he is right. I can't bring her back but I'm so sorry. I would kill myself except maybe that would hurt you even more. He told me that you would still love me but not what I did and that life is still worth living. I hope so. I've been able to live with it for a while, but I can't ignore it. It's too much for me and I can't be that deceiving. I've spoken to a priest but I still can't take it. I need to turn myself in, with you if you would come, today. Please forgive me. I need you. I'm so sorry that I've been a disappointment to you in every way. I'm even worse than words can describe and I hate myself. And after all I've done, I still have demands but I don't know what else to feel. I need your love, please still love me. I can't live unless you love me. I've ruined my life and yours and I don't know what to do and I'm so ashamed and scared. I love you.*
>
> *Bernadette*

Elaine Protti told her husband that "I wanted one last chance with my daughter." She drove alone to Miramonte High, where Bernadette was waiting outside, sitting on the curb by the parking lot.

A reporter who visited Miramonte on the day Bernadette's picture appeared on his newspaper's front page wrote that "students were wandering aimlessly in the halls, sobbing on one another's shoulders." Kris Johnson and several of Bernadette's other close friends went home.

"I think people at school would feel better knowing it was someone who was on drugs or not very well liked," said a junior girl, "but everyone feels terrible that it was Bernadette."

"When you hear that someone like her can do something like this," said a boy in the same class, "you think, well, anyone can do it."

Editorialized the *Sun,* "It would have been so much easier to bear if the suspect . . . had not been one of us . . . but instead . . . a tough from the other side of the tunnel."

Principal Yaich said that when told of the arrest "all I wanted to know was, was it either [Kathy Lang or Helena Hinton]."

Kathy was now attending St. Perpetua, the Catholic school from which Bernadette had transferred less than two years earlier. Kathy and Sharene Kacyra were riding to class when news of the arrest came over the car radio. "She said, 'I'm so glad.' But it was like the emotion all sort of hit her at once," Sharene remembered, and while Kathy said she was happy, "she looked sad."

"If it had been Kathy, you know, people would have all said, 'There, you see,' and been happy with themselves," Sharene said.

Within a few days of the arrest, Monsignor John McCracken, of Santa Maria Church, where Bernadette had been confirmed, let it be known that he was preparing a special sermon. "The attitudes of the parents in this community are being visited on the children," said McCracken. Bernadette Protti, the monsignor said, "may have felt the pressures of the community's standards," calling for "the best, the brightest and the most expensive. . . . This is a very close-knit community. Either you belong or you don't," McCracken said.

The monsignor's message was not well received, and the backlash helped the coalescence of the majority's sentiment that Bernadette Protti was an anomaly, one bad girl among the many good kids. "There is not a problem with materialism at Miramonte any more than there is anywhere else," said Principal Yaich. Orinda psychiatrist Stephen Heisler criticized "some" for seeking "easy answers" in socioeconomics while ignoring such important considerations as brain chemistry.

A story in the *Contra Costa Times* quoted local mental-health professionals who described Orinda's "community trauma": "Some communities have identities of being high-crime areas and others don't," one said. Only psychologist Suzanne Allen broke through the babble: "There's something wrong with our adolescents out there," she said. "There's too much focus on external achievement and success and not enough attention to the people inside." What she saw in practice was "tremendous pressure on kids to be successful. The kids have to step on one another to get ahead. There's a feeling that there's not enough to go around."

She only wanted to be friends with Kirsten, Bernadette had told Hilley and Weckel. Her plan was to talk to Kirsten in private, "to get to know her." It was Kirsten's idea to drive to the Presbyterian church, Bernadette said. Kirsten wanted to smoke a joint before the party, "but I didn't want to," Bernadette said, and Kirsten "made me feel really dumb" about it. The two of them talked in the Pinto for at least twenty minutes, Bernadette said, before Kirsten told her "you're weird," got out of the car and ran down the hill to the Arnold house. She followed on foot, to tell Kirsten she would take her home, Bernadette said, then ran back to the Pinto. As she tailed the Volvo to Kirsten's house, Bernadette told Hilley and Weckel, she grew frightened, imagining the things Kirsten would say to the other girls. By the time they made the turn at the nursery, her fear had become anger.

She found the knife between the Pinto's bucket seats, Bernadette said. Her sister Virginia, a bank examiner and a vegetarian, carried kitchen knives in the car to cut the tomatoes and cucumbers she ate for lunch.

She meant to hurt Kirsten, Bernadette told Hilley and Weckel, not to kill her. When she got home, she flushed the marijuana down the toilet, washed the knife and returned it to her mother's kitchen drawer, Bernadette said. She did not know for sure that Kirsten was dead until the next morning, when Gigi called.

Reporters made one last sweep across the Miramonte campus on the day Judge Edward Merrill convicted Bernadette Protti of second-degree murder. Virtually every student they interviewed said she should never come back to Orinda.

"I want her put away for life," said a girl from the junior class; her boyfriend suggested that Bernadette's family "move a long ways away."

"I don't think anyone here ever wants to see her again," said Rinda Cleary.

"Her classmates apparently don't relate to being an outsider, a loser, a loner," said Charles James, the public defender who represented Bernadette at her trial. "There's a smugness in Orinda," he said. "They're all happy with their situation—'I've got mine.' Weakness is not easily understood."

In the Miramonte principal's office, Branislav Yaich, recently named Orinda's Citizen of the Year, described the murder as "an isolated event," which had "no effect that I can see" on the school's students. He had read "only one good article on the whole affair," Yaich said, offering a column by the *Contra Costa Times'* Marcy Bachmann, entitled "Verdict on Orinda—Not Guilty." The thesis was that the problem all along had been Bernadette Protti, and since Bernadette was gone, so was the problem. It had been Bachmann, back in December, after Bernadette's arrest, who had produced a piece entitled "The System Works."

Fear of Frying

TIM CAHILL

MANY AND EXTREME WERE THE REASONS FOR A MAN
TO VOLUNTEER TO HIKE ACROSS DEATH VALLEY. JOHN
WAYNE GACY WAS BUT ONE OF THEM.

When Bob Wallace, my old friend from ROLLING STONE, called sometime in the early spring of 1984, I was living in a ranch house on Poison Creek in south central Montana, and was not, psychologically speaking, in the best of shape.

My wife had just pointed out that she had married me and me alone. She didn't really need to sleep with John Wayne Gacy every night as well. John Gacy was a serial killer who had murdered thirty-three young boys and buried most of them in the crawl space under his suburban Chicago home. Sometimes he doused the corpses in muriatic acid to speed decomposition.

Gacy wasn't there physically with us, of course. No, he was simply on my mind, day and night. I was writing a book about his crimes, which I had been researching for three years. Originally, I had imagined that anyone who committed such incomprehensibly cruel crimes must necessarily be insane. After three years, however, I had arrived at the discomforting conclusion that John Gacy killed rationally, shrewdly. Insanity, I had come to believe, is a curious cold comfort. We postulate insanity in cases like Gacy's in order to deny the existence of evil.

It is fair to say that, in the spring of 1984, I was obsessed with the existence of evil.

Additionally, winter in Montana had conspired to stick around for a few more months than was absolutely necessary. The cattle were frozen stiff in the fields, hooves pointed to the sky, or so it seemed. Drifts accumulated on the portion of my road the county did not plow. My car was parked half a mile from the ranch house. A trip to town was a survival trek.

And the wind: the wind was a constant tribulation. It whistled and boomed and battered the isolated house with sixty- and seventy-mile-an-hour gusts; it set my perfectly useless television antenna humming like a giant tuning fork. This irritating whine inspired my three dogs to howl along, in helpless harmony.

Things weren't going well up there on Poison Creek. The water from my spring box was tainted—there were little black wormy things flowing from the tap, a dozen or more to an eight-ounce glass. I'd have to wade through thigh-deep snow, chop ice for an hour or so and then dig around in the half frozen muck of the spring in order to install a filtering screen. And I'd have to do that pretty soon: the next time I was thirsty, in fact.

So when Bob Wallace called, my spirits soared. A little.

Bob had come to ROLLING STONE sometime in the early 1970s. He was hired as a fact checker. I was an associate editor in those days. Worked right there in the San Francisco office, under the watchful eye of editor-publisher Jann Wenner, who inspired me with such memorable epigrams as "you're fired." Apparently, when Bob Wallace arrived at the San Francisco office, I was between epigrams.

Bob was delighted with his new job at ROLLING STONE. He had last worked at the Stanford Poultry lab where he had manipulated roosters to assess their reproductive potential.

"How do you mean, 'manipulate,' " I asked Bob one night over a beer at Jerry's bar, across the street from the ROLLING STONE office.

The purpose of the experiment, as Bob explained it, had to do with pinpointing the exact moment when the roosters "burned out."

"Okay." I was interested in this. "So how do you 'manipulate' a rooster?"

"Don't egg him on," someone sitting on the next stool said.

"It's sort of an art," Bob Wallace explained. "The first thing you do, you put the rooster's head under your armpit. That gets them in the mood. Then—and this is hard to do at first, but it's like riding a bicycle: once you get the knack you never forget—you take your thumb and forefinger and gently squeeze just under the neck. You feel a kind of cord. That's the vas deferens. And you just run down the body on that cord. Collect what you get in a little vial."

A little vile, indeed.

Bob said that manipulating roosters for a living was a good way to learn to hate the whole damn chicken race.

"What did the roosters think about it?" I asked.

"Loved me," Bob said sadly. "I'd walk in, sit down on a chair, twenty roosters are trying to jump in my lap. 'Me first! Me first!' I began to loathe and despise them."

"You didn't, uh, form any lasting attachments?" I asked.

"No," Bob said. "I mean, roosters do have rudimentary personalities. There are some you like better than others."

"But all in all you'd rather work at ROLLING STONE than be a chicken jacker at a major American university?"

"Precisely," Bob agreed. There was another aspect of his job that he hadn't told me about. "When the roosters burned out, I had to kill them." And really, his antipathy toward poultry wasn't absolute: Bob sorta liked one or two of his charges. There were even a couple of polite roosters, ones that didn't clamor to sit on his lap, that had minimally endearing personalities.

"The professor'd come by," Bob said, "and he'd say, 'Looks like Big Red isn't producing anymore.'" If Big Red happened to be one of Bob's favorites, he'd "take a little out of Brown Buck's vial and put it in Red's."

There were, I thought, wells of compassion in Bob Wallace that a man had to admire. He was also one of the funniest human beings I had yet had the opportunity to meet. And he was odd enough to fit right in with the men and women who comprised ROLLING STONE magazine in the mid-seventies. Charlie Perry, for instance, whose passion was gourmet food and dead languages. You'd find Charlie in his office pouring over a parchment concerning the preparation of medieval Arabic condiments, some of which—this part excited Charlie—were prepared putrescent. Or David Felton, who was fired more times than I was and who kept a cryptic letter pinned to his bulletin board. It was from someone in Perris Valley, California, and consisted of a single remarkably mournful sentence: "Sad but true: masturbation gave me the face of an ox."

Ben Fong-Torres, the best of our music reporters, had papered his office with fan letters enquiring about his ethnicity. "Is Fong-Torres a Chinese or a Spanish name?" When Sarah Lazin, chief of research, looked out on the parking lot one day, she didn't see her new English car. "Where's the yellow Rover?" she asked the office at large. "I'm in my office," Ben shouted.

There was Paul Scanlon and Joe Eszterhas and Grover Lewis and Harriet Fier; there was Big John Crowell in the mail room, and Judy Lawrence at the front desk. It had been a big, loud, strange, obsessed, hardworking and fully dysfunctional family at the San Francisco ROLLING STONE offices.

When the magazine moved its offices to New York in 1977, I relocated in a small town in northern California, then jumped to Montana. Sometimes, it seemed lonely on the ranch. I seldom saw yellow Rovers or heard about rotted medieval condiments.

Bob Wallace had moved to New York, worked a spell for *Newsweek*, and was now the managing editor of ROLLING STONE. When Bob called in the spring of 1984, while the house hummed and the dogs howled, we talked about the old days.

Bob asked me how I was doing on the serial killer book.

"I used to be against capital punishment," I said.

Bob, a man who had saved many a burnt-out rooster from the axe, sensed the oppressive desperation in my voice. It was like the kitchen faucet in the house: dark wormy things coming out every time I opened my mouth.

"Maybe," Bob said, "you ought to do a story for us. Clear out your mind."

The story, we decided, should be healthy and hearty and fun. Something to contrast with my book project. Maybe something outdoorsy. Bob, who had visited the ranch on Poison Creek, knew I liked that sort of stuff. Fishing. Hiking.

It occurred to me that many of the people I knew in Montana were engaged in physical activities that pushed the limits of their chosen sports. Rock climbers. Mountaineers. Kayakers. Cavers. Extreme skiers.

Maybe, Bob and I agreed, there was a trend here. Perhaps I should document that trend. That's what ROLLING STONE had always done, after all. It had covered the people who worked the edges. The folks who went to extremes.

I'd do a series of articles, then. It'd be called "Going to Extremes."

The first story, Bob thought, ought to be a first-person account of some absurd and extreme venture. I pointed out that I was a poor climber, a bad skier, and had never been in a kayak. There was nothing in the realm of outdoor sports that I could do extremely well. Mostly I liked walking around in the mountains with a pack on my back.

So, Bob wondered, was there some extreme walk I might take?

That question generated the following story, which concerns itself, as you will see, with a stroll through Death Valley.

The long walk was meant to be a frame for the stories that were to follow, a way of thinking about the perfectly preposterous idea that physical fear was somehow cleansing. Indeed, in those hours when Death Valley had its hands around my neck, I failed entirely to think about John Wayne Gacy, the problem of evil, or the fact that I still needed to fix my spring box. Humor seemed possible, even mandatory.

The Gacy manuscript, *Buried Dreams*, became a national bestseller. I finished it in a burst of energy generated out of the Death Valley walk. My next several books, however, were about travel and adventure and laughter: *Jaguars Ripped My Flesh*, *A Wolverine Is Eating My Leg*, *Pecked to Death by Ducks*.

Occasionally, interviewers ask about the derivation of these titles. They are, I tell them, the Chicken Jacker's fowl legacy.

RS 457

SEPTEMBER 26TH, 1985

I am as low as a man can get in the United States, and I am slowly sinking lower. Death Valley, 550 square miles of it below sea level— all scalding salt flats and dunes—is surrounded by mountains: by the Amargosa, the Panamint and the Last Chance ranges, which rise from 4000 to 11,000 feet above the valley floor. These mountains catch what rain the westerly air currents didn't drop on the Sierras, and water rolls down the mountainsides into the valley, where it immediately evaporates, leaving the accumulated mineral residue of chlorides, sulphates and carbonates.

Not all of the water is lost, however. Some of it skulks in a steaming, muddy bog that lies just under a brittle salt crust out toward the center of the valley. Somewhere near the lowest point in the continental United States, the salt crust refuses to support the weight of a man; it takes the boot to the ankle, then the leg to the calf, the knee. Walking becomes a crack-splash affair, and the sharp, crystalline salt crust scrapes and cuts the shins. The bog below is a musty-gray combination of hot mud and salt that clings to boots and legs like hot clay. First the valley chews up your legs, then it rubs salt in your wounds.

There are rumors that "in some places in the middle of the bog, the soft salty area in the bottom of the valley, a team of horses or a man walking have been instantly sucked down out of sight." This bit of cheerful information comes from Daniel Cronkhite's well-researched book *Death Valley's Victims*. The author acknowledges that the story may be apocryphal and goes on to quote Old Johnnie, who told of "finding a dead man's face looking up at him out of the ground. 'He was a Swede with yellow hair, and he stared at the sun. He sank standing up.'"

This is a report to brood upon when walking across Death Valley around two in the morning with a photographer from ROLLING STONE. You want to crack-splash through the steaming mud about thirty feet apart, so that if one should go down, the other can more efficiently panic and go lurching off into the desert night, hands in the air, screaming and gibbering.

When the photographer, Nick Nichols, and I reached what we supposed was the nadir of life in the United States, the absolute pit, Nick also discovered that he had dropped his strobe, "back there." He began trudging along our back trail, muttering malign imprecations and leaving me standing knee-deep in hot, salty mud. There was no place to sit down, unless I wanted to take a scalding mud bath, and the Van Gogh stars spun madly overhead. The desert sky was impossibly clear, and I could make out the colors of various stars and planets, so that, glancing up, I felt as if I were stranded in space.

Thick, muddy water was draining back into our post-hole footprints— it was a sick sort of squishing sound—and the dead of a Death Valley night swallowed up Nick's receding light. Alone, in the darkness, I stared down at the unbroken salt crust of the valley floor. There were innumerable pillars of salt standing in inch-high clusters. Some formations, like certain tropical corals, took on the shapes of crystalline flowers, and they wound about in baroque curlicues, snaking across the floor like endless meandering rivers.

The mountains—waiting to reveal themselves in the light of the rising moon—whispered to one another in warm, gusting breezes that swept across the valley. The hot salt crust of the valley floor, under the cold light of swirling stars, emitted a faint glow, like the radium dial of a watch. The world was an ocean of salt and sand, so flat the eye saw a ridge, nuclear white, that rose on all sides.

I stood stock-still, wondering if I was sinking any deeper. The hot mud had been knee-deep on me, or so I thought, but now my legs felt braised to midthigh. It seemed hard to breathe out there, alone, in the middle of the night. I felt slightly faint and realized that in this condition I could very well commit philosophy.

'Death Destroys a Man, but the Idea of Death Saves Him'
—William Forester

Every life offers certain challenges that require grit, intelligence, spirit, spunk, careful planning and nifty interpersonal skills. Try cashing an out-of-state check in New York City on a Sunday. Buy a used car from a friend of your brother-in-law. Ask for a promotion. Or a divorce.

Few of the challenges we face every day, as a matter of course, are physical, however, and a growing number of people seem to feel that lack keenly. Some have taken up individual sports as a kind of antidote to physical stagnation. People run marathons, they compete in triathlons, cycle the breadth of the country nonstop or attempt to get their names in the *Guinness Book of World Records* by doing cartwheels across the state of Nebraska.

My problem with most athletic challenges is training. I am lazy and find that workouts cut into my drinking time. The thought of a new personal best no longer fills me with ambition or a burning desire to win. I need incentives.

Consequently, every once in a while, I like to flirt with some physical challenge in which the price of failure is death. Amazing how easy training becomes in such a situation, how carefully one plans, how intently the mind focuses.

Nothing is safe in a world where lawyers define what is dangerous. As it happens, a growing number of people have discovered that they enjoy a view unencumbered by guardrails and warning signs. These folks feel that they have enough sense not to fall off the nearest cliff. In point of fact, many of them search out spectacular cliffs for the sole and specific purpose of seeing them without plunging to their doom.

The Indiana Jones of Photography

"I know what you did," Nick Nicholas raged. We were kneeling on the floor of a hotel room in San Francisco, and topographical maps of Death Valley were spread out on the floor. The bed was littered with desert-survival books, wide-brimmed hats, long-sleeved shirts, heavy cotton jeans, homemade turbans, backpacks, cookstoves, canteens and cameras. "You were sitting in some editor's office in New York and came up with this, this . . ."

"Idea?"

"This insanity. You can't propose a story on the girls of Tahiti. Oh, no. Or the four-star restaurants of France. Or the grand hotels of Europe. You come up with this, this . . ."

I could tell Nick loved the idea. Together we have made something of a living working the adventure-travel beat. We've trekked through sections of the Amazon and Congo basins; studied and lived with mountain gorillas in the Virunga volcanoes of central Africa; swum in the pool under Angel Falls; flown with the air force into the eye of a hurricane; and made the first rainy-season ascent of Arthur Conan Doyle's "Lost World," Mount Roraima, in Venezuela.

We studied the maps for a while. The Park Service officials we contacted had actively discouraged the hike. We would be trekking through a blast furnace, they said. Late June was deadly in the valley. Why didn't we hike from Mount Whitney down to the ocean?

Trekking from the highest point to a pretty low point, we said, seemed to lack the proper emotional resonance. Chief Ranger Dick Rayner sighed and said that we'd have to file an itinerary with him and that we'd have to have a support vehicle, a four-wheel-drive rig driven by a third party. If we failed to reach the vehicle at the proper points and times, the driver would report to the rangers and a search party would be dispatched.

Frank Frost, a Northern California photographer, agreed to drive the support vehicle, and we were in business. Dick Rayner had said that natural springs in the valley were undependable and fouled with diarrhea-producing *Giardia*. It was best to stash water, to bury it in plastic jugs. We should plan on two gallons a day, minimum.

Nick and I formulated a set of rules. It was okay to make our packs as light as possible by burying food along with the water. We'd avoid roads and bushwhack cross-country as much as possible. Since the Park Service required a support vehicle anyway, it was okay to pack it full of cold water and iced beer.

"We're pretty psychological," I pointed out.

Nick didn't reply. He was studying a copy of *Death Valley's Victims*, looking at the photos of desiccated corpses baking out on the valley floor.

"We're going to die," the Indiana Jones of photography said.

Hot Damn

We managed to slog through the crusted, steaming bog before dawn, according to plan, and found the water and food Nick had buried. Our campsite was Tule Spring, on the valley floor, at the foot of Panamint Mountains. We pitched the rain flies from the one-man tents we carried and settled down for a long, windless sleep. The tents would provide shelter from the sun: we had tested them out on the grass at the Death Valley Visitors Center, in the village of Furnace Creek. The temperature inside the tents had been twelve degrees cooler than the outside air.

By eleven that morning I felt like a side of beef, and my skin was the color of medium-rare prime rib. The pores on the back of my hand were the size of quarters, or so it seemed, and dozens of tiny but cruel dwarfs were building a condominium inside my skull. The thermometer registered 128 inside the tent. The record high temperature in the United States is 134, recorded on July 10th, 1913, in Death Valley. If it was 12 degrees hotter outside of the tent—140 degrees—I was dying through the hottest American day on record.

But I found the temperature outside was only 113. It didn't make any sense. I laid the thermometer down on the ground, next to my boots, and the mercury pegged at 150 degrees. The thermometer wasn't made to measure temperatures any higher. What we'd failed to consider, Nick and I, is the fact that gravel and sand—like white cement highways under the summer sun—get hot. Real hot. A lot hotter than grass or even the air itself. The Indian name for Death Valley, Tomesha, means "ground on fire." In 1972, a record ground temperature of 201 degrees was recorded on the valley floor.

Instead of protecting us from the 113-degree outside air, the tents were concentrating the 150-plus-degree ground temperature and literally baking us. Nick and I moved outside. We sat on foam pads, under lean-tos we had made with space blankets. With the noonday sun directly overhead, the blankets provided perhaps two square feet of shade. It was now 121 degrees. Hot air, rising off the superheated sand and salt, scalded our lungs. Sleep was impossible.

"The tents were a dumb idea," Nick said.

"Poor planning," I muttered.

Then we didn't say anything for nine hours.

I could feel the hot air rising all around us. The laws of physics demand that heavier, cooler air should fall from the heavens, and that is what happens in Death Valley. It falls, comes into contact with the ground, becomes superheated and rises. The mountains surrounding the valley allow no air to escape, so that as the day wears on, the upper levels of air—which have made several passes over the ground—are not really cool anymore, only less hot than air at ground level. In effect, the valley is a giant convection oven.

All this rising and falling air whistles across the valley floor in gusting waves of arid wind that suck the moisture out of a man's body the way a hand wrings water from a sponge. You sweat, of course, but you do not feel sweat on your body in Death Valley, even at 121 degrees. The killing convective wind will allow no moisture to form, but all that rapid evaporation is a cooling process, so the wind feels good, almost pleasant, as it desiccates the body. And that is why people who die in the desert are often found naked, lying face down on the skillet of the valley floor.

Some victims have been found with a quart or two of water in their possession. Apparently, they intended to save the water until they felt they really needed it. Staggering, suffering from dehydration or heat exhaustion or heat stroke, they fell unconscious, and the ground on fire killed them in a matter of hours. Other victims, too weak to walk, simply fell to the sand and couldn't rise to their feet. In 1973, Death Valley killed three people this way.

Unpleasant thoughts. Huddled there in my small square of shade with the circumstances of various tragedies stumbling slowly through my mind like terminal winos, I began dreaming of the Man in the Freon Suit. What a guy! In Death Valley, certain legends exist and have the ring of truth about them because everyone knows them, everyone repeats them, and they are so poetically morbid as to live in memory, whether one wills them to or not.

In my mind's eye, I could see the foot-long icicle, blue white under a molten sun. Slowly, the thing began to grow, and it floated dumbly out into the shimmering salt pan of the valley floor, where it stood like a massive religious icon, a monolithic icicle plunged into the heart of Death Valley.

I wondered if Nick was hallucinating too.

There was poor planning involved, all right. The next water stash was only five miles away, at a place where a scrubby bush grew beside a rocky four-wheel-drive road. Unfortunately, in that area there had been a number of springtime flash floods. Water had thundered down the mountainsides in several temporary rivers, and each wash, in the light of our headlamps, appeared to be a four-wheel-drive road. We couldn't find the water. Poor planning.

The evaporative wind had cranked up to about forty miles an hour. This was serious. We retraced our steps, searching for the stash, walking like a pair of Frankenstein monsters in our adobe boots. We both were developing severe blisters, but there was no stopping now. Finding the water was more important than some little excruciatingly crippling pain.

About 2:30 that morning we stumbled over the water and food. We had been out on the valley floor for twenty-six hours, in temperatures sometimes exceeding 120 degrees. My feet looked and felt like I'd been walking across hot coals. We both carried extra boots, but walking over ground on fire makes feet expand. Mine looked sort of like big red blistered floppy clown feet. My second pair of boots simply didn't fit, not even a little bit. Another bit of poor planning that meant I'd have to walk forever in cruel shoes, limping pathetically.

We'd made too many mistakes, Nick and I, and the errors had compounded themselves exponentially, so that we had completely lost the will to push on. In the distance, seventeen miles away, we could see the lights of Furnace Creek. We doctored our feet—break the blister, apply the antiseptic, coat with Spenco Second Skin tape—and discussed complete capitulation. In our condition, with blisters and thirty-pound packs, we could probably make two miles an hour. It would take six and a half hours to walk to Furnace Creek just to surrender.

Into the Fire

We were perhaps 1500 feet up into the Panamints, walking up a long, bare slope littered with sage. There was no shade anywhere on the slope.

We had miles to walk before the rock would rise above us and provide some protection from the sun. Quite clearly, neither of us could survive another day crouched under a space blanket.

Nick was wearing shorts, and I could see the muscles in his thighs twitching spasmodically. It was only two hours until sunup. There was a full moon that night, and in its light I suddenly saw, sloping off to my right, a long, narrow valley. In that valley, almost glittering in the moonlight, was a town full of large frame houses, all of them inexplicably painted white. The houses seemed well maintained but were clearly abandoned. There was nothing on the map that indicated a ghost town here in Trail Canyon.

"Jesus, Nick, look." I pointed to the ghost town, perhaps 250 feet below us.

"What?"

"We can hole up down there."

"Where?"

"Down there."

Nick stared down into the valley for a full thirty seconds. "You're pointing to a ditch," he said finally. "You want to hole up in a ditch?"

I squinted down at the ghost town. Slowly, it began to rise toward me. The neatly painted white houses became strands of moon-dappled sage in a ditch perhaps five feet deep.

"I been having 'em, too," Nick said.

Nick wouldn't say what his hallucinations were like. I had to coax it out of him.

"Graveyards," Nick said finally. "I been seeing graveyards."

A Post Card of the Rescue

In the rocks above the bare sage slope, we found a narrow S-shaped canyon, where we lay down to sleep. Throughout the day, the sun chased us around the bends of the S, but there was always shade somewhere. We shared the canyon with a small, drab, gray sparrowlike bird that seemed to be feeding on some thorny red flowers that grew in the shade. I loved Death Valley. It was, as the ranger said, psychological, this place. It slammed you from one extreme to another. My heart seemed to expand inside my chest, and I could feel tears welling up in my eyes. I turned away from Nick, and we sat like that for a time, back to back.

"Nice here," I said finally. "Comfortable."

"Birds and shit," Nick agreed. His voice was shaky.

We slept for twelve hours, ate at nine that night, then slept until six the next morning. The swelling in our feet had gone down after twenty-one hours of sleep, and we could wear our extra boots. I felt like skipping. By noon that day we had reached an abandoned miner's cabin where we had stashed six gallons of water.

"How do you feel," I asked Nick.

"Real good."

"Me too."

"We're going to make it," he said.

"I know."

It was cool enough to cook inside the cabin, and Nick was whipping up one of his modified freeze-dried Creole shrimp dinners when we heard the plane.

It was moving up the slope, circling over the route we had given Dick Rayner, and we couldn't believe they were looking for us now that we felt like gods of the desert. It was still twenty-four hours to the first checkpoint. Why were they searching for us? I laid out a yellow poncho so the rangers could spot us. Beside the poncho I arranged several dozen rocks to read "OK" in letters ten feet high. The plane came in close and dipped a wing. The pilot looked like Rayner. He circled twice more, then flew back down Furnace Creek.

It was an odd sensation, having them out spending taxpayers' money searching for us. I felt like some boy scout had just offered to help me cross the street.

Apotheosis

We had, it seemed, acclimated to the desert. It was easier, now, to walk during the day and sleep in the cool of the evening. We took the Panamint Valley at midday in temperatures that rose to 115 degrees. The next day, climbing another range of mountains, we came upon a series of enclosing rock walls that reminded us of our good friend the S-shaped canyon. It rose up into the mountains, and there was a small, clear creek running down the middle of the canyon where green grass and bulrushes and coyote melons and trees—actual willow trees—grew. Ahead, water cascaded over some boulders that had formed a natural dam. The pool beyond the boulders was clear green with a golden sandy bottom. It was deep enough to dive into, and the water was so cold it drove the air from my lungs like a punch to the chest. Above, several waterfalls fell down a series of ledges that rose like steps toward the summit of the mountain.

The same sun that had tried to kill us in Death Valley offered its apologies, and we laid out on the rocks, watching golden-blue dragonflies flit over the pool. It was 111 degrees, and we were sunbathing.

The Kindness of Rangers Revisited

When we walked into Dick Rayner's office, I had a copy of the *Death Valley Gateway Gazette* under my arm. The chief ranger agreed that, yes, according to the plan we'd filed, we hadn't been late. What had happened, he said, was that Frank Frost, in the support vehicle, had climbed to the top of a mountain with a commanding view of our route and had spent a day scanning the trails with high-powered binoculars. It was the day we had spent sleeping in the S-shaped canyon. Frank couldn't find us anywhere.

He reported to the rangers, who had immediately set out to save our lives. The foul-up hadn't been anyone's fault really, and I suppose I was glad that the Park Service employs men like Dick Rayner who are willing to leave an air-conditioned office to save a couple of nincompoops like us.

Still, I couldn't help zapping him a little. "The article says we were more than twenty-four hours overdue. I mean, look at our trip plan. We still had twenty-four hours to the first checkpoint."

Rayner said, "I didn't write the article."

"They quote you directly, though. You say we were in 'good but fatigued condition.' "

"Well, we saw your footprints across the valley," Rayner said. "That's a tiring walk. And we could see you were in good condition when we flew over. So: 'good but fatigued condition.' "

The chief ranger seemed a little embarrassed. He recounted some of the rescues he'd participated in, and one of the deaths he knew about. Rayner seemed to be saying that he'd just as soon nobody walked across Death Valley in the summertime. It was his job to discourage such treks — to put guardrails along the cliffs — and he apparently felt that newspaper articles about half-dead dumbshits in the desert were something of a public service. He was a good man who just purely hated the idea of people getting hurt in his park.

"Would you do it again?" Rayner asked.

I glanced over at the Indiana Jones of photography, who was smiling in a manner that made him look somewhat psychological. "We could change the rules," he said. "No stashes. We walk from spring to spring and carry portable water purifiers. Badwater to Tule Spring to Trail Canyon . . ."

Dick Rayner seemed intrigued. Certainly against his better judgment, he pointed to the map on his desk and said, "There's a spring here that would get you into the canyon in better shape."

4OO Years in a Convent, 50 Years in a Whorehouse

P.J. O'ROURKE

PHILIPPINES PRESIDENT FERDINAND MARCOS WAS IN TROUBLE, SO WE SENT OUR CORRESPONDENT STRAIGHT TO MANILA. HE GOT THE SCOOP FROM WHORES, THUGS AND THE CITY JAILER.

Ah, "the story behind the . . ." This is the lifeblood, the inspiriting force, the *anima bruta* of every drunken bore of a foreign correspondent. And I am one. The bombs burst louder with each telling. The bullets fly closer. The villains grow viler. The heroes gain such stature that they're drafted by the NBA. The warm camaraderie among journalists becomes a boiling fondue pot of eternal brotherhood. And the local girls get so pretty it's a wonder *Sports Illustrated* hasn't done swimsuit issues in Tbilisi and Kuwait.

Me telling you how it *really* was—that's when I turn into a hell of a fellow with broad perspectives, brilliant foresight and a physical bravery I'd hardly dreamed of three drinks ago. Let me freshen this up and I'll suddenly remember I could speak the native lingo. Once I get started on the story behind the story, why, I've had people leap off bar stools, knock me to the floor, pry open my jaws and jam in a whole bowlful of those salted Goldfish crackers, trying to get me to shut up.

Fortunately for you, the reader, there is no story behind my story of the fall of Ferdinand Marcos. The advantage of the casual and unstructured (not to say pointless and sloppy) style of reporting presented here is that I was telling you the whole truth—lies and all—in the first place. That said, some things were omitted from "400 Years in a Convent, 50 Years in a Whorehouse"—some for lack of space, some for decency's sake. But most of what was left out was left out because I didn't know what it meant, if it meant anything at all. For example, in 1942 the victims of the Bataan Death March were led through the little town of Capas, north of Manila Bay. On the outskirts of that town forty-four years later was the sign CAPAS DEATH MARCH JAYCEES. "Bergen-Belsen Gas Chamber Boys Club?" "Sub-Saharan Starved Millions Softball League?"

I took notes on an NBC-TV interview with a resident of Manila's worst slum, the squatter settlement in the city dump. The dump resident was a firm supporter of Marcos's.

NBC-TV: Why?

DUMP RESIDENT: He lets me live here!

And I got hooked up somehow with a hugely alcoholic lying Australian who said he was the former head of security at the presidential palace, a personal friend of Ferdinand Marcos's, the godfather of the Pilar Street sex-club strip, the owner of three islands given to him by his Filipino father-in-law and a colonel in the Confederate Air Force. The Australian was so drunk he admitted these were lies. The man made no sense, had no information and was treated like a pariah everywhere he went. But as a result of letting him drag me on a daylong inane and frenetic tour of Manila, I met the city jailer, the bar-owning thug, the *mama-sans* and a number of other characters featured in my article. There's a lesson for young journalists in this somewhere. Though come to think of it, the jailer, thug and *mama-sans* didn't have any information or make much sense either.

I say the Australian was treated like a pariah, but not by Filipinos. They were as unfailingly affable to the Aussie toss-pot as they were to everyone else. Even in the midst of berserker violence, mob law and riot, there was a cheerful, wholesome courtesy to Philippine manners. People are so good-natured and obliging, it's sometimes all you can do to keep from strangling them.

Congenial atmosphere and sunny dispositions extended even into the most degenerate areas of the city's red-light district. A pretense of social as well as other kinds of intercourse was maintained. No sexual arrangements were concluded without the rudiments of flirtation. The young lady who took you upstairs was your "girlfriend," and she was going on a "date." You'd better not be making eyes at any of the other young ladies, either, or your girlfriend would get as jealous as any girlfriend—though on an hourly basis, of course.

It's heartbreaking—and terrifying—to think about all that now. This was 1986, the year before AIDS manifested itself in Manila. As of the election, only two or three cases had been diagnosed in the whole Philippine archipelago. Now hundreds of those Pilar Street women (and no few of their clients) must be dying. I say women, but most weren't twenty. They were very poor, very full of hopes and very beautiful with the undifferentiated beauty of extreme youth. The wages of sin have always been death, I guess, but the salary didn't used to be paid in cash.

This sad and desultory reminiscing, however, begs the question of whether there's any reason to read "400 Years in a Convent, 50 Years in a Whorehouse." Marcos is long gone. Cory Aquino is about to go. And so are the U.S. military and all its formerly vital, previously strategic interests in the area. Imelda is back, but as a sort of Saturday-morning-cartoon version of herself. Meanwhile the Philippine people are, as ever, put upon, shoeless and eating wind soup.

My article remains, I think, a fair portrait of Third World political turmoil. But it doesn't contain any answers. What makes a pleasant, decent and deeply religious society so corrupt and violent? How can a nation rich in resources, opportunities and willing, educated citizens stay amazingly poor? Why can't a new and honest government made up of intelligent people change these things? Let me say three words you've probably never heard from a journalist before: "I don't know."

I don't know the answers to those questions. And I don't know if there's any reason to dredge up this hoary wad of reportage. But I do think it behooves us to learn a little about the rest of the world even if we don't learn much. Americans are famous for international ignorance (pretty strange in a nation of immigrants, if you think about it). It's gotten us in trouble before.

There was a quiet period after the '86 election, while everyone waited for the votes to be miscounted. An ABC-TV producer friend of mine, Betsy West, and I decided to take the day off. Betsy had a car and a driver, and we traveled down into Laguna to a famous beauty spot called the Pagsanjan Falls. From the town of Pagsanjan we were taken in a dugout canoe up the river through the jungle to the waterfall itself. While good-natured boatmen poled us along, Betsy and I discussed the Philippine situation. Revolutionaries infested the hills, gangsters ran the government, street protests were growing, and out at Subic Bay and Clark Air Force Base, the American military stood ready. "It's like Vietnam," I said, although I'd never been to Vietnam.

"It's getting really tense, like Vietnam," said Betsy, although she had never been to Vietnam either.

"I wonder if we're getting into another Vietnam?" I said.

"It really could be like that, a Vietnam-type situation," said Betsy.

"It even *looks* like Vietnam," I said, gazing into the triple-canopy foliage along the riverbanks.

"You're right," said Betsy, "it *does* look like Vietnam."

"Oh, God," I said, "another Vietnam." And just as I said that, we rounded a bend in the river and there—all tattered papier-mâché and weathered plastic—was Kurtz's temple. Another Vietnam, indeed. We were boating through the *Apocalypse Now* set.

RS 471

APRIL 10TH, 1986

The day before the Philippine election, a Manila bartender tells me this one: President Marcos and General Ver find themselves in hell. General Ver is up to his neck in boiling tar. President Marcos is up to his knees. General Ver says: "Look, I've been your right-hand man for twenty years, and I've done some terrible stuff, but it's nothing compared to what you've done. How come you're only up to your knees?"

President Marcos says, "I'm standing on Imelda's shoulders."

A taxi driver tells me this one: Imelda and her kids, Irene, Imee and Bongbong (this is, no kidding, what Marcos' twenty-seven-year-old son, Ferdinand Jr., is called), are flying over the Philippines in their jet. Irene says: "Mommy, the Philippine people really hate us. Isn't there something we can do?"

"I've got an idea," says Bongbong. "We'll drop 10,000 packages out of the airplane. Each package will have 50 pesos in it. The people can buy rice and fish, and they'll love us."

"I've got a better idea," says Imee. "We'll only drop 5000 packages out of the airplane. But each package will have 100 pesos in it. The people can buy chicken and pork, and they'll love us even more."

"I've got the best idea," says Imelda. "We'll drop just one package out of the airplane, and the people will love us forever."

"What's in that package, Mom?" say the kids.

"Your father."

In Tondo, Manila's largest slum, I see a cigarette boy with a picture of President Marcos on the front of his vending tray. My companion, who speaks Tagalog, the local dialect, asks him, "Why do you have a picture of Marcos there?"

The boy runs his thumbnail across the president's profile and says, "I like to scratch his face off."

In a bar on Pilar Street, in the red-light district, some fellow journalists and I are surrounded by B-girls. Liquor cannot be served to Filipinos the night before an election, and the place is dead. A dozen smooth-skinned, peanut-butter-colored girls in tiny white bikinis are rubbing against us like kittens. Somebody orders them a round of five-dollar orange juices. In an attempt to somehow get this on my expense account, I ask, "Who are you going to vote for?" The girls make an L sign, thumb out, index finger up. It's the symbol of UNIDO/PDP-LABAN, the coalition backing Corazon Aquino.

My favorite B-girl, Jolly, who has the face of a pouty Hawaiian beauty queen and a body that could cause sins of commission at a hundred yards, takes a playful punch at my nose. "*Laban!*" she says. It means "struggle" in Tagalog. "I vote for Cory."

The other girls giggle. "She's not old enough to vote," says one.

"We're all for Cory," says another. "Even the *mama-sans* are for Cory." The *mama-sans* are the combination madams and bunny mothers of these establishments. They hire the girls, make sure you buy drinks and charge you a "bar fine" if you take anybody home.

I ask a *mama-san*, and she agrees. "Everybody here is for Cory. Only owners are for Marcos."

And I wouldn't be so sure about that. I visit an owner, an Aussie thug who runs one of the B-girl joints on Pilar Street. He's about forty, blond, thick chested, with mean blue eyes and an accent as broad as the space I'd give him if he were swinging a chair in a bar fight. His office is a windowless upstairs room. The desk is covered with thousands of pesos, bundled in rubber bands.

"The tourist trade has gone to hell," says the Aussie. "And it'll get worse with all the crap you reporters are turning out about the election. But something's got to be done for the Flips, doesn't it? They can only take so much, can't they? Now they'll be up in the hills with the New People's Army or some bloody thing."

Thugs, whores, cabbies, street Arabs, gin jockeys—these are by nature conservative folk. When you lose this bunch, your ass is oatmeal. You'd better pack your Dictator-model Vuitton bags and pray the U.S. Air Force will Baby Doc you someplace nice.

To think that they had an "election contest" in the Philippines is to get it all wrong. It was a national upchuck. It was everybody with sense or scruples versus everybody corrupt, frightened or mindlessly loyal.

Marcos, like any good crime boss, knew how to command loyalty. He co-opted the two traditional political parties and formed them into his own nonideological New Society party, the KBL. He declared martial law to avoid giving up office in 1972 and then changed the constitution so he could rule by decree and be reelected in perpetuity. He sent hit men after some of his enemies, jailed others and forced the rest into exile. Then he ruined the Philippine economy by granting monopolies on everything from sugar milling and copra processing to grain importing and by pumping oceans of government money into lame and corrupt corporations — a system known as crony capitalism.

According to *Newsweek*, American and Philippine economists estimate that Marcos and pals shipped as much as $20 billion out of the country. We're not talking about Michèle Duvalier's fur collection. Twenty billion dollars is more than half the Philippine gross national product, enough money to turn the archipelago into Hong Kong II. By comparison, total U.S. aid to the Philippines since independence in 1946 has been less than $4 billion.

Reporters who do duty in the third world spend a lot of time saying, "It's not that simple." We say, "It's not that simple about the Israelis and the PLO," or "It's not that simple about the *contras* and the Sandinistas." But in the Philippines it was that simple. It was simpler than that. Ferdinand Marcos is human sewage, an evil old power-addled flaming Glad Bag, a vicious lying dirtball who ought to have been dragged through the streets of Manila with his ears nailed to a truck bumper.

Manila: Pearl of the Orient

Spain owned the Philippines from 1521 to 1898, and America from 1898 to 1946. Pundits summarize this history as "400 years in a convent, 50 years in a whorehouse." Manila today looks like some Ancient Mariner who has lived through it all. The boulevards are tattered and grim and overhung with a dirty hairnet of electrical and phone wires. The standard-issue third-world concrete buildings are stained dead-meat gray by the emphysematous air pollution. Street lighting is haphazard. Ditto for street cleaning. The streets themselves are filled with great big holes. Fires seem to be frequent. Visits from the fire department, less so. There are numerous burned-out buildings. Every now and then you see what must have been charming Old Manila architecture — tin-roofed houses with upper stories that jut over the streets and windows boxed by trelliswork. Now these houses sag and flop. They don't seem to have been painted since the Japanese occupation. In fact, the first impression of Manila is of a defeated city, still occupied and exploited by some hostile force. Which has been more or less the case — Imelda Marcos was governor of the Metro Manila region for the past decade. You see her handiwork in occasional pieces of huge, brutish modernism rising uninvited from Manila's exhausted clutter. There is, for instance, the Cultural Center Complex, plopped on some landfill disfiguring Manila Bay. One of its buildings is the Manila Film Center, which Imelda rushed to completion in time for a 1982 international film festival. The story goes that the hurriedly poured concrete roof collapsed, burying forty or more workers in wet cement. No attempt was made to rescue them. This would have meant missing the deadline. The floor was laid over their corpses. Supposedly, Imelda later held an exorcism to get rid of the building's malevolent ghosts.

During the election, standard journalistic practice was to go to Forbes Park in the Manila suburbs, where Marcos' cronies were wallowing in money, then make a quick dash to the downtown slums — "Manila: City of Contrasts." My photographer, Tony Suau, was shooting a polo match in Forbes Park when one of the players trotted over between chukkers and said, "Going to Tondo next, huh?"

I visited one pretty rough place myself. It was occupied almost entirely by gang members, teenage boys with giant tattoos over their arms, legs, backs and I don't know where else. The gangs have names like Sigue-Sigue Sputnik and Bahala Na Gang. (*Sigue-sigue* means "go-go"; *bahala na* means "I don't care.") Members slash themselves on the chest to make ritual scars, one for every person they've killed. Each gang's turf is blocked off, with one or more kids guarding the entrance with clubs.

Actually, things were pretty clean around there. Nice vivid religious murals had been painted on the walls. Fishponds had been dug and vegetable gardens planted for the residents.

What I'm describing, however, is the Manila city jail. It's a relaxed place where friends and family come and visit all day. There are no cells, just long barracks where prisoners sleep on low wooden platforms. If they like, they can build their own tiny huts.

Hard to know what to say about a country where the only decent low-income housing is in the hoosegow.

The warden, a cheerful stomachy man, greeted me in his office while he pulled on his Adidas sweat pants. He was the only solid Marcos supporter I met. "What an open, free society to have such democratic debate," said the warden about the elections. I complimented him on his jail. He bought me a Sprite.

The real slums are another matter. The bad parts of Tondo are as bad as any place I've seen, ancient, filthy houses swarmed with the poor and stinking of sewage and trash. But there are worse parts — squatter areas where people live under cardboard, in shipping crates, behind tacked-up newspapers. Dad would march you straight to the basement with a hairbrush in his hand if he caught you keeping your hamster cage like this.

The world's a shocking poor place and probably always has been. I think I'm no hairless innocent about this. But the Philippines is an English-speaking nation with an eighty-nine-percent literacy rate. It has land, resources and an educated middle class. It has excellent access to American markets, and it's smack on the Pacific Rim, the only economic boom region in the world right now. It used to have one of the highest standards of living in Asia. There can't be any excuse for this.

And when you think you may actually get sick from what you've seen, you come to Smokey Mountain.

This is the main Manila trash dump, a vast fifty-foot hill of smoldering garbage, and in that garbage people are living—old people, pregnant women, little babies. There is a whole village of dirty hovels, of lean-tos and pieces of sheltering junk planted in the excrement and muck. These loathsome homes are so thickly placed I could barely make my way between them. The path in some places was not a foot wide, and I sank to my ankles in the filth.

People are eating the offal from this dung heap, drinking and washing in the rivulets of water that run through it. There are children with oozing sores, old people with ulcer-eaten eyes, crippled men lying in the waste. They live worse than carrion birds, pulling together bits of old plastic to sell. There's not much else of value in the rubbish. Not even the good garbage gets to these people.

In Smokey Mountain you don't feel disgust or nausea, just cold shock. I looked up and saw an immense whirlwind of detritus spiraling away from the dump's crest, something that would take a malnourished Dorothy off to the Dirt Oz.

I went back to the hotel and put on a pair of Bass Weejuns. I'd been told that Imelda wouldn't let anyone into the presidential palace in rubber-soled shoes. She is reputedly as crazy as a rat in a coffee can, and the statuary on the palace grounds bore that out. It looked like she had broken into a Mexican birdbath factory.

You got a whiff around Malacanang Palace that you were dealing with people a few bricks shy of a load. At the gate, there was intense inspection of footwear and pocket tape recorders. I had a borrowed press ID with Tony Suau's picture on it hanging around my neck. Tony and I look about as much alike as Moe and Curly, but this bothered the guards not at all.

The reception hall had obviously been decorated by a Las Vegas interior designer forced to lower his standards of taste at gunpoint. I mean, it had a parquet *ceiling*. There were red plush curtains and a red plush carpet and red plush upholstery on gold-leaf fake-bamboo chairs. The chandeliers were the size of parade floats, all wood, hand carved, and badly, too. And the air conditioning wasn't working.

It was the day after the election, and President Marcos was holding a press conference. It was completely uninteresting to see him in person. His puffy face was opaque. There was something of Nixon to his look, but not quite as nervous, and something of Mao, but not quite as dead. Marcos predicted how much he'd win by, which turned out to be how much he won by after his KBL-dominated legislature tallied the count. He blandly lied away, accusing the press of making things up and the other side of threats and cheating. One member of the press asked him about threats and cheating of his own. Said Marcos, "Why hasn't the opposition brought this to the attention of the authorities?" (Which were him.)

A reporter from the pro-Aquino *Manila Times* asked, "What will happen if there's no agreement about who won the election?"

"What do you think will happen?" said Marcos. For just a moment I thought that he wasn't making a threat, that he really didn't know.

I dozed in my fake-bamboo chair and was startled awake at the end of the session by Marcos saying, "When you see a nun touch a ballot box, that's an illegal act."

The stuff of nightmares, this country. And as every horror-movie director knows, it takes an element of the friendly and familiar to make a real nightmare. It has to be *Mom* eating snakes in the rec room.

In the Philippines, the element of the friendly and familiar is the Filipinos, remarkably nice people, cheerful, hospitable, unfailingly polite. Even the riot police and Marcos thugs were courteous when not actually terrorizing somebody. The gang members smile at you in jail. The dying smile at you in Smokey Mountain. When you ask a cab driver what the fare is, he says, "Ikaw ang bahala" ("It's up to you"). In the worst red-light dive the atmosphere is like a Rotary lunch.

There was an antiimperialist demonstration in front of our embassy. One of the protesters came up to Betsy West, an ABC-TV *Nightline* producer, and said, "If you could please wait five minutes, we'll burn the American flag."

Where were the guerrillas, the New People's Army, the question mark in Aquino's future, while all this was going on? Having Winter Carnival? Nobody seemed to know. I talked to Oswaldo Carbonell, Manila chairman of Bayan, the left-wing umbrella group with close ties to the NPA. Bayan and the NPA had urged a boycott of the election, but no one boycotted it. Now Oswaldo was leading a not very sizable demonstration by student radicals. "We welcome the NPA," he told me in one breath. "The Cory people are with us," he told me in another.

And while the communists were doing nothing, Marcos was doing too much.

Why did the old slyboots invite a congressional observer team, an international observer team and two battalions of newsmen to an election that was supposed to give him legitimacy and then cheat like a professional-wrestling villain? There he was; bent over, pants around his ankles, with his ass pressed against the window of public opinion.

And Marcos left behind a sizable body of crooks and collaborators armed to the teeth, with plenty of money. One thing the deposed president couldn't cram into the American transport planes was all the cats he'd fattened. Will the super-*tutas* sell their polo ponies to buy house trailers for the folks in Smokey Mountain? Will the thugs march off merrily to reeducation camps singing lewd parodies of "Bayan Ko"?

Then there's the economy. As far as I can figure, there's no one anywhere who knows anything about fixing a third-world economy. The last three underdeveloped nations to become relatively prosperous were Taiwan, South Korea and Singapore, and they all did it under hard-assed dictators like . . . well, sort of like Marcos.

Time for the Santo Niño. It's a small charm that's popular among the Philippine poor, a brass Baby Jesus with a hard-on. You wear it around your neck, and if you're in physical danger, you're supposed to put it in your mouth.

By Saturday, February 15th, eight days after the election, protest enthusiasm seemed to have ebbed. Cory Aquino hadn't been seen in public for two days. That night the Philippine National Assembly declared Marcos the winner. I rushed down to the palace for the riots, but there were none, just Bongbong and a BMW full of "junior cronies" driving none too steadily out the palace gate after the private victory party. In the back seat, the son of the Philippine ambassador to the Court of St. James was so blasted he was falling out of the car window.

An Aquino rally had been called for the next day. Cory supporters were to march to Rizal Park, in the center of Manila. I went out to one of the staging points in Quezon City, a middle-class suburb that is perhaps the most fervently anti-Marcos place in town. Only several hundred protesters were there at the appointed hour, milling around rather pointlessly. Eventually the crowd grew to about a thousand. The caskets of two murdered Aquino supporters were driven by, signaling the start of the march. (Carrying martyrs all over the place in their caskets is a big thing in the Philippines—sort of waving the bloody shirt and what's in it too.)

The marchers, chanting in a desultory way, began to move toward downtown Manila. By the time they'd gone a kilometer, the crowd had quintupled. In another kilometer, it had quintupled again. Only once, at the University of Santo Tomas, did I see a group join the march in an organized way. People just materialized. And all along the six-kilometer route, cheering crowds were hanging banners, flags, selves out of windows and throwing yellow confetti that they'd made by tearing up the Manila Yellow Pages.

By the time we reached Rizal Park—and it wasn't long because the marchers moved at a jog-trot—there were a half million people gathered around a ramshackle portable stage.

The crowd was squeezed even thicker than it had been at Baclaran church. I was with Tony and Betsy West from ABC. When people saw we were reporters, they somehow made way, moved where there was no room to move. "Foreign press!" they yelled. "Make way! Foreign press!"

We were handed through the mob, right to second row front on the center aisle.

The crowd chanted, "COR-EEE! COR-EEE!" in a fearful thunderous rumble that made your heart, lungs and liver swing like bell clappers in the rib cage. Then they began to sing. To hear half a million people sing "Bayan Ko" is . . . is like hearing half a million people sing anything. Even the theme song to *The Jetsons* would have been stirring.

Cory Aquino stepped to the microphones. The crowd was in the kind of frenzy, passion, rapture, transport, wild excitement or enthusiasm that sends a man to the thesaurus.

But did Cory give a rousing speech, calling for the head of Ferdinand Marcos and telling her countrymen, "Cry havoc, and let slip the dogs of war"?

She did no such thing. In her calm, high-pitched voice and best head-librarian manner she outlined a program of tame dissent. There'd be a national day of prayer, when people should take off work and go to church, she said. She asked the audience to boycott seven banks and certain other "crony corporations," including the San Miguel brewery. She asked them to delay paying their electric and water bills. And she requested a "noise barrage"—a traditional Philippine protest—each evening after she'd spoken to them over a church-owned AM station. "And you should experiment with other forms of nonviolent protest yourselves," she said, "and let us know how they work."

That was it. Keep your money in a sock. Don't drink beer. And bang garbage-can lids together when you listen to the radio. Betsy, Tony and I walked away scratching our heads. The crowd dispersed quietly.

Ten days later, they had the country.

Back in Black

DAVID FRICKE

IN THE LATE EIGHTIES, A GROUP OF YOUNG BLACK MU-
SICIANS FOUGHT FOR THEIR RIGHT TO ROCK. AND THE
CRITIC WAS ON HAND FOR THE NEXT BIG THING.

There is no greater joy in a rock critic's life than being able to say, "I told you so." The second greatest joy is being able to say, "You shoulda been there," to brag about those pivotal gigs and epiphanic nights that changed the music or at least fried your own circuits. The first night I saw Living Colour at CBGB, in New York, in mid-February 1987, I scored on both counts.

Of course, to any self-respecting critic living in New York, CBGB isn't just a club or a hangout. It's church, Our Lady of Feedback on the Bowery. It's where you go to be rebaptized in sweat and noise, to escape the suffocating pack mentality of the rock-press circus and to have your fan's instincts resharpened. The beers are cheap, and the thrill of discovery is always on tap. I've worshiped there regularly since I moved to New York in 1978.

Best known as the original House of Punk, where Television, the Ramones, Patti Smith and Talking Heads first declared war on rock's mid-Seventies sloth, CBGB has also endured as a dark, dank bowling-alley-shaped refuge for the young, the hungry and the scorned. For Living Colour, formed by guitarist Vernon Reid in 1985, CBGB wasn't just a regular gig. It was a sanctuary, a place for the band members to kick up their black-rock storm — resonant with the rainbow vitality and apocalyptic immediacy of Little Richard, Jimi Hendrix and Sly Stone — even while they were getting the bum's rush from record companies with pathetically short memories about where rock *really* comes from.

At CBGB on the night of February 16th, 1987, Reid, vocalist Corey Glover, drummer Will Calhoun and bassist Muzz Skillings laid out exactly where they thought rock was going and who was making delivery. It was also clear that they were not alone. The band was actually performing at the club as part of a two-day festival rich with young local black-rock and avant-soul talent and put together by the Black Rock Coalition, a New York-based collective co-founded by Reid for the same reasons that he'd started Living Colour: to put the color back in rock. I went to CBGB to check out the buzz on one band and walked into a full-scale mutiny.

I went home at 3:00 a.m. and transcribed my hastily scribbled notes. By the end of the week, I was interviewing Reid over a late breakfast of eggs, grits and superfine biscuits at a Harlem restaurant. My piece "Back in Black" was published in September and helped to sound the black-rock alarm in the great ROLLING STONE tradition of you-ain't-heard-'em-yet-but-you-will stories like our late-Sixties trumpeting of Johnny Winter and the MC5.

That, in the end, is what makes the rock-crit life worth living: the rapture of the chase, the glory of the score and the pleasure of seeing talent get its just reward. In a business that favors mediocrity and artistic expediency, the writing game isn't an art. It's war — pen-to-paper combat against complacency, hype and the crushing disappointment that always comes when you end up, after a long night on the tiles, with just another earful of crap. The best shows are not the ones that simply make you go home and spew superlatives; they're the ones that make you want to keep going out for more. My own paper trail is littered with more transcendent nights than one typewriter jockey rightly deserves.

Here are a few: the unsigned Patti Smith's stunning, opening set with her still-drummerless band at a suburban Philadelphia coffeehouse in 1974. Or the night in December 1978 that I stumbled (literally) down the steps of the Hope and Anchor, in London, a sweaty basement pub, to get bombed on the acid-flaked power pop of the Soft Boys and the band's gifted singer and songwriter, the future college-radio god Robyn Hitchcock. Or the spunky air-guitar celebration put on at the Lyceum, in London, in April 1980 by Def Leppard, a band of hard-rock pups from Sheffield, England, who sang a lot about America but had yet to set foot on it.

Revelation has often been just a subway ride away: the pre-*Chronic Town*

R.E.M. in high-twang gear at New York's Danceteria; New Order's emotionally charged performance at Hurrah's, only months after the band shed its original sound and name, Joy Division, in the wake of singer Ian Curtis's suicide; the dizzying early Eighties round of brilliant local debuts by the Dream Syndicate, the Minutemen, Hüsker Dü and the Violent Femmes.

I don't take any credit for the rock history and success stories that I've been party to; reveling in it all is groove enough. Which is why I was back at CBGB one ungodly humid night last July when Living Colour paid a not-so-secret visit to the club to test some new material on the faithful before going into the studio. Corey Glover, whose flailing shoulder-length braids had become an MTV fixture, showed up with short henna-dyed hair. The band's formidable new bassist, Doug Wimbish, a former member of the legendary Sugar Hill Records rhythm section, nailed the beat into the floor with explosive authority. As for the new tunes, it was a glorious ear-bleed evening of monster thrash, slam-dunk funk, snarling discontent and droll humor (chorus of the night: "Everybody loves you when you're bi").

You shoulda been there.

RS 509

SEPTEMBER 24TH, 1987

Michael Hill had given up. Ever since he'd seen Jimi Hendrix at the Fillmore East in the late Sixties, the Bronx-born guitarist had had a rock & roll dream—of plugging the blues into his amplifier and, like Jimi, sending it screaming into the future. Up in the Bronx, though, dreams like that don't often come true. Last year, Hill, by then in his thirties, was spinning his wheels and wasting his impressive chops on the covers circuit, playing local bars and weddings for a living.

Andre Anthony was no better off. For three years, the young guitarist and songwriter had led his own band, the Deed, confident that the world was hungry for an exciting new group that would fuse the dance-floor thump of funk with the bristling angularity of punk rock, the heady complexity of avant-jazz and the exhilarating slam of heavy metal. He knew it would work. He'd heard the applause and seen the smiling faces at the Deed's periodic club and college gigs in northern New Jersey. But by late 1985, all Anthony had to show for his faith was a shrinking gig sheet and universal rejection of the Deed's demo tapes by record companies. The music, they sniffed, wasn't "black enough."

Andre Anthony *is* black. So is Michael Hill. They also have a couple of other things in common. One is that they are members of the Black Rock Coalition, a New York organization devoted to combating racial stereotypes in the music business and creating a forum for undiscovered cutting-edge black talent. The other is that they were both recruited by another young black guitarist who quite literally changed their lives — Vernon Reid.

The Deed had only worked once in nine months when Andre Anthony happened to catch Reid and his group, Living Colour, at New York City's Village Gate. What he saw and heard blew his mind — a black rock & roll band whipping up a superstew of genuinely atomic funk that was equal parts hard-core punk, sledgehammer metal and Hendrixian soul, led by a guitarist who shared Anthony's own fondness for heady soloing and volcanic power chords. Somebody had done it! And he was getting paid for it! "I saw it all," Anthony says, "and loved it right away. I got Vernon's number, called him up and gave him a tape." Wowed by Anthony's demo, Reid begged him not to break up the Deed. Reid also invited him to a meeting of the Black Rock Coalition, of which he is the chairman and founder.

The BRC meeting was, for Anthony, as enlightening as the Village Gate show. Here was a roomful of other frustrated black musicians, rejected because they didn't conform to the record industry's established black-music molds — glitzy synthetic funk, gushy love ballads, copycat rap. But what impressed Anthony the most was that the members of the Black Rock Coalition believed that, united, they could do something about it.

"The moral support was quite significant," Anthony says of Reid's belief in the Deed and the solidarity he felt at that BRC meeting, "because that allowed me to go back and rehearse again with a purpose, to write a song with purpose. It allowed me to sing my lyrics with more conviction."

Michael Hill shares his euphoria. He had just scored a gig backing an experimental poet named Sekou Sundiata when he first met Reid, who had also played with Sundiata on occasion. Hill talked about his dream. Reid talked about the BRC and Living Colour, of his dreams coming true. "I finally saw the band at CBGB," Hill says. "There they were in an original music venue, a black band doing their own stuff entirely. That really motivated me. Seeing Vernon opened me up about what I could really do. I'd talk to him about playing, and he'd say, 'Yeah, but I want to see you playing your own music!'"

Today, Hill is doing just that. After seeing Living Colour, he went back to the Bronx and put together the Michael Hill Blues Band with his brother Kevin and four other pals. He is now determined to be the first black artist to make a platinum blues album.

Welcome to the exciting, ambitious, revolutionary, troubled but hopeful world of Vernon Reid and the Black Rock Coalition.

*   *   *

Reid knows all too well what Anthony and Hill have been through. He's heard the same jive from record companies over and over.

"People telling me, 'You gotta do something that's funky, you gotta play funk,'" he grumbles over lunch in a Harlem restaurant. "People telling me my music wasn't black enough. That was weird. Because I *am* a black person, aren't I? Where I'm coming from is black. I relate to music that way, as opposed to straightening my hair and going through all that thing. This *is* me."

In fact, Reid's understanding of the word "black" is quite different from what would appear to be the accepted definition within the American record industry—that is, the absence of color. In their eagerness to strike gold in the white-pop mainstream, major-label A&R squads have narrowed their sights on two particular types of black performers. One is the inoffensive balladeer or sex kitten peddling sweet nothings over vanilla funk and bedroom bounce arrangements (Luther Vandross, Gregory Abbott, Whitney Houston). The other is the tough-talking rapper who laces his street braggadocio with crossover doses of white-metal crunch and cartoon flamboyance (Run-D.M.C. and their descendants). There are notable if isolated exceptions: bluesman Robert Cray, soul thrush Anita Baker, guitarist Jon Butcher, the punk-funk band Fishbone. Other than that, there is almost nothing in-between. As Andre Anthony puts it, "You could either be Freddie Jackson or Jam Master Jay. And that feels weird to someone who grew up listening not only to Hendrix and the Ohio Players but Ginger Baker and Eric Clapton."

Prince, Reid claims, is the exception that actually proves the rule. "He's played up the quasi-mulatto angle," says Reid, "which I have a problem with. 'I'm not black, I'm not white, that's why everyone can relate to me.' Why should you have to be that for people to relate to you? If you say something truthful, it'll connect anyway.

"A lot of people say, 'What are you complaining about? Talking Heads has all these black members. Sting's band has a lot of black people in it.' But essentially, these people are employees. It's really good that good musicians are getting work. But even though what Sting did was pretty nervy for him, those guys in his band were still in the background. I don't want to be the guy who is brought into add some funk to the proceedings, to add some soul to the mix."

It was that refusal to be just another ghost in the chart machine that led Reid to start the Black Rock Coalition. "At first, I didn't think of this grouping as an organization," he says, "I was thinking of it as just getting together to compare notes. 'Hey, we're all dealing with this stuff. Let's talk about it.'"

There was a lot to talk about. There still is. No one in his right mind can deny that rock & roll is a product of the black experience in America. Its roots are found in the oppressive sorrow and poetic defiance of the blues, in the spiritual release and eternal hope of gospel, in the sexual frenzy and poignant-heart plays of rhythm and blues.

Vernon Reid and Living Colour, together with the twenty other bands and sixty individual performers and nonmusicians that make up the Black Rock Coalition, are only reclaiming what is already theirs. "Rock and roll is black music and we are its heirs," states the Black Rock Coalition manifesto, drawn up in the fall of 1985 by Reid and Greg Tate, a prominent critic for the weekly New York newspaper the *Village Voice* and a founding father of the BRC. "We too claim the right of creative freedom and total access to American and International airwaves, audiences and markets." Reid and the BRC, in other words, are fighting for nothing less than the right to rock.

That determination fuels every number in the Living Colour repertoire. Not long ago, at a downtown Manhattan club called Tramps, Reid and Living Colour wasted a roomful of rockers with their frenzied fusion of jackhammer punk, AOR hooks and booty-bouncing R&B. One minute, Reid was ripping up a Prince-like gasser called "What's Your Favorite Color?" with switch-blade chording and orgasmic feedback screams. The next, bassist Muzz Skillings and drummer Will Calhoun were deftly negotiating the hyperfunk changes of "Desperate People" with soulful aplomb.

The audience, mostly white collegians, probably didn't appreciate the irony of singing along with Living Colour's powerhouse vocalist Corey Glover during "Which Way to America?," an aggressive demand by a young black man for his piece of prosperity pie ("I look at the TV/Your America's doin' well/I look out my window/My America's catchin' hell/I just wanta know/Which way do I go/To get to your America"). But the standing ovation that followed was proof enough that the audience liked what it heard—and wanted more.

In the beginning, the problem facing the BRC wasn't how to put this music in America's face; rather, it was how to make non-mainstream black acts realize that, in spite of industry prejudice, chiseling club owners and radio indifference, they still had a future in music. If they couldn't penetrate the white-rock network, hell, they could start their own.

The first order of business at the inaugural meeting of the BRC, held in September 1985, was to lick wounds. "The key word was frustration," says Greg Tate, who attended that first session. But Tate notes that as the weekly BRC meetings progressed and attendance grew, "the mood of the meeting became more dominated by a sense of community, that we all shared a cultural history. We had all come of age in the Seventies, what we describe as the first black-rock movement—Mandrill, Funkadelic, the

Ohio Players. It was a generation that had a lot of the political and cultural ideas but had also been exposed to American pop culture."

One stumbling block was finding a name for the organization. "We thought of the Black Rock Collective, but we thought it sounded too communist," Reid says with a laugh. "There was a big argument about whether or not to use the term 'rock,' to just use 'music.' I said that 'black music' was too all-encompassing. We needed an image that would make people sit up, to upset them. Some people refused to join because it was called 'black rock,' not 'black music.' "

Guitarist Ronnie Drayton, a veteran of road and studio work with the Chambers Brothers, Wilson Pickett and Nona Hendryx, was one artist who declined, although for a much different reason. He treasured his independence. "When I was younger," he says, "I was in the Black Panther party. I've already evolved through that. I felt I could say more and do more as a black rock & roll guitar player working all sides of the marketplace."

Nevertheless, Drayton is one of a number of sympathetic outsiders who have not officially joined the coalition but have participated in BRC-sponsored concerts and seminars. Vernon and Greg, Drayton says, are "the spokesmen. But if I can come to a gig and play a few high harmonics that might pull a few more people in, that's okay for me."

To date, precious little BRC music has been available on records. But thanks to rave word-of-mouth reviews on the New York club circuit and the unexpected patronage of Mick Jagger—who was so knocked out by a Reid gig at CBGB that he paid for and produced two demos for the band—Living Colour became the subject of intense record-company negotiations this summer. As this story went to press, the group was about to ink with Epic Records, becoming the first coalition band to get a major-label deal.

The hopes, wishes and fears of the BRC go with them.

To some people in New York music circles, Vernon Reid isn't just a prominent member of the Black Rock Coalition—he is its very heart and soul. This judgment is true to some extent. Without question, Living Colour is the BRC's flagship band, the symbol not only of what the coalition stands for but of what its members hope to achieve in their careers. And Reid is the BRC's most persuasive salesman. When other musicians approach Ronnie Drayton for information on the coalition, he sends them straight to Reid. "'Cause if he can't sell you, nobody can," says Drayton. "He's a great salesman. I think he's got some kind of used car dealership somewhere."

As both a musician and music fan, Reid is a direct product of the black music heritage that the Black Rock Coalition is trying to preserve. His musical history is basically the history of black rock in microcosm. And in black rock, all roads eventually lead to Jimi Hendrix. Almost two decades after Hendrix's death, the legacy of rock's first superstar black guitarist still towers over Reid and his generation. Hendrix's reinvention of the electric guitar over a big rock beat, his dramatic lyric expansion of old blues themes and charismatic stage presence opened new vistas of musical and theatrical possibility for black pop acts like War, the Ohio Players, the Isley Brothers and George Clinton and his two-prong rhythm army, Parliament-Funkadelic.

By playing with white musicians, Jimi Hendrix also set a dramatic example of how integrated rock & roll could be. So did Sly Stone and his interracial Family Stone. The combined strengths of black R&B muscle and white rock experimentation had a lasting impact on the young black generation that would eventually come to form the Black Rock Coalition. "Rock is not a foreign thing for me and a lot of black musicians in my generation," says Reid. "It's what we grew up with. I grew up thinking and feeling music that way."

Born in London in 1958, of West Indian parents, Reid was raised in Brooklyn with the sound of music all around him—Sarah Vaughan and Xavier Cugat records, seminal calypso sides by the Mighty Sparrow and Lord Kitchener, hits by Elvis Presley and the Dave Clark Five. "My mother has every James Brown single," Reid says proudly, "all of them!"

Hendrix, of course, melted Reid's mind. "He'd do a thing with the feedback that sounded like voices crying," says Reid, "and then he'd hit the springs on the back of the guitar so it sounded like a big clock. That got to me." But Reid learned to make his own guitar talk that way only after long, diligent study. Bowled over by Led Zeppelin, he backtracked to the blues, joined a hardcore soul band when he was seventeen ("to get my funk thing together") and then took a sharp left into serious jazz, absorbing technique as well as musical ideas from horn players like John Coltrane, Ornette Coleman and Eric Dolphy. Reid's growing command of jazz forms and his ability to jam in almost any genre led in 1979 to his first major pro gig, with Ronald Shannon Jackson and the Decoding Society; he eventually recorded six critically acclaimed albums with them. In 1985, he formed Living Colour.

Vernon Reid realizes that as the founder and leader of the Black Rock Coalition as well as its most publicly outspoken member, he jeopardized Living Colour's future from time to time, putting music-industry people on their guard at the same time he was pursuing a record deal and trying to get gigs. But he insists there is a big difference between demanding equal opportunity and calling some A&R guy a racist motherfucker. "What people have to realize about me is that I'm not out to bait them," says Reid. "I'm looking for an honest shot. I'm not trying to bust people's balls. But this is about my life. And it's not just about my life. It's about the lives of a lot of black people, people that those radio guys don't know about.

"On a certain level, I want to reassure people that I ain't no Mau Mau. But I ain't gonna punk out. I'm not gonna smile and grin in people's faces. Because that's what we've been doing all along. We've been nice and friendly, and people then feel there's no problem—'We can go on doing what we've always done. The formulas are set, everything is cool.'

"Everything is not cool."

Nevertheless, the Black Rock Coalition has struck a major nerve, and not just in New York. After reading about the coalition in *Billboard* magazine, ex-Prince guitarist Dez Dickerson—frustrated in his own attempts to start a solo career—became a card-carrying member. The organization has also been receiving letters from young black musicians asking how they can start a BRC in their own town. The impetus to start an organization like the Black Rock Coalition may have been greatest in New York, the capital of the U.S. record industry, but the resentment and indignation of black musicians is universal.

"This is a creative crisis," Reid says, "not in terms of people being creative, but in being heard. Who knows what we could have if we let these people be heard? We don't know what kind of future we're cheating ourselves out of."

False Messiah

LAWRENCE WRIGHT

WHEN JIMMY SWAGGART WAS CAUGHT WITH A PROSTI-
TUTE, IT WAS JUST ANOTHER LOST BATTLE IN HIS LIFE-
LONG STRUGGLE TO SAVE HIS SOUL.

When I drove into Baton Rouge on Easter morning in 1988, joining the press mob that was already camped in the Sheraton, I enjoyed two advantages that would help me understand this story. The first was that I was pre-pared to believe what Jimmy Swaggart said about himself.

As is the case with most such events, there was already an accepted wisdom that would guarantee that nearly every article published on the Swaggart affair would take the same line: He was just another comic-opera evangelist playing out a farce in the swamps. At that level, there was nothing electric about this story. But what interested me about Swag-gart from the beginning was that essentially he appeared to be telling the truth. Yes, he was hedging about the details—he would admit only to the single episode of depravity, when his rival Marvin Gorman captured him on film with a prostitute named Debra Murphree. He was still hiding all those earlier occasions when he had wandered down to New Orleans in his Lincoln to pick up women, and one knew that because he was not ready to let go of his secret self, he would sin again. Nonetheless, he had stood in the pulpit bawling and begging forgiveness, confessing his sinfulness. He had even admitted to the elders of his denomination that he had been a sexual pervert since the age of ten. These were mighty admissions to make in any age, but especially so at a time when TV evangelists were making themselves synonymous with sanctimonious sleaze. Suppose, then, that this man had also been telling the truth when he said that he alone was divinely inspired to evangelize humanity. How else could one account for the fact that in just a few brief years Swaggart's broadcasts had covered the globe and that through his vast network of cable and satellite feeds he had become, however briefly, the most visible man in the world? Consider the possibility that Swaggart really did believe he was infested with demons. From the beginning, I had the sense that there was a larger story. That was the story Swaggart himself was telling us: It was the titanic struggle for his soul.

The second advantage I enjoyed was that I was representing ROLLING STONE. It is a peculiar passport to carry: One is expected to be unexpected. ROLLING STONE has made its reputation by approaching stories from odd angles. One might fairly say that its writers made the magazine what it is. I had grown up reading Joe Eszterhas, Tim Cahill, Jonathan Cott, Thomas Powers, Chet Flippo, Hunter S. Thompson, Timothy Crouse—to name a few of those literary hellcats who brushed aside journalistic conventions and social taboos to get at new ways of telling the truth. Back in its early days, the whole point of ROLLING STONE was to let a new generation talk to itself in its own language. It was a forum not just for the rock & roll generation, but for the Vietnam generation, the drug generation, the sexual-freedom and women's-liberation generation. These were powerful social currents, and although other magazines were standing on the banks observing the changes, ROLLING STONE was in the flow. It was a part of the experimentation. Although the journalism it practiced was sometimes inflammatory, hallucinatory and even chaotic, it was also surprising and real and often truer than the detached, sophisticated voices one heard elsewhere.

When I first began writing for the magazine, in 1985, it was already approaching its third decade, and by then it had become enough of an institution that it had begun to shape its writers as well as vice versa. One accepts a ROLLING STONE assignment knowing that not only must it be the final word on a subject; it must be freshly seen and powerfully told. The magazine presents the writer with a challenge to exceed himself, to break the shell of the story he might have written for another publication and invent a new way of telling it. In the first piece I wrote for the magazine, about the death of writer (and former ROLLING STONE contributor) Richard Brautigan, I told the story from the vantage of Brautigan's ghost. That sort of narrative inventiveness is rarely invited in other magazines.

There are some stories that the writer understands immediately to be a "perfect ROLLING STONE story." I don't know that the elements have ever been formally stated, but as I understand them, they include generational struggle, a clash between individuals and established institutions, an appreciation of the bizarre and the outré and—this is the secret ingredient, the cayenne that spices the mix—moral conflict. Every great ROLLING STONE story has these elements. It helps if there is a single compelling character riding outside the boundaries of convention who is passionately engaged in the question of how to live in our time. In every respect, I knew that Jimmy Swaggart's downfall was a perfect ROLLING STONE story the moment I entered Baton Rouge.

There was the immediate problem of access. Swaggart was refusing all interviews. It was unlikely that he would make an exception for me; after all, he had personally waged a campaign against rock magazines, which he saw as one of the devil's tools. (This was despite his boast that "my family invented rock & roll"—a reference to his cousin Jerry Lee Lewis.) After being stonewalled by his attorney and his publicist, I was determined that Swaggart should at least have the opportunity to tell me face to face that he wouldn't talk. After one of his services, I noticed that hundreds of his parishioners were lined up to receive his blessing. This involved hugging him and then stuffing money into the pockets of his suit. I got in line. When my turn came, Swaggart put his big arms around me and pulled me close. "God bless you," he said. I whispered in his ear, "I'm from ROLLING STONE." "ROLLING STONE—my Lord!" he cried. He jumped back as if he had stuck his toe in an electric socket. I left the podium. The next person in line was Marvin Gorman's private investigator, who stuck a subpoena in Swaggart's pocket.

I left Baton Rouge and drove north to Ferriday, Louisiana, Swaggart's hometown—and that of his cousins Jerry Lee Lewis and Mickey Gilley, the country singer. This part of Louisiana is copiously supplied with Swaggart's kin and childhood friends. It is also haunted by the stark fundamentalism that would shape Swaggart's view of himself and the world. The cousins had grown up spiritually hypnotized by their mothers; Swaggart and Lewis had been marked at an early age by their allegiance, respectively, to God and to Satan; both cousins would follow opposing spiritual paths, although in earthly terms their destinies were similar: fame, fortune and catastrophe. This was a parable involving good and evil, salvation and damnation, the judgment of God. That, at least, was how these men saw the struggle of their lives. My challenge was to write the article in a way that told the story from Swaggart's perspective as well as my own.

In this, I was aided immensely by my editor, Robert Vare. Writers always get the credit, but the truth is that every article is a collaboration.

The editor, however, is often caught between loyalty to his writer and the constraints of the magazine—for instance, the limitations of space, the boundaries of what it deems acceptable taste, the demands of the art department. These considerations factor into every story, and it is up to the editor to balance them wisely and considerably. When he gets a story he really believes in, he often has to become its advocate; he has to fight for space against other competing and worthy interests. Robert was a world-class campaigner.

The editor's main function, however, is to milk the best possible story out of his writer. For the Swaggart piece, this involved literally entire days of telephone conversations. In the meantime, the copy editor is scouring the piece for grammatical problems, the fact checker is calling sources to corroborate the assertions the writer has made, and the art director is overseeing the graphics to go with the piece. This, of course, is a common process that one finds at most serious magazines. The difference at ROLL-ING STONE is that there is one last hurdle. It's called "getting it by Jann."

I don't live or work in New York, so this last bit of business has always been a mystery to me, although from the tone of the editors I've talked to over the years, I gather it's just as enigmatic for them. There is a Vati-canesque air of puzzlement and acceptance that decisions that might seem arbitrary are somehow—if not infallible—probably right. The magazine is still, after all this time, an expression of Jann Wenner's intuitive judg-ments about the culture we live in. When, after the Swaggart story came out, I said that I wanted to write a series on religious figures, no one thought we could get it by Jann. He surprised all of us by endorsing the project enthusiastically. The series, "True Believers," went on to include profiles on Will Campbell, Anton LaVey and Father Matthew Fox.

As we revisit Swaggart in 1992, his empire is collapsing under the weight of a second public scandal. When he was ticketed in California last October for driving violations, he was in the company of another prosti-tute. He took a leave from his ministry. He had been booted off the air in all but a few cable markets in any case. His Bible college, which has lost nearly all of its enrollment and most of its staff, has dropped his name. His personal fortunes have been sinking since Gorman won a $6.4 million judgment against him. The Jimmy Swaggart saga is in its final act. We told the story of how his tragedy began.

RS 530/531

JULY 14TH–28TH, 1988

Some of the reasons that Jimmy Swaggart would destroy himself may be found in Ferriday, Louisiana—"my beleaguered little town," he would call the place of his birth, ten miles from Natchez across the Mis-sissippi River Bridge. It has been rather routinely described by passing journalists as a "typical" Southern crossroads town—an adjective weighed by the natives with a sense of disbelief, for even in the Deep South, Ferriday has the reputation of being one of the darker and more Gothic pockets of humanity.

Here Swaggart grew up with his cousins Jerry Lee Lewis and Mickey Gilley—all of them were born within a year of one another in the mid-1930s. Back then the town was run by their uncle Lee Calhoun, a "vile, vulgar, profane old man," as Jimmy later described him, whose name was carried forward by both Jerry Lee and Jimmy Lee. Although Uncle Lee made his fortune from bootlegging and cattle rustling, he seemed to float eerily above the world of law and consequence. "He was well respected in the community," Jimmy writes in his autobiography. *To Cross a River* (co-written by Robert Paul Lamb). "He never seemed to have the problems all my other relatives had. His house was constantly full of people looking for money, politicians asking for favors, and preachers hoping for some kind of contribution." Lee Calhoun's example would powerfully affect his namesakes.

In 1936, a woman called Mother Sumrall and her daughter Leona wandered into Ferriday from Laurel, Mississippi. They went around the village knocking on doors and inviting people to attend their "church"—an overgrown vacant lot with benches and chairs set among the weeds. Eventually they erected a tent in that lot, which was across the street from the Community Hall, where Sun Swaggart and his wife, Minnie Bell, would play community dances, he on the fiddle and she on the rhythm guitar. In that same hall, Sun's amateur boxing career had come to a sudden halt one night when a professional slugger separated him from consciousness. But by then he had raised enough money to own a small gas station a block away, on the main highway. He had been to church only one time in his life, for a Catholic funeral, but as he sat in his gas station, the music from Mother Sumrall's tent came tugging at him. One night Sun and Minnie Bell picked up their instruments, and the Swaggart family entered the Assemblies of God.

That night they became a part of a religious movement that already was profoundly changing the country and much of the world. It was the great Pentecostal revival, which began in Topeka, Kansas, on New Year's Eve 1900, when a young Bible student named Agnes Ozman prayed aloud in a language she had never heard before. Some syllables were later identified as Chinese, and for the next three days she was unable to communicate in any other language. Soon other students began speaking in tongues; their words were variously identified as French, German, Swedish, Czech, Japanese, Hungarian—twenty-one languages were counted.

Derided as Holy Rollers, the Pentecostals nonetheless represented a powerful and growing counterforce to scientific thinking and the belief in social progress that had taken over the cities and universities. The Pentecostals lived in a world of miracles. They saw science turned on its head by the triumph of faith. Science, for its part, looked upon Pentecostalism as a kind of mass psychosis. Linguists who studied these prayer languages easily showed that they were not French or Japanese, as the speaker might claim, but a "façade of a language" like Sid Caesar's French or the Japanese of John Belushi's samurai tailor. Linguists admitted, however, that the sounds were not gibberish; they had the shape and form and sound of languages, and other Pentecostals who heard the sounds could interpret them and agree upon their meaning.

The Assemblies of God was one of the several Pentecostal denominations to come out of the Azusa Street revival. Founded in Hot Springs, Arkansas, in 1914, the Assemblies would become the fastest-growing denomination in America, at a time when mainstream Protestant churches were in decline. Its roots were in the rural congregations like the little white church in Ferriday that was built on Mother Sumrall's lot and paid for by that old reprobate Lee Calhoun.

It was in this church that the Swaggarts, the Lewises and the Gilleys all came to find God. The women were particularly fervent. Mamie Lewis and Irene Gilley and Jimmy's grandmother Ada Swaggart would all become evangelists, as would Jimmy's father. The boys, Jimmy, Jerry and Mickey, were in the same Sunday-school class, which was taught by Sun Swaggart, and they each cut their names into the pew in the back of the church. Jimmy enjoyed the Bible stories. "David and Goliath was my favorite. Many times I sat pretending it was me hitting the giant with the rock."

Minnie Bell Swaggart had been saved for about a year when she began praying for her son. Jimmy preferred to spend his time with Jerry and Mickey, going to see Hopalong Cassidy or Johnny Mack Brown movies at the Arcade Theatre. "You really shouldn't go," his mother would tell him. She herself had given up going to movies when she became a Christian. Jimmy went anyway. He was standing in line to buy a ticket when "an entreating voice suddenly spoke to me. 'Do not go in this place. Give your heart to me. I have chosen you a vessel to be used in my service.'" Jimmy began to cry. He was eight years old.

Still, he resisted the call. Once during a revival, both Irene Gilley and Mamie Lewis fell to the ground and began speaking in tongues. These demonstrations alarmed Minnie Bell. "This shouting and hollering is ridiculous. I'll never do it." But the Spirit seized her during that revival. Jimmy had not gone to the meeting that day; he was playing with Jerry Lee and some other boys several blocks from the church when they all heard someone shouting at the top of her lungs. "A dread swept over my heart," Jimmy writes. "I knew it was my mother." He ran home in shame.

But that summer the Spirit came over him too. A woman came from Houston to preach. "The last night of the services something finally released within me," Swaggart writes. "Kneeling at the altar, praying as usual, I became aware of what seemed to be a brilliant shaft of light descending from heaven and focusing on me. Moments later I was speaking in tongues.

"For days afterwards, I spoke very little English."

Jerry Lee and Jimmy were closer than brothers. "At times it seemed as if we were twins," Jimmy notes, and indeed their lives would be intertwined in complex ways. It was almost as if they were opposing halves of a single person, neither of them complete by himself. Jimmy was fiercely shy; Jerry was hilariously boisterous. Jimmy was afraid of girls; Jerry was a teenage Casanova. Jimmy was a frugal, sanctimonious teacher's pet; Jerry was a profligate, untamed hellion. Anyone in Ferriday could assemble a list of such personality traits, marking Jimmy at one extreme and Jerry at the other. The only characteristics they had in common were an intense competitiveness with each other, a boiling need to get out of Ferriday and a tendency, as the world would see later, to live symbolic lives.

Each was fanatically devoted to his mother, and perhaps this would affect the twisted relationships with women that awaited the boys when they would become men. "These boys were mama's babies," says Frankie Jean, who lives in the five-bedroom brick house in Ferriday that once belonged to Lee Calhoun and then to Elmo and Mamie Lewis. The house has been carefully preserved, at her brother's insistence. "Jerry didn't even want me to put a microwave in the kitchen," says Frankie Jean. "He won't let me vacuum in her old bedroom because it's got her heel prints in the carpet."

In their ninth year, the lives of each boy would be forever changed. During Christmas, Jerry Lee sat at the piano in Lee Calhoun's parlor and picked out "Silent Night," mostly on the black keys. Jimmy and Mickey would also play their first notes on that piano—a small historical oddity, since the three cousins would one day rise to separate peaks of musical prominence in rock & roll, gospel and country music. Jerry Lee must have made an impression, because three months later his father mortgaged his house for $900 and bought him a used Stark upright. Eventually the bank foreclosed on the house, but Jerry Lee kept the piano—by then he had worn the ivory off the keys. His musical training ended after four piano lessons when his teacher slapped him across the face. The rest of his education came from Haney's Big House, a black nightclub Jerry and Jimmy would slip into on Friday and Saturday nights to hear B.B. King and Muddy Waters and a local piano player named Old Sam play the devil's music.

Jimmy was drawn to the piano as well. He had been moved by the performance of Brother Cecil Janway, a traveling evangelist who came through Ferriday and lifted the roof off the little frame church with his righteous piano style. Jimmy sat as close as he could to Brother Janway, and while he watched, he prayed aloud. "Lord, I want you to give me the gift of playing the piano," he said again and again, sometimes so loudly his father punched him. "If you give me this talent, I will never use it in the world. . . . I will always use the talent for your glory. If I ever go back on my promise, you can paralyze my fingers!" As soon as brother Janway stepped away, Jimmy walked directly to the piano and began to pick out chords.

"Jimmy wasn't very talented," Frankie Jean says, "but he prayed all day and night for that talent, and it came to him. I was about as shocked as the rest of them. I thought the days of miracles were behind us."

That summer, in 1944, Mickey's mother held prayer meetings in her home above the pool hall. The war raging in Europe and the Pacific seemed far, far away, but it grew closer when little Jimmy Swaggart began to prophesy in tongues. According to his father, Jimmy spoke for five days in German and Japanese (the languages were verified by war veterans who were drawn to the meetings) and then gave his own interpretations in English. His father says, "It would make cool chills run up and down your spine, because he's speakin' in the supernatural; he wasn't speakin' like just an ordinary person. He was a child in third grade, y'see, and yet he spoke as a college graduate."

"I didn't know what was happening," Jimmy writes in his autobiography. "I felt like I was standing outside my body. Then I began to describe exactly what I saw '. . . a powerful bomb destroying an entire city . . . tall buildings crumbling . . . people screaming.' "

Each day more prophecies poured forth. The crowds that gathered to hear this entranced, flaxen-haired child grew larger and forced the meetings to be held in the church. "Many outsiders, wandering into the little church on Texas Street, were saved after hearing the prophecies," Swaggart writes. "Some dismissed the whole matter because I was only nine years old. But a year later, when the two Japanese cities of Hiroshima and Nagasaki were destroyed, nobody thought the prophecies were childish any more."

Despite this potent evidence that God's hand was on him, Jimmy resisted the call; instead, he turned to crime. He and Jerry Lee began to break into local stores. "It was a lark to us," Jimmy writes. "We even stole some scrap iron from Uncle Lee's own back yard and sold it back to him." Jimmy's only interests then were playing the piano and boxing— his ambition was to become the heavyweight champion of the world. Already he sensed inside himself some raw force that could dominate the world of men. The only opponent he couldn't conquer was God.

"I no longer considered myself a Christian," he has said of this period. He and Jerry Lee worked up a stage act, where Jimmy played the bass line on the piano and Jerry played the treble, and together they swept talent contests around the state. One night each played separately, and Jimmy began a romping version of "Drinkin' Wine Spo-dee-o-dee," one of Old Sam's numbers at Haney's Big House. "A strange feeling came over me," Jimmy writes. "I was able to do runs on the piano I hadn't been able to do before. It seemed like a force beyond me had gripped me. My fingers literally flew over the keys." The crowd in the auditorium stomped and cheered. "For the first time in my life, I sensed what it felt like to be anointed by the Devil." Remembering his promise to the Lord never to play for the world, Jimmy felt a sudden rush of fear.

At this juncture in their lives, in their early teens, the future careers of Jimmy and Jerry Lee might have changed places. Each saw the choices of life as being all good or all bad. The roads out of Ferriday led only to good or evil, toward God or toward Satan, and each boy was standing at the crossroads. At the age of fifteen, Jerry Lee got a job playing the piano in the notorious Blue Cat Club, in Natchez, "the meanest, lowest-down, fightin'-and-killingest place in the world," he said later, but on Sundays he was preaching in Ferriday. When he was sixteen, he married the first of his six wives, a preacher's daughter named Dorothy Barton, and dropped out of school. Uncle Lee paid to send Jerry Lee to a Pentecostal Bible college in Waxahatchie, Texas, but he lasted only three months before he got kicked out for playing a boogie version of "My God Is Real" during chapel. He came home and started preaching at the church on Texas Street.

Jimmy would remember this period as "the darkest time of my life. God had called me to preach, but as the world drew me, I wanted less and less to obey Him." One day, to Jimmy's horror, his father declared that he was giving up his successful grocery business to go into the ministry full time, along with his wife. Jimmy began to cry and plead for them not to do it. For the first time in the history of the Swaggart family, they had become financially comfortable. Now all that was being thrown away in the pursuit of a pulpit in a little Holy Roller church in the dismal neighboring town of Wisner. Jimmy was profoundly ashamed. "For years after that," he writes, "when I had to fill out a school form listing my parents' occupation, I left it blank." Whenever his father and mother and sister Jeanette went to preach revivals in the little towns around Ferriday, Sun would ask Jimmy to come along. "We need you on the piano," his father said, but Jimmy refused. Jerry Lee went instead.

There is a pattern here. God calls, Jimmy resists. As why should he not? God wanted his soul, but Jimmy wanted his identity. His mother had told him repeatedly that he was going "to walk with God," that he would be "perfect." His cousins thought he was close to perfection already. "Jimmy to us was like Jesus walking on the face of the earth again," Mickey Gilley would say years later, after the scandal broke. To be perfect, to be Jesus, was a role Jimmy wasn't quite ready to play. Later, when he was a middle-aged man trapped inside this holy persona and God was making one dramatic demand upon him after another, what was left of the real Jimmy would conspire to break free. It was no accident that the route of his escape was through women.

Women became spiritual metaphors for his relationship with God. They were holy vessels of God's love, and the holiest vessel of all was Minnie Bell Swaggart. It was she who had led Jimmy to Jesus, and Jimmy's estrangement from his mother made him feel his separation from God most acutely. Minnie Bell and Sun would be off preaching out of town and would come home late at night, then she would slip into Jimmy's room. "I would not open my eyes when she kissed me on the cheek," Jimmy writes, "but after she left, I would remember the prayer she whispered over me. Many nights I would lay awake for hours, crying."

Other nights this haunted child would awaken "in the wee, still hours of the morning. The house would be quiet, and I would not hear a sound. I would suddenly be assailed with a terrifying thought: 'Jesus has come, everyone is gone, *and I'm left!*' "

Where had everyone gone? They had been raptured. They had risen to meet Christ in the clouds of heaven. Those who were left behind, the unsaved, would, according to the Book of Revelation, endure the seven years of the Great Tribulation, a period marked by the appearance of that dark figure of prophecy, the Antichrist. This was the very core of Jimmy's belief. "When I was a boy," he writes in *Armageddon: The Future of Planet Earth*, "every other sermon that was preached from behind our pulpits was based on the rapture. We were continually cautioned to be *ready*. Jesus was coming at any minute."

Had he come and left Jimmy behind? "More than once, I slipped out of bed and crept to my parents' bedroom door. There I would kneel and put my ear to their door in the hope that I would hear my mother breathing or, as she would so often do in her sleep, say the name of Jesus out loud. . . . I knew if I could hear them, the rapture had not as yet taken place—and there would still be a chance for me."

At the age of seventeen, Jimmy followed Jerry's lead and dropped out of high school, then married Frances Anderson, a pretty girl with dark hair and a crafty face who sang in the choir in Sun's church. "She was fourteen," Frankie Jean says. ("She was fifteen," Swaggart has said, "and not pregnant.")

"I couldn't believe Jimmy made the fatal step," Frankie adds. "Of course, I had gotten married myself when I was twelve. We're all kind of earthy, to say the least." Until he met Frances, Jimmy had never expressed interest in girls. Thirty-five years later he was still describing her as "the only woman I ever kissed."

Through Frances, Jimmy found the Spirit once again. He began preaching on street corners. Once when he was sermonizing in Ferriday, he spotted Mickey and Jerry Lee standing in the back of the crowd, with tears streaming down their faces. "I wish I had the guts to do that," Mickey told him. Jerry Lee said, "Jim, I just want you to know, me and Mickey are going out and hit the big time — and help support you in the ministry."

That was a prophecy that would soon come to pass. In 1954 another young communicant of the Assemblies of God, a nineteen-year-old truck driver from East Tupelo, Mississippi, named Elvis Presley, cut a record titled "That's All Right," and the age of rock & roll was born. Soon after that, Jerry Lee's dad drove him to Memphis to audition for Sam Phillips, who had produced Elvis at Sun Records. Jerry sang "Crazy Arms" on a demonstration record, and two months later the song had sold 300,000 copies. Jimmy was digging ditches at the time. He was sitting in a diner when he first heard his cousin's voice come over a jukebox. "My thoughts drifted back to the times Jerry Lee and I had played piano together, the times we had talked about making lots of money, the times we had planned to leave Ferriday for the big time," Swaggart writes. "Now it looked as if Jerry Lee had finally realized his part of the dream."

The lives of Jimmy Swaggart and Jerry Lee Lewis would begin a curious seesaw in which the fortunes of one would rise as the other's fell.

While he was in Memphis, Jerry Lee has said, he prayed to God for "one hit record, an' I'll take the money an' set up a li'l church an' dedicate the rest of my life to you, like Jimmy Lee." God had more than granted that wish. By 1957, Jerry Lee had sold 21 million records. "Whole Lotta Shakin' Going On" had made him a sensation. "Great Balls of Fire" was the hottest-selling single in the country. Jimmy, a father now, was still draining swamps, preaching the backroad churches, living in a house trailer and driving a crummy old Plymouth with faulty valves that he claimed to have "healed" with an anointing of oil on the hood ornament. One Sunday in early December 1957, Jerry wheeled into Ferriday, driving a new Cadillac. He seemed to be on top of the world, but that night in church he held the pew so tightly his knuckles turned white, and he wept, Jimmy has recalled, "as though his heart was shattered."

Jerry Lee's career, which had risen so high so quickly, was about to take a calamitous fall. On December 12th, Jerry Lee married his third wife, his thirteen-year-old second cousin, Myra Gale Brown, a wide-eyed seventh grader who still believed in Santa Claus. That spring Mr. and Mrs. Lewis flew to London to perform, but when the British press uncovered his "child bride" and the fact that he had never been divorced from his previous wives, he was booed out of England as a bigamist and a cradle robber. When he got home, he found his bookings canceled. Disc jockeys dropped his songs from their playlists. Barred from television and most major concert halls, dogged by a jeering press, he was reduced to one-night stands in the beer halls and ballparks of Waycross and Sulphur Dell.

In the meantime, Jimmy's career as an evangelist was picking up—thanks to Jerry Lee's notoriety. "Back in those days, he made posters saying, COME HEAR THE FIRST COUSIN OF JERRY LEE LEWIS," says David Beatty, himself a cousin and a rival evangelist. Despite his increasing popularity, Jimmy was still driving his rattletrap Plymouth, and he had begun to pray that God instruct Jerry Lee to give him an Oldsmobile. Jerry had made some careless promises before he went to Memphis. According to David Beatty, Jerry had promised to buy him a car if he sold a million records. "I made a fatal error," Beatty says. "I told Jimmy about it."

With the gift of an Oldsmobile 88, the genie of success passed out of Jerry Lee's hands and into Jimmy Lee's. Jerry would never again know the wild popular acclaim that had once been his. He watched Mickey Gilley, whom he would deride forever after as "an imitator," become a popular country singer, with three Number One records in a single year (a feat Jerry never accomplished), and the owner of the colossal nightclub in Houston that was the setting of the movie *Urban Cowboy*. Jimmy eventually recorded forty-six albums and claims he's sold 15 million copies. (Since most of them have been sold through his mail-order business, the Recording Industry Association of America has no figures to support the claim.) "I have sold more long-play albums than any gospel singer on the face of the earth," Swaggart would boast, and he lined the walls of his office with gold and platinum records that he had printed and awarded to himself. At the peak of his success, Jimmy was the sexual phenomenon that Jerry Lee had been thirty years before. To see him strut and dance on the stage, full of juice, his voice rippling with insinuation, was to be reminded of the young Jerry Lee, his wavy blond locks flying, as he gave himself up to ecstasy.

During those thirty years, Jerry Lee would see two of his children die, one in a car accident and the other drowning in Jerry's back-yard swimming pool. He would descend into a bitter midnight of the soul, going through women, wrecking cars, shooting his bass player, drinking, taking pills by the gross, beating his wives and, finally, getting arrested outside Elvis Presley's mansion with a gun in his hand.

And all of this time Jerry Lee would watch Jimmy Swaggart grow mightier, and more censorious, until he appeared as some volcanic prophet from the Old Testament. Jerry would be sitting in another hotel room in another city, and he would see Jimmy on television thundering like some new Isaiah, clothed with the garments of salvation and covered with the robe of righteousness, proclaiming a day of vengeance. Despite the confusion of narcotics, Jerry trembled in the sight of his cousin's judgment. He was tortured by the idea that he was playing Satan's music. "A man can't serve two masters," he would often say. "Satan has power next to God. You ain't loyal to God, you must be loyal to Satan. There ain't no in-between. Can't serve two gods. I'm a sinner; I know it. Soon I'm gonna have to reckon with the chillin' hands of death."

In February 1982, Jimmy preached the sermon at the graveside of Mickey's father. Jerry Lee was there, a bitter man. At the end of the sermon, Jimmy asked of the mourners, "Whosoever among you believes you wouldn't go to heaven with Uncle Arthur if you died today, come forward." Jerry Lee walked up and stood right in Jimmy's face. "Will you accept Christ as your savior?" Jimmy asked.

Jerry just stared at him, then turned away.

Their paths would cross again in Dayton, Ohio. Jimmy was there on a crusade. He would later tell a reporter for the Nashville TV station WSMV that he was surprised when Jerry's fourth wife called him. "She said, 'You've got to do something. He's in serious shape, and there's nobody else that can.' She was sobbing and almost hysterical."

Jimmy went to the auditorium. Jerry was playing "Meat Man," one of those dirty honky-tonk ditties, but his words were scarcely intelligible; he might as well have been speaking tongues. Jimmy walked onstage and took the mike out of his hands. "He was the most astonished human bein'," Jimmy said. "The music kinda just stopped, kinda just drifted off on its own, and the crowd—you coulda heard a pin drop. I was shakin' all over; I was scared to death. I said, 'Jerry Lee's my cousin, as most of you know, and I've come to get him.'" When the promoter protested, Jimmy pulled out a wad of cash and paid him off on the spot.

He flew Jerry to Baton Rouge in his private plane and fed him malted milk and shrimp for the next seven days. Jerry left a sober man, but it didn't take. Nor did Jimmy's plea to join him in the ministry. Because by now the cousins had been absorbed by forces larger than themselves. "Satan," Jerry mumbled in a radio interview. "He got power next to God. He'll drag you . . . to the . . . depths of . . . agony."

"How does Satan benefit from your entertaining people?" the puzzled interviewer asked.

" 'Cause I'm draggin' the audience to hell with me."

In the meantime, God was speaking to Jimmy. He came to him in a dream. There was an enormous field of cotton below a gloomy sky. God told Jimmy that the field needed harvesting before the storm came. Then he said, "If you fail, there is no one else to do it. I have many laborers, but none to reach the masses, and *you must not fail!*"

No one else! This was the stark commandment that Jimmy lived with. He had become the new Messiah. "I must do it," he writes. "God has called me to do it. He has laid His hand on my life to do it. . . . If you think there are many others out there — or even one other person — who can do it, you are so sadly mistaken. . . . So if I do not do it, it will not be done. I know that to be the truth."

It was this awesome responsibility, the very fate of the world itself, the salvation of the planet, that would eventually lead Jimmy Swaggart to ruin himself on Airline Highway.

Nowhere to Run

ELLEN HOPKINS

RENEE LINTON TOOK ALL THE RIGHT STEPS TO SAVE
HERSELF FROM AN ABUSIVE, BATTERING HUSBAND.
OUR STORY TRACED THE FAILURE OF THE SYSTEM THAT
LEFT HER TO DIE.

"Why didn't she leave?"
"Why didn't she call the authorities?"
"In the name of God, why did she keep talking
to him?"

This isn't yet another recap of the Clarence Thomas-Anita Hill debacle
but a sampling of typical reactions I encountered whenever I tried to
describe the short, unhappy life of Renee Linton, the battered woman I
had set out to memorialize.

It was 1988, and *The Burning Bed* and the Joel Steinberg-Hedda Nussbaum tragedy notwithstanding, the words *battered woman* didn't instantly
evoke sympathy—much less understanding. All most people had gleaned
from the first was that Farrah Fawcett allowing herself to look so terrible
on TV meant she was a *serious actress*. And Hedda Nussbaum wasn't a
crowd pleaser. Yes, it's true that children weren't the only victims in that
hellhole on West Tenth Street in New York City, but it's also true that

abuse doesn't absolve a woman of all societal obligations. If anything, Nussbaum may have set back the battered-woman cause.

Renee Linton was different. Renee, who was thirty-two when her husband shot her to death, never forgot who she was. She was a model mother to her three children—guarding them, cuddling them, pestering them to mind their manners and do their homework. She was a hard worker who took pride in her ability to support her family and maintain a home, all the while being stalked by a psychotic killer. She even dressed spiffily to the end, dying in a brand-new red jogging suit. In truth, she was somewhat unusual for a battered woman. Not just because of her dignity and her strength but because she had, in fact, called the police, had separated from her husband, Michael, and was doing her best to sever all contact with him.

But because she didn't do "the right thing" from the start, because she didn't hide that well or run that far, her story was often met with suspicion. I'll never forget one man's scorn when I tried to explain Renee's refusal to leave Westchester County, New York, where Michael and his large extended family lived. "Anyone who wants to can disappear," he said. "If she really wanted to save herself, why didn't she go to Europe?"

I wrote this article so that people would understand why women like Renee can't go to Europe, why in the end they truly have nowhere to run.

I found out about Renee from an old friend who sat on the jury that convicted Michael Linton of murdering his estranged wife. My friend was so haunted by what Renee had endured that once the trial was over, he insisted on telling me every scrap of her life story that he remembered— all that the justice system, with its elaborate rules of evidence, had allowed the jury to know.

Despite the many gaps, his rendition lasted the better part of an afternoon. The story, with its flourishes of prophetic Jamaicans, ominous BMWs and dying words heard on a phone, screamed Hollywood. I couldn't believe that a local journalist didn't already have a piece in the works.

Months went by, and nothing appeared in print. Still bewildered by this inattention to a great yarn, I ran the idea past a few editors I knew at various publications. No one was interested.

"Face it, Ellen," said one, "Renee was black and working-class. Her husband had had run-ins with the law. She isn't someone our target audience is going to identify with."

Another had an off-putting (if *Real-politik*) suggestion: "She worked in Scarsdale and had a Jewish-sounding name—why don't you imply in your proposal that Renee was a Jew? Then you'd have every editor in New York City wanting to know what happened to her."

Renee didn't make a posthumous conversion to Judaism. After months of shopping her story around I was fortunate enough to meet Robert Vare (who was then an editor at ROLLING STONE), a compassionate man with some funny notions about what the word *newsworthy* means. The horrific death of an ordinary black woman somehow met his criteria.

But getting Renee's story into print required much more than an adventurous editor, much more than a magazine that was oddly willing to run more than 14,000 words on a topic that had nothing to do with sex, drugs or rock & roll. It required immense courage on the part of Renee's friends and family members who agreed to talk to me. Threats against various witnesses had been made during the trial; one woman had had her windows shot out before she could testify. Another witness simply disappeared. The fact that Michael Linton now lived behind bars was cold comfort to those who knew Michael's cohorts, some of whom were still at large.

I got glimpses of the miasma of fear that must have poisoned Renee's final days whenever I tried to persuade someone who loved her to talk. I got used to late-night calls from women who wouldn't tell me their names or their phone numbers. All they wanted to do was to bear witness to the courage of a woman they couldn't forget. I remember interviewing the director of the shelter for battered women where Renee and her children sought refuge. We had to meet in a neutral location. The director wouldn't tell me the shelter's address.

One day I took a walking tour of Renee's life. I began with the tiny apartment in Yonkers where she had barricaded herself the last few months. I had expected a dark, cramped place. Instead, it was horribly airy and light. Nearly every wall had a window. Nearly every window had a fire escape. The only true hiding place was the closet.

I drove from there to the Scarsdale Agency, the insurance company where Renee had worked. Westchester parkways, with their narrow lanes and wooded backdrops, have a chummy way about them. Renee would often see Michael's bright orange BMW beside her on the Cross County Parkway. Imagine being watched on the way to work.

I sat at Renee's old desk at her office. It was set in the middle of a large picture window, on the first floor, facing the street. During office hours, Michael liked to drive back and forth along that street, often calling Renee later to tell her what she had worn to work that day, how many coffee breaks she had taken, what a laughably easy target she would be, how many days were left before he would put her out of her misery.

Renee spent half her life in love with the man who would kill her. They were childhood sweethearts. Virtually every lesson of adulthood they learned side by side. The hallmarks of their marriage were passion, children, dancing and more than 100 occasions on which Michael informed his wife how much he longed to blow her away. What is it like having a killer take up residence in your heart?

Since Renee's death, in 1987, battered women have come out of the closet somewhat. Stories about them appear with some frequency in magazines and newspapers. They get interviewed on morning talk shows. Sometimes they even use their real names. The battered-woman defense has become a commonplace in the courtroom. It would seem that battered women are being accorded long overdue respect.

Respect, though, still counts for little if you're dead. In 1988 approximately thirty percent of the 4611 female murder victims in America were killed by their husbands or boyfriends. Today those figures have not appreciably changed. Since domestic violence and unemployment often go hand in hand, the recession will likely keep these killings on a steady keel. Every fifteen seconds an American woman is beaten by her husband or boyfriend. The surgeon general has declared the home a more dangerous place for American women than our city streets. Six years after Renee Linton's heart, liver, left breast and left lung were torn apart by bullets from her husband's gun, six years after Michael Linton stuffed the earthly remains of his bride into a smoking oven, battering remains the single largest cause of injury to women in this country.

RS 550

April 20th, 1989

Assistant district attorney Jeanine Ferris Pirro is a snappy dresser with a great pair of legs, a lush mop of curly black hair, scarlet nails painted to match her bee-stung lips and a penchant for ankle bracelets — a real looker. She is also a smart, impassioned advocate for battered women who for the last eleven years has headed up the Westchester County D.A.'s Domestic Violence and Child Abuse Bureau. Pirro's appearance flouts expectations on such a grand scale, it's hard to believe her flamboyance isn't, at least in part, a deliberate message: Just because a woman's a hot tamale, buster, doesn't give you any rights to mess with her.

She's a woman possessed. When an exasperated man, lost in the bowels of Westchester County Court, burst into Pirro's office one day and begged for directions to the property-dispute office, Pirro patiently obliged, then, when the man exclaimed, "How can I thank you?" she snapped out, "Sir, do you have a wife, any children?"

"Yes," said the man, bewildered.

"Don't beat them. That's how you can thank me. Have a nice day, sir."

Pirro never met Renee Linton, though in the course of helping Renee get her order of protection, members of her staff did. And while all crimes against women infuriate Pirro, her rage increases exponentially when the victim has done just what she was supposed to do.

There are easier things in the prosecution world than seeking justice for a battered woman—especially when the battered woman has been killed and the killer is still at large. In the months following the murder of Renee, Pirro discovered that people with any knowledge of the case had a distressing tendency to clam up any time she mentioned going to court. Everyone who knew Renee knew about Michael's threats. Everyone knew, more or less, how, when, where and why he had killed her. But no one wanted to testify.

There was even a deep-throat caller who was willing to assist Pirro on the phone but repeatedly refused to come forward and be identified. "What carrot does a prosecutor have to make someone risk their life?" Pirro wondered.

A few weeks after the murder, Pirro went to the home of a friend of Renee's. The friend, who'd previously indicated she was willing to help, now refused to talk. The night before, one of her windows had been shot out. "Don't you understand?" said the friend, putting a hand on Pirro's shoulder. "People's lives are in danger. You're in danger too. God be with you."

In the twelve months between the murder and the trial, six key witnesses left town or simply couldn't be found. Right before the trial, one witness got an odd letter from a man in jail whose name she didn't recognize. All the letter said was he'd "heard of her." The witness decided it was time for an extended vacation at an undisclosed location.

As a possible eyewitness, Michael Anthony Anderson, who had dated Renee and was in her apartment the night of the murder, was particularly reluctant to talk. He would meet Pirro only at a place of his choosing. He wouldn't let her show him police photos in public. No matter how often she asked him, Anderson insisted all he'd seen was a flash of gunfire.

"As far as I'm concerned," he said, "it could have been Big Bird coming through that window."

Then Pirro got a call. A woman Renee had met in the shelter for battered women was outraged by newspaper reports that police had no leads (police were merely being cautious about releasing information to the press). "Whaddaya mean, no leads?" said the woman. "I knew Renee. That lunatic husband of hers was threatening her from day one."

Pirro asked the woman about the threats, about Renee's flights to the shelter, about the orange BMW. The woman obliged. She told Pirro how upset Renee would get whenever she saw the car, how much she'd cry.

"Did you ever *see* the BMW?" Pirro finally asked.

"Yeah," said the woman. "A real pimp car if you ask me."

"Congratulations. You're going to court."

The woman burst into tears. "I've got kids," she said. "Please, I'll sign anything you like to put that bastard away, just please don't put me on the stand."

"Sorry," said Pirro. "You've no choice. You're being subpoenaed." Then her voice softened. "I want you to understand this. We desperately need you."

The first day of the trial for the murder of Yvonne Renee Linton was February 8th, 1988. The fourth witness called to the stand was Michael Anthony Anderson, a man of average build, a few inches taller than Michael Linton. The timing of the trial had made Anderson even more jittery than he might otherwise have been: Four months earlier a car dispatcher in Queens, a witness in an unrelated case, had been shot by a sniper.

"And you people think you can protect *me*?" Anderson asked Pirro. He finally agreed to testify, but only with a police escort, highly unusual even in criminal court.

The reason for his nervousness became apparent once he told the court what had happened the night of February 10th, 1987:

. . . Around ten o'clock, Anthony glanced at his watch. He didn't want to be out too late; tomorrow was a working day. But Carol Burnett had just come on the TV. He slipped off his loafers, lay back on the cushions and decided to stay a little longer.

Just after 11:00 p.m., the phone rang. Renee answered and began chatting. Anthony paid little attention. The phone had been ringing all night. He closed his eyes.

He stopped dozing fast. There was a crash, a flash of gunfire, and then Anthony was running. He heard Renee scream, he wasn't quite sure from where. All Anthony knew was the gun was still shooting, and he had to get out. He headed in the direction of Renee's front door, but realizing it was locked, he dashed left into the bathroom and slammed the door behind him.

That turn, police believe, saved his life. There wouldn't have been time to unbolt the three locks on the front door. Shots followed him, two bullets lodging in the bathroom door. Anthony clambered into the tub and, with bare hands, smashed through the bottom pane of the bathroom window. Then he dove through a window the size of a toaster oven, down to the ground, about thirteen feet below.

He found himself shoeless, covered with blood, in a tiny concrete shaft. Behind him was the building. In front was a high chain-link fence. The area was entirely fenced in. He started to climb but then jumped back down into the shaft, leaving one sock behind. The fence was at least ten feet high. If Anthony reached the top, he'd be almost level with Renee's apartment—a marksman's dream of a target.

Anthony turned back to the building. Directly below the window he'd jumped from was another one, similar in size, only a few feet above the ground. Again with his bare hands, he smashed through the window and crash-landed in a tangle of baby clothes that were hanging over a slippery tub. Ripping through the layette barricade, he ran out of the bathroom past a screaming woman. Anthony never noticed the bullet lodged in the living-room floor, which had been fired from Renee's apartment above and landed just a few feet from his escape route.

He was surprised at how easily he found his way out. "Normally," he said, "in other people's homes, you cannot get out." Leaving a trail of blood behind, Anthony ran up the stairs from the basement apartment, out onto the street and, with one sock on, one sock off, ran up Mulberry Street toward the White Eagle Tavern. . . .

Total time elapsed: about two minutes. An intricately choreographed affair. Somehow, Anderson and the killer managed not to cross paths outside 21 Mulberry.

Throughout his testimony, Anderson insisted he saw nothing more than a silhouette, that he couldn't even tell if the intruder was male or female. Defense lawyer Michael Beatrice, a round-faced man with a light, sweet voice, didn't dwell on this. Beatrice seemed far more interested in the witness's name. Did Anderson ever tell the police his friends called him Anthony? What about the grand jury last March? Over and over, Beatrice urged Anderson to abandon this Anthony pretense, to own up to his given name of Michael.

There were too many Michaels in this case, Anderson protested. He even made a joke about it: "Everybody appears to have that name, even defense counsel."

Jurors were bewildered by this exchange. Was Beatrice trying to suggest Anderson was the killer? Just because his given name was the same as the defendant's?

Then Billie Carroll came to the stand—also accompanied by police escort. After relentless lobbying by Pirro, Judge Colabella had made an exception to the hearsay rule. As Aunt Billie related the last phone conversation Renee Linton had, her face contorted, her fluting voice grew shrill.

. . . At 11:02 Aunt Billie dialed 914-965-4281. A few rings, then Renee picked up.

"Hi, Renee," said Aunt Billie. "How are you?"

"Fine," said Renee.

"How are the kids?"

"Fine," said Renee. "We didn't go to court yesterday. He has to go tomorrow. I don't have to go. I'm taking the children to school. I'm going for my W-2 forms. I think I'll be safe."

Then, through more than 700 miles of fiber-optic cable, stretching from Fayetteville to Yonkers, Aunt Billie heard the troubled marriage of Michael and Renee Linton come to an end. All it took to cleave husband to wife was a few minutes in a church; all it took to release them was a few seconds, face to face, in the corner of Renee's kitchen. One shot was fired. Two. Renee screamed, "Michael, Michael, murder, murder!" The line went dead. Aunt Billie gripped the receiver tight. "Renee?" she said. "Hello?" No answer. "Hello? Renee?" No answer. . . .

Before Billie Carroll could finish her testimony, a woman in the courtroom cried out, "How could you lie, Aunt Billie? I told you what happened. How can you lie? How can you lie?"

"Take the jury out! Take the jury out!" yelled Judge Colabella.

"How can—"

"Just hold her there," said the judge, indicating the shouting woman.

The woman was Michael Linton's sister, Beverly. After a stern warning from the judge, she agreed to be quiet and was allowed to remain in the courtroom. All she'd accomplished by her outburst was to enable the jury, now back in court, to hear Aunt Billie wail once more her previously interrupted testimony—"Michael, Michael, murder, murder!"

But much of what Billie Carroll had to say the jury never heard. They heard nothing about Renee's middle-of-the-night call to Aunt Billie in 1982, asking for help because Michael was beating her; or Renee's calls from the shelter in 1986 and 1987, explaining why she was hiding out; or Renee's descriptions of Michael's banging on her door at 6:00 a.m. on January 8th, 1987, telling her he'd kill her before the divorce was final; or the phone call from Renee on February 8th, 1987, when Renee said that she'd left the shelter—scared stiff but determined to face up to her husband. If Michael killed her, she said, he'd kill her. She was tired of running.

All of this was deemed hearsay, inadmissible.

In fact, other than Renee's cry of "Michael, Michael, murder, murder!" (dying words are often exceptions to the hearsay rule), Aunt Billie's testimony was ultimately not allowed to include anything Renee had said the night she was killed.

In cross-examination, defense counsel Beatrice seemed strangely preoccupied with the elderly woman's health. "Do you need any water, or are you on any medication that you'd like?" he asked.

"No," said Aunt Billie.

Beatrice is a solicitous man. He asked Paulette Sullivan, Renee's downstairs neighbor, how many months pregnant she was; former assistant D.A.

Joseph Abinanti how private practice was going. The defense counsel was particularly interested in how the little people work, asking Officer Dennis Keidong what his duties were the night of the murder, when he'd seen the orange BMW.

"What were you doing in the parking lot at that time?" asked Beatrice.

"Objection," said Pirro.

"Overruled," said the judge.

"We were on surveillance," replied Keidong.

"What type of surveillance?" asked Beatrice.

"Objection."

"Overruled."

"Parking meters," said Keidong.

"I'm sorry?" asked Beatrice.

"Parking meters."

"Parking meters?"

"Yes," said Keidong.

On February 10th, a year to the day after Renee's murder, a parade of somber women came to Westchester County Court. In all, five women took the stand, one right after another—three from the Northern Westchester Shelter, one from the Department of Social Services, another from the D.A.'s domestic-violence bureau. Their testimony was severely restricted. All they were allowed to say was that they had known the victim, that she'd requested emergency shelter and that she'd gotten it. Not much else.

Renee's reasons for seeking refuge in the shelter were ruled inadmissible. It hardly mattered. The grim faces of the witnesses made a powerful impression throughout the courtroom. Mary Hartman, Joanne James, Karen Staffeld, Anne Marie Murray and Sharon White seemed to regard themselves as witnesses testifying not just at a murder trial but for all battered women. Renee Linton had been transfigured into their patron saint.

The following week, Mary Ann Smith, a co-worker of Renee's, testified that the sight of the orange BMW driving past Scarsdale Agency had made Renee cry—over Beatrice's sarcastic objections. ("What is the connection between the . . . BMW and the defendant in this case?" Beatrice asked. "Are we talking about the Flying Dutchman?") Smith's chats with Renee over the coffee machine about Michael's wanting to blow his wife away were ruled hearsay.

Later that afternoon, Pirro called pathologist Darly Jeanty to the stand. It was Ash Wednesday, the day Catholics atone for the vanities of the flesh. Pirro, her forehead smudged with black, took Dr. Jeanty through the autopsy report, asking him to describe what had become of Renee

Linton's earthly remains, to tell the jury how Renee had been burned in an oven after her heart had stopped beating.

At a judge's sole discretion in the state of New York, children as young as six may appear as sworn witnesses in criminal court. Michael Manley Linton Jr. was now eleven. Because of the hearsay rules, he was the only witness able to testify at length about the threats. Unlike most of the other witnesses, who'd only heard Renee's retelling, Mikey had actually heard what his father had said. There were, of course, restrictions on Mikey's testimony: He couldn't tell how his mother yelled at his father to get off the fire escape two nights before the murder. The judge ruled this incident inadmissible, making the odd argument that "a dry run" for murder was implausible.

Kecia didn't testify. Since the night of her mother's murder, she had barely mentioned her father's name, even omitting "God bless Daddy" from her nightly prayers. There was no point in putting her on the witness stand. And five-year-old Billie was too young. Without Mikey there was hardly any case at all.

Fortunately for Pirro, Mikey wanted to testify. Pete Intervallo, however, had warned him: "Hey, Mikey, you know if you testify and if your father goes to jail, it may be a long time before you see him again."

"I don't care," Mikey replied. "I want everyone to know what he did to Mommy." His main concern was whether he'd have to look at his father. Pirro assured him that other than identifying Michael Senior, there was no reason Mikey had to make eye contact with his father at all.

Mikey's day in court didn't begin auspiciously. As he entered the building, his grandfather saw him and in a Jamaican accent yelled something across the hall. The child burst into tears. As Mikey was escorted to the witness box, a wave of young children, his cousins, leaned forward in their seats, squealing, "Mikey, Mikey, Mikey," in high-pitched glee, stretching out their arms, motioning him to join them.

Mikey smiled sheepishly. He shifted a little in the witness box, partly pleased to see his cousins, partly embarrassed to be where he was. He was just like a kid who'd been sent to the head of the class, and all the other kids were goofing on him.

"In my opinion, and, of course, this is only my opinion," Judge Colabella later observed, "this was done to make the child feel like a rat."

The court reporter cried throughout Mikey's testimony. Mikey cried just a little himself—mainly when he told the court how his father had pulled a gun on his mother in North Carolina. He also got teary-eyed repeating certain threats: "He would call her asshole and all that. Because she would go out the house and go to work and take Billie to school, and he said that he could have killed her, and she's an asshole because he could have killed her right then and there, but he's going to make her suffer."

Jeanine Pirro treated Mikey with dignity. Even when he broke down, she never once offered her handkerchief or her sympathy. She merely waited for him to compose himself, and then, when Mikey was ready to resume his job, he went on.

Mikey had little to say about the night of the murder. "I thought I heard like a glass break," he said. "But I wasn't sure, and then I went back to sleep."

Michael Beatrice made a valiant effort to discredit Mikey. In his sweetest voice, Beatrice fired questions at the child: "How long did you live in Fayetteville, North Carolina?" "How old were you when you went to Fayetteville, North Carolina?" "And what's the name of the school you went to [in North Carolina]?" "Do you remember the year [you moved to North Carolina]?" (Mikey was about a year old at the time of the move south.)

Mikey got confused. A number of times he repeated, "I don't know," "I don't remember." The child seemed to clutch at the number 2 as a safe answer.

"Did [your father] give you money more than once?"

"No, about twice."

"Where did he take you to go out to eat?"

"He took us to McDonald's two times."

"How many times did he come to visit you when you lived at your Aunt Shug's house in Mount Vernon?"

"Twice."

"How many times did you see [Anthony]?"

"Twice."

There was one question Mikey didn't want to answer at all: "Where do you live?"

Mikey remained silent.

But when Beatrice began questioning the child about his mother, the child's voice grew stronger. He became more exact. Beatrice suggested Mikey hadn't really seen a gun in his father's hand that night in Fayetteville. Or if he had, maybe it was a toy gun, maybe it was plastic. "Do you remember anything about it, like the color?" Beatrice asked.

"No," said Mikey.

Maybe it was a BB gun, suggested Beatrice.

"It wasn't a BB gun," said Mikey with assurance. Mikey knew the difference. BB guns, he said, were what his daddy used to shoot at trucks.

People in the courtroom exchanged looks. Mikey's father smiled—as he'd done through most of his son's testimony.

Beatrice tried to demonstrate that the child had been prepped. He cited the fact that Mikey had referred to him earlier as "my father's attorney."

"And how did you know that I was your father's attorney if you never saw me before?" asked Beatrice.

"Because you were sitting beside him, okay," said Mikey.

"Did somebody tell you that your father's attorney would be sitting next to him?"

Mikey looked exasperated. "No," he said, "but I watch TV."

Everyone laughed, even the judge. One courtroom observer shook his head and said, "*That's* why you don't cross-examine a child."

When Mikey had finished, the judge escorted him out. A tall man, Judge Colabella strode through the halls like Jove, his black robes billowing about him, his hand on the shoulder of the eleven-year-old boy who'd just done his best to convict his father of the murder of his mother. Mikey and the judge went into an anteroom. The door closed. Behind it came the sound of a child weeping as though his heart would break.

Mikey's father didn't take the stand in his own defense. Michael Beatrice made a motion for dismissal — after eight previous motions for a mistrial (the average number in a murder case is one). Judge Colabella denied Beatrice's motion, as he had all prior ones.

In his summation, Beatrice offered a revisionist view of Renee's flights to the shelter. The reason Renee went, he explained, was because she'd run out of money. She had to exaggerate the threats in order to gain admittance. After all, he argued, she'd never shown any bruises or broken bones to shelter workers, had she? "People need shelter, people need food. When a person's back is up against the wall, they are going to do what they need to survive." Beatrice neglected to mention that Renee paid for each of her stays in the shelter about what it would have cost her for living expenses on the outside.

Beatrice also provided his own validation of Michael's innocence. If Michael Senior was the killer, he argued, "wouldn't he have taken the simple step of looking in the bedroom to see if his children were there?"

Beatrice then sounded his leitmotif of the many Michaels. Perhaps Michael Anthony Anderson, who'd come "bearing gifts" of whiskey and a rose, was the real killer. Or perhaps less obvious suspects should be considered. "They [Mikey, Kecia and Billie] slept through the entire incident," said Beatrice. "Is that fact a little unusual?"

The defense counsel ended his summation with a flat voice and stony face that belied his words: "[Michael Linton is] screaming right now, he's sitting there but he's screaming at you, screaming at you that he is not guilty, that he wasn't there, that he didn't do it. . . ."

The summation of the prosecutor was an exercise in controlled rage. "[Was] Renee Linton less of a person because somebody brought her a rose and a bottle of liquor?" Jeanine Pirro demanded. "Does it mean that she is not entitled to the equal protection of the law? . . ."

Pirro scorned Beatrice's suggestion that Anthony Anderson was the murderer. "Keep in mind that it was Renee Linton who was the hunted, and you know who she was running from," said Pirro. Not Anthony Anderson, shoeless and covered with blood, "caught like a rat" in the concrete shaft. It wasn't a barefoot man whom Vito Markowski had heard that night clattering past his window to a getaway car. Renee's murderer, Pirro said, was a man who had been trained to make commando hits, a man who knew guns well enough to kill quickly and tidily, with almost no blood. Her killer was a man who hated her so much that riddling her body with five bullets wasn't enough. He had to stuff what was left into a scorching oven.

Pirro attacked Beatrice's claim that Renee had embellished her husband's threats in order to get a roof over her head. "The only time Renee had her back up against the wall was when this defendant was shooting her," she said. "I ask you, in your deliberations, to recall what little you know about this thirty-two-year-old mother of three children who is now dead. . . . I say Renee Linton is entitled to justice. . . ."

Deliberations lasted all of an hour and twenty-six minutes, including a break for lunch. The jurors found Michael Linton guilty of murder in the second degree. Mikey's testimony, they agreed, obliterated all reasonable doubt.

Michael showed no emotion. As court officers handcuffed him, he turned to his father and shouted in his thick Jamaican accent, "Colonel! Not to worry, *mon*. Is small twirl in big swirl."

On May 11th, three months after the verdict, Judge Colabella disregarded Michael's protestations of innocence and sentenced him to the maximum of twenty-eight-and-a-half years to life. "I have before me now accomplished facts," said Colabella, "that point to one of the most heinous crimes I have ever been involved with as a trial judge."

A few weeks later, Mikey stopped by Jeanine Pirro's office. He was dressed the way Renee would have liked—gray flannel pants, white shirt and red tie. "You look great, Mikey," said Pirro. "Can I take your picture?"

Mikey thought this was a wonderful idea. He asked her to send him a copy. Then he said with shy formality, "I want to thank you, Jeanine, for what you did for me and my sisters. Now I can keep Kecia and Billie safe."

Michael Linton is currently appealing his conviction. His defense argues that Judge Colabella erred in allowing Billie Carroll to testify that she'd heard Renee's final cry. While dying words are often permitted as exceptions to the hearsay rule, dying words heard on the phone rest on far shakier legal ground—especially, Beatrice points out, when the witness is elderly and possibly unreliable. The defense also objects to Colabella's allowing the testimony of Mikey, whom Beatrice characterizes in court papers as an "infant witness . . . who didn't comprehend the actual events."

Michael Senior, who declined to be interviewed for this article, continues to maintain his innocence. His children continue to live in protective custody.

"Do you have a mommy?" Billie, now six, recently asked a family friend.

"I had a mommy," said the friend. "But she's in heaven now. Like yours is, sugar."

Billie digested this, then wanted to know, "Who bang, bang, banged yours?"

Mikey later confided to a relative that, contrary to what he'd said in court, he'd actually heard his mother scream the night of the murder—as well as a series of shots. Kecia, Mikey said, probably heard everything, start to finish—she's a light sleeper.

"But screaming, shots, I thought it was TV," said Mikey. "I wanted it to be TV, so I went back to sleep."

The Devil and John Holmes

MIKE SAGER

JOHN HOLMES WAS A PORN STAR. EDDIE NASH WAS A DRUG LORD. THEIR ASSOCIATION ENDED IN ONE OF THE MOST BRUTAL MASS MURDERS IN THE HISTORY OF LOS ANGELES.

His name was—well, never mind his name, he was keen on legal action—but his claim to a Hollywood portfolio seemed to rest in the fortuitous and oft-recounted happenstance of his affair of the heart with Miss Bette Davis, as he called her fondly, some twenty or thirty years ago, a fact confirmed by a liver-spotted rummy of his acquaintance, with whom I would later visit at his run-down Hollywood SRO.

This guy, Mr. Bette Davis, lived in Arizona. By day he worked for a home-security service. By night he was self-employed. He had a fax machine, exclusive rights to a pair of characters, a screenwriter in mind. He was a producer. He wanted to make a deal.

The year was 1988. Bob Love, my editor, had heard of the AIDS death of porn star John Holmes. Holmes had been involved in the bludgeoning murders of four Hollywood lowlifes known as the Wonderland Gang.

He'd been acquitted of the murders, but with his death, the case had been reopened. A Palestinian coke dealer and his bodyguard had been indicted.

And so it was that my journalistic mission began. The action was to be on three fronts. There was the story of the life of a man with a fourteen-inch penis. There was the story of the porn industry that Holmes had helped define. And there was the murder story—a tale of the freewheeling pre-Betty Ford days in L.A., when a gram and a couple of Valiums were *de rigueur* as handbag accessories on the golden West Coast.

As it would turn out, my war on the Holmes story took place on a front I had never expected, for 1988 was also a year when the face of news gathering had begun to change.

Previously, when you said you were a journalist, people pictured Bob Woodward. It was honorable to be a member of the Fourth Estate. And it was honorable for citizens to talk and tell the truth.

But by the summer of 1986, with the first airing of Fox's *Current Affair*, a new era of news had dawned. With a clarion of sensationalist graphics, special effects and theme songs, journalism began to give way to something new. The focus was gloom and doom, tragic scrapings of real lives. The format was headlines and generalization. The feeling was, you are there: ambush, re-creation, hot adjectives, prurient detail.

Late in '88 the dominant form in this fledgling permutation was called True Crime. The model was Truman Capote's landmark book *In Cold Blood*, a social and psychological exploration of the murder of a small-town, Midwestern family by a pair of drifters. Insightful, literary, horrific, its gruesome force lay in its nouns and verbs rather than in its adjectives; by layering detail upon detail, by doing exhaustive research, by entering the minds of all the characters, by telling a story with a moral for the times, Capote was able to convey true horror through understatement, through the mystical interplay between words on paper and pictures in the minds of readers. Importantly, he spun his tale to the good reviews of the people he wrote about. They didn't like everything he'd said, but they had to admit he'd understood. He'd gotten it right.

With the explosion of cable and the exponential growth of TV tabloid and True Crime, the job and the perception of a journalist began to change. With the report of each new crime in America, TV and film people flew out first-class to get the story. The tools of their trade—unlike the traditional legs, pad and tape recorder—were the lawyer, the checkbook, the rights agreement. Now, as I was to learn while doing the Holmes piece, a reporter showing up at the door was perceived as Geraldo rather than Woodward, and everyone had an agent or a lawyer or a producer claiming rights. Everyone wanted to get paid.

Mr. Bette Davis claimed rights to Holmes's first wife and his mistress. He wanted money. He wanted to share my byline. A Century City lawyer represented Misty Dawn, known once as the anal queen of porn, Holmes's second and surviving wife. A former drug dealer turned porn producer wanted a percentage in exchange for an interview. Another lawyer represented a writer who had begun a biography of Holmes. They wanted a percentage too. Two other guys, Wonderland Gang satellites, negotiated from prison cells for rights to their own pitiful tales.

As time goes by, things only get worse. I've shown up at a murder scene in the mountains of coal country only to find three lawyers, three production companies and a woman named Aphrodite writing a book. The members of the family that had lost a daughter to murder were feuding. They'd each sold rights to different companies. In Los Angeles the plumber who shot the video of Rodney King's beating was being represented by the same PR man as Ed McMahon. When I lived with a crack gang for six weeks, I encountered homeboys who—between drive-bys and drug binges—worked regularly on anti-drug commercials and music videos. Monthly I receive letters from men in prison, long rambling appeals not for habeas corpus but for six-figure book and movie deals.

These days working on a story, I no longer go out and knock on doors. Chances are, by the time I arrive, anyone involved has already found cameras peeking into their living-room window. If they did give an interview, they saw their six hours of heart pull boiled down to a twenty-second bite, accompanied by dramatic tears. Now I write each person a letter, enclose some of my work. I promise, in writing, to listen carefully, not to sensationalize, not to fuck them over. Ten percent of the time, it works.

With this tabloidization of the news, we face grave times in America. In a world where information is the major product, the average reader or viewer is being fed high concept instead of understanding, gory detail instead of insight, hype instead of truth. Back in 1984 when Bob Wallace took the helm at ROLLING STONE, he told me that the job of a magazine journalist was to find an event, wait for the dust to settle, then go in, look around, try to explain the event in the context of our times.

Today journalists play a new role. The questions we ask shape the world's agenda; our portrayal of events sets a mood. Orwell was close but not exactly right in his predictions. The tube is always on, but it is not the government that is playing the message. Rather, it is the producers, the journalists, the marketeers. If all seems hopeless and grim, perhaps it is because we get gloom and doom all day long from the morning newspapers, the afternoon talk shows, the news, the movies, the late-night analyses.

In "The Devil and John Holmes," we were able to tell a squalid tale in human terms. We wrote about prurient and base instincts without resorting to hyperbole. We went in and tried to tell the truth as best we could, to shed a little light, to explain, to entertain.

Not too long ago, I wrote a story in these pages about a man called the Pope of Pot. His views about life were a bit unworkable, I thought, and I think he is beginning to feel that way too, spending as he has the last several months in jail at Rikers Island. But he did say one thing I will always remember. One's goal, said Mickey the Pope, should be to "win by example—you can't make society change the way it does things, but you can show it a better way."

RS 554

JUNE 15TH, 1989

Deep in Laurel Canyon, the Wonderland Gang was planning its last heist. It was Sunday evening and the drugs were gone, the money was gone, things were desperate. They'd sold a pound of baking soda for a quarter of a million dollars; there were contracts out on their lives. Now they had another idea. They sat around a glass table in the breakfast nook. Before them were two pairs of handcuffs, a stolen police badge, several automatic pistols and a dog-eared sheet of paper, a floor plan. They needed a score. This was it.

There were seven of them meeting in the house on Wonderland Avenue, a jaundiced stucco box on a steep, winding road in the hills above Hollywood. Joy Audrey Miller, forty-six, held the lease. She was thin, blond, foul-mouthed, a heroin addict with seven arrests. She had once been married to a Beverly Hills attorney. Her lover, Billy DeVerell, forty-two, was also a heroin addict. He looked "like a guy in a dive bar in El Paso," according to a neighbor. The third roommate was Ronald Launius, thirty-seven. A California cop called him "one of the coldest people I ever met."

The house at 8763 Wonderland rented for $750 a month. A stairway leading from the garage to the front door was caged in iron. There was a telephone at the entrance, two pit bulls sleeping on the steps. Though elaborately secure, the house was paint-cracked and rust-stained, an eyesore in a trendy neighborhood. Laurel Canyon had long been a prestige address, an earthy, woodsy setting just a few minutes from the glitter and rush of Tinseltown.

Things at the house were always hopping, someone was always showing up with a scam. Miller, DeVerell and Launius needed drugs every day.

At the moment, on this evening of June 28, 1981, Wonderland Avenue was quiet. Five men and two women were meeting in the breakfast nook, sitting in swivel chairs, leaning against walls. The floor plan before them

showed a three-bedroom, high-end tract house on a cul-de-sac in the San
Fernando Valley. It had a pool, a sunken living room, jade and art and
most appealing of all, large quantities of money and drugs.

The man who owned the house was named Adel Nasrallah. He was
known as Eddie Nash. A naturalized American, Nash came to California
from Palestine in the early Fifties. In 1960 he opened a hotdog stand on
Hollywood Boulevard. By the mid-Seventies, Nash held thirty-six liquor
licenses, owned real estate and other assets worth over thirty million dollars.

Nash had clubs of all kinds; he catered to all predilections. The Kit
Kat was a strip club. The Seven Seas was a bus-stop joint across Hollywood Boulevard from Mann's Chinese Theaters. It had a tropical motif,
a menu of special drinks, a Polynesian revue. His gay clubs were the first
in L.A. to allow same-sex dancing. His black club was like a Hollywood
Harlem. Los Angeles police averaged twenty-five drug busts a month at
the Starwood. One search of the premises yielded a cardboard box containing four thousand counterfeit Quaaludes. A sign on the box, written
in blue Magic Marker, said, FOR DISTRIBUTION AT BOX OFFICE.

Nash was a drug dealer and a heavy user. His drug of choice was
freebase, home-cooked crack cocaine, and he was smoking it at the rate
of two to three ounces a day. His bodyguard, Gregory DeWitt Diles, was
a karate expert and convicted felon who weighed a blubbery three hundred
pounds.

Now, in the breakfast nook, a tall, gaunt man with curly hair and a
sparse beard pointed to the floor plan he had sketched.

"You sure about this, donkey dick?" asked Tracy McCourt, the gang's
wheelman.

"Hey, it's cool," said John Holmes, thirty-six, the man with the plan.
"Nash loves me. He thinks I'm famous."

John Holmes was famous, at least in some circles. What he was famous
for was his penis.

In a career that would span twenty years, Holmes made 2274 hard-
core pornographic films, had sex with 14,000 women. At the height of his
populrity, he earned $3000 a day on films and almost as much turning
tricks, servicing wealthy men and women on both coasts and in Europe.

Since the late Sixties, Holmes had traded on his natural endowment.
His penis, when erect, according to legend, measured between eleven and
fifteen inches in length. Recently, however, Holmes's biggest commodity
had been trouble. He was freebasing one hit of coke every ten or fifteen
minutes, swallowing forty to fifty Valium a day to cut the edge. The drugs
affected his penis; he couldn't get it up, he couldn't work in porn. Now
he was a drug delivery boy for the Wonderland Gang. His mistress, Jeana,
who'd been with him since she was fifteen, was turning tricks to support

his habit. They were living out of the trunk of his estranged wife's Chevy Malibu. Holmes was stealing luggage off conveyers at L.A. International, buying appliances with his wife's credit cards, fencing them for cash.

Holmes was into Nash for a small fortune. Now Holmes owed the Wonderland Gang, too. He'd messed up a delivery, had a big argument with DeVerell and Launius. They'd taken back his key to Wonderland, and Launius punched him out, then hit Holmes with his own blackthorn walking stick. They told him to make good. He tried to think. Addled synapses played him a picture: Eddie Nash.

John Curtis Holmes had the longest, most prolific career in the history of pornography. He had sex onscreen with two generations of leading ladies, from Seka and Marilyn Chambers to Traci Lords, Ginger Lynn and Italian member of Parliament Ciccolina.

Holmes started in the business around 1968, a time when porn was just beginning to surface from the underground of peep shows and frat houses into mainstream acceptance. The sixties, the pill, "free love," communes, wife swapping, the perverse creativity of mixed-media artists who were pushing the limit, trying to shock—all of these things created an atmosphere in which porn could blossom.

In a way, Holmes was everyman's gigolo, a polyester smoothy with a sparse mustache, a flying collar and lots of buttons undone. He wasn't threatening. He chewed gum and overacted. He took a lounge singer's approach to sex, deliberately gentle, ostentatiously artful, a homely guy with a pinkie ring and a big dick who was convinced that he was every woman's dream.

Holmes's voice was sly and ingratiating. He sounded a lot like Eddie Haskell on "Leave It to Beaver" and bore some resemblance to the actor who played him. Above all, he said, he loved his work: "A happy gardener is one with dirty fingernails, and a happy cook is a fat cook. I never get tired of what I do because I'm a sex fiend. I'm very lusty."

John was born to Mary and Edward Holmes on August 8, 1944, in Pickaway County, Ohio, the youngest of three boys and a girl. Edward, a carpenter, was an alcoholic. Mary was a Bible-thumping Baptist. John remembered screaming, yelling, his father puking all over the kids. He lost his virginity at age twelve to a thirty-six-year-old woman who was a friend of his mother's.

After three years in the army, at age nineteen, Holmes went to work as an ambulance driver, and soon thereafter he met Sharon Gebenini. Sharon was a nurse at USC County General, working on a team that was pioneering open-heart surgery. In 1965, the two were married.

One summer day in 1968, Sharon came home a little early from work. She'd gone to the market, and planned a special dinner for her husband.

Recently, Holmes had been drifting from job to job, trying to find a niche. He quit the ambulance service and sold shoes, furniture, Fuller brushes door-to-door. Currently he was training to be a security guard.

Now, Sharon left her purse in the foyer, squeaked down the hall to the bathroom of their apartment in Glendale. The door was open. Inside was her husband. He had a tape measure in one hand, his penis in the other.

"What are you doing?" she asked.

"What does it look like I am doing?"

"Is there something wrong?"

"No, I'm just curious," said Holmes.

Sharon went to the bedroom, laid down, read a magazine. Twenty minutes later, Holmes walked into the room. He had a full erection.

"It's incredible," said John.

"What?"

"It goes from five inches all the way to ten. Ten inches long! Four inches around!"

"That's great," said Sharon, turning a page of her magazine. "You want me to call the press?"

Unbeknownst to Sharon, Holmes had recently started in porn following an encounter with a professional photographer named Joel in the bathroom of the poker parlor in Gardina. Holmes was doing sex pictorials, dancing in clubs.

Now her husband fixed her with a long stare. Finally he said, "I've got to tell you I've been doing something else, and I think I want to make it my life's work."

And so began the loops and the stags, and then Johnny Wadd was born. Holmes let his hair grow, started wearing three-piece suits. He and Sharon settled into a strange hybrid of domesticity. She paid for food and household expenses, did his laundry, cooked for him when he was home. John kept his porn money and spent it on himself. By 1973, John and Sharon were sharing the same house, even the same bed, but they were no longer having sex. Sharon had gone so far as to stop physical relations, but she couldn't bring herself to kick him out. "Let's face it," she says. "I loved the schmuck. I just didn't like what he was doing."

John bought himself an El Camino pickup and a large diamond solitaire that became his trademark in films. Then he designed a massive gold and diamond ring in the shape of a dragonfly, and a gold belt buckle, measuring eight by five inches. The buckle depicted a mother whale swimming in the ocean, her baby nursing beneath. John was into Save the Whales.

Holmes was an inveterate collector of junk. He picked wire out of dumpsters and sold the copper. He went to garage sales and bought old furniture. He could repair anything, liked sketching and working in clay.

He also collected animal skulls. Once, Sharon says, he got a human head from UCLA. He boiled it clean in a pot on Sharon's stove. They called it Louise. At Christmas, they decorated it with colored lights.

Jeana Sellers (not her real name) arrived in Holmes's life in 1976. She was a teenager, and her parents had just divorced. She'd driven out from Miami with her father and younger sister. Mr. Sellers had no particular plan; they pulled into the apartment complex managed by Sharon Holmes.

Soon after, the courtship of Jeana began. Whenever he returned from days or weeks away, Holmes would bring gifts: stuffed animals, roses, a ring. One night Holmes told Jeana to meet him at the van. They went to the beach. "I didn't know what was going to happen, but I knew what might," she says. "We sat on the rocks, the moon was just right. We sat for a long time, and he was very, very quiet. He just stared. I played in the water. When I got out, he said, 'Let's go,' and we drove toward home. And then, just as we got to this intersection, he slammed on the brakes. It was dark, and there wasn't any traffic. He said, 'Would you make love to me?' I literally shook to death. I said yes. I loved him. We did it in the van. After that I was his."

By 1978, Holmes was freebasing cocaine all the time. He'd been turned on to the drug on a movie set in Las Vegas and had been smoking ever since. Now he never went anywhere without his brown Samsonite briefcase. Inside were his drugs, his glass pipe, baking soda and a petri dish for cooking cocaine powder into rock base, a bottle of 151 rum and cotton swabs for lighting the pipe. Jeana was doing freebase too, almost every night.

"When he did coke," says Jeana, "he'd do it until it was all gone, and then he'd scrape the pipe and smoke all the resin he could find, and then he'd take a bunch of Valium. He'd have me make these peanut-butter chocolate-chip brown-sugar butter cookies. All the sugar helped him come down. He'd have a big glass of milk, and we'd turn on the cartoons and then he'd go to bed in Sharon's room. I'd usually fall asleep on the couch."

By this time, Sharon had befriended Jeana. "The poor girl was emaciated. I knew the whole picture," says Sharon. "He was picking on a kid that didn't know any better. I had to let her know there was another world out there, that John was not God Almighty.

"John was terrified that I was going to confront her. But I had no reason to confront her. Why? Why would I confront her? He meant nothing to me in that way."

John was gone now more and more, making films in Europe, San Francisco and Hawaii, doing private tricks, traveling to film openings across the country. On sets, he was harder and harder to deal with. He'd lock himself in bathrooms, in closets. People who worked with him joked that you had to leave a trail of freebase from the bathroom to the bedroom to get Holmes to work.

*   *   *

Tracy McCourt turned right on to Dona Lola Place, drove a hundred yards into the cul-de-sac, parked, cut the engine. While McCourt waited, Lind, Launius and DeVerell entered Nash's house through a sliding glass door Holmes had left open according to plan. Lind took the lead and charged down the hall, a short-barreled .357 Magnum in one hand, a stolen San Francisco police detective's badge in the other. Diles and Nash were in the living room. Diles was wearing sweat pants, carrying a breakfast tray. Nash was wearing blue bikini briefs.

"Freeze!" yelled Lind. "You're under arrest! Police officers!"

DeVerell and Launius covered Nash. Lind made his way behind the shirtless, blubbery bodyguard. He shifted the badge to his gun hand, his left, then took out the handcuffs with his right. As he fumbled with his paraphernalia and Dile's thick wrists, Launius came over to help, tripped, bumped into Lind's arm. The gun discharged. Diles was burned with the muzzle flash. Nash fell to his knees. He begged to say a prayer for his children.

"Fuck your children!" said Launius. "Take us to the drugs."

Lind rolled Diles onto his stomach, handcuffed him, threw a Persian rug over his head. Then he joined the others in Nash's bedroom. Everything was where Holmes had said. Lind put his .357 to Nash's head, asked for the combination to the floor safe. Nash refused. Then Lanius forced the stainless-steel barrel of his gun into Nash's mouth.

In the floor safe were two large Zip-lock bags full of cocaine. In a gray attaché case were cash and jewelry. In a petty-cash box were several thousand Quaaludes and more cocaine. On the dresser was a laboratory vial about three-quarters full of heroin.

Lind taped Nash's hands behind his back, put a sheet over his head. He found a Browning 9-mm under Nash's bed, then went to Diles's room, where he found more weapons. Meanwhile, Launius asked Lind for his hunting knife. He went over to Diles, pulled the rug off his head, edged the knife against his neck.

"Where's the rest of the fucking heroin?" he demanded.

"I don't know," said Diles.

Launius pulled the knife slowly across Diles's neck. Blood flowed.

Suddenly, outside, Tracy McCourt began honking the horn of the getaway car.

"Forget it!" said Lind. "Let's get out of here!"

At 10 A.M., Lind, McCourt, Launius and DeVerell walked through the door of the Wonderland house.

Holmes jumped up from the couch. "So what happened? How did it go down?"

"Don't tell him anything," snapped Lind.

Launius, DeVerrel and Lind went into Launius's bedroom. They'd decided, before leaving Nash's, that they would short Holmes and McCourt in the division of the loot. Working quickly, Launius removed about $100,000 in cash from the briefcase and hid it in his room. Everyone got busy. Holmes and Lind weighed the cocaine. Launius counted the Quaaludes. DeVerell counted the money. On the table were eight pounds of cocaine, five thousand Quaaludes, a kilo of high-quality China White heroin and $10,000 in cash. The jewelry would later be fenced for $150,000. Lind, Launius and DeVerell, the three who'd carried out the robbery, were to receive 25 percent each. Holmes and McCourt went halves on the last share.

As soon as the weighing was done, Holmes went to the kitchen to cook some cocaine powder into rock, then went into the bathroom to smoke. The rest of the Wonderland people took turns injecting heroin and cocaine. After a while, Holmes came back into the living room. He complained about his share of the money. It was only about $3000. He knew that Nash had a lot more than that lying around the house.

An argument ensued. Launius punched Holmes in the stomach. "Get the fuck out of here!" he screamed.

Gregory DeWitt Diles, six feet four, 300 pounds, barged through the front door of Eddie Nash's house, dragging John Holmes by the scruff of his neck.

"In here," said Nash.

Diles shoved, Holmes skidded across the carpet. Nash shut the bedroom door.

Wednesday afternoon, July 1, two days after the robbery. Jeana was tucked into a motel in the Valley. An hour before, Holmes had run into Diles. Holmes was wearing a ring that had been stolen from the boss.

Eddie Nash was fifty-two years old, six feet tall, gray haired, strong and wiry. His family had owned several hotels before the creation of Israel in 1948. Nash told a friend that he missed the moonlight and the olive trees of his homeland, that he'd spent time in a refugee camp, that his brother-in-law was shot by Israeli soldiers.

The youngest son in the family, Nash arrived in America with seven dollars in his pocket. He worked for others for a time, then opened Beef's Chuck, a hotdog stand on Hollywood Boulevard. Nash was on the job day and night, wearing a tall white chef's hat, waiting tables himself.

By the mid-Seventies, Ade Nasrallah had become Eddie Nash and had amassed a fortune. He was also a drug dealer and a heavy user: His drug of choice was freebase; sometimes he mixed the crack with heroin. Nash was missing part of his sinus cavity, one of his lungs had been removed, and he had a steel plate in his head.

For the last several years, Nash had rarely left his white-stone ranch house in Studio City. At home, Nash walked around in a maroon silk robe, or sometimes in bikini briefs, his body covered with a thin sheen of sweat. His voice had a smooth Arabic lilt, "You want to play baseball?" he'd ask his ever-present guests, lighting his butane torch, offering a hit off his pipe.

"The consumption of alcohol and drugs was an ongoing, everyday affair," says an attorney who is a long-time acquaintance of Nash's. "The cast of characters would go from two or three to ten or more. It was amazing, the haphazard way in which people would come and go. You'd walk into the house, there were various girls walking around in various states of undress. Some were quite attractive. Others looked like they'd been sucking on the pipe a little too long.

"When you met with Eddie, you met at his place, on his terms. I believe that cocaine paranoia created within him the desire to stay within that closed environment that he had control over. If anything, one of the themes in Eddie's life has always been control. He wanted to be in charge. He wanted to be the Arab man in his tent. The master, the giver of hospitality. All his lawyers—I think he had maybe six or seven working on different things—all his managers, employees, customers, everyone, would come to him. He'd have Jimmie, the cook, prepare these elaborate spreads. You could walk up, whisper something in his ear, and he'd make it available. Whatever. You just had to ask, and he'd give."

During his six or seven years of heavy drug use, said the attorney, "Nash lost over a million a year directly attributable to drugs. His business empire totally atrophied as a result of coke. What really cracks me up is people believe he was a dope dealer. That's bullshit. He was consuming it. At an alarming rate."

On the afternoon of Wednesday, July 1, 1981, Eddie Nash was again consuming drugs at an alarming rate. He'd been ripped for eight pounds of cocaine, but the Wonderland Gang hadn't found his private stash, and now he was bubbling his glass pipe furiously. He'd sent two of his minions out to score more drugs, but they hadn't yet returned. Two customers waited. They did hits off Eddie's pipe, eyed the door.

Now Holmes was in Nash's bedroom. Diles smacked Holmes, threw him across the room, shoved him against a wall. "How could you do this thing!" Eddie Nash screamed. Diles hit him again. "I trusted you! I gave you everything!"

Nash and Holmes had met three years earlier at the Seven Seas. Nash was a big fan of porn. He invested in movies, leased office space to several porn-related operations. Holmes was one of the greats in the business. Nash liked having him around. He introduced him to all his guests. "I'd like you to meet Mr. John Holmes," he'd say.

For his part, Holmes did anything he could for Nash. Frequently, he brought him girls. On Christmas Day 1980, he'd even presented Jeana. Nash reciprocated with a quarter ounce of coke. Holmes thought Nash was the most evil man he'd ever met, but he couldn't quite figure him out, so he respected him.

Now things were not so friendly. Holmes was crumpled on the floor. Diles leveled a gun at his head. Nash was leafing through a little black book that Diles had taken from Holmes's pocket.

"Who's this in Ohio?" Nash screamed. "Who's Mary? Your mother? Who's this in Montana? . . . Is this your brother? . . . I will kill your whole family! All of them! Go back to that house! Get my property! Bring me their eyeballs! Bring me their eyeballs in a bag, and I will forget what you have done to me! Go!"

Thursday, July 2, 3:30 A.M. Sharon Holmes switched on the porch light, spied through the peephole. Christ, she thought, John. She hadn't seen him for three months. His clothes were ripped, he was bloody from head to toe. He stared straight ahead, unblinking. She opened the door, folded her arms against her chest.

"Well?"

"Accident . . . car . . . um . . ." he stammered. "Can I . . . come in?"

They went to the bathroom. Sharon, a registered nurse, rummaged through a well-stocked medicine cabinet, brought out iodine and cotton swabs. She reached up and took John's chin in her hand, turned his head side to side. Funny, she thought, no cuts, no abrasions. Just blood. "You had an accident in the Malibu?"

John looked down at Sharon. His eyes blinked rapidly. They'd been married sixteen years. Sharon always knew when he was lying. That's probably why he always came back. "Run me a bath, will you?" he said.

John eased into the tub. Sharon sat on the commode. "What now?" she thought. He dunked his head, put a steaming washcloth over his face. Then he sat up. "Murders," he said. "I was there."

"What murders? What do you mean you were there?"

"It was my fault," John said, his eyes welling with tears. "I stood there and watched them kill these people."

"What are you talking about?"

"I was involved in a robbery," John began, and he told the story. The setup, the robbery, Nash's threat to kill his whole family, Sharon included. "So I told him everything," John said. "I told where the robbers lived and how to get there. I had to take them there."

"Who?"

"Three men and myself."

"Okay, you took them there."

"I took them there. There was a security system at the house. I called up and said I had some things for the people inside and to let me up. They opened the security gate, and the four of us went up the stairs, and when the door opened, they forced their way inside. Someone held a gun to my head. I stood there against the wall. I watched them beat them to death."

"You stood there?"

"There was nothing I could do."

"John, how could you?"

"It was them or me. They were stupid. They made him beg for his life. They deserved what they got."

"Blood! Blood! So much blood!" Holmes was having a nightmare. Tossing and moaning, punching and kicking. "So much blood!" he groaned over and over.

Jeana was scared to death. She didn't know what to do. Wake him? Let him scream? It was Thursday, July 2, 1981. After bathing at Sharon's, Holmes had come here, to this motel in the Valley. He had walked through the door, flopped on the bed, passed out.

Jeana sat very still on the edge of the bed, watching a TV that was mounted on the wall. After a while, the news. The top story was something about a mass murder. Four bodies. A bloody mess. A house on Wonderland Avenue. Jeana stood up, moved closer to the tube. *That house,* she thought. Things started to click. *I've waited outside that house. Isn't that where John gets his drugs?*

Hours passed, John woke. Jeana said nothing. They made a run to McDonald's for hamburgers. They watched some more TV. Then came the late-night news. The cops were calling it the Four on the Floor Murders. Dead were Joy Miller, Billy DeVerell, Ron Launius, Barbara Richardson. The Wonderland Gang. The murder weapon was a steel pipe with threading at the ends. Thread marks found on walls, skulls, skin. House tossed by assailants. Blood and brains splattered everywhere, even on the ceilings. The bodies were discovered by workmen next door; they'd heard faint cries from the back of the house: "Help me. Help me." A fifth victim was carried out alive. Susan Launius, twenty-five, Ron Launius's wife. She was in intensive care with a severed finger and brain damage. The murders were so brutal that police were comparing the case to the Tate-LaBianca murders by the Manson Family.

Holmes and Jeana watched from the bed. Jeana was afraid to look at John. She cut her eyes slowly, caught his profile. He was frozen. The color drained from his face. She actually saw it. First his forehead, then his cheeks, then his neck. He went white.

*   *   *

On July 10, police knocked down the door of their motel room and arrested Jeana and Holmes. For the next three days, John, Jeana and Sharon were held in protective custody in a luxury hotel in downtown Los Angeles. Armed guards in the lobby, in the hallway. Room service. John tried to make a deal with the cops. He wanted witness protection, a new name, money, a home. He wanted new names for Sharon and Jeana too. He offered the police secrets. Names of mobsters, drug dealers, prostitutes, pimps. The police wanted to know who killed the Wonderland Gang. Holmes wouldn't tell. They cut him loose.

The three went back to Sharon's house. Sharon cooked dinner. John picked up Sharon's two dogs from the kennel. Later, the women dyed John's hair black, and John and Jeana painted the Malibu gray with a red top. They used cans of spray paint. The finish was drippy and streaked, but it didn't matter. They were going underground.

Now it was midnight in the parking lot at a Safeway in Glendale. The Malibu was idling. Jeana sat in the front seat. John leaned up against the back bumper, smoking a cigarette. Sharon stood with her arms crossed.

"Change your mind. Come with us, Sharon."

"No way, John."

"It can be the three of us, Sharon, like old times."

"You've got to be joking."

"You can't do this to me," he said.

"Why? Why can't I?"

"Because I love you."

Sharon looked at him. On their first date, he'd brought a bottle of Mateus and a handful of flowers. Sharon had watched through the window as he'd picked them from a neighbor's front yard. Now she shook her head slowly, walking around the car to the passenger side. Jeana leaned out the window, and they hugged. Over the years, they'd become like mother and daughter. "Take care of him," Sharon said.

"Hello, Jeana."

"Chris? Is that you?"

"How are you, sis?"

"Fine. Where are you calling from? You sound close."

"I'm here."

"In Miami?"

"Yeah."

"What are you doing here?"

"Well, I, I, ah, came . . . with a friend. Listen. Tell me where you are. I'll pick you up."

Jeana hung up the phone. Her brother Chris, sixteen, lived in Oregon.

She hadn't heard from him in, what, six months? Now it was December 4, 1981. After leaving California, Jeana and John had gone to Vegas, then Montana, then headed south, visiting the Grand Canyon, the Painted Desert. Holmes broke into cars along the way, financing the trip with stolen goods.

The couple ended up in Miami, at a small, run-down hotel on Collins Avenue. Everyone there was on some kind of slide. Big Rosie, the manager, let Jeana work the switchboard and clean rooms in exchange for rent. Holmes went to work for a construction company, painting a hotel down the strip. For extra money, Jeana solicited tricks on the beach.

"Everybody at the hotel got to know us," Jeana says. "We were real friendly. John was doing a lot of drawing. Drawings of the dog, of me. We'd have dinner with other people at the hotel, go to movies. We were like a normal couple. After a while, I said I didn't want to go out on the beach anymore. We had a big fight. I ran out the door, down to the pool, and he ran after me, the fool. Everybody was down there. He beat the shit out of me, then walked back up to the room. Everybody was just shocked."

Now her brother was in town; something weird was going on. Chris didn't have a driver's license. How could he rent a car?

They picked up a six-pack, went to a park, sat by a pond.

"Jeana, I've got to tell you. See that car over there? It's the cops."

When the cops got to his hotel room, Holmes was there. "I've been expecting you," he said. He invited them in for coffee.

Following his arrest in Miami, Holmes was tried for the murder of the Wonderland Gang. His defense was simple: John Holmes was the "sixth victim" of the Wonderland murders, and Eddie Nash was "evil incarnate." "Ladies and gentleman," his lawyer told the jury at the outset, "unlike some mysteries, this is not going to be a question of 'Who done it?' This is going to be a question of 'Why aren't the perpetrators here?'"

In the end, the most damaging evidence the prosecution could produce was a palm print on a headboard above one of the victims. Holmes refused to testify. The jury found him innocent.

With all the publicity from the murders, John Holmes had achieved almost mainstream celebrity. The video boom was just beginning, and Holmes became a kind of Marlon Brando of porn. No longer the leading man, he was now the featured oddity. In *California Valley Girls,* for instance, he had one scene. He came in, sat on a couch. A girl entered stage right. Then another girl, another. At the end, there were six working at once on his penis.

Early in 1983, Holmes was shooting *Fleshpond* at a studio in San Francisco. One of the actresses in the cast was Laurie Rose. Laurie was nineteen; she came from a small town outside Vegas. In the business she was billed as Misty Dawn, the anal queen of porn.

"That first time, we didn't get to work together," says Laurie, "but we were attracted. It sounds silly, but you know how you can meet someone for the first time and it's like you know them already?"

After the film, John and Laurie, who looked like Jeana, began dating. Usually, they smoked freebase and had sex. Then, says Laurie, "the third time I went up there, he came up to me with the mirror and said, 'You want a hit?' and I turned to him and said no. He looked shocked. He said, 'Why not?' and I said, 'Because it makes me feel funny and I can't talk.' So he went in the bathroom, and he locked himself in. He stayed in there like three hours, and I'm just sitting there, you know, twiddling my thumbs. Finally he came out and said, 'You know what? This stuff makes me feel funny too. I'm going to quit.' "

Apparently, Holmes made good his promise and stopped doing drugs. John and Laurie stayed home a lot and watched videos. On weekends they went to swap meets and yard sales.

Then, in the summer of 1985, John tested positive for AIDS.

"When he came back," says Laurie, "he was laughing about it. We closed up the office and went to the beach. We played our favorite songs, walked, talked. John said he felt like he was chosen to get AIDS because of who he was, how he lived. He felt like he was an example."

John Holmes died on March 13, 1988. "His eyes were open," says Laurie, "and it looked like he had looked up to Death and said, 'Here I am.' It was the most peaceful look I ever saw in my life. I tried to shut his eyes like in the movies, but they wouldn't stay shut."

Holmes didn't want a funeral, but he did have a last wish. "He wanted me to view his body and make sure that all the parts were there," says Laurie. "He didn't want part of him ending up in a jar somewhere. I viewed his body nekked, you know, and then I watched them put the lid on the box and put it in the oven. We scattered his ashes over the ocean."

Six months later, on September 8, 1988, Diles and Nash were charged with the murders on Wonderland Avenue. They were later acquitted.

Paradise Lost

TOM HORTON

THE EXXON OIL SPILL IN ALASKA WAS A CRIME AGAINST THE ENVIRONMENT, BUT IT MAY HAVE CAUSED GREATER DAMAGE TO THE HUMAN SPIRIT.

The call from ROLLING STONE came a few days after the biggest oil spill in American history. Minutes after midnight, March 24th, 1989, the supertanker *Exxon Valdez* had grounded on Bligh Reef, disgorging 11 million gallons of North Slope crude into the pristine waters of Alaska's Prince William Sound.

I wondered how ROLLING STONE editor Susan Murcko had ever heard of me, let alone decided to offer the environmental story of the year to a relative unknown. After a dozen years on the environment beat for the Baltimore *Sun*, I had been two years in semiexile, running an education center in a tiny fishing village on a marsh island twelve miles out in the Chesapeake Bay.

Murcko said she had read my book of nature essays, *Bay Country*. The essay on advanced waste-water treatment was particularly compelling, she said. She figured anyone who could make sewage readable could distill meaning from the often technical charges and countercharges flying about the mammoth spill and the cleanup facing Alaska.

Coming after twenty months of teaching seventh graders to differentiate among marsh grasses, the offer to jet off to Alaska seemed a refreshing change of pace at the least. I told Murcko I wanted to think about it for a day.

I really wasn't sure what I was getting into. I hadn't read ROLLING STONE regularly since my college days, in the Sixties. Would I be expected to produce a "Fear and Loathing in Valdez" piece, à la Hunter Thompson? I was a nice boy, brought up journalistically to pass the *Sun*'s "breakfast test," which forbade imagery that might roil the morning digestion of readers in areas populated by the paper's owners and top management. And my family now lived in one of America's most traditional, God-fearing communities this side of the Amish, where *Grit* was the newspaper of choice and the only local government was that of the Methodist church. The night before I would leave on assignment, my son returned from evening services. "Dad," he said, "the whole town is praying for you"—whether for my safe journey or because of my affiliation with a decadent New York journal, he was uncertain.

Also, there was the matter of money. I called a friend who used to freelance for magazines and told him I was prepared to bargain tough, not a penny less than $2500. That would be ten times my previous high, freelancing for local magazines. He said to go for $5000. That seemed astronomical, but this was the big time. Not a penny less than $5000, I told Murcko the next day. There was a silence. I was about to promise to take a sleeping bag and eat sparingly when she said, gently, "Ah, we were thinking of $10,000 for about 10,000 words." "Sounds fine," I managed to say without a stutter. My salary at the time was $18,000 a year.

Murcko and I talked a long time that day about how we should cover the spill. She must be Hunter Thompson's polar opposite—calm, reasoned, therapeutic in her willingness to let a writer prattle on, injecting advice painlessly. The hardest decision we made was that I *would not* rush to the scene of the disaster. It would be a howling mob of press, and most of my potential sources would be overwhelmed trying to respond to the crush of events. I would use the time to gather background on the history and ecology of oil spills.

There was a matter I was nervous about broaching with Murcko but felt compelled to settle upfront. She should realize that the environmental impacts of this spill almost surely would not be as horrible as the public already was convinced they were. I had covered lots of disasters—famines in Africa, Three Mile Island, an oil-well blowout in Mexico even bigger than the Valdez spill. What you often found was that long before you were ready to write, television already had sought out and conveyed around the world the direst and most compelling fragments of the disaster.

It was not that these images were untrue—indeed, they often galvanized public opinion and support for needed disaster relief—but they distorted reality as a telephoto lens compresses a few people into a crowd. More than once, in famine-stricken Ethiopia and Sudan, I had found it surprisingly hard to find anything to match the horrific pot-bellied, dead-by-the-time-this-film-airs children that had been filling viewers' screens for days. The broader story—chronic malnutrition and its underlying causes—was at least as important as these tragic worst cases, but I had seen the pressure to make the disaster measure up to its early televised images affect the judgment of more than one editor.

Murcko said sensationalism was not what she was after. I told her I thought if we could tell the story of all the ways this spill affected Alaskans, sociologically and philosophically as well as economically and environmentally, we would have something special. It would take time, and it would take space to tell it so that readers would understand the subtleties. Murcko said she thought she could get the space we needed.

Dawn was just erasing stars in the eastern sky when I left my island for Alaska one chilly April morning. My skiff parted flocks of wild swans and geese as I shot the winding marsh channel and keyed on a red-blinking navigational buoy to set a course for the mainland. I often try to write my story in my head before I get to the scene. Usually this amounts to mental nail biting, a security blanket against the fear that you won't be able to produce, but as I passed that red blinker, still some 3000 miles from Valdez, a critical chunk of the eventual narrative I would write fell into place.

"Red right returning"—everywhere in North America it is one of the most basic tenets of navigation; you always keep the red channel markers on your right when returning to a port and, conversely, keep them on your left when leaving. Bligh Reef, in Prince William Sound, on that fateful midnight was marked with a red flasher just like the one I was passing at sunrise in Chesapeake Bay. How could a modern supertanker with a trained crew, world-class navigational gear and clear weather fail to do as I was doing—how could it go to the wrong side of a bright red light flashing so clearly against the total blackness of the Alaska night?

In Valdez I soon arrived at a dual-passport routine for extracting information. A ROLLING STONE writer got immediate attention from the fishermen and most Alaskans (despite a lot of disappointment that I did not know Hunter Thompson—hell, I didn't even know P. J. O'Rourke). This same affiliation caused visible anguish among the Exxon crowd, which was so sure I was a son of gonzo they did not dare to ask about Hunter Thompson. They unbent slightly when I hauled out my Baltimore *Sun* press card (I was at the time on leave from the paper). So it went: To U.S. senators, congressmen, state-government types over fifty and anyone from corporate America, I turned *Sun*-ny side up; for the kids, the environmentalists and the free-spirited fishermen, why, hell yes, it was just one wild and crazy time after another back at the STONE.

None of this established rapport with the Indians, whose subsistence livelihoods were grievously threatened by the spill. Some came out of their shells when I began to talk about the island community where I lived in mid-Chesapeake, but I consider it my failure that I was never able to put in perspective native Alaskans' perceptions of the spill.

I stayed in Alaska four weeks—stayed mostly away from the official press briefings and handouts and news conferences. Those I could read about later. My plan was to stay out on Prince William Sound as much as possible. In a wilderness, getting anywhere can take inordinate amounts of time. The sound, which many people envisioned as totally oil covered, encompasses tens of thousands of square miles of water and unpopulated coastline. Currents and tides had sent oil throughout it, but it was quite possible to travel for hours by boat or plane without seeing a trace of either oil or the massive cleanup activities.

There were whole days I spent dozing and pacing in my orange survival suit on remote shorelines where a float-plane or fishing boat had dropped me with assurance that another ride would be along any hour. I tried not to dwell on the fact that Exxon's cleanup crews were often accompanied by guards armed to shoot any hungry bears just then coming out of hibernation.

The best of times I spent with the fishing people of Cordova, just down the sound from Valdez. In poetry and song at community gatherings, in candid interviews and in stopping sometimes in their daily activities just to cry, they were so eloquent about the pain they felt over the spill—a loss, a sense of violation and broken trust that I am convinced will be of longer-lasting impact than any hydrocarbon analysis of the sound's sediments will ever show. I thought those feelings were as important as any "news" I reported.

Four weeks. I could have stayed longer, but I knew in advance I would not. I've found on other stories in faraway places that a month without a break is about my limit. After that period the dashing correspondent just gets homesick. He misses his wife and kids and begins babbling to baffled interviewees about the good old Chesapeake Bay.

I stopped in New York on the way home—the first time Murcko and I had ever met face to face. Jann Wenner, as kinetic as Murcko is phlegmatic, debriefed me from a toilet stall as I peed in the men's room. It was a little odd, but his questions were to the point, and I liked his enthusiasm. I suppose that is one way very busy people cram it all in.

Cramming it all in came to occupy Murcko and me as weeks rolled by. I knew when I ended up with 350 pages of notes, typed, single-spaced, that we would need more than 10,000 words. Keep writing, my noble editor said. It was May by now, and writing had to cope with the spring crab run. The fishermen's pumps in the crab holding tanks sucked so much electricity that my computer suffered constant brownouts.

At some point around 15,000 words, just when I was thinking I'd soon own a Volvo, the powers that be at the magazine served notice that their dollar-a-word payment had reached its limits. By then I would have paid *them* not to make me cut that mother back to the agreed-upon 10,000 words. At 18,000 words, I figured I'd better send Murcko what I had and hold my breath. Let's see the rest, said that woman of ultimate good taste and literary generosity. To make a long story short, the fever ran its course at about 32,000 words, and ROLLING STONE, bless its hide, swallowed the whole thing. I calculate I spent more than fifty hours just going over it all with the fact checker, Bradley Bloch.

After the piece ran, I decided it was self-indulgent to think I could not cover an oil spill in less than half a book. A reader from Ohio wrote that the piece "lasted longer than the spill." Then I got a note from a family in Cordova whom I had come to respect immensely. "You hit it just exactly right," they said.

Many people told me after the spill that with so much research invested, I should write a book, but I felt then and feel now it was a very good long article and a very thin book. I think we see all too many thin books that really should be wonderful long articles, because almost no one publishes long articles anymore. Perhaps that includes ROLLING STONE, squeezed as are most magazines by the recession. My last piece for them, about Greenpeace, began at 10,000 words and had to be cut to under 7000. Anyhow, I can say that once upon a time, in the pages of ROLLING STONE, I wrote till I could write no more.

RS 567/568

DECEMBER 14TH–28TH, 1989

Time and again, when I have gotten numb trying to sort claim from counterclaim about responsibility for the spill and its cleanup, I go visit the animals, the birds and otters, oiled by the spill, brought from all over the sound to rehab centers hastily erected here. They are the only true innocents in this whole, sad business. They are not consumers of petrochemical products, nor sellers of salmon. They are neither regulators nor environmentalists, are not in any way responsible for what happened. They just are, and now many of them aren't anymore.

Over at the bird center, auburn ponytail flipping as she moves swiftly about business, Jessica Porter is tubing a murre. Each of the several dozen birds recovering in the converted classrooms of the Prince William Sound Community College gets tube-fed three times a day. Murres, pretty, little waterfowl that appear to fly underwater when diving for food, took a heavy hit from the oil. Hundreds will be recovered, thousands likely died and were not recovered, says Porter, one of the veterinarians here. (The total estimate of birds killed by oil will eventually go over 100,000.) Another murre, which arrived several hours ago looking like a sullen tar ball, has been resuscitated and cleaned with a one-percent solution of Dawn in warm water. Dawn, says Porter, after years of experimentation, is still the only product that cuts the grease and is still gentle. "We get lots of ambulance-chasers at these spills, trying to sell us all sorts of products, but nothing beats Dawn," she says.

Soaping the murre has taken two volunteers working with toothbrushes and Water Piks nearly an hour and fifteen tubs of soapy water. Next comes another session of forty minutes, rinsing the murre with high-pressure hoses until, improbably, its feathers become dry. "It sounds crazy," explains Porter, "but what the oil does is disrupt the integrity of the feathers, which form a protective basket around the bird, trapping air. As the oil is removed, the feathers actually become so dry you can blow in them as you rinse." The murre, pinioned by beak and wing and one webbed foot, is pissed . . . but fluffing nicely now under the water jets. "Hang on, murre, hang on!" says Jim Noland, one of the washers, but no, "back off, he's had it for the day. . . . See his eyelids coming over his eyes, his heartbeat's up, too." They will try again tomorrow with the murre. The birds coming in now, says Porter, are goopier but healthier than in the early days of the spill, as the more toxic elements of the crude, the light ends, like toluene and xylene, evaporate, leaving the heavier asphaltenes, waxes and paraffins.

Porter, raised at Tenth Avenue and Fifty-second Street in New York City, worked her first spill in 1964, in the marshes of East Anglia, at age fifteen. "It was horrible—we were using acetone, a solvent, for God's sake," she says. "It cut the oil, but the inhalation was toxic to both the birds and the rescuers." Nowadays she rehabs hummingbirds, otters, foxes, raccoons, muskrats, deer, elephant seals and other wildlife at her Wolf Hollow Wildlife Rehabilitation Center in the San Juan Islands of Washington State. "It doesn't pay like doctoring poodles in Honolulu, but it's a living," she says.

Bird rescue, says Porter, has always been the orphan of oil-spill cleanup, "getting the most PR and the least money. Originally, it was unscientific, and it got this image of little old ladies whose kids left them with an overabundance of maternal instinct and lots of spare time. But the people running it these days are professional zoologists, biologists, vets. Wildlife rehabilitating is becoming a science." Her employer here, the International Bird Rescue and Research Center (IBRRC), was contacted by Alyeska, for which Alice Berkner, the founder of the IBRRC, did training sessions two years ago. "What Alice has done is standardize techniques for cleaning birds and making sure they are ready for release that can be applied anywhere in the world," says Porter.

I asked Porter how she justified the cost, estimated at more than a quarter million dollars to date, of paying boats to range the huge sound, chasing down a few hundred birds, many of whom will die, all of whom together, whether they live or die, will not affect the ecological balance of the region. Her answer was good enough to serve for all future spills: "Because they are citizens of this planet, too, and we are responsible for them . . . their right to do what they do in a healthy, clean, free environment. I think more people are recognizing these spills as a crime against creatures with no redress in Congress or the courts. This is just taking responsibility for what we did, all of us who drive cars and use plastic cups."

In the background as we talked, a volunteer was busy converting shot glasses to cc's. She figured it would help fishermen who were picking up the birds under contract to Exxon calculate how much fluid was needed to hydrate the victims on the way into the center. Another volunteer supervised a day-care center for the children of rescue workers. The bird rescue center, for all its makeshift surroundings, smacked of organization, training and single-minded devotion to its purpose rarely seen in other sectors of the spill response.

"IBRRC was called two or three hours after the spill," said Porter. "I was contacted at 6:30 a.m. Friday [March 24th] and given half an hour to catch a plane. Four of us were in Valdez setting up operations on Saturday morning. I think we need the same kind of SWAT-team type of response to the spills themselves."

Perhaps it would work. But why is it I can just see Alyeska and Exxon, if they ran the bird operation, rejecting volunteers just as they rejected help from fishermen on the spill; citing the danger of bird bites, risks of infection, corporate liability, inadequacy of housing? . . . What I think is really the secret of the bird people's getting up here and bending to work so wholeheartedly is not just organization, or experience—it is because they care so damn much.

From the bird rescue center, it's a short walk between dirty, bulldozed banks of old snow to the Growden-Harrison Elementary School, which more resembles a keening, squalling MASH unit these days. It is home to some seventy or eighty otters just now, in all stages of recovery and disintegration from the dark kiss of the *Exxon Valdez*. Early on, things were a lot worse, says Terrie Williams, a marine-mammal expert up here from the Sea World Research Institute, in San Diego. One large otter came in, bleeding and duct-taped from head to toe because the fishermen who found it had nothing to restrain it with. It died soon after. The rescuers knew that oil would disrupt the otters' insulating fur, and the mammals, which have no insulating layer of subcutaneous fat, as do seals, would die in the icy water that is otherwise their natural home.

But that didn't prepare them, say workers, for what they got—otters rattling and gasping, contorting, foaming at the mouth, excreting blood. Autopsies revealed that the real damage often was internal—livers that crumbled to the touch, lungs blown like broccoli, immune systems defused, all from those light ends, the toxics coming off the crude in the initial days of the spill. The otters inhaled the fumes, absorbed them through their skin. The pain they suffered, says a vet, "must have been indescribable."

"We know a lot more now than we did about the logistics of trying to save animals in a big spill," says Terrie Williams. "We know now it's a nightmare."

Things at this point are more settled. There have been no deaths for days among the inmates, which are housed in pens under the score clock and backboards of the gym. A sign on the wall reads: ALL SIX OTTERS THAT WENT TO TACOMA ARE DOING FINE. . . . THEY HAD A GOOD TRIP AND ARE ALL EATING. YEA! Many of the otters have been named— Fat Albert, Ollie, Otteri, Garfield, Odie, Kimmer; one, fur slicked heavily with crude, has been dubbed John Tower. Exxon has given the recovery center here "a blank check," say the vets.

"The critical thing," says Williams, "is to get them grooming their fur again to get the air layer back into it, get their natural oils flowing. If they don't groom, they die of exposure." As of late April the center has handled about 140 otters, of which about half have died or been euthanized. Long-term survival is still questionable for many of the living. Estimates of otter deaths in the sound are running as high as 6400—perhaps half of the local population. Some commercial fishermen in Cordova, when they first heard of the otters' plight in a meeting with Exxon, stood and applauded. They are convinced that the expanding otter population (otters are federally protected from hunting or trapping) is adversely affecting their catch. Others recognize that nothing, including their own endangered livelihoods, has so mobilized public sentiment about the tragic nature of the spill as the travail of oiled otters on the world's television screens. The crush of media at the recovery center in the early days of the spill probably killed some otters or hastened their demise, workers here acknowledge.

The last otter I saw in Valdez was a pregnant female that had come in days earlier with corneas scarred shut from the fumes. She had been moved to an outdoor cage, a good sign, but now she has just aborted her pup. The female lies listlessly on the floor of the plywood and wire cage, as another otter licks and grooms about her sightless eyes and—there is no other word for it—cuddles her. I know the journalistic pitfalls of the Bambi syndrome, of attributing human emotions to dumb animals, but I also know that the great ethologist Konrad Lorenz, after a lifetime of scientific study of animal behavior, felt strongly that "in terms of emotions, animals are much more akin to us than is generally assumed." I haven't the least trouble believing that.

I think it would be fitting to invite some of the executives of Alyeska and its owner companies, and maybe a few tanker captains who haven't yet got as careless as Joe Hazelwood—invite them to spend some time as volunteer otter handlers. The men who can ram one of the world's biggest pipelines across untrammeled Alaska and navigate superships through the planet's stormiest ocean then could try something really challenging, like putting the natural oil back in a wild creature's fur, or figuring out what to do with a blinded otter.

Oil Is a Natural Substance

Let me make a modest confession here. I don't believe that this oil spill, and oil spills in general, damage the environment as badly as most people think they do. Granted, the Exxon spokesman who announced early on that "oil is a natural substance" was colossally insensitive, as though telling a rape victim that sex is a natural act; but the fact is, more than a decade of close scientific attention to oil spills has shown the marine environment is more capable of degrading and assimilating crude oil than was generally assumed. Studies by a wide range of interests, from the oil industry to the National Academy of Sciences, suggest that biological impacts from large spills are seldom as extensive or as long-term as the public perceives. Marked exceptions are the tragic impact on birds and otters that encounter oil.

Perhaps the worst-case spill in history, from the standpoint of damage to the ecosystem, was from the *Amoco Cadiz* in 1978, when six times as much crude oil as from the *Exxon Valdez* went directly ashore on the coast of Brittany. The extensive salt marshes there are generally a more fragile habitat than the rocky shores and gravel beaches hit in Prince William Sound and less easily cleansed by either nature or man. (The NOAA ranks the nation's coastlines by sensitivity to oil spills, with 10—protected coastal marshes—being the most sensitive. A sheer, rocky headland subjected to high wave energy would be an example of a 1 ranking. None of the shores hit here ranked higher than 8, and at least seventy percent of them ranked lower.) At the *Amoco Cadiz* spill site, which was much harder hit, fishing was normal again in less than three years, mollusks and clams on the bottom recovered in six years. The longest-term impacts were associated with the marsh areas that had been immediately cleaned of oil, sometimes with heavy machinery. Marshes left alone recovered virtually 100 percent within five years, while cleansed marshes took years longer.

The waters of Prince William Sound are mostly hundreds of feet deep, often nearly to the shore, and relatively devoid of suspended sediment, the latter due to the lack of soil washing off its forested, rocky watershed. "That's excellent news for the environment there and bodes well for the fisheries," said James R. Payne, who has done extensive studies for the NOAA on the fate of North Slope crude oil in cold-water environments like the sound. He explained that it seemed almost certain the area would escape one of the biggest long-term problems of oil spills—the burial of toxic portions of the oil in bottom sediments. These can subsequently leach out over time or possibly work their way up the food chain as they are consumed by lower life forms on the bottom, which are eaten by higher predators, and so on. "The two major ways you get that is with sandy beaches, which we didn't have here, and with high loads of suspended sediment in the water [that can take the hydrocarbons to the bottom]," said Payne. He said sediment loads need to be at least 100 parts sediment suspended in every 1 million parts of water for that to happen. Prince William Sound had levels last spring of about .4 to 4 parts per million.

As far as toxicity in the water itself, a good deal of the nastiest portions, the so-called light ends of the spill, evaporated in a matter of hours or a couple of days—so much so that the spill probably lost fifteen to twenty percent of its total mass in that period, according to NOAA scientists. The highest level of toxicity scientists at the spill were able to measure in the water was .24 parts hydrocarbons to 1 million parts of sound water— that in readings taken in heavily oiled shoreline areas about two weeks after the spill. Readings from a week later found these toxicities reduced to about .04 parts per million. "The lowest levels at which we get any effects on sensitive organisms like larval fish and shellfish are from .1 ppm to 1 ppm, so I would not expect to see any widespread impacts [in the water]," said John Robinson of the NOAA.

"I think effects from [oil in the water] are going to be very, very difficult to measure, They will be so low, and given the naturally occurring variations in any species, it'll be extremely difficult statistically to ever show the long-term effect on fisheries," said Payne.

No one, of course, argues that the spill was benign or says that Exxon should leave off its beach-cleaning efforts—although the smart money is mostly on nature to finish the bulk of the job. And it seems likely that there are areas where oil has become trapped so deeply within the gravels and boulders of beaches that occasional sheens will be oozing out for years, maybe a decade or more; but the problem will be a lot closer to a nuisance than the catastrophic. "With a few exceptions, I'd be surprised two or three years from now if you can see much impact either analytically or visually," said David Kennedy, Robinson's colleague at the NOAA.

On a national scale, look at what Congress *did not* say about oil and the environment in its December 1988 oversight report *Coastal Waters in Jeopardy*, the first time that body had focused attention on the "pervasive . . . damage and loss" of environmental quality in the bays and inlets and harbors of America's shores from Maine to Alaska. The report devoted one word to oil and none to oil spills or, for that matter, other disasters. Rather, it detailed the degradation of our waters from the constant, everyday flows of sewage, farm fertilizers, sediment from development and deforestation and plowing; toxics deposited by automobiles into the air and onto streets; power-plant emissions, acid rain, herbicides, pesticides from urban lawns, marsh filling for marinas and seaside condos.

Ultimately, it is not by disasters, terrible and mediagenic though they may be, that we lose our natural heritage but by humdrum incrementalism. The Three Mile Island nuclear fiasco, on the Susquehanna River in Pennsylvania, just upstream from my native Chesapeake Bay, galvanized national attention for weeks in 1979 with the specter of radioactive water spreading downstream, poisoning the rich aquatic life of one of the world's most productive estuaries. Years later the Chesapeake is indeed increasingly polluted from upstream in Pennsylvania, but it is no nuclear meltdown that did it. It is decades of inattention to controlling the millions of pounds of cow manure and other fertilizers flowing quietly, incessantly off poorly managed farms, clotting the waters with algal growth, overwhelming the natural balance of life in the great bay.

So what does it all mean? Have we overreacted? If the studies, which assuredly will be done, find no measurable diminution of algal productivity, no untoward elevation of sediment hydrocarbons, nor any bankrupt crabbers, salmon netters and tour-boat operators a year or two hence, then how do we regard the spill of the *Exxon Valdez*? How far is society justified in going to assure it never occurs again?

John Fowles, in his 1983 essay "The Green Man," proposed that while we worry with some justification about our potential for harming the environment, we exaggerate the degree to which nature has already been overwhelmed: "It is far less nature itself that is yet in true danger than our attitude to it." His point, well taken, was that we are resigned to a continuing indifference, even hostility, toward nature unless we comprehend it must be, in part, forever unquantifiable, beyond lucid and rational discussion, unconnectable with any human purpose. "There is something in the nature of nature, in its presentness, its seeming transience, its creative ferment and hidden potential, that corresponds very closely with the wild, or green man in our psyches; and disappears as soon as it is relegated to a . . . merely classifiable *thing*," concluded Fowles. I would add a corollary—that if we do not treat as a serious crime the disruption of that green man within us, indefinable, unquantifiable though it be, then we will never assign full and proper weight to the damage from events such as occurred on Good Friday in the state of Alaska.

I had been thinking for several days how to express adequately what a lot of the fishing community seemed to feel over the soiling of their sound; how it went so much deeper than even their worst (and probably overestimated) fears of damage to the fisheries.

"There's a deep emotional attachment to our land and water here that's been broken, been violated," said Rick Steiner, a university fisheries adviser resident in Cordova. Indeed, though they are here because of the great numbers of fish, there is far more than the catch statistics operating on the psyches of fishermen these days. Listen to David Grimes and others talk about the beauty in their spring harvest of herring roe, which is deposited like nacreous pearls on the leaves of underwater kelp; about how you can't separate the catching from the spring sights of diving eagles, lengthening daylight, receding snow on the mountain peaks and the phosphorescence of nighttimes: "The herring moving through the plankton blooms like the northern lights, with sea lions and orcas feeding on them, moving like green rockets," said Grimes.

"You gotta crab to know, but it's exciting being out there," said Skip Mallory, a top captain out of Cordova who wrestles giant traps in the stormiest winter weather on the sound for dungeness, tanner and king crab. "You don't just set a pot for crab, you gotta chase 'em, psyche out where they're at, and when you get right on 'em . . . well, it's a challenge, and you're doing it in some of the most beautiful waters in the world."

"Yeah, every fisherman has a little area of the sound that's their special place . . . where they've learned the tides, and the holes, the 'lay' of the place," said Laurie Honkola. "You can't homestead the land around here much anymore, but fishermen kind of homestead favorite spots on the water. Over on the Copper River flats there's certain people you associate with certain spots—the Kikerhenik boys, the Softuk boys the Grass Island boys."

"I feel the social-psychological impacts will far outweight the ecological ones," said Jim Brady. "There's such an anticipation to fishing each spring, and this [spill] came when hopes were at a peak. These people are businessmen, but they've also gone a long way out of their way to make this something they can deeply enjoy. . . . They identify so strongly with certain beaches, bays and inlets."

"For this to happen here, where there were beaches you'd walk on and who knew if another human being had ever been there before you—just look out there," said Sheelagh Mullins, pointing out her living-room window. "There's a whole range of mountains and no one's in them. They've never been defiled . . . that's why people are here. When it [pollution] can happen here, it makes you feel the whole damn planet must be out of control."

Mullins and many other men and women in Valdez and Cordova would tell me days would go by and they would feel all right, then they would be in the middle of shopping, or doing the dishes, or eating, and they would just cry, they weren't even sure why. I kept coming back to rape as an analogy for what had happened. The physical damage would heal, maybe quickly, but the emotional and psychological trauma, I was convinced, might never go away entirely. I could see a lot of "blaming the victim" occurring: "Well, we all use too much oil, so we shouldn't complain"; "We're all guilty for being part of a consumer society"; and so on. And, thinking about Exxon's controversial efforts so far to clean up the spill— would you assign the rapist to nurse the victim back to health?

One April Sunday, a month to the day after the big spill, a gale was building out over Orca Inlet as townspeople walked, bent against the rain, into the "Home of the Wolverines," at Cordova High, for the first Prince William Sound Day. The signs I had originally seen in Valdez advertised that today was to be Prince William Sound *Memorial* Day, and I had heard some talk about turning it into some good old-fashioned Exxon bashing— "sign of the double cross" and all that. But inside the school the townspeople had turned it into something really beautiful, no memorial, or bitterness. The theme was "Sound Love," and the stage was open "to anyone and everyone who wants to share from their heart to create a vision of and for the sound."

Letters and drawings from kids festooned the walls of the gym—from Auke Bay and Wasilla, from Willow, Juneau, Nome and even San Diego—lots of pictures of whales and otters with big red hearts drawn around them: "Did all the animos diey?"; "Wee love our water to bee clean." I've read so many books about the complexities of man-nature relationships. These kids just cut through all the bullshit—Sound Love. Later we'll teach 'em how much more complicated it all is. Brownie Troop 255 handed out bright bouquets of paper flowers. We had poets, recitations, singing, good and bad; a woman read the Declaration of Independence, no one was sure just why, but it seemed fine.

John McCutcheon, a fine folk singer and songwriter who came all the way from Virginia to help out his friends in Cordova, sang a special composition about the salmon called "Silver Run": "One hundred miles, maybe more, along that living, leaping shore/Oh, we'll cast our nets and dream of better times/All along Prince William Sound, where the silvers run and bound/And our lives meet in the tangle of the lines."

At 2:00 p.m. there was five minutes of silence, which was to be observed by people all over Alaska. Then a pretty woman with the richest long black hair talked to us about the years she and her husband, Ray, spent aboard his old gill netter the *Little Queen.*

"Those were lean years, monetarily," she said, "and the only vacations we had were when we loosed our lines from the dock and left all cares and worries in town and went out for weeks at a time for salmon seining and herring seining. In the summer we would go ashore on the closures [of the fishery] to pick arm-load bouquets of wildflowers to fill the cabin all week long . . . exploring old copper and gold mines and herring canneries . . . hiking up to go trout fishing in beautiful, silent lakes . . . beachcombing and clam-digging for that quick, short burst of pure flavor. And in winters, deer hunts I can never forget . . . winter skies etched in my mind as the most delicate turquoises and palest peaches . . . the pinks and powder blues . . . the flaming oranges and deepening nights . . . the storms . . . when only sure boatmanship forged from a lifetime's experience on the sound, coupled with divine protection, saw us through back home safely."

And she read this poem she wrote to Prince William Sound:

> *There is a shadow,*
> *dark as death,*
> *lying over this land and sea.*
> *A place where gods are born*
> *and men to privilege see.*
> *I long to enclose you in my arms,*
> *protect you from the large society,*
> *which grunts with hunger for the oil,*
> *and counts the risk of you*
> *too late spent*
> *and then it is too late*
> *and I sorrow to see*
> *your great and final purity.*
> *This is your last hour,*
> *how I would change it if I could,*
> *perhaps instead your water should.*
> *But nothing can remake your essence*
> *once they begin to take*
> *their greed and poison:*
> *Your death will be their fate.*
> *Stripped of your trees,*
> *your beaches black and lifeless,*
> *I will remember the day*
> *it was not so.*
> *And I will love you*
> *all the more.*

It was fifteen years ago she wrote that, Christine Honkola said the next morning as seven children, some hers, played around her cheery mountainside log home. It was the pipeline that brought her here, she says, "because when it began, I didn't feel like Anchorage was a place any longer for a woman alone. . . . It seemed like a rape a day there." Her husband, out on the spill cleanup, has heard fourth hand that an Exxon skimmer filled up, had no place to unload and was told to dump it back and skim it up again—apocryphal perhaps, but it will go into the lore that's building. The poem she read yesterday seemed remarkably prescient, I said. "Well, we all felt it was inevitable, but it hasn't made what happened easier to take," she said, adding, "If any message goes out to the world, it's that people have to have more say for their concerns about environmental protection, because they are the ones who have the most to lose, not the corporations."

What was lost? Much that can never be adequately articulated, if Fowles is right. Ultimately, it is the poets and singers, and not the scientists, who will come closest to telling us. The true verdict will be rendered in art, in the gut, not in the lab, and I suspect it will be less exonerating than the ten-year follow-up study that is reported at the 1999 Oil Spill Conference in Houston or New Orleans. And to the extent we do not sense that, heed it, we will be vulnerable to future oil spills. We need the numbers, the biological and financial and legal accountings of what happened here and who was responsible, but those alone will not save us from another Joe Hazelwood. A bigger voice in the future of Alaska for those with Sound Love might, though, along with a fuller understanding of what the spill meant to them.

Johnny Clegg's War on Apartheid

SAMUEL G. FREEDMAN

SOUTH AFRICA'S BEST-KNOWN MUSICIAN HAS DEDI-
CATED HIS LIFE TO CROSSING THE LINES SEPARATING
WHITE AND BLACK.

As a storyteller, every journalist strives for wholeness and symmetry, for a narrative that after all its circumnavigation returns to the beginning, as if to say, "Here, enclosed, is an entire world." In both the subject and the assignment itself, my profile of Johnny Clegg—the pop star and political activist in South Africa—afforded a remarkable sense of coming full circle.

It was in the late Seventies, in the years immediately after the Soweto uprising, that I became fully aware of both the racial tragedy of South Africa and the magazine for which I would ultimately describe one part of it. I was working on a newspaper in the suburbs of Chicago, covering nearly fifty school districts and wondering if this was where the rainbow ended, when I read Jan Morris's essay about South Africa in ROLLING STONE. To this day I can remember riding the el toward a friend's apartment, completely absorbed in her words.

Part of the appeal was Morris's sure grasp of the South African psyche, as symbolized in her prolonged and precise description of the Voortrekker

Monument. It is, she wrote, "no place for conciliations or second thoughts. It is more like a setting for *Götterdämmerung*, and all around it there stands a barricade of sculpted ox wagons, encircling the shrine in perpetual watchful laager, as if to imply that the Battle of Blood River is not over yet."

Just as Morris's subject influenced me, so did her prose. It possessed an elegance, a density of detail, an intellectual heft, that reassured me there was some reason to keep honing my craft on 700-word dispatches from the mundane world of DuPage County, Illinois. I never felt I held the imaginative power to create fiction, but Jan Morris, more than any other writer, demonstrated to me that nonfiction could be every bit as literary, every bit as morally urgent, as a novel.

Fortunately, I was not isolated in these aspirations. The paradox of my tenure at the *Suburban Trib* was that next to an editor who chain-smoked, picked his nose and ate Twinkies in a single bite sat a petite and brilliant young woman named Cissi Falligant, who had intended to become a professor of comparative literature. The three or four reporters with whom Cissi worked most closely as an editor called her Max, short for Maxwell Perkins. Besides inspiration and dreams, the most lasting gift she gave me was her copy of *The Rolling Stone Reporting Style,* an anthology by such first-generation RS writers as Ben Fong-Torres, Timothy Crouse and Joe Eszterhas. By the time I finished with it, the book had to be held together by tape, glue and staples.

As I moved from the *Suburban Trib* to the *New York Times,* the fascination with South Africa that Jan Morris had kindled grew into a campaign of self-education. I devoured the novels of André Brink, J.M. Coetzee and Nadine Gordimer and the plays of Athol Fugard, Barney Simon and Mbongeni Ngema. As a cultural reporter on the *Times,* I was able to interview many of these artists. Which only heightened my desire—my obsession, really—to report from South Africa itself.

Since the *Times* considered me too inexperienced to entrust with such an important foreign posting, I made my own plan. I would write a book about the shared tragedy of apartheid, and in 1986, I discovered an ideal scenario. A year and a half earlier, a young woman from Johannesburg had driven her maid home to the black township of Sebokeng. There her car crossed the path of a funeral procession mourning a ten-year-old boy who had been killed during random army strafing. Seeing the white woman, some of the marchers began pelting her car with stones, and one rock struck and killed her infant, seated beside her. Two deaths, two innocents: Here was the paradigm.

The dilemma was that I could never attain a visa. I visited the South African embassy in Washington to plead my case. I enlisted contacts ranging from a senator and a congressman to a colleague of the notorious Roy

Cohn, who was defending the South African government in a civil suit in New York. Four different times I was rejected. From a source I learned what I already suspected: My articles in the *Times* about dissident South African artists had established me as a foe of the regime, an unacceptable risk.

I left the *Times,* started writing a different book and, with an introduction by a *Times* colleague to a ROLLING STONE assistant managing editor named Robert Vare, developed a rich working relationship with the magazine. I wrote mostly about the nexus between popular music and social forces, profiling Los Lobos as emblems of the Mexican immigrant experience and following a Chicago blues band on a tour of Midwestern college towns, where it introduced young whites to the world of black culture. And so, from ROLLING STONE's perspective, it made sense to have me write about Johnny Clegg and his immersion into both African music and the struggle against apartheid.

"Sounds great," I told Jim Henke, the managing editor, when he called me with the assignment in December 1989. "The only problem is I probably can't get into the country. Maybe you ought to ask Rian Malan to write this."

After I summarized my previous thwarted efforts, Jim encouraged me to reapply for a visa anyway, even as the magazine planned to have a staff writer put in for a visa in case I failed again. The schedule was extraordinarily tight. Clegg was playing South Africa for two weeks in early January 1990 before beginning a world tour. A flight was booked for me and a photographer, David Katzenstein, on the evening of January 10th, giving us barely enough time to see Clegg's last two shows. And for three weeks, the South African consulate in New York prevaricated, approving David but insisting my application had to be vetted in Pretoria. Only on January 8th was my visa granted. And as I later learned, it was awarded only because, as a favor to a friend who worked for Clegg's record label, a South African woman who had never met me had assured the Department of Home Affairs she would take personal responsibility for my conduct.

Still, as I debarked at Jan Smuts Airport on a glorious summer morning, I expected to be turned away at customs. Instead, I ambled through without incident and was met by Clegg's indefatigable aide, Denzyl Fiegelson, clad in a tropical-print shirt. What was most shocking about South Africa was its ordinariness, its normalcy. The vivid footage on American newscasts of protests and tear gas and gunfire and death hardly prepared me for the shopping malls and glass skyscrapers and gardens of protea and jacaranda, for a landscape less reminiscent of war-ravaged Lebanon than sybaritic Southern California.

The story of white South Africa, as I discovered, was the story of seduction. The ease and pleasure that apartheid guaranteed—with job set-asides, cheap household labor, rights to the most fruitful land and countless other legal protections—whispered incessantly into white ears: "You are living in Paradise. You are living in Eden. Why surrender it for some abstract concept of right?"

Yes, insurrection raged, but in townships hidden over hillsides, tucked inside valleys. Yes, concrete walls and razor wire guarded the mansions, but affluence always seeks protection. Yes, blacks in ragged clothes carrying the tools of manual labor trudged along every street, but after a while they became merely part of the ambient radiation. For a white person in South Africa, living with apartheid required no more blindness than most white Americans muster as they neatly skirt townships called Brownsville and Lawndale and South Central.

It was Johnny Clegg's refusal to be seduced that made him such an impressive person. In America, it cost anti-apartheid activists nothing to campaign for divestment or erect a shantytown, all the while ignoring their own nation's rampant race hate. But in South Africa, holding to ideals meant paying a price—being arrested and spied upon, having songs banned and shows canceled, mourning friends murdered by the state. I remember the matter-of-fact way Clegg's mother, Muriel Pienaar, told me she knew her phone was bugged because she could hear the tape reels being changed each morning at ten. I remember the prosaic tone with which Clegg's friend and associate Jabu Ngwenya pointed to the bullet holes in his Soweto home, left by a Special Branch assassination squad.

The Johnny Clegg I met and profiled had been pushed to a nearly suicidal despair, and yet he had shielded the pilot light of his hope. Now, in January 1990, events were finally moving toward him. State President F.W. DeKlerk was dismantling the legal scaffolding of apartheid and preparing to release Nelson Mandela. The opposition press was reemerging from hiding. A heady excitement, a Prague Spring sort of feeling, infused every conversation, because the long and hard work of establishing democracy under majority rule had not yet intruded on the ebullience.

And Clegg's music provided the underscoring for the moment. All day, with unceasing eloquence, he would submit to interviews with journalists from the United States, West Germany and South Africa. He led reporters and photographers into Soweto and Sebokeng, to the migrant workers' hostels on the fringes of Johannesburg. To satisfy camera crews and photographers, he performed Zulu dances and taught his son, Jesse, the tribal sport of stick fighting. Meanwhile, he was playing host to a houseful of relatives.

Yet when he mounted the stage in the Standard Bank Arena, with an energy that belied the day's exhaustion, something more than the performer's spirit animated him. He answered to a genuine sense of mission, and I answered to my own in transmuting his moral courage into words.

O ne evening when Johnny Glegg was twelve years old, his mother
sent him to buy a loaf of bread. Beneath the street lights outside
the store stood a black man playing a guitar, and the sound from his
strings halted the boy. Something in that African song reminded Johnny
of the Celtic music he adored, adored because he associated it with the
English father who had vanished from his life before his first birthday.

"Please teach me," Johnny asked.

The black man nodded yes.

After school the next day, with his mother still safely at her job, Johnny
went to the apartment building where the musician worked as a janitor.
The superintendent, an Afrikaner, asked the boy's purpose and, learning
what it was, ordered him to return home. Johnny retreated out the door,
then sneaked to the servants' entrance and scaled the fire escape to his
new teacher's room.

His name, Johnny now learned, was Charlie Mzila. He was a Zulu. He
was a warrior. He was a migrant worker, forced by laws Johnny had only
begun to comprehend to live apart from his family eleven months each
year. The room smelled of sweat and a paraffin stove. Pictures of saints
hung on the wall. Beneath the mattress, Mzila stored what was most dear,
the traditional tribal machete and fighting sticks and a photo album whose
every snapshot had been bent and smudged. Mzila seated Johnny on the
one chair—a cardboard box covered with newspaper—and played songs
in Zulu of the itinerant's life. With their minor keys and 6/8 time signatures, they were jaunty and mournful all at once.

"It was as if some very powerful disclosure was being made to me,"
Clegg recalls, "and I didn't understand it. And that freaked me out. Those
songs seemed to be from another place, another time. And yet they were
discussing something about the world. There was a secret locked in there.
And then I knew that I had to know the secret."

Mzila taught Johnny the Zulu language and dances. He led him into
gambling dens and migrant hostels and the township bars called shebeens,
all the places where racial pride refused to be crushed by the passbook
laws, which rendered blacks aliens in their own land, and by the utterance
a thousand times a day of "Yes, me baas." Johnny asked his mother for a
Gallo-tone guitar, the cheapest brand made but the one that for its economy had become central to modern Zulu music. For three months he
made the backstairs pilgrimage to Mzila's room for lessons, until one day
the superintendent burst through the door, drunk.

"Out," he shouted, grabbing Johnny by the shirt. "Get out. Never come back." Mzila shoved the man away from Johnny, and the man shoved Mzila back. And then the Zulu warrior did the perilous, the almost unthinkable: He turned his fists on a white man, an Afrikaner, his baas, and drove him from the room in defeat. And in the super's wake hovered the unspoken presentiment of dismissal, arrest, exile.

"It was a terrible thing," Clegg remembers. "All I'd wanted to do was play music. And yet I was terribly moved. Because this was the first time anyone older than me had stood up for me. Just to be with me."

All he had wanted was to play music. All he had wanted was the approval of a father, who would initiate him into the mysteries of manhood. It had been that simple. It had had nothing to do with anything as abstract as politics. But Johnny Clegg was white and Charlie Mzila was black and South Africa was South Africa, where in matters of race nothing was simple and everything was political, inescapably and tortuously political. Others, to be sure, could cross the line and then withdraw behind it, withdraw into the protective laager that is the governing metaphor of white South Africa. They could love their black nannies and their black houseboys and grow up to call them "kaffirs" and march with the army through their townships. It was an emotional dynamic that tore one apart, if one happened to have both white skin and a working conscience.

Johnny Clegg, however, did not enjoy the option of rejection. By age twelve he had been sundered not only from his father but from his stepfather as well. He had lived in three countries, attended six schools. He only felt at peace camping in the bush, sighting birds in the parks and singing and dancing with Charlie Mzila and the other migrants. Then as now he considered himself a "marginal man," and in their marginality be found fellowship. He could hardly imagine where such an elemental human instinct would ultimately lead.

The police surged into the Wemmer Hostel, a brick barracks for 3000 migrants, on a routine search for stolen goods and workers without passbooks. They found thirty or forty men dancing and humming in a space cleared between the bunks and barely lit by one bulb. Only when they herded the group outdoors did the officers notice that one of its members was a white teenager, his tank top and khakis augmented by Zulu beads and sandals.

"*Wat gaan heir aan?*" one officer demanded of fourteen-year-old Johnny Clegg, incredulous. "What's going on here?"

"I'm dancing here," he began to answer before the *isango*, the dance leader, stepped forward to speak for him, according to tribal protocol. The leader proceeded to tell the officers that the white boy had been dancing with this troupe for a long time. The Zulu men, in fact, had given

Johnny the nickname Madlebe, from the word for the large earrings Zulu men wear. This so incensed the police they dragged Johnny to their car. The migrants assumed he was being taken to jail, though the officers decided instead to bring him to his mother.

"This is your son," one told Muriel Pienaar when she opened her door ten minutes later. "Do you know where we found him?"

"Must've been one of the hostels."

"You mean to say you *allow* him?"

"Why, yes. He's studying Zulu dancing."

"Do you know how dangerous those places are?" the officer persisted. "There are weapons. There are drugs. We have four or five murders there every weekend. We don't go in there without a gun on."

"It's a bit different for Johnny," Pienaar explained sweetly. "He's their friend."

"Your son is crazy," the officer concluded. "You must look after him." Turning to leave, he added, "And what he's doing is illegal."

That Pienaar remained calm should have been no surprise. She and Johnny had been called worse than crazy by her own mother, a Lithuanian Jew who had settled in Rhodesia. "Oy, vay," she said on her periodic visits to Johannesburg. "What will become of him, running around barefoot with his *shvartzer* friends? What a disgrace. What sort of mother lets him grow wild?"

Yet it was largely because her own parents had discouraged her musical ambitions that Pienaar so nurtured those of her son. Before Johnny's stepfather moved away, he had filled the house with African music and contempt for apartheid. And when the family had lived in Zambia for two years in the early Sixties, just as that nation was gaining its independence, Johnny had attended an integrated school. Racial isolation was simply at odds with his most intimate and formative moments.

But the older Johnny grew, the less the authorities saw his hostel evenings as harmlessly perverse. He was arrested more than a dozen times, and Pienaar grew afraid they might both be deported. (She carried a Rhodesian passport, Johnny a British one, since he had been born in Manchester.) Short of trying to halt Johnny's visits to Wemmer, she forced him to carry a letter from the South African Folk Music Association assuring the police that his business there was strictly apolitical. The Zulus at the hostel, however, could hardly have been prouder. Going to jail was part of coming of age; jail was called *urela emadobenr*, "the place of men."

By day, it was true, Johnny was forced to inhabit segregated schools and cinemas and parks, and he was bound by his late teens for the University of the Witwatersrand, where he would receive an education available to virtually no blacks. Yet it was not in any of those settings that his political and musical enlightenment truly commenced. It was in the migrant hostel—the institution that was, paradoxically, integral to both apartheid and the vibrant urban African culture.

The hostel system was designed to supply white South Africa with a permanent pool of cheap black labor that itself would be deprived of the benefits of permanence. A family's breadwinner needed a work permit, which by law expired on a regular basis; the rest of the family remained hundreds of miles away in the tribal "homeland." So with the push of joblessness and the pull of blood, every migrant had to leave the city every year or two, uncertain whether he would be permitted to return.

At the same time, however, the hostels gave birth to a distinctively citified culture, one that subverted the apartheid ideal. The musical instruments of the hostels and townships were ones borrowed and adapted from their white rulers—a concertina with its buttons rearranged to suit African scales, a guitar restrung to carry bass and treble lines, a penny whistle turned from toy into woodwind. The choral music lately popularized by Ladysmith Black Mambazo and Paul Simon's *Graceland* grew from the encounter of African worshipers and the Christian church. So as he learned the tribal dances, Johnny also learned the urban music, the *kwela* and *mbaqanga*, and came to hear between the bars a language of perseverance and resistance.

If he had achieved Zulu manhood with his maiden arrest, then Johnny accomplished musical brotherhood the evening not long after when he first met Sipho Mehunu. Sipho was only twelve then, newly arrived in Johannesburg from Natal and serving without passbook or work permit as a white family's gardener. He had learned tales back home of a white who spoke and sang and danced like a tribesman, but he did not believe them.

Then one evening as he played guitar on a street corner, Sipho heard someone whistle in Zulu fashion. When he looked up, all he saw was a white boy on a bike. Then the boy spoke in *fanakalo*, the migrant's pidgin mix of Zulu and English, inviting him home to take tea. Once there, Johnny set up a tape recorder, the first Sipho had ever seen, and asked his guest to sing. Then he rewound the tape and played it back. "This boy has *umlingo*," Sipho thought. "This boy has magic."

Soon Sipho took on Charlie Mzila's role of musical guide, but he also became a friend in a way Mzila as a father figure necessarily could not.

In 1976 the two recorded their first single. They pieced together uniforms at the Saturday flea market, learned and arranged Zulu songs and started to write their own. One of Johnny's first was the bittersweet internal monologue of a migrant returning home after his months away. Then, in 1979, Johnny and Sipho formed a full band named Juluka, Zulu for "sweat."

Folkish in tone, painfully earnest in intent, Juluka aroused remarkable controversy solely by being the first racially mixed band in South Africa. For in 1965 the government had adopted laws protecting "cultural purity" by balkanizing the media not merely into black and white but into Afrikaans, English, Zulu, Sotho and similar sectors. At almost any white setting except the Witwatersrand campus, a stronghold of English liberalism, Juluka's shows were likely to be forcibly canceled. Their songs were barred from the government's English station for having Zulu lyrics and from its Zulu station for having English lyrics. From time to time, a spectator would grow so incensed at Clegg, the *kaffirboetjie*, that he would leap onstage to take a swing at him. Even Johnny's best white friend told him he had no right to write about the black lives, lives he could not possibly understand.

As if to contradict that friend, Juluka found a devoted audience in the townships like Soweto, Sebokeng and Alexandria. Outside of Johannesburg, the solution to censorship was simpler: drive down the dirt lanes, announce the show out of the windows of a moving van, set up in a tumbledown municipal hall and start playing. Juluka sold at least half of its early records to black listeners, and several of the albums went gold with sales exceeding 20,000. Three Zulu clans formally inducted Johnny, and when his son Jesse was born years later, Clegg was married in a Zulu ceremony to his wife, Jenny, a former dancer. (Zulu practice is not to perform a marriage until the wife has proven her fertility.) To this day men and women from the townships will hail Clegg not by his own name but with the salutation "Juluka!"

But the plight of the South African moderate is to be flayed from both flanks of the racial divide. And in the aftermath of the 1976 Soweto uprising, the inauguration of the modern era of resistance, Juluka endured enormous pressure from black intellectuals and activists. The Black Consciousness philosophy articulated by Steve Biko, like America's black nationalism, instructed sympathetic whites to work solely among those of their own color. In any racially integrated enterprise, however admirable its goals, white presence would retard black development. Only when the races could meet as equals—however many decades in the future that might be—would they meet at all.

"They talking politics all the time," Sipho Mchunu recalls. "Some people they come to me, say, 'You're wasting your time. Why you play with this white guy? You can play with your own.' I said, 'What I started I cannot give up. Johnny is a friend.' "

"There was an argument I shouldn't sing in Zulu, because English was the international language," says Clegg. "There was criticism that what we were doing was 'conservative.' But I said culture by itself isn't 'liberal' or 'conservative.' It's what you *do* with it. And I wasn't interested in struggling against anything. I was interested in establishing an African identity."

Here, then, was a new definition of marginality for a man obsessed with transcending it. The songs Clegg wrote about itinerants took on another level of metaphor amid the increasing insurrection. In context, if not in original design, they became the *cri de coeur* of all the decent South Africans whose good intentions appeared irrelevant, whose democratic dreams seemed obsolete. As Clegg put it in one 1982 composition: "They are the scatterlings of Africa/Each uprooted one/On the road to Phelamanga/Where the world began/I love the scatterlings of Africa/Each and every one/In their hearts a burning hunger/Beneath the copper sun."

Juluka disbanded in 1985 when Sipho Mchunu, tried of the road, returned to KwaZulu to tend his family's livestock. And in some respects that was a blessing, because when State President P.W. Botha declared a state of emergency the following year, the entire idea of making music seemed pointless. By the end of the decade, some 5000 South Africans had perished, either in army assaults or internecine black violence, and another 35,000 had been detained by the authorities. The resistance, in turn, aimed to render the townships ungovernable, and any band that dared schedule a performance would find its crowd stoned and its equipment burned. There was no time for concerts, the comrades said, there was only time for the struggle.

Whatever distance Clegg as an artist had tried to maintain from politics closed with a crash. The Botha regime, adroitly exploiting tribal rivalries, used the Zulu nation that Clegg considered his own to divide, politically and physically, the black resistance. In the vicious intraracial bloodshed that followed (and that continues in Natal), Zulu migrants whom Clegg recognized from Juluka's audiences were slain by the score. Then a white social worker from Durban, whom Clegg had known since she housed him and Mchunu during the 1978 Natal Folk Festival, was seized by the Special Branch, the notorious political police.

Charged with aiding the African National Congress (ANC), the woman disappeared into a series of prisons, where she was placed in solitary confinement and interrogated without cease. Clegg joined a detainees' support committee, sent his friend letters and tapes, tried to locate her in the security labyrinth. Three months after her arrest, the friend was released without explanation. Alive and physically unscarred, she was luckier than most. But Clegg was nearly shattered.

"I had a sense of hopelessness," he says. "I felt paralyzed. Desperate. There were these two opposing factions—the securocrats and the young black militants—neither of whom gave any quarter. There's always been a hidden, invisible middle ground in South Africa of connections between people and cultures. That was being incinerated. Music was the most effective way I could work out my feelings. It was a way of trying to understand what I was experiencing."

The sidemen Clegg assembled to help him—including two Juluka alumni, percussionist Dudu Zulu and drummer Derek De Beer—evolved into Savuka. The songs Clegg wrote and recorded became the band's first record, *Third World Child*, a despairing personal history of the times.

Clegg and Savuka achieved gold or platinium designation for *Third World Child* and its successor *Shadow Man* in South Africa and several European countries. As Clegg's music metamorphosed from Juluka's folkloric stylings to a more accessible interweaving of Celtic and African influences, Clegg found himself last spring in Los Angeles recording the album intended to secure him stardom in the United States.

Several weeks into the sessions, the telephone rang in Clegg's bedroom. The voice was that of the friend who had been detained.

"Johnny," she said, "the most terrible thing has happened. They shot David. David Webster."

Clegg hardly needed the surname to know. Webster had been Clegg's mentor from the moment they had met eighteen years earlier at the University of the Witwatersrand. Webster was teaching an anthropology course on Zulu culture, and Clegg stuck out as the one freshman fluent in the language. With Webster's encouragement, he earned his degree in anthropology and went on to become a junior lecturer in the field.

It was impossible for Clegg to picture this man as the woman on the telephone described him—struck as he strolled home from jogging, bleeding to death in his wife's arms. No, perhaps it was all too easy to conceive and that was far more disturbing.

"I felt like I'd been axed, like a cleaver had come into my brain," Clegg recalls. "I was seized once again by this fucking paralysis, an impotence, a real fright. In a death like this, you realize the contingency of history, the reality of existing in chaos. We have a superficial web of order we place over things. This smashed my web."

For three weeks, Clegg could not write a word. "I felt lost in the world," he says. "I didn't trust the universe anymore."

Trying to salvage both the album and Clegg's spirits, producer Hilton Rosenthal hastily arranged a short European tour. The evening after the final show, Clegg flew to New York, where he was to deliver the keynote address at the New Music Seminar. As he crossed the night sky, he scribbled notes on his topic, the history of progressive music in South Africa, a history otherwise undocumented and largely forgotten.

The more Clegg wrote, the more absurd he felt. Had these events really taken place? Or did they exist only in his imagination? And even if they had occurred, what did it matter? Amid detention and emergency and sidewalk assassination, who cared?

Yet as he spoke the next afternoon, and the audience listened, Clegg felt lifted by some small catharsis. Perhaps in declaiming this history of persecution, he had made the musicians' sacrifices not less real, but more. He knew then he would be able to continue. "There's no going back," he says. "I can't stand still; I've done it. I can only move forward."

Shorn of naiveté but not an existential need to believe, Clegg renamed the album *Cruel, Crazy, Beautiful World*. The first song he wrote was "One (Hu)'Man, One Vote." He dedicated it to the memory of David Webster.

As the sound of a talking drum poured from the speakers at the Standard Bank Arena in Johannesburg, before the lights even rose on Johnny Clegg and Savuka, the capacity crowd shrieked with an abandon that bordered on Beatlemania. There were black and colored and Indian listeners among the 6000, but with a ticket price of seven dollars, relatively high for South Africa, most were whites in surf shirts and designer jeans. They would not have seemed alien in Orange County, except that when one looked closer, especially at those nearest the stage, one saw a banner declaring, WE ARE ONE WORLD, and a T-shirt emblazoned with the ANC Freedom Charter and another bearing a photograph of David Webster.

They burst into delirium when Clegg unstrapped his guitar and stepped back from the microphone to dance with Dudu Zulu. The men dropped to their haunches, spun on their heels, arms outstretched for balance; they stood straight and then kicked each leg high into the air; and then they fell backward as if in rapture. Theirs was a warrior dance of the Zulus, and together, black and white, they had slain the enemy.

In the crowd boys with baggy shorts and tank tops mimicked their moves. Girlfriends jumped into the air for a glimpse of the stage. And what did it mean? What did their joy mean? Their clenched fists and swaying arms? For gestures so direct, their meaning remained elusive. Were these young white inheritors simply riding in that moment the forbidden pleasure of an African beat? Or were they truly attending Clegg and his message, accepting an empowerment that meant surrendering their privilege?

"We all want change," said James Kamp, a thirty-eight-year-old supplier of engineering equipment, after the show. "But not so fast as Clegg says. It'll be a bloody blood bath. They'll run amok. They'll chase us out of our homes."

"Why not one man, one vote?" said Bernd Globisch, an eighteen-year-old high-school student. "As long as the minority isn't oppressed."

"What he says about one man, one vote is right," said Ashley Cohen, a twenty-three-year-old computer-systems manager. "But it's scary, because it's different and it's unknown."

Clegg himself has no illusions, but he does have some faith. There are, after all, only four destinations for a white in the land of apartheid—faith, racism, exile or madness. Faith has cost some their freedom, others their lives. Clegg has been fortunate enough to survive essentially unscathed and to embody finally a spirit in which others can invest their own faith.

"I've fought against being seen as a symbol, a messiah, who could never deliver the goods," Clegg says. "So I've been pragmatic. But if I'm someone's hero, that's wonderful. It's wonderful to play music that does more than give people a good time. Every time I come offstage, I feel, 'Another nail in the coffin.'"

Warren Beatty

BILL ZEHME

WHEN YOU'RE INTERVIEWING THE LAST MOVIE STAR,
IT'S NOT WHAT HE SAYS THAT MATTERS BUT HOW HE
DOESN'T SAY IT.

There are nights I dream of him, and it is still horrible. We are sitting there, and he says nothing. He begins to say something, and then he stops. He pauses that pause of his: *the Pause!* Like eternity is the Pause. I feel my hair fall out in clumps. I feel my teeth rot. At once I have aged—what?—forty, fifty years. Waiting for him to finish. To say something. But what can he say? We have both forgotten the question. He tries to respond, anyway. Blinking at me, smiling, shrugging, ageless in hesitation. There is no sound, nothing, just him, knowing what he knows and keeping it to himself. Somewhere a clock ticks as the Pause expands. . . .

Then I awaken and remember that it was all true—*it really happened!*—except for the hair-and-teeth part, that is. I remember those Pauses the way other men remember mortar fire. And yet, because survival has a way of breeding nostalgia, I often find myself missing the Reticent One.

Warren Beatty *is* the Reticent One. It is art, the way he withholds! To this day I remember everything he never told me. Many people read our published conversations and summarily proclaimed Warren Beatty to be the ultimate Impossible Interview. I pity those people. They missed everything. They were ill equipped to marvel at his wry ellipses. They could not grasp the eloquence of his vast silences. After all, it is not what Warren Beatty says but how he doesn't say it.

This was Warren's first serious print interview in twelve years, and he had stored up a wealth of topics not to speak about. He had last spoken somewhat in *Time* in 1978, and before that he had publicly said not much of anything after having said too much to Rex Reed in a famous 1967 *Esquire* piece called "Will the Real Warren Beatty Please Shut Up?" (He obeyed, forcing journalists to thereafter pay for the sins of Rex Reed, which as you can imagine is an indignity of no small proportion.) In 1982, Warren appeared on the cover of ROLLING STONE as the subject of a memorable profile by Aaron Latham, to whom Warren never spoke. That piece, executed in the witness style of the just-released film *Reds* (which Warren triumphantly produced, directed, co-wrote and starred in), deftly interwove the voices of many people who knew Warren well enough to have heard him say things. For eight years after *Reds*, however, Warren all but disappeared from public view, except for costarring with Dustin Hoffman in the legendary bomb *Ishtar*. During that period, he was quoted as saying, "I'd rather ride down the street on a camel *nude* . . . in a *snowstorm* . . . *backwards* than give what is sometimes called an in-depth interview." But this was to change in the spring of 1990. Perhaps fearing that a new generation of filmgoers had no idea who he was, Warren agreed to end his silence as best he could. He would sit for interviews on behalf of his forthcoming auteur project, *Dick Tracy*, in which he was to star opposite his new love, Madonna.

As is customary, a tremendous fight erupted over which magazine would get Warren's first definitive interview. I am told that many people lost their lives in that battle, and certain publicists were forced to enter witness-relocation programs. But what matters is that Warren chose ROLLING STONE to be his forum, a decision that may have forever altered the course of his life.

Now let me say this: Actors are for the most part not terribly interesting. They are paid to not be themselves, which would limit any of us, if you think about it. But most actors are not Warren Beatty. Warren has seen everything and done everything, especially with actresses. More than just a fabled Lothario, he is a Movie Star in a time when there are no more Movie Stars. He is a repository of Hollywood history, an icon who knew the icons that came before him (He played cards with Marilyn Monroe the night before she died.) His knowledge of women, all by itself, must be encyclopedic. He would seem to be a fellow who could tell you a thing or two. Someone who could bend your ear and give you something to think about.

To Warren, however, such matters are trifling, and of course, he is right. More impressive than any knowledge are his skills as a brilliant diplomat, and I would eventually learn that few things equal the sheer entertainment value of listening to a diplomat circumvent truth. Our sessions, therefore, fairly rollicked with clever deflections and escapes. To ensure that none of his nuance would be misrepresented in print, Warren always had a tape recorder of his own running next to mine. While this could be construed as a sign of paranoia—Jerry Lewis has, after all, long made it his practice—I now believe Warren did it because he cared. He assured me: "It's for *your* safety." I returned this gesture of friendship by often letting him "borrow" my extra blank tapes. Sometimes we would both run out of tape simultaneously, and those, I think, were some of our best times together.

Warren did share my concern about the seemingly futile quality of our conversations. I remember how we would pace around his swimming pool, fretting together. "Let's keep moving around from subject to subject," he said, "and maybe I'll not be boring on something." Often I would try to engage him by sharing tidbits from my personal life: I told him how an actress had recently wreaked havoc on my heart. He asked her name, then said, by way of consolation, "I never dated her." Whereupon he imparted staggering wisdom on the perils of dating actors and actresses, but this was during an off-the-record break. I asked him to repeat himself when the tape was going, but all he said after a long silence was "I don't know what you're talking about." That always struck me as one of his finest moments.

Now, about those Pauses: Never had I encountered silence to match the breadth and scope of Warren's silences. Historically, silence, like odorlessness, is difficult to portray in print, which is understandable, since there is not a lot you can really say about it. Still, I could not cheat readers out of Warren's astonishing silences. You needed to *experience* them to fully appreciate their richness. But how to communicate this? A solution came to me on a flight to Chicago. Upon deplaning, I called my transcription service back in Burbank, where a team of typists was about to begin work on the interview tapes. "Time them," I said. "Time what?" said the chief transcriber. "The Pauses," I said. And so a roomful of women in headphones set about clicking stopwatches on and off, measuring one man's reluctance.

It is no secret that, as a result, Warren's Pauses became something of an international sensation. Because modesty had always prevented Warren from bragging about the length of his Pauses, I seized the opportunity to help. I took the hard numbers and salted them throughout the published article. Readers could endure Warren as authentically as I did, by simply consulting the second hand of any timepiece. Hubbub ensued. *USA Today* reported that Warren's longest Pause was fifty-seven seconds. (There were, in fact, longer ones, but they preceded responses so bland they were unpublishable.) VJ Martha Quinn did dramatic readings from the piece on MTV. When Madonna was handed the magazine in a limousine, she reportedly recited the story aloud, repeating favorite comic passages over and over. She then included a tribute to Warren's Pauses in at least one of her Blond Ambition concerts. (She would ask a leering question of a dancer dressed as Dick Tracy, then turn to the audience and announce, "Pause, twenty-seven seconds.") Several weeks later she expressed her glee over the piece by giving me the high five at a party. Clearly, she was grateful that I had shown readers the Warren she knew so well. But when I asked her where he was that night, she said, a tad bitterly, "Who knows?" Such is love's mercurial way.

As for Warren, I was told he read the piece on a flight to New York and pretended to be unmoved. "I don't hate it," he told his travel companion, "and I don't like it." (Always the diplomat!) Still, I am certain that impact was made. After all, there comes a time in every man's life when being cagey gets dull. Confronted with his own excellent Pauses, Warren could only reassess his dedication to Avoidance. Soon thereafter, he began work on another film, the splendid *Bugsy*, and fell in love with his costar Annette Bening, herself a woman of great reticence. Next, news came that she was expecting Warren's baby. There was talk of marriage. When it was time to promote *Bugsy*, a different Warren emerged in interviews, a Warren who actually spoke sentences of merit and color, of self-revelation and candor. He hardly even Paused! Then his daughter, Kathlyn, was born, and he got awards for *Bugsy*. Warren had stopped running away from truth, and suddenly he had much to show for it.

It is not my nature to take credit, but I have lately placed many calls and sent several faxes to his home, in order to congratulate him on the new openness in his life. His assistant assures me that Warren has gotten all of my messages. I'm sure I will be hearing from him.

RS 579

MAY 31ST, 1990

He is a ghost. He is human ectoplasm. He is here, and then he is gone, and then you aren't sure he was ever here to begin with. He has had sex with everyone, or at least tried. He has had sex with someone you know or someone who knows someone you know or someone you wish you knew, or at least tried. He is famous for sex, he is famous for having sex with the famous, he is famous. He makes mostly good films when he makes films, which is mostly not often. He has had sex with most of his leading ladies. He befriends all women and many politicians and whispers advice to them on the telephone in the dead of night. Or else he does not speak at all to anyone ever, except to those who know him best, if anyone can really know him. He is an adamant enigma, elusive for the sake of elusiveness, which makes him desirable, although for what, no one completely understands. He is much smarter than you think but perhaps not as smart as he thinks, if only because he thinks too much about being smart. He admits to none of this. He admits to nothing much. He denies little. And so his legend grows.

You hear Warren Beatty stories. They get around as he gets around. What you hear is carnal lore, possibly embellished, certainly superfluous. Warren Beatty, you hear, is gentle and respectful and never pushy, but he would not mind having sex right now, right this very microsecond. He loves women profoundly. Unsolicited, women tell me this and men corroborate. When Warren first meets a woman, he says [befuddled], "Now, I forget your name." Or [bedazzled], "You're the most beautiful woman I've met who's not an actress or model." One famous director remembers having a conversation with him during which Warren, the director says, "had his hand up a woman! She didn't seem to mind, and he acted as though it seemed a perfectly natural thing to do." Another scenario: Warren calls an actress late on a Saturday night. Her husband answers the phone. She gets on the line, and Warren invites her up to his house right away to read for a movie role widely reported as already cast. She puts him off but takes his home number anyway. Next to the number, her husband notices, she mistakenly writes, "Warren Beauty." Many note pads have likely known this error.

Madonna has his number. She may have his number like others have not. He told someone at lunch last year, "Sometimes I look at myself in the mirror and say, '*I'm with Madonna!*' " He is reborn in love, restored to public persona. For we only see Warren when he loves deeply (we only *hear* about him when he prowls). From the Sixties onward, we saw him most clearly (but never too well) with Joan Collins, Natalie Wood, Leslie Caron, Michelle Phillips, Julie Christie, Diane Keaton, Isabelle Adjani. Madonna is more famous than any of them; she is more famous than he is; she is more famous than everyone, more or less. By loving him, she makes him more famous than he was before. Theirs is a sort of vampire love: She needs his credibility; he needs her youth. He is fifty-three, and she is thirty-one, and they are evenly matched legends; hers is louder, his is longer. It works out.

Warren Beatty is paranoid. He is an occluded Hollywood god, one who

shuts up and off and imagines himself invisible. Afraid of being misunderstood, he says nothing and is more misunderstood. He likes it that way.
Unlike, say, Brando's silence, Beatty's silence is showy. Puckish and
smooth, he phones up journalists to inform them *at length* and with sly
humor that he doesn't cooperate with the media. He would rather eat
worms. In a dozen years, he has said nothing. Maybe a few hollow words
in behalf of *Ishtar*. Maybe a futile endorsement now and again for his
crony—the presidential infidel Gary Hart. It was Warren who nudged him
back into the election, post-Donna Rice. Otherwise, Warren has been so
mum, he has all but evaporated. *Reds* did limp business, theory goes,
because Warren gave no interviews. If *Dick Tracy*, his newest film, dies, so
too might his career. Posturing has its limitations.

And so he has talked. And talked. For days, I have listened to him talk.
I have listened to him listen to himself talk. I have probed and pelted and
listened some more. For days. He speaks slowly, fearfully, cautiously, editing every syllable, slicing off personal color and spontaneous wit, steering
away from opinion, introspection, humanness. He is mostly evasive. His
pauses are elephantine. Broadway musicals could be mounted during his
pauses. He *works* at this. Ultimately, he renders himself blank. In *Dick
Tracy*, he battles a mysterious foe called the Blank. In life, he is the Blank
doing battle with himself. It is a fascinating showdown, exhilarating to
behold.

To interview Warren Beatty is to want to kill him.

It is also to become fond of him. He seduces anything that is not
mineral. He is impossible, but charming. Jack Nicholson, his neighbor on
altitudinal Mulholland Drive, calls him the Pro. Meaning Warren knows
what he is doing: I am invited one Friday night to watch him score. (*See
Beatty score! Not unlike seeing Picasso draw, Astaire twirl, DiMaggio swing!*)
Alas, there are musicians present; he is supervising *Tracy's* musical score
on an old MGM orchestra stage in Culver City.

"I told you never to meet me here," Warren says, meeting me for the
first time. (An opening line.) He looks tousled, untucked, an aging boy
barely aging, with drooped shirttails and sweet comportment. He is at
once good and bad and will do anything to make up for it. He fusses—
dithers, really—eager to get me a chair, to get me liquids and solids, to
get me.

One week later, on the night of his fifty-third birthday, the interroga-
tions begin. Feeling celebratory, he orders in Big Macs and El Pollo Loco
chicken ("Hang the expense!"). There is much for him to avoid discussing. We hole up for the first session in a Hollywood sound-mixing studio,
where he's been toiling on *Tracy*. Further conversations take place in his
home, that bestilled sanctuary on his private Olympus, and on the phone,
his instrument of choice. Because what he doesn't say is often more re-

vealing than what he does, this interview will frequently pause (as will Warren), so that necessary detail, commentary and homicidal impulses can be noted.

Okay, you and Madonna—the truth!
Art is truth.
That's all? You want to go with that?
[*Grins*] Okay by me.
Describe the qualities she possesses that convinced you to cast her as the sexpot temptress Breathless Mahoney in 'Dick Tracy.' How does she qualify?
Madonna is [*21-second pause*] simultaneously touching and more fun than a barrel of monkeys. [*11 seconds*] She's funny, and she's [*21 seconds*] gifted in so many areas and has the kind of energy as a performer that can't help but make you engaged.
You mean sexual energy?
[*47-second pause*] Um, she has it all.
Do you think that your reluctance to give interviews has inflated your personal mythology?
I can't accept your flattering premise of me. To do so is unattractive or self-serving. It's hard to misquote someone who doesn't say anything. There's almost nothing that hasn't been said about me. But there's an awful lot that I haven't said. I don't talk about private things.
You don't talk about anything. What's the most ridiculous rumor you've read about you?
Really an adroit question, because if I repeat a ridiculous rumor here, it gives fifty-percent credence to the rumor, whatever it is. [*Ponders, 57-second pause*] If I tell you I saw an item that said I was actually born on Pluto, fifty percent of the people will say, "*I wonder. . . .*" It's a sin, you know, starting a rumor. You'll notice I picked a really outlandish one. I had to think for a minute.
All things considered, it could be true.
[*Smiles*] You know I wasn't born on Pluto. I'd get much more attention had I been.

Warren, I would learn, has a habit of going off the record, and when he is off the record, he is almost like a person. At these times, one gets a greater sense of his playfulness. The lines blur occasionally. At one point, when we are neither on nor off the record, just sort of pacing around, he suggests that we depants his lovely young publicist. He thinks it might ease tension. It is also during such off-the-record spates that he reveals his pet term for scurrilous articles written about his sexual profile: "fuck and suck." He asks me if I know about any such pieces that may be currently in the works. The prospect seems to neither disgust nor please him. He is resigned to his reputation. He has never sued for libel and, moreover, feels there should be no libel laws: "Since the public is vaguely aware that there is some recourse in court, they figure what is printed about you must be sort of true." For instance, there is a tony British catalog of celebrity sex partners called *Who's Had Who*, in which Beatty's long section is billed thusly: FASTEN YOUR SEAT BELTS, AND HOLD YOUR HATS—THIS IS THE BIG ONE!!! Among the alleged conquests listed: Britt Ekland, Goldie Hawn, Kate Jackson, Brigitte Bardot, Diana Ross, Liv Ullmann, Candice Bergen, Carly Simon. (Diane Sawyer is one notable omission.) Also quoted in the book is his sister, reincarnated actress Shirley MacLaine, who says she wishes she could do a love scene with Warren. "Then," she states, "I could see what all the shouting was about."

Do you think you're eccentric?

Anybody who becomes a movie star when they're twenty-two, or whatever I was, is going to be eccentric. It's an eccentric situation. You become rich and famous out of proportion to that which is anticipated. Quite a candy store there.

You make movies slowly. You speak slowly. What do you do fast?

Prevaricate. [Note: defined by Webster's as "to evade the truth . . . to lie."]

What else?

I can dial a telephone number faster than anybody you know. [*He demonstrates—his hand falls onto a touch-tone panel, his fingers perform instant symphony, he passes me the receiver, an operator answers at the Beverly Wilshire hotel, where he kept a suite for many years. Dialing time: exactly 1 second.*] Want me to do it again? Want to see it again? [*He dials once more, full of swagger.*] That was quick, wasn't it?

That was breathtaking.

Thank you.

Do you drive fast?

I've been trying to drive at a sane speed. The other day I was driving along Mulholland and thinking about how sedately I was driving. Then around the turn came two cars side by side, and it's a two-lane road. On my right was a cliff, a steep drop. Straight ahead I faced a head-on collision. I didn't have time to fear for my life. It was a moment of realizing that there's going to be a very serious choice to make. So I tried to split the difference. Fortunately, the guy on the left slowed down, and the car passing him swerved and hit [my car] just behind my head.

This put me into a temporary state of manic elation. I got out of my car, and this kid who had hit me leapt out of his car and started to berate himself. I put my arms around him and said, "Don't worry, nobody's hurt." Then the people in the other cars came over, and they were all from Italy and Switzerland. They all had portable phones, and when they saw me, they called their mothers in Switzerland and wherever. So they put me on the phone with these lovely women, who were fans of mine. I stood there making transatlantic calls—how did I get into this?

If there is a moral here, it is this: Not only does Warren Beatty know how to cheat death, he gets to talk on the phone afterward to Swiss women. The telephone, of course, is Warren's second most legendary appendage. Rarely is he phoneless. It is said that he will make and take calls even while engaged in animal rapture. His mind swirls with phone numbers, memorized for the ages. His phone voice is a mellifluous purr, instantly conspiratorial. He is at home in the ear. He has been inside all the best ears. On Easter, I call and ask, among other things, if he has been hunting eggs. "Just laying them," he replies, a bit luridly.

Warren's fact file—here are some things Warren won't discuss: Himself (in emotional terms). Where he keeps his Oscar (Best Director for *Reds*). How to successfully date an actress. The most fun he can have with his clothes on. Misconceptions about himself. ("I can't talk about public perceptions of me. I have no idea how to focus on that.") The irony of his having produced *The Pick-up Artist* (dreadful Robert Downey Jr. film). Warren Beatty jokes. Accomplishments of, attractions to, relationships (of any sort) with other human beings. For instance, on fatherhood (as in, would he like to have done it? Would he want kids?), he says, "Um, to address this subject, by implication, I might be talking about some other people that I've known who may not want to be talked about." On what he sees when he looks in the mirror: "Why don't you get a little tougher, rather than ask me this open-ended kind of stuff, which I really can't do. I'm not gonna be the kind of guy who rambles on, particularly in these areas where the subject of the interview is left to muster up and exhibit a high level of personal narcissism."

It was Warren's wish, incidentally, to do this interview in the question-answer format. He felt it would protect him from misquotation. "Getting tougher," for Warren, involves asking him questions whenever possible that can be answered with yes or no. "If it's not entertaining," he says, "we can do some more later."

Robert Towne, with whom you wrote 'Shampoo,' says you "are a man who is deeply embarrassed by acting." True?
   [*Puzzled*] He said that about me? I'm very embarrassed by my own *bad* acting.
   Could you, at this point, still act in other people's movies?

Oh, sure, I would prefer to be directed by someone else. It's almost impossible to act and direct at the same time. We pretend to do it. But in fact, when you're acting, you ideally are out of control. In control of being out of control, but out of control. And when you are directing, you should be in control. Somewhat out of control of being in control. But in control. And if you're trying to be out of control and somewhat in control of being out of control but out of control and, at the same time, in control but somewhat out of control of being in control but still in control, it makes you crazy [*beams stupidly*].

Well, then. Let's talk politics. You pushed your friend Gary Hart back into the presidential race after he dropped out over his entanglement with Donna Rice. Why? How did you expect the public to respond?

[*Pauses 26 seconds*] I felt that he should not have gotten out. I get very irritated with people who are so condescending about political candidates. Gary Hart is a sensitive man with a high level of love and concern for his family. He didn't want them to be subjected to any more of that kind of humiliation, and it [*27 seconds*] was a tragic event for the country. It was not only a terrible thing to happen to him, but it deprived the country of its leading conceptualist presidential candidate at a time when that kind of detailed thinking was urgent. And I felt that if he and the family could take any more of it, that [getting back in] was the right thing to do.

You were a key member of his brain trust. What exactly did you do for him? I heard you actually wrote speeches for him.

Well, here's the way I participate in politics: I respect politics. And I respect the privacy of the people in politics with whom I am involved. I don't kiss and tell.

Didn't Ronald Reagan tell you that he wished 'Reds' had a happier ending after you showed him the film at the White House?

[*Startled*] Where did you hear that? I wouldn't want to . . . um, well, you know he has a great sense of humor. He's a funny guy. [*Pauses 21 seconds*] I guess I have a lot of feelings about Reagan that I am not articulating. He is an actor and a very, very likable man. But I guess you know I'm not a conservative Republican.

Reagan did, in fact, wish for a happy ending. Warren tells many colorful Reagan stories, none of them for attribution. My favorite has to do with the former president lecturing him about the marble of meat, but I can reveal no more. Warren will, however, talk hard-core politics until eyelids calcify and plummet. Much of it he will say for the record and with great insight and invective. In fact, he would prefer we spoke of nothing else in this interview. But Warren is, with all due respect, an actor, and an actor filibustering on politics is a little like a plummer dispensing Buddhist dogma. Noble, to be sure; but who really cares?

Instead, I will describe his house: Is it stark and Bauhausian, sprawling and all white, with no pictures on the walls of the main rooms, just lots of windows peering down on the basins of Los Angeles. His floors are polished oak, which give the sanctum its echo. On tables: big flower arrangements and piles of books about communism and comic strips. Very tidy: Toilet paper is always folded to a point. Piano (he can play quite decently) in the living room. Unseen, down a long corridor, is the Bedroom, where he frequently retreats to take lengthy calls. He mostly holds forth in an electronically glassed-in room, just off the pool, where the sun bears down. Here, a young British fellow appears every fifteen minutes with phone messages. Handsome meals are impeccably served by the young woman who is paid to prepare them. Warren will occasionally lope into the kitchen, foraging for custards. One day an actor friend of Warren's named Marshall Bell emerges from the gym downstairs, and mildly lascivious chatter erupts. It is only then that one gets the irrefutable impression that this is, indeed, the home of the right Warren Beatty.

How old do you feel?
Eleven.
Have you had a midlife crisis yet?
Many, I'm sure. They started when I was about eighteen. Ultimately, I learned that the secret to overcoming them is to not see them as crises. But I suppose the real answer to your question is, I don't know what you're talking about.
What's the most important thing to know about women?
[*Pauses 21 seconds*] That they're not very different from men.
What do you mean?
That's eight pages.
Eight classic pages. What do you mean?
[*Pauses 14 seconds*] Well, I'm lucky that I grew up in an atmosphere in which I was taught to treat women as respectfully as I would treat men. I don't differentiate. Sometimes people don't treat themselves very seriously, but that might happen more often when this business of sexual attraction rears its head and we all get a little giddy.
Describe what love feels like to you.
Do unto others.
Romantic love.
Define romantic love.
When you're in love.
Well, as soon as you use the word *romantic*, then the word *fiction* begins to peep around the corner, or the word *bullshit* begins to lurk in the shadow. But if you say *sexual love*, which I think is not bullshit and not

fictitious, that's something else. But I think there's a certain amount of do unto others even in that.

How do you know you're in love? What incites your love?

I don't know if you ever figure that out. If you're smart, you don't figure it out. Of course, you always try to figure it out. But if you're smart, you know you can't. I take great pride in my stupidity in this area. I have no clear way of being able to define at what point [*21 seconds*] passion for loyalty has overcome me.

Has your heart been broken?

Sure.

How many times?

[*Laughs richly, then 17-second pause*] I'm sure I've reached my quota. I'm not at liberty to disclose my quota. But then you'd have to define *break* and *heart.*

How do you mend yours? Give advice.

To the lovelorn? There is no away. Nobody goes away. Except the Big Away, and there's nothing you can do about it. If you really love someone [*17 seconds*] and they're healthy and happy . . . you ought to be able to live with that.

Can you always be that philosophical?

[*24 seconds*] Pretty close.

A musicial question. As per legend: "You're so Vain"—did you think the song was about you?

[*Laughs, 15-second pause*] *Who* wrote that?

Helicopter attack! Right over Warren's glass room, right when he is trying to avoid the subject of Carly Simon's pop wrath, a helicopter divebombs us! "Press!" Warren announces, both panicked and thrilled. This is a game he's played before. He runs for cover, ducking into the living room. "Let's see if they're taking pictures," he hollers above the prop wash and moves intrepidly from window to window, his gaze arched skyward. The British assistant runs up from his office below and watches with us. "I don't think it's press," the assistant says after a while. Warren is uncertain but says, "I don't see a guy hanging out of the helicopter with a camera. That's usually the tip-off." "No," says the Brit, "it must be something else." Both seem a tad disappointed. They conclude that it's probably some local law-enforcement mission. Perhaps to cheer himself, Warren then performs for me his impersonation of Walter Lippmann, the great political journalist, reacting to being interviewed by Warren himself (while doing *Reds* research). Warren leans forward and pushes his face very close to mine. "Ask me a question," he says. "Can you cook?" I ask. He simply grins a reproachful grin. And stares into my eyes. And keeps grinning. And says nothing. Which is Warren's canny way of saying that he knows the feeling. He knows.

Anarchy in the U.S.S.R.?

ANTHONY DeCURTIS

GORBACHEV HAD LOST CONTROL. THE SOVIET ECONOMY WAS BRAIN DEAD, THE PARTY PRIMED TO SELF-DESTRUCT. AN EYE-WITNESS ACCOUNT OF REAL LIFE IN RUSSIA IN THE WANING DAYS OF COMMUNISM.

He made me an offer I couldn't refuse.

It was early in January of 1990, a month or so after I had turned down a job at—gasp!—another magazine. After three and a half years, I had been feeling overworked, underpaid, unappreciated, driven crazy at ROLLING STONE—what else is new? The job had become that strange phenomenon of the hip publishing world; a glamorous grind. Writing stories had become a frantic afterthought to jumping on planes to go report them. I had been put in charge of the record review section in October, but never had the time to give it the attention it required. The offer to go elsewhere came, and I was seriously considering it.

Jann's performance, when he learned I was thinking about leaving, was masterful. He actually entered my office, braving the clutter that normally provokes violent discomfort in him ("He does care," I immediately thought). He sat down and looked at me for a moment, as if to assess whether I had simply lost my mind and was, therefore, beyond persuasion. He then said, with a sense of purpose worthy of Hannibal, "Anthony, what are you doing?"

What followed was an aria of unprecedented emotional range. I was alternately, and sometimes simultaneously, flattered, chided, charmed, cajoled and denounced. Didn't I realize that I had one of the best magazine jobs in the country, that I was the record review editor of ROLLING STONE? Was it the money? (He seemed hurt that I might let money turn my head. Also sheepish—he *knew* what I was making.) That could be taken care of. Was it the writing or the editing that was bothering me— why didn't I chose one or the other? How could he help me if I didn't tell him what the problem was? In fact, why hadn't I come to him in the first place?

As for the honchos at that other company, what had they ever done for any of their writers? Maybe I thought they would make me a star. Ha! He could barely keep their writers straight, tell one from another. Could anyone? No, ROLLING STONE was the place where I could truly distinguish myself—couldn't I see that?

This went on for three days, I agonized, wondering what I should do, what really would be the best decision for me. But Jann always seemed energized, absolutely at the top of his game, a swagger in his step, a smile never far from his lips. "He's enjoying this," I thought to myself. He loved the air of competition, the sense that something was at stake, the fight. I'd never really seen this scrapper side of him. It made me think about how he'd started a magazine at twenty-one and brought it, day by day, to this point, about how many fights he'd had to fight to get where he is.

Dear reader, I stayed.

So when I was called into Jann's office that January to meet with him and Bob Wallace, I had no idea what was up. Characteristically, Jann came directly to the point, even before I had sat down: "Anthony, how would you like to go to the Soviet Union for three weeks?"

ROLLING STONE had been approached about doing an exchange by *Arguments & Facts,* one of the most popular weeklies in what was then still known as the Soviet Union. ROLLING STONE would send a writer to Moscow for up to three weeks; *Arguments & Facts* would send one to New York sometime later. The publications would serve as home bases to the writers, providing an office, contacts, an interpreter and travel assistance. I was the writer chosen to go for ROLLING STONE. And I knew why when Jann asked, in what can only be described as a tone of taunting gratitude, "Aren't you glad you stayed now?"

At that time, the Soviet Union was going through tumultuous upheavals, though the nature of those changes was profoundly unclear to me. I followed the international news carefully, but I was not by the furthest stretch of the imagination a Sovietologist. Only ROLLING STONE, I remember thinking at the time, would send its record-review editor to cover one of the most important political stories of the century.

Like most Americans, I assumed that Mikhail Gorbachev was as revered in the Soviet Union as he was in the rest of the world. I would soon get a rude awakening. The product of a Cold War upbringing and my own studiously acquired left-wing views, I assumed that Moscow was a fully supplied, sophisticated, world-class city and that the Soviet Union was a daunting power, awesome in every respect. I assumed that the "shortages" dutifully reported in the Western press meant that not every brand was in stock. None of the research I did before I left prepared me for what I found when I got there.

When I returned I was so happy to be home I blasted Chuck Berry's "Back in the U.S.A." and immediately ran out to my favorite neighborhood pizza place. Back at work, Jann asked me two questions. The first was, "So what was it like?" I spoke for twenty minutes, uninterrupted— a first (and only) for a discussion with Jann. When I was done, he simply said, "What do you want to write?" I told him I wanted to write a story that would convey the feelings of a people who were desperately struggling to envision a future beyond the disintegration of everything they had ever known.

"Sounds great," he said. "Do it."

RS 582/583

JULY 12TH–26TH, 1990

I magine the Sixties, the Depression, Watergate and the Civil War going on all at the same time, and you'll get some sense of what's happening in the Soviet Union. All verities have been destroyed, and nothing has risen to replace them. No one can sense where things are heading. No one mood prevails; every social current generates an equally strong counterresponse. These are not the best of times; they are possibly the worst of times.

A journalist friend in Moscow whose English was serviceable, but no better, kept referring to my assignment in his country as a story about "real Soviet life." In the course of my three-week visit as a guest of the Soviet weekly newspaper *Arguments and Facts*, I could never tell if he was serious or just kidding me, mocking my ambitions as an American magazine writer looking—between museum visits and expense-account meals— for the inside story of the country he has lived in his whole life.

All I know is that he'd use the phrase whenever the grimly funny, daily surrealism of Soviet society would manifest itself. "This is real Soviet life," he'd say with an exasperated laugh when we were inexplicably refused tables at half-empty restaurants, when I discovered mice in the room of my supposedly top-of-the-line hotel in Moscow, when drunk American tourists, having failed to produce the requisite pass, sloppily grappled with armed guards—"What the fuck *is* this? I *live* here!"—outside their hotel in Leningrad. "'What the fuck *is* this,'" he'd say, laughing, mimicking their American accents and their outrage. "This is not America," he'd say, as if in answer to the question. "This is real Soviet life."

In fact, among the people I met, the term *soviet* served essentially as a synonym for "fucked up." I'd been in the country about three days when a car that was sent to take me to an interview failed to start. After several attempts to get it going, the driver turned to me, smiled wearily and explained: "Soviet car." By that time, that was all the explanation I needed.

The depth of the Soviet people's bitterness about conditions in their country is profound. They've been living for the past seventy-three years under socialism as it might have been conceived of by Groucho, not Karl, Marx, as it might be depicted in a novel by William Buckley. Quite simply, nothing in the country works. Broken chairs, for example, became something of a slapstick motif during my visit. A woman went to sit down at an editorial meeting: The chair crumbled. A young man picked up a chair in a restaurant to move it to his table: The seat fell off. Lights in public places flickered on and off with distressing unpredictability. Phone service was spotty at best. Domestic mail was problematic, and sending something by overseas mail was considered tantamount to throwing it away.

What has brought matters to this extreme pass? "The October Revolution," Sergei Troitsky, the genially obnoxious twenty-three-year-old bass player for a Moscow band called Metal Corrosion, declared, alluding to Lenin's 1917 coup d'etat. One afternoon Troitsky was kind enough to show me a videotape of Moscow's first Thrash Metal and Sex Festival, which took place last year. The event achieved perfection of a sort when, during a song called "Let's Go Shake Shake" (the chorus, sung in English, ran: "Let's go shake shake/Let's go fuck and shake"), ten or so Soviet lovelies took the stage, stripped to bikini underpants, garter belts and stockings and cavorted with Troitsky and his leering band mates before a crowd of 5000 ecstatic young people. With unerring, if unintended, Soviet irony, the Moscow authorities had granted a permit for this show under the guise of its being an AIDS-awareness event—this, in a country in which condoms, not to mention disposable syringes, are virtually impossible to come by.

Understandably, Troitsky sees his country as gripped by decadence. His solution: the restoration of the monarchy. "At every concert, we play the old Russian hymn 'God Save the Czar,' " he said proudly through an interpreter. "We write out the lyrics of the hymn to give to our fans, and they sing with us." Troitsky's father, meanwhile, works at the Institute of Marxism-Leninism, an organ of the Central Committee of the Communist party. What does Dad think about his doings? "He has his own problems to keep him busy," Troitsky said wryly.

A far more serious critic of the current system than Troitsky is Alexander Podrabinek, the editor in chief of the *samizdat* journal *Express-Khronika*. "The biggest problem of our society is socialism," said Podrabinek. "And as we liberate ourselves from this, our problems will be solved." Podrabinek is a veteran of the days when papers like *Express-Khronika*—which routinely covers issues like the independence movements in the Baltic states, terrorist actions in the Soviet republic of Azerbaijan and antigovernment actions in the Georgian capital, Tbilisi—could only be distributed in secret and at great risk.

As it is, the journal has moved its offices seventeen times in the past three years to keep a quick step ahead of the authorities; only a week before my visit, the para-military police entered the curent offices, which are on the ground floor of a run-down apartment complex in Moscow, and questioned the staff for three hours while a police bus stayed parked ominously in the lot outside. Even so, the lean, intense Podrabinek was able to look around his office and smile. "Now to publish *samizdat*, we have computers, fax machines, telephones," he said.

Podrabinek does not mince words in describing the state of the Soviet Union. "All of our problems have one source: The reluctance and inability of the Soviet leadership to give the society political initiatives," he said. "It concerns everything—economics, the free definition of national policy.

"With the example of Lithuania," Podrabinek continued, "we see the central powers are reluctant to give power to the republics to pursue their policies independently. So everywhere you see a dictatorship from the center. Now the authorities give many possibilities to the society, but within very clear-cut boundaries. Those who try to traverse those boundaries are going to be punished."

The limitations on the freedoms of the Soviet people after the heady initial promises of *glasnost* and *perestroika* have combined with the paralyzing shortages and inefficiencies of the Soviet economy to undermine President Mikhail Gorbachev's national standing completely. One European writer recently described Gorbachev as a centrist in a country that no longer has a center, and in capturing the degree of the president's isolation in a land that is flying apart in every conceivable direction, that description is apt. Virtually no one has a good word to say about him. Perhaps the only person less popular than Gorbachev is his wife, Raisa, who is seen as intrusive and uppity in a country in which it is assumed that, as one woman explained only half-jokingly, "Russian women are very obedient." The most sympathetic view of Gorbachev's plight is that *glasnost* and *perestroika* have opened a Soviet Pandora's box.

"It's a lot of mess going on," complained Sasha Gradsky, a trailblazer in the creation of Soviet rock & roll more than two decades ago and a prominent figure on the music scene today. "Those things that Gorbachev intended to do, that's not quite what we have in the results. I think he wanted to start with some slight reforms, but he didn't take into account that the people are awaiting permission to shout — and very much awaiting it. He half opened the door, and the people stuck their foot in. People say that he is unstable, unsteady, that he changes his views very often, because it is not he who has chosen the way. On the contrary, the way has chosen him."

Vladislav Starkov, the editor of the Moscow-based *Arguments and Facts*, was nearly removed from his position by Gorbachev late last year after the paper published a survey that suggested the leader's popularity was slipping. The paper's editorial board, heartily supported by more than 30 million subscribers, held firm, and Starkov was permitted to retain his position. Now the Communist party refuses to allot adequate paper and printing facilities to *Arguments and Facts* — a decision the paper's editors see as political, the paper shortage in the Soviet Union notwithstanding. Starkov remains a politic supporter of *perestroika* — and Gorbachev — nonetheless.

"Two alternatives are possible, and as often happens in life, they can overlap," Starkov said about the immediate future of his country. "I'll start with the worst one. The worst may come if the leadership and the conservative part of our society manage to curtail *perestroika*. That will mean a return to the previous way: to a dictatorship of the ministries, to censorship, to tightening things up, to wasting the national wealth.

"Such measures can work for a very short time, but, after all, they will end in failure, because it is like curing a malignant tumor with anaesthetic injections. The way out of such a situation is only in civil war, because the population has accepted *perestroika* and is looking forward to the results of *perestroika*. If the conservative forces try to interfere with and hinder *perestroika*, of course, civil war will become inevitable.

"The way that Gorbachev follows is to go along a very uneven road in a cart that goes very slowly," Starkov continued. "Sometimes it stumbles, sometimes it loses its wheels, but still it goes slowly forward. Of course, it's a very slow way, but it is the right way. It does not leave any room for civil war, and it allows for the expectation among the people that at some time in the future, they will go along the paved, even road."

* * *

Such moderate views are uncommon in the two major cities of the Soviet Union, where the failures of the old system and the shock of the new generate extremes. Tensions are running uncomfortably high, as worlds collide. People are feeling the strain. I understood this in an abstract sense even before I arrived, but it became dramatically clear on a personal level about halfway into my visit when, on a bright, cool April afternoon, my driver and my interpreter got into a fistfight as we drove down a broad, heavily trafficked avenue in Leningrad.

They hadn't been getting along since they'd met the previous day, and before the fight broke out, they'd been shouting at each other for some time. Since I don't understand Russian, couldn't fathom the problem and was equally dependent on both of them, I maintained a diplomatic silence in the back seat. The din subsided for a moment, and then the interpreter, who was sitting next to me, uncorked two rights to the driver's shoulder, and our car careened into the next lane. I shouted at them to stop and, feeling a combination of shock and terror, bolted out of the car as it paused at the next traffic light.

I stood on the street, trying to collect myself amid the crowd of pedestrians strolling by. The interpreter leaped out of the car, ran over to me and offered a terse apology. Evidently, he'd been called a motherfucker; "I don't like bad things said about my close relatives" is how he more delicately explained it. The two of us rode public transportation—buses, trolleys and subway trains—in near silence for the rest of the afternoon.

For the remainder of the time I was in the Soviet Union, and for weeks after I returned to New York, I wondered about this incident. The sense of having been in physical danger far from home is one obvious reason the event stayed with me. But I also wondered about the pressures that could have driven these two men—each perfectly friendly in his own way—to violate so outrageously the strict Russian code of hospitality, not to mention risk their own lives and the life of their American guest.

I thought about how, one day before the fight, the interpreter—a proper, punctilious man in his early forties with blond, closely cropped hair—had returned from his first trip to the United States. The resident of a city in which you need to carry an identity card to purchase the few goods available in the shops, he had reeled at the world of consumer plenty he had encountered in Washington, D.C., New York, Boston and Chicago.

Just a few hours after his return to Leningrad from the United States, he'd gotten a call asking if he could do some freelance work, beginning that afternoon, as an interpreter and guide for an American visitor. Though suffering from jet lag and still on vacation from his full-time job, he accepted. Having had to watch his money "like a calculator" while in America, and given the current state of the Soviet economy, how could he pass up the chance to pick up a few extra rubles?

The driver, meanwhile, had his own complex story—really, no story in the Soviet Union is simple. In contrast to the rather prim interpreter—a fiend for efficiency, a true product of *perestroika*—the driver was a portly, white-haired, insanely garrulous man who had served in the Russian navy for thirty-five years. A great deal of fun and almost willfully useless as a driver—he refused to take directions and talked far too much to keep track of where he was going—he was obsessed with his car and its Italian-made engine, a virtually priceless commodity given the heaps of Soviet-made junk the vast majority of his countrymen felt lucky to own.

Fuel, it seems, was suddenly in short supply—perhaps because of the recent shutdown of oil pipelines to nearby Lithuania; typically, no one could say for sure. So when, on that fateful morning, we passed a queue of perhaps fifty cars at an apparently well-stocked gasoline station, the driver unilaterally decided that regardless of our schedule, he needed to tank up.

The interpreter, steaming at the delay, and I got out, hitched a ride to a hotel a few miles away in exchange for a pack of Marlboros, and had lunch. After we finished, we waited another hour or so before the driver turned up. He was late, he explained, because the attendants at the gas station—in perfect Soviet fashion—had decided to break for lunch themselves, despite the long line. On the drive back, the two men went at each other.

Mysterious shortages, short tempers, long lines, unnecessary problems, misunderstandings, visiting foreigners, old people in a changing world, glimmering visions of Western-style prosperity, opportunities for earning extra money in the *perestroika* economy, flirting with complete catastrophe: Welcome to the old, new Soviet Union, a huge, disunited giant of a nation balanced on a high, thin tightrope.

Contradictory impulses within Soviet society fuel the instability of contemporary times. The Communist party has been entirely discredited, while, particularly among older people, there remains an almost heartbreaking nostalgia for the certainties the party has provided. In the wake of Afghanistan and the upheavals in the outlying republics, the Red Army may be seen as an oppressive force, but any resident of Moscow or Leningrad will tell you the history of every war memorial in those cities. Older men proudly wear their military decorations on their suit coats, and the army's heroism in World War II is palpably felt. The nation's horrifying history has been revealed; Stalin is now vilified, and even the officially sacrosanct Lenin is despised by many Soviet citizens. But people are beginning to tire of the sordid revelations and wonder why all the purgative truth telling isn't making their hard, everyday lives any easier. There is an ardent desire for more freedom but a hatred for leaders who vacillate. There is a dangerous yearning for order that some seem to believe only the iron hand of the past can provide.

The free market is seen as a panacea. It's really almost shocking to hear Russians, in their ravaged circumstances, spout all the hucksterisms of a Chamber of Commerce buffoon, to hear them go on and on about joint ventures, economic development, multinational deals, business infrastructures. "You have to understand the extremism of the Russian character," one woman explained to me. "If ten years ago everybody was an agent or a spy, today everybody is an entrepreneur."

The free market is also viewed with tremendous apprehension. After all, the price of bread, maintained at an artificially low level by the government, hasn't risen here in thirty years—though it will this summer. Housing conditions are by and large appalling, but everyone is guaranteed a place to live. The economy is absurdly inefficient, but everyone is guaranteed a job—and no one watches the clock too closely if you need to knock off work for a couple of hours to go stand on line for shoes or soap. Despite the current fascination with capitalism, people are deeply suspicious of individually acquired wealth and often associate the profit motive with the omnipresent black marketeers who run what amounts to an obscenely lucrative second economy. Everyone is eager for the consumer goods that capitalism seems able to provide so effortlessly in the envied West; no one is eager to face the hardships, social dislocation and instability that the transition to an open market will bring.

There is a sense that people have suffered enough. How could they, *why should they*, be expected to suffer more? "It seems to me that in the United States, they do not take account of suffering as one of the most important themes of art," said Mikhail Levitin, chief producer of the aesthetically adventurous Hermitage Theater, in Moscow. "But we are suffering too much here. And this is probably the way we have shared the spheres in culture and art. You take the joy of life, and we take the suffering."

Suffering, of course, is an essential theme of traditional Russian art; it is the kiln in which the Russian soul was forged, and the Russian soul is a hot ticket these days. While Americans primarily hear of the more fashionable nationalist movements in the Baltic republics, the most fiercely—and dangerously—nationalistic group in the Soviet Union is the Russians. With the seven decades since the revolution largely perceived as an unmitigated failure, a longing for the purity of the noble Russian past is in the air. That past is viewed as Slavic and Christian—a point of view that does not signal good times ahead for Jews, Asians or other non-Russian ethnic groups, who aren't exactly having a picnic even under the current conditions. Pamyat, the Russian nationalist group that is frankly antisemitic and fascist, has garnered a following, but even Russians who stop well short of such extremism openly speak of darker-skinned Georgians, for example, with a contempt just a hair shy of racism.

In line with those developments, Russian mysticism is experiencing a big revival, accompanied by an extraordinary fascination with the occult. Faith healers, astrologers, psychics and fortunetellers are much in demand. Odd rumors abound, like those that float through America about Elvis or JFK. Cosmonaut Yuri Gagarin didn't really die when it was reported he did, one such story ran; he was held in a mental institution in the provinces and only died recently.

Because Russians tend not to come at things very directly, such interests often emerge in odd contexts. For example, a series of rock concerts along the Volga River was planned to raise awareness about environmental problems in the Soviet Union—a good idea, given that the air in Moscow is pretty much three-dimensional and many of the country's waterways are horribly polluted. (One Russian I met asked if he would be able to buy a Geiger counter on an upcoming visit to the United States, so concerned was he about exposure to radiation in the wake of Chernobyl.)

Rather than addressing any specific environmental problems, however, the money raised from this series of rock concerts would go toward the establishment of a Center for Nontraditional Healing—the broad connecting idea being "health."

What exactly is nontraditional healing, I asked. "It's becoming more and more popular," a spokesman explained. "There are these people who have the ability to heal with their hands, with herbs. They can heal with energy. It comes from an interaction with nature. They say that they get the energy from space, and then they can influence you with their energy in such a big amount that it makes your organs operate in the right way. That's major league!"

As an American, I was assumed by most Soviets to be an uncritical fan of *glasnost* and *perestroika*, an unquestioning supporter of Gorbachev. They took enormous, friendly delight in indulging my perceived illusions and then disabusing me of them.

"Do you want me to say what you want to hear from me, or do you want me to say what I think?" asked Mikhail Levitin with a broad smile when I asked his opinion about the effects of *glasnost* and *perestroika* and about his country's prospects.

First what I want to hear, I replied, then what he really thinks. "Very good," he said, laughing heartily. "So I will answer in the way you'd like it to be: 'There are great changes, of course, and they are irreversible! There is no way back.' The next is my answer: 'There have been no real changes, and life will be as it is now.'"

Alexander Podrabinek of *Express-Khronika* is similarly harsh in his assessment, echoing Vladislav Starkov's worries about the possibility of a civil war. "It is very difficult to make prognoses, to forecast under this regime," he said. "You'd need to be a fortuneteller or an astrologist in this situation. For the immediate future, I would say that the society demands possibilities for itself that the authorities do not provide. If they continue to resist those demands, it might end in civil war.

"To a certain extent, Gorbachev is a symbol of what is going on here, that is true," Podrabinek continued. "But in the West, they do not see everything that is happening here; they see only what propaganda presents. There are no structural changes in the state whatsoever. All the changes are within the framework of the policy of today. If the government changes, if policy changes, everything can easily go back to what we had. Of course, we ourselves *want* it to be irreversible, so our *wishes* are the same. But the world surrounding us, we look at it with different eyes, because it is closer to us. We know it better. And we see that there are no irreversible changes."

Foreigners often remark that the dreadful food shortages evident in Russian shops bear no relationship to the bounteous hospitality one receives in Russian homes. At the home of Olga Kalinina, a film archivist, and her husband, Alec, who directs a puppet theater, this contrast could not have been more dramatic. What was supposed to be, on my last night in Leningrad, a quick interview about the conditions of Soviet life was soon overwhelmed by endless offerings of splendid food and paralyzing amounts of vodka.

The conversation—Alec, Olga and I were joined by the couple's daughter, a sister-in-law, my interpreter and a Russian journalist—turned instead to the relative merits of American and Russian women, the beauty of Leningrad's Venice-style canals, the superiority of Leningrad (to this partisan crowd, at least) to Moscow. Eventually, however, the talk returned, as all talk eventually does in the Soviet Union, to politics. "Gorbachev is a product of the old system who wants to introduce new realities into society," Olga said.

"If we look back into history, we will see that the Soviet people have been frightened by that kind of experiment," Alec added. "As history shows, there has never been a single man who could turn things upside down and create something better. That's why people are so cautious about Gorbachev." So, once again, things could be changed back?

"We simply wait for that," Olga said, with matter-of-fact sadness. "We don't wait, we *expect* it," said Alec. "Unfortunately, a lot of things repeat themselves," said Olga. "This frightens us, because if it happens, things will go backwards." Then she gathered herself, brightened and raised her glass. "So let us drink that things will go forward," she said. "If the way things develop depends on this table, there will be no problems."

But there will be problems, and they will be ravaging. The redefinition of Soviet history sparked by *glasnost* has given the past a new, more immediate life—and, in something of a reverse prophecy, made it a threatening vision of the possible future. "It's rather dramatic," said Svetlana Makurenkova, a prominent Russian translator, "that this experience, accumulated through blood and tears, is coming back to us, also to bear new blood and new tears."

New blood and new tears. Leaving Moscow I was homesick and heartsick—avid to come home to my loved ones, to my familiar life in America, troubled by the ruthless days lying in wait for my friends who must continue to live in real Soviet life. Some are born to endless night, wrote Blake. Good night, Moscow.

The Lonesome Drifter

WILLIAM GREIDER

THE REAL WASHINGTON SCANDAL OF THE EIGHTIES?
RONALD REAGAN DIDN'T CARE ABOUT LEADING THE
COUNTRY. SO WHY DID WE LOVE HIM LIKE WE DID?

A decade ago, when I was assistant managing editor for national news at the *Washington Post*, some colleagues thought I was having a nervous breakdown when I announced that I was leaving the *Post* for ROLLING STONE. A lot of people outside the newsroom figured I must have been fired. Why else would anyone abandon the inner circle of Washington media heavies to write for a rock & roll magazine? It *was* a bizarre midlife career change, I admit. My decision might be explained with Tom Cruise's immortal line from *Risky Business*: "Sometimes you gotta say, 'What the fuck.'"

Dr. Hunter S. Thompson claimed afterward that the idea was his. He says he was standing at his toilet late one night, taking a leak, and thought of me. Hunter then made one of his nocturnal phone calls to Jann Wenner and explained his inspiration: This was the dawning of the Reagan era, and ROLLING STONE needed someone in Washington to keep track of the damage. Roughly speaking, that's what I've been doing ever since.

Departing from the A list of Washington journalists was much easier than it may look. From afar, people imagine that the Washington reporters, columnists and editors (at different times, I had been all three at the *Post*) have great influence in the capital. Certainly, many of those journalists pretend that they do. Up close, I knew this was ninety-eight percent illusion or self-delusion.

The truth is that what the Washington reporters usually influence is not the big decisions of government but the city's parlor politics—its endless gossip and argument. After many years of writing for the *Post*'s elite readership, I had a feeling that my precious insights were merely providing more fodder for the self-important chatter at dinner parties. I certainly hadn't seen any great deviations in events because of anything I had written.

At ROLLING STONE, as I told my friends, I would be speaking to a vast new audience across the country—young and diverse and mostly disengaged from the tricky-track news of government and politics. I told myself that I was giving up the intimacy of Washington's high-powered audience in exchange for the freedom to write what I really think is true, without the usual stunts and evasions of orthodox news.

I was mistaken about the intimacy. Despite differences of age and geography, I eventually felt closer to RS readers than I ever had to *Post* readers because I experienced the hot breath of their reactions in my mail and occasionally in person. RS readers tend to claim a proprietary interest in the magazine, and they swiftly let you know when they think your prose has cluttered or besmirched its pages. Some of the letters are droolingly mindless screeds; others are astute critiques that often nail the weaknesses in my own analysis.

For a writer, the overall effect is stimulating—a sense that someone is actually listening to what you are saying and prepared to respond forcefully, either positively or negatively. I have been refreshed by both. Ironically, I have also heard from the elites of Washington—senators, White House officials, important journalists—often because their teenage children have confronted them at the dinner table with something provocative I have written in RS. It is perversely satisfying to me that I occasionally jerk the chain of powerful personages not through the august columns of an important newspaper but through their own subversive children.

As it happened, the bulk of my columns formed a running critique of the Reagan regime at the very moment when a major segment of RS readers was falling in love with the Gipper. The young Reagan fans did not appreciate my dissenting views, to put it mildly, and they regularly denounced me in the most colorful terms. As faithful readers know, I did not back down, but the corrosive fan mail was, well, invigorating like a cold shower.

In time, I learned to appreciate the different context in which many RS readers were seeing Reagan. From my vantage point, he was a talented and cynical illusionist—using his video-genic skills to gull the country into destructive fantasies that evaded deeper social and economic problems. For many younger readers, he was the first good thing they had seen in politics—an idealistic leader who exuded patriotic values and a sure sense of the nation's destiny.

When Reagan became ensnared in the Iran-*contra* scandal in 1986, his deceitful, lawless qualities became painfully clear even to those who had been believers, and their palpable sense of betrayal was also reflected in my mail. The letters expressed real pain and regret. Much as I detested Reagan's guileful leadership, I recognized at that moment that he had been providing young people with something valuable—a sense of optimism and unblemished idealism about the nation. Now his image too was exposed as illusion, and I found myself joining in the lament.

"American idealism is probably the most important asset we have as a nation, a strength steadily eroded by disillusioning scandals in the White House." I wrote at the time. "If Americans become as cynical as Europeans about the supremacy of law, then we will inevitably lose something vital and binding. Our national innocence gives us a kind of energy. It allows people to dream and invent and change things peaceably, even to change themselves. We don't ever want to lose our youthful sense of optimism. . . . The trick for the nation is how to become wiser about the world without becoming cynical, how to look at ourselves more honestly without losing our faith in the future."

Whatever the topic, that message is still the theme of my RS columns: the need to get smart about things without losing hope, to be honest about the nation's condition while remaining optimistic about our possibilities.

RS 495

MARCH 12TH, 1987

It could hardly be called a secret, because so many Washington insiders knew it. Ronald Reagan, they said, was not functioning as the president of the United States, though he held the title and performed on television behind the seal of office. The real president was James A. Baker III, Reagan's chief of staff, who presided over the quarrelsome White House staff and decided what the president should be told about his own administration. When Baker left, in 1985, to become the secretary of the treasury, the new de facto president was his successor, Donald Regan.

An exaggeration perhaps, but with some truth to it. During the last six years, the stress of bearing the responsibilities of the Oval Office became visible in the faces of Baker and Regan. They changed dramatically, aging and graying before our eyes, as had earlier presidents, because it was they who were running the country. Ronald Reagan, meanwhile, remained forever young.

Often baffled and bored by the demands of governing, the president remained stubbornly detached—so much so that some defenders of his role in the Iran-*contra* affair are now claiming that he really didn't know what his own national-security staff was doing down the hall and in the basement. It has also been suggested that Reagan was told about the shuffling of arms and money between Iran and Central America but simply forgot. That seems even more plausible.

The unfolding scandal has forced the nation to face the truth about Ronald Reagan. He is a man who projects an image of strength and idealism, a bold and optimistic leader who stands by his principles and stands up to the world. But seated behind his desk at the White House, he hardly leads at all. He is a passive man who floats along in his own world, cajoled and managed by subordinates who occasionally bluff and bully him into doing what they think is needed. Like any good actor, he listens to the director and sticks to the script.

And yet for years the true story was not told. Some have blamed the press for this. The news media did not cover the leadership crisis that was occurring in the White House, although many reporters caught a glimpse of it. The Washington press seemed to have decided shortly after the 1980 election that the public didn't want to read anything unpleasant about Ronald Reagan, and so it stopped reporting the facts. By 1984, the press itself had been seduced by the president's larger-than-life image.

Even so, the story got out—most candidly in the memoirs of Reagan's former aides. In *Caveat: Realism, Reagan and Foreign Policy,* published in 1984, the former secretary of state Alexander Haig broadly sketched the president's fuzzy understanding of foreign policy and his constant manipulation by his advisers. And in *The Triumph of Politics,* published last spring, the former budget director David Stockman provided a devastating firsthand account of presidential incompetence. Reagan, Stockman wrote, never really grasped the elementary features of his own economic program. He had no idea why the federal debt was doubling under his stewardship and never quite believed it was happening. When confronted by a hard policy choice, Reagan would often deflect it with another hoary anecdote from his bank of charming stories.

Reagan's apparent role as a cat's-paw in the Iran-*contra* scandal reminds me of a scene from Stockman's book. The budget director and Caspar Weinberger, the secretary of defense, had been tenaciously arguing over a proposed $30 billion cut in the Pentagon budget. Unable to resolve the dispute, Jim Baker—knowing that Reagan had no stomach for such dis-agreements—decided to send the two men in to see the president. As the cabinet officers entered the Oval Office, the president was reading heart-warming letters from admiring citizens. Stockman and Weinberger argued the $30 billion question furiously; neither would yield. The president ap-peared distressed and confused by their fighting and pleaded with them to come to an agreement. But he refused to make his own decision on the issue. As they left, Stockman looked back and saw the president, with a smile on his face, return to his fan mail.

If Ronald Reagan's inability to lead was no secret, then the explanation for its never becoming an issue must run deeper than a failure of the press. It certainly couldn't have been that the voters liked the way the government was being run: the Reagan record, both at home and abroad, is studded with the kinds of failures and contradictions that would have sunk another president. The public, we know from countless opinion polls, has never agreed with Reagan's right-wing agenda, from waging war in Nicaragua to the trashing of food assistance for the poor. Yet in spite of this, his popularity swelled during the last six years.

I suspect that most voters were aware of Reagan's limitations and loved him anyway. In fact, I think his detachment was part of his appeal. He seemed as fed up as the rest of the country with the complexities of government and the world. He, too, made light of the eye-glazing details of Washington and rebelled against them. He clung to the simple verities and insisted that they were all he needed to guide the country.

This was a reassuring, self-indulgent fantasy, and most people bought into it. A real man with his heart in the right place didn't have to under-stand all this complex stuff to be president. If he stood by the American dream, he could lead our country bravely into the future and leave the details to others. Now the fantasy has collapsed. It's as though the nation has been rudely awakened from a pleasant sleep.

The question that fascinates me is why the vast majority of Americans needed to suspend disbelief and embrace the make-believe Ronald Reagan. The answer, I think, reveals dangerous weaknesses in our national char-acter, flaws that the president was a master at exploiting.

Reagan played the strong, innocent American for an audience that deeply wanted to believe these same qualities characterized the entire nation. A guy takes a shot at him and he ad-libs jokes in the hospital operating room. The brave cowboy as president. He gets caught on the air wise-cracking about bombing Russia. But, hey, he's only kidding. People espe-cially loved it that Reagan never regretted anything—unlike some of his predecessors.

What could be more American? It is exactly how we like to see ourselves in the world. Tougher than the other kids on the block—but also easygoing and lovable. America sees itself as the free spirit of the world, uncorrupted by history, unencumbered by complexity and compromise. We do as we please, disregarding the complaints of friends and foes alike. How morally satisfying it is to confront the troublemakers of the world—the Qadaffis and ayatollahs and commies—with a real American as commander in chief, a white-hatted cowboy who never backs down, never makes deals.

Virtually every significant episode in the history of Reagan's foreign policy started from the premise of American innocence—and ended disastrously. Reagan sent marines into Lebanon, as though the warring factions there would simply lay down their arms before the Stars and Stripes. Instead they slaughtered our marines. Reagan pumped hundreds of billions of dollars into defense budgets, as though the United States could buy back its old hegemony in the world. America would be respected again if only the nation would acquire more tanks, fighters, nuclear missiles and aircraft carriers. When this approach didn't work, Reagan proposed an even simpler one—Star Wars, a miraculous, though horribly expensive, solution to the real-world complexities of national security.

The real world, alas, will not cooperate in this nonsense, not in Moscow or in the capitals of Western Europe, not in the Middle East or in Central America. It goes forward with its own messy claims and contradictions—and American frustrations deepen. Why can't our allies cooperate? Why don't third-world countries behave? Why isn't the world the way Ronald Reagan says it is, the way it used to be? The complaint is like the whine of a child who doesn't want to grow up.

A nation that lives in the past is on dangerous ground. The most damaging thing about Reagan's nostalgic vision is that it blinds us to the present. One can make a rather impressive checklist of the ominous problems the Reagan presidency has refused to deal with. The debt crisis that threatens to topple Latin American economies and our own banking system. The burgeoning arms race that invites smaller nations to acquire their own nuclear arsenals. The economic warfare that leads to the export of American production and jobs to the countries of Europe and Asia (while America pays the bill for their national defense). Reagan has dealt with these problems and many others by pretending they don't exist—and the country has gone along with him.

But the realities are getting harder to ignore. Our cities' streets are lined with the homeless. Home ownership has declined among American families in the Eighties for the first time since the Great Depression. The economy is performing more poorly in the 1980s than it did in the 1970s. Deflation has torn apart broad sections of the country—the farm belt, the oil states, the factory towns. Reagan's answer — to tell a funny anecdote and change the subject — seems to be losing its charm. The Democrats did not recapture the Senate last year because of their own brilliant solutions; they won because more and more Americans recognize that something is terribly wrong with the Reagan revolution and that the president is unwilling and unable to do anything about it.

Instead of developing serious strategies for confronting real problems, Reagan's men invent safe little melodramas: liberating Grenada; bombing Qadaffi; trying to make the Sandinistas "cry uncle," as the president put it. The end result of this brand of strength is, ironically, weakness.

In the Middle East, for instance, Reagan has now bombarded the citizens and soldiers of three Arab countries — Lebanon, Syria and Libya. Yet he is the first president in forty years to make absolutely no progress toward a genuine peace in the region. Negotiating in the Middle East is terribly difficult and frustrating, a politically unrewarding chore. Bombing is quick and easy and provides instant gratification.

In Latin America, Reagan has boiled down daunting economic and political complexities to a single, satisfying objective: beating the commies in Nicaragua. Yet this obesssion has created only more poverty and instability in the region and has pushed the chances for peace further into the future.

Carried away by the president's image of innocence and strength, the public went along with his simplistic view of the world and pushed his popularity to record levels. But the Iran-*contra* scandal has changed that. We have seen the real Ronald Reagan. He portrayed himself as tough and idealistic, but suddenly he looks as weak and cynical as the most deceitful of politicians. He promised the people he would not grovel before the bad guys of the world. Now it turns out he was lying — manipulating public opinion while at the same time giving away the farm to the ayatollah. The president's fall-back defense is his ignorance — "Gosh, I didn't know" — which is not the same as innocence. Worst of all, the president was snookered in the deal, like any hayseed who tries to do business with con men.

The audience is embarrassed for the aging actor. His character has lost its credibility, and people are withdrawing their suspension of disbelief. The audience, I suspect, is also a little embarrassed for itself. People did, after all, bite hard on the story.

As the various investigations of the Iran-*contra* affair proceed and the guilty are eventually punished, it's important that we remember how popular the Reagan fantasy was. Individuals, perhaps even the president, are to blame for breaking the law, and they should be held accountable, but this scandal contains a larger message that shouldn't be ignored. These events did not stem solely from the inadequacies of Ronald Reagan or his aides, any more than the Watergate scandal was uniquely attributable to Richard Nixon's twisted character.

In both instances, a larger political culture encouraged lawless behavior in the White House and convinced arrogant men that they needed to do these things and that they could get away with them. Our willingness to condone immoral or illegal activities by our government is rooted in the cold war, the American obsession with worldwide ideological conflict. The Central Intelligence Agency is essentially licensed to wage semisecret wars round the globe without the knowledge or approval of Congress and the people. Despite occasional congressional qualms, the CIA is authorized to break laws in the name of national security, and it regularly does. When the president's men routinely violate international law—by secretly mining the harbors of a foreign country, by bribery and subversion of sovereign nations—it is an easy step for them to disregard domestic law as well.

The American public is implicated, too. By faithfully responding to the cold-war rhetoric and acceding to corrupt methods, we have allowed our innocence to become a form of self-deception. Our national idealism is twisted into a simple-minded world view that is not only stupid but dangerous. Ronald Reagan played masterfully on this weakness. He told us that the complex problems of this world—and our own future—could be reduced to a simple moral struggle between a good America and, on the other side, an evil empire.

Most Americans know better, I think, but this is such an attractive story line—so simple and easy to enjoy compared with the complexities of the world. Good guys and bad guys. Rambo in action. No need to make messy compromises, no need to understand the ambiguities of real life. This, of course, is how Ronald Reagan sees things himself. There is no debt crisis threatening Latin America and the world's financial system. There is only this war to be won against the Soviet puppets in Nicaragua. We don't have to worry about the problem in international trade and the disaster in farming and manufacturing. Everything will be swell if America just rolls up its sleeves. I think the country is finally coming out of its trance—waking up at last to the fact that Reagan's magic is unreal.

American idealism is probably the most important asset we have as a nation, a strength steadily eroded by disillusioning scandals in the White House. If Americans become as cynical as Europeans about the supremacy of law, then we will inevitably lose something vital and binding. Our national innocence gives us a kind of energy. It allows people to dream and invent and change things peaceably, even to change themselves. We don't ever want to lose our youthful sense of optimism.

But Americans need to grow up a bit, to get a lot smarter about the world and our own role in it. The public has to start resisting the simple-minded nonsense that passes for U.S. foreign policy. Voters have to stop falling for political slogans that reduce a complicated reality to corny cowboy stories. Americans are smarter than that, surely. The trick for the nation is how to become wiser about the world without becoming cynical, how to look at ourselves more honestly without losing our faith in the future. This is something Ronald Reagan couldn't do.

Contributors

DAVID BLACK is a novelist, screenwriter and producer. He has been awarded a fiction grant from the National Endowment for the Arts, and the story excerpted in this book won the National Magazine Award for Reporting. He is currently executive producer and writer for Columbia Pictures/Fox's *The Good Policeman.*

DAVID BRESKIN is a ROLLING STONE Contributing Editor. He has produced records for Vernon Reid, Bill Frisell, Ronald Shannon Jackson and John Zorn, and he is the author of a novel, *The Real Life Diary of a Boomtown Girl,* and *Inner Views,* a compilation of his ROLLING STONE interviews with film directors.

TIM CAHILL is a founding editor of *Outside* magazine and is currently that magazine's editor-at-large. He is also a ROLLING STONE Contributing Editor and the author of *Buried Dreams, Jaguars Ripped My Flesh, A Wolverine is Eating My Leg, Road Fever,* and *Pecked to Death by Ducks.* He lives in the shadow of the Crazy Mountains in Montana.

MARCELLE CLEMENTS is the author of pieces, *The Dog Is Us,* and a novel, *Rock Me.* She is currently working on another novel.

RICHARD BEN CRAMER is the author of *What It Takes,* a book about the 1988 presidential candidates. He lives in Paris.

ANTHONY DeCURTIS is a writer and Senior Features Editor at ROLLING STONE, where he oversees the album-review section. He is also the pop music critic for the weekend edition of "All Things Considered," on National Public Radio. He is the editor of *Present Tense: Rock & Roll and Culture* and coeditor of *The Rolling Stone Illustrated History of Rock & Roll* and *The Rolling Stone*

Album Guide. His essay accompanying the Eric Clapton retrospective *Crossroads* won a Grammy Award in 1989 and in 1992 he received a ASCAP Deems Taylor Award for excellence in writing about music. He holds a PhD in American literature from Indiana University and has taught at Emory University.

ERIC EHRMANN was a twenty-three-year-old Contributing Editor to ROLLING STONE in 1969. His columns on international affairs have appeared in the Baltimore *Sun*, the *Boston Globe*, the *Chicago Tribune*, the *Christian Science Monitor*, the *New York Times* and *USA Today*. He has lectured on the media and politics at the Indiana University School of Journalism and at the University of Virginia.

JOE ESZTERHAS was formerly a Senior Editor of ROLLING STONE. He is now a screenwriter; his credits include *The Music Box, Betrayed, Flashdance, Jagged Edge* and most recently, *Basic Instinct*. He lives in Northern California.

CHET FLIPPO is a former Senior Editor of ROLLING STONE and the author of *Your Cheatin' Heart: A Biography of Hank Williams; Yesterday: The Unauthorized Biography of Paul McCartney; It's Only Rock & Roll*; and *Everybody Was Kung Fu Dancing*. He is now working with Waylon Jennings on Jennings' autobiography.

SAMUEL G. FREEDMAN is a former *New York Times* staff reporter; he has written for ROLLING STONE since 1987. He is the author of *Small Victories: The Real World of a Teacher, Her Students*, and *Their High School*, a finalist for the 1990 National Book Award, and *Upon this Rock: The Miracles of a Black Church*. He was the McGraw Distinguished Professor of Writing at Princeton University and currently teaches journalism at Columbia University.

DAVID FRICKE is the Music Editor of ROLLING STONE. He joined the magazine in 1985 as a Senior Writer. He is also the American correspondent for the English weekly *Melody Maker* and has written about music for *Musician, People* and the *New York Times*. He is the author of *Animal Instinct*, a biography of Def Leppard, and wrote the liner notes for the box set *The Byrds*, released in 1990.

ROBIN GREEN has been writing for television for the past five years; she is presently supervising producer of *Northern Exposure.*

ROBERT GREENFIELD is the author of *S.T.P.: A Journey Through America With the Rolling Stones; The Spiritual Supermarket; Haymon's Crowd; Temple* and coauthor, with Bill Graham, of *Bill Graham Presents.*

WILLIAM GREIDER is the National Editor of ROLLING STONE; he was formerly an assistant managing editor of the *Washington Post*. He is the author of *The Trouble with Money; Secrets of the Temple; The Education of David Stockman and Other Americans*; and *Who Will Tell the People.*

DAVID HARRIS began his career in journalism as a ROLLING STONE Contributing Editor. Born and raised in Fresno, California, Harris was a leader in the movement against the Vietnam War, spending two years in prison for resisting the draft and refusing induction into the military. The author of six books, including *The League*, he lives in the San Francisco Bay Area and is currently at work on an account of the conflict over California's last remaining virgin redwood forest.

GERRI HIRSHEY is a ROLLING STONE Contributing Editor. She also writes for *GQ* and *Vanity Fair* and is the author of *Nowhere to Run: The Story of Soul Music*.

CHRIS HODENFIELD is the former editor of *American Film* magazine and is now a feature editor at *Golf Digest*.

ELLEN HOPKINS is a ROLLING STONE Contributing Editor. She lives in New York.

TOM HORTON is an environmental writer formerly at the Chesapeake Bay foundation. He has written for the *New York Times Magazine* and *Audubon*, and he is the author of *Swanfall* and *Water's Way*. Currently, he writes an environmental column for the Baltimore *Sun*.

KEN KESEY is the author of *One Flew Over the Cuckoo's Nest*; *Sometimes a Great Notion' Garage Sale*; *Demon Box*; *Little Tricker the Squirrel Meets Big Double the Bear*; *The Further Inquiry*; *The Sea Lion*; and *Sailor's Song*. He is also coauthor of *Caverns*.

JOE KLEIN writes the Public Lives column for *Newsweek* magazine and is a consultant for CBS News. He was formerly the political columnist for *New York* magazine and is the author of two books, *Woody Guthrie: A Life* and *Payback: Five Marines After Vietnam*.

HOWARD KOHN is a ROLLING STONE contributing Editor and the author of *Who Killed Karen Silkwood?* and *The Last Farmer*, which was Pulitzer Prize finalist in 1989. He produces documentaries for radio and is an associate of the Center for Investigative Reporting and a freelance writer. He lives in Maryland and is now at work on a social history of racism in modern times to be published by Simon & Schuster.

KURT LODER was an editor at ROLLING STONE from 1979 to 1988 and is still a Contributing Editor. He is the author of *I, Tina*, a best-selling biography of Tina Turner. He is currently the anchor of *MTV*.

GREIL MARCUS is a ROLLING STONE Contributing Editor and the author of *Mystery Train*; *Lipstick Traces*; and *Dead Elvis*. He writes music columns for *Artforum* and *Interview*, and is working on *Ranters & Crowd Pleasers: Punk in Pop Music, 1977–1992*, to be published by Doubleday. He lives in Berekely, California.

DAVE MARSH was an Associate Editor of ROLLING STONE from 1975 to 1980 and has since written a number of books about music, including two bestsellers about Bruce Springsteen: *Born to Run* and *Glory Days*. He now edits *Rock & Roll Confidential*, a newsletter about music and politics.

DAISANN MCLANE, a former ROLLING STONE Assistant Editor, currently writes the Global Beat and World Music columns for ROLLING STONE. Her articles about Latin, African and Caribbean cultural affairs frequently appear in the *New York Times* and *The Village Voice*, where she is a contributing editor. She is now studying for her doctorate at Yale University and working on a memoir of her years as a calypso singer in Trinidad and Tobago.

P.J. O'ROURKE is the former editor of the *National Lampoon* and the author of *The Bachelor Home Companion*; *Holidays in Hell*; *Republican Party Reptile*; *Modern Manners*; *Parliament of Whores*; and *Give War a Chance*. He is at work on *All The Trouble in the World*, which will be published by Atlantic Monthly Press in the fall of 1994. He is the foreign Affairs Desk Chief for ROLLING STONE.

ROBERT PALMER started writing for ROLLING STONE in 1970 while playing for the band Insect Trust; he is presently a Contributing Editor. He is the author of four books, including the award-winning *Deep Blues*, and a former pop critic for the *New York Times*. He has also made a film and a CD of Mississippi juke-joint music under the sponsorship of Eurythmics' Dave Stewart, and written and codirected *The World According to John Coltrane*.

MIKE SAGER is a longtime ROLLING STONE Contributing Editor who writes the "Living in the USA" column. He is a former staff writer at the *Washington Post*, and has read and lectured at Columbia University's Graduate School of Journalism and at the Yale Law School. He is at work on a book, *Deviant Behavior*, to be published by Atlantic Monthly Press.

RANDALL SULLIVAN is a former ROLLING STONE Contributing Editor and *Los Angeles Herald-Examiner* columnist. He is the author of the forthcoming book *The Price of Experience*, to be published by Atlantic Monthly Press.

MICHAEL THOMAS is V.V. Panno. He was the Caribbean correspondent for ROLLING STONE. For reasons too twisted to go into here, most of his stuff appeared under an alias. It's all collected in his book *Okker Chic*. He's published a couple of books on Jamaica and written a heap of movies, including *The Hunger*, *Ladyhawke*, *Scandal*, *Ruby Cairo*, *Countryman* and *Sex Kittens of Saigon*.

HUNTER S. THOMPSON is a humble man who writes books for a living and spends the rest of his time bogged down in strange and crazy wars. He is the author of many violent books (see below) and brilliant political essays, which his friends and henchmen in the international media have managed for many years to pass off as "Gonzo Journalism."

The reasons for this are myriad, and we will speak of them later. In the meantime, Dr. Thompson lives the life of a freelance country gentleman in Woody Creek, Colorado, and exists in a profoundly active Balance of Terror with the local police authorities. He is the author of *Hell's Angels*; *Fear and Loathing in Las Vegas*; *Fear and Loathing on the Campaign Trail '72*; *The Great Shark Hunt*; *The Curse of Lono*; *Songs of the Doomed*; *Generation of Swine*; *Better Than Sex*; *Fear and Loathing on the Campaign Trail '92*; the long-awaited sex book, *Polo is My Life*; and other major statements of our time.

DAVID WEIR is a cofounder of the Center for Investigative Reporting and is currently investigative editor of *Mother Jones*. He is the author of *The Bhopal*

Syndrome and coauthor of *Circle of Poison* and *Raising Hell*, and teaches investigative reporting at University of California, Berkeley, Graduate School of Journalism.

TOM WOLFE is the author of *The Kandy-Kolored Tangerine-Flake Streamline Baby*; *The Pump House Gang*; *The Electric Kool-Aid Acid Test*; *Radical Chic and Mau-Mauing the Flak Catchers*; *The Painted Word*; *The Right Stuff* (which was developed from the article excerpted here); *From Bauhaus to Our House*; and most recently, *The Bonfire of the Vanities*, which was originally serialized in ROLLING STONE.

LAWRENCE WRIGHT, a former Contributing Editor of ROLLING STONE, is a staff writer for *The New Yorker* and the author of *In the New World: Growing up with America from the Sixties to the Eighties*. *Saints and Sinners*, a collection of profiles of religious personalities, including the piece on Jimmy Swaggart excerpted here and many others that originally appeared in ROLLING STONE, was published in 1993.

CHARLES M. YOUNG was formerly an Associate Editor of ROLLING STONE and is currently the executive editor of *Musician* magazine.

BILL ZEHME has been a ROLLING STONE Senior Writer since 1989. He is the author of *The Rolling Stone Book of Comedy* and coauthor of *The Bob Book: A Celebration of the Ultimate Okay Guy*. He is currently working on a collection of his ROLLING STONE pieces.